JANE'S
ALL THE WORLD'S AIRCRAFT
1919

JANE'S
ALL THE WORLD'S AIRCRAFT
1919

A Reprint of the 1919 Edition of All The World's Aircraft

Founded by

FRED T. JANE

Edited and Compiled by C. G. GREY

ARCO PUBLISHING COMPANY, INC.
New York

First published by Sampson Low Marston in 1919

This edition published 1969 by ARCO PUBLISHING COMPANY, INC.
219 Park Avenue South, New York, N. Y. 10003

Library of Congress Catalog Number 69-14964
ARCO Book Number 668-01955-7

Printed in Great Britain

ALPHABETICAL LIST OF ADVERTISERS.

CLASSIFIED LIST OF ADVERTISERS.

12 adv.

VICKERS LIMITED.

The First Direct Flight between Newfoundland and Ireland
was accomplished by this aeroplane in 15 Hours 57 Minutes.

Aeroplanes

for

Commercial

and

Military Use.

□□□

Aviation Department :
Imperial Court, Basil Street,
KNIGHTSBRIDGE. S.W.3.

"VICKERS—Vimy—ROLLS"

Flying Boats

for

Commercial

and

Naval Use.

□□□

Telephone :
Kensington 6520 (4 lines).
Telegraphic Address :
Vickerfyta, Knights, London.

PIONEERS in aeronautical construction, the BRITISH and COLONIAL AEROPLANE CO., LTD., to-day hold a leading position amongst the world's aircraft designers and constructors.

THE war has proved the unfailing soundness of design, and the all-round excellence in construction of the "BRISTOL" aeroplanes. Just as the first two years of fighting saw the "BRISTOL" Scout ahead of all other models, so the close of hostilities saw the "BRISTOL" Fighter supreme amid the aeroplanes of all designs and all nations.

IN the machines evolved for the requirements of commerce, the "BRISTOL" aeroplanes maintain their high repute. For the conveyance of cargo and passengers, the "BRISTOL" Triplanes have no superiors. The four engines with which these machines are fitted, ensure the highest measure of safety and reliability.

FOR the carriage of passengers, mails and light general cargo, other machines have been evolved of the aeroplane, hydro-plane and flying-boat types, for use under all conditions, and in all climates. To small aeroplanes, for commercial and sporting purposes, considerable attention is being paid.

Enquiries concerning the " BRISTOL " aeroplanes addressed to the Designer and constructors at FILTON, BRISTOL, will receive prompt and careful attention.

The " BRISTOL " Pullman, fitted with Four 400 H.P. Liberty Engines.

THIS machine has been designed for passenger and freight carrying work. For the comfort and convenience of the fourteen passengers which the machine conveys, in addition to two pilots, a special Pullman has been constructed. Seven feet in height and wholly enclosed, and fitted with electric heating and lighting, richly upholstered armchairs are installed on each side of a central gangway. For each passenger Triplex glass windows are provided. Any, or all the seats can be removed, and over 500 cubic feet of space made available for cargo. The machine has a maximum speed of 125 miles per hour and can cruise with two pilots, 2700 lbs. of cargo in fuel, for 5 hours at an economical speed of 105 miles per hour.

Catalogues or further particulars will be supplied on application to :—

The BRITISH & COLONIAL AEROPLANE
COMPANY, LTD.,
FILTON, — BRISTOL.

Telegrams:—AVIATION, BRISTOL
Codes:—A1, A.B.C., & MOREING,

Telephone :—
3906, BRISTOL,

16 adv.

THE FORWARD GONDOLA AIRSHIP R33.

RIGID AIRSHIPS FOR MAIL & PASSENGER SERVICE.

SIR W. G. ARMSTRONG, WHITWORTH & CO., Ltd.,

NEWCASTLE-UPON-TYNE.

LONDON OFFICE : 8, GREAT GEORGE ST., WESTMINSTER, S.W. 1.

TELEGRAMS : "ZIGZAG PARL.. LONDON."
TELEPHONE : VICTORIA 4010.

WORKS: BARLOW, NEAR SELBY. YORKS.

THE FAMOUS AIRSHIP R 33 ON HER TRIAL TRIP.

— RIGID AIRSHIPS FOR WAR SERVICE. —

SIR W. G. ARMSTRONG, WHITWORTH & CO., Ltd.,

NEWCASTLE-UPON-TYNE.

LONDON OFFICE : 8, GREAT GEORGE ST., WESTMINSTER, S.W. 1.

TELEGRAMS : "ZIGZAG PARL. LONDON."
TELEPHONE : VICTORIA 4010.

WORKS: BARLOW, NEAR SELBY, YORKS.

18 adv.

Chairman (and Founder, 1911):   **G. HOLT THOMAS.**

The Largest Aircraft Enterprise in the World

THE Aircraft Manufacturing Company, which, with its associated Companies, is the largest aircraft enterprise in the world, is in a unique position to undertake the construction and complete equipment of aircraft for every kind of commercial, scientific and administrative purpose.

While many firms are dependent upon outside industries for essential parts of their output, the vast Airco resources and experience enable the associated Companies to carry out practically every phase of modern aircraft construction in their own works and under their own skilled supervision. The importance of this fact will be appreciated by those responsible for the inauguration and development of public air services.

Among the highly specialised products of the associated Companies are:

HIGH-SPEED AEROPLANES, AIRSHIPS AND KITE BALLOONS, SEAPLANES AND FLYING BOATS, AERO-ENGINES, PROPELLERS, INSTRUMENTS OF PRECISION, etc., etc.

THE AIRCRAFT MANUFACTURING Co., Ltd.

AIRSHIPS, LTD.   GNOME & LE RHONE ENGINE CO. (Peter Hooker, Ltd.).   MAY, HARDEN & MAY, Seaplane Base, HYTHE.   INTEGRAL PROPELLER CO., LTD.

London Offices: 27, BUCKINGHAM GATE, LONDON, S.W.1.

THE CENTRAL AIRCRAFT COMPANY,

179, HIGH ROAD, KILBURN, LONDON, N.W.

HAVE been engaged in the Aircraft Industry since 1909. During the War, the Company were engaged in manufacturing Aeroplanes to official designs, and to the designs of various firms. Are now engaged in manufacturing Aeroplanes to their own design. The following three types of commercial and pleasure machines have been designed and manufactured since the armistice, November, 1918, and have proved extremely successful in performance. The Central Aircraft Co. have also opened a school of Aviation, where instruction, both theoretical and practical, is given on the finest training machines yet produced.

The School is under the personal management of Mr. Herbert Sykes, O.B.E., assisted by a fully qualified staff of instructors. The fee for the whole course is £125, for which a pupil is guaranteed the Royal Aero Club's Certificate and not less than 10 hours actual flying.

Type C/F 4. This machine has been specially designed for school work, and with a view to low cost of maintenance and ease of repair. To this end, it embodies many valuable features, amongst which is the interchangeability of component parts. The machine is safe, simple, and easy to fly, at the same time possessing inherent stability to a marked degree. Its low landing speed and wide range are features which render it particularly suitable for instructional purposes.

GENERAL SPECIFICATION.

Motor	...	...	...	Renault 80 h.p.	Weight per sq. ft.	...	...	4.2 lbs.	Speed Range	...	...	...	32-75 m.p.h.
Tankage	...	...	...	3 hours.	Weight per h.p.	...	...	18.65 lbs.	Petrol consumption per hour	7.5 galls.
Span	...	...	...	34 ft. 3 in.	Total weight	...	...	1400 lbs.	Oil	do.	do.	1.5 galls.
Length	...	...	...	24 ft. 8 in.	Unladen weight	...	...	900 lbs.	Control ...	...	...	...	Dual.
Surface	...	...	...	331 sq. ft.	Useful load	...	...	500 lbs.					

THE CENTRAL AIRCRAFT COMPANY.

Type C/F 5.   100 h.p. Sporting or Touring Model.

This machine has been designed to cater for the requirements of those who desire an aeroplane for Sporting or Touring purposes. Simplicity and strength of construction are the outstanding features of the design, whilst by the employment of folding wings, a great objection to the present day type of machine—viz., the large amount of space required for storage—has been effectually overcome. Side-by-side seats are provided, and the comfort and convenience of passengers has been carefully studied. The workmanship and finish are beyond criticism, whilst the flying qualities of the machine are admirable in every way. It is inherently stable, yet exceptionally light and easy on control. It possesses a very wide range of speed, and is capable of making remarkably slow landings, a very important consideration to the private owner. The machine has been designed throughout with a view to providing sportsmen with a thoroughly efficient and excellent flying machine at a minimum cost for upkeep and maintenance.

Motor	Anzani 100-110 h.p.	Weight empty	1100 lbs.
Tankage	3 hours.	Weight laden	2060 lbs.
Span	33 ft. 4 ins.	Speed	40-80 m.p.h.
Length	23 ft. 3 ins.	Petrol consumption per hour	8 gallons.
Surface	350 sq. ft.	Oil do. do.	1.5 galls.
Width with wings folded	12 ft. 3 ins.	Control	Wheel.

Type C/F. 2a.   320 h.p. Twin engine 9 seater Passenger or Commercial Model.

A thoroughly efficient and economical machine for passenger carrying or commercial use. By the use of two engines, the risk of forced landings is reduced to a minimum, a valuable consideration when carrying passengers for hire. The machine provides accommodation for two pilots and seven passengers, who are seated within a luxuriously appointed and electrically warmed cabin, with sides of Triplex non-splintering glass, or when passengers are not carried, for half a ton of mails or goods. With a fuel capacity of three hours and a maximum speed of 90 m.p.h., it should prove a most useful and economical vehicle for the purposes specified above. The machine possesses the same excellent flying qualities as our smaller models, while the beauty and strength of construction are altogether exceptional. This model is provided with folding wings which enables it to be housed in a small hangar or shed.

Motor	2-160 h.p. Beardmore	Total weight	5400 lbs.
Tankage	3 hours.	Unladen weight	3160 lbs.
Span	63 ft.	Useful load	2240 lbs.
Width, with wings folded	30 ft.	Speed range	40-90 m.p.h.
Length	39 ft.	Petrol consumption per hour	25 galls.
Wt. per sq. ft.	6 lbs.	Oil do. do.	2 galls.
Surface	900 sq. ft.	Control	Duplicate.
Weight per h.p.	16.9 lbs.		

100 h.p. 2 or 4 Seater Sporting or Touring Biplane.

320 h.p. Twin Engine 9 Seater Passenger or Commercial Biplane.

MARTINSYDE L^{TD.}

BROOKLANDS.

DESIGNERS and
MANUFACTURERS
.. of ..

The famous F4 Fighter

which established a WAR RECORD

for CLIMB and SPEED at Height.

This Machine holds the

LONDON–PARIS SPEED RECORD.
75 Minutes.

And of the

COMMERCIAL TYPE "A"

for MAIL, PASSENGER

and CARGO CARRYING.

JOHN DAWSONS

G. H. HUMPHREY,
Governing Director.

Having booked this space in 1918 for Aircraft, have to use it to announce that they are turning all their Aircraft organisation over to the manufacture of Furniture.

Contributory to the Nation's Need for Aircraft during the War, they now contribute to the Nation's Need in Furniture in the re=establishment of England's Homes— in the firm conviction that War shall be no more.

Victoria Works, NEWCASTLE-ON-TYNE

THE secret of the success of Boulton & Paul Aircraft, lies in the fact of sound scientific research, and the highest practical experience of the craftsmen employed.

Here is illustrated just one of the valuable aids to designing—the wind channel fitted with all instruments necessary for collecting valuable data.

BOULTON & PAUL, LTD.

MAKERS OF AIRCRAFT,

NORWICH.

THE policy of employing first-class specialists and highly qualified experts is a guarantee of watchful improvement in aeronautical design. Everything that ability can do towards attaining a certainty in safety and reliability of performance is carried out under careful supervision.

Our new types of machines (the details of which are given elsewhere in this volume), embody the last word in aircraft design.

Prospective purchasers are invited to make inspection of our Laboratories and Experimental Workshops, and to see our Machines put to practical test in the air.

Compare them with others before placing your orders.

Telegrams : "Boulton, Norwich." Telephone : Norwich 851.

THE
GLOUCESTERSHIRE AIRCRAFT Cᵒ Lᵀᴰ
CHELTENHAM
CONTRACTORS To HIS MAJESTY'S GOVERNMENT

DESIGNERS & MANUFACTURERS
OF ALL TYPES OF HEAVIER
THAN AIR MACHINES.

TELEGRAPHIC ADDRESS,
"SUNNINGEND"
TELEPHONE
1161 (5 LINES) CHELTENHAM

HEAD OFFICES & WORKS

SUNNINGEND
WORKS, CHELTENHAM

31 adv.

34 adv

Beardmore
Aero Engines

THE ENGINE THAT HELPED MOST
WHEN THE NEED WAS GREATEST.

BEARDMORE ENGINES are to the fore now that the Commercial struggle has started.

They hold records in height, efficiency, time and distances. The Newest Designs, the results of War experiences, outclass all that engine construction has hitherto achieved.

A Designer of one of the most prominent Aircraft Factories writes :—

"You may be interested to know that we consider your engine would be more suitable for commercial work than any other engine that has been used in the War."

THE BEARDMORE
AERO ENGINE LTD.

London Showrooms & Depots :—

**112, GT. PORTLAND ST.,
LONDON, W.1.**

Telephone : 238 Gerrard.

C.D.C.

37 adv.

12 Cyl. 275 H.P.
Sunbeam - Coatalen
"Maori" type Engine with direct drive

This type of Engine is fitted on all the later Admiralty Airships.

SUNBEAM-COATALEN AIRCRAFT MOTORS

THE SUNBEAM MOTOR CAR CO., LTD., WOLVERHAMPTON.

AEROPLANE ENGINES

"WASP"
Specification.

Type of Engine	7 Cylinder static radial.	**Oil Recommended**	Wakefield Castrol R.
Type of Cylinder	Steel, fins A.B.C., copper coated, 3 overhead valves, 2 exhaust and 1 inlet.	**Oil Consumption**	4 pints per hour.
		Oil Consumption per B.H.P.	.02 pints.
		Carburettors	2 A.B.C. 48 m/m.
Bore	4¾	**Petrol Consumption**	.56 pints per B.H.P. hour.
Stroke	6¼ ins.		
Normal B.H.P.	200.	**Magnetos**	2 P.L. 7 type. 2 Spark.
Rotation	Anticlock, facing propeller.	**Speed of Magnetos**	1¼ Engine Speed.
		Magneto Rotates	Clockwise facing driving end of armature.
Normal Speed	1800 r.p.m.	**Rev. Counter Rotates**	Anticlock facing driving shaft.
Lubrication	2 Rotary Plunger Pumps, 1 feeding through hollow c/shaft to Crankpin, centrifugal feed to big end and thence splash. 1 feeding to nose, dropping into cam and forming a permanent sump for gears in bottom of nose.	**Speed of Rev. Counter Drive**	¼ Engine Speed.
		Weight of Engines including Prop. Boss but without Oil or Fuel	350 lbs.
		Weight of Engine per B.H.P.	1.75 lbs.

"GNAT"
Specification.

Type of Engine	2 Cylinder Horizontally opposed.	**Oil Consumption**	1.7 Pints.
Type of Cylinder	Steel, Fins A.B.C. Copper Coated.	**Oil Consumption per B.H.P. Hour**	.037 Pints.
		Carburettors	1 A.B.C. 48 m/m.
Bore	4.75.	**Petrol Consumption**	.56 Pints per B.H.P. Hour.
Stroke	5¼.		
Normal B.H.P.	45. Max. 50.	**Magnetos**	1 M.L. Magneto. Type K2.
Rotation	Anticlockwise facing Propeller.	**Speed of Magnetos**	½ Engine Speed.
		Mag. Rotates	Anticlockwise facing driving end of armature.
Normal Speed	1800 r.p.m. Max. 2000.	**Weight of Engine including Prop. Boss but without Oil or Fuel**	115 lbs.
Lubrication	One Rotary Plunger Pump from tank to crankcase, and then splash to cylinders.	**Weight of Engine per B.H.P.**	2.3 lbs.
Oil Recommended	Wakefield Castrol "R."		

To realise the wonderful advance which has been made in aero-engine design and construction, investigate the Selsdon products.

The WASP II is developed from the war-tried Wasp I, with a special eye to the requirements of commercial flying. It is the lightest engine of its power, 350 lbs. in a 200 H.P. engine, representing 1.75 lbs. per B.H.P.

Suitable for passenger - carrying machines, machines engaged on postal work, or for taxi-planes.

The GNAT is essentially the engine for the sporting flyer, small and compact. Weighs only 115 lbs. yet develops 40 H.P. This engine is exclusively fitted by the Blackburn Aeroplane and Motor Co., Ltd., in their sporting two-seater monoplane.

The petrol consumption of both engines is remarkably low.

SELSDON AERO & ENGINEERING Co., LTD.,

1, Albemarle Street, Piccadilly, London, W.

"WASP" AERO ENGINE.

"GNAT" AERO ENGINE.

SELSDON

SELSDON AERO CROYDON

GWYNNES

LIMITED.

AERO ENGINES OF THE FINEST WORKMANSHIP.

SOLE LICENCEES

AND

MANUFACTURERS

OF THE

"CLERGET"

GWYNNES LTD.,
CHURCH WHARF, CHISWICK, LONDON
AND HAMMERSMITH,

AND

OTHER TYPES

OF

AERO

ENGINES.

GWYNNES LTD.,
CHURCH WHARF, CHISWICK, LONDON.
AND HAMMERSMITH,

THE ENGLISH ELECTRIC Co., Ltd.

 Phoenix
BRADFORD

Designers and Constructors of all Classes of Aircraft, School Machines, Land Bombers, Chasers, Patrol Machines, Torpedo Carrying Seaplanes.

SPECIALITY:

LARGE FLYING BOATS.

CONTRACTORS TO H.M. GOVERNMENT.

THE ENGLISH ELECTRIC Co. which incorporates the works of MESSRS. COVENTRY ORDNANCE, DICK KERR and PHŒNIX DYNAMO MFG. Co., has consolidated the joint aircraft experience and plant of the three concerns in one large central factory, having exceptional manufacturing and testing facilities.

Telephone:
BRADFORD 3700 (7 lines).
Private Branch Exchange.

WORKS:—THORNBURY AND SCOTSTOUN.
AIRCRAFT OFFICES:—THORNBURY WORKS, BRADFORD.
CENTRAL OFFICES:—QUEEN'S HOUSE, KINGSWAY, LONDON.

Telegrams:
DYNAMO, BRADFORD.

Machine Designed and Built by the Coventry Ordnance Works in 1911.

The Phœnix Flying Boat 1918.

The Coventry Ordnance Military Trials Machine 1912.

43 adv.

SDEB 14. GENERAL UTILITY TYPE.
(DESIGNED BY SERGE DE BOLOTOFF.)

SDEB 14

DE BOLOTOFF, LTD., ENGINEERS.

SIDDELEY AIRCRAFT ENGINES.

The Siddeley Aircraft Engine.

THE Siddeley aircraft engine is the standard six-cylinder water-cooled engine of the Royal Air Force. More than 6,000 of these engines have been supplied to the British Government.

This engine formed a large part of the engine equipment of the Independent Air Force on the Western front. Its reliability and consistency are well established, and make it an ideal engine for commercial aeronautics.

General Particulars.

Six-cylinder vertical engine, 160 m/m. bore by 180 m/m. stroke.

Dual ignition by two 6-cyl. magnetos.

Weight complete without water 700 lbs.

Normal revolutions 1500 per minute; maximum 1700 per minute.

Horse-power at normal revolutions 300.

      ,,   ,, maximum   ,,   350.

Petrol consumption ·5 to ·55 pints per horse-power per hour.

The Siddeley-Deasy Motor Car Co., Ltd., Coventry.

Contractors to H.M. Air Ministry.

SIDDELEY AIRCRAFT ENGINES.

The Siddeley "Tiger" Motor.

THE Siddeley "Tiger" engine of 600 horse-power is a twelve-cylinder water-cooled motor of robust construction. The propeller is driven at a reduced speed to ensure efficiency, and to make the unit suitable for large aeroplanes, either for war or peace. An electric starting motor is provided with automatic friction clutch gear.

General Particulars.

12-cylinder vertical motor, 160 m/m. bore by 180 m/m. stroke. Dual ignition by two magnetos or by one magneto and battery ignition.

Weight complete, without water 1400 lbs.

Normal revolutions 1500 per min.

Maximum   ,,   1700 ,, ,,

Horse-power at normal revolutions 600.

   ,,   ,,   ,,   maximum   ,,   660.

Revolutions of propeller at normal revs. of engine 835.

Petrol consumption ·5 to ·55 pints per horse-power per hour.

 The Siddeley-Deasy Motor Car Co., Ltd., Coventry.

Contractors to H.M. Air Ministry.

SIDDELEY AIRCRAFT ENGINES.

The Siddeley Radial Motor.

THE Siddeley radial motor is intended for high speed aeroplanes where performance is the first consideration. It is capable of giving 300 horse power at an altitude of 10,000ft., and weighs 670 lbs. complete.

It is fitted with the Siddeley system of forced induction, comprising a turbine air compressor and patented drive. The lubrication is on a novel system, and the aluminium and steel construction of the cylinders ensures thorough cooling by air.

The Siddeley-Deasy Motor Car Co., Ltd., Coventry.

Contractors to H.M. Air Ministry.

Rudge-Whitworth

Rudge-Whitworth, L^{td}..

Rudge-Whitworth
Britain's Best Bicycle

Britain's Best Bicycle. 50 years' experience in making high grade bicycles. Finest materials—British workmanship.

The Rudge Motor Bicycle was the first single cylinder motor bicycle to do over 60 miles in the hour. Rudge Multi, winner of the Senior Tourist Trophy Race, Isle of Man, May 21st, 1914.

Rudge-Whitworth Detachable Wire Wheels are fitted to all high grade makes of cars and aeroplanes.

Rudge-Whitworth
Detachable Wire Wheels

Aeronautical Dept.

Our four years' experience of Government Work building complete components.
Specialists in:

Planes.	Tails.	Fins.
Rudders.	Skids.	Undercarriages.
Ailerons.	Elevators.	Airshipcars.
Radiator Shutters.		Tierods.
Metal Fittings.	Metal Wing Spars.	

Ball Bearings.

We established the manufacture of the highest possible class for use in Aeroplane engines during the war.

We invite enquiries from Motor and Engineering Industries.

Rudge ⊙ Multi

For full particulars write to

Rudge-Whitworth, Ltd.
(Dept. 703.)

COVENTRY, England.

25/30 H.P. R.F.C. MODEL.

CROSSLEY MOTORS LIMITED,

Builders of Quality Cars,

Telephone:
City, 4611 (3 lines).

MANCHESTER.

Telegrams:
MOTORS, GORTON.

London Office & Service Depot: 50, PACE STREET, WESTMINSTER, S.W.1.

" Let us remember those who belong to the most recent military arm.

The Keen-eyed, Swift-winged knights of the air, who have given to the World a new type of daring and resourceful heroism."

(*The King's Speech*).

That the Crossley should be chosen by those whom the King describes as " keen-eyed and swift-winged " is eloquent testimony to the qualities that are combined in the 25/30 h.p. R.F.C. Crossley model.

Both the business and pleasure motorist will find comfort, refinement and economy, carried to their highest development in the Crossley 25/30 h.p. R.F.C. model.

Chassis Price (including electric starter and lighting) **£850.**

Touring Car (as illustrated, fully equipped) **£995.**

Write for full particulars and name of agent for your district.

51 adv.

"RYLARD" VARNISH.

SUPREME.

"*RYLARD*" *Varnish, which was adopted by the Air Ministry, has proved itself to be unaffected by the changing temperature of the Air, the action of sea water, and the wear and tear of the road.*

Llewellyn Ryland, Ltd.,
Varnish and Paint Manufacturers,
Birmingham.

"SHELL"

THE

AVIATION

SPIRIT.

Every Airman is eager to fly on "Shell."

'Rok' Roofing is British-Made

by British Labour, backed by British Capital. It forms a permanent and easily applied roof-covering, and can be used instead of Slates, Tiles, or Corrugated Iron. It is laid on close-jointed wood boards.

'ROK' is supplied in rolls of 72 feet by 3 feet wide, in the following grades—

½-Ply averaging	50	lb. per roll.
1-Ply ,,	72	,,
2-Ply ,,	82	,,
3-Ply ,,	104	,,

Sufficient nails and cement are supplied free with each roll to fix it. It is easily applied, and can be fixed by the buyer without skilled assistance.

'Rok' Roofing may also be used on concrete roofs fixed with special 'Rok' Mastic. 'Rok' Roofing as supplied is a uniform Grey Colour, but special Paint known as 'Rokolor' can be furnished by the manufacturers in Red, Green, or Black to paint over it. Extremes of temperature do not affect it in any way.

ROK ROOFING

D. ANDERSON & SON, LTD., LAGAN FELT WORKS, BELFAST.

66 adv.

Allen FRICTIONLESS
PISTONS AND RINGS

Gudgeon Pins, Pressings, Gun Mounts and Castings.

"ALLEN" RINGS are made on scientific lines, and "STRESSED" by a single mechanical operation, guaranteed true to dimensions.

ALLEN PATENT FILLING-UP and SECURING RING overcomes the difficulties of machining narrow piston ring grooves. Eliminates groove wear in aluminium pistons. Securely locks the piston ring and prevents it turning in the groove.

CAST IRON AND ALUMINIUM PISTONS OF ANY DESIGN, with or without the "ALLEN" Hardened Gudgeon Pin Bush.

GUDGEON PINS, etc., of all descriptions. CASE HARDENING by SCIENTIFIC and MOST UP-TO-DATE METHODS.

PRESSINGS of ALL KINDS, and for ALL DESIGNS OF AIRCRAFT.

GUN MOUNTS "ALLEN" PATENT SAFE AND SURE. CASTINGS of all descriptions.

THE ALLEN PATENT FRICTIONLESS PISTON RINGS, SO SUCCESSFUL IN THE WORLD OF STEAM, WILL SHORTLY BE AVAILABLE FOR AERO AND MOTOR CAR ENGINES.

Allen & Simmonds, Ltd., Engineers, Reading, Eng.

80 adv.

86 adv.

91 adv.

99 adv.

CONFIDENCE

in anything you undertake is half the battle! PRIOR TO AUGUST 1914 we pointed out the possibilities in Aviation.

MANY REALIZED OUR CONTENTIONS and CONSISTENTLY USED OUR PAGES. Since the ARMISTICE many have wavered, but the argument we put forward has induced 95 per cent. of our advertisers to GO ON! We say—and with authority—*Aviation will be the Biggest Industry in the World!* It is merely in its infancy, but enormous developments are even now in progress.

Now that we HAVE BEATEN the Huns—Fighting Machines are done with—our attention will be devoted to entirely new designs. Think what has been accomplished since 1914, and we are certain these will sink into insignificance the next 4 years. The resources of every Branch of Engineering will be required, and thousands of trades will find a Market in this Great Industry. Here are a few:

Acetylene Weld. Plant	Clothing	Glues	Office Furniture	Steel
Almn. Press Work	Copper & Brass Rods	Hangers	Parachutes	Tanks & Cowls
Ball Bearings	Covering & Doping	Instruments	Petrol Storage	Timber
Beltings	Dopes	Leather Goods	Photographic Appl.	Time Recorders
Brass & Copper Alloys	Electrical Appliances	Machine Tools	Plywood	Tools of all kinds
Buildings	Engines & Parts	Magnetos	Press Tools	Varnishes & Colours
Calculators	Felting & Roofing	Metal Parts	Radiators	Woodworking Mach'y
Castings	Furnaces	Motor Cars	Sparking Plugs	

Do YOU want some of the Trade? If so, we ask your Confidence in

AERONAUTICS

THE TRADE PAPER OF THE INDUSTRY.

Send for a Specimen Copy and Advertisement Rates.

Telephone—City 9852 (4 lines).
Telegrams—"Allangas," Fleet, London.
New York Address—1790 Broadway.

Editor : Major C. C. TURNER (late R.A.F.)
A.F.Ae.S.

J. P. H. BEWSHER, Avertisement Manager.
AERONAUTICS
6 and 8 Bouverie Street - London, E.C.4.

Published Every Thursday by **BENN BROTHERS**, LD., 6 and 8 Bouverie St., E.C.4.

104 adv.

Published Annually.

ALL THE WORLD'S AIRCRAFT.

(ORIGINALLY KNOWN AS "ALL THE WORLD'S AIRSHIPS.")

FOUNDED BY

THE LATE FRED T. JANE,

FOUNDER AND EDITOR OF "FIGHTING SHIPS" (ANNUAL) ETC.

EDITED AND COMPILED BY C. G. GREY,

(*Editor of "The Aeroplane"*).

PART A.—ALL THE WORLD'S AEROPLANES.

PART B.—ALL THE WORLD'S AERO-ENGINES.

PART C.—ALL THE WORLD'S AIRSHIPS,

TENTH YEAR OF ISSUE.

(FOUNDED 1909.)

LONDON & EDINBURGH:

SAMPSON LOW, MARSTON & COMPANY, LTD.

1919.

CONTENTS.

CONTENTS—*continued.*

———

PREFACE.

BY C. G. GREY, EDITOR OF "THE AEROPLANE."

WHEN one began the compilation of "*All the World's Aircraft*" for 1919, one did so with a light heart. Though Peace had not been declared, the War was manifestly over, and all lets and hindrances due to the necessary, and one may add, the kindly and sympathetic, censorship of a publication entirely concerned with war material were removed. It was to be assumed that all would be the plainest of plain sailing.

But as the work progressed one found, as many people have found in other occupations, that Peace was by no means an unmixed blessing, and one almost wished for the simple condition of war, when there was a fixed regulation for everything. One began to sympathise with the dog whose muzzle is removed at the end of a prolonged Muzzling Order, and who does not quite know what to do with himself.

During the War it was fairly easy to judge what one might safely put into the book. In these days the difficulty is to know how to get into it all the matter that obviously ought to be in it, for there are limits to the amount of paper and printing which can be expended on a publication of this nature, even at a slightly increased price. Also there are limits to the size of book which a cover will hold without bursting asunder in the midst. Also there are limits to the time which can be allowed for printing and binding if the book is not to consist entirely of ancient history.

Therefore the problem became largely one of what to leave out of the book rather than what to put into it. In order to make room for the mass of illustrations, specifications and technical descriptions which are now available it was necessary to cut out something else. Consequently the whole of what was "Part A" of last year's volume, consisting of the Dictionary, the International Glossary, the Table of Records, and so forth, has been omitted bodily. The Dictionary has been published separately, for the benefit of those who are still unfamiliar with aeronautical phraseology. The whole of the Historical Section has also been eliminated, for if one were to attempt to do justice to All the World's Historical Aircraft one would need a volume nearly as big as this. Also the List of Pilots and the R.A.F. Honours' List have been omitted, for they also have grown to such a size that if they were included most of the Aeroplane Section of the book would have to be excluded.

The removal of all these sections of the previous volume has left room for many more illustrations and descriptions of aeroplanes, airships and engines than have ever appeared in any other publication, but even so the task of compilation has not been easy. Naturally one has wished to give the fullest possible descriptions of British and Allied machines. As a matter of interest, and also of education for our own designers, one has endeavoured to describe as fully as possible the machines of our erstwhile enemies, the Germans.

And here, be it said, there is much to learn from the German aeroplanes and engines. Though British aeroplanes have had the finest performance of any in the world during the war, there are many German machines which beat the majority of our own in pure "eyeability." And it is an axiomatic fact that if an aeroplane *is* right it *looks* right, though it is by no means true that conversely if an aeroplane *looks* right it *is* right. Many German machines *look* right, but are constructionally bad.

It may be noticed that British aeroplanes have during the past two years become more and more "Hunnish" in appearance. Long before the end of the war one of the greatest compliments one could pay an aeroplane was to say that it looked "very like a Hun," and the attitude of mind among aviators which was indicated by this state of affairs showed that the Germans had developed an eye for the aeroplane that looked right. Where they failed was firstly in detail of construction, and secondly in certain points of aerodynamic science which need not be specified, for we are now commercially at war with Germany.

For this reason the German section of this volumn is well worth study, and one is glad to acknowledge the fact, that thanks to the enterprise of Mr. Hildesheim, the compiler of the Scandinavian pages of this book, one was able to secure at the last moment before printing a number of photographs of German aeroplanes which have not hitherto been published out of Germany. Taking these in conjunction with the constructional details of German machines which have been reproduced from the reports of the Technical Department, Aircraft Group, Ministry of Munitions, much may be learned about German aircraft design.

As regards the French section, it has been extremely difficult to obtain information from the French firms, chiefly, one believes, because there has been so little new in French design for the past two years. The French aircraft designers and constructors blame "*l'Administration*" for holding back their best designs in the effort to produce enormous output during the last year of the war. The fact remains that during 1918 very little of interest was produced in France.

The British section is naturally the most voluminous of all, but here, the keen enquirer will see serious anomalies. Hardly any details will be found about some machines, and there are profuse descriptions of others. The reader must blame the firms and not the present writer. About the end of 1918 precisely the same letter was sent to each and every firm in the Aircraft Industry asking for information about its products. Some sent full details, with photographs and scale drawings, some sent photographs without descriptions, some sent descriptions without photographs, and some sent drawings without descriptions. Others again sent blue prints of drawings on such a scale that they could not be reproduced. Yet others refused to send any details of their machines, for fear lest their competitors might copy them.

In each case the material available has been used, and one hopes that it has been displayed to the best advantage of the British Aircraft Industry. But the disparity apparent between the information acquired concerning one firm and that acquired from another may be taken as representing the views of the various firms on the desirability of publishing details of their products.

Nevertheless one believes that on the whole the British Industry makes a good display.

An additional difficulty this year has been the fact that one has had to mix together war aeroplanes and commercial aeroplanes. It is true that with about two exceptions all so-called commercial aeroplanes are merely war aeroplanes with a species of conservatory added in which to carry an extra passenger or two, but it would have been distinctly more instructive if it had been possible to separate them. Doubtless this will become possible in future as the design of war aeroplanes diverges from that of commercial aeroplanes. But at present much space is occupied by obsolete war machines, which are included simply because it has not been permissible to publish them sooner, and by peace machines which are merely converted war machines.

A certain amount of extra information has been gathered this year concerning several countries which in previous volumes made but little showing in aeronautics. One is particularly indebted to the Japanese, Swedish and Argentine representatives in this country, and to certain Brazilian naval officers for their kindness in assisting one to procure information concerning aviation in their countries.

Finally one would like a word with one's friends the critics. One's only complaint against them is that they were too kind to the last volume. It is one's ambition to make "All the World's Aircraft" an absolute necessity to anybody who has to do with aircraft in any shape or form, and one would be grateful for any criticisms of this volume, and suggestions for improvements in future volumes which will make the book more valuable and therefore more necessary to the aeronautical world in general.

Meantime one hopes that the professional critics will be moderately pleased with those review copies which they acquire without cost, and that the buyers of the book will feel that it gives them value for their money. One can at any rate assert truthfully, as a certain famous comedian remarked about motoring, that there is nothing like it.—C.G.G.

THE WORLD'S AEROPLANES.

ARRANGED IN ALPHABETICAL ORDER OF NATIONALITY.

(WITH NOTES ON THE DEVELOPMENTS OF NAVAL AND MILITARY AERONAUTICS IN EACH NATION).

AND A PREFACE ON AIRCRAFT IN THE WAR BY

MAJOR W. E. DE B. WHITTAKER,

(LATE THE KING'S REGIMENT AND GENERAL STAFF.)

AIRCRAFT IN THE WAR.

By Major W. E. de B. WHITTAKER, Late of the King's Regiment and General Staff.

THE last piece in this series was written when the fate of the allies was in the balance. Through the dark days in the spring of 1918 there seemed to be a possibility of final victory falling to the Central Powers. At the best the end might be indecisive and all the blood and treasure wasted to no apparent good.

A brief six months after the most critical period all was over save the talking and the reconstruction. The unity of the Central Powers, so powerful a factor in the continuance and course of the great war, had dissolved, the Kaiser, powerless before the rising disloyalty of his people, had gone sadly into Holland and an armistice giving victory to the allies had been signed by the responsible military authorities.

It is not uncommon in great wars of the past for the culminating effort on both sides to be greater in determination and vigour than any of the earlier stages of hostilities. Waterloo, which ended a quarter of a century of conflict, surpassed in grandeur and decision all the battles of the Revolutionary and Napoleonic eras. The hardest fighting in the American Civil War came at the end. The Russo-Japanese war drew to its close in a blaze of fury which almost rivalled M. Bloch's worst prophecies as to the horrors of modern war. The throw of the dice for the last time is generally for the largest stakes and is directed by a desperation not unallied with tragedy.

In those operations which brought the war successfully to its close the Royal Air Force, the newest of the King's Services, took a primary part. While the Royal Air Force units with the troops in the field carried out their duties with loyalty and efficiency, impressing their personality on the enemy, the Independent Air Force was busily engaged destroying the moral of enemy civilians far behind the battle line by means of bombs distributed impartially by day or by night. At sea the enemy submarine campaign had ceased to be a serious menace to allied shipping almost entirely as a result of the aeroplane, airship and kite-balloon patrols carried out by R.A.F. units attached to the Navy. In each theatre of war the Royal Air Force can regard with pride its fighting records during the first and most vital period of its existence.

RECONNAISSANCE.

In that work which one cannot help regarding as the most important duty which fell to the R.A.F. during the war, the final year of hostilities saw no marked change. The principles of aerial reconnaissance had been well defined in earlier days and experience had shown but little reason for any amendment. The methods and the means employed improved but that is all. The photographs taken were better and the number produced was greater. More efficient wireless equipment was issued and the training and knowledge of pilots and observers showed marked improvement.

The improved types of aeroplanes available for reconnaissance in the latter days of the war extended the area over which it was possible to carry out with a proper degree of security the work of strategical scouting. Before the output and efficiency of aircraft had increased strategical reconnaissance was only possible under conditions of high risk and at great expense in casualties. It is one thing to fly a hundred miles behind the enemy lines on an aeroplane with all the appearance and many of the attributes of a Christmas tree and fitted with an engine on which but little reliance could be placed but there is greater joy and more profit in making the same journey in machines possessing both speed and reliability and equipped in such a manner as to make aerial fighting less one-sided in its results.

Tactical reconnaissance had improved greatly in the later stages of the war as a result of the increased knowledge of both pilots and observers in matters concerning military operations. There is a great art in reading correctly the movements of an enemy and before it can be attained those engaged in the work must have a close understanding of the principles of war and their concrete application. It is not possible to report everything seen—life and a flight are too

A Bristol Two-seater Fighter and Reconnaissance Machine in the air.

short for that, but it is necessary to record everything that is of importance. It is not always the obvious that is of value and many a pilot has wasted valuable time to report manœuvres which in the light of events could be read quite as easily from the ground and from behind the lines.

The value of photography in tactical reconnaissance cannot be overestimated. By its aid a daily map can be prepared and changes in enemy dispositions can be recorded in detail and with accuracy. It provides a check on visual observation and is invaluable in all artillery preparations. During the war aerial photography has grown from an experiment to an exact science. It provides a valuable means of correcting maps in areas where imagination rather than exactitude has directed the delineation of the ground. Some day when the official history of the war is produced it will be possible for the first time in history to illustrate each stage of hostilities by actual photographs taken during the conflict.

ARTILLERY OBSERVATION.

When first it was decided to employ aircraft to "spot" for the guns, the gunner officer was a little sceptical as to the value of aerial observation. Such ideas looked very well on paper, but would they work out equally well in practice? And he was not greatly encouraged by the first experiences of "spotting" during the war. Inexperience coupled with the inefficiency of the aeroplanes in use, made the first observations a little erratic and disconnected. Wireless was not available and the then prevailing method of using Véry light signals was cumbrous and slow. To-day all has changed. Wireless equipment is fitted in all "spotting" aircraft and is dependable and rapid in action. Observers understand their work and are in close liaison with the artillery at all times. No gunner to-day would dream of setting to work without the aid of aircraft when aircraft is available.

The introduction of the wireless telephone is another improvement which increases the speed and accuracy of "spotting." It will be possible for artillery brigade, group or battery to communicate direct in open speech with the observers "spotting" for them. There is less chance of error in the conveyance of messages and targets can be changed at will either from the ground or from the air without the delay consequent even in the use of the wireless telegraph. It must be remembered that in the case of the wireless telegraph it was not the custom to fit receiving apparatus in the machines, consequently replies or requests from the ground had of necessity to be sent visually. In any case speech is simpler to the ordinary man than is the Morse Code.

AERIAL FIGHTING.

The production of aeroplanes definitely designed for aerial fighting proceeded with vigour up to the end of the war both in the British and the German armies. Others of the allies on both sides paid attention to this matter but the results were not striking. None compared favourably in all round fighting efficiency with those produced in Germany and England. In the air as on the land

A Patrol of Bristol Fighters Starting in Formation.

Part of a Squadron of Reconnaissance Machines in Formation.

and sea the two great antagonists in the war developed their material of war on similar lines and with almost equal success.

It is a matter of high interest to follow throughout the war the progress of aerial fighting from the days when contests were few and were almost in every case accidental to the last phase when it had become an exact science and was a deliberate and vital part of war. There is not space for any recapitulation of the stages of this progress and it has been done in various manners before but it cannot be stated too often how important in modern warfare is the employment of a strong aerial fighting arm. By degrees the aeroplane is becoming the eyes of an army in the fullest sense of the phrase. Cavalry is restricted in its speed of action and in the area over which it can operate. The tank and the armoured car also adversely affect the operations of the mounted arm. Hence the aeroplane alone can carry out with efficiency and speed the work of scouting. The new principle is accepted and the greatest reliance is placed in the reconnaissance work of the Royal Air Force.

Should aerial reconnaissance fail from any cause there is nothing to replace it with adequacy and the army whose aerial arm has even temporarily been defeated is almost completely blinded. The transition from a great volume of intelligence to an entire lack of information is paralysing in its effect. A force operating entirely in the dark would be less liable to disaster—though victory would not be a common incident—than would a body of troops suddenly deprived of all information.

Thus the maintenance of a strong force of aeroplanes whose sole duty is that of fighting is essential in modern war. More and more will it be necessary to obtain an actual fighting supremacy in the air before the routine duties of the flying service can be carried out. At one time failure in the air was a drawback, an inconvenience which had to be compensated for in other ways, but to-day and in the future the success of a ground operation will depend largely on what happens in the air.

CONTOUR FIGHTING.

The use of aeroplanes in the attack on lines of communications troops, reserves and so on will grow until the tactical conditions of war have undergone fundamental variation. During the actions of the last two years of the war it was common practice for aircraft to be employed on contour fighting against infantry and other arms in the field but the lack of machines and more particularly of specially designed machines, prevented the growth of these tactics to a stage when they would influence the entire movements of an army.

An army strong in itself but harassed continually over all its area of operations by continual attack from low flying aircraft would be unable to carry any detailed plan into effect with that degree of certainty which is essential in manoeuvres on a large scale. The staffs of the army would be unable to work in peace unless buried well below the earth, communications would be constantly interrupted, movements in column would become well-nigh impossible and above all the fighting troops would never be permitted to rest.

Certain important nerve centres of an army could it is true be accommodated in dug-outs sufficiently deeply cut into the ground as

No. 23 Squadron R.F.C. (Spads) ready to start for the Somme Front on March 23rd, 1918.

A Captured German "Albatros" Single-seater Fighter.

5a

A 2

to give them comparative safety from aerial attack but it is manifestly impossible to bury an entire army and expect it still to spread terror upon the earth. The obtaining of security by measures of passive defence is clearly limited.

Hence other measures must be taken to prevent ground forces being reduced to impotence by the somewhat impertinent attentions of hostile pilots. There is always a solution to every problem. When the steam engine was first adopted as a means of propulsion in ships there were those who foretold the entire destruction of somebody's navy because of the superior mobility inherent in steam-ships. And destruction would certainly have fallen on any navy which cared to rely entirely on sail power when attacked by ships which owed their ability to manœuvre to Mr. Watt's curious interest in the eccentricities of a tea kettle. The answer in that case was to adopt similar measures to those of the enemy. And it is invariably so in war. The tank will be countered by the tank as the rifle was met by the rifle. So too must the contour fighting aeroplane be met in its own element by weapons of its own class.

Anti-aircraft guns and machine guns specially equipped for the purpose cannot be an entire answer or even an adequate answer. They are not ubiquitous nor is it possible to supply sufficient of them with the necessary personnel to cover all sections of the territory occupied by troops. Therefore it is essential to defend by means of a vigorous aerial offensive. Both sides endeavouring to attain the same ends by the same means will deflect the contour fighting aeroplane from its specified duties to an aerial battle in self defence. Engagements will take place at all levels and in all places.

FUTURE DEVELOPMENTS.

A definite system of strategy and tactics is growing imperceptibly. The time is rapidly approaching when it will be no longer possible for the aerial arm of an army to carry out a series of sporadic raids unrelated to each other in general principles. Every move of aircraft units will be in accordance with the plan and the ultimate purpose will be kept always in sight.

It is a little difficult at this moment to foretell the influence of aircraft on the form of future war. There are some who think that trench warfare will remain the constant habit in great conflicts owing to the necessity of providing adequate cover for vital sections of an army. Trenches are a necessary protection in ground warfare and they are still more necessary when a large proportion of the attack comes from the air. The greatest protection for the greatest numbers is quite a possible theory in the future. There are many attractions in immobile warfare. The preparation of operation orders is simplified, the element of surprise is reduced and the maintenance of communications is not difficult. There is less necessity for quick decision and enemy attacks can more easily be countered in a short space of time.

But trench warfare implies defensive warfare. The duration of hostilities is prolonged and the final victory is rarely decisive. Attrition and weariness determine the period and success is not entirely due to the sword. Victory, if conclusive, should be decided in the field and in action. Its after effects are then healthier and

less provocative of future trouble. The starving of a nation rouses the worst spirit of revenge, and sooner or later the world is again bathed in blood because the sword failed in its duty.

Trench warfare simplifies the duties of the aerial arm. There is little difficulty in conducting orderly operations over an extended fortified line. Each change is recorded from day to day and all positions are registered. The daily work proceeds almost as a matter of routine. There is little opportunity for the unexpected

without which life lacks its chief charm. Aerodromes can be maintained in reasonable security and in a degree of comfort which cannot fail to react favourably in the efficiency of pilots and observers. Aeroplanes worked under these conditions can be kept in a constant state of fitness for service. To the aerial arm there are distinct attractions in trench warfare.

It is because of this simplification of the work of aircraft that we imagine future wars will not be immobile in nature and that siege

A Formation of Fokker Biplanes, of the late 1918 period.

6a

warfare will become exceptional. The old days of open contest will return and generalship will once again hold the field. In a war of manœuvre the work of the aeroplane, as shown in Mesopotamia, Palestine and Egypt, will be of the highest importance and will in the hands of an efficient general be a weapon of vast possibilities. But with an increase in the importance of its duties, the aerial arm will meet with far greater difficulties than have been common in the present war. The advanced squadrons must be highly mobile and the quantity of stores carried will of necessity be small. No lengthy

A German Junker-Fokker "Contour-Fighter" or "Ground-Strafer" loading up with food and ammunition for conveyance to German troops in trenches which were cut off from other communication.

Bourlon Wood and the open country to the South of the Bapaume-Cambrai Road, showing the trench lines.

tenure of any aerodrome can be guaranteed and change of position will be constant. Conditions will arise which have not been common in the past.

Strategical reconnaissance will become of first and immediate importance. Information as to enemy movements must then be instantly forthcoming and of high accuracy. One's own movements must be screened by offensive action or by a feint which will draw enemy squadrons over many objectives. Bombing will be arranged as counter measures to enemy tactics with exclusive attention to such moves as are read to be essential parts of a coming attack in the culmination of strategical dispositions which are in successful progress.

In a war of movement, aircraft, even in the vast numbers certain to be employed in future wars, will have no easy task and that reason is one of those which, it seems, may sound the knell of trench warfare.

THE INDEPENDENT FORCE R.A.F.

During 1918, the Independent Force R.A.F., operating in accordance with the plans of the Supreme Command, but a separate entity of the British Armies in the Field, came into its own. Day by day, night by night, in fine or even in stormy weather, the large bombing aeroplanes of this force flew far beyond the enemy lines and past the frontiers into Germany bombing with discrimination, munition areas, rail-heads and dumps, until life in the back areas was deprived entirely of happiness. Many tons of bombs were dropped with startling frequency on such places as the railway triangle at Metz-Sablon and in towns as far removed from apparent danger as Karlsruhe and Cologne.

The moral of the German people was disturbed by this incessant and successful bombardment and the depression and dismay reacted unfavourably on the fighting troops with results which undoubtedly helped in the final collapse of the German arms.

Berlin would have been bombed before the year was out had it not been for hostilities ending with depressing suddenness. Many machines were completed and waiting opportunity, all of which could have reached the enemy capital with comparative ease.

In the previous year and in the first few months of 1918 German bombing squadrons had operated with a high degree of success against the Allies' back areas, attacking dumps, towns, junctions, army and corps' headquarters with equal impartiality. The menace at one time became serious and the damage done was seriously affecting the course of the war.

Night flying units were sent from England to join in the defence, the anti aircraft organisation overseas was improved and was equipped with unwonted liberality, and the advanced fighting squadrons made special preparations to carry the offensive into enemy territory. The new measures were successful and by the summer of 1918 enemy back-area bombing by night had dropped from intensity to a desultory series of rather aimless raids.

A Scene at an Aircraft Depot in France, at which damaged aeroplanes were rebuilt and re-issued to the Mobile Supply Parks nearer the Front Line.

KITE BALLOONS.

A high standard of efficiency in the employment of observation balloons on land had been attained at an earlier stage in the war and few improvements save in detail equipment were made in the last year of hostilities. The use of balloons was understood and their value appreciated in a proper degree. During the final retreat of the Germans on the Western Front many balloon companies achieved fame by the manner in which, undeterred by the heavy risks, they carried their balloons so far forward that they were within reach of enemy rifle fire. The value of the work done during those last days cannot be over estimated and the balloon *personnel* have aided ably in the creation of tradition in the newest of the King's Services. There was at one time a feeling among pilots that the balloon sections were a suitable home for enervated warriors unwilling to face the greater risks of war. The casualty list has supplied an adequate answer and all who know will regard those who have chosen the balloon service as their path in war with the respect due to those who have fought bravely and well.

The use of observation balloons as a part of the balloon apron system is dealt with later in this paper.

The enemy have not neglected balloons in their scheme of war. In fact at one time they made use of an infinitely greater number of observation balloons than did the allies. The duties in both cases were similar. primarily in artillery observations, secondarily in watching and reporting on movements of their own infantry. These balloons were well protected by anti-aircraft guns both small and large, and the work of destroying them was not simple.

ANTI-AIRCRAFT DEFENCES AT HOME AND ABROAD.

At the beginning of the war anti-aircraft defences did not exist in this country and were particularly inadequate in other countries. Firstly there had been no experience on which to base the necessary organisation, and secondarily the necessity of putting all available material into the field prevented the allocation of guns, searchlights and aeroplanes to what then seemed a somewhat problematical duty.

The Zeppelin airship was the only aerial menace to English territory in 1914 and it does not seem to have been considered a formidable enemy in those days. We were all so deeply convinced that the aeroplane was the master of the airship in every way that the possibilities of aerial attack by airship were largely discounted.

With 1915 came a series of Zeppelin attacks growing steadily in intensity as the enemy began to realize not only the inadequacy but the non-existence in any practical sense of anti-aircraft defences in this country. A few isolated guns of small calibre on improvised mountings permitting of high elevation do not and cannot constitute a defence.

In view of the shortage of military *personnel* the Admiralty undertook the aerial defence of London and the Home Counties. Admiral Sir Percy Scott, K.C.B., who had been interested in gunnery, was posted in command. Little however was done to prevent enemy air raids, largely owing to the shortage of material, and in 1916 the War

The Italian Avorio-Prassone Kite-Balloon, the most efficient kite-balloon of the war. Introduced into the British Services for Balloon-Apron Work.

Office took over responsibility for what was in truth a military matter. Squadrons of night flying aeroplanes were at once organised and vulnerable points were protected in some degree by guns and searchlights. In the autumn of that year success was achieved against raiding Zeppelins by aeroplanes and the airship menace ceased for a space. The credit of the organisation which they formed under almost incredible conditions of difficulty, yet supplied the answer to the airship attack, was due to General Headquarters, Home Forces in general and in particular to the Anti-Aircraft Branch of that Headquarters.

In 1917, as was foreseen, attack by aeroplane became common. First in broad daylight, later by night German aeroplanes made a series of air raids over the Home Counties inflicting heavy damage at but little cost in machines or *personnel*. It was considered necessary to form a separate command responsible directly to General Head-quarters Home Forces in order to co-ordinate and direct the anti-aircraft defences of London and the South of England. Guns, searchlights and aeroplanes were supplied with a generosity unknown in the earlier stages of hostilities. Guns were disposed in accordance with considered tactical plans and the system of specifically defending vulnerable points was relinquished in favour of a general scheme. Searchlights, highly important in anti-aircraft defences, were sited with the guns and in positions in which they could co-operate effectively with aeroplanes. Night flying aeroplane squadrons were based in areas over which they could patrol without being in danger of injury from the defending shell fire. Each part of the defences was arranged in such manner as to co-operate most easily with other parts of the command. Elaborate communications were established and the system of control was unified while entire discretion was left to subordinate commanders as to action in cases of emergency.

A new form of defence was also devised and produced. The balloon apron which mystified so deeply such of the public as had heard rumours of its existence came to take its effective part in the defences. After rapid experiments, the balloon apron was brought to a stage of usefulness which, if immature, had its very real value in war. The final scheme was that three balloons of the latest type, without car and of any desired dimensions, were placed equidistantly over a space of 1,000 yards. These balloons were connected by a cable to which depended a series of streamers 1,000 feet long. The apron thus constructed was elevated to such a height that aeroplanes flying in its vicinity had perforce to fly at their extreme altitude in order to avoid the risk of entanglement.

The aprons were disposed on sites distributed in vital parts of the London Air Defence Area and all intelligence indicates that their moral effect was considerable among enemy pilots. There are few who fly and would care to travel through a sky dotted with obstructions of this nature. No aeroplanes capable of carrying an effective supply of bombs could fly at a height at which they were immune from risk in regard to balloon aprons. It is always natural to exaggerate the dangers of the entirely unknown and it is possible that raiding pilots had greater fear of balloon aprons than of high explosive shell or aeroplane attack.

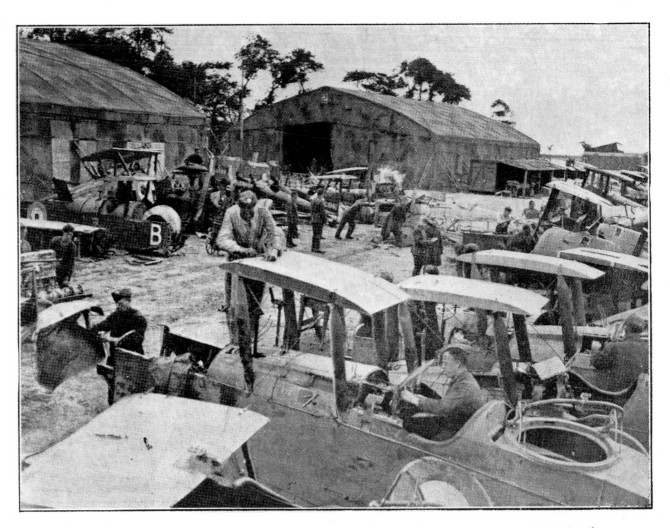

Another scene at an Aircraft Depot in France, showing Reconnaissance Machines in process of reconstruction.

It is known that enemy aircraft were damaged by these aprons and it is possible that one machine was destroyed through collision with a cable though the final blow was dealt by a defending aeroplane. The aprons covered but a small area in a vast sky and it would be absurd to expect any high rate of positive destruction. Moral effect is in itself a vital asset in war and that the enemy, brave though he undoubtedly was, had no pleasure in encountering aprons is a sufficient gain to the defences.

Incidentally the existence of balloon aprons in a thickly populated area for over eighteen months without the public knowing either their form or uses is proof of the standard of secrecy which can be maintained when necessary in His Majesty's Forces.

Other nations adopted or had adopted systems of balloon screens which were no very close relations to those used in London. Venice eager to preserve its historic beauty organised an aerial defence of high efficiency, a part of which was a screen of small balloons in single cables. These balloons were independent and were not connected by aprons. France had a somewhat similar system round various vulnerable points behind the lines.

Germany, never far behind in the great game of war, also protected in this manner many of the towns threatened by aerial attack but in these cases again the balloon apron was not put into use.

It is the fashion in some quarters to scoff at anti-aircraft gunners apparently because enemy aircraft are not destroyed by each round fired. It is a new science vastly different from gunnery in the horizontal plane. Questions of height finding and range finding complicate the issue in addition to a mass of technical troubles unsuitable for discussion in this paper. The four years of war have brought the science from birth to a high stage of efficiency and the public would be surprised, if surprise still exists in humanity, at the successes gained by anti-aircraft gunnery in the war.

The aeroplane is naturally the mainstay of any system of aerial defence. It alone can engage enemy aircraft in any part of the area defended and it alone can continue the fight until success or defeat

At an Aircraft Depot in France, showing air mechanics endeavouring to start a reconstructed engine in a repaired aeroplane.

The Bow of a German "Giant" Bombing Aeroplane, showing the two pilots, and the position of the Commanding Officer behind them.

ends the contest. At one time it was thought that flying and fighting by night would be highly expensive in *personnel* and machines. Yet in truth the casualties by night have been no greater than those by day. In home defence with many dozens of aeroplanes in the air during any night raid the total casualties in the five years of war can almost be counted on the fingers of the two hands. It was even rare for a machine to be damaged in landing even though emergency landings under conditions of great difficulty were by no means uncommon.

The searchlight, which though a thing of beauty to the public has attracted no great appreciation for its services, is the third essential part of anti-aircraft defences. Here, too, efficiency has greatly increased and the training has improved to such a degree that whereas at one time the illumination of every aeroplane from the ground was a matter of charming accident, to-day aircraft are located and passed from beam to beam with great frequency. Each succeeding year will raise the standard of success until it will be possible to locate and hold all "aircraft" passing over the illuminated areas.

The Engineers looking out of the forward engine-room window of German five-engined "Giant" aeroplane.

But to no branch of the service is all the credit due. The secret of success in anti-aircraft defence is co-operation. The aeroplane, the gun, the heightfinder, the balloon apron, the searchlight and the sound locator have each their respective places in the scheme, but all are inter-dependent. One helps the other and it is the entire united effort which leads on to victory.

Future wars may begin by aerial attack. Commercial aircraft can be converted to war machines in a few hours and consequently all an enemy country's aeroplanes are its potential fleet in War. A swift aerial blow well timed and well placed might cripple the attacked country before mobilisation was completed. The centres of government in a country are no more immune from attack than is the smallest and most remote village.

Hence the importance of fixed anti-aircraft defences will increase in the future and it will probably be necessary to retain a strong force under war conditions.

Anti-aircraft defence in the field has to face very different conditions. The constant change in position of an army in open warfare or even in trench warfare make it necessary for anti-aircraft defences to be highly mobile. The maintenance of communications is a primary difficulty. Efficient communications are naturally of the first importance as an aerial attack may be made at any time and in any place. The anti-aircraft guns in the forward area are subject to constant and often heavy shell fire. Thus frequent changes of position are necessary. Communications also are destroyed with disconcerting regularity. As an instance of the strenuous nature of the life, in one Army alone in France the casualties during one year to the *personnel* manning the anti-aircraft guns in the forward area amounted just to 100 per cent. of their establishment. The route of the attackers can be altered at will, a freedom of movement which is rare in land warfare. Secondly, in a constantly moving number of units it is difficult to keep to the necessary standard of co-operation which must be assured if the defence is to be effective. In attacks on countries such as England or Germany there are certain definite objectives on which the attackers must concentrate if any real damage is to be inflicted. Towns, harbours, dockyards, munition areas and railway junctions each has its attraction to the invading pilot. He has no desire to waste effort by bombing sparsely inhabited areas. The defences have therefore the advantage of knowing what they have to defend, and they know moreover the probable lines of approach of enemy attack.

In the field the position is more difficult. The entire back area of an army is crowded with *personnel*, material and transport. Countless roads and railways feed the front line. There is little that is not of importance and the possibilities of doing damage are limitless. Then to this the troops and guns in the line must be added and it will be seen that the attacking aircraft are rather in the advantage as to the power of inflicting injury on the attacked.

It is manifestly impossible to defend with equal strength the whole of the area now occupied by an army in the field—at least until the relative strength of anti-aircraft defence to other arms be adjusted in the light of future experience in air war. It therefore falls to the

Supreme Command in the Field so to lay out his defences as to protect definite zones over which defending aircraft will endeavour to drive the enemy if the attack is by night or by day.

NAVAL AERONAUTICS.

The aeroplane designed and produced for work over the sea has developed greatly during the past eighteen months until at the present time the seaplane and flying boat are not very far behind the land machine in efficiency. The flying boats of various sizes produced from designs drawn out at Felixstowe have been employed incessantly on patrols over the seas surrounding Great Britain with such success as greatly to reduce the risks to shipping from submarine attack.

The Germans did not devote much time to the development of flying boats but the seaplanes produced by the navy and certain firms which specialised in this work were very effective. In the early part of 1918 the Brandenburg seaplane, a monoplane of somewhat curious design, began to appear in quantities and waged very successful war against our shores and less handy flying boats. Day after day they with other classes of seaplanes crossed the British coast fighting and destroying all manner of aircraft which they were fortunate enough to encounter. They escorted torpedo carrying seaplanes whose efforts were directed entirely against shipping entering the Thames or the great ports on the East coast.

The Engine Arrangement of a five-engined German "Giant" aeroplane.

The answer to the Brandenburg type of machine was presumably found in the use of land machines flying from the decks of ships of war. The higher power of manœuvre inherent in land machines, owing to the lack of floats and the head resistance resulting therefrom and to the necessarily heavier construction of machines destined to alight in the sea, gives them the mastery over the seaplane in action.

It was also common practice for land machines to patrol long distances over the sea despite the high risks attendant on such procedure. The machines employed were not always the most satisfactory type and the patrolling squadrons have paid the price in casualties of their silent and unadvertised work.

During the year the Navy added to its lists two specially designed seaplane carriers, the "Furious" and the "Argus." Originally built as fast cruisers with a long range armament they were adapted shortly after launch to their new work. The upper deck in either case was free from encumbrances—in the "Argus" entirely so and in the "Furious" forward and aft the bridge and funnels. It was intended that aeroplanes should fly from the decks and after the flight alight again on the decks, the ship heading into the wind to simplify the task. In practice it would seem that most pilots preferred to alight in the sea alongside. The machine was then lifted on board and was re-fitted with wings and such other parts as were damaged by the sea water. Pilots are more expensive than aeroplanes and the cost of new wings, tailplanes, etc., is but little in the general expenditure of a great war.

As the high value of the aeroplane in naval warfare began to be understood it became the practice for the bigger ships of war each to carry one or two aeroplanes (not seaplanes). These were launched by the method indicated in the article on the R.A.F. A platform was laid down over two big guns and from this the aeroplane took to flight, the ship steaming into the wind to reduce the necessary run. The aeroplane on the completion of the reconnaissance either alighted in the sea or flew to the nearest land.

Other Navies, the French and the Italian, also employed seaplane carriers but in each case one understands that only flying boats and seaplanes were carried. The land aeroplane was not used. An illustration is given in the Italian section of an Italian seaplane ship with her cargo festooned round her sides.

The Germans apparently made no use of seaplane ships as far as one can gather, though individual ships of war carried aeroplanes on occasion. The Wolff, at one time an elusive terror of the seas, had one or two aeroplanes as part of her equipment though little is known as to when and where they were used. German naval effort except in regard to isolated raiders and to submarines was confined to the North Sea, consequently the airship served the purpose of reconnaissance better than would an aeroplane.

One of the London Balloon-Aprons.

13a

AIRCRAFT IN THE WAR.

THE AIRSHIP.

The airship improved steadily in so far as Germany is concerned until the armistice stopped all military effort. The principal use of the airship is undoubtedly for naval reconnaissance and for raiding by night. At one time the aeroplane provided a satisfactory answer to airship attack made under cover of darkness as the heights attained by airships were not great—13,000 to 14,000 feet. Towards the end of hostilities the Zeppelin was capable of reaching a height of 20,000 feet and could cruise at that height for lengthy periods. Hence the task of the defences both on the earth and in the air was greatly increased. It is conceivable that raiding under these conditions might have been profitable to the enemy. The attack now known as "The Silent Raid" was arranged in accordance with this principle of flight at extreme altitudes but it failed entirely as a result of the entirely unsuitable weather encountered when at a height of 20,000 feet over England.

Anti-aircraft defence would be quite capable of dealing with the new menace after the necessary modifications in materiel had been made. The chief drawback in home defence during a war in which aircraft were undergoing their first trial, lay in the fact that the best machines were required in the field until construction caught up to the demand.

The British while designing and constructing large rigid airships of the Zeppelin type were unable during the war to produce any which would have been of use in operations. Time sets a limit on all things and war invariably ends when equipment and organisation is about to attain perfection. England made great use of the non-rigid airship which had been developed in this country to a stage not yet attained elsewhere. The small "Blimps" and the larger S.S.'s and North Sea types each proved of high value in sea warfare, though their value in land operations was negligible. No German Submarine Commander had much liking for the airships which dogged his path through European waters.

KITE BALLOONS AT SEA.

The Kite balloon, at one time discredited because it was expected to carry out work for which it was not designed, found one of its

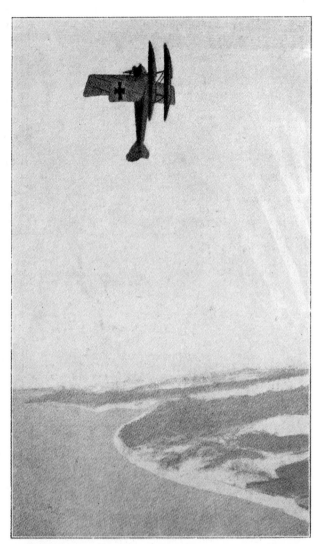

A Brandenburg Seaplane looping over the coast. Machines of this type for a time gave the Germans the Command of the Air over the North Sea.

H.M.S. Furious, Seaplane-Carrier, showing the long forward launching deck.

principal uses in one branch of sea warfare. Towed behind a ship of war it flew as a protective eye over the movements of the great convoys of ships which brought food and men to Europe.

At one time the shipping losses—especially in the Mediterranean which the gallant and resourceful Otto von Hersing had made his hunting ground—rose to a dangerous figure and every plan to reduce them failed or was only of moderate success. The kite balloon was then employed and with almost startling suddeness the losses decreased and convoy after convoy passed from port to port unscathed.

Improvements in design made it possible for these balloons to be drawn through the air at high speeds without resultant instability.

ARMAMENT AND ARMOUR IN AIRCRAFT.

The most common form of armament in British aircraft was a machine gun of the Lewis type, the design of which is peculiarly suitable for aerial work. These guns were mounted in various manners, some fixed rigidly along the fuselage in front of the pilot and firing between the propellor blades by means of special gearing. In this case the aeroplane itself was used in aiming at enemy targets. In the rear seat of two-seaters and in the bows of multiple engined machines and flying-boats the Scarff rotating mounting was used, the observer thus having a large arc of fire. There was in truth very little difference in the manner of mounting guns in any of the great armies.

The French made extensive use of the Hotchkiss automatic gun which, while not entirely satisfactory in land warfare, did excellent work in the air, and they also used with some success towards the the end of the war a " cannon " of 37 mm. bore, which fired through the airscrew-boss of a geared-down V-type engine.

The German aerial arm used in general either the Spandau or Parabellum machine guns, which resembled closely the Vickers and Lewis machine guns common in Allied armies. The larger German aircraft and contact patrol machines were fitted with a 22 mm. automatic gun firing an explosive or incendiary shell six inches in length. These shells were clipped into chargers holding twelve rounds, the charger sliding into the top of the breech. As in the case of the Vickers gun it is operated by recoil action. This gun which has shown its value during the closing operations of the war is about 3' 6" in length, and weighs complete with mounting and one charger, under 100 lbs.

There is evidence that a larger gun is employed in giant aeroplanes but few details have been permitted to leak out as to its form and capabilities.

As the size and reliability of aircraft increases there is little doubt that guns of considerably greater calibre will be fitted. The day is not far off when three inch and larger guns specially designed for the purpose will be mounted in aircraft and will be employed against other aircraft and against land defences. There is naturally no limit to the size of guns which it will be possible to carry at a future date.

As with armament so with armour. Tentative attempts were made in early machines to protect the pilot but the armour in such

H.M.S. Argus, a Seaplane-Carrier in which the funnels are led horizontally aft, thus giving a flush deck.

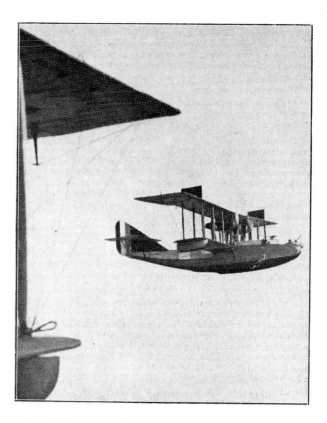

A British Flying Boat, of the F.2a. type made practicable by Lieut.-Col. John Porte, photographed from another boat.

cases rarely consisted of more than a steel seat-plate which did little more than retard the passage of the projectile without entirely stopping its progress save at extreme ranges and in the case of glancing shot. Machines in the beginning of the war were already sufficiently laden with all manners of instruments and gear without the additional weight even of a small steel plate.

Later, as the efficiency of aircraft increased, efforts were made by the Germans to put adequate armour on the aeroplanes set aside for contour fighting. Such armour was intended only to protect against rifle and machine gun fire and not in any way against anti-aircraft guns. There are no aeroplanes yet in existence capable of carrying armour of such thickness as would deflect or stop shells or large shell fragments.

In the British Forces a certain amount of armour was placed round the engine or engines in some machines, as it was held that the smallest fragment of a projectile often sufficed to put an engine out of action and it was known that many pilots paid special attention to inflicting injury on motors. The engine provides a bigger and not less vulnerable target than does the aviator.

Little detail is available to those not employed in the Air Ministry as to the manner in which armour was fitted, nor is it possible easily to find what grades or thickness of steel were employed.

The aeroplane of the future, large, swift and easy of manœuvre, will, when equipped for war, almost certainly be comparatively heavily armoured. Possibly, as in the case of the Navy, the newer theory will be that effective gun power and speed will more than counterbalance the risks attendant on light armouring. The contrary view that increased gun power should be met by increased armour protection may perhaps be held, but one thinks this to be unlikely.

THE END.

The war is over and the lethargy of peace is again with us for a space. The forced progress in aeronautics brought about by the demands of the fighting forces has ceased and the Industry is groping for direction into the necessities of civil aviation.

Little is known as to what can be done or what is required. The time is however comparatively distant when the design of the commercial aeroplane will be so individual in character as to make it of little use for warlike purposes. For years to come the large commercial aeroplane will be a potential bomb dropper possessed of wide range and a high ceiling. Even the fast sporting aeroplanes will not be without value as scouts or as fighting aircraft for the adventurous.

The future is hidden from our sight, but it is almost a platitude to say even at this date that aeronautics will bring about a fundamental change in the daily habits of our lives. We have seen what aircraft can do as a weapon of war while yet in an early stage of development. Can any doubt that the future possibilities of aeronautics in war and peace are so immense as to be beyond all human vision?

A British Fighting Pilot changing a double Lewis drum on the top gun of an S.E.5a.

ARGENTINE.

Aerial Journals :—

Boletin del Ae. C. Argentino, Avenida de Mayo, 646, Buenos Ayres. Monthly.

Aerial Societies :—

Aero Club Argentino, Avenida Alvear, 1325, Buenos Ayres.

MILITARY AVIATION.

The Argentine Government decided in 1912, in collaboration with the Aero Club, Argentino, to establish a military flying school and balloon school on a sound basis.

First of all, the military school at Palomar was established and several pilots were trained, the ground at Villa Lugano being used for balloons. It was hoped to have at the end of 1914 a perfectly organised military aviation service.

The Military Aerodrome of El Palomar is equipped with half-a-dozen *Henry Farman* 50 h.p. Gnôme biplanes, for primary training, and about a dozen Blériot and Morane-Saulnier type 80 h.p. Gnôme monoplanes, for advanced training.

Most of these machines were built at the carpentry attached to the aerodrome, only the motors being imported from Europe.

The aerodrome is under the command of Commandante Alejandro Obligado.

The carpentry and repair works are in charge of Sr. Edmundo Lucius.

Fifty-three aero-engines were available on Jan 1st, 1918, in the Argentine.

BEST ARGENTINE FLIGHTS IN 1918.

13th of April : Crossing of the Cordillera de Los Andes by Teniente Luis C. Candelaria, piloting a Morane-Saulnier Parasol of 80 H.P. from Zapala (R. Argentina) to Cunco (Rio de Chile). Distance, 200 km. Maximum height, 4000 metres.

23rd of May : Flight from El Palomar (Province of Santiago del Estero) to Tucumán on a Voisin, Salmson engine, 140 h.p. Pilot Teniente Benjamín Matienzo ; passenger, Edmundo Lucius. Distance, Palomar to Tucumán and back, total 1400 km. Total time, 12 hours. Mean height, 900 metres.

ARGENTINE FLYING SCHOOLS.

El Palomar. Escuola Militar de Aviadión. Director Tet. Coronel Uriburu, actualmente Teniente Coronel Alejandro Obligado.

San Fernando : Civilian School Director-Founder, Aviador Marcel Paillete and Aviador Teodoro Fels.

Villa Lugano : Civilian School Director-Founder, Aviador Pablo Castaibert.

Quilmes : Civilian School Director-Founder, Aviador Edmundo Marechal.

José C. Paz : Civilian School Director-Founder, Aviador Luis A. Pardo.

Longchamps : Civilian School Director-Founder, Aviador

ARGENTINE MILITARY AVIATION,

The following have passed through the Military School :—

First Course, begun Nov. 4, 1912 :

Teniente de Navio Melchor Escola, Capitán Raúl E. Goubat, Capitán Anibal Brihuega, Teniente Pedro Zanni, Teniente Baldomero Biedma, Teniente Saturno Perez Ferreyra, Teniente Carlos

The Military School at El Palomar in 1918.

Officers of the Argentine Air Service—Capitan Anibas Briuhega, Tte. Leopoldo Casavega, Cap. Raul E. Goubat, Tte. Baldomoro Biedma, Tte. Pedro Zanni, Tte. S. Ferreyra.

17a

ARGENTINE AVIATION.

Gimenez Kramer, Teniente Leopoldo Casavega, Teniente Carlos Ferreyra, Sargento 1° Francisco Sanchez.

Teniente 1° Alfredo Agneta (killed 18 of October, 1914, in an accident in a Nieuport 100 H.P.)

Sub-Teniente Manuel Origone (killed 19 of January, 1913, in an accident on a Blériot 50 H.P. during a flight to Mar del Plata.)

Second Course, begun in August, 1913 :

Capitán Juan M. Pueta, Teniente 1° Elisendo Pissano, Teniente 1° Edgardo Benavente, Teniente 1° Enrique Padilla, Teniente 1° José E. Campos, Teniente 1° Agustin Varona.

Third Course, begun in June, 1914 :

Capitán Angel Zuloaga, Teniente 1° Alberto Gonzales Albarracín, Teniente 1° Antonio Parodi, Teniente 1° Atilio Cataneo, Teniente 1° Mario Godoy, Teniente 1° Julio García Fernandez.

Sargento 1° Ramón Alderete, Sargento 1° Segundo Gomez.

Cabo 1° Abraham Jalil (killed on 27th of November, 1914. Killed while practising on a Farman.)

Fourth Course, begun in August of 1915.

Teniente 1° (Oriental) Cesareo Berisso, Alferez Esteban Cristi.

Sub-Teniente (Reserva) Martín Pico, Sub-Teniente (Reserva) Edmundo Lucius, Sub-Teniente (Reserva) Alfredo Sosa, Sub-Teniente (Reserva) Enrique Molina, Sub-Teniente (Reserva) Enrique Torres.

Fifth Course, begun in September of 1916.

Capitán (Bolivian) José Alarcón (killed on 23rd of January, 1917, while flying for his certificate on a Farman). Capitán (Bolivian) René Parejas, Teniente (Bolivian) Horacio Vasquez, Teniente (Peruvian) Enrique Ruiz (killed on 13th of March, at Mercedes, while flying over the triangular Military Course in a Blériot 50 H.P. No. III), Teniente (Peruvian) Guillermo Protzel, Guardia Marina (Peruvian) Ismael Montoya, Guardia Marina (Peruvian) Roberto Velazco, Teniente 1° (Argentine) Jorge Manni, Teniente José Rosasco, Teniente Martín Salinas Gomez, Teniente Luis Candelaria, Teniente Benjamín Matienzo, Teniente Valentin Campero, Teniente Argilioo T. Vadela Orito, Teniente Victoriano Martinez de Alegria, Teniente Adolfo C. Udry, Teniente Otón Mantovani, Teniente Florencio D. Parravicini.

Also the following N.C.O.'s :

Sargento 1° Dante Ferrari, Sargento Pedro Mendez, Sargento Próspero Sianja, Sargento Liborio Fernandez, Sargento José A. Sábatto, Sargento Luis T. Romero, Cabo 1° Juan C. Goggi, Cabo 1° Pedro Oyarzabal, Sargento 1° Luis Barruffaldi, Sargento Angel C. Albornóz (killed on 26th of December, 1917, while training on a 50 h.p. Blériot).

NAVAL AVIATORS,

Teniente de Navio Melchor Z. Escola : Passed tests 23rd of October, 1912.

Condestable Joaquín Oytabén : Began training on 2nd of September, 1915. Died at Berisso on 16th of October, 1915.

Teniente de Navío Ricardo Fitz Simón ⎫ Joined the U.S.A.
Alferez de Navío Geferino Ponchán ⎬ School at Pensacola,
Alferez de Navío Marcos Zar ⎭ on 19th of Sept., 1917.

Teniente de Navío Raúl M. Moreno : Joined the Naval School at La Plata, on 29th of January, 1918.

Mecánice Electricista Principal José A. Pennaecki : Joined the Naval School at La Plata on the 5th of February, 1918.

PILOTS UP TO 1914—Private Aviators.

J. M. P. Arseno, (killed), J. A. Both, A. de Bruyn, G. E. C. England, L. Eusebione (killed), T. Fels (killed), C. A. Goffre, C. Foel, A. R. Madcias, J. Newberry (killed), F. Parravicini, Dr. J. A. Roth.

Officer Pilots of the Argentine Air Service.

Argentine N.C.O. Pilots—Sargente I° D. Ferrari, Sargente Pedro Oyargatal, Sargente I° J. Sabathe, Sargente I° Fernandez, Sargente Luis T. Romere, Sargente I° L. Baruffaldi, Sargente I° Pedro Mondez, Sargente I° P. Seaya, Sargente Juan C. Coggi.

AUSTRO-HUNGARIAN.

The Empire of Austria-Hungary having been broken up into various ungoverned sections, there is now no Air Service or Aircraft Industry to be described.
The following matter brings the record of Austro-Hungarian aircraft up to the end of the War.

MILITARY AVIATION : GENERAL.

In June, 1912, a central aeronautical committee was created, under the presidency of Prince Fürstenberg, to deal with the creation of a national aerial fleet. One of the objects was the perfection of the Austrian machines and factories.

In July, 1913, it was proposed to acquire six *Zeppelins*, to be stationed respectively at Vienna, Budapest, Innsbruck, Prag, Lemberg and Sarajewo.

In February, 1914, the military aviation corps was reorganised and formed into a battalion of four companies stationed at Vienna, Cracow, Sarajewo and Goerz.

In March, 1914, a prize of 12,000 kroner was offered by the Minister of War as follows :—Armed two-seater, gun to have arc of fire 120 degrees, 30 degrees elevation and 60 degrees depression. Useful load 1764 lbs. (800 ks.). Minimum climb 6,500 ft. (2,000 m.) in 45 minutes from times of starting, to alight in ploughed field.

A prize of 13,000 kroner for the machine with the best speed variation.

In June, 1914, the airship *Korting* (*M 3*) was wrecked by collision with an aeroplane. All were killed in both.

ARMY SECTION.

At end of July, 1914, there were :—

60 monoplanes.—*Etrich-Taube, Albatros, Lohner-Daimler.*

50 biplanes.—*Lohner-Daimler* and *Albatros.*

The majority of the aeroplanes used by the Austrians on active service have been of German make, or have been made by Austrian branches of the big German firms, and have frequently had German pilots.

NAVAL SECTION.

A large number of seaplanes were in use. Most of them are of German make, and others built by the Lohner Aircraft Works of Vienna, or by Austrian branches of German firms.

The Austrian naval pilots have done much consistently good flying, from the purely naval point of view.

THE AUSTRO-HUNGARIAN AIRCRAFT INDUSTRY.
(BY A FOREIGN CORRESPONDENT.)

The German journal " Motor " contained recently a report on the Austrian-Hungarian aircraft trade during the War, as rendered below, leaving an impression of the retardment of aeroplane developments in that country too from official Government efforts of pushing their own products, inferior to private results, and showing further that Austria differed in one respect from most other countries, and thus in being not held up in output for lack of aero-engines, but rather from the insufficient number of works turning out planes.

When war started, Austria-Hungary was the least prepared aeronautically of all the big powers, lacking financial support going no further than for a few Etrich " Taube " monoplanes and Lohner " Arrow " biplanes of national manufacture, besides

a few German-made aeroplanes. Only the Lohner Body Works and the Albatros and Aviatik branches built aircraft in quantity, and not till during the War the Ufag (Ungarische Flugzeugwerke A. G.) in Assod and the Lloyd Works in Hungary were formed, the former building *Lohner* biplanes under license, the latter the *D.F.W.* type.

So the army authorities required German support highly, a large number of *Albatros, Rumpler* (*RuC1*), *D.F.W.* (*Mars*) and *Aviatik* biplanes being supplied, while the home-produced aero-motors, Austro-Daimler and Hiero (by the Ersler, Warschalowski Co.) proved efficient.

The C.O. of the airship department, Colonel Uzelac, had few officer pilots, engaged some German civil aviators, as Kriger (Bill) and conscripted some in the service of German firms, like the Fokker pilot Franz Kuntner and the L.V.G. one, Alois Stiplocheck.

The Russian opponent air service was, however, not too effective for a start, and so the home industry, which proved a necessity, found time to develop. The Lloyd works brought out types of their own, and the Albatros establishment went especially ahead, managed by the former chief engineer, Gabriel, of the Johannisthal plant, thanks to good workmanship.

Large contracts were executed too by Fokker, and thus twelve flight companies had been established when Italy entered the War. The fighting troops were separated from the home, being centralized as a " Flight Arsenal " under the command of Major Leidl.

The Aspern aerodrome, by Vienna, was the chief acceptance point, further ones being erected later at Vienna Neustadt and Budapest.

To introduce new types, the *Brandenburg* biplane was ordered, Commerce Councellor Camillo Castiglione forming a combine of the Hansa, Brandenburg, Vienna Albatros and Ufag companies, being all turned to the production of Brandenburg aircraft.

The large Skoda works (known for their 305 mm. howitzers) financed the " Oeffag " works in Vienna Neustadt (Oesterreichische Flugzeugfabrik A. G.) which produced a type of their own, as did now the Lloyd works, theirs being also manufactured by Dr. Guttmann's W.F.K. works (Wiener Karosseric Fabrik) changing from body to aeroplane work.

All before-mentioned types did well on active service, which cannot, however, be said of the aircraft designed by Professor Knoller, which was pushed by the Government Factory, and which the Aviatik, Lohner, W.F.K. and Thone & Fiala (a former engineering works), were forced to build against their will. The result was that large sums were expended and several good pilots killed in test flights before the *Knoller* aeroplanes were sent unflown to eternal sleep in the stores.

So far, all aeroplanes had been two-seaters, with the exception of a few *Fokkers*. The Ufag made twin-engined aircraft to Brandenburg pattern and proved a failure, as did a giant aircraft to the design of Professor Dr. Richard von Mieses, of which much was expected, and only cost lots of money.

But the period of aerial engagements came, and the *Brandenburg K. D.* single-seater proved to some extent a success, but was superseded by the *DIII*, borrowed from the German Albatros Company, and built in hundreds for active service by the Oeffag.

Next the Hungarian General Engine Works " Mag " (Allgemeine Maschinen Fabrik), in Budapest, acquired the licence for building *Fokkers*, and not till 1917 did a pure Austrian product put up a good performance, this being the biplane scout of Engineer Berg, at the Vienna Aviatik works, of a speed of 190-200 kilometres per hour and climbing to 3,000 feet in 2¼ minutes, with a 185 h.p. Daimler motor. So the " Berger " commenced, the type being ordered from almost every Austrian and Hungarian aircraft works.

A good single-seater was turned out, too, by the Phönix works, being the new manufacturing establishment of the Austrian Albatros Company, remaining a plant for turning out experimental craft.

During the last part of the War, big aeroplane orders were again given to Germany, more than 100 twin-engined *Gothas* (*GIV*) being ordered from the L.V.G. firm, and some experimental aeroplanes from Rumpler, Pfalz and Fokker.

The Oeffag acquired the rights for the twin-engined *Friedrichshafen*, but Austria broke down so quickly that only some *Gothas* saw active service.

The War did not help the Austro-Hungarian aircraft works to a strong financial position, as neither of the active C. O. of the " Flight Arsenal," Major von Petroczu, nor his successor, Colonel von Prochaska, succeeded in speeding office matters. Thus the works had to wait for months, or even years, to have their accounts paid, the lack of raw materials was in a hopeless position, the lack of skilled workmen felt still more hardly, and private activities were hampered by petty official inspection.

When the War ended, the Government refused to take over half-finished products, or materials only employable in aeroplane construction, in spite of all agreements. The Austrian does not pay any accounts later than August, the works having thus perforce to reduce their staffs, Phönix, for instance, from 1,700 to 100 workmen, while the Hungarian Government continued to pay, but then did not allow any dismissals, the result being only that the men did no work for high wages.

Finally, the Government " Aeraric " aircraft works should be referred to, a giant plant, formed in Fischamend under military control, two more in Aspern and Szeged.

Later, so-called " flight parks " in Vienna Neustadt and Graz-Thalerhof, showing an output of Lohner and Brandenburg biplanes that would have ruined any private enterprize. These establishments were to supply cheap school machines for the training, being exclusively carried out military in 22 " Ersatz " reserve companies, but in fact hampered the school service, being unable to cope with the breakages, and three private-produced aeroplanes could have been made at the cost of one Government aircraft.

A.M.A. Allgemeine Maschinen Aktien Gesellschaft Aircraft department in Budapest, Vaczi-ut 141/43.

LLOYD Aircraft Co., Ltd., Budapest.

Managed by the well-known military pilot Oberlieut. Bier, former director of Deutsche Flugzeug Werke in Liepzig, and building as branch " D.F.W's " under license.

The altitude record with three passengers stands to the credit of Oberlieut. Bier on a *Lloyd* biplane since the Vienna 1914 Meeting.

LOHNER, Jacob & Sons, Aircraft and Body Builders, Vienna.

Creator of the tractor *Arrow* biplane, generally adopted by Germany. Since the Etrich Dove Manufacturing Company is defunct, the only producer of an original Austrian model and chief supplier of the Army with a pre-war yearly output of 100-150 machines.

Piloted by Oberlieut Blaschke, the *Lohner* biplane won second place in the Berlin-Vienna race, 1911, and all later national competitions up to the Schicht circuit, 1914, as well as leading place in the various Vienna meetings.

Features : One single cock-pit for pilot and passenger, the latter sitting behind ; a special tube landing chassis and streamlined front body part and propeller cap, adopted too in the later *Etrich* " Tauben."

Numerous "flying boats" of the types shown herewith have been built by the Lohner firm during the war, and are said to have a very good performance.

THE LOHNER FLYING-BOAT—1917-18.

This is an enlarged machine of the *Lohner* type, retaining the swept back wings, which are typical of the *Lohner* aeroplanes.

There are six steel struts on either side and, two by two, are connected in transverse planes with steel tubes of 40 mm. outside diameter. The distance between two struts in the direction of the brace is 1.30 m., and in the direction of the spar 2.17 m.

General Dimensions.

Span : Upper Plane, 9.70 m.
Span : Lower Plane, 7.20 m.
Chord : Upper Plane, 2.70 m.
Chord : Lower Plane, 2.20 m.
Hull : Maximum Length, 12.50 m.
Bomb Carrying Capacity : 400 kg.
Motor : Austro-Daimler, 300 h.p.

In form the ailerons are trapezoidal. Length of ailerons, 3.47 m. ; mean width, 0.90 m.

A 1915-16 Lloyd Two-Seater Biplane.

A Lohner Single-Bay Flying Boat.

M.L.F. Motorluftfahrzeug Gesellschaft, Vienna. Oldest Austrian aircraft works, having built *Etrich* dove monoplanes and *Lohner* arrow biplanes, now manufacturing only the latter.

Ö-ALBATROS. Oesterreichische-Ungarische Albatros Flugzeug Werke G.m.b.H., Vienna, XXI Stadlar.

Owned by the former Ober-engineer Gabriel of the Berlin *Albatros* firm. Remained during the war as an experimental plant, with the allied Phönix firm as the production plant.

Ö-AVIATIK. Oesterreichische-Ungarische Flugzeug-fabrik Aviatik, G.m.b.H., Vienna.

Branch of the German firm. Towards the end of the war produced the famous Berg scout to the Oesterreichische Flug-zeugfabrik, A.G., Wiener-Neustadt (known as the *Oeffag*). Founded during the war and financed by the Skoda Works.

OESTERREICHISCHE FLUGZEUG-FABRIK, A.G. Vienna-Neustadt.

Known as the *Oeffag.* Financed by the Skoda Works.

PHÖNIX AEROPLANE WORKS.

Vienna XXI–Stadlau.

Formed during the war by the engineer Gabriel, formerly of the Berlin Albatros Company, who upon the outbreak of hostilities transferred his activities to his native country, starting the Austrian Albatros works and now running the two concerns so that the Phönix firm undertakes the quantity production, while the Ö-Albatros carries out the experimental work.

A Brandenburg Two-Seater Biplane, built by the " Oeffag " in 1916.

The first Austrian war-product Scout—The Brandenburg K Model and K.B. built by the Phönix Co.

A Phönix 1918 type Single-seater. A Phönix Two-seater is seen in the background.

A Phönix Two-seater " C " Class Biplane. (230 h.p. Hiero Engine.)   A4

The " Star-Strutter " Brandenburg Scout, built by the Phönix Works.

PHÖNIX—*continued.*

General Arrangement Drawings of the 1918 Model Phönix Biplane.

THÖNE & FIALA. Aircraft Engineers, Vienna.

UNGARISCHE FLUGZEUGWERKE, A.G.
Budapest. Albertfalva. (Known as the *Ufag*). Formed during the war by Baron von Skoda, the owner of the Skoda Gun Works, in connection with Hungarian Banks, with a capital of 600,000 kroner.
Built Lohners under license.

UNGARISCHE MASCHINENFABRIK GESELLSCHAFT. Hungarian General Engine Works, Budapest-Mátyásföld.

Manufacturing *Fokker* aircraft and aero engines. Capital raised from 3–5 million kroner.

W.F.K. (Wiener Karroserie Fabrik.) Vienna Body and Aeroplane Works of Dr. W. Gutmann.
Licencees of Lloyd aeroplanes as sub-contractors.

A. WEISER & SON, Ltd., Vienna XIX.
Manufacturers of Aviatik aircraft as sub-contractors.

BELGIAN.

Flying Grounds :—(All were in possession of the German Army, but are now reinstated as Belgian aerodromes.)

Berchem—St. Agathe.

Brasschaet (Military).

Camp de Casteau.

Etterbeek, near Brussels.

Kiewit.

St. Job (formerly private property of Baron de Caters).

Tenplaux (Military).

MILITARY AEROPLANES.

At the outbreak of war, the military air force consisted of twenty-four 80 h.p. Gnôme *H. Farman,* also various old school machines.

The military school was at Brasschaet, near Antwerp.

The course was as follows :

1.—*Theoretical Course.*—Lectures on meteorology, structure of aeroplanes, aviation motors, etc.

2.—*Practical.*—This, in addition to flight, consists of dismounting and replacing parts of aeroplanes and aerial motors, all general repairs, erecting hangars and aerial photography.

The school possessed nine hangars, of which three were Bessonneau type, three wooden, and three metal.

For 1913, the sum of £20,000 was expended for purchase of aeroplanes and the establishment of aerial squadrons at Antwerp, Liege, and Brasschaet.

These were organised into six squadrons of four units each. The full complement of each squadron is eight aviators, fifteen to twenty mechanics, etc., and six citizen soldiers.

A small but fairly efficient force had been created. It was almost extinguished. Later on new Belgian pilots were trained in France and England, and were equipped with French machines, largely Moranes, Voisins, Farmans. British machines such as B.Es., R.Es., and Sopwiths have also been supplied to the Belgian Army. On various occasions they have proved a useful adjunct to the Allies' forces operating in Flanders.

AEROPLANE FACTORIES.

Destroyed or adopted by the Germans.

BOLIVIAN.

MILITARY AVIATION.

A start in this direction was made in 1917, when Capts. Jose Alarcon and Renato Parejas, and Sub-Lieut. Horacio Vasquez were sent to El Palomar (Buenos Ayres) for training as aviators.

The first-named officer unfortunately lost his life on Jan. 23rd, 1917, while training, but the two others successfully graduated.

An aero-engine was imported during 1917 from the Argentine, apparently for the purpose of instruction.

CENTRAL AMERICAN, ETC.

General Note.—Nicaragua and S. Domingo have both purchased one or two aeroplanes for their military forces : but nothing appears to have been done with them.

Gautamela had one aeroplane flown by Nannini, who was appointed military flying instructor.

Cuba had one, flown by Paris.

CHILEAN.

Aerial Societies:—

Aero Club de Chile, Santiago de Chile.

Aerial Journals:—

Auto y Aero. Santiago de Chile. (Monthly.)

MILITARY AVIATION.

Three engines were imported during 1917 from the Argentine for the construction of training machines.

MILITARY AEROPLANES.

The available force consisted of **18** machines when last communications were received :—

8 *Bleriots,* **4** *Brequets,* **1** *Voisin,* **4** *Sanchez-Besa,* **1** *Deperdussin.*

Aerodrome:—

Lo Espejo. (Four sheds and some portable hangars).

Flying Grounds:—

Lo Espejo. (Military Aerodrome.)

AVIATORS.

Military Flying Corps.

Concha, General, Inspector-Gen. of Aeronautics.	Leon, 1st Lt. A. G., Adjut.
	Larrain, C., Quarter-master.
Donoso, Dr. R. U., Surg.	Prado, Copt. M. V., Command.

Military Pilots.

Ampuero, Sergt. A.	Page, Sergt. L. O.
Bello, Lt.	Perez, 1st Lt. E.
Cabezas, M.	Rojas, Sergt. F.
Cazarino, Lt.	Torres, 2nd Lt. J.
Conberas, Lt.	Verscheure, Sergt.
Conzalez, Sergt. F.	Valenzuela, 1st Lt. G.
Menadier.	Urgua, 1st Lt. A.

Private.	Killed.
Cadezas, M.	
Donoso, P. L.	1914.
Figuroa.	Mery, Lieut.

Note.—No fresh information has been obtainable during 1919, beyond the fact that in 1917 six Bristol monoplanes with Le Rhône engines of 110 h.p. were sent to Brazil by the British Government in part payment for two battleships building for Chile in British yards at the outbreak of war and taken over by the British Navy. On one of these a Chilean officer flew over the Andes to Argentina.

Lieut. Cortinez, Chilean Army, crossing the Andes on April 4th, 1919, on a Bristol monoplane.

CHINESE.

FIRST AVIATORS.

Gunn, T. (*Instructor*).	Tsai Tao, Prince	Wee Gee.
Lym, A. (*Instructor*).	Tsing, Col.	Yoa, Lt.
Lee, Y. L.	Poa, Lt.	

MILITARY AVIATION.

In March, 1913, orders were placed for six 80 h.p. *Caudrons*, also for six 50 h.p., and a decision arrived at gradually to acquire a large force. A home-made aeroplane was built at Nanuan, in 1913.

In January, 1914, Art Lym was appointed flying instructor to the Chinese Army.

In the "White Wolf" operations, 1914, four of the *Caudrons* were employed, and found very effective in locating the enemy. No casualties to the machines occurred.

AERODROME.

The military school (*Caudron*) is at Nanyuen, Peking.

The chief instructor is Mr. Zee Yee Lee, who learned to fly at the Bristol School on Salisbury Plain.

The Officer Commanding is Sao K. Y. Chen.

Two snapshots at a Chinese Aerodrome near Peking.

BRAZILIAN.

Aerial Societies :—

Aero Club Brazileiro, 31, Rua do Theatre. Rio de Janeiro. Founded 1911.

Aerial Journals :—

Aerophilo (Orgas Official do Aero Club).
Aviacao Nacional Avenida Rio Branco, 110, Rio de Janeiro. (Subscription : 5 milreis per annum, Brazil ; 8 milreis, foreign.) Monthly.

Flying Grounds :—

Ilha dos Euxadas, Bay of Guanabara, Rio. (Naval Air Stations and Flying School).

Aerodromo dos Affonssos, Rio de Janeiro. (Flying Ground, School of the Aero Club.)

Aeroplane Factories :—

Newspapers state that the Brazilian Government has been in "pourparlé" with Italian firms to make a big one in Rio, and the shopwork of the Naval School, Ilha dos Euxados, is fitting for to produce aeroplanes for the Navy.

Airscrew Factories :—

Internacional Fabrica de Helies, 139-145, Rua dos Invalidos, Rio de Janeiro.

NAVAL AVIATION.

Nine naval aviators, graduates of the naval flying school at Euxadas, were sent to England in January, 1917, for a course of advanced training and to be attached to the R.A.F. for war active service.

A number of naval officers also went to Italy for war experience.

MILITARY AVIATION.

This is still in the experimental stage, but plans are maturing for the development of the fifth arm of the Army, and it is contemplated to create in each state of the Union one, or several, federal flying grounds. To hasten this achievement, several state organisations have started public subscriptions tending to present to the federal government a number of military aeroplanes.

A big French commission arrived in Rio last October to create the aviation for the Army.

BRAZILIAN AVIATORS.

The following are the names of the Brazilian aviators (end of 1918) :—

Civil :—Santos Dumont, Edu. Chaves Bergmann, Cicero Marques.

Naval Aviators :

Araujo (O. de, Lieut.), Baudiera (R. V. F., Lieut.), *Barbedo (H. de), *Borges (Leitao), de Lamare (V. B., Lieut.), Epaminondas dos Santos (Sub-Lieut.), Filleto dos Santos (Sub-Lieut.), Godiuho (M. da C., Sub-Lieut.), Possolo (Eugenio), Lieut., killed through collision in the air in Eastbourne. Sá Earp (Fabio de, Lieut.), Silva Junior, Schoreth (Augusto), Lieut. Com.-Mecanico, Trompowsky (Armando), Lieut., Varady (Heitor), Lieut., Vasconcellos (M. A. P. de), Lieut.-Com., Victor de Carvalho (Sub-Lieut.), *Vieira de Mello.

* Those marked thus are Army Officers trained at the Naval School.

Machines (types flown in Rio) :—*Curtiss* Flying Boats (seaplane), *Standard* (seaplane), *Farman, Morane.*

Since September of 1918 aviation in Brazil has made great advances, but detailed information is lacking.

INSTRUCTORS AND PUPILS AT THE BRAZILIAN CHIEF FLYING SCHOOL AT ENXADAS.

BRITISH.

MILITARY AERONAUTICS.

THE British Flying Services have grown out of what was originally The Balloon Company, Royal Engineers, therefore it is necessary to deal with Military Aviation first, despite the correct precedence of the older Services. The Balloon Company was first commanded by Colonel Templer, R.E., then by Colonel Trollope, R.E., and, when flying first began, by Colonel Capper, R.E. (now Major-General).

In 1908, Colonel Capper did his best to encourage the production of an aeroplane by the late Samuel Franklin Cody, then employed at the Balloon Factory, R.E., at South Farnborough, Hants, on the production of War Kites. Colonel Capper and Mr. Cody had previously produced an airship.

Mr. Cody's aeroplane began to fly in 1909, and in the same year a Wright biplane was also acquired by the Army from the late the Hon. Charles Rolls. Mr. Cody then left the Balloon Factory to experiment by himself, during 1910, on Laffan's Plain, Aldershot. Mr. Mervyn O'Gorman was appointed chief of the Balloon Factory.

On March 1st, 1911, The Air Battalion, R.E., was formed, to operate five aeroplanes and one or two small experimental airships.

No. 1 Aeroplane Section of The Air Battalion was formed later, with Captain J. D. B. Fulton, R.F.A., in command, the Airship and Balloon Company being under the command of Major Sir Alexander Bannerman, Bart, R.E. The Aeroplane Section was stationed at Lark Hill, on Salisbury Plain, officers and men living in the Artillery Camp at Bulford. Various French aeroplanes were purchased, including *Farmans*, *Bleriots*, and *Nieuports*, but no encouragement was given to British enterprise.

In the same year, the Army Aircraft Factory was formed, on what had been the Balloon Factory, R.E., and Mr. Mervyn O'Gorman remained in charge. The chief control of Army aircraft of all kinds was in the hands of Brigadier-General David Henderson, D.S.O., then Director of Military Training at the War Office.

THE FORMATION OF THE R.F.C.

During 1912, various developments took place. The Royal Flying Corps was formed from the old Air Battalion, and General Henderson became Director-General of Military Aeronautics. The Aircraft Factory was exalted into The Royal Aircraft Factory, ostensibly as an experimental workshop, though its subsequent growth before the war was so great as to give rise to the belief that it was intended to build all the Army's aeroplanes there, a belief increased by the fact that hardly any British aeroplanes of designs other than those produced by the R.A.F. were purchased, though a number of French machines were bought. Up to the outbreak of war, all engines on British Army aeroplanes were of French make, except for one or two Austrian engines, but from 1912 onwards, the R.A.F. was endeavouring to produce an aero-engine of its own design.

In the autumn of 1912, a Military Aeroplane Competition, open to the world, was held on Salisbury Plain, and the £5,000 prize offered for this was won by the late S. F. Cody, on a machine of his own make, with an Austro-Daimler engine.

When the R.F.C. was formed, it was supposed to consist of a Naval Wing and a Military Wing, each wing supplying pilots and machines to the other when required. Major F. H. Sykes was appointed Commandant Military Wing, and Captain Sueter, R.N., was made Director of the Air Department at the Admiralty. Also a joint Central Flying School was formed on Salisbury Plain (at Upavon), with Captain Godfrey Paine, M.V.O., R.N., as Commandant, and Lieut.-Col. Cooke, R.A., D.S.O., as Assistant-Commandant. In 1913, Major Hugh Trenchard, D.S.O., Royal Scots Fusiliers, became Assistant-Commandant.

In practice, Naval pilots assisted at Army Manœuvres in 1912 and 1913, but no Army pilots ever took part in Naval Manœuvres. The Central Flying School also held a large

Official Photograph.

THE R.F.C. in 1918. A group of Flying Officers of the R.F.C. on active service. It is stated officially that each of the pilots and observers in this group has brought down at least three German machines. The increasing altitude at which fighting now takes place is indicated by the pseudo-Arctic costumes worn by the crews of fighting machines.

majority of Army pupils, and ultimately became entirely Military.

By the beginning of 1913, the R.F.C. possessed thirteen aeroplanes in flying order—as proved by Mr. Joynson-Hicks, M.P., in the House of Commons early that year. At Army Manœuvres, in the Autumn of that year, something like fifty aeroplanes were got together, including half-a-dozen Naval machines attached to the " White " Army. During this year, the Aeronautical Inspection Department was formed, under Major Fulton, C.B., and became one of the best organised departments in the King's Services. Major Fulton (by then Lieut.-Col.) died in 1916, and his death was the most severe blow the R.F.C. has suffered by the death of any one officer.

THE ESTABLISHMENT.

In 1913, it was laid down that the establishment of the R.F.C. was to consist of seven squadrons of aeroplanes of 12 machines each, with 12 pilots, and a reserve of 12 machines and 12 pilots for each squadron. This figure was never reached up to the outbreak of war. Headquarters were built at Farnborough.

At the beginning of 1914, No. 1. Squadron, R.F.C., was stationed at Farnborough, No. 2 Squadron at Montrose, No. 3 and No. 4 Squadrons at Netheravon, on Salisbury Plain, but all squadrons were still below the establishment laid down.

In June of 1914, a concentration camp of these four squadrons, with the nucleus of a fifth squadron, then in process of formation at Farnborough, was formed at Netheravon. Representatives of all foreign powers, including Germany and Austria, visited the camp. The maximum number of aeroplanes capable of taking the air on one day did not exceed thirty, which may be taken as representing the effective strength of the R.F.C. at the outbreak of war.

WAR.

When war broke out, four squadrons of the R.F.C. were raised almost to establishment—but without the 100% reserve—by calling up civilian pilots who had previously joined the Corps as Special Reserve officers, and by taking over the best machines from the Central Flying School. Brigadier-General Henderson took command in the field. Major Trenchard left the C.F.S. and took command of R.F.C. Headquarters at Farnborough, and Major Brancker acted as Assistant Director at the War Office. A fifth squadron came into being soon after the outbreak of war.

The increase of the personnel of the R.F.C. was begun and continued with energy, and enormous expansions took place. Aeroplanes, chiefly to designs produced by the R.A.F., were ordered in large quantities from firms which, at the outbreak of war, were on the verge of closing down, and all sorts of firms who had never made aeroplanes were induced to come into the Aircraft Industry. Motor firms were turned on to make engines, also largely of R.A.F. designs.

Later on, General Henderson returned from the front, and Major Trenchard, promoted by successive steps to Major-General, commanded until the end of 1917. He has been on various occasions thanked in despatches from the Commander-in-Chief in France for the excellent work done by the R.F.C., under his able leadership.

In 1915, Major Brancker, after seeing active service in France, was promoted to Brigadier-General, and in 1916 was appointed Director of Air Organisation. In April, 1917, he was further promoted to Deputy-Director General of Military Aeronautics, and Lieut.-Col. L. E. O. Charlton, D.S.O., was appointed Director of Air Organisation, with temporary rank of Brigadier-General.

At the end of 1915 and beginning of 1916, agitation was raised in Parliament and out on account of the superiority in speed and climb of the German machines over the British. This agitation was led by Lord Montagu, of Beaulieu, Mr. Pemberton-Billing, M.P., Mr. Joynson-Hicks, M.P., Captain Bennet-Goldney, M.P., and others. As a result, a Committee of Enquiry was appointed to investigate the affairs of the R.F.C., and its report, published at Christmas, 1916, disclosed various defects, many of which have since been remedied. Another Committee visited the Royal Aircraft Factory, at Farnborough, and advised drastic changes, which have been more or less effected.

General Henderson during 1916, had been promoted to Lieut.-General, and had been appointed a member of the Army Council. An enquiry into the administration of the Royal Naval Air Service was refused.

At the beginning of 1917, a fresh agitation arose for the better equipment of the R.F.C., as the Germans had put a number of " destroyers " of a new type into the air towards the end of 1916, which did considerable damage to the older types of British aeroplanes.

During 1915-1916-1917, the whole organisation of the R.F.C. was altered and expanded out of all recognition. The old five squadrons were vastly extended. Wings containing a number of squadrons apiece and commanded by a Lieut.-Colonel were formed. Wings were assembled into Groups, with a full Colonel in command. Groups again were formed into Brigades, each with a Brigadier-General in command. And Brigades were grouped into Divisions, each under a Major-General.

The R.F.C. in France remained during 1917 under the command of Major-General Trenchard. Lieut.-General Sir David Henderson, K.C.B., remained Director General of Military Aeronautics. The Headquarters work of the R.F.C. grew to such an extent that De Keyser's Hotel, at Blackfriars, was taken over, renamed Adastral House, and turned into a species of War Office on its own account during 1916.

Later the administration of the R.F.C. was removed to the Air Board Office at the Hotel Cecil, Strand, W.C., and, as towards the end of 1917 even this proved too small for the various combined departments of the R.N.A.S. and R.F.C. and Ministry of Munitions (all operating under the Air Board, q.v.), other premises were also commandeered for the ever-growing mass of officers in home billets.

The growth of the R.F.C. warranted the expansion. Flying schools on a big scale were opened in Canada, in Egypt, and in France.

During the early part of 1917, the Germans, as stated by Mr. Ian MacPherson on March 13th, in the House of Commons, " reinforced and rested during the winter, put up a serious opposition," but, thanks to the high *moral* of the R.F.C. under General Trenchard, the R.F.C. continued to do its Army work. As newer machines of superior types were produced, the Corps regained its mastery in the air, and, despite heavy losses during the fighting at Easter, 1917, before Arras, by the end of the year had definitely established its complete superiority over the enemy.

By April 1st, 1918, when the Royal Air Force came into being, the R.F.C. was incomparably the finest aerial fighting force in the world, and by common consent in the Corps the credit for its efficiency and *moral* was given to General Trenchard.

In July of 1917, Brig.-Gen. Brancker was promoted to Major-General, while holding the post of Director-General of Military Aeronautics, and in September, Brevet Lieut.-Col. (temp. Brig.-Gen.) J. M. Salmond, D.S.O., was promoted to Major-General, on the expansion of the Home Training Brigade to the size of a Division.

In October, Major-General Salmond was made Director-General of Military Aeronautics, Lieut.-General Sir David Henderson being " deputed to undertake special work "—the duty in question being the drawing up of the organisation of the new Royal Air Force. General Brancker was sent to Egypt. Brig.-General Charles Longcroft was promoted to temp. Major-General, Commanding Home Training Division, with Brig.-Gen. Ludlow-Hewitt as Inspector of Training. General Salmond also became a member of the Army Council.

In December, Brig.-General E. L. Ellington was gazetted Deputy-Director-General of Military Aeronautics.

In the last few days of December, Major-General Trenchard, C.B., D.S.O., was promoted to K.C.B., and at about the same date he handed over the command of the R.F.C. in the Field to General Salmond, he himself coming back to England to take over the office of Chief of the Air Staff in the newly formed Air Ministry.

The R.F.C. continued in existence, daily increasing its superiority over the enemy, until March 31st, when it ceased to exist, and became a part of the Royal Air Force, which came officially into being on April 1st.

ANTI-AIRCRAFT DEFENCES.

During the latter part of 1917, great alterations were made in the organisation of the London Air Defence Area by Major-General Ashmore, C.M.G., M.V.O., R.A., formerly a Brig.-General, R.F.C. Proper gun and searchlight co-operation was established. Special " destroyer " squadrons of the R.F.C. were stationed in suitable positions, and operated highly effectively against German raiders. The proof of the efficacy of the organisation was given on Whit Sunday, 1918, when a raiding squadron lost five machines, certainly observed, and probably others which fell in the sea. This proved to be the last German raid over this country. The efficacy of the London Air Defence Area seems to prove that a permanent Air Defence organisation for the whole of the British Isles, concentrated

BRITISH AEROPLANES.

under a single command, is one of the military necessities of the future.

THE R.N.A.S.

Naval flying began in 1911, when three Naval officers and a lieutenant of the Royal Marine Light Infantry were permitted by their Lordships of the Admiralty to draw full pay while being taught to fly at the Royal Aero Club ground at Eastchurch, on three *Short* biplanes lent by Mr. Frank McClean, a member of the Club. Mr. G. B. Cockburn, another member of the Club, gave his services gratuitously as instructor for some six months, while teaching these officers to fly.

When the Royal Flying Corps was formed in 1912, these officers, and some three or four others who had learned to fly at their own expense, were located at Eastchurch as the Naval Wing, R.F.C. An Air Department was formed at the Admiralty, under Captain Murray F. Sueter, R.N., who had already been concerned with airship work. (See Airship Section.)

From this nucleus, the Naval Wing expanded. Coast defence and experimental stations were formed before the war at Calshot, Isle of Grain (Kent), Felixstowe, Yarmouth, and Dundee. Much development and experimentation with seaplanes was carried on.

Seaplanes took part in Naval Manœuvres of 1913, in the North Sea, and many excellent flights far out to sea were made.

On July 1st, 1914, the Naval Wing, R.F.C., became by Royal Warrant the Royal Naval Air Service, and was dissociated from the Army entirely. Captain Sueter was promoted to Commodore.

Prior to this, all the Army airships had been handed over to the Navy, and several military officers who had been concerned with the development of airships went over to the Navy with the ships, and were given rank in the R.N.A.S. corresponding to their R.F.C. rank.

At the Spithead Review in July, immediately before the war, the R.N.A.S. concentrated all its seaplanes at Calshot, about a dozen in all, and all its land-going aeroplanes at Gosport—about another dozen.

After the outbreak of war, many new coast stations were formed and many aeroplanes and seaplanes were ordered. The personnel of the Service was expanded largely, and R.N.A.S. pilots operated all over the world.

During 1917, the R.N.A.S. continued its amphibious duties. The activities of seaplanes, airships, and naval kite-balloons against submarines, became more and more developed, and by the end of the year were having very considerable effect. Seaplanes and airships definitely sank a number of submarines. Convoys of ships escorted by aircraft, and by other ships equipped with kite-balloons, were hardly ever, if at all, attacked by submarines, and it gradually became recognised that here was the real reply to the submarine menace.

R.N.A.S. shore-going squadrons at Dunkerque carried on bombing and fighting expeditions against German forces in Flanders. Fighting squadrons operated with the R.F.C. in France. Bombing squadrons bombed German towns from aerodromes on the Eastern French frontier. Sea and land squadrons operated in the Eastern Mediterranean, in the Red Sea, and in Mesopotamia, in alliance with the R.F.C. During May, 1917, a Naval Handley-Page biplane flew from London to an aerodrome in the Balkans, and thence, after re-fitting, bombed Constantinople with good effect on July 9th.

When the new Air Board was formed at the beginning of 1917, Commodore Godfrey Paine, C.B., M.V.O., R.N., was appointed Director of Air Services by the Admiralty, and was made a member of the Board of Admiralty with the title of Fifth Sea Lord. He remained in command of the R.N.A.S. till it too became merged in the Royal Air Force on April 1st.

KITE BALLOONS.

Kite-balloons, a German invention, were introduced into the Royal Naval Air Service by officers at Dunkirk, who had opportunities of watching the operation of the solitary kite-balloon possessed by the Belgian Army. Several K.B. Sections were formed, and proved so successful that the R.F.C. also adopted kite-balloons, and had a large number in operation by the end of 1916. Kite-balloons were also used largely by the Navy for spotting for Naval guns, the balloons being carried on ships specially fitted out for the purpose.

The uses of kite-balloons have been greatly increased during 1917 and 1918. They were particularly useful in repelling submarine attacks, and it is stated as a fact that no convoy of merchant ships equipped with K.Bs. ever lost a ship, or was ever attacked, whether escorted by destroyers or not.

THE AIR BOARD.

The Air Board came into being on Jan. 2, 1917, with Lord Cowdray, better known perhaps as Sir Weetman Pearson, as President, to control the supply of aircraft for both Services, and to co-ordinate the work of the Services. The Board was composed of Commodore Godfrey Paine, who was also made Fifth Lord of the Admiralty, representing the R.N.A.S.; Lieut.-General Sir David Henderson, representing the R.F.C.; Mr. William Weir, as Controller of Aeronautical Supplies, representing the Ministry of Munitions; and Mr. Percy Martin, as Controller of Aero-Engines, also representing the Ministry of Munitions. Major J. G. Baird was appointed Parliamentary Under-Secretary. The technical departments of the R.N.A.S. and R.F.C. were removed from the Admiralty and Adastral House.

Officers of the Royal Naval Air Service as they were before the War.

Photograph by F. N. Birkett.

22a

BRITISH AEROPLANES.

House respectively, and located at the Hotel Cecil, which was made the Air Board Office, and much of the administrative work of the Flying Services was also transferred to the Hotel Cecil.

Mr. William Weir was knighted on February 11th, and one may safely say that seldom, if ever, has a knighthood been more fully deserved. As Controller of Aircraft Supplies, during 1917, he increased output to an extraordinary extent. To him and to Sir Hugh Trenchard may be ascribed the dominance in the air possessed by the R.F.C. in 1918.

On May 23rd, 1918, the formation of a Civil Aerial Transport Committee, to study after-the-war problems, was announced in the House of Commons. Lord Northcliffe was made Chairman; Major Baird, Deputy Chairman; and among the members were the Duke of Atholl, Lord Montagu, Lord Sydenham, Mr. Balfour Browne, Mr. Berriman, Mr. G. B. Cockburn, Mr. Holt-Thomas, Mr. Claude Johnson, Mr. Joynson Hicks, Mr. Lanchester, Lieut.-Col. O'Gorman, Maj.-Gen. Ruck, Mr. Siddeley, Mr. Sopwith, Mr. H. G. Wells, Mr. H. White-Smith, Mr. Dyson Wilson, Sir Laurence Guillemard, Col. Pringle, Lord Drogheda, Mr. Murray, Sir Thomas Mackenzie, Mr. W. P. Schreiner, Mr. Grindle, Capt. Vyvyan, and General Brancker. The Secretary was Mr. D. O. Malcolm.

Much was expected of the Committee, but little came of it. Various sub-committees were formed and met at various times. A voluminous report was issued late in 1918, which gave evidence of much work, which appears to have been of some service to drawing up the Regulations for Civilian flying in 1919.

The Air Board carried on its work very effectively till the end of 1917, when it was superceded by the Air Ministry. Before the end, however, several changes were made. Sir William Weir was made Director-General of Aircraft Production, with all the Technical Department under him. Mr. Henry Fowler, O.B.E. (later K.B.E.) was made Assistant D.G.A.P. Lieut.-Col. Alexander became Controller of the Supply Department, and Lieut.-Col. J. G. Weir, Controller of the Technical Department.

THE AIR FORCE BILL.

The Air Force Bill was introduced in the House of Commons on November 8th, and passed its third reading on November 13th. It passed its third reading in the House of Lords on November 27th, and received the Royal Consent on November 28th, 1917. This Act established the Air Council and the Royal Air Force.

THE AIR MINISTRY.

The Air Council, under the Secretary of State for the Air Force, came into being by an Order in Council of January 2nd, 1918. It was constituted as follows:—

Lord Rothermere—Secretary of State and President of the Council.

Major-General Sir Hugh Trenchard, K.C.B., D S.O.—Chief of the Air Staff.

Rear-Admiral Mark Kerr, C.B., R.N.—Deputy Chief of the Air Staff.

Commodore Godfrey Paine, C.B., M.V.O., R.N.—Master-General of Personnel.

Major-General W. S. Brancker—Comptroller-General of Equipment.

Sir William Weir—Director-General of Aircraft Production in the Ministry of Munitions.

Sir John Hunter, K.B.E.—Administrator of Works and Buildings.

Major J. G. Baird, C.M.G., D.S.O., M.P.—Parliamentary Under-Secretary of State.

Lieut.-General Sir David Henderson, K.C.B., D.S.O.—Additional Member of Council and Vice-President.

With the R.A.F. in the Field:—A R.A.F. Padre preaching to officers and men of the R.A.F. from the nacelle of a F.E.2b Night-bomber. It will be noted that the men still wore R.F.C. uniform. This custom still prevailed in many parts until the middle of 1919, when nearly all the men were demobilised.

Mr. W. A. Robinson, C.B., C.B.E.—Permanent Secretary to the Council.

Mr. H. W. McAnally—Assistant-Secretary.

Sir Henry Norman was appointed an Additional Member of the Air Council by Lord Rothermere.

Under this arrangement, the Air Council had no representative either on the Board of Admiralty or on the Army Council. However, an officer of the R.N.A.S., Wing-Capt. F. R. Scarlett, D.S.O., was appointed Director of the Air Division at the Admiralty, presumably to act as a link between the Air Council and the Navy. No analogous appointment has been announced at the War Office, but an Army Council Instruction, issued in March, makes it clear that so far as the Army is concerned the Air Ministry has merely to supply men and machines, and that for all practical purposes, when once they are supplied, they then become part of the Army.

On March 15th, it was notified in the *London Gazette* that the Air Force, to be created under the recent Act, was to be known as the Royal Air Force. The name roused considerable comment, as its initials were the same as those of the Royal Aircraft Factory—an institution which was not popular with the Services. At a later date, the name of this institution was changed to "The Royal Aircraft Establishment," to prevent confusion. Mr. Sydney Smith, formerly Chief Inspector of Factories under the Home Office, was appointed Superintendent in March, in succession to Sir Henry Fowler, K.B.E., who had become Assistant D.G.A.P.

On Sunday, April 14th, it was made known publicly that Major-General Sir Hugh Trenchard had resigned his post as Chief of the Air Staff, and that Major-General F. H. Sykes, C.M.G., had been appointed in his stead. The announcement raised the biggest storm in Parliament, and out, ever known in connection with a purely Service appointment, for it was well known that the resignation of General Trenchard was caused by personal disagreement with the Air Minister. No objection was raised to General Sykes, who, though he had not been concerned with aviation for some two years, was recognised as one of the pioneers of Military Aeronautics, but the Services strongly resented the removal of General Trenchard, who was acknowledged to be the soul and inspiration of the R.F.C., and the organiser of victory in the air.

As the result of these changes, Lieut.-General Sir David Henderson also resigned from the Air Council, giving as his reason that he felt himself unable to work with the new C.A.S.

On April 25th, Lord Rothermere resigned his position as Air Minister. Sir William Weir was appointed Air Minister in his stead, and the appointment gave general satisfaction. Sir Arthur Duckham, K.C.B., of the Ministry of Munitions, was appointed to supervise the production of aircraft, in place of

Sir William Weir, who, after being made Air Minister, was justly rewarded for his earlier work by being made a Peer of the Realm.

By the end of May, 1918, the affairs of the Air Ministry seemed to have settled down, and the organisation appeared to be working smoothly.

THE R.A.F. IN 1918.

The Royal Air Force came into being officially on April 1st, 1918. It embraces all personnel and matériel of the R.N.A.S. and the R.F.C.

The Home Command was at first divided into five areas, as follows :—

London Area.—Maj.-Gen. F. C. Heath-Caldwell, C.B.

North Eastern Area.—Maj.-Gen. The Hon. Sir Frederick Gordon, K C.B., D.S.O.

South-Western Area.—Maj.-Gen. Mark Kerr, C.B., M.V.O. (Rear-Admiral, R.N.)

Midland Area.—Brig.-Gen. J. F. A Higgins, D.S.O., R.A.

Scottish Area.—Maj.-Gen. G. C. Caley, C.B. (Rear-Admiral, R.N.)

Maj.-Gen. J. M. Salmond remained G.O.C., R.A.F. in France and Germany, and Maj.-Gen. G. H. M. Salmond—his brother—G.O.C., R.A.F. in the Eastern Areas until June, 1919.

At a later date the North Eastern Area and the Scottish Area were amalgamated into one. A separate Irish Area was also created, An Irish Officer, Brig.-Gen. E. L. Gerrard (Lt.-Col. R.M.L.I.) was made the first G.O.C., Ireland.

Maj.-Gen. Sir Hugh Trenchard, greatly to the satisfaction of the Services, was appointed in May, 1918, to command "an important part " of the R.A.F. in France. After some months it was made known that this was the Independent Force R.A.F., which was formed by Lord Weir to operate independently from the Navy and Army and to carry aerial warfare into Germany.

An important adjunct to the R.A.F. was created in May by the organisation of the Women's Royal Air Force, under the Hon. Violet Douglas-Pennant—as Commandant. The W.R.A.F's are to the R.A.F. what the W.A.A.C.'s are to the Army, and the W.R.N.'s to the Navy. Shortly afterwards Miss Pennant was dismissed, and her dismissal became the subject of a Special Committee of the House of Lords late in 1919.

THE DEVELOPMENT OF THE R.A.F.

Perhaps the most peculiar thing about development of the R.A.F. in 1918 is the fact that no attempt was made to divide it definitely into three distinct branches for Naval, Military, and purely Aerial operations respectively. On the contrary, officers and men of the former R.N.A.S. were deliberately mixed up with those of the R.F.C., and *vice versa*, with, as the natural result, a marked drop in the efficiency of the two branches.

Young officers and men trained for the R.F.C. were drafted to seaplane work, and those trained for the R.N.A.S. were sent to the squadrons in the field. The natural result was that the young men found that, except for the mere fact of being able to fly, all the months they had spent in training had been practically wasted, as the manners, customs and operations of seaplane stations differ entirely from those of squadrons with the Army in the Field, or at aerodromes at home, precisely as the manners, customs and operations of the Navy differ from those of the Army. The experienced air mechanics of the two Flying Services who were mixed up in this way also lost efficiency through having to unlearn what they had previously learned of Service routine and to learn anew the routine of another Service.

This chaotic and inefficient state of affairs occurred because the R.A.F. naturally had no customs or routine of its own, and each individual station, ship, aerodrome, or squadron was run on the lines chosen by its Commanding Officer, according to whether he happened to have been of the R.N.A.S. or of the R.F.C. It was impossible for even the Air Council, if warlike operations were to continue, to be logical and thorough in mixing the two Services, and to complete the job by putting sailors in command in the Field and soldiers in command at sea, so operations at sea, from ships or coast stations, still remained in the hands of R.N. and R.N.A.S. officers, generally down to the grade of Squadron-Commander, and those in the Field were commanded by R.F.C. officers—except for a few R.N.A.S. squadrons which had been specially trained for land fighting and bombing in Belgium.

The result, as might have been expected, was a grave loss in the efficiency of many units. Nevertheless, owing to the enormous numbers of British aviators, as compared with those of the enemy, owing to the marked superiority of British aeroplanes, and owing to the individual skill and bravery of the British aviators, aided by the excellent organising ability of many experienced General Officers in the Field and by the gallant leadership of wing, squadron and flight commanders in action, the R.A.F. on the West and East fronts was more than able to hold that Command of the Air which was won by the R.F.C. in 1917, despite the *dicta* of highly-placed officials who sneered at the idea of the Command of the Air as impossible to achieve.

In the Summer of 1918, His Majesty the King visited his Armies in the Field, and on August 13th, in a letter to Field-Marshal Sir Douglas Haig, he wrote :—" Its prowess and established superiority over the enemy make me proud to be General-in-Chief of this last creation in the fighting forces of the World."

This established superiority was maintained until the end of the War, and for the last two months of fighting, the German aviators were practically driven out of the air.

THE COMMAND IN THE FIELD.

At the date of the Armistice, the R.A.F. with the Army in the Field was commanded by Major-General J. M. Salmond, C.M.G., D.S.O., and his Brigade-Commanders were Brigadier-Generals T. I. Webb-Bowen, C.M.G.; C. A. H. Longcroft, D.S.O.; E. R. Ludlow-Hewitt, D.S.O., M.C.; L. Charlton, C.M.G., D.S.O.; D. le G. Pitcher, C.M.G.; and R. Hogg, C.I.E.

Brigadier-General C. L. Lambe, D.S.O. (Post Captain, R.N.), commanded another brigade (composed entirely of R.N.A.S. shore-going squadrons) in Belgium, but, though operating with the Army at the end of the War, this was theoretically under the Admiral Commanding Dover Patrol.

The Independent Force R.A.F., under Major-General Sir Hugh Trenchard, K.C.B., D.S.O., was operating on the Franco-German frontier, with Headquarters near Neufchateau. This force was still only in process of formation, and consisted of a single brigade, under Brigadier-General C. L. N. Newall. Preparations were well in hand for the bombing of Berlin in November, but the Armistice occurred a few days too soon.

Nevertheless, the I.F., R.A.F., had already had a very considerable effect on the *moral* of civilians in Western Germany, and on that of the German troops in the regions around Metz and Luxemburg, so that it contributed very materially to that break-up on the Western front which was on the verge of occurring when the Armistice was signed just in time to enable the German Army to say truthfully in the future—as we said of our Army after the Retreat from Mons—that though it was a beaten army it was never a broken army.

Major-General W. G. H. Salmond, C.M.G., D.S.O.—elder brother of General J. M. Salmond—continued to command the R.A.F. in the Near and Middle East, his forces being distributed over the Balkans, Palestine, Egypt, East Africa, the Soudan, Mesopotamia and India. Despite the fact that the oldest machines, of types obsolete or obsolescent on the Western Front, were sent to him to be used up, the R.A.F. in those war areas maintained the same command of the air as was held by their better-equipped brethren in the West. Also, a vast training establishment in Egypt maintained a constant supply of well-educated pilots and observers for the Eastern Areas.

The R.A.F. Brigade detached for service with the British Army in Italy was at first commanded by Brigadier-General Webb-Bowen. When that officer returned to command in France (at the special request of General Plumer, it is understood) the command in Italy was taken over by Colonel P. B. Joubert de la Ferté, D.S.O.

SEA WORK.

The sea work of the R.A.F. consisted chiefly of patrolling the coasts of Great Britain, the North Sea, and the Mediterranean, in search of mines and submarines. Some few bomb-raids were made, including one successful one on the Zeppelin sheds at Tondern, in Slesvig, several across the Adriatic on Austrian ports, and some on Turkish positions in Palestine and Asia Minor.

The machines used for coast patrols at home were very largely land-going machines which were unfit for use at the front. They were generally fitted with floatation bags, but frequently not. Many of them fell into the sea and were lost, but in most cases the crews were saved. These crews were generally officers and/or men who had been trained for the R.F.C. and knew nothing about sea work.

Officers of a Unit of the Independent Force, R.A.F., in France, showing the mixture of Naval, Military, and R.A.F. uniforms in vogue on Active Service.

25a

THE R.A.F. AT SEA :—H.M.S. Furious, arranged as a Seaplane Carrier and Aircraft Ship. In the bows may be seen an aeroplane of the type adapted to fly off a ship's deck. Round it is a removable stockade, which acts as a wind-breaker. Aft may be seen an S.S. Airship (or "Blimp"), which has alighted on deck. Forward of the airship is a scaffold arrangement which is intended to act as a screen to prevent aeroplanes which alight on the deck from over-shooting their mark and running overboard.

BRITISH AEROPLANES.

The North Sea patrols were chiefly done by big flying-boats of the type originated in America by Mr. Glenn Curtiss and developed into highly-efficient flying machines by Lieut.-Col. J. C. Porte, C.M.G. (formerly Lieutenant, R.N.). These are known as *F* Boats, having been produced at Felixstowe, where Colonel Porte was in command of the R.N.A.S. Experimental Station as well as the War Station.

During 1918, the Experimental Station produced, to the designs of Colonel Porte, a triplane flying-boat, with five Rolls-Royce engines. This was, at the end of 1918, the biggest aeroplane in the world.

It was intended originally, when the Armistice was signed, that this boat should fly the Atlantic. The scheme was quashed on the score of expense, though the boat's tests proved that she was capable of carrying fuel for the distance, whether flying from East to West or from West to East.

The speed and lifting power of the "Felixstowe Fury" are both very much higher than would be expected from so big a craft.

DECK FLYING.

The units of the R.A.F. operating with the Grand Fleet developed during 1918 the art of flying aeroplanes off and onto the decks of ships. H.M.S. *Furious*, which had proved to be useless as a super-battle-cruiser, was turned into a seaplane carrier, her forward deck being used as a starting platform and her after deck being rigged up with catching gear, so that ordinary aeroplanes with wheels might alight thereon with comparative success.

H.M.S. *Argus* was constructed with a flush deck along her whole length, her funnels being led horizontally aft to permit of this construction.

A number of battleships and cruisers were fitted with platforms on their gun-turrets, the out-board ends of the platforms resting on the guns, and from these turret-platforms aeroplanes were flown in the manner illustrated. In these cases no provision was made for the machines to alight again, and the plan was that when their flight was finished they should come down in the sea and be picked up as opportunity might serve.

The experiments in "deck-flying" as it was called, which produced these schemes, were chiefly carried out at the R.N.A.S. Experimental Station, Isle of Grain, at first under Wing-Commander John Seddon, and later under Wing-Commanders L'Estrange Malone, Featherstone Briggs, and Harry Busteed.

If these experiments had received more support from their Lordships of the Admiralty in the early and middle days of the War, there is no doubt that bomb-dropping and torpedo-carrying aeroplanes flown from the decks of seaplane-carriers would have played a very important part in the War, for it was a single flight of such machines which destroyed several Zeppelin sheds at Tondern, in Slesvig, in 1918, and all these schemes, now mentioned for the first time in this book, were actually proposed before the War and reached the early stages of experiment in 1915 or 1916. In fact, aeroplanes had been flown off and onto ships by British and American aviators in 1912, and special launching gears for use on ships were illustrated in 1913 or earlier.

An R.A.F. Flying-Boat of Lieut.-Col. Porte's design, and known as the F2a Type. Dazzle-painted, in accordance with Naval custom.

BRITISH AEROPLANES.

FURTHER HISTORY OF 1918.

On August 22nd, further changes took place in the organisation of the R.A.F. at home. Major-General Sir Godfrey Paine, Master-General of Personnel, was made Inspector-General R.A.F. Major-General W. S. Brancker was appointed M.G.P., and Major-General E. H. Ellington, C.M.G., was appointed Controller General of Equipment.

In September, Mrs. Gwynne-Vaughan, C.B.E., commanding W.A.A.C. in France, was appointed to command the W.R.A.F.,

The following are the chief figures concerning the machine:— Span 123 ft. (two upper planes); Length (including tail) 60 ft.; Height (from keel) 27 ft. 6 ins.; total weight 23,400 lbs. Power Plant, Five "Eagle" Rolls-Royce engines, driving two tractor and three pusher air-screws.

in place of Miss Violet Douglas-Pennant. Miss Pennant demanded an official enquiry into the cause of her dismissal, and at the time of going to press that demand was about to be satisfied.

On November 11th, the Armistice was signed, and on November 26th the Air Council transmitted its thanks to the R.A.F. for services in the War.

THE WAR EFFORTS OF THE DOMINIONS.

The assistance given by the British Dominions Over Seas to the Empire during the War is given full credit in an official resumé published early in 1919. This reads as follows :—

GENERAL SURVEY.

In 1915, the Dominion Governments, foreseeing the inevitable development of aerial co-operation in land and sea operations, initiated their support by offering to organise their own flying formations and by generally encouraging their younger men to volunteer and take up flying. Even prior to this many who aspired to qualify as pilots and observers were coming over to join the Royal Flying Corps and the Royal Naval Air Service, and during the whole course of the War service of the highest

Side and Three-quarter Bow View of the Big Porte Boat, known officially as the " Felixstowe Fury."   28a

BRITISH AEROPLANES.

value has been performed by pilots from the Dominions who were destined to play an important part in building up and maintaining the air-fighting forces in every theatre of war. The following details give some idea of the extent of the efforts of the principal Dominions :—

AUSTRALIA.

The inauguration of the Australian Flying Corps in 1915 was the result of an offer by the Australian Government to form a flying unit for co-operation with our Indian forces in Mesopotamia. Four flying officers and sixty other ranks arrived at Basra in May, 1915, and took part in the Kut operations. The first complete Australian squadron left Australia for Egypt in March, 1916, and later played an important part in the work of the 40th Wing in the Middle East Brigade. Three additional squadrons were organised for service in France, the first arriving there in August, 1917 ; these were responsible for the destruction of over 400 enemy machines between that time and the signing of the Armistice. Further, four training squadrons were formed in

England in which most of the Australian pilots were trained, the entire personnel being drawn from Australia or from the Australian Imperial forces in France. Some months ago a central flying school was created at Melbourne, and the aeroplane industry has now been definitely established in Australia.

The strength of the Australian Flying Corps in November, 1918, amounting to over 250 pilots and a total personnel of

considerably over 3,000, gives an impression of the part played by Australia in gaining aerial supremacy.

CANADA.

In the early days of the War a large number of Canadians came over to join the Royal Flying Corps and the Royal Naval Air Service, and as many as 800 officers and cadets had been enrolled in the former corps up to the time when a training centre for flying cadets was organised in Canada itself. A total

A "Ship-Plane," flying off a turret platform.

An Aeroplane on the Turret of a Warship, showing the out-board portion of the platform folded back. This portion rests on the supports which may be seen fixed to the barrels of the guns.

of 1,239 Canadian officers have been seconded or attached to the Royal Flying Corps, Royal Naval Air Service, and the Royal Air Force, and, since training in Canada was begun, over 4,000 Canadian cadets have been commissioned in the flying services, while the number of other ranks transferred and subsequently commissioned is about 2,750. Altogether, over 8,000 Canadians have served as officers in our flying services, and at the date of the Armistice there were nearly 2,500 in the Royal Air Force, while 1,200 Canadian cadets were undergoing training in England and in Canada. It may be added that several Canadian firms have maintained a large output both of machines and engines ; Canada was producing, in November, 1918, about 350 light machines and eight large flying-boats per month.

NEW ZEALAND.

Over 300 New Zealanders have served as officers in the British Flying Services during the War, and at the time of the Armistice there were 142 cadets in training.

The Dominion has presented six aeroplanes to the Imperial Government and lent two others.

Since the outbreak of War, two Schools of Instruction in Aviation have been established in New Zealand.

SOUTH AFRICA.

On the outbreak of War many South Africans came to England to take up flying, and by the beginning of 1916 nearly 2,000 were serving in England or Egypt as probationary flight officers. When the 28th Squadron Royal Flying Corps was sent to co-operate with the Forces in East Africa, it was largely composed of South Africans, and came to be known as the South African Squadron.

The total number of South Africans who have been commissioned in the Flying Services is about 3,000, who have taken part in the campaigns in France, Egypt, Palestine, and Africa.

The Colony presented a large number of machines to the Imperial Government during the War.

ASSISTANCE TO THE ALLIES.

The same official resumé gives an account of the assistance given by the R.N.A.S., R.F.C., and R.A.F. to the Allies and the United States. This reads as follows :—

AMERICA.

The Government of the United States has paid a striking tribute to the British Air Service by adopting our system of training. The first 500 American officer cadets to be trained went through the School of Military Aeronautics at Oxford, subsequently graduating at various aerodromes in England. These officers formed the nucleus of American schools which were eventually started both in the United States and in France. In addition to this training of American pilots, 10 American squadrons were partially trained in Canada under a reciprocal agreement whereby Canada obtained the use of certain American aerodromes at seasons when weather conditions rendered some of the Canadian aerodromes temporarily unavailable. Four of these squadrons completed their training in England, and were then attached to the R.A.F. in the field to gain experience under Service conditions for six to eight months. The remaining six went direct to the American authorities in France. In all, about 700 American pilots have passed through our schools and graduated at our aerodromes.

An agreement was also entered into under which a pool of American mechanics up to a maximum of 15,000 at a time was maintained in England. This arrangement was mutually advantageous, as, while relieving the demand for skilled tradesmen in the R.A.F., it also assisted the Americans to train their own squadrons for service in the field. This personnel, coming from America untrained, was attached to training units for three to eight months, being then sent to France from time to time in the form of complete squadrons until a total of 59 squadrons was reached in accordance with the demands of the American Command in France.

We have also supplied large numbers of aeroplanes of modern standard type, and when the question of producing a standardised engine was considered, every facility was given and all our experience placed at the disposal of the American Government, with the result that the Liberty engine was evolved. Some 95 officers were sent out to the United States to assist in an advisory capacity, and a large number of American officers have both visited and undergone courses at most of the schools and training stations of the Royal Air Force. In addition, a very large amount of material, supplies, samples, drawings, and technical information was supplied to both the American Army and Naval Aviation Services.

FRANCE.

We have assisted the French Government to a considerable extent in training her pilots, more especially in aerial fighting. For this purpose four Gosport instructors together with four mono-Avro aeroplanes were sent to France. We have supplied 48 complete machines and various new types of engines to the French Government, and an order for 150 Sunbeam engines is on the point of completion.

About 600 Hythe gun cameras were also supplied during 1917-1918 to the French schools for training purposes.

French officers have constantly visited this country with a view to studying our methods, and have been given every facility for visiting schools, training centres, and technical establishments.

ITALY.

Immediately after the Italian retreat in November, 1917, four British aeroplane squadrons were sent to the Italian Front to co-operate with the Italian Air Service and with the British Forces in Italy ; these four squadrons have been maintained and a fifth squadron has recently been added.

The brief record of the work performed by these squadrons, given in the Appendix, illustrates the valuable assistance they have rendered to our Ally.

During 1918, the Italian Government were supplied with 150 Vickers guns each month, and with upwards of 2,000 Lewis guns.

A number of Hythe gun cameras have been sent out, and between 200 and 300 sights and lenses, as well as photographic chemicals.

BELGIUM.

In 1916, a number of Sopwith 1½ strutters were provided by the R.N.A.S. In 1917, 22 more machines of this type were supplied, and 22 R.E. 8s for artillery co-operation. In 1918, 36 " Camel " and 18 D.H.9 machines were furnished to the Belgian Aviation Corps.

GREECE.

The Greek Government have been supplied with 20 seaplanes, 40 D.H.6 machines and 6 Sopwith " Camels," together with complete equipment and transport, had been allotted and were ready for dispatch, but have been held back owing to the cessation of active hostilities.

RUSSIA.

In 1916, a mission was sent to Russia to assist in training and organising the Russian Flying Corps, and during the latter part of 1916 and during 1917 Russia was supplied with 251 aeroplanes.

In May, 1918, orders were issued for the dispatch of a R.A.F. contingent in conjunction with a special mission which was being sent to Northern Russia to operate from Archangel. The Force consisted of 8 D.H.4 (R.A.F.3a) machines with a complement of personnel and stores. On arrival at Archangel, sufficient machines were collected from those which had previously been sent to Russia to form two squadrons of Nieuports and 1½ strutters.

In August, 1918, reinforcements were dispatched to Archangel, consisting of a proportion of British officers, N.C.Os, and men, a wing headquarters, an Intelligence Section, one flight of R.E.8s, and two Repair Sections for engines and aircraft respectively. On November 12th, 1918, a further reinforcement of six Sopwith scouts and a six months' supply of stores were dispatched.

JAPAN.

Several officers have been undergoing courses on aeroplanes and seaplanes.

BRAZIL.

Seventy-seven complete machines and 100 Le Rhone engines have been supplied.

Several officers have graduated as pilots under the tuition of our instructors. Two flying-boats have been supplied to the Brazilian Government.

ROUMANIA.

Several officers have been given instruction and have graduated as pilots. Twenty Sopwith machines have also been supplied.

Air Ministry, January 1st, 1919.

BRITISH AEROPLANES.

FIGURES FOR THE FLYING SERVICES.

The tables which follow hereafter give, in easily visible form, some interesting comparative figures illustrating the accomplishments of the Flying Services in the War.   They are taken from the official resumé to which reference has already been made.

PERSONNEL.

	August 1914.			December 1916.			December 1917.			October 1918.		
	Officers.	Other Ranks.	Total.	Officers.	Other Ranks.	Total.	Officers.	Other Ranks.	Total.	Officers.	Other Ranks.	Total.
R.F.C.	147	1,097	1,244	5,982	51,915	57,897	15,522	98,738	114,260	..	..	..
R.N.A.S.	50	550	600	2,764	26,129	28,893	4,765	43,050	47,815	..	..	..
R.A.F.	..	..	..	..	..	..	..	..	..	27,906	263,842	291,748
Total	..	..	1,844	..	..	86,790	..	..	162,075	..	..	291,748

MACHINES AND ENGINES ON CHARGE.

	August 1914.		January 1917.		January 1918.		October 1918.	
	Machines.	Engines.	Machines.	Engines.	Machines.	Engines.	Machines.	Engines.
R.F.C.	179	..	3,929	6,056	8,350	14,755	..	..
R.N.A.S.	93	..	1,567	3,672	2,741	6,902	..	..
R.A.F.	..	..	..	..	..	..	22,171	37,702
Total	272	..	5,496	9,728	11,091	21,657	22,171	37,702

OUTPUT OF MACHINES AND ENGINES.

	August 1914 to May, 1915 (10 months).		June, 1915 to February, 1917 (21 months).		March 1917 to December, 1917 (10 months).		January 1918 to October, 1918 (10 months).	
	Machines.	Engines.	Machines.	Engines.	Machines.	Engines.	Machines.	Engines.
R.F.C.	530	141	7,137	8,917	12,275	..	..	..
R.N.A.S.	No record.	No record.	No record.	No record.	1,246	..	..	..
R.A.F.	..	..	..	..	..	..	26,685	29,561
Total	530	141	7,137	8,917	13,521	13,979	26,685	29,561

BRITISH AEROPLANES.

EXPANSION OF MOTOR TRANSPORT.

Motor Transport. (All Types.)	R.F.C. Only.				Royal Air Force.
	August 1914.	August 1915.	August 1916.	August 1917.	October 31, 1918.
On charge ..	320	2,469	5,282	8,584	23,260

SQUADRONS MAINTAINED.

	Service.			Training. (1 Training Depot Station reckoned as 3 Squadrons.)	
	August 1914.	October 31, 1918.		August 1914.	October 31, 1918.
Western Front	4 (R.F.C.)	84 & 5 flights	Home	1 (R.F.C.)	174
Independent Force ..	..	10		2 (R.N.A.S.)	
5 Group ..	..	3	Egypt	..	10
India	..	2	Canada	..	15
Italy	..	4			
Middle East ..	..	13			
Russia ..	..	½			
Home Defence ..	..	18			
Naval Units ..	1 (R.N.A.S.)	64			
Total ..	5	198½ & 5 flights	..	3	199

RESULTS OF OPERATIONS IN THE AIR.

	July 1916 to Nov. 11, 1918	January 1, 1918, to November 11, 1918.									
	Western Front.	Indepen-dent Force.	Home Forces.	5th Group and Naval Units.	Italy.	Egypt.	Mesopo-tamia.	Salonika.	Palestine.	India (Aden).	Total.
Enemy aircraft accounted for, i.e., brought down or driven down	6,904	150	8	470	405	25	6	59	81	..	7,908
Our machines missing ..	2,484	111	..	114	44	9	13	8	24	..	2,810
Bombs dropped .. (tons)	6,402	540	..	662	59	43	25	130	74	30	7,945
Hours flown	889,526	11,784	..	39,102	25,206	7,022	7,862	13,417	21,848	579	1,016,346
Rounds fired at ground targets	10,238,182	353,257	..	..	222,704	50,937	107,563	193,354	735,550	7,527	11,858,137
Photographs taken ..	401,375	3,682	..	3,440	14,596	8,135	66,720	15,587	27,039	542	501,116
Enemy balloons brought down	258	..	..	..	..	..	..	..	..	..	258

NOTE.—Records are not available of the results obtained by Expeditionary Force, Western Front, prior to July, 1916, or by 5th Group and Naval Units, or in Eastern Theatres prior to January, 1918. The absence of these records, however, will not materially affect the totals shown as regards enemy aircraft accounted for, our machines missing, or the weight of bombs dropped, owing to the comparatively recent growth in intensity of aerial fighting and the smaller number of aircraft engaged.

NOTE BY EDITOR OF "ALL THE WORLD'S AIRCRAFT."—It should be noted that the number of British machines recorded as "missing" does not represent our losses as compared with those of the enemy, as it does not include machines shot down in our own territory, or crashed on landing. An official statement published in November, 1918, states that the Total Losses of the Flying Services were 7,589 killed, wounded, and missing, of whom 1,551 officers and 1,129 other ranks were definitely reported as killed.

BRITISH AEROPLANES.

Aerial Societies:—

The Royal Aero Club.—(Governing Body of the Sport of Aviation).
Address: 3, Clifford Street, Bond Street, W.1.

The Royal Aeronautical Society. (Premier Society, founded 1866. Represents the scientific side of Aeronautics and Aviation).
Address: 7, Albemarle Street, W.1.

The Royal Air Force Club. (Residential Club for officers of the Royal Flying Corps).
Address: Bruton Street, W.1. (Temporarily).

The Aerial League.—(Propagandist body).
Address: 46, Dover Street, W.1.

The Society of British Aircraft Constructors. (The Manufacturers' Organisation).
Address: 1, Albemarle Street, W.1.

Aerial Journals, etc. :—

Aeroplane, The. 6d. every Wednesday. 175, Piccadilly, London. (The recognized organ of the Flying Services and of the Aircraft Industry.)

Aeronautical Journal, The. Monthly. (The organ of the Royal Aeronautical Society.) 7, Albemarle Street, W.1.

Aeronautics. 6d. weekly. 6 & 8, Bouverie Street, E.C.4.

Flight. 6d. every Friday. 36, Gt. Queen Street, Kingsway, W.C.2.

Flying. 6d. weekly. 5, Chancery Lane, E.C.

All the World's Aircraft. 30/-. Annual. 100, Southwark Street, London, S.E. (The annual work of reference on Aeronautical Affairs.)

Aerodromes :—

The following list includes the majority, so far as ascertainable, of the aerodromes and landing grounds employed by the Royal Air Force during the war. Some of these places are not now occupied by Air Force Units, some also have been or may be relinquished by the authorities, but in each case alighting ground (or water) for aircraft is available.

In accordance with the terms of the Air Navigation Regulations, a landing ground which is regularly used as such by aircraft must be licensed. At the date of compiling this list, in the transition period between war and peace, it has been found impossible to indicate which of the places mentioned is, or may be, licenced, except those officially designated for civil use; that certain other well-known and safe aerodromes will be licenced is obvious. Many other grounds also will be licenced temporarily for exhibition and "joy-ride" flying.

N.B.—Places marked in heavy type are recognised civil or semi-civil aerodromes, where landing and refueling facilities may be expected to exist. They are under the control of the Air Ministry, and were established provisionally on May 1st, 1919.

Places marked † are Airship Stations. Care must be exercised in landing or taking off at these Stations with aeroplanes.

Places marked * are Seaplane Stations.

Places marked § are "appointed aerodromes" for traffic with foreign countries when the ban on flying to or from places abroad is removed.

Acton (Middlesex).
Aldergrove (nr. Belfast.)
Andover (Hants)
†Anglesey (Isle of)
Atwich (Yorks.)
Ayr (Ayrshire).
Baldonnel (Dublin).
Bangor (Carnarvon).
†Barlow (Yorks.)
†Barrow (Lancs.)
Beaulieu (Hants.)
†Bedford
Bekesbourne (Kent).
*Bembridge (I. of W.)
Berehaven (Cork).
Beverley (Yorks.)
Biggin Hill (Kent).
Bircham Newton (Norfolk).
Blackpool Sands (Lancs.)
Boscombe Down (Wilts.)
Bracebridge (Lincs.)
Brighton—Ladies Mile (Sussex).
Brooklands (Surrey).
Buckminster (Lincs.)

Cairncross (Berwick).
*Calshot (Hants).
Castlebar (Co. Mayo).
Castle Bromwich (B'ham).
Catterick (Yorks.)
Cattewater (Devon).
Coal Aston (Sheffield).
Collinstown (Dublin).
Copmanthorpe (Yorks.)
Coventry (Warwick).
*Cowes (I. of W.)
Cramlington (Northumberland).
†Cranwell (Lincs.)
Croydon (Surrey).
Curragh (Co. Kildare).

Detling (Kent).
Doncaster (Yorks.)
Donibristle (Kinross).
*Dover (Kent).
Driffield (Yorks.)
*Dundee (Forfar).
Duxford (Cambs.)

†East Fortune (Haddington).
Eastbourne (Sussex).
Eastchurch (Kent).
Eastleigh (Hants).
Easton on the Hill (Northants).
Elmswell (Suffolk).
Fairlop (Essex).
*Felixstowe (Suffolk).
Feltwell (Norfolk).
Fermoy (Cork).
Filton (Bristol).
*Fishguard (Pembroke).
Folkstone (Kent).
† „ „ (Capel.)
Fowlmere (Cambs.)
Freiston (Lincs)

Gormanston (Co. Neath).
Grain, Isle of (Kent).

§**Hadleigh (Suffolk).**
Hainault Farm (Essex).
Halton Camp (Bucks).
*Hamble, Southampton (Hants).
Harlaxton (Lincs.)
Harling Road (Norfolk).
Harpswell (Lincs).
Hawkinge (Kent).
Hendon (London Aerodrome).
Hendon—Stagg Lane (Middlesex).
Hooton Park (Cheshire).
Hornchurch—Sutton's Farm (Essex).
*Hornsea Mere (Yorks).
§**Hounslow (Middlesex).**
†Howden (Yorks.)
Hucknall (Notts).
Hylton (Sunderland).
†Inchinnan (Dumbarton).

Joyce Green (Kent).

Kenley (Surrey).
†Killeagh (Co. Waterford).
*Killingholme (Yorks.)
†Kingsnorth (Kent).
Kirton Lindsey (Lincs).

Lake Down (Salisbury Plain).

Lark Hill (Salisbury Plain).
Lee-on-Solent (Hants).
Leighterton (Glos.).
Leuchars (Fife).
Lilbourne (Northants).
London Colney (Hants).
Longridge (Hants).
†Longside (Aberdeen).
Lopcombe Corner (Hants).
*Lough Foyle (L'derry).
†**Luce Bay (Wigtown).**
Lydd (Kent).
§**Lympne (Kent).**
Manchester—Didsbury.
Manchester—Alexandra Park.
Manston (Kent).
Manywell Heights (Nr. Bradford).
Marham (Norfolk).
Marske (Yorks).
Martlesham Heath (Suffolk).
Merifield (Devonport).
Minchinhampton (Glos).
Montrose (Forfar).
†Mullion (Cornwall).
Netheravon (Wilts).
Newcastle-on-Tyne.
*Newhaven (Sussex).
§**New Holland (Yorks).**
*Newlyn (Cornwall).
Newmarket (Suffolk).
New Romsey (Kent).
Northolt (Middlesex).
North Queensferry (Linlithgow).
North Shotwick (Cheshire).
North Weald Bassett (Essex).
Norwich (Norfolk).
Old Sarum (Salisbury).
Oranmore (Co. Galway).
Ordfordness (Suffolk).
Owthorne (Yorks).
Padstow (Cornwall).
†Pembroke.
Penston (Haddington).
*Peterhead (Aberdeen).
†Polegate (Sussex).
Porteholme (Hunts).
*Portland (Dorset).
Prawle Point (Devon).
†Pulham (Norfolk).
*Queenstown (Co. Cork).
Rathmullan (Co. Donegal).
Redcar (Yorks).

Rendcombe (Glos).
Renfrew (Nr. Glasgow).
Retford (Notts).
Ripon (Yorks).
Rochford (Essex).

Scale Hall (Lancs).
Scampton (Lincs).
Scopwick (Lincs).
Sea Houses (Roxborough).
Seaton Carew (Durham).
Sedgeford (Norfolk).
Shawbury (Salop).
South Carleton (Lincs).
South Farnborough (Hants).
Southport (Lancs).
*Southsea, Portsmouth.
Spittlegate (Lincs).
Stonehenge (Wilts).
Stow Maries (Essex).
Strathbeg (Aberdeen).

Tadcaster (Yorks).
Tallaght (Nr. Dublin).
Tangmere (Sussex).
*Tees Bay (Yorks).
Ternhill (Salop).
Throwley (Kent).
*Torquay (Devon).
*Tresco (Scillies).
Turnberry (Ayr).
Turnhouse, Edinburgh.
Tynehead (Edinburgh).
Tynemouth (Northumberland).

Upavon (Salisbury).
Upwood, Ramsey (Hunts).

Waddington (Lincs).
Waterloo Sands (L'pool).
West Ayton (Yorks).
*Westgate (Kent).
Weston-super-Mare Sands (Somerset).
Weston-on-Green (Oxford).
Westward Ho (Devon).
*Wexford (Ireland).
Whiddy Island (Co. Cork).
Whiteburn, (Berwick).
Whitney (Oxon).
Wittering (Northants).
Wormwood Scrubbs (London).
Wye (Kent).
Wyton (Hunts).
*Yarmouth (Norfolk).
Yatesbury (Wilts).

ROYAL AIRCRAFT ESTABLISHMENT.—(Late Royal Aircraft Factory).

[The R.A.F. aeroplanes hereafter illustrated and described are those which were in use at the end of the war. The earlier types have been described in previous issues of "All the World's Aircraft."—*Ed.*].

THE F.E. 2b. With Beardmore engine of 120 h.p.

This machine was the fore-runner of the Rolls engined type, which it resembles in general design.

This machine, with slight modifications and a 160 h.p. Beardmore engine, was still in use at the end of the war, as a night-bombing machine.

A

AIRCRAFT ESTABLISHMENT, ROYAL. (New name for The Royal Aircraft Factory, South Farnborough.) This establishment was engaged in airship construction and repairs. During the war the Factory has been at work on experiments in various types of aeroplanes, and has been turning out a certain number of spare parts for existing machines. It is not used for the production of aeroplanes in quantities, the designs produced from its experiments being built by numerous "contractors."

As the result of the Air Defence agitations of early 1916, a Committee, composed of Sir Charles Parsons, the late Sir Richard Burbidge, and the late Sir Frederic Donaldson, investigated the management of the Royal Aircraft Factory. In 1916, Mr. Henry Fowler, late of the Ministry of Munitions, and previously Chief Mechanical Engineer of the Midland Railway, was appointed to be Superintendent.

In 1917, Mr. Fowler was created a Knight of the Order of the British Empire, and, as Sir Henry Fowler, K.B.E., he was appointed Assistant Director-General of Aircraft Production under the Air Ministry. Mr. Sydney Smith, formerly Chief Inspector of Factories, took his place as Superintendent.

THE F.E. 2b. Viewed from below.

ROYAL AIRCRAFT ESTABLISHMENT.

"F.E." indicated "Farman Experimental," M. Henri Farman being credited with having originated the "pusher" type. It is now taken to mean "Fighting Experimental." This has been developed along various lines, the "F.E. 2b" being a big fighting machine with a 160 h.p. Beardmore engine, and the "F.E. 2d" still bigger, with a 250 h.p. Rolls-Royce engine. One may state this without giving away secrets, as samples of both types have been captured by the enemy.

The "F.E. 8," on the other hand, is a small single-seat fighting machine.

"R.E." indicates "Reconnaissance Experimental." These also have been developed as "R.E. 2," "R.E. 3," up to "R.E. 7," "R.E. 8," and so forth, with various engines.

"S.E." indicates "Scouting Experimental."

The Royal Aircraft Factory was so known until, on April 1, 1918, the Royal Air Force came into being. In order to prevent confusion over the initials the name of the Factory was then changed to The Royal Aircraft Establishment.

THE R.E. 8. With 130 h.p. R.A.F. engine (Side view.)
This machine was still in use at the end of the war, as an artillery observation machine and as a night bomber.

The R.A.F. "type-letters" have the following significance :—

"B.E." at first indicated "Bleriot Experimental," M. Blériot being credited with having originated the "tractor" type machine. It is now taken to mean "British Experimental."

The original B.E. was designed by and built under the supervision of Mr. Geoffrey de Havilland, now Captain R.F.C., and chief designer for the Aircraft Manufacturing Co., Ltd. A later type of the same general design was numbered "B.E. 2." Developments of this type were the "B.E. 2b," "B.E. 2c," "B.E. 2d," and "B.E. 2e," the two last being built in very large quantities, but the "B.E. 2c" is now chiefly used for school purposes.

The "B.E." general type was also developed along different lines, as the "B.E. 3," "4," "5," "6," and so forth, up to the "B.E. 12," which cannot be here described, as it is in war use. One may perhaps say that it has been successful in destroying *Zeppelins*, and is very much more powerful than the "B.E. 2c."

THE R.E. 8. With 130 h.p. R.A.F. engine.
Note the big engine, the heavier aileron strut, and the less overhang to the upper planes than in the B.E. 2e. The pilot sits in front, and the gunner has a gun-ring ·round the after seat.

E

(Reproduced from " Flugsport.")

Side view of a S.E. 5 Biplane, captured by the Germans.

BRITISH AEROPLANES.

ROYAL AIRCRAFT ESTABLISHMENT.

Above the angle of incidence is 5 deg. mean, below by the body 6 deg., by the struts 5 deg.

Both plane spars show sections of I shape, whereas the longerons of the rudiment pieces, running through the body are steel tubes of 1.75 millimetre thickness, and 45 mm. outer diameter. The plane ribs show the usual construction of most British air craft.

There are no compression struts between the spars, some of the ribs being solid struts instead.

The interior wiring of the planes between the body and the struts is carried out in simple profile wire, that of the over-hanging ends of thick-end wire.

A wood strip forms the back edge of the planes. Further, two auxiliary ribs ranging from the leading nose edge to the main spar are arranged between each two ribs.

The fabric is sewed together with the ribs, and is painted yellow below, browned above, as is the fabric of the body. Shoe-eyes are arranged on the underside of the trailing edge of the plane to assess the pressure.

The centre section struts are covered steel tubes. The plane spruce struts rest in long stampings, serving as fixing points of the vertical wiring.

Profile wire is employed for the plane cross wiring with twin wires for those carrying load and single for counter ones.

The two spars of the upper planes are strengthened further between the centre section and the struts with two wires each. Unbalanced ailerons are hinged to the back crossbar of the upper and lower planes.

THE S.E. 5a.

A Neutral Correspondent writes :—

Following is a translation of the description of the British S.E.v.A. (scouting, experimental) fighting single-seater, published in the March issue of the German Airmen's Journal, "Luftwaffe," reading thus :—

The aeroplane in question was built by Vickers, Ltd., and numbered B.507, wearing further as recognition initial or that of a squadron, an A as well as a white circle. The propellor is marked : S.E.v.A., which leads to the idea that the older model of this same aeroplane type with the 150 h.p. Hispano motor not geared down is called S.E.v.

The biplane has a surface of 22.8 square metres, and both planes, connected with but one pair of struts to each side, have a span of 8.15 metres, and a chord of 1.52 metres, the gap from the top of the fuselage amounting to 0 45 metre.

No arrow-shape prevails. The V-shape of the equal-sized ends of the upper and lower planes mounted on the centre section and respective body rudiments amounts to 1.71 degrees.

The sight field of range is improved by cutting the centre section in the middle and the lower planes near the body.

Three-quarter rear view of a S.E. 5 Biplane, captured by the Germans.

ROYAL AIRCRAFT ESTABLISHMENT.

The body shows the usual strut-cum-wire combination, being rounded above with half-circle frames and fairings, and having three-ply wood planking of 4 millimetre thickness to the pilot's seat. Fuselage longitudinals and struts have sections of I-shape, except the vertical struts behind the pilot's seat, which are worked out round.

The tail-plane is curved to both sides and fixed to the body, so that the angle of incidence can be varied during the flight within the limits + 4.5 deg. and — 3 deg. To this end the front spar is turnable, while the rear spar, with its wiring, is fixed to a tube, arranged shiftable to the body stern post. This tube rests with a piece of thread in a gear nut, again resting in the stern-post fixed, yet turnable.

When the nut is turned from the pilot's seat by means of wheel and cable, the tube is displaced upwards or downwards, transferring thereby the same manœuvre on the rear spar of the tail plane, and thus its angle of incidence changes. The elevator hooked to the fixed tail-plane partakes in this movement. The wires for operating the elevator are led through the body and tail-plane, which certainly saves air resistance, yet makes twice a 20 deg. direction change of each wire necessary. Main and tail-planes are equipped with cellon windows, rendering a control of the rollers possible.

The under-carriage shows the normal form. The through-running axle rests between two auxiliary ones. There is no limit of the springing range.

The tail skid shows an unusual construction, being arranged turnable behind the stern-post and connected with the rudder cable by intermediance of springs. A brass skid bow is sprung by means of two spiral pressure springs which are prevented from sideway turning by inserted telescope tubes.

According to the firm's sign board the Wolseley-Hispano-Suiza engine gave the 30th August, 1917, on brake 206 h.p. = 203 P.S. at 2005 revolutions. The r.p.m. of the four-bladed airscrew is geared down in the ratio of 4 to 3.

The exhaust gas is led behind the pilot's seat in two tubes to each side of the body. The motor sits so that there is free accessibility after removing the bonnet. The radiator forms the bow of the body.

A cover arrangement makes it possible to uncover the body about half-way from the pilot's seat.

The main petrol tank of 120 litres' capacity is placed behind the motor on the upper fuselage longitudinals. A gravity tank of 17 litres capacity is arranged in the centre section between the leading edge and the main spar. The oil tank of a capacity of 14 litres lies across in the engine frame below the rear edge of the motor.

The fuel suffices for a flight of about two hours duration.

Following instruments are arranged in the pilot's seat :—

To right : A box for the light pistols ; a contact breaker for the self-starter ; a contact breaker for the two magnetos ; a triple led cock for the gravity and pressure petrol ; a triple led cock for the hand and motor air-pump ; a thermometer for the water of the radiator ; the petrol gauge placed on the back side of the main tank, and a manometer for air-pressure.

To left : Gas lever ; lever for regulation of the gas in altitude flights ; lever for operating the radiator blinds, clip for three light cartridges. On the bottom is further arranged a hand-pump for the hydraulic machine-gun gear ; two boxes for drums for the moveable machine-gun and self-starter.

E 2

A square windshield of Triplex glass is placed in front of the pilot's seat. Behind it a box is arranged in a queer position to the body with access from outside.

The fixed Vickers' machine-gun lies to left of the pilot inside the body fabric. The cartridge girdle is of metal. The firing of the machine-gun takes place hydraulically by means of a control arrangement, placed in front of the motor and connected with the machine-gun through a copper main, as well as driven from the air screw by a gear set. The firing lever sits on the stick.

On the bow-shaped iron band lying on the centre section rests a Lewis gun, which can be pulled down during the flight to permit vertical firing.

The empty weight of the aeroplane was worked out at 706 kilos, distributed as follows :—

	kilos.
Engine	225.0
Exhaust collection	12.0
Self-starter	3.6
Radiator	23.8
Radiator water	31.0
Air screw	26.6

Main petrol tank	17.8
Gravity petrol tank	6.5
Oil tank	3.9
Motor equipment	6.4
Body with seat and plate covers	151.0
Tail-plane angle of incidence change arrangements	1.9
Under carriage	40.8
Tail skid	3.7
Pilotage arrangement	5.4
Planes with wiring	112.2
Vertical and horizontal wiring	21.0
Body equipment	14.0
	706.0

The fuel weight amounts with fully loaded tanks to 111 kilos., so that the total useful load can be calculated at 250 kilos., the total weight working out at 956 kilos.

The load of the planes is thus : $\frac{956}{22.8} = 42$ kilos per square metre.

The performance load is then : $\frac{956}{200} = 4.78$ kilos per horse power.

Hohenflossen — verstellvorrichtung des S.E.

Elevator and variable tail-plane arrangement, with steerable tail-skid of the S.E.

(This and the two following illustrations are taken from "Luftwaffe.")

Engl. S. E. V. A.

Der englische S. E. V. A.-Kampf-Einsitzer

Steuerungsschema

Querschnitt a b

Größter Querschnitt
Inhalt 0,224 m²

Rumpf: Holzdrahtboot
Hintersteven   Rumpfholme Holz
Höhe 250 mm   Rumpfstiele. Holz
Breite 50 mm   Rumpfverspannung. Draht
           Rumpfaussenhaut Stoff.

Einstellwinkel

420 bei wagerechter Flugelsehne

Einstellw. d. Höhenflosse
(−3,0° ÷ +4,5°)

Rippe vom Ober- und Unterflügel

Höhenflosse

Holmquerschnitte der Flügel
Material Spruce

vorn

hinten

Flacheninhalt. m².	Motor	Luftschraube.	Kühler.	Fahrgestell.
Oberfl. 11,8, Unterfl. 11,0 + 2,2,8 mit Querrud.	200 PS Hispano Suiza	Holz 4 flüglig	Stirnkühler	Streben Federung Gummischnur
Querruder 4 × 0,7 = 2,8.	Bremsleistung	Durchmesser 236 cm.	mit Abdeckvorrichtung	Federungsweg. Ohne Anschlag.
Höhenflosse: 1,4, Höhenruder. 1,4.	N = 200 PS.	Blattbreite. 26 cm.	Kühlwasser einschl.	79·29 Reifen: 700 × 100 mm.
Kielflosse 0,6, Seitenruder 0,5.	n = 2000 Umdr/min.	Steigung.	Motor + Leitungen	13 Stahlrohr Nabe Breite 180 mm
		n ≈ 1500	31,0 l.	ohne Fütterung Innerer ⌀ 45 mm.

Engl. S.E.V.A.

Fuselage Details of the S.E. 5a. from "Luftwaffe."　　39a

A—continued.

AIRCRAFT MANUFACTURING Co., Ltd.

47, Victoria Street, London, S.W. Works: Hendon, London, N.W. This Company, established in 1912 by Mr. G. Holt Thomas, holds all the British rights for the *H. & M. Farman* types.

During 1914 Mr. Holt Thomas secured the services of Capt. Geoffrey de Haviland, R.F.C., as the firm's designer-in-chief, and has produced the series of extraordinarily successful machines which have made Capt. de Haviland's initials famous.

As a matter of general interest, and for purposes of reference, specifications of the whole of the "De H." series are included in the following descriptions, but no illustrations are given of the older types of this make. These aeroplanes are now known as "Airco" machines.

AIRCO DE H.1.

The first of the series, produced just before the declaration of war, was a two-seater Renault-engined "pusher" machine.

Specification.

Type of machine	Biplane ("Pusher.")
Name or type No. of machine ..	De H.1.
Span	41 ft.
Gap, maximum and minimum ..	5 ft. 7 in.
Overall length	28 ft. 11⅝ in.
Maximum height..	11 ft. 4 in.
Chord	5 ft. 6 in.
Total surface of wings, including centre plane and ailerons ..	409.3 sq. ft.
Span of tail	12 ft. 5½ in.
Total area of tail (empennage) ..	80.45 sq. ft.
Area of elevators..	11.0 sq. ft. each.
Area of rudder	16.15 sq. ft.
Area of fin	4.05 sq. ft.
Area of each aileron	18.0 sq. ft.
Engine type and h.p. ..	80 h.p. Renault.
Airscrew, diam., pitch and revs.	9.03 dia. ; 9.2 pitch; 870 revs.
Weight of machine empty ..	1,356 lbs.
Weight of machine full load ..	2,044 lbs.
Load per sq. ft.	4.99 lbs.
Weight per h.p. full load ..	25.5 lbs.
Tank capacity in gallons ..	30 gallons.

Performance.

Speed low down	78 m.p.h.
Landing speed..	41 m.p.h.

Climb.

To 3,500 feet	11¼ minutes.

Disposable load apart from fuel .. .. .. 420 lbs.
Total weight of machine loaded .. .. .. 2,044 lbs.

AIRCO DE H.1A.

This was a modified De H.1 fitted with a 120 Beardmore engine in place of the original Renault.

Specification.

Type of machine	Biplane ("Pusher.")
Name or type No. of machine ..	De H.1a.
Span	41 ft.
Gap, maximum and minimum ..	5 ft. 7 in.
Overall length	28 ft. 11¼ in.
Maximum height..	11 ft. 2 in.
Chord	5 ft. 6 in.
Total surface of wings, including centre plane and ailerons ..	409.3 sq. ft.
Span of tail	12 ft. 3 in.
Total area of tail (empennage) ..	79.9 sq. ft.
Area of elevators..	11.0 sq. ft. each.
Area of rudder	15.6 sq. ft.
Area of fin	4.05 sq. ft.
Area of each aileron	18.0 sq. ft.
Engine type and h.p. ..	130 h.p. Beardmore.
Airscrew, diam., pitch and revs.	9.03 diam., 9.2 pitch, 1,350 revs.
Weight of machine empty ..	1,672 lbs.
Weight of machine full load ..	2,400 lbs.
Load per sq. ft.	5.87 lbs.
Weight per h.p. full load ..	18.45 lbs.
Tank capacity in gallons.. ..	33 gallons.

Performance.

Speed low down	89 m.p.h.
Landing speed..	49 m.p.h.

Climb.

To 3,500 ft.	6.45 mins.

Disposable load apart from fuel .. .. .. 420 lbs.
Total weight of machine loaded .. .. .. 2,400 lbs.

AIRCO DE H.2.

The De H.2 was produced in 1915 to meet the need for a high-speed single-seater fighter.

At that time the synchronised machine-gun fire through the airscrew had not been developed in this country, and consequently the high-speed tractor single-seater was of very little use for fighting purposes.

This machine was therefore an attempt to combine a high performance with the unobstructed use of a machine-gun firing straight ahead, which is possible with a machine of the "pusher" type.

In this respect the De H.2 was extraordinarily successful. During 1915 and the early part of 1916 this type of machine gave an excellent account of itself on the Western Front, but was displaced by machines of the "tractor" type when the use of synchronised guns became general.

Specification.

Type of machine	Biplane ("Pusher.")
Name or type No. of machine ..	De H.2.
Span	28 ft. 0½ in.
Gap, maximum and minimum ..	4 ft. 6 in.
Overall length	25 ft. 2½ in.
Maximum height..	9 ft. 6½ in.
Chord	4 ft. 9 in.
Total surface of wings, including centre plane and ailerons ..	228.0 sq. ft.
Span of tail	10 ft. 3 in.
Total area of tail (empennage) ..	56.5 sq. ft.
Area of elevators..	6.8 sq. ft. each.
Area of rudder	13.5 sq. ft.
Area of fin	2.4 sq. ft.
Area of each aileron	9.7 sq. ft.
Engine type and h.p.	100 Gnôme.
Airscrew, diam., pitch and revs.	8.0 dia., 7.7 pitch, 1,350 revs.
Weight of machine empty ..	896 lbs.
Weight of machine full load ..	1,320 lbs.
Load per sq. ft.	5.8 lbs.
Weight per h.p. full load ..	13.2 lbs.
Tank capacity in gallons.. ..	22.4 galls.

Performance.

Speed low down	93 m.p.h.
Landing speed..	45 m.p.h.

Climb.

To 6,500 ft.	8.40 mins.

Disposable load apart from fuel .. .. .. 213 lbs.
Total weight of machine loaded .. .. .. 1,320 lbs.

AIRCRAFT MANUFACTURING CO., Ltd.
—*continued*.

AIRCO DE H.3.

This machine, produced in 1915, was never put into service. It is of interest, however, as one of the earliest attempts at building a twin-engined machine and as the ancestor of the De H. 10.

Specification.

Type of machine	Biplane "Pusher" (2 engines)
Name or type No. of machine ..	De H.3.
Span	60 ft. 10 in.
Gap, maximum and minimum ..	7 ft.
Overall length	36 ft. 10 in.
Maximum height	14 ft. 6 in.
Chord	6 ft. 9 in.
Total surface of wings, including centre planes and ailerons ..	790.0 sq. ft.
Span of tail	23 ft. 2 in.
Total area of tail (empennage) ..	164.0 sq. ft.
Area of elevators..	25.5 sq. ft. each.
Area of rudder	22.0 sq. ft.
Area of fin	13.0 sq. ft.
Area of each aileron	30.7 sq. ft.
Engine type and h.p.	Two 130 h.p. Beardmore.
Airscrew, diam., pitch and revs..	9.03 diam., 9.18 pitch, 1,400.
Weight of machine empty ..	3,982 lbs.
Weight of machine full load ..	5,776 lbs.
Load per sq. ft.	7.3 lbs.
Weight per h.p. full load ..	22.2 lbs.
Tank capacity in gallons.. ..	140 gallons.

Performances.

Speed low down	95 m.p.h.

Climb.

To 6,500 ft.	24 mins.
Landing speed..	53 m.p.h.
Disposable load apart from fuel	711 lbs.
Total weight of machine loaded	5,776 lbs.

AIRCO DE H.4.

The De H. 4 was the first really high-speed British general utility machine of the medium weight type fitted with a high-power stationary engine. In the original form produced in 1916 —fitted with a B.H.P. engine of 240 h.p.—the De H. 4 had a speed greater than, and a climb and speed little, if at all, inferior to, that of the best of the rotary-engined single-seater fighters of that date.

It was thus possible to use these machines for reconnaissance and photographic work over the lines without the need for a fighter escort, since their excellent performance and the fact that they were fitted with a gun ring in the after seat in addition to a synchronised gun firing through the airscrew, put them upon at least equal terms with any existing type of enemy fighter.

The later editions of the same type fitted with "Eagle" Rolls-Royce engines, were considerably more valuable, and were extensively used for day bombing in addition to reconnaissance work.

41a

The Aircraft Manufacturing Co.'s De H.3 (2-160 h.p. Beardmore engines).

The De H. 4 Biplane, with Rolls-Royce "Eagle" engine, 375 h.p.

AIRCRAFT MANUFACTURING CO., Ltd.
—continued.

From a structural point of view this machine is chiefly remarkable for the very extensive use which is made of three-ply wood in the fuselage.

From the nose to aft of the passenger's seat the fuselage is devoid of wire bracing, a three-ply covering serving the purpose. Not only is this the case, but the whole of the engine mountings are built of ply-wood, which takes the place of the metal plates commonly used for such purposes.

It is thus possible to put bullet holes through almost any part of the front end of the fuselage without seriously impairing the strength of the structure—whereas with the usual methods of construction a single lucky shot may destroy an important bracing or cut out the flange of an engine plate, and seriously weaken the structure.

Specification.

Type of machine	Biplane "Tractor."
Name or type No. of machine ..	De H.4.
Span	42 ft. 4⅝ in.
Gap, maximum and minimum ..	5 ft. 6 in.
Overall length	30 ft.
Maximum height	11 ft. 4½ in.
Chord	5 ft. 6 in.
Total surface of wings, including centre plane and aileron ..	434.0 sq. ft.
Span of tail	14 ft.
Total area of tail (empennage) ..	81.1 sq. ft.
Area of elevators	12.0 sq. ft. each.
Area of rudder	13.7 sq. ft.
Area of fin	5.4 sq. ft.
Area of each aileron	20.5 sq. ft.
Engine type and h.p.	240 h.p. B.H.P.
Airscrew, diam., pitch and revs.	8.75 diam., 8.2 pitch, 1,355 revs.
Weight of machine empty ..	2,302 lbs.
Weight of machine full load ..	3,400 lbs.
Load per sq. ft.	7.84 lbs.
Weight per h.p. full load ..	14.35 lbs.
Tank capacity in gallons.. ..	66 gallons.

Performance.

Speed low down	120 m.p.h.
Landing speed	52 m.p.h.

Climb.

To 6,500 feet	8 minutes.
To 10,000 feet	14.10 minutes.
To 15,000 feet	29.15 minutes.
With R.R. engine	136½ m.p.h.
To 6,500 feet	5.15 minutes.
To 10,000 feet..	9 minutes.
To 15,000 feet	16.30 minutes.

Disposable load apart from fuel	578 lbs.
Total weight of machine loaded	3,400 lbs.

An "Airco" De H.4 (375 h.p. "Eagle" Rolls-Royce) Converted to Passenger Carrying Purposes.

A Passenger-Carrying De H.4 in the air.

An "Airco" De H. 4 transformed for
Passenger-carrying.

De Havilland IV

Fuselage Construction of the "Airco" De H.4.

From a German Print.

43a

F

AIRCRAFT MANUFACTURING CO., Ltd.—*continued.*

General arrangement of the "Airco" De H. 4.   *(From a German Print.)*

44a

AIRCRAFT MANUFACTURING CO., Ltd.
—continued.

AIRCO DE H.5.

This machine, produced late in 1916 and extensively used at the front in 1917, was in the main an effort to produce a single-seater fighter in which the pilot's view upwards and forward was not entirely blanketed by the top wing.

For this reason the top wing was staggered backwards very considerably, and the pilot's cockpit was put beneath the leading edge of that wing. In spite of the loss of efficiency which results from this backward stagger, Capt. De Haviland, by careful attention to the reduction of head resistance and weight, succeeded in producing a machine with a very good all-round performance.

Specification.

Type of machine	Biplane " Tractor."
Name or type No. of machine ..	De H.5.
Span	25 ft. 8 in.
Gap, maximum and minimum ..	4 ft. 9 in.
Overall length	22 ft.
Maximum height	9 ft. 1½ in.
Chord	4 ft. 6 in.
Total surface of wings, including centre plane and ailerons ..	212.1 sq. ft.
Span of tail	8 ft. 4½ in.
Total area of tail (empennage) ..	34.1 sq. ft.
Area of elevators	6.1 sq. ft. each.
Area of rudder	6.3 sq. ft.
Area of fin	2.2 sq. ft.
Area of each aileron	11.6 sq. ft.
Engine type and h.p.	110 h.p. Le Rhône.
Airscrew, diam., pitch and revs.	8.5 diam., 8.33 pitch, 1,295 revs.
Weight of machine empty ..	1,012 lbs.
Weight of machine full load ..	1,492 lbs.
Load per sq. ft.	7.03 lbs.
Weight per h.p. full load ..	13.57 lbs.
Tank capacity in gallons ..	25 gallons.

Performance.

Speed at 10,000 feet	102 m.p.h.
Speed at 15,000 feet	89 m.p.h.
Landing speed	50 m.p.h.
Disposable load apart from fuel	260 lbs.
Total weight of machine loaded	1,492 lbs.

Three-quarter Front View of the " Airco " De H. 5 (110 h.p. Le Rhône engine).

AIRCRAFT MANUFACTURING CO., Ltd.—*continued.*

Fuselage Construction of the "Airco" De H. 5.
(From a German Print.)

AIRCRAFT MANUFACTURING CO. Ltd.,

—continued.

AIRCO DE H.6.

The De H. 6 was produced as an elementary training machine for pilots, and, to meet requirements, fundamentally different from those which are desirable ·in machines for war use.

High performance was not desired, was in fact rather to be avoided. Cheapness and simplicity and strength of construction, together with ease in repair and a low landing speed, were of primary importance.

As a result of these considerations, the De H. 6, vulgarly known alternatively as the " Clutching Hand " or the " Sky Hook " has very few of those rather expensive refinements of form which characterise most modern machines.

It has, in fact, rather the appearance of having been built by the mile and cut off to order, which is, of course, a testimony to the thoroughness with which the desired simplicity has been reached in the design.

Specification.

Type of machine	Biplane " Tractor."
Name or type No. of machine	De H.6.
Span	35 ft. 11 in.
Gap, maximum and minimum ..	5 ft. 8½ in.
Overall length	27 ft. 3½ in.
Maximum height..	10 ft. 9½ in.
Chord	6 ft. 4 in.
Total surface of wings, including centre plane and aileron ..	436.3 sq. ft.
Span of tail	12 ft.
Total area of tail (empennage) ..	81.0 sq. ft.
Area of elevators..	13.0 sq. ft. each
Area of rudder	12.0 sq. ft.
Area of fin	5.5 sq. ft.
Area of each aileron	19.0 sq. ft.
Engine type and h.p.	100 h.p. R.A.F. 1A.
Airscrew, diam., pitch and revs.	9.085 diam., 10.0 pitch, 1,800 r.p.m.
Weight of machine empty ..	1,460 lbs.
Weight of machine full load ..	2,027 lbs.
Load per sq. ft.	4.64 lbs.
Weight per h.p. full load ..	20.27 lbs.
Tank capacity in gallons ..	26 gallons.

Performance.

Speed low down	66 m.p.h.
Landing speed	39 m.p.h.

Climb.

To 6,500 feet	29 minutes.
Disposable load apart from fuel	360 lbs.
Total weight of machine loaded	2,027 lbs.

A De H. 6 Biplane, with R.A.F. engine (90 h.p.)

AIRCRAFT MANUFACTURING CO., Ltd.
—continued.

AIRCO DE H.9.

This machine is a modification of the De H. 4, intended for bombing work. The main alterations are that the pilot's cockpit has been moved from beneath the centre section to just behind the trailing edge thereof leaving space for bombs in the fuselage, that the engine centre line has been slightly raised and the chassis somewhat shortened, and that the nose radiator has been replaced by a vertical water tank and a radiator in the bottom of the fuselage.

The total weight empty has been reduced by about 100 lbs., the tank capacity is somewhat increased, and the total load carried has been increased by about 500 lbs., at the cost of a slight loss in speed and climb and an increase in the landing speed.

Specification.

Type of machine	Biplane "Tractor."
Name or type No. of machine ..	De H.9.
Span	42 ft. 4⅝ in.
Gap, maximum and minimum ..	5 ft. 6 in.
Overall length	30 ft. 10 in.
Maximum height	11 ft. 2 in.
Chord	5 ft. 6 in.
Total surface of wings, including centre plane and ailerons ..	434.0 sq. ft.
Span of tail	14 ft.
Total area of tail (empennage) ..	81.1 sq. ft.
Area of elevators	12.0 sq. ft. each.
Area of rudder	13.7 sq. ft.
Area of fin	5.4 sq. ft.
Area of each aileron	20.5.
Engine type and h.p.	240 h.p. B.H.P.
Airscrew diam., pitch and revs. ..	9.5 diam., 6.9 pitch, 1525 revs.
Weight of machine empty ..	2,200 lbs.
Weight of machine full load ..	3,890 lbs.
Load per sq. ft.	8.95 lbs.
Weight per h.p. full load ..	16.2 lbs.
Tank capacity in gallons	74 gallons.

Performance.

Speed at 10,000 feet	110½ m.p.h.
Speed at 15,000 feet	102 m.p.h.
Landing speed	57 m.p.h.
Disposable load apart from fuel	1,121 lbs.
Total weight of machine loaded	3,890 lbs.

A Standard Type De H.9 (240 h.p. B.H.P. engine).

A De H.9 with a Napier "Lion" engine (450 h.p.)

PLAN.

STARBOARD.

PORT.

SPAN 42'-4⅝"

10'-0"

20'-0⅜" (FLAT)

20'-0⅜" (FLAT)

2'-11"

1'-8½"

5'-6"

27'-11"

10'-10"

1'-9"

3'-1"

2'-0"

14'-0"

1'-0"

AREA OF AILERONS, 20·5 SQ.FT. EACH.

AREA OF MAIN PLANE, 85 SQ.FT.

AREA OF CENTRE PLANE, 12 SQ.FT.

TOTAL AREA OF MAIN PLANES, AILERONS & CENTRE PLANE, 434 SQ.FT.

TOTAL AREA OF EMPENNAGE, 81·1 SQ.FT.

AREA OF TAIL PLANE, 38 SQ.FT.

AREA OF ELEVATORS, 12 SQ.FT. EACH.

FRONT ELEVATION.

11'-2"

GAP 5'-6"

19'-11¾"

2'-5⅝"

19'-11¾"

6'-0"

750 × 125 ᵐ/ᵐ WHEELS.

DIHEDRAL ANGLE 3°

SIDE ELEVATION

DeH.9.

5'-3¾"

AREA OF RUDDER 13·7 SQ.FT

AREA OF FIN 5·4 SQ.FT

CHORD 5'-6"

INCIDENCE ANGLE 3°

30'-10"

11"

5'-11"

SCALE OF FEET
0 1 2 3 4 5 6 7 8 9 10

FORD-JONES/19

AIRCRAFT MANUFACTURING CO., Ltd.

—*continued.*

AIRCO DE H.9.A.

This machine is an enlarged De H. 9, designed for the 375 h p. Rolls or the 400 h.p. Liberty. The span and the total surface have been somewhat increased, and the nose radiator has returned. Otherwise there is little alteration.

Specification.

Type of machine ..	Biplane "Tractor."
Name or type No. of machine ..	De H.9a.
Span	45 ft. 11⅜ in.
Gap, maximum and minimum ..	5 ft. 6 in.
Overall length	30 ft. 3 in.
Maximum height	11 ft. 4 in.
Chord	5 ft. 9 in.
Total surface of wings, including centre plane and ailerons ..	486.73 sq. ft.
Span of tail	14 ft.
Total area of tail (empennage) ..	80.1 sq. ft.
Area of elevators.. ..	12.0 sq. ft. each.
Area of rudder	13.7 sq. ft.
Area of fin	5.4 sq. ft.
Area of each aileron ..	18.59 sq. ft.
Engine type and h.p. ..	375 h.p. Rolls-Royce or 400 h.p. Liberty.
Airscrew, diam., pitch and revs.	10.0 diam., 12.3 pitch, 1,780 r.p.m.
Weight of machine empty ..	2,656 lbs.
Weight of machine full load ..	4,815 lbs.
Load per sq. ft.	9.89 lbs.
Weight per h.p. full load ..	12.8 lbs., 12.03 lbs.
Tank capacity in gallons ..	112 gallons.

Performance.

R.R. engine.   Speed at 10,000 feet   110½ m.p.h.
Landing speed .. 59 m.p.h.

Climb.

To 6,500 feet .. .. .. 11 minutes.
To 10,000 feet .. .. .. 20.6 minutes.

Disposable load apart from fuel .. .. .. 1,199 lbs.
Total weight of machine loaded .. .. .. 4,815 lbs.

Note.—If less weight is carried a speed of 125½ m.p.h. is attained at 10,000 feet, and 116 m.p.h. at 15,000 feet.

Three-quarter View from Rear—" Airco " De H.9A (400 h.p. Liberty engine).

Another View of the " Airco " De H.9A (400 h.p. Liberty engine).

AIRCRAFT MANUFACTURING CO., Ltd.—*continued* .

A De H.9A, with Liberty engine.

The Pilot's and Gunner's Cockpits of a De H.9A,
with Napier Lion engine. 450 h.p.

Three-quarter Front View—The De H.9A (Liberty engine).

STARBOARD.

PORT.

45'- 11 ⁷⁄₈"

9'-6"

10'- 3¾"

1'-0"

FRONT ELEVATION.

5'-6"

11'-4"

21'- 8¹¹⁄₁₆"

21'- 8¹¹⁄₁₆"

3'- 0⁹⁄₁₆"

2'-0"

14'-0"

2'-5½"

3°

3°

SIDE ELEVATION.

30'- 2¹³⁄₁₆"

SCALE OF FEET.
0 1 2 3 4 5 6 7 8 9 10

DEH9A.
(400 H.P. LIBERTY "TWELVE")

Ford-Jones, 19.

AIRCRAFT MANUFACTURING CO., Ltd.
—continued.

AIRCO DE H.10 AND 10A.

The De H. 10 was designed as a high-speed day bomber and made its first appearance towards the end of 1917. As has been already stated, it is essentially a development of the De H. 3, from which it differs in that whereas the De H. 3 was fitted with pusher airscrews, the De H. 10 has tractor airscrews.

The most noticeable feature of this machine is the extremely low position of the fuselage, which is mainly below the bottom wing, and the curious mounting of the engines, overhung from one side of the outer centre section struts.

The De H 10 is a somewhat later type of the same machine. They differ mainly in that in the De H. 10 the twin engines are mounted well up in the gap between the planes, and in the De H 10a, the engine nacelles are actually on the bottom plane.

The alterations have resulted in a very marked increase in the speed of the type 10a, accompanied by an increase in the empty weight of the machine of nearly 140 lbs.

Both types proved their qualities on active service, before the cessation of hostilities, and it may be expected that with suitable modifications they will show their value even more fully as commercial machines in the near future.

Specification.

Type of machine	Biplane "Tractor."
Name or type No. of machine ..	De H.10.
Span	65 ft. 6 in.
Gap, maximum and minimum ..	7 ft.
Overall length	39 ft. $7\frac{7}{16}$ in.
Chord	7 ft.
Total surface of wings, including centre plane and ailerons ..	837.4 sq. ft.
Span of tail	22 ft.
Total area of tail (empennage) ..	144.3 sq. ft.
Area of elevators..	16.54 sq. ft. each.
Area of rudder	25.75 sq. ft.
Area of fin	10.0 sq. ft.
Area of each aileron	29.5 sq. ft.
Engine type and h.p.	Two 400 h.p. Liberty.
Airscrew, diam., pitch and revs.	10.0 diam., 7.3 pitch, 1,625 revs.
Weight of machine empty ..	5,355 lbs.
Weight of machine full load ..	8,500 lbs.
Weight per h.p. full load ..	10.6 lbs.
Tank capacity in gallons.. ..	215 gallons.

Performance.

Speed low down	$117\frac{1}{2}$ m.p.h.
Speed at 10,000 feet	115 m.p.h.
Speed at 15,000 feet	110 m.p.h.
Landing speed..	62 m.p.h.

Disposable load apart from fuel .. .. .. 1,381 lbs.

Front View of a De H. 10 (two 400 h.p. Liberty engines) without wings.

Three-quarter Front View—"Airco" De H.10 (two Rolls-Royce "Eagle" engines, each 360 h.p.)

G

AIRCRAFT MANUFACTURING CO., Ltd.
—continued.

AIRCO DE H.10 A.

Type of machine	Biplane "Tractor."
Name or type No. of machine ..	De H.10a.
Span	65 ft. 6 in.
Gap, maximum and minimum ..	7 ft.
Overall length	39 ft. $7\frac{7}{16}$ in.
Maximum height	14 ft. 6 in.
Chord	7 ft.
Total surface of wings, including centre plane and ailerons ..	837.4 sq. ft.
Span of tail	22 ft.
Total area of tail (empennage) ..	144.3 sq. ft.
Area of elevators..	16.54 sq. ft. each.
Area of rudder	25.75 sq. ft.
Area of fin	10.0 sq. ft.
Area of each aileron	29.5 sq. ft.
Engine type and h.p.	Two 400 h.p. Liberty.
Airscrew, diam., pitch and revs.	10.0 diam., 7.3 pitch, 1,625 revs.
Weight of machine empty ..	5,488 lbs.
Weight of machine full load ..	8,500 lbs.
Weight per h.p. full load.. ..	10.6 lbs.
Tank capacity in gallons.. ..	215 gallons.

Performance.

Speed low down	128 m.p.h.
Speed at 10,000 feet	124 m.p.h.
Speed at 15,000 feet	117 m.p.h.
Landing speed	62 m.p.h.
Disposable load apart from fuel	1,248 lbs

Three-quarter View from Aft—The De H. 10A (two 400 h.p. Liberty engines).

STARBOARD

65'-6"

7'-0"

14'-8"

10'-0"

5'-9"

22'-0"

7'-4¾"

PLAN.

PORT

15'-6⅛"

2½°

1'-0"

13'-0"

FRONT ELEVATION

4½°

SIDE ELEVATION
DeH—10.

39'-7⁷⁄₁₆"

14'-6"

7°

SCALE OF FEET

Ford Jones 19/

A—continued.

ALLIANCE. The Alliance Aeroplane Co., Ltd.

Registered Offices : 45, East Castle Street, London, W.1.

Works : Cambridge Road, Hammersmith, London, W.14.

Aerodrome : Noel Road, Acton, W.

Founded by Mr. Samuel Waring, of Waring & Gillow, Ltd. (now Sir Samuel Waring, Bart.).

Originally at works of Waring & Gillow, Ltd., but soon expanded into new works, and embraced various subsidiary works in various parts of England.

Engaged during the War entirely in producing aeroplanes and spares to official specifications.

After the Armistice, turned attention to the trans-Atlantic Competition, and produced a biplane, designed by Mr. Peters, to enter for the contest. This machine is illustrated herewith. As the trans-Atlantic prize was won before it was ready, the machine was flown to Madrid in a non-stop flight. This was the first non-stop journey between the two capitals. It is fitted with a 450 h.p. Napier " Lion " engine.

ALLIANCE " SEABIRD."
Specification.

Type of machine	Two-seater Biplane.
Name of type No. or machine ..	Alliance " Seabird."
Purpose for which intended ..	Commercial.
Span	53 ft.
Overall length	33 ft. 6 in.
Engine type and h.p. ..	Napier " Lion." 450 h.p.
Weight of machine empty ..	2600 lbs.
Weight per h.p.	16.4 lbs.
Tank capacity in gallons ..	500 gallons.
Tank capacity in hours ..	21 hours.

Performance.

Speed low down	140 m.p.h.
Landing speed	45 m.p.h.
Disposable load apart from fuel	4800 lbs.
Total weight of machine loaded	7400 lbs.

Three-quarter Front View of the Alliance Co.'s "Seabird" (450 h.p. Napier "Lion" engine).

The Alliance Biplane (450 h.p. Napier "Lion" engine). This machine flew non-stop from London to Madrid.

A--continued.

ARMSTRONG-WHITWORTH.

Sir W. G. Armstrong, Whitworth & Co., Ltd., of Gosforth, Newcastle-on-Tyne (Aeroplane Works), and Barlow, nr. Selby (Airship Works).

Captain I. F. Fairbairn-Crawford, who is general manager of the aircraft department, founded the aeroplane department in 1913 and the airship department in 1915. Lieut.-Commander R. G. Lock, R.N., was assistant to the general manager. Mr. F. Murphy is chief designer and works manager of the aeroplane department, Gosforth. Mr. H. H. Golightly is works manager of the airship department, Barlow Aircraft Works, Selby.

Both departments have been working at full pressure during the period of the war, and over 1,300 aeroplanes for military purposes and three large rigid airships for the Navy have been completed and delivered.

The following types of aeroplanes have been delivered :—

B.E.2a., B.E.2b., B.E.2c., biplanes to R.A.F. design.

The 70 h.p., 90 h.p., 120 h.p., and 160 h.p. F.K. type Armstrong-Whitworth two-seater biplanes, which were designed by Mr. Frederick Koolhoven.

A 250 h.p. triplane.

Several 130 h.p. quadruplanes.

220 h.p. B.R.2, F.N. type, single-seater scout biplanes. (The " Armadillo.")

320 h.p. A.B.C., F.M. type, single-seater scout biplanes. (The " Ara.") Etc., etc., etc.

The following Naval rigid airships.

H.M.R.25, with four 250 h.p. Rolls-Royce engines.
H.M.R.29, with four 250 h.p. Rolls-Royce engines.
H.M.R.33, with five 270 h.p. Sunbeam engines.
Cars for fifteen S.S. and coastal type non-rigid airships.
Larger rigid airships are in course of construction and design.

THE ARMSTRONG-WHITWORTH F.K.3.

The Armstrong-Whitworth F.K.3 was designed by Mr. Frederick Koolhoven, and was built at the time when B.E.2cs were being produced in large numbers and was an improvement on this type of machine.

In general appearance there is very little difference from the B.E.2c, the fuselage being of the same long, narrow type, with the exception that the pilot is placed in front of the observer, who is equipped with a swivel gun-mounting.

A 90 h.p. R.A.F. air-cooled engine is carried in the nose.

The undercarriage consists of an axle hinged in the middle to a central skid which is carried in two Vees from the fuselage, the two side struts from the axle being mounted on oleo-pneumatic shock-absorbers inside the fuselage.

Three-quarter Front View of the Armstrong-Whitworth F.K.3 (90 h.p. R.A.F. Engine).

Three-quarter Rear View of the Armstrong-Whitworth F.K.3 (90 h.p. R.A.F. Engine).

ARMSTRONG-WHITWORTH—*continued*.

The main planes are staggered with a wide gap, and have two sets of struts on each side of the fuselage. The rudder is balanced. The machine was used on active service for some time, but was eventually used as a training machine in conjunction with the B.E.2c and d.

Specification.

Type of machine	Two-seater Biplane.
Name or type No. of machine ..	Armstrong-Whitworth F.K.3.
Purpose for which intended ..	Sport and Training.
Span	40 ft.
Overall length	28 ft. 8 in.
Maximum height..	10 ft. 2½ in.
Engine type and h.p. ..	90 h.p. R.A.F.
Weight of machine empty ..	1,900 lbs.
Tank capacity in hours ..	3½ hours.

Performance.

Speed at 1,000 feet	85 m.p.h.
Landing speed..	38 m.p.h.

Climb.

To 10,000 feet in minutes ..	23 minutes.

THE ARMSTRONG-WHITWORTH F.K.8.

The Armstrong-Whitworth F.K.8, also designed by Mr. Koolhoven, was a heavier and improved F.K.3. It had a deeper fuselage, a similar type of undercarriage except that the central skid was cut short in front of the front Vee, and a 120 h.p. Beardmore engine was enclosed in a cowling, with two radiators, one on either side of the fuselage and meeting in the form of an inverted Vee at the upper plane.

There is no centre section, the two upper planes being attached to two inverted Vees over the fuselage.

This machine was used to a large extent on various fronts for contact patrols, artillery spotting, light bombing, photography and reconnaissance work up to the signing of the Armistice, although it was gradually being superseded by machines of improved design.

About half-way through its active service life the F.K.8 was slightly modified by having a Vee-type undercarriage fitted and the engine mounting altered to take a 160 h.p. Beardmore and smaller radiators of improved efficiency, fitted on the sides of the fuselage only A long exhaust pipe was also added to carry the exhaust fumes well clear of the crew.

Accommodation was made for two guns, camera and wireless installation to be carried.

The F.K.8 Type Armstrong-Whitworth Biplane. With 120 h.p. Beardmore engine.

Three-quarter Front View of the Armstrong-Whitworth F.K.8 (160 h.p. Beardmore engine).

ARMSTRONG-WHITWORTH—*continued.*

Specification.

Type of machine	Two-seater Biplane.
Name or type No. of machine ..	Armstrong-Whitworth F.K.8.
Purpose for which intended ..	Military and Commercial.
Span	43 ft. 4 ins.
Overall length	31 ft.
Maximum height	10 ft. 6 in.
Engine type and h.p.	160 Beardmore.
Weight of machine empty ..	2,500 lbs.
Tank capacity in hours	3½ hours.

Performance.

Speed at 1,000 feet	104 m.p.h.
Landing speed..	45 m.p.h.

Climb.

To 10,000 ft. in minutes ..	17½ minutes.

THE ARMSTRONG-WHITWORTH "ARMADILLO."

This machine was designed by Mr. Murphy as a single-seater fighter and was produced about the middle of 1918, the trial flights taking place in September of that year.

The chief characteristics of the machines are a square fuselage and the top plane resting on the upper longerons. Two pairs of interplane struts are fitted on each side of the fuselage.

A 200 h.p. B.R.2 engine is carried in the nose of the fuselage and is enclosed in a circular cowl in the top of which is a peculiar box-like hump, which is actually a continuation of the upper part of the fuselage brought round and finished off on the cowling. In this box-like arrangement are two fixed Vickers guns, mounted to fire through the airscrew with the usual form of fire control gear.

Specification.

Type of machine	Single-seater Biplane.
Name or type No. of machine ..	"Armadillo" (1918).
Purpose for which intended ..	Military and Sport.
Span	27 ft. 6 in.
Overall length	20 ft.
Maximum height	7 ft. 10 in.
Engine type and h.p. ..	220 h.p. B.R.2 Rotary.
Weight of machine empty ..	1,900 lbs.
Tank capacity in hours ..	2¾ hours.

Performance.

Speed at 1,000 feet	140 m.p.h.
Landing speed..	55 m.p.h.

Climb.

To 10,000 feet in minutes ..	4½ minutes.

Three-quarter Front View of the Armstrong-Whitworth "Armadillo" (220 h.p. B.R.2 Engine).

Front View of the Armstrong-Whitworth "Ara" (320 h.p. A.B.C. Engine).

ARMSTRONG-WHITWORTH—*continued.*

THE ARMSTRONG-WHITWORTH "ARA."

The Armstrong-Whitworth "Ara," although it was not produced until early this year, was designed as a single-seater fighter, but can be easily adapted as a sporting machine for one who desires something more than the low-powered, slow-speed machines which are being introduced by many firms at the present time.

The fuselage is of square section and carries a 320 h.p. A.B.C. "Dragonfly" engine in its nose, which is covered in by a conical cowl leaving the cylinder heads protruding, a continuation of the cowl forming a spinner on the propeller boss

An ordinary vee-type undercarriage is fitted. The upper plane is placed very low over the top of the fuselage thus giving the pilot an excellent view upwards.

Three Experimental Armstrong-Whitworths.—Two of the F.K.10 Type Quadruplanes and an F.K.8 with a Sunbeam-Coatalen "Arab" Engine.

Specification.

Type of machine	Single-seater Biplane.
Name or type No. of machine ..	"Ara" (1919).
Purpose for which intended ..	Military and Sport.
Span	27 ft. 6 in.
Overall length	20 ft.
Maximum height	7 ft. 10 in.
Engine type and h.p.	320 h.p. A.B.C. "Dragonfly."
Weight of machine empty ..	1,900 lbs.
Tank capacity in hours	3¼ hours.

Performance.

Speed at 1,000 feet	150 m.p.h.
Landing speed..	55 m.p.h.

Climb.

To 10,000 feet in minutes ..	5½ minutes.

The Armstrong-Whitworth "Ara" 320 h.p. A.B.C. "Dragonfly."

A—continued.

AUSTIN MOTORS, LTD. Northfield, Birmingham.

A motor-car firm which took up the manufacture of aircraft during the war. In addition to numerous machines to Government specifications, have built the machines hereafter described and illustrated to their own designs.

THE AUSTIN "BALL" SINGLE-SEATER BIPLANE.

The *Austin* "Ball" biplane was designed as a single-seater fighting scout to the ideas of the late Capt. Ball, V.C., D.S.O., M.C. The fuselage is very deep, reaching almost to the top plane, and carries in its nose a 200 h.p. Hispano-Suiza engine, which is well cowled in, the radiators being fixed on the side of the fuselage below the front centre section struts.

The planes are unstaggered and of equal length, having one pair of struts on either side of the fuselage. The tail unit is of standard type except that there is no fixed fin area. Undercarriage is of the Vee-type, the axle and wheels being slung at the apex of the Vee with rubber shock absorber. A small tail-skid pivoted to an extension of the rudder-post takes the weight of the tail, when the machine is at rest on the ground.

Front View of the Austin "Ball" (200 h.p. Hispano-Suiza Engine).

Side View of the Austin "Ball" Single-seat Fighter.

Specification.	
Type of machine	Single-seater Biplane, Scout, Fighter.
Name or type No. of machine ..	Austin "Ball."
Purposes for which intended ..	Scouting and Fighting.
Span	30 ft.
Gap	4 ft. 9 in.
Overall length	21 ft. 6 in.
Maximum height	9 ft. 3 in.
Chord	5 ft.
Wing surface	290 sq. ft.
Span of tail	11 ft. 3 in. (over elevators).
Total area of tail	32 sq. ft. (includes elevators).
Area of elevators	8 sq. ft. each.
Area of rudder	8 sq. ft.
Area of Ailerons	$7\frac{1}{2}$ sq. ft. each.
Total area of ailerons	30 sq. ft.
Engine type and h.p.	200 h.p. Hispano-Suiza "V" type, water cooled.
Weight of machine empty ..	1,426 lbs.
Load per sq. ft.	7 lbs.
Load per h.p.	9.25 lbs.
Tank capacity in hours ..	2 hours.
Tank capacity in gallons ..	Petrol $31\frac{1}{2}$ galls., oil 5 galls., water 9 galls.

Performance.
Speed low down	138 m.p.h.
Speed at 10,000 feet	126 m.p.h.

Climb.
To 10,000 feet..	10 minutes.
Total weight of machine loaded	2,075 lbs.

AUSTIN MOTORS, LTD.—*continued.*

THE AUSTIN "GREYHOUND."

The *Austin* " Greyhound " represents one of the latest efforts to produce a fast, quick-climbing two-seater, fighting and reconnaissance biplane. In general arrangement it follows standard practice. The fuselage carries in its nose a 320 h.p. A.B.C. " Dragonfly " engine. A conical cowling covers the engine in with the exception of the cylinder heads, the shape of the cowling being preserved throughout the length of the fuselage by fairing. There is almost equal fin area above and below the fuselage. The upper main plane trailing edge is cut away, and the lower plane is of lesser chord than the upper, thereby giving the pilot a good view. Accommodation is made for the machine to carry three guns, camera, wireless, oxygen apparatus and heating apparatus.

Specification.

Type of machine	Two-seater Fighter, Reconnaissance Biplane.
Name or type No. of machine ..	" Greyhound."
Purposes for which intended ..	Fighting and Reconnaissance.
Engine type and h.p. ..	A.B.C. " Dragonfly," 320 h.p.
Span	Top plane, 39 ft.; bottom plane, 36 ft. 7 in.
Gap	4 ft. 11⅞ in.
Maximum height.. ..	10 ft. 4 in.
Chord	Top plane, 6 ft. 4.8 in.; bottom plane, 4 ft. 3 in.
Total surface of wings ..	400 sq. ft.
Span of tail	12 ft. 9.5 in.
Total area of tail.. ..	47 sq. ft.
Total area of elevators ..	19.8 sq. ft.
Area of rudder	9.9 sq. ft.
Area of fin	Top, 2.76 sq. ft. bottom, 2.3 sq. ft.
Area of each aileron and total area	Two top, 14.8 sq. ft.; two bottom, 7.8 sq. ft ; total, 45.2 sq. ft.
Weight of machine empty ..	2,050 lbs.
Load per sq. ft.	7.72 lbs. per sq. ft.
Weight per h.p.	10.3 lbs.
Tank capacity in hours ..	3 hours.
Tank capacity in gallons.. ..	Petrol 66 galls., oil 8 galls.
Weight of machine full ..	3,090 lbs. (including guns, ammunition, &c.)

Performance (estimated).

Speed at 10,000 feet ..	..	130 m.p.h.
Landing speed.. ..	..	45 m.p.h.

Climb.

To 10,000 feet.. ..	..	11 minutes.

Three-quarter Front View of the Austin " Ball " Single-seat Fighter.

Three-quarter Front View of the Austin " Greyhound " 320 h.p. A.B.C. " Dragonfly " Engine.

Three-quarter Rear View of the Austin "Greyhound."

AUSTIN MOTORS, LTD.—*continued.*

In addition to these machines the firm propose to place upon the market a single-seater sporting type machine to the following specification :—

AUSTIN "WHIPPET."

Type of machine	Single-seater Biplane.
Purposes for which intended ..	General run-about for business and pleasure, forest patrol, etc.
Engine	A 45 h.p. twin cylinder horizontal opposed.
Weight of machine empty ..	500 lbs.
Weight of machine fully loaded..	730 lbs.
Tank capacity (sufficient for two hours' flight)	Petrol 6½ galls., oil 1½ galls.
Performance (estimated).	
Speed low down	90–95 m.p.h.
Speed at 10,000 feet ..	80 m.p.h.
Landing speed	About 30 m.p.h.

Climb.

To 5,000 feet in 6 minutes.
To 10,000 feet in 14 minutes.

General Particulars :—

Fuselage.—This is constructed throughout of steel tubes, bracing wires being eliminated.

Engine Mounting.—The engine is mounted on a special shock absorber device, consisting of four rubber buffers, making a connection between the fuselage and the engine bearers.

Wings.—These have been designed for a high factor of safety, and are of standard construction. They are made to fold back along the body, where they are automatically locked and sup-ported by supporting tubes attached to the fuselage. They are locked in flying position by a special positive locking device. The strut members consist of streamline tubes, tie rods only being used for the centre section.

Tail Plane, Elevators and Rudders.—These are of standard design, the tail plane being made adjustable to correct centre of gravity for different weights of pilots.

Landing Gear.—This is the ordinary "V" type, streamline tubes being used for the struts.

Side View of the Austin "Greyhound" Single-seat Fighter.

Controls.—These are of standard type, the usual joystick and rudder bar being fitted.

Rear Skid.—This is of the swivelling type, consisting of a compression spring working over telescopic tubes. In order to give a good wearing surface, a special arrangement of shoe is fitted, consisting of vertical laminated plates.

Seat.—A specially upholstered seat is fitted, and the cowling and wind-screen are arranged to give complete protection to the pilot.

Luggage.—A cupboard is provided under the seat to accommodate the pilot's luggage, and any tools it is required to carry.

Engine Controls, Instruments, etc.—For starting a small induction pump is fitted for pumping mixture into the cylinders. The pilot starting his engine from inside the machine by means of a starting magneto.

General.—The object of the designers has been to design a machine which will be stable in the air, and will require very little adjustment and attention on the ground, which has a low landing speed, and which can be housed in a motor garage or small shed. With wings folded, the machine can be comfortably housed in a hangar 18 ft. long, 9 ft. wide and 8 ft. high.

AUSTIN MOTORS, LTD.—*continued*.

An Austin-built S.E.5a.

Side View of an Experimental Austin Triplane.

64a

A—*continued.*

AVRO. *Aeroplanes.* A. V. Roe & Co., Ltd., Clifton Street, Miles Platting, Manchester.

A new factory, with its own aerodrome and experimental plant, has been established at Hamble, Hants, where Mr. A. V. Roe is in charge, assisted by his brother, the Rev. E. V. Roe.

The main output of the firm is produced at the Manchester Works.

Mr. H. V. Roe left the firm in 1917 and joined the Royal Flying Corps. He was injured in an accident in the Vosges while night-flying, and has now retired from the aircraft business.

The history of the *Avro* machine commences with the design in 1906 by Mr. A. V. Roe of a biplane, which by leaving the ground at Brooklands, in July, 1908, was the first British aeroplane to fly. In 1909, Mr. Roe flew a triplane with a 9 h.p. J.A.P engine at Lea Marshes. During 1910, Mr. Roe built two more triplanes, fitted with 30 h.p J.A.P. and 35 h.p. Green engines, and flew them at Wembley and at Brooklands.

Early in the summer of 1911 an *Avro* biplane made its first flights at Brooklands, piloted by Mr. Howard Pixton. At this period the embryo " Avro " firm was financed by Mr. H. V. Roe, who owned the firm of Everitt & Co., Webbing Manufacturers, of Manchester.

From this biplane of 1911 the development of the *Avro* machines is to be traced through a very pretty little machine with a 40 h.p. E.N.V. engine, built for Mr. Duigan, the first Australian aviator, an extremely efficient two-seater with a 60 h.p. E.N.V. engine, a series of 50 h.p. Gnôme-engined machines ordered by the War Office, which were actually the first aeroplanes designed and built by a British firm to be delivered to the British Army, to the totally enclosed biplane with the 60 h.p. Green engine which gave so good an account of itself in the British military trials at Salisbury Plains in 1912.

Early in 1913 the famous two-seater *Avro* with an 80 h.p. Gnôme engine made its appearance. This machine—unaltered in all its essential aerodynamic features and in its main dimensions—survives to this day as the *Standard Avro* training machine.

THE AVRO STANDARD TRAINING BIPLANE.

By a process of detailed improvement, which has led to increased strength and greater simplicity, and by the adoption of standardised methods of manufacture, the 80 h.p. machine of 1913 has evolved into the Type 504 K., a machine admirably adapted for the methods of quantity production.

General Remarks.

This machine is specially suitable for the purpose of training pilots, and has been adopted as the Standard Training Machine by the Royal Air Force.

Front view.—The Standard Avro Training Machine.

Three-quarter front view of the Avro Standard Training Machine.

AVRO—*continued*.

In the 504 K. Type the nose of the machine has been altered and the engine mounted overhung from the bearers. The machine will now take any of the existing rotary engines up to 150 h.p. This has been accomplished by suitably designing the engine mounting and fitting adaptors to take the different engines. It will be seen that this is a great advantage from the engine supply point of view.

The machine retains its characteristics of simplicity, strength and controllability, and one of its chief advantages is the ease with which it can be repaired at School Workshops where interchangeable spares can be obtained readily.

Specification.

The following tables give the main features of this machine :

Type of Aeroplane ..	..2 Seater Biplane (Training Machine).
Aeroplane Specification	.. " Avro " Type 504K.
Engine	..100 Mono Gnôme, 110 Clerget, 110 Le Rhône, or 130 Clerget.
Revolutions of engine for stated b.h.p. ..	..1250 r.p.m.

Estimated speed with full load and with all fittings in position.

Maximum speed for the above horse power and revolutions.
At ground level	.. 95 m.p.h.
At 8,000 feet	.. 87 m.p.h.
At 10,000 feet	.. 85 m.p.h.

Duration of flight at this speed.
At ground level	.. 2 hrs.
At 8,000 feet	.. 2.14 hrs.
At 10,000 feet	.. 3 hrs.
Minimum speed with full load near ground	.. 40 m.p.h.
Estimated speed at ¾ power at 8,000 feet	.. 74 m.p.h.
Estimated speed at ¾ power at 10,000 feet	.. 71 m.p.h.
Estimated duration at ¾ power at 8,000 feet	.. 3.7 hrs.
Estimated duration at ¾ power at 10,000 feet	.. 4.25 hrs.

Estimated climb with full load and with all fittings in position.
To 3,500 feet	.. 5 mins.
To 8,000 feet	.. 10 mins.
To 10,000 feet	.. 16 mins.

Seating Accommodation.
Pilot, position ..	Level with trailing edge of lower wing.
Passenger's position	.. In front of pilot.

Airscrew.
Type	.. 2 bladed " Avro."
Pitch (110 Le Rhône)	.. 8 ft. 8 in.
Diameter	.. 9 ft. 0 in.

Overall Dimensions.

Span of upper wings	.. 36 ft. 0 in.	Length overall .. .. 29 ft. 5 in.
Span of lower wings	.. 36 ft. 0 in.	Chord top wing .. .. .. 4 ft. 9 in.
Span of tail plane	.. 10 ft. 0 in.	Chord second wing .. .. .. 4 ft. 9 in.
Height overall	.. 10 ft. 5 in.	Chord tail plane .. .. .. 2 ft. 8⅜ in.
		Chord elevator.. .. .. .. 2 ft. 4 in.

The Avro Seaplane—Front view.

Three-quarter view from rear—The Avro Standard Training Machine.

AVRO—*continued*.

Details of Weight.

Component.		Weight in lbs.
Tail Unit.		
Tail plane with supports	.. ..	$21\frac{1}{2}$
Elevators	.. .. ..	12
Rudder with levers and wires	.. .. ..	$8\frac{1}{2}$
	Total ..	42 lbs.
Main Lift Structure.		
Wings with flaps with centre section	.. ..	$260\frac{1}{2}$
Interplane struts	.. .. ..	41
Interplane wires	.. .. ..	$24\frac{1}{2}$
	Total ..	326 lbs.
Alighting Gear.		
Undercarriage with axle and skid	.. ..	65
Main Wheels 100 × 700 ..	.. .. ..	40
Wing skids	.. .. ..	2
Tail skids	.. .. ..	6
	Total ..	113 lbs.
Hull.		
Body and Engine Housing ..	.. ..	270
Aeroplane control gear and wires	.. ..	30
Other details, flying instruments, lighting set, etc.		25
	Total ..	325 lbs.
Power Plant.		
Engine with magnetos 110 h.p. Le Rhône ..	..	330
Airscrews, boss and bolts ..	.. ..	41
Oil tanks, cooler and piping..	.. ..	15
Petrol tanks, piping and air pressure system	..	39
	Total ..	425 lbs.

Total weight of machine bare with water in radiators 1231 lbs.

Military Load.

Crew of 2 at 180 lbs. each .. .. 360 lbs.

Weight of Machine in Flying Trim.

(*a*) Weight of machine bare with water in radiators		1231
(*b*) Military load	.. ..	360
(*c*) Petrol $25\frac{1}{2}$ galls.	.. ..	184
(*d*) Oil 6 galls.	.. ..	54
	Total ..	1829 lbs.

Areas. Wings and Ailerons.

Top	.. ..	173 sq. ft.
Second	.. ..	157 sq. ft.
	Total ..	330 sq. ft.

AVRO STANDARD   TRAINING MACHINE

36 - 0"

4' - 10"

2' - 2"

FORD JONES

SCALE of FEET

General arrangement of the Standard Avro Type 504 K.

AVRO—*continued*.

Wing Flaps.

Top	..	..	..	..	..	22.7 sq. ft.
Second	..	..	..	..	..	22.7 sq. ft.

	Total	..	45.4 sq. ft

Tail Plane	..	..	..	..	..	26 sq. ft
Elevators	..	..	..	..	..	18 sq. ft.
Rudder	..	..	..	..	..	9 sq. ft.

Dihedral.

Top wing	..	..	..	..	..	$2\frac{1}{2}°$
Second wing	..	..	..	..	..	$2\frac{1}{2}°$

Loading.

Loading on wing surface per sq. ft ..	..	5.57 lbs.
Weight fully loaded per h.p. (nominal)	..	16.7 lbs
Weight carried on tail in flight	..	..	nil.
Movement of C. G. with total variation in load during flight		4.2 ins.

Side view of the Avro Seaplane.   This machine is the Standard Training Machine in all essentials, fitted with a float.
under-carriage.

Control.

Type		Control pillars and foot bars.
Positions from which aeroplane may be controlled		Complete dual control.
What control provided for crew other than pilot		
Position of engine controls		On left hand side of body.
No adjustment of rudder bar is provided		
Tail skid		Can be controlled if desired.
Load on tail skid when loaded ready for flight		100 lbs.
Tail plane adjustable on the ground but not in the air from pilot's seat		

Bracing.

Wings—(*a*) Internal		H.T. Steel Wire.
(*b*) External		Cable or streamline wires.
Body		H.T. steel wire.
Undercarriage		Cable.
Other parts		Wire and cable.

Undercarriage.

Type		Special "Avro."
Size of standard wheels fitted	..	100 m/m × 700 m/m.

AVRO —continued.

Materials.

Wing spars	Spruce.
Wing struts	Spruce.
Body struts	Spruce and ash.
Undercarriage struts	Steel tubes.
Longerons in body	Ash.
Shock absorber	Rubber cord.

Tanks.

Petrol. Position.	Pressure or Gravity.	Capacity (gallons).	Material.	Weight empty
(a) Behind engine. Pressure.		21 galls.	Tinned steel.	27
(b) In centre section. Gravity.		4½ galls.	Tinned steel.	10
Oil. Behind engine. Gravity.		6 galls.	Tinned steel.	12

Factor of safety. Machine had a factor of safety of 7 on sand test.

Range of movement of centre of pressure   .3 to .5 of Chord.

THE AVRO SEAPLANE—TYPE 504 L.

The *Avro* seaplane 504 L is practically the standard *Avro* 504 K land machine fitted with two pontoon single-step floats, which are attached to the fuselage by four struts, as shown in the accompanying photographs. A small tail float is also fitted direct to the fuselage.

The fairing of the sides of the fuselage has been improved, so that the shape throughout now more or less conforms with the shape of the engine cowling.

The machine is a two-seater, is fitted with dual control, but it is also being made as a three-seater, the pilot then being situated in front with single control.

It is arranged to take all rotary engines up to 150 h.p. and also the A.B.C. 175 h.p. "Wasp" radial engine, by means of an engine mounting designed to take adaptors for the various engines.

It can be looped, spun, side-slipped, stalled, etc., like the standard *Avro* 504 K. A speed of 90 m.p.h. was obtained with a 130 h.p. Clérget flying at sea level.

THE AVRO TWO-SEATER FIGHTER.—Type 530.

This machine was originally designed by Messrs. A. V. Roe and Co., in 1915, to meet the needs of the R.F.C. for a fast two-seater fighter. For some reason or other (presumably because it was so much better than the contemporary R.A.F. product—ED.) the machine did not obtain the approval of the authorities, and has never been put into production.

In its design special attention has been given to securing the best possible view for both pilot and passenger.

The upper centre section is arranged to be level with the pilot's eye, thus obstructing his view to the smallest possible extent. The lower plane is staggered back and gives him a view downwards and forwards at a very steep angle.

The rear gunners' seat is aft of the trailing edge of the lower wing, so that both occupants have a very wide range of vision.

The following tables give the essential details of the machine :—

The Avro 504 L. type Seaplane "taxying."

Specification.

Type of machine..	Two-seater Biplane.
Name or type No. of machine ..	Avro 530.
Purpose for which intended ..	Fighter or fast two-seater.
Span	36 ft.
Gap, maximum and minimum ..	5 ft.
Overall length	28 ft. 6 in.
Maximum height	9 ft. 7 in.
Chord	5 ft. 6 in.
Total surface of wings ..	325⅓ sq. ft.
Span of tail	12 ft.
Total area of tail	52.2 sq. ft. (including elevators).
Area of elevators	23.8 sq. ft.
Area of rudder	8.8 sq. ft.
Area of fin	4.5 sq. ft.
Area of each aileron and total area	4 × 14.5 sq. ft. = 58 sq. ft.
Maximum cross section of body .	14.0 sq. ft.
Horizontal area of body.. ..	63⅓ sq. ft.
Vertical area of body	100 sq. ft.
Engine type and h.p.	200 h.p. Hispano-Suiza or Sunbeam "Arab."

Airscrew, diam., pitch, and revs..	Avro Tractor D. 2.97, p. 2.82; r.p.m. 1,200
Weight of machine empty ..	1,695 lbs.
Load per sq. ft.	8.23 lbs.
Weight per h.p.	13.4 lbs. (assuming 200 h.p.)
Tank capacity in hours ..	4 hours at 10,000 ft.
Tank capacity in gallons ..	40 gallons.

Performance.

Speed low down	114 m.p.h.
Speed at 10,000 feet	102 m.p.h.
Speed at 20,000 feet	
Landing speed..	58 m.p.h.

Climb.

To 5,000 feet in minutes ..	6½ min.
To 10,000 feet in minutes ..	15 ,,
To 20,000 feet in minutes ..	Ceiling, 18,000 ft. in 40 mins.
Disposable load apart from fuel	574 lbs.
Total weight of machine loaded	2,680 lbs.

AVRO—*continued.*

THE AVRO "MANCHESTER" TWIN-ENGINED BIPLANES.

The two "Manchester" types hereafter described differ mainly in respect of their power plant.

Both have a common origin in the *Avro* "Pike," a twin-engined three-seater fighter-bomber built and designed for the Royal Naval Air Service by the Avro firm in 1916.

This machine, fitted with two 160 h.p. Sunbeam engines, performed exceedingly well in spite of the insufficient power plant, and was undeniably one of the cleanest twin-engined designs which has yet been produced.

The "Manchester" Mark 1 and 2 machines differ very little in their general arrangements and outline from this original.

One very interesting feature which is shown in the scale drawings reproduced of the Mark 1 machine, is the method of balancing the ailerons which is employed.

To the top of the upper king-post of the top plane aileron a small plane is fixed. When an aileron is pulled down this plane is given a positive incidence by the movement of the king-post, and gives an appreciable lift. As the plane is ahead of the aileron hinge, this lift assists in holding the aileron down, and so partly balances the aileron.

When the aileron is pulled up the balancing plane is given a negative incidence, and exerts the required balancing force tending to hold the aileron up.

Both types are three-seaters with pilot's cockpit under the leading edge of the wings, observer's seat and gun turret in the nose of the fuselage, and a rear gunner's cockpit well aft of the main planes, whence a very wide field of fire is obtained.

THE TWIN-ENGINED AVRO.—"Manchester Mark 1."

Type of machine	Three-seater Twin-engined Biplane
Name or type No. of machine ..	Avro "Manchester Mark I."
Purpose for which intended ..	Photography, reconnaissance. bombing.
Span	60 ft.
Gap, maximum and minimum ..	7 ft. 3 in.
Overall length	37 ft.
Maximum height	12 ft. 6 in.
Chord	7 ft. 6 in.
Total surface of wings ..	843—30 (area of nacelles).
Span of tail	13 ft.
Total area of tail	82 sq. ft. (including elevators.)
Area of elevators	32 sq. ft.
Area of rudder	19 sq. ft.
Area of fin	11.7 sq. ft.
Area of each aileron and total area	31 sq. ft.; total 124 sq. ft.
Maximum cross section of body .	14.3 sq. ft.
Horizontal area of body	80 sq. ft.
Vertical area of body	111 sq. ft.
Engine type and h.p.	A.B.C "Dragon-fly"; 320 h.p. at 1,650 r.p.m.
Airscrew, diam., pitch, and revs..	Avro Tractor D. 2.9m., P. 2m., r.p.m. 1600.
Weight of machine empty ..	4,049 lbs.
Load per sq. ft.	8.06 lbs.
Weight per h.p.	10.3 lbs.

Three-quarter front view of the Avro Two-seater Fighter, Type 530. (200 h.p. Hispano-Suiza).

Side view, the Avro Two-seater Fighter, Type 530.

AVRO—*continued.*

Tank capacity in hours .. .. 5¾ hours, at 10,000 ft. (including climb).

Tank capacity in gallons .. 183 gallons.

Performance.
Speed low down .. .. 128 m.p.h.
Speed at 10,000 feet .. .. 122 m.p.h.
Speed at 15,000 feet .. .. 115 m.p.h.
Landing speed .. .. .. 45 m.p.h.

Climb.
To 5,000 feet in minutes .. 4½ mins.
To 10,000 feet in minutes .. 11 mins.
To 20,000 feet in minutes .. Service ceiling, 40 mins.

No bombs carried for this performance.

Disposable load apart from fuel.. 1,007 lbs.
Total weight of machine loaded.. 6,586 lbs.

THE TWIN-ENGINED AVRO.—"Manchester Mark II."

Type of Machine	Three - seater Twin - engined Biplane.
Name or type No. of machine..	Avro "Manchester Mark II."
Purpose for which intended	Photography, reconnaissance, bombing.
Span	60 ft.
Gap, maximum and minimum	7 ft. 3 in.
Overall length	37 ft.
Maximum height..	12 ft. 6 in.
Chord	7 ft. 6 in.
Total surface of wings	843—26 (area of engine nacelles)
Span of Tail	13 ft.
Total area of Tail	82 sq. ft. (including elevators).
Area of elevators	32 sq. ft.
Area of rudder	19 sq. ft.
Area of fin	11.7 sq. ft.
Area of each aileron and total area	31 sq. ft.; total 124 sq. ft.
Maximum cross section of body..	14.3 sq. ft.
Horizontal area of body	80 sq. ft.
Vertical area of body	111 sq. ft.
Engine type and h.p.	Siddeley "Puma" (boosted); 300 h.p. at 1,600 r.p.m.
Airscrew, diam., pitch and revs.	Avro Tractor D. 2.9m., P. 2m., r.p.m. 1,600.
Weight of machine (empty)	4,574 lbs.
Load per sq. ft. ..	8.76 lbs.
Weight per h.p. ..	11.93 lbs. (assuming 600 h.p.)
Tank capacity in hours..	3¾ hrs. at 10,000 ft., including climb.
Tank capacity in gallons	116 gallons.

Performance.
Speed low down .. .. 125 m.p.h.
Speed at 10,00 feet.. .. 119 m.p.h.
Speed at 15,000 feet .. 112½ m.p.h.
Landing speed .. .. 45 m.p.h.

Climb.
To 5,000 feet in minutes .. 6½.
To 10,000 feet in minutes .. 16⅓, 15,000 ft. in 32 mins.
To 20,000 feet in minutes .. Service ceiling 17000 ft. in 43 minutes.

Disposable load apart from fuel .. .. .. 1,614 lbs.
Total weight of machine loaded .. .. .. 7,158 lbs.

AVRO TYPE 530.

General arrangement of the Avro Two-seater Fighter. (200 h.p. Hispano-Suiza.)

71a

PLAN.

60'-0"

7'-6"

7' 3"

FRONT

SIDE ELEVATION

AVRO MANCHESTER MARK 1.

2 - A.B.C. DRAGONFLYS.

FORDJONES/19.

AVRO—*continued.*

Three-quarter front view of the Avro " Pike " (two 230 h.p. B.H.P. engines).

Side view of the Avro " Pike " (two 230 h.p. B.H.P. engines).

AVRO—*continued.*

THE AVRO "SPIDER."

The *Avro* "Spider" is one of the very few examples amongst British aeroplanes of the so-called "wireless" type. The wing structure is entirely supported by a triangulated system of steel tubes, and has neither flying nor landing wires.

The front end of the fuselage is identical in all respects with the forward portion of the type 504 *Avro*; but it has been shortened up aft of the cockpit. The tail unit is also of the same design as that of the standard training machine, so that fittings already being produced in quantity can be used for the whole of this part of the machine.

This machine has been specially designed as a single-seater fighter. Great attention has been paid to the question of view and manœuvrability. It is extraordinarily quick and light on the controls, and in mock flights, for which it has so far been used, has easily out-manœuvred other machines which have been standardised.

Although the first machine has only been fitted with 110 Le Rhône, it is proposed to fit a much higher-powered engine, so as to get a still better performance.

The view in every direction is excellent, as the pilot sits between the main spars of the top plane, and has a perfect view both upwards and downwards, the dimensions of the bottom plane being so small as hardly to obstruct the view at all.

The pilot's cockpit is very roomy and comfortable, and full use can be made of the controls without any obstruction.

The guns are conveniently placed and the ammunition boxes and chutes well arranged.

The engine controls are placed in a convenient position on the pilot's left-hand side, and the hand-pump is in a comfortable position for use.

Specification.

Type of Aeroplane	Single-Seater "Fighter."
Aeroplane specification	Avro "Spider."
Engine	180 h.p. B.R. 2.
Revolutions of engine for stated b.h.p.	1250 r.p.m.

Estimated speed with full load and with all fittings in position.

Maximum speed for the above horse-power and revolutions.

At ground level	124 m.p.h.
At 8,000 feet	121 m.p.h.
At 10,000 feet	122 m.p.h.
At 15,000 feet	115 m.p.h.

Duration of flight at this speed.

At 10,000 feet	2 hrs.
At 15,000 feet	2½ hrs.

Minimum speed with full load near ground .. .. 45 m.p.h.

Front view of the Avro "Spider" Showing the wing bracing system. (110 h.p. Le Rhône.)

Side view of the Avro "Spider." (110 h.p. Le Rhône.)

AVRO—*continued.*

Estimated climb with full load and with all fittings in position.

To 3,500 feet .. .. 2·2 mins.
To 8,000 feet .. .. 5 mins.
To 10,000 feet .. .. 7 mins.
To 15,000 feet .. .. 13½ mins.
To 18,000 feet .. .. 20 mins.
To 20,000 feet .. .. 26 mins.
Pilot, position .. .. Between main spars of top plane.

Air-screw.

Type .. .. "Avro."
Pitch .. .. 9 ft.
Diameter .. .. .. 8 ft. 6 in.

Overall Dimensions.

Span of top wings .. .. .. 28 ft. 6 in.
Span of bottom wings.. .. .. 21 ft. 6 in.
Span of tail plane .. .. .. 8 ft. 6 in.
Height overall .. .. 7 ft. 10 in.
Length overall .. .. 20 ft. 6 in.
Chord top wing .. .. .. 6 ft.
Chord bottom wing .. .. .. 2 ft. 6 in.
Chord tail plane .. .. .. 2 ft. 8 in.
Chord elevator.. .. .. .. 1 ft. 6 in.

Details of Weight.

Component.	Weight in lbs.
Tail Unit.	
Tail plane	12
Elevator	10
Rudder	10
Total	32 lbs.
Main Lift Structure.	
Wings with flaps	170
Interplane struts	70
Interplane wires	5
Total	245 lbs.
Alighting Gear.	
Under carriage	25
Main wheels and axle	34
Tail Skids	6
Total	65 lbs.
Fuselage.	
Body and engine housing	186
Aeroplane control gear and wires	15
Other details, flying instruments, lighting set, etc.	25
Total	226 lbs.
Power Plant.	Centre
Engine with magnetos	500 lbs.
Airscrews, boss and bolts	35
Oil Tanks, cooler and piping	10
Petrol tanks, piping and air pressure system	35
Total	580 lbs.
Total weight of machine bare	1,148 lbs.

Three-quarter rear view of the Avro "Spider." (110 h.p. Le Rhône.)

Rear view of the Avro "Spider." (110 h.p. Le Rhône.)

AVRO—*continued*.

Armament and Military Load.

Pilot's gun	70
Mounting and ammunition box	20
Belt and ammunition, 800 rounds	60
Total Gun Load ..	**150 lbs.**
Véry Pistol with cartridges	8
Total reconnaissance load ..	**8 lbs.**

Military Load.

Total of Gun, bomb and reconnaissance loads ..	158
Crew of 1 at 180 lbs	180
Total military load ..	**338 lbs.**

Weight of Machine in Flying Trim.

(*a*) Weight of machine bare	1148
(*b*) Military load	338
(*c*) Petrol 26½ gallons	194
(*d*) Oil 6 gallons	54
Total ..	**1734 lbs.**

Areas.—Wings.

Top	122 sq. ft.
Second	45 sq. ft.
Total ..	**167 sq. ft.**

Wing Flaps

Top	22 sq. ft.
Total supporting surface ..	**189 sq. ft.**

Tail Plane..	17.5 sq. ft.
Elevators	11 sq. ft.
Rudder	7.8 sq. ft.

Loading.

Loading on wing surface per sq. ft. ..	9.15 lbs.
Weight fully loaded per h.p.	9.65 lbs.
Weight carried on tail when in flight ..	Nil.

Control.

Type of aeroplane controls	Stick and V foot bar.
Position of engine controls	On left hand side of body.
Rudder bar adjustable	
Tail skid controllable..	
Load on tail skid when loaded ready for flight	100 lbs.
Tail plane adjustable on the ground but not in the air from pilot's seat	

Bracing.

Wings—(*a*) Internal	High tensile wire.
(*b*) External	Steel struts.
Body	High tensile wire.
Undercarriage	Cable.

Undercarriage.

Type	"Vee" Type.
Size of Standard Wheels fitted ..	700 m/m × 78 m/m.

Materials.

Wing spars	Built up spruce.
Wing struts	Steel tubes.
Body struts	Spruce.
Undercarriage	Steel tubes.
Longerons in body	Spruce.
Shock absorber	Rubber cord.
Petrol tank	Behind pilot.
Pressure feed capacity	26½ gallons.
Material	Tinned steel.
Weight empty..	20 lbs.

	Top.	Bottom.
Minimum factor of safety—front spars	13	9½
rear spars	13	
Rear wing bracing.		
front struts	6	6
rear struts	6	6
Range of movement of centre of pressure	.20 to .5 of chord.	

General arrangement of the Avro "Spider." (110 h.p. Le Rhône.)

AVRO—*continued*.

THE AVRO " GREEN " SPORTING BIPLANE.

Since the cessation of hostilities Messrs. A. V. Roe & Co., Ltd., have produced a single-seater machine designed for the pilot owner which is hereafter described and illustrated.

As will be seen its lines follow the very latest modern practice and the machine has proved herself on test to be very highly efficient, controllable and stable. The general design and construction follows closely the Standard *Avro* practice and the same care has been expended on this machine as in all the productions of A. V. Roe and Co., Ltd.

The engine is a 4-cylinder water-cooled 35-40-h.p. " Green." Everyone connected with aviation will remember the large amount of work which this little engine performed in the early days of aviation and it is interesting to note that the identical engine used in the experimental model was twelve years old and was used by Captain Pixton in the early *Avro* biplane at Brooklands in 1912. The engine has been considerably improved by the Green Co., and has been fitted with aluminium pistons, new-type camshaft, valves and valve cages and with an oil pressure regulator which regulates the amount of oil used by the engine according to the throttle opening. The engine has been found to run very smoothly and without vibration, and although a considerable amount of flying and testing has been already carried out with this machine, no adjustments have been necessary to the engine since it was installed in the plane. Although this particular engine is somewhat heavy for its horse-power, the production engines will be lighter and A. V. Roe and Co., Ltd., are of the opinion that the slightly extra weight of this type is more than compensated for by its extreme reliability and economy.

Three-quarter front view of the Avro " Baby " (35 H.P. Green engine.)

Front view of the Avro " Baby."

AVRO—*continued*.

Specification.

Type of machine	Single-seater
Name or type No. of machine	Avro Baby.
Purpose for which intended	Sporting Model.
Span	25 ft.
Gap	4 ft. 6 in.
Overall length	17 ft.
Maximum height	7 ft. 6 in.
Chord	4 ft.
Total surface of wings	180 sq. ft.
Span of tail	7 ft. 6 in.
Total area of tail and elevator	21 sq. ft.
Engine type and h.p.	35 h.p. "Green"
Engne revs.	1,500 r.p.m.
Weight of machine empty	625 lbs.
Load per sq. ft.	4.75 lbs.
Weight per h.p.	21.4 lbs.

Performance.

Speed low down	80 m.p.h.
Landing speed	32 m.p.h.

Climb.

To 3,000 ft. in minutes	6 minutes
To 10,000 ft. in minutes	24 minutes
Total weight of machine loaded	857 lbs.

The Engine Installation in the Avro "Baby."

Three-quarter view from aft of the Avro "Baby."

AVRO
SINGLE-SEATER
BIPLANE.
35 H.P. GREEN.

Span of Main planes 25' 0.

Span of Tail plane 7' 6"

B

B.A.T. The British Aerial Transport Company. Head Office, 38, Conduit Street, London, W.1. Works, Hythe Road, Willesden, London, N.W.10.

Founded by Mr. Samuel Waring (now Sir Samuel Waring, Bart.) in 1917, when the firm took over, purely as an experimental works, not as a production factory, the premises in Hythe Road, formerly occupied by the Joucques Aviation Co.

Chief designer, Mr. Frederick Koolhoven, who, in conjunction with M. Béchereau, was responsible for the design of the 1913 "Gordon Bennet" *Deperdussin* monoplane, the first machine to cover 120 miles in an hour. Mr. Koolhoven was also responsible for the design and construction of the British *Deperdussin* machine built for the British Military Trials of 1912, which machine was still flying in 1917, and for a number of the *Armstrong-Whitworth* machines, including the type F.K. 8, one of the very few 1914 designs which continued to be used on active service till the signing of the Armistice.

THE B.A.T. "BANTAM."

The B.A.T. "Bantam" is a small single-seater fighter, and although it was never adopted by the Air Board, it certainly had the finest performance for its type of any machine constructed at the time. The fuselage is of the monocoque type, built up of formers covered with three-ply, dispensing entirely with any form of internal bracing. The main planes have a very small gap, which is practically filled by the fuselage, and the pilot is seated between the centre section spars, with his head protruding above the top plane. The sides of the cockpit are cut away, thus giving him a good view downwards.

Two sets of struts are fitted, one either side of the fuselage. The under-carriage consists of two Vees, one under each of the inner sets of interplane struts. Two tubes hinged to the under side of the fuselage and rubber spring to the Vees form axles for the two wheels.

The armament consists of two fixed Vickers guns fitted low down on either side of the pilot, and firing between the two lower pairs of cylinders.

Specification.

Type of machine			Biplane
Name and type No.			"Bantam" F.K. 23.
Purpose			Single-seater Fighter.
Span			25 ft
Gap			3 ft. 3½ in.
Overall length			18 ft. 5 in.
Maximum height			6 ft. 9 in.
Chord			3 ft 11¼ in.
Total area of wings			185 sq. ft.
Span of tail			9 ft. 2 in.
Total area of tail			23 sq. ft.
Area of elevators			6.3 sq. ft
Area of rudder			4.4 sq. ft.
Area of fin			2.85 sq. ft.

Side View of the B.A.T. "Bantam" (A.B.C. 200 h.p. "Wasp" engine).

Rear View of the B.A.T. "Bantam" (A.B.C. 200 h.p. "Wasp" engine).

B.A.T.—continued.

THE B.A.T "BANTAM."—continued.

Area of ailerons..	4.5 sq. ft. each; 18 sq. ft. total.
Max. cross sectional area of body	8.7 sq. ft.
Horizontal area of body.. ..	32 sq. ft.
Vertical area of body	30 sq. ft.
Engine type and h.p.	A.B.C. "Wasp."
Airscrew	"Bat" dia. 7 ft. 10½ in.; pitch 5 ft. 4 in.
Weight of machine empty ..	830 lbs.
Load per sq. ft.	7.2 lbs.
Load per h.p.	7.85 lbs.
Tank capacity, hours	3½
Tank capacity, gallons	22.

Performance.

Speed at ground level ..	138 m.p.h.
Speed at 10,000 feet	134 m.p.h.
Speed at 15,000 feet	127 m.p.h.
Speed at 20,000 feet	121 m.p.h.
Landing speed..	50 m.p.h.

Climb.

To 5,000 feet in minutes ..	3 mins. 10 secs.
To 10,000 feet in minutes ..	7.20 minutes.
To 20,000 feet in minutes ..	21.48 minutes.
Disposable load apart from fuel	378 lbs.
Total weight of machine loaded	1,333 lbs.

Front View of the B.A.T. "Bantam" (A.B.C. 200 h.p. "Wasp" engine).

18'-5

25'-0"

4'-0"

9'-2"

The British Aerial Transport Cº Lᵀᴰ
Type. F.K.23. "Bantam".
Single Seater Biplane.
170. H.P. A.B.C. Wasp. I.

Two Views of the B.A.T. "Bantam" in the air.   80a

B.A.T.—*continued.*

THE BAT "BASILISK."

The "Basilisk" is a slightly enlarged form of "Bantam." The principal alterations are the installation of the 320 hp. A.B.C. "Dragonfly" engine, an increase in the gap, and the placing of the pilot in rear of the main planes.

Specification.

Type of machine	Biplane.
Name and type No.	"Basilisk" F.K. 25.
Purpose	Single-seater Fighter.
Span	25 ft. 4 in.
Gap	4 ft. 4 in.
Overall length	20 ft. 5 in
Maximum height	8 ft. 2 in.
Chord	4 ft. 6½ in.
Total area of wings	212 sq. ft.
Span of tail	9 ft. 10 in.
Total area of tail..	22 sq. ft.
Area of elevators..	8.3 sq. ft.
Area of rudder	4.5 sq. ft.
Area of fin	2.6 sq. in.
Area of ailerons	7.5 sq. ft. each; 30 sq. ft. total.
Max. cross sectional area of body	9.2 sq. ft.
Horizontal area of body	29.5 sq. ft.
Vertical area of body	47 sq. ft.
Engine type and h.p.	A.B.C. "Dragon-fly," 320 h.p.
Airscrew..	"Bat" dia. 8 ft. 8in.; pitch 8 ft.; 1,650 r.p.m.
Weight of machine empty ..	1,350 lbs.
Load per sq. ft.	9.25 lbs.
Load per h.p.	5.77 lbs.
Tank capacity, hours	32.
Tank capacity, gallons	40.

Performance.

Speed at ground level ..	162 m.p.h.
Speed at 10,000 feet	154 m.p.h.
Speed at 15,000 feet	141 m.p.h.
Speed at 20,000 feet	132 m.p.h.
Landing speed	52 m.p.h.

Climb.

To 5,000 feet in minutes ..	2 minutes.
To 10,000 feet in minutes ..	5 minutes.
To 20,000 feet in minutes ..	16.40 minutes.
Disposable load apart from fuel	448 lbs.
Total weight of machine loaded	2,085 lbs.

Side View of the B.A.T. "Basilisk" (320 h.p. A.B.C. "Dragonfly" engine).

The Dashboard of the B.A.T. " Basilisk."

Front View of the B.A.T. " Basilisk."

Three-quarter Front View of the B.A.T. " Basilisk " (320 h.p. A.B.C. " Dragonfly " engine).

B.A.T.—*continued*.

THE BRITISH AERIAL TRANSPORT. Cº Lᵀᴰ.

TYPE. F.K. 25. BASILISK.

Single Seater Biplane.

320. H.P. A.B.C. DRAGONFLY.

B.A.T.—*continued.*

THE B.A.T. "BABOON." TYPE F.K. 24.

A small dual control two-seater, designed for training purposes.

Very great attention has been paid in design to ease of manufacture and interchangeability of parts.

As an instance of this it may be noted that ailerons, rudder and elevators are all identical and interchangeable.

The following are the leading particulars.

Specification.

Type of machine	Two-seater Biplane (dual control).
Name or type No. of machine ..	B.A.T. F.K. 24 " Baboon."
Purpose for which intended ..	Training.
Span	25 ft.
Chord	5 ft. 7 in.
Gap, maximum and minimum ..	4 ft. 8½ in.
Stagger	Nil.
Dihedral	2° upper and lower planes.
Overall length	22 ft. 8 in.
Overall height	8 ft. 10 in.
Total area of planes	259 sq. ft.
Ailerons	On upper and lower planes.
Area of each and total area of ailerons	Each 6 sq. ft. Total 24 sq. ft.
Span of tail	9 ft. 10 in.
Total area of tail	27.75 sq. ft. (including elevators).
Area of elevators	12 sq. ft.
Area of rudder	6 sq. ft.
Area of fin	5.25 sq. ft.
Max. cross sectional area of body	7.5 sq. ft.
Side area of body	52 sq. ft.
Engine (type and B.H.P.) ..	170 A.B.C. Wasp I.
Revs. at nominal b.h.p. ..	1850 r.p.m.
Propeller (make and type, etc.)	B.A.T. 2 blade Tractor dia. 7 ft. 10 in., pitch 5ft.
Weight of machine empty ..	950 lbs.
Load per sq. ft.	5.2 lbs.
Weight per h.p.	7.95 lbs.
Tank capacity in hours	2 hours.
Tank capacity in gallons ..	12 gallons.
Disposable load, apart from fuel	400 lbs.
Armament.	
Weight of Instruments	12 lbs.
Total weight of machine fully loaded	1350 lbs.
Performance.	
Speed (at ground level) ..	90 m.p.h.
Landing speed	40 m.p.h.
Climb.	
To 10,000 feet..	12 mins.

Front View of the B.A.T. "Baboon."

Rear View of the B.A.T. "Baboon."

The B.A.T. " Baboon " Two-seater Training Machine (170 h.p. A.B.C. " Wasp.")

Three-quarter Front View of the B.A.T. " Baboon " Training Machine (170 h.p. A.B.C. " Wasp " engine).

B.A.T.—*continued.*

22 8"

25'-0 Span

5'-2 Chord

9'-10"

The British Aerial Transport Co Ltd
Type. F.K. 24 "Baboon"
Two Seater Biplane
A.B.C. 170 H.P. Wasp.

B.A.T.—continued.

THE B.A.T.—F.K. 26.

The B.A.T.—F.K 26, produced by the British Aerial Transport Co., Ltd., to the designs of Mr. Frederick Koolhoven, is the first aeroplane primarily designed as a commercial machine.

It is a tractor biplane, and is capable of carrying in the specially designed cabin either four passengers or their equivalent weight in goods or mails.

The fuselage is very deep and embodies two forms of construction, the front half being made up of six formers covered with three-ply, the rear half following normal practice in wire-braced girder construction.

The power unit, a 375 h.p. " Eagle " Mark VIII Rolls-Royce engine, is mounted on ash engine bearers carried between the first and second formers. Between the second and third formers, which are more or less bulkheads, are carried the petrol tanks. which have a capacity sufficient for six hours' flying.

The space from the third to the fifth formers forms the cabin, the fourth former being left open, that is, it has no cross members or three-ply filling, as in the second, third, and fifth formers, the last two forming the front and rear " walls " of the cabin.

Aft of the cabin the wire-braced construction begins, and consists of a girder of six bays, the pilot's seat being situated between the second and third cross members and well up in the fuselage, thus giving him an excellent view all round.

From the cabin aft the sides of the fuselage are fabric-covered, with a top fairing of three-ply.

The controls are similar to those of the old *Deperdussin* monoplanes, and consist of an inverted U-shaped member pivoted at the flooring of the cockpit, on which is mounted a wheel which has two segments cut from it top and bottom, as shown in the sketch of the pilot's cockpit.

The elevators are operated by two oval section tubes connected at their front ends to point one on either side halfway up the inverted U and at their rear end to crank-arms on the underside of the elevators, thus giving direct pull and push action.

Aileron cables pass from the control " wheel " down the sides of the U member round the pulleys, under the floor of the cabin to points in rear of the front main spars, where they pass over pulleys and out through the fuselage and along the wings to the ailerons. The ailerons are inter-connected by balance cables between the right and left-hand ailerons.

The rudder control consists of the usual foot-bar.

The tail plane is adjustable, the actuating gear being operated by a wheel situated low down on the left-hand side of the pilot's

Front View of the B.A.T.—F.K. 26 Passenger Machine (375 h.p. Rolls-Royce engine.)

B.A.T.—continued.

THE B.A.T.—F.K. 26—continued.

seat, which is connected to a threaded spindle by a continuous cable. Above the tubular nut on the spindle is a collar connected to the front main spar of the tail plane by means of four tubes, two inside the fuselage on either side of the central tube, and two streamline tubes running out on either side of the fuselage to a point on the front main spar of the tail plane.

The under-carriage consists of two Vees set across the fuselage, the apices of which are connected by a member, and from the Vees two divided axles, two on either side, meet at a wheel hub. From the hubs two tubes run up to two levers which just project through the sides of the fuselage and which are pivoted at their innermost ends to the centre of the third fuselage former. The levers are connected near their outer ends to an oleo and elastic shock-absorber. A sketch is given of the general arrangement of the under-carriage and also of the shock-absorbing device.

The main planes are of equal span, and are connected to upper and lower centre sections, the latter consisting of two small false wings attached to the side of the fuselage which, with the width of the fuselage, are the same span as the upper centre section, thus the upper and lower main planes are of the same length and consequently interchangeable.

The spars of the lower centre section pass right through the fuselage and are built into the third and fourth formers.

Two pairs of interplane struts are fitted on either side of the fuselage, traced with streamline wires.

The empennage, of which a sketch is given, is of conventional design, except in plan form.

The tail skid is pivoted to the base of the rudder and a pair of telescopic tubes containing a spring run from the toe of the skid to a lug some distance up the rudder post,

The engine-cooling system consists of two long honeycomb radiators which were carried on either side of the fuselage and connected to two water-tanks inside the fuselage, the temperature therein being controlled by two shutters operating at the back of the radiator.

The oil-tank has an extension which projects through the side of the fuselage and which has a series of tubes passing through it, thus forming an oil-cooler.

The following table gives the main particulars of this machine :

Specification.

Type of machine	Five-seater Biplane (Pilot and 4 Passengers).
Name or type No. of machine ..	B.A.T. Type F.K. 26.
Purpose for which intended ..	Passenger or mail carrying.
Span	46 ft.
Chord	6 ft. 6 in.
Gap	6 ft. 6 in.
Stagger	Nil.
Dihedral	2° on both wings.
Overall length	34 ft. 8 in.
Overall height	11 ft. 3 in.
Total area of wings	580 sq. ft.

The B.A.T.—F.K. 26 Passenger Carrier.   View showing entrance to cabin.

B.A.T.—*continued.*

THE B.A.T.—F.K. 26—*continued.*

Ailerons	Top and bottom.
Area of each aileron and total area	4 × 13 sq. ft. = 52 sq. ft.
Span of tail	15 ft. 9 in.
Total area of tail ..	66.6 sq. ft. (including elevators).
Area of elevators	23.6 sq. ft.
Area of rudder	10.8 sq. ft.
Area of fin	8 sq. ft.
Maximum cross sectional area of body	20.5 sq. ft. approx.
Side area of body	142 sq. ft. approx.
Engine (type and max. b.h.p.) ..	350 h.p. Rolls Royce "Eagle 8."
Revolutions at max. b.h.p. ..	1450 r.p.m.
Propeller (make, type, etc.) ..	B.A.T. Tractor, 4 bladed, 11 ft. dia.; 8 ft. 6 in. pitch; 1025 r.p.m.
Weight of machine empty ..	2,700 lbs.
Load per sq. ft.	7.7 lbs.
Weight per h.p.	13 lbs.
Tank capacity in hours at $\frac{3}{4}$ throttle	6 hours.
Tank capacity in gallons ..	100 gallons.
Disposable load apart from fuel	1000 lbs.
Total weight of machine fully loaded .. :.	4500 lbs.

Performance.

Speed low down	122 m.p.h.
Speed at 10,000 feet	110 m.p.h.
Landing speed	50 m.p.h.

Climb.

To 5,000 feet	4 mins.
To 10,000 feet..	10 mins.
Ceiling	18,000.

The Cabin.

Tail Skid.

Chassis and Radiator.

The B.A.T.—F.K. 26 Passenger Carrier. Pilot's seat and controls.

The B.A.T. F.K. 26
Passenger Carrier.

Some Details.

The Internal Shock Absorbers.

The Tail Units.

The Elevator Lever.

THE BRITISH AERIAL TRANSPORT
Cº Lᵗᴰ.
TYPE F.K.23.
5.SEATER PASSENGER BIPLANE.
.ROLLS.ROYCE EAGLE 8.

THE B.A.T.—F.K. 27.

A really high performance two-seater sporting type machine, which follows generally the outlines of the *Bantam* and *Basilisk* in design.

The two seats are arranged *en echelon* in the fuselage just below the trailing edge of the upper wing.

The lower wing is of considerably smaller chord and rather less span than the upper.

The leading particulars are as given below :—

Specification.

Type of machine	Two-seater Biplane.
Name or type No. of machine ..	B.A.T. type F.K. 27.
Purpose for which intended ..	Fast sporting machine.
Span	Top plane, 26 ft. ; bottom plane, 22 ft. 10 in.
Chord	Top plane, 5 ft. 7 in. ; bottom plane, 3 ft.
Gap, maximum and minimum ..	3 ft. 11 in.
Stagger	8½ in. on leading edges.
Dihedral	3° top and bottom plane.
Overall length	20 ft. 7 in.
Overall height	7 ft. 10 in.
Total area of wings	200 sq. ft.
Ailerons	Top only
Area of each aileron and total area	2 × 7.5 sq. ft. = 15 sq. ft.
Span of tail	9 ft. 2 in.
Total area of tail	23.4 sq. ft. (including elevators).
Area of elevators	6.3 sq. ft.
Area of Rudder	4.4 sq. ft.
Area of fin	2.8 sq. ft.
Maximum cross sectional area of body	10.5 sq. ft. approx.
Side area of body	40 sq. ft. approx.
Engine (type and max. b.h.p.) ..	200 A.B.C. " Wasp II."
Revolutions at max. b.h.p. ..	1,850 p.m.
Propeller (make, type, etc.) ..	B.A.T. Tractor, 2 bladed. 7 ft. 10 in. dia. ; 5 ft. 4 in. pitch ; 1850 r.p.m.
Weight of machine empty ..	800 lbs.
Load per sq. ft.	7 lbs.
Weight per h.p.	7 lbs.
Tank capacity in hours at ¾ throttle	4 hrs.
Tank capacity in gallons ..	30 gallons.
Disposable load apart from fuel	400 lbs.
Total weight of machine fully loaded	1400 lbs.

Performance.

Speed low down	142 m.p.h.
Speed at 10,000 feet ..	130 m.p.h.
Landing Speed	50 m.p.h.

Climb.

To 5,000 feet	2 mins.
Ceiling	24,000.

The British Aerial Transport Cº Lᵗᵈ

Type. F.K. 27

2 Seater Sporting Biplane

200.H.P. A.B.C. Wasp II

Some Products of the B.A.T. Co. From left to right : The "Bantam," the Commercial Passenger Carrier (F.K. 26), and the "Basilisk."

From left to right : The B.A.T. "Bantam," F.K. 26, and the "Basilisk." 92a

B—*continued.*

BEARDMORE. Wm. Beardmore & Co., Dalmuir, nr.

Glasgow, Scotland. The world-famous firm of engineers and shipbuilders, proposed, just before the war, to construct under license the *D.F.W.* biplane (see GERMANY) fitted with Beardmore Daimler motors.

Mr. G. Tilghman Richards (late lieut. R.N.V.R.) is in charge of the design and technical department of the aircraft works.

In addition to the manufacture of a number of machines of external design, this firm has produced a number of machines of its own design. Particulars of the more important types are given herewith.

THE BEARDMORE BIPLANE W.B.1.

This was a large two-seater bomber, from which the type W.B. 1a was developed later. The following gives the main particulars of this machine :—

Specification.

Type of machine	Biplane.
Name or type No. of machine ..	W.B. 1.
Purpose for which intended ..	Bomber.
Span	61 ft. 6 in.
Gap, maximum and minimum ..	7 ft.
Overall length..	32 ft. 10 in.
Maximum height..	14 ft. 9 in.
Chord	7 ft.
Total surface of wings, including ailerons	796 sq. ft.
Span of tail	18 ft.
Total area of tail	106 sq. ft.
Area of elevators	40 sq. ft.
Area of rudder	20 sq. ft.
Area of fin	14.2 sq. ft.
Area of each aileron and total area	28.32 sq. ft., 113.26 sq. ft.
Maximum cross section of body..	15.2 sq. ft.
Horizontal area of body	88 sq. ft.
Vertical area of body	81.6 sq. ft.
Engine type and h.p.	240 h.p. Sunbeam or 230 h.p. Beardmore Adriatic.
Airscrew, diam., and revs. ..	10 ft. 6 in. dia., 1,075 revs. (with Sunbeam)
Weight of machine empty ..	3,410 lbs. (with Beardmore).
Load per sq. ft.	7 lbs.
Weight per h.p.	23 lbs.
Tank capacity in hours	7.3 hours.
Tank capacity in gallons.. ..	137 gallons.

Performance.

Speed low down	91 m.p.h.
Landing speed	48 m.p.h.

Climb.

To 5,000 feet in minutes ..	26 minutes.
To 10,000 feet in minutes ..	44 minutes.
Disposable load apart from fuel	1,100 lbs.
Total weight of machine loaded	5,600 lbs.

Front View of an early Beardmore Experimental Single-seater Biplane.

Side View of a Beardmore Type W.B.1 "Adriatic" (230 h.p. B.H.P. Engine).

BEARDMORE—continued.

THE BEARDMORE BIPLANE W.B. 1A.

The *Beardmore* two-seater biplane W.B. 1a. was designed as a long-distance bomber equipped with a 500 h.p. Beardmore Atlantic engine. The main planes are heavily staggered, are of large span, and have four pairs of interplane struts at either side of the fuselage. The pilot and observer are placed very much in rear of the main plane, the pilot being midway between the main and tail planes and the observer is immediately in advance of the fixed fin which emerges from the fairing round the observer's cockpit.

Specification.

Type of machine	Biplane.
Name or type No. of machine ..	W.B. 1a.
Purpose for which intended ..	Bomber.
Span	70 ft.
Gap, maximum and minimum ..	7 ft.
Overall length	32 ft. 10 in.
Maximum height	15 ft. 8 in.
Chord	7 ft.
Total surface of wings, including ailerons	946 sq. ft.
Span of tail	19 ft.
Total area of tail	110 sq. ft.
Area of elevators	33.5 sq. ft.
Area of rudder	20 sq. ft.
Area of fin	14.2 sq. ft.
Area of each aileron and total area	29.5 sq. ft., 118 sq. ft.
Maximum cross section of body..	22.5 sq. ft.
Horizontal area of body ..	105 sq. ft.
Vertical area of body ..	131 sq. ft.
Engine type and h.p. ..	Beardmore Atlantic 500 h.p.
Airscrew, diam. and revs. ..	14 ft , 900.
Weight of machine empty ..	4,537 lbs.
Load per sq. ft.	9.4 lbs.
Weight per h.p.	17.3 lbs.
Tank capacity in hours ..	6.5 hours.
Tank capacity in gallons ..	214 gallons.

Performance.

Speed low down	110 m.p.h.
Speed at 10,000 feet	101 m.p.h.
Landing speed	65 m.p.h.

Climb.

To 5,000 feet in minutes ..	12 minutes.
To 10,000 feet in minutes	27 minutes.

Disposable load apart from fuel	2,700 lbs.
Total weight of machine loaded	8,900 lbs.

THE BEARDMORE FIGHTER W.B. 2 AND 2A.

The *Beardmore* W.B. 2 is a conventional two-seater fighter equipped with a 230 h.p. Hispano-Suiza engine. The main planes are heavily staggered. The pilot is situated under the trailing edge of the top plane and the observer over the trailing edge of the bottom plane, giving both an excellent view all round.

The type W.B. 2a. is a modified version of this machine fitted with a Beardmore " Adriatic " engine of 230 h.p and with increased tank capacity.

The following tables give the details of both machines :—

BEARDMORE BOMBING AEROPLANE
TYPE W.B. 1.A
515 HP BEARDMORE PACIFIC ENGINE.

BEARDMORE—*continued.*

THE BEARDMORE BIPLANE W.B. II.

Type of machine	Biplane.
Name or type No. of machine ..	W.B. II.
Purpose for which intended ..	Fighter.
Span	34 ft. 10 in.,
Gap, maximum and minimum ..	5 ft. 6 in., 5 ft. 6 in.
Overall length	27 ft. 3 in.
Maximum height	10 ft. 11 in.
Chord	5 ft. 6 in.,
Total surface of wings, including	
ailerons	354 sq. ft.
Span of tail	13 ft.
Total area of tail	49 sq. ft.
Area of elevators	21 sq. ft.
Area of rudder	11.5 sq. ft.
Area of fin	6 sq. ft.
Area of each aileron and total area	16 sq. ft., 64 sq. ft.
Maximum cross section of body ..	11 sq. ft.
Horizontal area of body	65 sq. ft.
Vertical area of body	64 sq. ft.
Engine type and h.p.	Hispano Suiza 200 h.p.
Airscrew, diam., and revs. ..	9 ft.; 1,186.
Weight of machine empty ..	1,765 lbs.
Load per sq. ft.	7.5 lbs.
Weight per h.p.	13.25 lbs.
Tank capacity in hours	2.8 hours.
Tank capacity in gallons	41.5 gallons.

Performance.

Speed low down	120 m.p.h.
Speed at 10,000 feet	111 m.p.h.
Landing speed	50 m.p.h.

Climb.

To 5,000 feet in minutes ..	7 minutes.
To 10,000 feet in minutes ..	15 minutes.
Disposable load apart from fuel	540 lbs.
Total weight of machine loaded	2,650 lbs.

THE BEARDMORE BIPLANE W.B. II A.

Type of machine	Biplane.
Name or type No. of machine ..	W.B. IIa.
Purpose for which intended ..	Fighter and Reconnaissance.
Span	Top 34 ft. 10 in.,
	bottom 34 ft. 10 in.
Gap, maximum and minimum ..	5 ft.
Overall length	27 ft. 7 in.
Maximum height	10 ft. 1 in.

Chord	Top 5 ft. 6 in.,
	bottom 5 ft. 6 in.
Total surface of wings, including	
ailerons	354 sq. ft.
Span of tail	13 ft.
Total area of tail	49 sq. ft.

Area of elevators	21 sq. ft.
Area of rudder	11.5 sq. ft.
Area of fin	8.1 sq. ft.
Area of each aileron and total area	16 sq. ft., 64 sq. ft.
Maximum cross section of body ..	11.7 sq. ft.
Horizontal area of body	66 sq. ft.

BEARDMORE FIGHTER M/C
TYPE W.B. II A.

Ford Jones/19

0 1 2 3 4 5 6 7 8 FEET.
SCALE

BEARDMORE—*continued*.

Vertical area of body	.. ..	75 sq. ft.
Engine type and h.p.	..	Beardmore Adriatic, 230 h.p.
Airscrew, diam. and revs.	..	10 ft., 1,350 r.p.m.
Weight of machine empty	..	1,650 lbs.
Load per sq. ft.	.. ..	7.6 lbs.
Weight per h.p.	.. ..	11.7 lbs.
Tank capacity in hours	..	4.5 hours.
Tank capacity in gallons..	..	75 gallons.

Performance.

Speed low down	..	125 m.p.h.
Speed at 10,000 feet	..	117 m.p.h.
Landing speed ..	..	50 m.p.h.

Climb.

To 5,000 feet in minutes	..	5 minutes.
To 10,000 feet in minutes	..	12 minutes.

Disposable load apart from fuel	.. ..	460 lbs.
Total weight of machine loaded	.. ..	2,700 lbs.

THE BEARDMORE BIPLANE W.B. III.

The *Beardmore* W.B. III. was evolved from the *Sopwith* "Pup" in an effort to turn this machine into a ship-plane, the principal modifications being folding planes and a retractable under-carriage, in order to simplify stowage on board ship. The fuselage and tail unit are practically of Sopwith design, the overall length being only slightly increased.

Instead of four short centre-section struts, four long struts, two on either side of the fuselage, are fitted with a short horizontal strut connecting them with the upper longeron of the fuselage. The main planes are unstaggered and hinged at the main rear spar close up to the fuselage.

Two sets of interplane struts are fitted to each set of main planes one set being placed at the inner edge of the plane in order to preserve the truss when the wings are folded.

Ailerons are fitted to upper and lower planes and are operated on the Nieuport principle, the upper and lower ailerons being inter-connected by a strut.

An ordinary Vee-type under-carriage is fitted, the front members of the Vee being hinged, and the rear members equipped with a release device operated from the pilot's seat which allows the under-carriage to collapse into the fuselage, leaving half the wheels exposed. The armament consists of a Lewis gun fitted on a special mounting in front of the pilot's cockpit to allow it to fire through an opening in the centre section.

Particulars of this machine are given in the following table :—

Type of machine	.. .. ..	Biplane.
Name or type No. of machine	..	W.B. III.
Purpose for which intended	..	Ship's Scout.
Span	.. .. ..	25 ft.
Gap, maximum and minimum	..	4 ft. 9 in., 4 ft. 9 in.
Overall length	.. ..	20 ft. 2.5 in.
Maximum height ..	..	8 ft. 1.25 in.
Chord	.. .. ..	5 ft. 1.5 in.
Total surface of wings, including ailerons	.. .. ..	243 sq. ft.
Span of tail	.. ..	10 ft. 1 in.
Total area of tail ..	..	34.5 sq. ft.
Area of elevators ..	..	11.5 sq. ft.
Area of rudder	..	4.5 sq. ft.
Area of fin	..	3.5 sq. ft.
Area of each aileron and total area	5.75 sq. ft., 23 sq. ft.
Maximum cross section of body..	4.6 sq. ft.
Horizontal area of body ..	..	17 sq. ft.
Vertical area of body	..	39 sq. ft.
Engine type and h.p.	..	Clerget or Le Rhône 80 h.p.
Airscrew, diam. and revs.	..	8 ft. 6 in. ; 1,200 r.p.m.
Weight of machine empty	..	880 lbs.
Load per sq. ft.	.. ..	5.3 lbs.
Weight per h.p.	.. ..	16.1 lbs.

Tank capacity in hours ..	..	2.75 hours.
Tank capacity in gallons..	..	18 gallons.

Performance.

Speed low down	..	103 m.p.h.
Speed at 10,000 feet	..	88 m.p.h.
Landing speed ..	..	40 m.p.h.

Climb.

To 5,000 feet in minutes	..	9 minutes.
To 10,000 feet in minutes	..	24 minutes

Disposable load apart from fuel	.. ..	300 lbs.
Total weight of machine loaded	.. ..	1,290 lbs.

THE BEARDMORE BIPLANE W.B. IV.

The *Beardmore* W.B. IV. is a single-seater ship's scout designed with flotation gear in the fuselage and a dropping under-carriage. In order to keep the size of the flotation gear which is actually built into the fuselage, down to a minimum, the power unit is placed under the centre-section and over the centre of gravity, the pilot being seated in front astride the airscrew shaft in a watertight cockpit.

The under-carriage is of the Vee type and is so arranged that by means of a control in the pilot's cockpit the whole under-carriage can be released.

Two wing-top floats are fitted as additional stabilizers when the machine is resting on the sea.

The Beardmore Type W.B. III Folding Ship plane (80 h.p. Le Rhône Engine) with wings and chassis folded for stowage.

BEARDMORE—*continued*.

Specification.

Type of machine	Biplane.
Name or type No. of machine ..	W.B. IV.
Purpose for which intended ..	Ship's Scout.
Span	35 ft. 10 in.
Gap	4 ft. 9 in.
Overall length	26 ft. 6 in.
Maximum height	9 ft. 10.5 in.
Chord	Top 6 ft. 3 in., bottom 4ft. 9 in.
Total surface of wings, including ailerons	350 sq. ft.
Span of tail	11 ft. 9 in.
Total area of tail	50.5 sq. ft.
Area of elevators	24 sq. ft.
Area of rudder	12 sq. ft.
Area of fin	8 sq. ft.
Area of each aileron and total area	18.8 sq. ft. each, 37 ft. 6 in. total.
Maximum cross section of body ..	12.5 sq. ft.
Horizontal area of body	73 sq. ft.
Vertical area of body	51 sq. ft.
Engine type and h.p.	Hispano-Suiza 200 h.p.
Airscrew, diam. and revs. ..	9 ft., 1,500 r.p.m.
Weight of machine empty ..	1,960 lbs.
Load per sq. ft.	7.5 lbs.
Weight per h.p.	13 lbs.
Tank capacity in hours ..	8.5 hours.
Tank capacity in gallons	37 gallons.

Performance.

Speed low down	110 m.p.h.
Speed at 10,000 feet	102 m.p.h.
Landing speed	45 m.p.h.

Climb.

To 5,000 feet in minutes ..	7 minutes.
To 10,000 feet in minutes ..	18 minutes.
Disposable load apart from fuel	340 lbs.
Total weight of machine loaded	2,600 lbs.

THE BEARDMORE BIPLANE W.B. V.

This machine was also designed as a ship single-seater fighter, and was of very much the same overall dimensions as the W.B. IV.

Instead of placing the engine over the C.G. and driving the propeller by a shaft passing between the pilot's legs, and designing the fuselage to provide the necessary buoyancy for flotation after alighting on the sea, the conventional engine in front arrangement was adopted, and the necessary buoyancy had to be provided by external air bags.

Specification.

Type of machine	Biplane.
Name or type No. of machine ..	W.B. V.
Purpose for which intended ..	Ship's Scout.
Span	35 ft. 10 in.

The Beardmore Ship plane, Type W.B. IV (200 h.p. Hispano-Suiza Engine).

The Beardmore Type W.B. V Ship plane (200 h.p. Hispano-Suiza Engine.

BEARDMORE—*continued.*

THE BEARDMORE BIPLANE W.B. V.—*continued.*

Gap	4 ft. 9 in.
Overall length	26 ft. 7 in.
Maximum height	11 ft. 10 in.
Chord	6 ft. 3 in.
Total surface of wings, including ailerons	394 sq. ft.
Span of tail	11 ft. 9 in.
Total area of tail	50.5 sq. ft.
Area of elevators	24 sq. ft.
Area of rudder	12 sq. ft.
Area of fin	8 sq. ft.
Area of each aileron and total area	18.8 sq. ft. each, 37.6 sq. ft. total.
Maximum cross section of body ..	11.5 sq. ft.
Horizontal area of body	46.5 sq. ft.
Vertical area of body	58 sq. ft.
Engine type and h.p.	Hispano-Suiza 200 h.p.
Airscrew, diam. and revs. ..	9 ft., 1,500 r.p.m.
Weight of machine empty ..	1,860 lbs.
Load per sq. ft.	6.33 lbs.
Weight per h.p.	12.5 lbs.
Tank capacity in hours ..	2.5 hours.
Tank capacity in gallons ..	37 gallons.

Performance.

Speed low down	112 m.p.h.
Speed at 10,000 feet	103 m.p.h
Landing speed	45 m.p.h.

Climb.

To 5,000 feet in minutes ..	6 minutes.
To 10,000 feet in minutes ..	17 minutes.

Disposable load apart from fuel	340 lbs.
Total weight of machine loaded	2,500 lbs.

THE BEARDMORE TORPEDO CARRIER W.B. VI.

The *Beardmore* single seater torpedo-carrying, folding ship-aeroplane, type W.B. VI., was the result of one of the many efforts to produce a satisfactory, fast torpedo-carrier. The general arrangement is on conventional lines, with the pilot well back in the fuselage.

The under-carriage is arranged to permit the stowage and dropping of a torpedo under the centre of gravity.

Specification.

Type of machine	Biplane.
Name or type No. of machine ..	W.B. VI.
Purpose for which intended ..	Torpedo Carrier.
Span	Top 53 ft. 6.5 in., bottom 47 ft. 10.5 in.
Gap	7 ft. 6 in.
Overall length	34 ft.

Maximum height	12 ft. 6 in.
Chord	Top 8 ft. 10 in., bottom 7 ft. 9 in.
Total surface of wings, including ailerons	796 sq. ft.
Span of tail	15 ft. 9 in.

Total area of tail	80 sq. ft.
Area of elevators	32.4 sq. ft.
Area of rudder	12 sq. ft.
Area of fin	10 sq. ft.
Area of each aileron and total area	47.75 sq. ft. each, 95.5 sq. ft. total

58'-0"

9'-0"

BEARDMORE SINGLE SEATER TORPEDO CARRYING FOLDING SHIP

AEROPLANE

TYPE W.B. VI.

Ford-Jones 19

0 1 2 3 4 5 6 7 8 FEET

SCALE

BEARDMORE—*continued.*

TORPEDO CARRIER W.B. VI—*continued.*

Maximum cross section of body..	10 sq. ft.
Horizontal area of body	62 sq. ft.
Vertical area of body	100 sq. ft.
Engine type and h.p.	Rolls-Royce Eagle 350 h.p.
Airscrew, diam. and revs. ..	12 ft., 1,080 r.p.m.
Weight of machine empty ..	3,027 lbs.
Load per sq. ft.	7 lbs.
Weight per h.p.	15.6 lbs.
Tank capacity in hours ..	3 hours.
Tank capacity in gallons.. ..	70 gallons.

Performance.

Speed low down	102 m.p.h.
Speed at 10,000 feet	91 m.p.h.
Landing speed..	47 m.p.h.

Climb.

To 5,000 feet in minutes ..	15 minutes.
To 10,000 feet in minutes ..	41 minutes.

Disposable load apart from fuel	2,060 lbs.
Total weight of machine loaded	5,637 lbs.

THE BEARDMORE TRIPLANE W.B. VIII.

The *Beardmore* three-engine passenger and cargo triplane is designed on similar lines to the *Caproni* triplane long-distance bomber. There are two fuselages, with passenger compartments in the nose of each, and a central nacelle carrying the crew and one power unit.

Three power units, each a 500 h.p. Beardmore "Atlantic" engine, are carried, the two outer ones driving geared airscrews through shafts running along the top inside longeron of each fuselage, and the central engine driving a single pusher in the rear of the nacelle.

The tail is a biplane, with three comma-shaped balanced rudders.

Specification.

Type of machine	Triplane.
Name or type No. of machine ..	W.B. VIII.
Purpose for which intended ..	Passenger and Cargo Carrier.
Span ·	Top 120 ft., bottom 118 ft.
Gap, maximum and minimum ..	8 ft.
Overall length	62 ft.
Maximum height	23 ft.
Chord	10 ft.
Total surface of wings, including ailerons..	3,260 sq. ft.
Span of tail	37 ft.
Total area of tail	430 sq. ft.
Area of elevators..	72 sq. ft.
Area of rudder	105 sq. ft.
Area of fin	77 sq. ft.
Area of each aileron and total area	55 sq. ft. each, 220 sq. ft. total.
Maximum cross section of body..	132 sq. ft.
Horizontal area of body	645 sq. ft.

Vertical area of body	490 sq. ft.
Engine type and h.p.	Three Beardmore Atlantic, 500 h.p. each.
Airscrew, diam. and revs. ..	15 ft., 900 r.p.m.
Weight of machine empty ..	14,262 lbs.
Load per sq. ft.	8.37 ibs.
Weight per h.p.	18.2 lbs.
Tank capacity in hours ..	6 hours.
Tank capacity in gallons.. ..	660 gallons.

Performance (estimated).

Speed low down	92 m.p.h.
Speed at 10,000 feet	81 m.p.h.
Landing speed..	53 m.p.h.

Climb.

To 5,000 in minutes	15 minutes.
To 10,000 feet in minutes ..	41 minutos.

Disposable load apart from fuel	7,450 lbs.
Total weight of machine loaded	27,320 lbs.

BEARDMORE PASSENGER CARRYING AEROPLANE.

TYPE W.B.8.

B—continued.

BEATTY. The Beatty Aviation Co., Cricklewood, London, N.W.

Mr. G. W. Beatty, one of the earliest American pilots, came to England in 1912 to exhibit the Gyro engine. He returned in 1913 and started a school of flying at the London Aerodrome, Hendon, where he trained a large number of pupils, very many of whom have done good work in the Flying Service.

In 1916 he produced a small biplane, his idea being to provide a fast single-seater school machine for the use of pupils who have already taken their certificates and wish to continue their training. The machine was also of use for military pupils as a cheap substitute for the more costly types of military aeroplanes, which have been largely used and broken in the later stages of training.

The first example of machine had a 35 h.p. Anzani air-cooled engine, but this was later changed for a 60 h.p. 4-cylinder air-cooled engine of Mr. Beatty's own make. With that engine the machine had a speed of 80 miles an hour and a climbing rate of about 800 feet per minute, carrying a pilot and fuel for 2½ hours.

On the Hendon Aerodrome being taken over by the Army, Mr. Beatty removed to new works and an aerodrome of his own at Cricklewood. He closed his aerodrome early in 1918 and is now engaged in manufacturing aeroplanes and parts and on general motor Engineering.

BLACKBURN Aeroplanes. The Blackburn Aeroplane and Motor Co., Ltd., Olympia, Leeds, and Seaplane Works, Brough and Hull. Mr. Robert Blackburn produced his first machine early in 1910 (see 1911 edition for details). In the latter part of that year he designed the machine which ultimately developed into the *Blackburn* military monoplane. In 1911 other types were produced. The *Blackburn* monoplane was successfully flown by naval officers before the war.

The 80 h.p. *Blackburn* monoplane has done a great deal of work in the past. In October, 1913, one of these machines won the Inter-County 100 Miles "War of the Roses" Air Race for a Silver Challenge Cup presented by the "Yorkshire Evening News."

A machine of similar type was used in 1914 for passenger flying, and was in use at the end of 1915, fitted with floats and a 100 h.p. Anzani motor, as a school machine on Windermere.

The firm turned out during 1915 a number of B.E. 2c. biplanes and certain seaplanes and other machines for the Admiralty.

The firm's more recent work has been of a nature of high importance to naval and military flying, and is hereafter described.

BRITISH AEROPLANES.

The active directors of the firm are Mr. Robert Blackburn, one of the pioneers of British aviation, and Mr. Stuart A. Hirst, a well-known Leeds business man, and the combination is proving highly successful.

Mr. Bumpus (late major R.A.F.) and Mr. Harris Booth F.Ae.S. (formerly of the Admiralty), are the chief technical officials of the firm.

THE BLACKBURN POPULAR TWO-SEATER.

As a purely post-bellum product the Blackburn firm have produced a very small side-by-side two-seater, equipped with a small two-cylinder air-cooled engine, which it is proposed to sell complete for £450. The following table gives the main particulars :—

Specification.

Type of machine	Two-seater Monoplane.
Name or type No. of machine ..	Blackburn "Side-car."
Purpose for which intended ..	Sporting.
Span	27 ft. 3 in.
Overall length	20 ft. 6 in.
Maximum height	6 ft. 3 in.
Engine type and h.p.	A.B.C. "Gnat," 45 h.p.
Tank capacity in hours	4 hours.

Performance.

Speed low down	83 m.p.h.
Landing speed	48 m.p.h.

THE BLACKBURN "KANGAROO."

The Blackburn twin-tractor biplane was developed from a twin-float twin-engined seaplane built by the Blackburn firm for the Admiralty in 1916–17, of which a specification is given.

The machine was afterwards remodelled as a long-distance bomber, and has been used as such, and also to a considerable extent for anti-submarine patrols over the North Sea and elsewhere.

Two Views of the Blackburn Popular Two-seater
(45 h.p. A.B.C. Gnat Engine).

Three-quarter View from the Rear of the Blackburn "Kangaroo" (Two 250 h.p. Falcon Rolls-Royce Engines).

BLACKBURN—*continued.*

THE BLACKBURN "KANGAROO."—*continued.*

The central fuselage carries the pilot's cockpit well in advance of the leading edge of the planes and two gunner's cockpits, one right in the nose and the other about midway between nose and tail, well in the rear of the planes. The power units, two Rolls-Royce 250 h.p. "Falcon" engines, are carried (one on either side of the fuselage) in two streamline housings between the first two sets of interplane struts and just above the lower planes.

Under each power unit is a separate Vee-type chassis.

The upper plane has a considerable overhang, braced above from kingposts and below from the base of the outer set of struts. Ailerons are fitted to both sets of planes and are interconnected by a light strut.

The tail unit is of the biplane type with two fins, which are used as a fairing to the intertail struts.

Specification.

Type of machine	Blackburn Twin Tractor.
Name or type No. of machine ..	"Kangaroo."
Purpose for which intended ..	Long Range Bomber.
Span	74 ft. 10¼ in. top; 47 ft. 9½ in. bottom plane.
Gap	7 ft. 3 in.
Overall length	46 ft.
Maximum height	16 ft. 10 in.
Chord	7 ft. 3 in.
Total surface of wings	880 sq. ft.
Span of tail	17 ft. 6 in.
Total area of tail	143 sq. ft.
Area of elevators..	63.5 sq. ft.
Area of rudder	22.5 sq. ft.
Area of fin	25 sq. ft.
Area of ailerons	166.5 sq. ft.
Maximum cross section of body..	12 sq. ft.
Horizontal area of body.. ..	105 sq. ft.
Vertical area of body	115 sq. ft.
Engine type and h.p.	Falcon-Rolls, two 250 h.p.
Weight of machine empty ..	5,150 lbs.
Load per sq. ft.	9.21 lbs.
Weight per h.p.	16.2 lbs.
Tank capacity in hours	8 hours.
Tank capacity in gallons.. ..	230 petrol; 18 oil.

Performance.

Speed low down	87 knots.
Disposable load apart from fuel	1,710 lbs.
Total weight of machine loaded	8,100 lbs.

THE "BABY" SEAPLANE.

The "Baby" seaplane traces its origin back to the original *Sopwith* "Schneider," the winner of the International "Schneider" Cup for hydro-aeroplanes at Monaco in 1914.

Something over a year after the outbreak of hostilities the Air Department of the Admiralty awoke to the fact that a machine of this type might have uses, and, after a few experiments, a number of these machines, somewhat modified, were ordered from Messrs. Sopwith & Co. Ltd., and from a number of other makers. The original machines were all fitted with 100 h.p. monosoupape Gnômes. A later edition was fitted with 110 h.p. Clerget engines.

It was then attempted to use these machines as bomb carriers, with two 65 lb. bombs, with the result that in their overloaded condition they became distinctly unpopular.

Orders for the type were stopped, and a number of experimental machines were ordered from various sources with the idea of supplanting this type of machine.

Before any of the experimental types had reached a production stage an acute shortage of seaplanes, and particularly of seaplanes with any reasonable speed, occurred, and orders for large numbers of the "Baby" type, fitted with 130 h.p. Clerget engines were placed with various firms.

Messrs. Sopwith being at that time extremely busy with single-seater land fighters, the task of carrying out the modifications necessary for the new engine and of issuing all the new drawings was entrusted to the Blackburn Aeroplane and Motor Co.

The machine is of very simple and straightforward construction. The wings are of low aspect ratio, and have a gap less than the chord, and the overall length of the machine has been reduced to a minimum by placing the pilot's feet beneath the carburettor, and bringing the engine very close up to the leading edge of the wings.

In consequence, the machine has a very compact appearance and is extremely easy to manœuvre.

Specification.

Type of machine..	Tractor Single-seater Biplane Twin-float Seaplane.
Name or type No. of machine..	"Baby."
Purpose for which intended ..	Fighting Scout.
Span	25 ft. 8 in.
Gap	4 ft. 6 in.

Three-quarter View from Rear the Blackburn "Baby" Seaplane (130 h.p. Clerget Engine).

BLACKBURN—continued.

THE " BABY " SEAPLANE—continued.

Overall length	23 ft.
Maximum height..	10 ft.
Chord	5 ft. 2 in.
Total surface of wings ..	225 sq. ft.
Span of tail	9 ft. 5 in.
Total area of tail	34 sq. ft.
Area of elevators	15 sq. ft.
Area of rudder	7 sq. ft.
Area of fin	4 sq. ft.
Area of ailerons.. ..	23 sq. ft.
Maximum cross section of body	10 sq. ft.
Horizontal area of body ..	38 sq. ft.
Vertical area of body ..	42 sq. ft.
Engine type and h.p.	Clerget ; 130 h.p.
Weight of machine empty ..	1,226 lbs.
Load per sq. ft.	7.63 lbs.
Weight per h.p.	13.2 lbs.
Tank capacity in hours ..	2¼ hours.
Tank capacity in gallons	25 petrol ; 6 oil.

Performance.

Speed low down	87 knots.

Climb.

To 10,000 feet in minutes ..	35 minutes.
Disposable load apart from fuel	255 lbs.
Total weight of machine loaded	1,715 lbs.

THE BLACKBURN THREE-SEATER SEAPLANE.

Type of machine	Blackburn Twin Seaplane.
Name or type No. of machine ..	S. P.
Purpose for which intended ..	Long Range Bomber.
Span	74 ft. 10¼ in. top; 47 ft. 9½ in. bottom plane.
Gap	7 ft. 3 in.
Overall length	46 ft.
Maximum height.. ..	16 ft. 10 in.
Chord	7 ft. 3 in.
Total surface of wings ..	880 sq. ft.
Span of tail	17 ft. 6 in.
Total area of tail	143 sq. ft.
Area of elevators	63.5 sq. ft.
Area of rudder	22.5 sq. ft.
Area of fin	25 sq. ft.
Area of ailerons	166.5 sq. ft.
Maximum cross section of body.	12 sq. ft.
Horizontal area of body ..	105 sq. ft.
Vertical area of body ..	115 sq. ft.
Engine type and h.p. ..	Falcon-Rolls, two 250 h.p.
Weight of machine empty ..	5,840 lbs.
Load per sq. ft.	9.78 lbs.
Weight per h.p.	17.2 lbs.
Tank capacity in hours.. ..	8 hours.
Tank capacity in gallons ..	230 petrol; 18 oil.

Performance.

Speed low down	87 knots.	
Disposable load apart from fuel		1,710 lbs.
Total weight of machine loaded		8,600 lbs.

THE BLACKBURN " BLACKBURD."

This machine, designed as a torpedo carrier for use from aeroplane carriers working with the fleet at sea, was designed primarily with a view to ease of production.

The machine is generally on conventional tractor lines, with a chassis designed to allow of the dropping of a torpedo slung beneath the body.

The most noticeable feature, as far as appearance is concerned, is the side elevation of the fuselage, which is of the same depth from the leading edge of the lower wing to the sternpost.

Specification.

Type of machine..	Tractor Biplane.
Name or type No. of machine .	" Blackburd."
Purpose for which intended ..	Torpedo carrier, for use from ship or land.
Span	52 ft. 6 in.
Gap	7 ft.
Overall length	36 ft. 3 in.
Maximum height..	12 ft. 4½ in.
Chord	7 ft.
Total surface of wings	709 sq. ft.
Span of tail	17 ft.
Total area of Tail	82 sq. ft.
Area of elevators	34 sq. ft.
Area of rudder	9 sq. ft.
Area of fin	18 sq. ft.
Area of ailerons	85 sq. ft.
Maximum cross section of body	11 sq. ft.
Horizontal area of body ..	80 sq. ft.
Vertical area of body ..	126 sq ft.
Engine type and h.p.	" Eagle " Rolls-Royce ; 350 h.p.
Weight of machine empty ..	3,080 lbs.
Load per sq. ft.	7.53 lbs.
Weight per h.p.	15.3 lbs.
Tank capacity in hours ..	3 hours.
Tank capacity in gallons ..	69 petrol ; 9 oil.

Performance.

Speed low down	92 m.p.h.
Speed at 10,000 feet	84½ m.p.h.

Climb.

To 5,000 feet in minutes ..	11½ minutes.
To 10,000 feet in minutes ..	33½ minutes.
Disposable load apart from fuel	1,680 lbs.
Total weight of machine loaded	5,340 lbs.

Three-quarter Front View of the Blackburn Torpedo-carrying " Blackburd " (350 h.p. " Eagle " Rolls-Royce Engine).

B—*continued.*

BOULTON & PAUL, Ltd., Norwich.

Big firm of building constructors. Hence have undertaken with conspicuous success the construction of aircraft to War Office specification. Have developed under the management of Mr. Geoffrey ffiske into one of the most progressive of aircraft firms, and may be regarded as likely to occupy a big position in aviation after the war.

Mr. J. D. North, one of the best-known of British aeronautical scientists, is the firm's chief technician and designer.

The firm has produced the following machines :—

THE BOULTON & PAUL "BOBOLINK."

A small single-seat fighter scout on standard lines, with a high performance. The N-type interplane struts are a characteristic feature.

Specification.

Type of machine	Single-seater Biplane.
Name or type No. of machine	Bobolink.
Purpose for which intended	Fighting Scout.
Span	29 ft.
Gap, maximum and minimum	3 ft. $10\frac{5}{8}$ in.
Overall length	20 ft.
Maximum height	8 ft. 4 in.
Chord	Top plane, 5 ft. $4\frac{1}{2}$ in. ; bottom plane, 4 ft. $1\frac{11}{2}$ in.
Total surface of wings	266 sq. ft.
Span of tail	9 ft. 2 in.
Total area of tail	30 sq. ft.
Area of rudder	10 sq. ft.
Area of fin	2 sq. ft.
Area of ailerons	7.5 sq. ft.
Maximum cross section of body	7.5 sq. ft.
Horizontal area of body	30 sq. ft.
Vertical area of body	41 sq. ft.
Engine type and h.p.	230 h.p. B.R.2.
Airscrew, diameter and revs.	9 ft. 0 in. 1350 revs.
Weight of machine empty	1220 lbs.
Load per sq. ft.	7.25 lbs.
Weight per h.p.	8.35 lbs.
Tank capacity in hours	2.65 hours.
Tank capacity in gallons	38 gallons.

Performance.

Speed at 10,000 feet	125 m.p.h.
Speed at 15,000 feet	110 m.p.h.
Landing speed	50 m.p.h.

Climb.

To 10,000 feet in minutes	$9\frac{1}{2}$ minutes.
To 15,000 feet in minutes	18 minutes.
Disposable load apart from fuel	430 lbs.
Total weight of machine loaded	1920 lbs.

Three-quarter Front View of the Boulton & Paul "Bobolink" (236 h.p. B.R. 2 engine).

Three-quarter Rear View of the Boulton & Paul "Bobolink."

BOULTON & PAUL—*continued.*

THE BOULTON & PAUL "BOURGES."

This machine was designed late in the war as a fighter bomber.

Is remarkable for its small overall dimensions.

This machine combines the speed, climb, and manœuvring qualities usually associated with a small single-seat fighter, with the fuel and load capacity expected of a large bomber.

The appended specification gives the leading characteristics :

Specification.

Type of machine	Twin-engined Biplane.
Name or type No. of machine ..	Boulton & Paul P 7. "Bourges."
Purpose for which intended ..	Bomber-fighter.
Span	54 ft.
Gap, maximum and minimum ..	6 ft. 6 in.
Overall length	37 ft.
Maximum height	12 ft.
Chord	Top plane, 8 ft. ; bottom plane, 6 ft. 6 in.
Total surface of wings	738 sq. ft.
Span of tail	16 ft.
Area of tail plane	96 sq. ft.
Area of elevators	96 sq. ft.
Area of rudder	21 sq. ft.
Area of fin	14 sq. ft.
Area of ailerons	27 sq. ft.
Maximum cross section of body	5.3 sq. ft.
Horizontal area of body.. ..	73 sq. ft.
Vertical area of body	140 sq. ft.
Engine type and h.p.	2—320 h.p. A.B.C. "Dragonfly."
Airscrew, diameter and revs. ..	9 ft. 6 in. dia. 1650 r.p.m.
Weight of machine empty ..	3420 lbs.
Load per sq. ft.	8 lbs.
Tank capacity in hours ..	9.25 hours.
Tank capacity in gallons ..	190 gallons.

Performance.

Speed at 10,000 feet	124 m.p.h.
Speed at 15,000 feet	118 m.p.h.
Landing speed	50 m.p.h.

Climb.

To 10,000 feet in minutes ..	11 minutes.
To 15,000 feet in minutes ..	21 minutes.
Disposable load apart from fuel	1200 lbs.
Total weight of machine loaded	5920 lbs.

Front View of the Boulton & Paul "Bourges" Twin-engined Fighting Bomber (two 300 h.p. A.B.C. "Dragonfly" engines)

Half-side View of the Boulton & Paul "Bourges" Bomber (two 300 h.p. A.B.C. "Dragonfly" engines).

104a

BOULTON & PAUL—*continued.*

THE BOULTON & PAUL COMMERCIAL TYPE MACHINE.

A modified and somewhat enlarged edition of the "Bourges" bomber, equipped for commercial, cargo and passenger carrying, and fitted with Napier "Lion" engines instead of B.R. rotary engines fitted in the original model.

Two machines of this type have been adapted for attempts at the Transatlantic flight.

Specification.

Type of machine	Twin-engined Tractor Biplane.
Name or type No. of machine ..	Boulton & Paul P 8.
Purpose for which intended ..	Passenger and Commercial.
Span	59 ft.
Gap, maximum and minimum ..	6 ft. 6 in.
Overall length	40 ft.
Maximum height	12 ft. 4 in.
Chord	Top plane, 8 ft. ; bottom plane, 6 ft. 6 in.
Total surface of wings	770 sq. ft.
Span of tail	16 ft.
Area of tail plane	96 sq. ft.
Area of elevators	96 sq. ft.
Area of rudder	21 sq. ft.
Area of fin	14 sq. ft.
Area of ailerons	27 sq. ft.
Maximum cross section of body	22 sq. ft.
Horizontal area of body.. ..	108 sq. ft.
Vertical area of body ..	180 sq. ft.
Engine type and h.p.	2—450 h.p. Napier "Lion"
Airscrew, diameter and revs. ..	9 ft. 6 in. 1450.
Weight of machine empty ..	4000 lbs.
Load per sq. ft.	9.75 lbs.
Weight per h.p.	8.34 lbs.
Tank capacity in hours	4 hours.
Tank capacity in gallons ..	210 gallons.

Performance.

Speed at 10,000 feet	149 m.p.h.
Speed at 15,000 feet	142 m.p.h.
Landing speed	54 m.p.h.

Climb.

To 10,000 feet in minutes ..	8 minutes.
To 15,000 feet in minutes ..	15 minutes.
Disposable load apart from fuel	2000 lbs.
Total weight of machine loaded	7500 lbs.

Another View of the Boulton & Paul "Bourges" Bomber. (A.B.C. engines.)

BOULTON & PAUL—*continued.*

Three-quarter Front View of the Boulton & Paul " Bourges " Bomber (two 230 h.p. B.R. 2 engines).

Three-quarter View from Rear of the Boulton & Paul " Bourges " Twin-engined Bomber. (B.R. engines.)

BOULTON & PAUL—*continued.*

BOULTON & PAUL "P 6."

A small two-seater general utility machine of reasonable performance. As indicated by the attached illustrations, one of the types is in regular use by the firm's own Sales Department.

Specification.

Type of machine	.. ..	Tractor Biplane.
Name or type No. of machine	..	P 6.
Span	.. .. ..	25 ft.
Gap, maximum and minimum	..	5 ft.
Overall length	.. ..	19 ft.
Maximum height	.. ..	8 ft.
Chord	.. .. ..	5 ft.
Total surface of wings	.. ..	235 sq. ft.
Span of tail	.. ..	11 ft.
Total area of tail	.. ..	40 sq. ft.
Area of rudder	.. ..	9 sq. ft.
Area of fin	.. ..	2.5 sq. ft.
Area of ailerons	.. ..	7.5 sq. ft.
Maximum cross section of body		7.8 sq. ft.
Horizontal area of body	..	27 sq. ft.
Vertical area of body	..	44 sq. ft.
Engine type and h.p.	..	100 h.p. R.A.F.
Airscrew, diameter and revs.	..	9 ft. 3 in. 1000 revs.
Weight of machine empty	..	1100 lbs.
Load per sq. ft.	.. ..	7.35 lbs.
Weight per h.p.	.. ..	17.25 lbs.
Tank capacity in hours	..	2.37 hours.
Tank capacity in gallons	..	20.1 gallons.

Performance.

Speed at 1,000 feet	.. ..	103 m.p.h.
Landing speed	.. ..	45 m.p.h.

Climb.

To 5,000 feet in minutes	..	9 minutes.
Disposable load apart from fuel	.. .. ..	400 lbs.
Total weight of machine loaded	.. .. ..	1725 lbs.

Front View of the Boulton & Paul P 6 (100 h.p. R.A.F. engine).

o

BOULTON & PAUL—*continued*.

THE BOULTON & PAUL "P 9."

Apparently a slightly improved edition of P. 6.

Specification.

Type of machine	Tractor Biplane.
Name or type No. of machine ..	P 9.
Span	27 ft. 6 in.
Gap, maximum and minimum ..	5 ft. 6 in.
Overall length	25 ft.
Maximum height	10 ft.
Chord	5 ft. 6 in.
Total surface of wings ..	285 sq. ft.
Span of tail	12 ft.
Total area of tail	40 sq. ft.
Area of rudder	9 sq. ft.
Area of fin	2.8 sq. ft.
Area of ailerons	9.45 sq. ft.
Maximum cross section of body	7.8 sq. ft.
Horizontal area of body.. ..	37 sq. ft.
Vertical area of body ..	56 sq. ft.
Engine type and h.p.	100 h.p. R.A.F.
Airscrew, diameter and pitch and revs.	9 ft. 3 in. ; 1000.
Weight of machine empty ..	1244 lbs.
Load per sq. ft.	6.3 lbs.
Weight per h.p.	17.7 lbs.
Tank capacity in hours ..	3 hours.
Tank capacity in gallons ..	24 gallons.

Performance.

Speed at 1,000 feet	104 m.p.h.
Landing speed	42 m.p.h.

Climb.

To 5,000 feet in minutes ..	8½ minutes.
Disposable load apart from fuel	400 lbs.
Total weight of machine loaded	1770 lbs.

Side View of the Boulton & Paul P. 6 type machine, in regular use by the firm's Sales Department.

A row of " Camels " built by Boulton & Paul, Ltd.

B—*continued.*

BRISTOL. The British and Colonial Aeroplane Co., Ltd., Filton House, Bristol. The first great British aeroplane firm. Founded in 1910, by the late Sir George White, Bart., the pioneer of electric tramways. Have very extensive works on the outskirts of Bristol, where they manufacture "Bristol" aeroplanes of the firm's own design.

Chairman, Mr. Samuel White. Managing Director, Sir G. Stanley White, Bart. Secretary and Director, Mr. H. White-Smith. Works Manager, Mr. Herbert Thomas. Chief designer, Captain F. S. Barnwell, R.F.C.

The Bristol "Fighter" has been recognised, especially by the enemy, as one of the most effective and efficient fighter machines yet produced in any country.

BRISTOL SCOUT "D."

The Bristol scout, type "D," now commonly known as the Bristol "Bullet," was produced during 1914.

It was originally fitted with an 80-h.p. Gnôme and showed a remarkable performance for its date. At the outbreak of war it was used on service, from time to time being fitted with higher-power engines. When its period of active service work ceased it was adopted as one of the standard training machines in the R.N.A.S. It was fitted with either the 80 Gnôme, 100 Mono Gnôme, 110 Le Rhône, or 130 Clerget engines.

Specification.

Type of machine	Single-seater Biplane.
Name or type No. of machine ..	Scout D.
Purpose for which intended ..	Fighting and Reconnaissance.
Span	24 ft. 7 in.
Vertical gap	4 ft. 3 in.
Overall length	20 ft. 8 in.
Maximum height	8 ft. 8 in.
Chord	4 ft. 6 in.
Total surface of wings ..	200 sq. ft.
Area of ailerons	23·2 sq. ft.
Area of fixed tail	23 sq. ft.
Span of tail	10 ft.
Area of elevators	15 sq. ft.
Area of rudder	7 sq. ft.
Engine type and h.p. ..	80 h.p. Le Rhône.
Airscrew, diam., pitch and revs.	8 ft. 2½ in. diam., 7 ft. 10½ in. pitch, 1,300 r.p.m.
Weight of machine empty ..	760 lbs.
Load per sq. ft.	6.25 lbs.
Weight per h.p.	14.7 lbs.
Petrol tank capacity in gallons ..	27 gallons.
Oil tank capacity in gallons ..	5½ gallons.

Performance.

Speed low down ..	..	100 m.p.h.
Speed at 5,000 feet ..	..	94 m.p.h.
Speed at 10,000 feet ..	..	86 m.p.h.
Landing speed	..	44 m.p.h.

Climb.

To 5,000 feet	..	6.5 minutes.
To 10,000 feet	..	18.5 minutes.
Disposable load apart from fuel		240 lbs.
Total weight of machine loaded		1,250 lbs.

Front View of Bristol Scout, type "D," commonly known as the "Bullet" (80 h.p. Gnôme engine).

BRISTOL—*continued*.

THE BRISTOL SCOUT, TYPE F.1.

The Bristol scout, type F1, is a recent production of the Bristol firm and was about to be put in production when the Armistice was signed. The fuselage is very deep and carried in its nose a 200 Sunbeam " Arab." The main planes show the principal departure from standard Bristol practice in that the lower plane is of smaller chord than the upper one so as to improve the pilot's range of vision downwards. One set of three struts, in the form of an N, are fitted on either side of the fuselage and are inclined outwards from the base. Ailerons are fitted to the upper plane only. The tail plane and undercarriage are of normal type. Armament consists of two fixed Vicker's guns fitted on top of the fuselage and firing through the propeller with the usual form of fire-control gear. The machine shows a speed of 128 m.p.h. at 10,000 feet, to which height it climbs in 8½ minutes.

A later edition with a " Cosmos " engine of 315 h.p. has given a much better performance.

Specification.

Type of machine	Single-seater Biplane.
Name or type No. of machine	Scout F.
Purpose for which intended	Fighting and Reconnaissance.
Span	Top 29 ft. 6 in., bottom 26 ft. 2 in.
Gap	5 ft. 1 in.
Overall length	20 ft. 10 in.
Maximum height	8 ft. 4 in.
Chord	Top 5 ft. 7 in., bottom 4 ft. 11 in.
Total surface of wings	260 sq. ft.
Area of ailerons	30 sq. ft.
Total area of tail	15 sq. ft.
Span of tail	10 ft. 6 in.
Area of elevators	14.5 sq. ft.
Area of rudder	5 sq. ft.
Area of fin	4.1 sq. ft.
Engine type and h.p.	200 h.p. Sunbeam " Arab."
Airscrew, diam., pitch and revs.	9 ft. 2 ins., 9 ft., 1,155 r.p.m.
Weight of machine empty	1,300 lbs.
Load per sq. ft.	8.08 sq. ft.
Weight per h.p.	10 lbs.
Petrol tank capacity in gallons	32 gallons.
Oil tank capacity in gallons	5 gallons.
Performance.	
Speed low down	138 m.p.h.
Speed at 5,000 feet	135 m.p.h.
Speed at 10,000 feet	128 m.p.h.
Landing speed	49 m.p.h.
Climb.	
To 5,000 feet	3.7 minutes.
To 10,000 feet	8.5 minutes.
To 15,000 feet	16 minutes.
Disposable load apart from fuel	450 lbs.
Total weight of machine loaded	2,100 lbs.

Three-quarter Rear View of the Bristol type F.1., Single-seat Fighter. (Fitted with a " Mercury " Cosmos engine of 315 h.p.)

BRISTOL—*continued*.

Three-quarter Front View Bristol type **F.1.** (315 h.p. Cosmos " Mercury " engine.)

Side View Bristol Single-seater type **F.1.** (Cosmos 315 h.p. " Mercury " engine.)   111a

BRISTOL—*continued.*

THE BRISTOL MONOPLANE.

Contrary to the usual run of single-seater fighting machines, the majority of which pertain to the biplane breed, the British and Colonial Aeroplane Co., designed a monoplane which possessed a very good all-round performance, and which was used on active service in the Eastern theatre of war with great success.

The fuselage is of circular section, the shape of the cowling being preserved down to the tail plane by fairing composed of formers and laths covered with fabric. A 110-h.p. Le Rhône forms the power unit and a large circular spinner is fixed to the propeller.

The armament consists of one fixed Vickers gun firing through the propeller.

Specification.

Type of machine	Single-seater Monoplane.
Name or type No. of machine ..	Bristol Monoplane.
Purpose for which intended ..	Fighting.
Span	30 ft. 9 in.
Overall length	20 ft. 4 in.
Maximum height	8 ft.
Chord	5 ft. 11 in.
Total surface of wings ..	145 sq. ft.
Area of ailerons	18 sq. ft.
Total area of tail	20 sq. ft.
Span of tail	10 ft. 3 in.
Area of elevators	15 sq. ft.
Area of rudder	4.5 sq. ft.
Area of fin	5 sq. ft.
Engine type and h.p. ..	110 h.p. Le Rhône.
Airscrew, diam., pitch and revs.	8 ft. 6 in., 8 ft. 11 in., 1,350 r.p.m.
Weight of machine empty ..	850 lbs.
Load per sq. ft.	8.9 lbs.
Weight per h.p.	10.8 lbs.
Petrol tank capacity in gallons ..	20 gallons.
Oil tank capacity in gallons ..	5 gallons.

Performance.

Speed low down	130 m.p.h.
Speed at 5,000 feet	127 m.p.h.
Speed at 10,000 feet	117 m.p.h.
Landing speed	49 m.p.h.

Climb.

To 5,000 feet	3.5 minutes.
To 10,000 feet	9.0 minutes.
To 15,000 feet	19.0 minutes.

Disposable load apart from fuel	260 lbs.
Total weight of machine loaded	1,300 lbs.

Side View of a Bristol Monoplane. (110 h.p. Le Rhône engine.)

View from Rear—The Bristol Monoplane.

BRISTOL—*continued.*

Front view—Bristol Monoplane.

Three-quarter Front View of the Bristol Monoplane.

BRISTOL—*continued.*

THE BRISTOL F.2B. BIPLANE (FIGHTER).

The Bristol F.2B. biplane, more commonly known as the Bristol " Fighter," was designed as a fighter and reconnaissance two-seater biplane. The fuselage is square section and tapers to a horizontal knife edge aft. A Rolls-Royce " Falcon " engine is carried in the nose of the machine on steel tube engine bearers, with the radiator in front. Metal cowling covers the front of the fuselage as far back as the front top and bottom centre section struts, and the top of the fuselage back to the pilot's seat. The fuselage is slung midway between the planes, there being both top and bottom centre-sections.

The angle of incidence of the tail plane can be altered from the pilot's seat to offset varying weights carried. Partial dual control is fitted, the control column being duplicated in the observer's cockpit, but for the rudder control instead of the rudder bar two hand-grips are fitted to the rudder control which pass through the observer's cockpit.

The armament consists of one fixed Vickers gun inside the cowling firing through the propeller, and a Scarff mounting round the observer's cockpit which is capable of carrying either a single or twin Lewis guns. The 200-h.p. Sunbeam "Arab" and the 200-h.p. Hispano-Suiza engines have been fitted and used on active service in addition to the 250-h.p. Rolls-Royce "Falcon."

Specification.

Type of machine	Two-seater Biplane.
Name or type No. of machine	F.2.C.
Purpose for which intended	Fighting and Reconnaissance.
Span	39 ft. 3 in.
Gap	5 ft. 5 in.
Overall length	25 ft. 9 in.
Maximum height	10 ft. 1 in.
Chord	5 ft. 6 in.
Total surface of wings	405 sq. ft.
Area of ailerons	52 sq. ft.
Total area of tail	22.2 sq. ft.
Span of tail	12 ft. 10 in.
Area of elevators	23.2 sq. ft.
Area of rudder	7.2 sq. ft.
Area of fin	10.7 sq. ft.
Engine type and h.p.	Rolls-Royce " Falcon III.," 250 h.p.
Airscrew, diam., pitch and revs.	9 ft. 8 in. diam., 9 ft. 4 in. pitch, 1,220 r.p.m.
Weight of machine empty	1,750 lbs.
Load per sq. ft.	6.92 lbs.
Weight per h.p.	10.6 lbs.
Petrol tank capacity in gallons	45 gallons.
Oil capacity in gallons	4 gallons.
Performance.	
Speed low down	125 m.p.h.
Speed at 5,000 feet	122 m.p.h.
Speed at 10,000 feet	113 m.p.h.
Landing speed	48 m.p.h.
Climb.	
To 5,000 feet	5 minutes.
To 10,000 feet	11.5 minutes.
To 15,000 feet	21.5 minutes.
Disposable load apart from fuel	630 lbs.
Total weight of machine loaded	2,800 lbs.

Three-quarter Front View—A Bristol Two-seater Fighter. (Rolls-Royce " Falcon " engine.)

Three-quarter Rear View of the Bristol Two-seater Fighter.

114a

BRISTOL F2B.
AEROPLANE
PLAN.

25'-9"

13'-10

TOTAL WING AREA
405·6 ☐'

TAIL PLANE
22·250 ☐'

ELEVATOR
23·250 ☐'

SPAN 39'-5"

1300

FRONT ELEVATION

RUDDER
AREA
7·2 ☐'

TOP FIN AREA
6·9 ☐'

BOTTOM FIN
3·8 ☐'

SIDE ELEVATION

Ford Jones

BRISTOL—continued.

BRISTOL ALL-METAL M.R.I. BIPLANE.

The Bristol all-metal biplane is more or less an all-metal Bristol " Fighter " with sundry modifications and was designed primarily for use in countries where extremes of heat and cold might have a detrimental effect on woodwork.

Metal has entirely replaced wood in the construction, the fuselage being constructed of aluminium and steel and can be easily dismantled for transport and storage purposes. The wings, which are unstaggered are of all-steel construction. The fuselage is slung between the planes, as in the Bristol " Fighter," but the lower centre section is completely cut away, leaving the two main spar tubes, to which are attached the two lower centre section struts.

Specification.

Type of machine..	Two-seater Biplane.
Name or type No. of machine ..	All Metal M.R.I.
Purpose for which intended ..	Fighting and Reconnaissance.
Span ..	42 ft. 2 in.
Gap	5 ft. 11 in.
Overall length ..	27 ft.
Maximum height ..	10 ft. 3 in.
Chord ..	6 ft.
Total surface of wings ..	458 sq. ft.
Area of ailerons ..	39 sq. ft.
Total area of tail ..	27.8 sq. ft.
Span of tail	16 ft. 3 in.
Area of elevators ..	30 sq. ft.
Area of rudder ..	8.25 sq. ft.
Area of fin ..	7.8 sq. ft.
Engine type and h.p. ..	170 h.p. Wolseley " Viper."
Airscrew, diam., pitch and revs...	8 ft. 10 in. diam., 5 ft. 7 in. pitch, 1,700 r.p.m.
Weight of machine empty ..	1,700 lbs.
Load per sq. ft. ..	6.13 lbs.
Weight per h.p. ..	16.5 lbs.
Petrol tank capacity in gallons ..	50 gallons.
Oil tank capacity in gallons ..	5 gallons.

Performance.

Speed low down ..	110 m.p.h.
Speed at 5,000 feet ..	106 m.p.h.
Speed at 10,000 feet ..	98 m.p.h.
Landing speed ..	47 m.p.h.

Climb.

To 5,000 feet in minutes ..	8 minutes.
To 10,000 feet in minutes ..	20 minutes.
Disposable load apart from fuel	630 lbs.
Total weight of machine loaded	2,810 lbs.

Side View—The Bristol All-Metal M.R.I. (200 h.p. Sunbeam " Arab " engine.)

116a

BRISTOL—*continued*.

Front View—Bristol All-Metal Biplane.

Three-quarter Front View—The Bristol All-Metal M.R.I.

117a

Front View of the Bristol Braemar Triplane. (Four 400 h.p. Liberty engines.)

View from Rear of the Bristol Braemar Triplane.

THE BRISTOL TRIPLANE "BRAEMAR" MARK II.

The Bristol "Braemar" was originally designed as a long-distance bomber, but owing to the Armistice coming when it did the machine was never used on active service. It is now being slightly modified to do duty as a passenger-carrier and commercial machine.

It is a four-engined triplane with a single fuselage and with the four engines fixed in pairs tandem-wise driving two tractors and two pushers on either side of the fuselage.

In its original form the fuselage had accommodation for one gunner in the nose, two pilots just in advance of the main planes and another gunner's cockpit midway between the planes and the tail unit. The tail is a biplane with triple rudders.

The main planes are slightly swept back and ailerons are fitted to the two upper planes only.

The main planes are made to fold.

Side View of the Bristol Braemar Triplane.

Maximum height	..	..	..	20 ft. 8 in.
Chord	..	..	..	8 ft. 6 in.
Total surface of wings	..	..	1,905 sq. ft.
Total area of tail ..	..	..	Top 51.5 sq. ft., bottom 45 sq. ft.
Area of elevators ..	..	..	Top 42.5 sq. ft. bottom 42.5 sq. ft.
Area of rudder	..	..	25 sq. ft.
Area of fin	..	..	28.2 sq. ft.
Engine type and h.p.	..	..	Four Liberty engines, 1,640 h.p. (total).
Airscrew, diam., pitch and revs...			Front (two) 10 ft. 2 in. dia., rear (two) 9 ft. 2 in. dia., front (two) 6 ft. 11 in. pitch, rear (two) 7 ft. 5 in. pitch, 1,750 r.p.m.
Weight of machine empty	..	..	10,650 lbs.
Load per sq. ft.	..	..	8.6 lbs.
Weight per h.p.	..	..	10 lbs.
Petrol tank capacity in gallons ..			450 gallons.
Oil tank capacity in gallons	..		40 gallons.

Performance.

Speed low down	..	..	125 m.p.h.
Speed at 5,000 feet	..	..	122 m.p.h.
Speed at 10,000 feet	..	..	113 m.p.h.
Landing speed ..	..	..	55 m.p.h.

Climb.

To 5,000 feet	..	..	..	6 minutes.
To 10,000 feet	..	..	..	13 minutes.
Disposable load apart from fuel	..	..	..	1,940 lbs.
Total weight of machine loaded	..	..	16,500 lbs.

Specification.

Type of machine	..	..	..	Four-engined Triplane.
Name or type No. of machine	..		Braemar Mk. 2.
Purpose for which intended	..		Bomber or Passenger Carrier.
Span	..	..	..	Top 81 ft. 8 in., centre 81 ft. 8 in., bottom 78 ft. 3 in.
Gap	..	..	..	7 ft. 2½ in.
Overall length	..	..	..	51 ft. 6 in.

51'- 6"

8' 6"

PLAN
81'- 6"

FRONT ELEVATION

20' 8"

SIDE ELEVATION

51'- 6"

BRISTOL "BRAEMAR" AEROPLANE

B—*continued.*

DE BOLOTOFF. de Bolotoff Aeroplanes, Sevenoaks, Kent.

Prince Serge de Bolotoff will be remembered as the producer of a curious triplane in the very early days of aviation.

During the war he designed and has built the machine illustrated herewith. This is a two-seater machine of medium size (span about 36 feet), fitted with a 200 h.p. 12-Cylinder "Curtiss" Engine.

No detailed information as to dimensions or performance have been received.

As may be seen, the machine is generally on the lines of the early Albatros biplanes.

Front View of the de Bolotoff biplane.

Side View of the de Bolotoff biplane.

Three-quarter Rear View of the de Bolotoff biplane.

C

THE CENTRAL AIRCRAFT Co., Ltd.

179, High Road, Kilburn, N.W.

Built a quantity of aeroplanes and parts to official requirements during the war. The Brothers Cattle, proprietors of the firm, then decided to remain in the aircraft industry in time of peace.

The following illustrations and descriptions refer to the post war activities of the firm.

THE TYPE C.F.4. SCHOOL MACHINE.

The *C.F.* 4 has been specially designed for school work, and with a view to low cost and maintenance. A large number of the parts are made interchangeable, such as interplane struts, top and bottom main planes, and rudder and elevators. Dual control is fitted, and the machine has a very wide range of speed, the landing speed being extremely low.

Specification.

Type of Machine	Single Engine Tractor Biplane
Name	C/F.4
Purpose	School Machine
Span	34ft. 25in.
Gap	5 ft.
Overall length	24ft. 9in.
Chord	5 ft.
Total Surface of Wings	331 sq. ft.
Span of tail	10 ft.
Total area of tail	47.4 sq. ft.
Area of elevators	14.5 sq. ft.
Area of rudder	7 sq. ft.
Area of fin	5 sq. ft.
Area of Aileron	11.25 sq. ft. each 45 sq. ft. total
Maximum body section	2 ft. 6 in. x 2 ft. 2½ in.
Horizontal area of body	33.94 sq. ft.
Vertical area of body	39.95 sq. ft.
Engine Type H.P.	70 H.P. Renault Engine 1,800 revs.
Airscrew Revs.	900 Revs
Weight of machine empty	1,096 lbs.
Load per sq. ft.	4.84 lbs.
Weight per h.p.	22.8 lbs.
Tank capacity in hours	3
Tank capacity in gallons	21
Disposable load apart from Fuel	360 lbs.
Total weight of Machine loaded	1,600 lbs.

Performance.

Speed low down	70 m.p.h.
Landing Speed	28 m.p.h.

The Central Aircraft Co.'s type C.F.4 School Machine (70 h.p. Renault engine).

CENTRAL AIRCRAFT—continued.

TYPE C.F.5 TOURING MODEL

A side by side two-seater of simple and robust construction, fitted with folding wings to facilitate stowage.

Specification.

Type of Machine	Single Engined Tractor Biplane
Name or type No. of machine ..	C/F.5
Purpose for which intended ..	Sporting or Touring Model
Span	33 ft. 4 in. with wings folded 12 ft. 6 in.
Gap	6 ft.
Overall length	23 ft.
Height	9 ft. 3 in.
Chord	6 ft.
Total surface of wings ..	350 sq. ft.
Span of Tail	12 ft. 6 in.
Total area of tail	45 sq. ft.
Area of elevators	18 sq. ft.
Area of rudder	7 sq. ft.
Area of fin	5 sq. ft.
Area of ailerons	35 sq. ft. total (4)
Maximum body section ..	12 sq. ft.
Horizontal area of body..	48 sq. ft.
Vertical area of body ..	50 sq. ft.
Engine type and h.p.	Anzani—100 h.p. Air cooled radial
Weight of machine empty ..	1,120 lbs.
Load per sq. ft.	5.9 lbs.
Weight per h.p.	20.6 lbs.
Tank capacity in hours ..	3
Tank capacity in gallons ..	24 galls. petrol—4½ galls. oil
Disposable load apart from fuel	720 lbs.
Total weight of machine loaded	2,060 lbs.

Estimated Performances.

Speed low down	85 m.p.h.
Landing Speed	40 m.p.h.
To 5,000 ft. in minutes ..	8 minutes

The Central Aircraft Co.'s 2-seater touring model C.F.5. (100 h.p. Anzani engine.)

The Central Aircraft Co.'s C.F.4 School machine.

CENTRAL AIRCRAFT—*continued.*

TYPE C.F2A. 8 SEATER PASSENGER MACHINE.

The *C.F.* 2a is an eight-seater biplane built for passenger-carrying and commercial use. The general arrangement is that usual in most twin-engined biplanes. There is a central fuselage, carrying crew and passengers, and the power units are carried on either side of the fuselage, between the first sets of interplane struts.

Seats for two pilots are arranged in the nose of the fuselage, with duplicate controls.

Six passengers are allowed for in the fuselage, under the centre section in a main enclosed cabin fitted with Triplex glass windows which is electrically warmed. Instead of the six passengers, half a ton of goods or mails can be carried.

Specification.

Type of Machine	Twin Engine Tractor Bipiane
Name or type No. of machine ..	C/F.2.A.
Purpose for which intended ..	Passenger of Commerce
Span	63.5 ft.
Gap	7.5 ft. constant
Overall length	40 ft.
Height	12.5 ft.
Chord	7.5 ft.
Total surface of wings ..	8.95 sq. ft.
Span of tail	16.5 ft.
Total area of tail..	97 ft. sq.
Area of elevators	32 sq. ft.
Area of rudder	20 sq. ft.
Area of fin	15 sq. ft.
Area of aileron	35 sq. ft. each 140 sq. ft. total
Maximum body section ..	13.5 sq. ft.
Horizontal area of body ..	98 sq. ft.
Vertical area of body ..	110 sq. ft.
Engines	2 Beardmore 160 N.H.P. 175 B.H.P.
Air screw	Dia. 8.75 ft. Pitch 5 ft. Revs. 1,250
Weight of machine empty ..	3,850 lbs.
Load per sq. ft.	Full 6.6 lbs. per sq. ft. light 4.4 per sq. ft.
Weight per B.H.P.	16.7 lbs.
Tank capacity in hours ..	2 hours
Tank capacity in gallons ..	50 galls.
Disposable load	1,440 lbs.
Total weight loaded ..	5,850 lbs.

Estimated performances.

Speed low down	90 m.p.h.
Speed at 10,000 ft.	83 m.p.h.
Landing speed	42 m.p.h.

The Central Aircraft Co.'s type C.F.2A. twin engined passenger carrier. (2-160 h.p. Beardmore engines).

D

DARRACQ & Co.
Branch of famous French motor-car firm. Built during the war, aeroplanes and parts to Government orders.

E

E.A.C.
The Eastbourne Aviation Co., Ltd., Eastbourne.

Before the war this firm built biplanes to their own design. Since the war broke out, the building of these machines has been dropped, and work entirely confined to construction to Government specifications of a confidential nature. The Founder and Managing Director of the firm, Mr. F. Bernard Fowler, became in 1914 an officer of the Royal Naval Air Service (later major R.A.F.). The firm's aerodrome, outside Eastbourne, was taken over by the Navy.

Major Fowler has since returned to the firm, who have regained possession of their works and are building land machines and seaplanes for passenger work.

F

THE FAIREY AVIATION Co., Ltd.

Offices: 175, Piccadilly W.1. Works: Hayes, Middlesex, and Hamble, Hants.

Founded by Mr. C. R. Fairey in 1916 to develop the manufacture of seaplanes and aeroplanes to his own designs.

Mr. Fairey was one of the earliest British aircraft designers. He was associated in 1910-11 with Mr. Dunne in the construction of the experimental Dunne inherently stable machines, and afterwards with Messrs. Short Bros. at Eastchurch, played a very important part in the practical development of the seaplane.

Mr. Fairey's chief recent contribution to the art of aircraft design is the practical development of the use of trailing edge flaps as a camber changing device. This arrangement permits of the use of heavy wing loadings on an efficient wing section, which, when the flaps are pulled down, and the camber increased, becomes a high lift wing section, and makes it possible to land slowly.

The first machine upon which this device was successfully used was a modified " Baby " Seaplane—later produced by the firm as the " Hamble Baby."

Other types of the firms manufacture are described and illustrated hereafter.

THE FAIREY F2 TWIN ENGINE MACHINE.

The type F2 twin engine machine was one of the earliest of the large twin engine types built. It was designed in 1914, and was flying in 1916. It was actually the first twin engine machine fitted with folding wings.

The following table gives the main particulars :—

Specification.

Type of machine	Land Biplane.
Name or type No. of machine ..	F2.
Purpose for which intended ..	General.
Span, upper plane overall ..	77 ft.
Gap, Maximum and minimum ..	6 ft.
Overall length	40 ft. 6½ in.
Maximum height	13 ft. 5⅝ in.
Chord	5 ft. 6 in.
Total surface of wings ..	718.4 sq. ft.
Span of tail	17 ft. 6 in.
Total area of tail	103.9 sq. ft. (including (elevators).
Area of elevators	39 sq. ft.

ANTE-DATING THE ENEMY.—The Fairey Aviation Co.'s Twin-engined Folding-wing Biplane. Designed by Mr. C. R. Fairey in Dec., 1914; built in the summer of 1916; delivered in the autumn of 1916. It had a remarkably good performance.

Three-quarter Front View of the Fairey Twin-engined Folder Biplane. F.2 type.

124a

THE FAIREY AVIATION Co.—*continued.*

F2. TWIN ENGINE—*continued.*

Area of rudder (2 rudders, 10 sq.
 ft. each)   ..   ..   ..   20 sq. ft.
Area of fin (2 fins, 10.9 sq. ft.
 each)   ..   ..   ..   21.8 sq. ft.
Area of each aileron and total
 area   ..   ..   ..   47.8 sq. ft. each ; 95.6 sq. ft.
  total.
Maximum cross section of body   3 ft. × 2 ft. 6 in.
Horizontal area of body..   ..   97 sq. ft.
Vertical area of body   ..   ..   75 sq. ft.
Engine type and h.p. (2 engines)   190 h.p. Rolls-Royce.
Load per sq. ft. ..   ..   ..   6.8 lbs.
Weight per h.p. ..   ..   ..   13 lbs.
Tank capacity in hours ..   ..   3½ hours.

Performance.
  Speed low down   ..   ..   81 kts.
  Landing speed   ..   ..   38 m.p.h.
Climb.
  To 5,000 feet in minutes   ..   6 minutes.
Total weight of machine loaded   ..   ..   ..   4880 lbs.

THE FAIREY CAMPANIA Types F16, F17, & F22.

These machines were designed as patrol seaplanes with special reference to the stowage capacity and hatchway dimensions of H.M. Seaplane Currier " Campania."

The original F16 was designed for the Rolls-Royce " Eagle " engine.

F17 was a slightly modified version fitted with a more efficient wing section, and a later version of the Rolls " Eagle " engine.

The demand for Rolls " Eagles " at the time was considerably greater than the production thereof, and a further Campania type—the F22 was manufactured, fitted with a 260 h.p. Sunbeam engine.

All these machines were fitted with the *Fairey* variable camber device.

The leading particulars of all three types are as follows :—

CAMPANIA F16.

Type of machine   ..   ..   Seaplane.
Name or type No. of machine   ..   F16.
Purpose for which intended   ..   Patrol.
Span, upper plane overall   ..   61 ft. 7½ in.
Gap, maximum and minimum ..   6 ft. 6 in.
Overall length   ..   ..   43 ft. 3⅜ in.
Maximum height   ..   ..   15 ft. 1 in.
Chord   ..   ..   ..   6 ft. 4 in.
Total surface of wings   ..   639.8 sq. ft.
Span of tail   ..   ..   13 ft.
Total area of tail   ..   ..   75.1 sq. ft. (including
  elevators).

Three-quarter rear view of the Fairey Twin-engined Folding Biplane.

A Fairey Campania (260 h.p. " Sunbeam " engine), just before leaving the water.

125a

FAIREY AVIATION CO.—*continued.*

CAMPANIA F 16.—*continued.*

Area of elevators	28.1 sq. ft.
Area of rudder	22 sq. ft.
Area of fin	14 sq. ft.
Area of each aileron and total area	23.4 sq. ft. ; 46.8 sq. ft.
Maximum cross section of body	3 ft. 6 in. × 3 ft. 1 in.
Horizontal area of body	90 sq. ft.
Vertical area of body	88 sq. ft.
Engine type and h.p.	250 h.p. Rolls-Royce.
Load per sq. ft.	8.6 lbs.
Weight per h.p.	22.2 lbs.
Tank capacity in gallons	88 gallons.

Performance.

Speed low down	72 kts.
Landing speed	42 m.p.h.

Climb.

To 5,000 feet in minutes	14 minutes.
Disposable load apart from fuel	1026 lbs.
Total weight of machine loaded	5500 lbs.

A Fairey Campania just leaving the water.

CAMPANIA F17.

Type of machine	Seaplane.
Name or type No. of machine	F17.
Purpose for which intended	Patrol.
Span, upper plane overall	61 ft. 7½ in.
Gap, maximum and minimum	6 ft. 6 in.
Overall length	43 ft. 0⅝ in.
Maximum height	15 ft. 1 in.
Chord	6 ft. 4 in.
Total surface of wings	627.8 sq. ft.
Span of tail	13 ft.
Total area of tail	75.1 sq. ft. (including elevators).
Area of elevators	28 1 sq. ft.
Area of rudder	19 6 sq. ft.
Area of fin	16 2 sq. ft.
Area of each aileron and total area	23 4 sq. ft. ; 46.8 sq. ft.
Maximum cross section of body	3 ft. 6 in. × 3 ft. 1 in.
Horizontal area of body	90 sq. ft.
Vertical area of body	88 sq. ft.
Engine type and h.p.	275 h.p. Rolls-Royce.
Load per sq. ft.	8.7 lbs.
Weight per h.p.	19.5 lbs.
Tank capacity in gallons	88 gallons.

Performance.

Speed low down	78 kts.
Landing speed	43 m.p.h.

Climb.

To 5,000 feet in minutes	12.30 minutes.
Disposable load apart from fuel	1100 lbs.
Total weight of machine loaded	5560 lbs.

A Fairey Campania well off.

CAMPANIA F22.

Type of machine	Seaplane.
Name or type No. of machine ..	F22.
Purpose for which intended ..	Patrol.
Span, Upper plane Overall ..	61 ft. 7½ in.
Gap, maximum and minimum ..	6 ft. 6 in.
Overall length	43 ft. 0⅝ in.
Maximum height	15 ft. 1 in.
Chord	6 ft. 4 in.
Total surface of wings ..	627.8 sq. ft.
Span of tail	13 ft.
Total area of tail	75.1 sq. ft. (inc. elevators).
Area of elevators	28.1 sq. ft.
Area of rudder	19.6 sq. ft.
Area of fin	16.2 sq. ft.
Area of each aileron and total area	23.4 sq. ft. ; 46.8 sq. ft.
Maximum cross section of body	3 ft. 6 in. × 3 ft. 1 in.
Horizontal area of body.. ..	90 sq. ft.
Vertical area of body	88 sq. ft.
Engine type and h.p.	250 h.p. Sunbeam.
Load per sq. ft.	8.14 lbs.
Weight per h.p.	20.1 lbs.
Tank capacity in gallons ..	88 gallons.

Performance.

Speed low down	74 kts.
Landing speed	40 m.p.h.

Climb.

To 5,000 feet in minutes ..	18 minutes.
Disposable load apart from fuel	1026 lbs.
Total weight of machine loaded	5329 lbs.

THE FAIREY N9 TYPE F127.

The *Fairey* seaplane N9 was built in 1917 as a patrol seaplane for the R.N.A.S.

This machine has one set of struts on each side of the fuselage, and a top plane with a large overhang.

Owing to the Rolls-Royce "Falcon" engine being used in other types of machines in production, this type was never proceeded with. It is interesting to note that the original N9 remained in service to the middle of 1918, and was the first float seaplane to begin an actual flight by being thrown off a warship by a catapult gear.

Specification.

Type of machine	Seaplane.
Name or type No. of machine ..	F127.
Purpose for which intended ..	Ship work.
Span	50 ft.
Gap, maximum and minimum ..	5 ft. 7 in.
Overall length	35 ft. 6 in.
Maximum height	13 ft.
Chord	5 ft. 6 in.
Total surface of wings ..	420 sq. ft.
Span of tail	13 ft.
Total area of tail	34.2 sq. ft.
Area of elevators	34.2 sq. ft.
Area of rudder	9.8 sq. ft.
Area of fin	8.9 sq. ft.
Area of each aileron and total area	18 ft.
Engine type and h.p.	190 h.p. Rolls-Royce.
Load per sq. ft.	9.08 lbs.
Weight per h.p.	18.15 lbs.
Tank capacity in hours ..	5¼ hours.
Tank capacity in gallons ..	70 gallons.

Three-quarter Front View of the Fairey Seaplane. F 127 (N 9). (190 h.p. Rolls-Royce "Falcon" engine.)

Performance.

Speed low down	78 kts.
Speed at 10,000 feet	74 kts.
Landing speed	38 m.p.h.

Climb.

To 5,000 feet in minutes ..	9.30 minutes.
To 10,000 feet in minutes ..	38 minutes.
Disposable load apart from fuel	516 lbs.
Total weight of machine loaded	3812 lbs.

Side View of the Fairey F 127 (N 9).

FAIREY AVIATION CO.—*continued*.

THE FAIREY, Type 3.

The Fairey type 3 was the F127 fuselage, chassis and empennage, with wings of equal span, and fitted with a 260 h.p. Sunbeam engine. It was originally built as a float seaplane and was later converted to a ship-plane with wheel under carriage, as type 3A. This machine was put into production in both forms.

Specification.

Type of machine	Seaplane.
Name or type No. of machine	F128.
Purpose for which intended	Sea Scout.
Span	46 ft. 2 in.
Gap, maximum and minimum	5 ft. 7 in.
Overall length	36 ft.
Maximum height	13 ft.
Chord	5 ft. 6 in.
Total surface of wings	476 sq. ft.
Span of tail	13 ft.
Total area of tail	34.2 sq. ft.
Area of elevators	34.2 sq. ft.
Area of rudder	9.8 sq. ft.
Area of fin	9.8 sq. ft.
Area of each aileron and total area	16.5 sq. ft.
Engine type and h.p.	260 h.p. Sunbeam.
Load per sq. ft.	8.74 lbs.
Weight per h.p.	15.69 lbs.
Tank capacity in hours	4½ hours.
Tank capacity in gallons	76 gallons.

Performance.

Speed low down	90 kts.
Speed at 10,000 feet	82 kts.
Landing speed	41 m.p.h.

Climb.

To 5,000 feet in minutes	9.15 minutes.
To 10,000 feet in minutes	23 minutes.
Disposable load apart from fuel	584 lbs.
Total weight of machine loaded	4160 lbs.

3A.

Type of machine	Aeroplane.
Name or type No. of machine	F III A.
Purpose for which intended	General.
Span	44 ft.
Gap, maximum and minimum	5 ft. 7 in.
Overall length	31 ft.
Maximum height	13 ft.
Chord	5 ft. 6 in.
Total surface of wings	476 sq. ft.
Span of tail	13 ft.
Total area of tail	34.2 sq. ft.
Area of elevators	34.2 sq. ft.
Area of rudder	9.8 sq. ft.
Area of fin	9.8 sq. ft.
Area of each aileron and total area	16.5 sq. ft.
Engine type and h.p.	260 h.p. Sunbeam
Load per sq. ft.	7.76 lbs.
Weight per h.p.	13.93 lbs.
Tank capacity in hours	4½ hours.
Tank capacity in gallons	76 gallons.

Performance.

Speed low down	95 kts.
Speed at 10,000 feet	90 kts.
Landing speed	40 m.p.h.

Climb.

To 5,000 feet in minutes	7.10 minutes.
To 10,000 feet in minutes	17.30 minutes.
Disposable load apart from fuel	584 lbs.
Total weight of machine loaded	3694 lbs.

The Fairey type 3 Seaplane (260 h.p. "Sunbeam" engine).

The Fairey type 3 A Folding Aeroplane (260 h.p. "Sunbeam" engine).

128a

FAIREY AVIATION CO.—*continued*.

THE FAIREY Type 3 B.

The Fairey 3B was designed as a bomber with the same fuselage as the N10 but the upper plane was increased in span, and larger floats were fitted. The wings and chassis were interchangeable with those of the original type 3.

Specification.

Type of machine	Seaplane.
Name or type No. of machine	F.III.B.
Purpose for which intended	Sea Bomber.
Span	62 ft. 9 in.
Gap, maximum and minimum	5 ft. 7 in.
Overall length	36 ft.
Maximum height	13 ft.
Chord	5 ft. 6 in.
Total surface of wings	570 sq. ft.
Span of tail	13 ft.
Total area of tail	34.2 sq. ft.
Area of elevators	34.2 sq. ft.
Area of rudder	12.4 sq. ft.
Area of fin	12.4 sq. ft.
Area of each aileron and total area	23 sq. ft.
Engine type and h.p.	260 h.p. Sunbeam.
Load per sq. ft.	8.5 lbs.
Weight per h.p.	18.5 lbs.
Tank capacity in hours	4½ hours.
Tank capacity in gallons	76 gallons.

Performance.

Speed low down	83 kts.
Speed at 10,000 feet	76 kts.
Landing speed	42 m.p.h.

Climb.

To 5,000 feet in minutes	12.30 minutes.
To 10,000 feet in minutes	36 minutes.
Disposable load apart from fuel	1041 lbs.
Total weight of machine loaded	4892 lbs.

Front View of the Fairey type 3 B. Seaplane (260 h.p. " Sunbeam " engine).

The Fairey type 3 B. Seaplane (260 h.p. " Sunbeam " engine).

FAIREY AVIATION CO.—*continued*.

Rear View of the Fairey type 3 B. Seaplane (260 h.p. "Sunbeam" engine).

The Fairey type 3 B. Seaplane.

FAIREY AVIATION CO.—*continued*.

THE FAIREY Type 3C.

This machine was a further development of the F127 type. Wings and Chassis were still interchangeable with those of the F127 or the type 3B but a more powerful engine—the 375 h.p. Rolls-Royce "Eagle" was installed.

The actual wings were identical with those of the original type 3, and the chassis and floats were those of the type 3B

Specification.

Type of machine	Seaplane.
Name or type No. of machine	F.III.C.
Purpose for which intended	Reconnaissance.
Engine type and h.p.	360 h.p. Rolls-Royce.
Load per sq. ft.	10.6 ins.
Weight per h.p.	14 lbs.
Tank capacity in hours	6 hours.
Tank capacity in gallons	120 gallons.

Performance.

Speed low down	97 kts.
Speed at 10,000 feet	90 kts.
Landing speed	44 m.p.h.

Climb.

To 5,000 feet in minutes	6.40 minutes.
To 10,000 feet in minutes	17.30 minutes.
To 20,000 feet in minutes	
Disposable load apart from fuel	1030 lbs.
Total weight of machine loaded	5050 lbs.

The Fairey type 3 C. Seaplane (375 h.p. Rolls-Royce "Eagle" engine).

Half side view of the Fairey type 3 C. Seaplane.

FAIREY AVIATION CO.—*continued.*

THE "HAMBLE BABY" SEAPLANE.

Reference has already been made to this machine. The leading characteristics are as stated :—

Specification.

Type of machine	Seaplane.
Name or type No. of machine ..	F129.
Purpose for which intended ..	Reconnaissance.
Span, upper plane overall ..	27 ft. 9¼ in.
Gap, maximum and minimum ..	4 ft. 6 in.
Overall length	23 ft. 4 in.
Maximum height	9 ft. 6 in.
Chord	4 ft. 9 in.
Total surface of wings	246 sq. ft.
Span of tail	10 ft. 9 in.
Total area of tail	41 sq. ft. (including elevators)
Area of elevators	17 sq. ft.
Area of rudder	6.7 sq. ft.
Area of fin	4.3 sq. ft.
Area of each aileron and total area	14.1 sq. ft. ; 36.4 sq. ft.
Maximum cross section of body	3 ft. 2 in. × 2 ft. 7¾ in.
Horizontal area of body.. ..	39.4 sq. ft.
Vertical area of body	34 sq. ft.
Engine type and h.p.	110 h.p. Clerget.
Load per sq. ft.	7.8 lbs.
Weight per h.p.	17.21 lbs.
Tank capacity in hours	3½ hours.

Performance.
Speed low down	85 kts.
Landing speed	44 m.p.h.

Climb.
To 5,000 feet in minutes ..	8 minutes
Total weight of machine loaded	1900 lbs.

Front view of a Fairey type 3 B Seaplane.

Rear view of a Fairey type 3 B Seaplane.

G

THE GOSPORT AIRCRAFT Co., Ltd.

Gosport, Hants.

The Gosport Aircraft Company was formed early in the War by Sir Charles Allom, of White, Allom & Co., Ltd., who is the well-known owner of racing yachts, and Mr. Charles Nicholson, of Camper & Nicholson, the famous yacht builders, of Gosport.

The firm has constructed a number of flying boats to Government specifications, chiefly F.B.A's of the Norman Thompson type. More recently the firm has built complete, several F5 type boats of the kind developed by Lieut.-Col. John Porte, C.M.G., R.A.F. Another of the firm's achievements was the building of the hull illustrated herewith, for one of the biggest flying boats in the world (up to the middle of 1919). This hull was designed by Mr. Charles Nicholson, for a machine being completed by the Phœnix Dynamo Company, of Bradford.

The Gosport Company is now engaged on building various types of boats to its own designs for commercial purposes, and a number of these designs are illustrated hereafter.

The Hull of a large Flying Boat built by the Gosport Aircraft Co., Ltd.

A F5 Flying-boat (2—375 h.p. Rolls-Royce " Eagle " engines), built by the Gosport Aircraft Co., Ltd.

A F.B.A. Flying-boat (100 h.p. Gnome engine), built by the Gosport Aircraft Co., Ltd.

133a

The Hull of one of the biggest flying-boats in the world, being brought out of the works of the Gosport Aviation Co., Ltd. Additional interest is given to this picture by the fact that Lord Nelson's old flag-ship, H.M.S. Victory, appears in the right background.

GOSPORT—*continued.*

THE GOSPORT "SHRIMP."
Specification.

Type of machine	Single-seater Flying-boat.
Name or type No. of machine ..	Gosport "Shrimp."
Purpose for which intended ..	Sporting and Commercial.
Span	Top plane, 23 ft. ; Bottom plane, 17 ft. 3 in.
Gap	3 ft. 6 in.
Overall length	19 ft.
Maximum height	7 ft. 3 in.
Chord	Top plane, 4 ft. 6 in. ; Bottom plane, 3 ft.
Total area of main planes ..	140 sq. ft.
Engine type and h.p.	A.B.C. "Gnat." 45-50 h.p.
Load per sq. ft.	5.35 lbs.
Load per h.p.	15 lbs.
Tank capacity in hours	3¼ hours.
Tank capacity in gallons ..	10 gallons.

Performance.

Speed low down	65 m.p.h.
Landing speed	35 m.p.h.

Climb.

Ceiling with full load	10,000 ft.
Useful load (pilot, fuel and luggage)	270 lbs.
Total weight of machine loaded	750 lbs.

GOSPORT AIRCRAFT C⁰
GOSPORT - ENGLAND

SINGLE SEATER BOAT

SPORTING TYPE

SCALE

DRG N⁰ 445

GOSPORT—*continued*.

THE "GOSPORT" PATROL BOAT.

Specification.

Type of machine	Two-seater Flying-boat.
Name or type No. of machine ..	"Gosport" Patrol Boat.
Purpose for which intended ..	Fast Patrol or Police Boat.
Span	48 ft. 6 in.
Gap	6 ft.
Overall length	27 ft. 4 in.
Maximum height	10 ft.
Chord	5 ft. 6 in.
Total area of main planes ..	520 sq. ft.
Engine type and h.p. ..	280 h.p. "Falcon" Rolls-Royce. (Offset from centre line of boat.)
Load per sq. ft.	5.42 lbs.
Load per h.p.	10.07 lbs.
Tank capacity in hours ..	2¾ hours.
Tank capacity in gallons ..	50 gallons.

Performance.

Speed (fully loaded)	91 m.p.h.
Landing speed (fully loaded)	42 m.p.h.
Ceiling (fully loaded)	22,000 ft.
Useful load	880 lbs.
Total weight of machine loaded	2,820 lbs.

GOSPORT AIRCRAFT Cº

GOSPORT — ENGLAND

TWO-SEATER PATROL BOAT

EQUIPPED WITH WIRELESS.

SCALE.

DRG. Nº 478

GOSPORT—*continued.*

THE GOSPORT TOURING BOAT. (TAIL BOOM TYPE.)

Specification.

Span	Top plane, 40 ft. ; Bottom plane, 28 ft.
Gap, maximum and minimum ..	6 ft. 5 ft. 3 in.
Overall length	25 ft.
Maximum height	9 ft. 3 in.
Chord	5 ft. 6 in.
Total area of main planes ..	340 sq. ft.
Engine type and h.p.	160 h.p. Beardmore.
Load per sq. ft.	5.88 lbs.
Load per h.p.	12.5 lbs.
Tank capacity in hours ..	2½ hours.
Tank capacity in gallons ..	33 gallons.

Performance.

Speed (fully loaded)	75 m.p.h.
Landing speed (fully loaded) ..	25 m.p.h.
Ceiling (fully loaded)	14,000 ft.
Useful load (pilot, passenger, fuel and luggage) ..	650 lbs.
Total weight of machine loaded	2,000 lbs.

GOSPORT AIRCRAFT Cº
GOSPORT - ENGLAND

TWO-SEATER TOURING BOAT

TAIL BOOM TYPE.

SCALE

DRG Nº 442.

GOSPORT—*continued.*

THE GOSPORT "MAIL" BOAT.

Specification.

Type of machine	Six-seater (Two-engined) Flying Boat.
Name or type No. of machine ..	Gosport " Mail."
Purpose for which intended ..	Long-distance commercial and Mail Carrier.
Span	Top plane, 79 ft. ; Bottom plane, 66 ft.
Gap	7 ft. 6 in.
Overall length	41 ft.
Maximum height	15 ft. 7½ in.
Chord	7 ft. 6 in.
Total area of main planes ..	1,000 sq. ft.
Engine type and h.p.	2—280 h.p. " Falcon "—Rolls-Royce.
Load per sq. ft.	6.4 lbs.
Load per h.p.	11.42 lbs.
Tank capacity in hours ..	2½ hours.
Tank capacity in gallons ..	92 gallons.

Performance.

Speed (fully loaded)	100 m.p.h.
Landing speed (fully loaded)	45 m.p.h.
Ceiling (fully loaded)	15,000 ft.
Useful load (full mail and six passengers) ..	.. 2,000 lbs.
Total weight of machine loaded	.. 6,400 lbs.

GOSPORT AIRCRAFT Cº
GOSPORT - ENGLAND

TWIN ENGINED MAIL BOAT.

FOR FAST POSTAL & PASSENGER SERVICE

SCALE.

DRG Nº 430

GOSPORT—*continued.*

THE GOSPORT "FIRE-FIGHTER."

Specification.

Type of machine	Ten-seater, Two-engined Flying Boat.
Name or type No. of machine ..	Gosport " Fire-Fighter."
Purpose for which intended ..	Long Distance, commercial, &c.
Span	Top plane, 103 ft.
Gap	9 ft.
Overall length	49 ft.
Maximum height	19 ft.
Chord	8 ft.
Total area of main planes ..	1,380 sq. ft.
Engine type and h.p.	2—360 h.p. " Eagle "—Rolls-Royce.
Load per sq. ft.	9.05 lbs.
Load per h.p.	17.36 lbs.
Tank capacity in hours ..	4 hours.
Tank capacity in gallons ..	190 gallons.

Performance.

Speed (fully loaded)	89 m.p.h.
Landing speed (fully loaded)	42 m.p.h.
Ceiling (fully loaded)	14,000 ft.
Useful load (fuel, crew of 10, gear or supplies and wireless)	3,600 lbs.
Total weight of machine loaded	12,500 lbs.

GOSPORT AIRCRAFT C°
GOSPORT — ENGLAND

TWIN ENGINED 10 SEATER BOAT

DRG N° 461

GOSPORT—*continued.*

THE GOSPORT "POPULAR."

Specification.

Type of machine	Two-seater Flying Boat.
Name or type No. of machine ..	Gosport " Popular."
Purpose for which intended ..	Sporting.
Span	Top plane, 40 ft. ;
	Bottom plane, 28 ft.
Gap	5 ft.
Overall length	25 ft. 6 in.
Maximum height	10 ft.
Chord	5 ft. 6 in.
Total area of main planes ..	340 sq. ft.
Engine type and h.p.	160 h.p. Beardmore.
Load per sq. ft.	5.88 lbs.
Load per h.p.	12.5 lbs.
Tank capacity in hours	2½ hours.
Tank capacity in gallons ..	33 gallons.

Performance.

Speed (fully loaded)	80 m.p.h.
Landing speed (fully loaded)	35 m.p.h.
Ceiling (fully loaded)	14,000 ft.
Useful load	650 lbs.
Total weight of machine loaded .. .. .. 2,000 lbs.	

GOSPORT AIRCRAFT Cº

GOSPORT - ENGLAND.

TWO-SEATER TOURING BOAT.

SCALE

DRG Nº 441

G—*continued.*

GRAHAME-WHITE. The Grahame-White Aviation Co., Ltd., 32, Regent St., London, W. Works and Flying Ground : Hendon. Founded by Mr C. Grahame-White, the well-known aviator, who in 1909 commenced operations with a school at Pau. Later this was removed to England, and a general agency for the sale of aeroplanes, etc., established. This developed, and early in 1911 the Hendon Aerodrome was acquired, and a factory established, which has grown continually ever since. In April, 1912, a monoplane to special design was completed. By the close of the same year biplanes of advanced design were constructed. In 1913, the firm took up the agency for the *Morane-Saulnier* monoplanes, and had built a large number for the War Office, besides building machines of Government design for the Admiralty,

During 1916, the firm built war machines of various types under official supervision. The aerodrome was taken over by the War Office late in 1916, and all the schools were placed under Government control. Later, they were removed to other flying grounds and the Hendon Aerodrome was devoted entirely to the testing of Government aeroplanes.

Since the cessation of hostilities the firm has regained part use of the Hendon Aerodrome, and has emitted an ambitious programme of post-bellum types for future construction.

Particulars of the proposed machines, together with those of the "Ganymede" and the single-seater which are actually in existence, are given herewith.

THE GRAHAME-WHITE E.IV DAY BOMBER "GANYMEDE."

This machine was designed prior to the signing of the Armistice, as a long-range day bomber.

It is of the twin fuselage, three engine type, two motors, one in the front of each fuselage driving tractor air screws, and a third, in the rear end of a central nacelle, driving a pusher air screw.

Particulars of dimensions are given in the following table :—

Specification.

Fitted with three 270 h.p. Sunbeam "Maori" motors.

Type of machine	Twin fuselage, three-engined.
Name or type No. of machine ..	"Ganymede."
Purpose for which intended ..	Day Bomber.
Span	89 ft. 3 in.
Gap, maximum and minimum ..	9 ft. 3 in.
Overall length	49 ft. 9 in.
Maximum height	16 ft.
Chord	10 ft. 3 in.
Total surface of wings	1,660 sq. ft.
Span of tail	29 sq. ft.
Total area of tail	254 sq. ft.
Area of elevators..	114 sq. ft.

Side view of the Grahame White "Ganymede" (3/270 H.P. Sumbeam Maori Engines); and of the Grahame White "Bantam" (80 H.P. Le Rhône)

View of the Pusher Installation of the Grahame-White "Ganymede."

The Central Nacelle and One Tractor Engine unit of the Grahame-White "Ganymede."

GRAHAME-WHITE—*continued.*

"GANYMEDE"—*continued.*

Area of rudders	50 sq. ft.
Area of fin	30 sq. ft.
Area of each aileron and total area	200 sq. ft.
Engine type and h.p.	3 Sunbeam "Maori," 270 h.p. each.
Airscrew, diam., pitch and revs...	3.140 diam., 2.570 pitch, 1,050 r.p.m.
Weight of machine empty ..	11,500 lbs.
Load per sq. ft. fully loaded ..	9.65 lbs. sq. ft.
Weight per h.p. fully loaded ..	19.7 lbs. h.p.
Tank capacity in hours	9 hours at 10,000 feet.
Tank capacity in gallons.. ..	400 gallons.

Performance.

Speed low down	105 m.p.h.
Speed at 10,000 feet	93 m.p.h.
Landing speed..	52 m.p.h.
Disposable load apart from fuel	.. .. 3,100 lbs.
Total weight of machine loaded	.. .. 16,000 lbs.

The makers state that the machine had been designed for 3–400 h.p. Liberty engines, which would have increased the speed to 120 miles per hour.

THE GRAHAME-WHITE SINGLE-SEATER.

This machine is designed for the use of the sporting owner pilot, and follows fairly closely the conventional lines for light single seaters of small size.

Specification.

Type of machine	Single-seater Biplane.
Name or type No. of machine ..	"Bantam."
Purpose for which intended ..	Sporting.
Span	20 ft.
Gap, maximum and minimum ..	3 ft. ; 2 ft. 9 in.
Overall length	16 ft. 6 ins.
Maximum height..	6 ft.
Chord	4 ft. 6 in. top wing ; 3⅞ft. bottom wing.
Total surface of wings	130 sq. ft.
Span of tail	9 ft.
Total area of tail	19 sq. ft.
Area of elevators..	10 sq. ft.
Area of rudder	5.5 sq. ft.
Area of fin	3.75 sq. ft.
Area of each aileron and total area	8 sq. ft.; total 16 sq. ft.
Engine type and h.p.	Le Rhône, 80 h.p.
Airscrew, diam., pitch and revs.	7 ft. diam., 1,200 r.p.m.
Load per sq. ft.	7.51 lbs.
Weight of machine empty ..	640 lbs.
Weight per h.p.	12.45 lbs.
Tank capacity in hours	2.3 hours.
Tank capacity in gallons.. ..	15 gallons.

Performance.

Speed maximum	100 m.p.h.
Speed at 10,000 feet	93 m.p.h.
Landing speed..	40 m.p.h.
Disposable load apart from fuel	.. .. 200 lbs.
Total weight of machine loaded	.. .. 995 lbs.

PROJECTED GRAHAME WHITE TYPES.

GRAHAME-WHITE "DOMINIONS" TYPE FLYING BOAT.

Type of machine	Amphibious flying boat.
Name or type No. of machine ...	"Dominions" type.
Purpose for which intended ..	Passenger, mail, and goods carrying.
Span	80.29 ft.
Engine type and h.p.	Two 350 h.p. "Eagle" Rolls-Royce.
Tank capacity in hours	6 hours.

Three views of the Grahame White Sporting Single Seater (80 H.P. Le Rhône Engine.)

Estimated Performance.

Speed maximum	85 m.p.h.

10 Passengers will be carried excluding crew.

GRAHAME-WHITE INSTRUCTIONAL MACHINE.

Type of machine	Two-seater Biplane.
Purpose for which intended ..	Training.
Span	37 ft. 6 ins.
Total surface of wings	345 sq. ft.
Engine type and h.p.	80 h.p. Le Rhône.

Estimated Performance.

Speed maximum	85 m.p.h.
Landing speed..	40 m.p.h.

Dual control fitted.

GRAHAME-WHITE "EXPRESS AIR-MAIL" BIPLANE.

Type of machine	Single-seater Biplane.
Name or type No. of machine ..	"Express Air-Mail."
Purpose for which intended ..	Aerial mail carrying.
Engine type and h.p.	270 h.p. radial (type unstated).
Disposal load apart from fuel and crew	.. 100 lbs. (mail).
Total weight of machine loaded	.. .. 2,000 lbs.

GRAHAME-WHITE FOUR-SEATER AERO-LIMOUSINE.

Type of machine	Four-seater Biplane.
Name or type No. of machine ..	Aero Limousine.
Purpose for which intended ..	Passenger carrying.
Engine type and h.p.	Two 270 h.p. Rolls-Royce.

Estimated Performance.

Speed maximum	110 m.p.h.
Speed minimum	60 m.p.h.

GRAHAME-WHITE FIVE-SEATER AERO-LIMOUSINE.

Type of machine	Five-seater Biplane.
Name or type No. of machine ..	Aero-Limousine.
Purpose for which intended ..	Passenger carrying.
Engine type and h.p.	Two 270 h.p. Rolls-Royce.

Estimated Performance.

Speed maximum	105 m.p.h.
Speed minimum	60 m.p.h.

GRAHAME-WHITE TWENTY-PASSENGER TRIPLANE.

Type of machine	Twenty four-seater Triplane.
Purpose for which intended ..	Passenger and goods carrying
Span	100 ft.
Engine type and h.p.	Three engines (types unstated) Two 500 h.p., one 800 h.p.

Estimated Performance.

Speed maximum	110 m.p.h.
Speed cruising	100 m.p.h.
Total weight of machine loaded	.. .. 8—8½ tons.

BRITISH AEROPLANES.

H

HEWLETT & BLONDEAU, Ltd., Leagrave, Beds.

Founded in 1913 by Mrs. Maurice Hewlett, wife of the famous author, and herself the first British aviatrice, in conjunction with M. Gustave Blondeau, one of the earliest French aviators. Constructors of aeroplanes for the Admiralty. Employed entirely on work to Government specifications.

K

KENNEDY.

Kennedy Aeroplanes, Ltd., Cromwell Road, London, W.7.

Mr. C. J. H. MacKenzie-Kennedy.

Mr. Kennedy was one of the pioneers of aviation in Russia, and was largely concerned with the development of the Sikorsky biplane.

Returning to England soon after the outbreak of War, he was responsible for the design of the machine illustrated herewith, which was built by the Gramophone Company, Ltd., at their works at Hayes, and was erected in the open at Northolt Aerodrome, there being no shed in the country sufficiently large to house it.

The machine was equipped with 4—200 h.p. British-built Salmson engines, as the only ones which the authorities would issue, and the power was inadequate for more than straight flights.

The following are the leading dimensions :—

Span	..	..	..	142 ft.
Chord	..	..	..	10 ft.
Gap	..	..	..	10 ft.
Overall length	..	..	80 ft.
Maximum height	..	..	23 ft. 6 in.
Weight of machine empty	..	19,000 lbs.
Engine type and h.p.	..	4—200 h.p. Salmson.

L

LONDON AIRCRAFT Co., Ltd., Urswick Road, Lower Clapton, N.

Manager : Mr. J. S. Morch. Made aeroplanes and parts during the war to official specifications.

142a

A Front View of the Kennedy Giant, with a Bristol "Fighter" alongside.

Side View of the Kennedy Giant (4—200 h.p. Salmson Engines).

The Kennedy Giant being erected at Northolt.

L—*continued*.

LONDON & PROVINCIAL AEROPLANE
Co., Edgware, N.

Build machines of various types to order. Have produced several school machines of *Caudron* type, and also the tractor biplane, designed by Mr. Fletcher, which has performed well, described below.

Under the management of Messrs. F. W. Warren & Smiles, has trained many pilots for the Flying Services. Removed from the London Aerodrome to a new ground of their own at Edgware.

THE L. & P. SCHOOL BIPLANE.
Specification.

Type of machine	L. & P. Biplane.
Name or type No. of machine ..	"No. 4."
Purpose for which intended ..	School.
Span	32 ft. 6 in.
Gap, maximum and minimum ..	5 ft.
Overall length	25 ft. 3 in.
Maximum height..	8 ft. 9 in.
Chord	4 ft. 7½ in.
Total surface of wings	280 sq. ft.
Span of tail	10 ft. 6 in.
Total area of tail..	24¾ sq. ft.
Area of elevators..	16¼ sq. ft.
Area of rudder	6 sq. ft.
Area of fin	3 sq. ft.
Area of each aileron and total area	10 sq. ft. ; 40 sq. ft.
Maximum cross section of body..	Depth, 3 ft. 3 in. ; width, 2 ft. 9 in.
Horizontal area of body	42 sq. ft.
Vertical area of body	44 sq. ft.
Engine type and h.p.	Gnôme ; 50 h.p.
Airscrew	7 ft. diam. 1,200 r.p.m
Weight of machine empty ..	655 lbs.
Load per sq. ft.	3.82 lbs.
Weight per h.p.	27 lbs.
Tank capacity in hours	1½ hours.
Tank capacity in gals.	8 galls. petrol ; 4 galls. oil.
Performance.	
Speed low down	60 m.p.h.
Landing speed..	30 m.p.h.
Climb.	
To 5,000 ft.	20 minutes.
Total weight of machine loaded	1,070 lbs.

Owing to Air Ministry action in refusing to license the firm's post-bellum designs for passenger work, the L. & P. Co. has ceased its aeroplane works, and does not intend to begin again until such times as Air Ministry officials alter their views as to what constitutes a safe aeroplane. It is to be noted that no L. & P. machine has ever broken in the air, and that no accidents have ever happened owing to defective L. & P. machines.

Front view of the London & Provincial Aeroplane Co.'s School Biplane (50 h.p. Gnôme engine).

The London & Provincial Aeroplane Co.'s School Machine (60 h.p. Anzani).

M

MARTINSYDE. Martinsyde, Ltd., Brooklands, Weybridge, and Woking, Surrey.

Were among the pioneers of British aviation, Messrs. Martin & Handasyde having built a monoplane in 1908. Their big monoplanes of 1912 and 1913 flew magnificently, but failed to find approval for Service use.

Early in 1914 the firm built an enormous monoplane to the order of the late Gustav Hamel, who was being backed by Mr. Mackay Edgar, the Canadian capitalist, for the attempt on the trans-Atlantic flight, which was frustrated by the death of Mr. Hamel in the English Channel. The trans-Atlantic *Martinsyde* was designed for a 250 h.p. Sunbeam engine, and the tanks held a ton of petrol.

Late in 1914, the firm produced a small fast biplane " Scout," with an 80 h.p. Gnôme motor, which was an immediate success, and was promptly ordered in large quantities by the War Office. It played an important part in the war in 1915, till the increased speed of the German machines rendered it out of date. It was superseded by a more powerful type of *Martinsyde* scout, fitted at first with a 120 h.p. Beardmore engine and later with a 160 h.p. Beardmore.

As the result of the success of these machines, the firm acquired very big works near Woking, where the output of Martinsydes and other types exceeded anything thought possible before the war.

Since then the firm has produced some of the most valuable fighting machines, and some of those with the highest performance in any belligerent country.

THE MARTINSYDE F3 & F4.

The *Martinsyde* F3 single-seater scout biplane was designed in 1917, and, although it was far superior to any other machine of the period in speed and climb, was not put into production, owing to the difficulty in obtaining engines, in this case, the Rolls Royce " Falcon," which were earmarked by the Air Ministry for other machines actually in use.

It was then adapted to take the 300 h.p. Hispano-Suiza, and was put into production as the F4, but its appearance on active service was preceded by the Armistice.

The fuselage is very deep and carries enclosed in the cowling twin Vickers sychronised guns. One set of interplane struts are carried on either side of the fuselage, and are splayed outwards from the base.

The pilot is set well back, and fairly high in the fuselage, the upper plane being cut away and the lower plane staggered back, thereby giving him a good view both upward and downward.

The Martinsyde F3 Single-seat Fighter (Rolls-Royce " Falcon " engine, 275 h.p.

The Martinsyde F4 Single-seat Fighter (300 h.p. Hispano-Suiza motor.)

MARTINSYDE—*continued.*

THE MARTINSYDE F4.
Specification.

Type of machine	F 4.
Purpose for which intended ..	Fighter.
Span	Top plane, 32 ft. 9¾ in.; bottom, 31 ft. 2¾ in.
Gap, maximum and minimum	5 ft. 2⅝ in.
Overall length	25 ft. 5⅝ in.
Maximum height	10 ft. 4 in.
Chord	Top plane, 6 ft. 0½ in. ; bottom plane, 5 ft. 6¼ in.
Total surface of wings ..	320 sq. ft. (all in).
Span of tail	11 ft. 1½ in. (over elevators).
Total area of tail	36¾ sq. ft. (tailplane and elevators).
Area of elevators	8¼ sq. ft. each. Total 16½ sq. ft.
Area of rudder	9¾ sq. ft.
Area of fin	6½ sq. ft.
Area of each aileron and total area	Top, 11¾ sq. ft. each ; Bottom, 9¼ sq. ft. each. Total, 42 sq. ft.
Engine type and h.p.	Hispano-Suiza. 300 h.p.
Airscrew, diameter and pitch and revs.	Dia., 8 ft. 8⅞ in. ; Pitch, 6 ft. 6 in. ; Revs., 1850 r.p.m.
Weight of machine empty ..	1710 lbs.
Load per sq. ft.	7 lbs.
Weight per h.p.	7½ lbs.
Tank capacity in hours ..	3 hours.
Tank capacity in gallons ..	43 gallons.

Performance.

Speed low down	145 m.p.h.
Speed at 10,000 feet	143 m.p.h.
Speed at 20,000 feet	126 m.p.h.
Landing speed	45 m.p.h.

Climb.

To 5,000 feet	3.0 mins.
To 10,000 feet	6.30 mins.
To 20,000 feet	19.30 mins.
Total weight of machine loaded	2280 lbs.

The Martinsyde "Raymor" (Rolls-Royce 275 h.p. engine) being erected in preparation for the attempt on the trans-Atlantic flight.

Front View of the Martinsyde "Raymor" trans-Atlantic Machine (275 h.p. Rolls-Royce engine).

MARTINSYDE—*continued*.

THE MARTINSYDE.—Type A.

This is essentially the type of machine built for Mr. Raynham's attempt to win the " Daily Mail " trans-Atlantic Prize.

For this attempt the machine was fitted with petrol tanks up to the limit of the machine's carrying capacity.

As a commercial machine, with fuel for seven hours' flight, there is a large reserve of disposable load.

Specification.

Type of machine	" A."
Name or type No. of machine ..	Trans-Atlantic (Modified).
Purpose for which intended ..	Commercial.
Span	43 ft. 4 in.
Gap, maximum and minimum ..	5 ft. 6 in.
Overall length	27 ft. 6 in.
Maximum height	11 ft. 0 in. (on prop).
Chord	6 ft. 6 in.
Total surface of wings ..	500 sq. ft.
Span of tail	12 ft. 4 in. (over elevators).
Total area of tail	44 sq. ft.
Area of elevators	9.3 each. Total, 18.6.
Area of rudder	10 sq. ft.
Area of fin .. .. .:	6.68 sq. ft.
Area of each aileron and total area	17.36 sq. ft. each ; total, 69.44 sq. ft.
Engine type and h.p.	" Falcon Mark 3," 285 h.p.
Airscrew, diameter and pitch and revs.	10 ft. dia. ; 9 ft. pitch, approx. 1300 revs.
Weight of machine empty ..	1800 lbs.
Load per sq. ft.	9.2 lbs.
Weight per h.p.	16 lbs.
Tank capacity in hours ..	7 hours.
Tank capacity in gallons ..	110 gallons.
Performance.	
Speed low down	125 m.p.h.
Speed at 10,000 feet	118 m.p.h.
Landing speed	45 m.p.h.
Climb.	
To 5,000 feet	8 mins.
To 10,000 feet	.18 mins.
Disposable load apart from fuel	2000 lbs.
Total weight of machine loaded	4600 lbs.

MANN, EGERTON & Co., Ltd., Norwich, and at Euston Road, London, N.

Famous motor car firm building aeroplanes of various types to official specifications. Have built up a reputation for workmanship which promises well for their aeronautical future after the war.

Side View of the Martinsyde Trans-Atlantic Machine.

N

NIEUPORT & GENERAL AIRCRAFT Co., Ltd. Cricklewood, London, N.W.

The firm is under the direction of Major Heckstall-Smith late of the Royal Aircraft Factory.

The accompanying photographs illustrate the British-Nieuport "Nighthawk" with the 320 h.p. A.B.C. "Dragonfly" engine.

This machine is particularly interesting as having been built to the first specification issued by the Royal Air Force. When the R.A.F. decided that the time had come to concentrate on a limited number of types to finish up the war, they decided to concentrate for a single-seater fighter solely on the *Nieuport* "Nighthawk" for the "Dragonfly" engine.

The reasons why this machine was selected were :—

(1) That it fulfilled the performance required.

(2) That it was fully up to the required strength as demonstrated by loading tests on every part of the machine.

(3) That the general arrangement of the machine gave the very best facilities to the pilot for fighting—namely : for position and accessibility of guns, instruments, etc., and the minimum blind area.

(4) Because the general design of the machine was for quick production and the fact that complete engineering drawings and schedules had been prepared in advance.

The design was carried out by Mr. H. P. Folland, who is the chief engineer and designer to the Nieuport Company. Mr. Folland was assistant chief designer at the Royal Aircraft Factory, where he carried out the designs of *F.E.*2 and *S.E.*5.

Prior to the war, when Lieut.-Col. J. E. B. Seely, who was then Secretary of State for War, wished to make a world's record on behalf of the Royal Aircraft Factory, he instructed the superintendent of the R.A.F. to produce a machine for this purpose. This machine was known as *S.E* 4, and was fitted with 160 h.p. 18 cylinder Gnôme engine. The design of this machine was carried out by Mr. Folland, and the machine was flown by Maj. J. M. Salmond (now Major-General and K.C.B.), and, as mentioned in the House of Commons in 1914, the machine made a speed of 135 m.p.h. and climbed the first 1,500 ft. in one minute.

Major S. Heckstall Smith, general manager of the Nieuport Company, was at that time Assistant Superintendent at the R.A.F., and was largely responsible for such successes as the factory produced. The "Nighthawk" is a marked advance in detail design and construction on any of the R.A.F. work, and both he and Mr. Folland deserve to be congratulated on its production.

As will be seen, the machine somewhat resembles the *Sopwith* "Snipe" in general appearance and dimensions. It is designed as a production job, and a quantity of the fittings which are used in *S.E.*5s have been worked into the design, because these are stock fittings and can be procured easily and in quantities.

The photographs show that the machine is eyeable, and that it gives one an impression of speed. It will be interesting to notice how the official performance of the machine works out in practice.

THE NIEUPORT "NIGHTHAWK."

During 1918 the firm produced a high-performance single-seat fighter, known as the "Nighthawk," which was ordered on a large scale by the R.A.F. Particulars of this machine are given in the following table :—

Type of machine	Fighting Scout.
Name or type No. of machine ..	British Nieuport "Nighthawk."
Purpose for which intended ..	Fighting, airship destruction, convoying.
Span	28 ft.
Gap, maximum and minimum ..	4 ft. 6 in.
Overall length	18 ft. 6 in.
Maximum height.. ..	9 ft. 6 in.
Chord	5 ft. 3 in.
Total surface of wings ..	270 sq. ft.
Span of tail	9 ft.
Total area of tail	28 sq. ft.
Area of elevators.. ..	10 sq. ft.
Area of rudder	5 ft 3 in.
Area of fin	5 ft. 2 in.
Area of each aileron and total area	9.3 each; total 37.2 sq. ft.
Maximum cross section of body .	10 sq. ft.
Horizontal area of body	46 sq. ft.

Front view of the Nieuport "Nighthawk" (320 h.p. A.B.C. "Dragonfly" Engine).

T

NIEUPORT—*continued.*

THE NIEUPORT "NIGHTHAWK"—*continued.*

Vertical area of body	49 sq. ft.
Engine type and h.p.	A.B.C. "Dragon-fly," 320 h.p.
Airscrew, diam., pitch and revs...	9 ft. dia.; 7 ft. pitch; 1,650 revs.
Weight of machine empty ..	1,500 lbs.
Load per sq. ft.	7.75 lbs.
Weight per h.p.	6.62 lbs.
Tank capacity in hours	3 hours at 20,000 feet.
Tank capacity in gallons ..	40 petrol, 4 oil.

Performance.

Speed low down	151 m.p.h.
Speed at 10,000 feet	140 m.p.h.
Speed at 20,000 feet	121 m.p.h.
Landing speed	58 m.p.h.

Climb.

To 5,000 feet	3 minutes.
To 10,000 feet..	7 minutes.
To 20,000 feet..	20 minutes.
Disposable load apart from fuel	400 lbs.
Total weight of machine loaded	2,120 lbs.

Side view of the British Nieuport "Nighthawk" (320 h.p. A.B.C. "Dragonfly" engine).

P

HANDLEY PAGE.   Handley Page, Ltd.

110, Cricklewood Lane, N.W. Flying ground : Cricklewood. Established at the end of 1908. In June, 1909, it was turned into a Limited Liability Co., and after that it was busily employed in producing its own machines, also others to inventors' specifications.

The first successful H.P. monoplane was worth noting as it showed such remarkable resemblance to the German " Taube " monoplanes, which played so important a part in the early portion of the war. The first *Handley Page* tractor biplane was of somewhat similar type.

The biplane was taken over by the Navy at the outbreak of war and was used for instructional flying.

In 1916, the firm produced their now well-known twin-engined bomber, of the O/400 type, and in 1918 the four-engined V/1500 type.

HANDLEY-PAGE TWIN-ENGINED BIPLANE, TYPE O/400.

The general arrangement of the *Handley-Page* O/400 bomber is probably well-known to all by now, so it will suffice to say that the characteristics of the machine are—long fuselage with a biplane tail, twin engines carried in " power-eggs " half-way between the main planes, folding wings, extension to the upper plane fitted with balanced ailerons, and a rather complicated form of under-carriage consisting of three sets of Vees under each power unit, connecting to a short central skid, across the centre of which is a hinged axle. On the end of each axle, outside of the wheel hub, a telescopic strut with an inserted shock-absorber runs upwards to the front spar under the engine struts, which is enclosed.

The main petrol tanks are carried in the upper half of the fuselage between the planes. The accommodation is similar to most twin-engined bombers, viz. :—observer in nose, equipped with Lewis gun on Scarff ring, and bomb sights ; the pilot's cockpit, fitted with two sets of controls, just in rear of front observer and aft of main planes, a cockpit for a rear gunner fitted with two swivel gun mountings.

Specification.

Type of machine	Biplane.
Name or type No. of machine ..	O/400.
Purpose for which intended ..	Night bombing.
Span	100 ft.
Gap, maximum and minimum ..	11 ft.
Overall length	62 ft. 6 in.
Maximum height..	22 ft.
Chord	10 ft.
Total surface of wings ..	1,630 sq. ft.
Maximum cross section of body..	6 ft. 10 in. × 4 ft. 9 in.
Engine type and h.p.	2 R.R. Eagle VIII (Standard equipment.)
Airscrew, diam., and revs. ..	11 ft., 1,080 r.p.m.
Weight of machine empty ..	8,200 lbs.
Load per sq. ft. fully loaded ..	8.5 lbs.
Weight per h.p.	20 lbs.
Tank capacity in hours	8½ hours.
Tank capacity in gallons.. ..	300 gallons.

Performance.

Speed low down	.. ..	97 m.p.h. fully loaded.
Speed at 6,500 feet	.. ..	95 m.p.h.
Speed at 10,000 feet	.. ..	93 m.p.h.
Landing speed..	.. ..	50 m.p.h.

Climb.

To 5,000 feet	.. .. ..	10 minutes.
To 10,000 feet	.. .. ..	25 minutes.

Disposable load apart from fuel   ..   ..   .. 3,500 lbs.
Total weight of machine loaded   ..   ..   ..14,000 lbs.

Alternative Engines.

2 " Liberty's," 2 " Sunbeam Maori," 2 " Sunbeam Cossack," or 2 " F.I.A.T." etc.

The Handley Page Type O/400 (2—375 h.p. Rolls-Royce " Eagle " Engines) with the wings folded.

HANDLEY PAGE
TWIN LIBERTY MOTORED
TYPE O/400 BOMBER

Scale of feet

McLaughlin

HANDLEY PAGE—*continued.*

Front, Rear and Three-quarter Rear View of the Handley Page Biplane.

HANDLEY PAGE—*continued.*

HANDLEY-PAGE FOUR-ENGINED BIPLANE, V/1500.

Tho four-engined *Handley-Page* was a development of the smaller two-engined machine. It was designed principally for night bombing, its most spectacular " engagement " being the bombing of Berlin, which was only forestalled by the signing of the Armistice.

The fuselage remains the same in all its essentials and internal arrangements. The four engines are carried, two tandemwise, on either side of the fuselage, and are not enclosed in any cowling. The upper and lower main planes are of equal span, the upper main plane being flat and the lower plane having a dihedral, and both planes have a decided sweepback. The under-carriage consists of two pairs of Vees under each power unit ; the front legs of the Vees carries shock-absorbers enclosed in streamline fairing, the rear members being hinged.

Both the O/400 and V/1500 types can be converted to commercial vehicles by the mere elimination of the military apparatus—bomb gear and guns—and the refitting of the interior of the fuselage for the accommodation of passengers or goods. In the event of passengers, mails and goods all being carried by the same machine, each would be conveyed in a separate compartment.

In addition to the necessary crew of three men, and petrol, oil and water for a non-stop flight of 400–500 miles, the nett useful load of each machine would be :—

Type O/400 :—2,700 lbs. of goods or 18 passengers.

Type V/1500 :—10,000 lbs. of goods or 45 passengers.

The external ranges of these machines as commercial vehicles can be regarded as :—

Type O/400 :—800 miles non-stop with useful load of a half ton.

Type V/1500 :—1,300 miles non-stop with useful load of one ton

Front View of the Handley Page Type V/1500.

Fore Part of a V/1500 type Handley Page, shewing the mounting of the Rolls-Royce engines.

152a

HANDLEY-PAGE—*continued.*

Specification.

Type of machine	Biplane.
Name or type No. of machine ..	V/1500.
Purpose for which intended ..	Night bombing.
Span	126 ft.
Gap, maximum and minimum ..	15 ft. ; 12 ft.
Overall length	62 ft.
Maximum height	23 ft.
Chord	12 ft.
Total surface of wings ..	3,000 sq. ft.
Maximum cross section of body..	8 ft. ×6 ft. 2 in.
Engine type and h.p. ..	4 R.R. Eagle VIII.
Airscrew, diam. and revs. ..	13 ft. 5 in. (tractors) ; 10 ft. 4 in. (pushers). 1,080 ; 1,080.
Weight of machine empty ..	15,000 lbs.
Load per sq. ft. fully loaded ..	10 lbs.
Weight per h.p.	21 lbs.
Tank capacity in hours	14 hours.
Tank capacity in gallons.. ..	1,000 gallons.

Performance.

Speed low down	103 m.p.h. fully loaded.
Speed at 6,500 feet	99 m.p.h.
Speed at 10,000 feet	95 m.p.h.
Landing speed..	50 m.p.h.

Climb.

To 5,000 feet	8 minutes.
To 10,000 feet	21 minutes.

Disposable load apart from fuel .. .. .. 7,000 lbs.
Total weight of machine loaded .. .. ..30,000 lbs.

Alternative Engines.

4 b.h.p. "Atlantic's," each 500 h.p., or 4 Napier "Lion's," etc.

Side View of the
Type V/1500 Handley Page.

A Four-engined Handley Page (Rolls-Royce engines) Type V/1500.   153a

HANDLEY PAGE—*continued*.

Three-quarter Front View of a Handley Page Type V/1500 (Four 375 h.p. Rolls-Royce "Eagle" Engines). The standing figures indicate the size of this machine.

P—*continued*.

PARNALL & SONS (Proprietors : W. & T. Avery, Ltd.), Mivart Street, Eastville, Bristol. Wood-working firm of note. Designing and manufacturing aeroplanes and seaplanes of various designs, for the Air Force.

THE PARNALL "PANTHER."

The Parnall "Panther" was designed as a two-seater reconnaissance ship-plane. It is equipped with a water-tight bulkheaded fuselage, airbags, which are blown up when necessary by the pilot, and a small hydrovane fitted to two struts in advance of the undercarriage to prevent the machine turning over when landing in the sea.

The fuselage is built up of formers and three ply, minus any internal wire tracing (on the German principle), and is made to fold at a point just in rear of the observer's seat On top of the monocoque fuselage is a huge bulge in which is situated the pilot and observer s cockpits. The elevator controls are carried through the continuation of this hump to the tail, whereas the rudder control runs through a special compartment on the right hand side of the fuselage clear of the bulkheaded portion of the fuselage.

Main planes have no dihedral and have four ailerons inset in the trailing cage. A photograph shows the arrangement of the empennage. A Vee type undercarriage is fitted, the whole being released by the pilot automatically when the air bags are blown up.

Specification.

Type of machine	Two-seater Reconnaissance Ship Aeroplane.
Name or type No. of machine ..	Parnall "Panther."
Purpose for which intended ..	Flying off Carrier or Cruiser.
Span	29 ft. 6 in.
Gap, maximum and minimum ..	6 ft. 3 in. to 6 ft. 2½ in.
Overall length	In flying trim, 24 ft. 11 in.; folded, 14 ft. 6 in.
Maximum height	10 ft. 6 in.
Chord	6 ft. 3 in.
Total surface of wings	336 sq. ft.
Span of tail	12 ft.
Total area of tail	(Tail plane alone), 18.4 sq. ft.
Total area of elevators	(Two, balanced), 19.3 sq. ft.
Area of rudder	4.4 sq. ft.
Area of fin	6.85 sq. ft.
Area of each aileron and total area	Each 11.3 sq. ft., total 45.2 sq. ft.
Maximum cross section of body, including fairing	14.5 sq. ft.

Three-quarter front view of the Parnall " Panther " Ship Plane (230 h.p. B.R. 2 engine).   The machine is here shown with air bags inflated for flotation purposes, and the hydrovanes on the chassis can be clearly seen.

U

PARNALL & SONS—*continued.*

Engine type and h.p.	200 h.p. B.R.2. Actual h.p. about 210 at 1,300 r.p.m.	
Airscrew, diam. pitch and revs...	Diam. 2,775, pitch 2,416, 1,300 r.p.m.	
Weight of machine empty ..	1,420 lbs. (production machine).	
Load per sq. ft.	7.6 lbs.	
Weight per h.p.	12.2 lbs.	
Tank capacity in hours ..	See below.*	
Tank capacity in gallons.. ..	Petrol 58 galls., oil 10 galls.	

Performance.

Speed, ground	122 m.p.h. approx.	These are actual trials with all up weight of 2,480 lbs.
Speed at 6,000 feet	116 m.p.h.	
Speed at 10,000 feet	111 m.p.h.	
Landing speed	40 m.p.h.	

Climb.

To 6,000 feet	6 mins., 3 secs.	
To 10,000 feet..	12 mins., 29 secs.	

Disposable load apart from fuel .. .. .. .630 lbs.
Total weight of machine loaded .. .. .. 2,560 lbs.
(production machine.)

*The makers write :—" This figure is a misleading one, since the consumption in gallons per hour drops steadily with the speed at any given height. It is better to quote *maximum economical mileage*. This is found at approximate 100 m.p.h. when the consumption is 12 gallons per hour at 2,000 feet. Hence *maximum economic mileage*=480 miles."

Three-quarter rear view of the Parnall " Panther," with fuselage folded for stowage on shipboard.

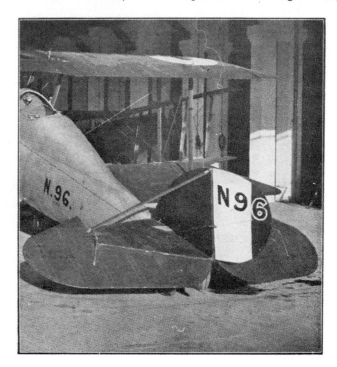

The curious Tail Unit of the Parnall " Panther."

P—*continued*.

PHŒNIX DYNAMO Co. Ltd. Bradford.

Managing Director. Mr. P. J. Pybus, C.B.E.; Managing Director of Aircraft Department, Capt. J. C. Crawshaw; Aircraft Designer, Mr. W. O. Manning (late lieut. R.N.V.R.), one of the pioneers of British aviation, having been the colleague of Mr. Howard Wright in the experimental work of 1908–09.

Amalgamated with Dick Kerr & Co. and the Coventry Ordnance Co. as the English Electrical Co. The aircraft work of the group is concentrated at the Phœnix Co.'s works.

Manufacturers of land machines and float and boat type seaplanes to Air Ministry and own designs. Speciality : Large flying boats.

THE PHŒNIX "CORK" FLYING BOAT.

One of the most successful of the large type of flying boat.

The machine is a twin-engined boat on well-tried and conventional lines, but special care has been devoted to detail design.

In particular the hull is of excellent form and of very low resistance.

Great attention has been paid to the duplication of all controls, and the whole of the petrol system, including the gravity tanks and the piping, is in duplicate. Both engines can be operated through either petrol system.

A noticeable feature of the later models of this type are the two nacelles mounted behind the rear spar in the upper wings, the occupants of which have an extremely wide angle of vision and of fire for the machine guns with which they are equipped.

Specification.

Type of Machine	Flying Boat.
Name or type No. of machine ..	"Phœnix Cork" P. 5.
Purpose for which intended ..	Submarine Patrol.
Span	85 ft. 6 in.
Gap .. .. { maximum	10 ft. 6 in.
{ minimum	10 ft.
Overall length	49 ft. 2 in.
Maximum height	21 ft. 2 in.
Chord	9 ft.
Total surface of wings	1,300 sq. ft.
Span of tail	25 ft.
Total area of tail	200 sq. ft.
Area of elevators	58 sq. ft.
Area of rudder	42 sq. ft.
Area of fin	31 sq. ft.
Area of each aileron and total area	42.75 each ; 85.5 total.
Maximum cross section of body..	27.75 sq. ft.
Horizontal area of body	202.5 sq. ft.
Vertical area of body	208 sq. ft.
Engine type and h.p.	"Eagle" Rolls-Royce, two 360 h.p.
Airscrew, diam., pitch and revs...	10 ft. diam., 10 ft. p., 1,080 revs. r.p.m.
Weight of machine empty ..	7,000 lbs.
Load per sq. ft.	8.85 lbs.
Weight per h.p.	16.1 lbs.
Tank capacity in hours	8 at full speed.
Tank capacity in gallons	360 galls.

157a

Side view of a Phœnix "Cork" Flying Boat.

A Phœnix "Cork" Flying Boat Afloat.

PHŒNIX—continued.

Performance.

Speed low down	.. ..	106 m.p.h.
Speed at 10,000 feet	.. ..	94 miles.
Landing speed..	.. ..	52 m.p.h.

Climb.

To 5,000 feet	.. ..	10 minutes.
To 10,000 feet ..	.. ..	30 minutes.
Disposable load apart from fuel	.. .. ..	2,000 lbs.
Total weight of machine loaded	.. .. ..	11,600 lbs.

Armament : 5 Lewis guns and 4—230 lbs. or 2—520 lbs bombs. Crew, 5,—Pilot, observer, wireless operator, engineer, and gunner.

A Phœnix " Cork " Flying-Boat (2—375 h.p. Rolls-Royce engines) on the Slipway.

Three-quarter Front View of a Phœnix " Cork " Flying Boat (two 375 h.p. Rolls-Royce " Eagle " engines.) Note the gunner's nacelles in the upper plane.

158a

S

FREDK. SAGE & Co., Ltd. 58-62, Gray's Inn

Road, London, W.C., also at Peterborough, and at 5, Boulevard des Italiens, Paris.

An old established firm of shopfitters who took up the manufacture of aircraft during the war of 1914-19.

During the period of hostilities, the Aircraft Department was under the control of Mr E. C. Gordon England, one of the earliest British experimental pilots and constructors. Mr. Clifford W. Tinson was the chief designer, under Mr. England's management, and retains that position at the time of writing.

Mr. England is now a consulting engineer to various aircraft and motor firms.

SAGE I.

Specification.

Type of machine	Biplane.
Name or type No. of machine ..	Sage I.
Purpose for which intended ..	Bombing.
Span	66 ft.
Gap, maximum and minimum ..	7 ft. 2 in.
Overall length	38 ft.
Maximum height	12 ft. 6 in.
Chord	7 ft.
Total surface of wings	778 sq. ft.
Span of tail	17 ft. 3 in.
Total area of tail	44 sq. ft.
Area of elevators	30 sq. ft.
Area of rudder	15 sq. ft.
Area of fin	20 sq. ft.
Area of each aileron	58½ sq. ft.
Total area of ailerons	117 sq. ft.
Maximum cross section of body	5 ft. × 3 ft. 10 in.
Horizontal area of body.. ..	115 sq. ft.
Vertical area of body	132 sq. ft.
Engine type and h.p.	(2) 190 h.p. Rolls.
Airscrew diameter and pitch ..	7 ft. d. × 6 ft. p.
Airscrew revs.	1327 r.p.m.
Weight of machine empty ..	3787 lbs.
Load per sq. ft.	77.71 lbs.
Weight per h.p.	15.8 lbs.
Tank capacity in hours ..	5¾ hours.
Tank capacity in gallons ..	100 gallons.

Performance.

Speed low down	93 m.p.h.
Landing speed	52 m.p.h.

Disposable load apart from fuel	500 lbs.
Total weight of machine loaded	6000 lbs.

THE SAGE NO. 2 SCOUT.

The Sage No. 2 Two-seater fighter was designed in the spring of 1916. The pilots and observers seats are enclosed in a Streamline cabin reaching to the upper plane, the top plane being left open so as to enable the observer to use a Lewis gun in a ring mounting on the top plane, for firing over the propeller.

Specification.

Type of machine	Biplane.
Name or type No. of machine ..	Scout.
Purpose for which intended ..	Fighting.
Span	32 ft. 2½ in.
Gap, maximum and minimum ..	5 ft. 6 in.
Overall length	21 ft. 1⅝ in.
Maximum height	9 ft. 6 in.
Chord	Top plane, 5 ft. ; lower plane, 2 ft. 8 in.
Total surface of wings	168 sq. ft.
Span of tail	9 ft. 5 in.
Total area of tail	20 sq. ft.
Area of elevators	14.5 sq. ft.
Area of rudder	9 sq. ft.
Area of each aileron	12½ sq. ft.
Total area of ailerons	25 sq. ft.
Maximum cross section of body	3 ft. 5 in. dia.
Horizontal area of body.. ..	44 sq. ft.
Vertical area of body	52.5 sq. ft.
Engine type and h.p.	100 h.p. Gnôme.
Airscrew diameter and pitch ..	8 ft. d. × 7 ft. p.
Airscrew revs.	1200 r.p.m.
Weight of machine empty ..	890 lbs.
Load per sq. ft.	9.2 lbs.
Weight per h.p.	15.46 lbs.
Tank capacity in hours	2½ hours.
Tank capacity in gallons ..	26 gallons.

Performance.

Speed low down	112 m.p.h.
Speed at 10,000 feet	100 m.p.h.
Landing speed	50 m.p.h.

Climb.

To 5,000 feet	6½ minutes.
To 10,000 feet	14¾ minutes.

Disposable load apart from fuel	96 lbs.
Total weight of machine loaded	1546 lbs.
Ceiling	16,000 ft.

Three-quarter View from Rear—Sage No. 2 (100 h.p. Mono Gnôme engine).

SAGE—continued.

THE SAGE NO. 3 TRAINING BIPLANE.

The *Sage No. 3* was designed in the autumn of 1916 as a primary training machine and was fitted with dual control with a full cut-out gear in the instructor's cockpit. The undercarriage is of the oleo-pneumatic type and has a pair of small wheels mounted on the front Vee in addition to the landing wheels.

Specification.

Type of machine	Biplane.
Name or type No. of machine ..	Sage 3.
Purpose for which intended ..	Training.
Span	34 ft. 6 in.
Gap, maximum and minimum ..	5 ft.
Overall length	26 ft. 6 in.
Maximum height	10 ft. 9 in.
Chord	4 ft. 9 in.
Total surface of wings ..	330 sq. ft.
Span of tail	11 ft. 4 in.
Total area of tail ..	26 sq. ft.
Area of elevators ..	24 sq. ft.
Area of rudder ..	10 sq. ft.
Area of fin	4 sq. ft.
Area of each aileron ..	18 sq. ft.
Total area of ailerons ..	72 sq. ft.
Maximum cross section of body	2 ft. 6 in. × 2 ft. 6 in.
Horizontal area of body..	59 sq. ft.
Vertical area of body ..	78 sq. ft.
Engine type and h.p. ..	75 h.p. Rolls.
Airscrew diameter and pitch ..	8 ft. d. × 6 ft. 4 in. p.
Airscrew revs.	1500 r.p.m.
Weight of machine empty ..	1390 lbs.
Load per sq. ft.	6.25 lbs.
Weight per h.p.	27.5 lbs.
Tank capacity in hours ..	4 hours.
Tank capacity in gallons ..	26 gallons.

Performance.

Speed low down	72 m.p.h.
Landing speed	38 m.p.h.

Climb.

To 5,000 feet	20 minutes.
Disposable load apart from fuel	119 lbs.
Total weight of machine loaded	2064 lbs.
Ceiling	9,500 ft.

THE SAGE NO. 4A SEAPLANE.

The *Sage No. 4a* was designed for sea patrol work in June 1917. It is similar to most float seaplanes and is fitted with a 150 h.p. Hispano-Suiza engine which gave the machine a considerably superior performance to any seaplane or flying boat of its power at the time. The *No. 4b* and *No. 4c* were similar to the *No. 4a*, but were fitted with dual control and 200 h.p. Hispano-Suiza and Sunbeam "Arab" engines. The *No. 4c* had staggered planes and folding gear, whilst the *4b* had fixed wings of slightly smaller area and a faster wing section. Both types could be rolled, spun, looped, &c., and have been used for advanced training for seaplane pilots.

Specification.

Type of machine	Seaplane.
Name or type No. of machine ..	Sage 4a.
Purpose for which intended ..	Patrol.
Span	34 ft. 6 in.
Gap, maximum and minimum ..	5 ft.
Overall length	26 ft. 8 in.
Maximum height	11 ft. 3 in.
Chord	4 ft. 9 in.
Total surface of wings ..	330 sq. ft.
Span of tail	11 ft. 4 in.
Total area of tail ..	26 sq. ft.
Area of elevators	24 sq. ft.
Area of rudder	9 sq. ft.
Area of fin	7 sq. ft.
Area of each aileron ..	18 sq. ft.
Total area of ailerons ..	72 sq. ft.
Maximum cross section of body	2 ft. 6 in. × 2 ft. 5 in.
Horizontal area of body..	59 sq. ft.
Vertical area of body ..	78 sq. ft.
Engine type and h.p. ..	150 h.p. Hispano.
Airscrew diameter and pitch ..	9 ft. d. × 7 ft. 3 in. p.
Airscrew revs.	1500 r.p.m.
Weight of machine empty ..	1620 lbs.
Load per sq. ft.	8.0 lbs.
Weight per h.p.	17.6 lbs.
Tank capacity in hours ..	4 hours.
Tank capacity in gallons ..	50 gallons.

Performance.

Speed low down	93½ m.p.h.
Speed at 10,000 feet ..	81 m.p.h.
Landing speed	50 m.p.h.

Side view of the Sage Training Machine, Sage 3 (75 h.p. "Hawk" Rolls-Royce engine).

SAGE—*continued*.

THE SAGE No. 4A.—*continued*.

Climb.

To 5,000 feet ..	..	..	12 minutes.
To 10,000 feet..	..	..	25 minutes.
Disposable load apart from fuel	..	..	.. 291 lbs.
Total weight of machine loaded	..	..	.. 2645 lbs.
Ceiling	..	..	.. 13,000 ft.

SAGE 4B.
SAGE 4C.
Specification.

Type of machine	Seaplane.
Name or type No. of machine ..	Sage Seaplane.
Purpose for which intended ..	Training.
Span	39 ft. 7¼ in.
Gap, maximum and minimum ..	5 ft. 3 in.
Overall length	37 ft. 6 in.
Maximum height	11 ft. 7 in.
Chord	5 ft. 3 in.
Total surface of wings ..	386 sq. ft.
Span of tail	11 ft.
Total area of tail	24 sq. ft.
Area of elevators	21 sq. ft.
Area of rudder	9 sq. ft.
Area of fin	7 sq. ft.
Area of each aileron ..	21 sq. ft.
Total area of ailerons ..	84 sq. ft.
Maximum cross section of body	2 ft. 6 in. × 2 ft. 5 in.
Horizontal area of body..	56 sq. ft.
Vertical area of body ..	70 sq. ft.
Engine type and h.p. (4. A.) ..	200 h.p. Hispano-Suiza ;
(4. B.)	200 h.p. " Arab " Sunbeam.
Airscrew diameter and pitch ..	9 ft. d. × 7 ft. 9 n. p.
Airscrew revs.	1500 r.p.m.
Weight of machine empty ..	2100 lbs.
Load per sq. ft.	7.45 lbs.
Weight per h.p.	14.4 lbs.
Tank capacity in hours ..	2½ hours.
Tank capacity in gallons ..	35 gallons.

Performance.

Speed low down	..	97 m.p.h.
Speed at 10,000 feet ..	..	94 m.p.h.
Landing speed	..	45 m.p.h.

Climb.

To 5,000 feet ..	..	..	8 minutes.
To 10,000 feet..	..	..	21 minutes.
Disposable load apart from fuel	..	..	.. 155 lbs.
Total weight of machine loaded	..	..	.. 2875 lbs.
Ceiling	..	..	.. 15,800 ft.

S. E. SAUNDERS, Ltd. East Cowes, Isle of Wight.

Famous makers of motor boats on Saunders' Patent principle. Made the hulls of the original Sopwith " Bat-boats " with marked success, and later specialised on hulls for flying-boats of various types. Took to making aeroplanes complete, and has won a high reputation for excellence of workmanship.

Later produced the famous " Consuta " system of sewing wooden sheets together. This has been used with much success in the hulls of flying boats.

Side View—The Sage No. 4A Seaplane (150 h.p. Hispano-Suiza engine).

BRITISH AEROPLANES.

S—continued.

SHORT BROS.
Works : Rochester, Kent. London Works : Queen's Circus, Battersea Park, S.W. London office : 29/30, Charing Cross, S.W.

The firm of Short Bros., which is the oldest established firm of aeroplane designers and producers in the United Kingdom, was founded by two brothers, Eustace and Oswald Short, in the year 1898, their work for some years being the manufacture of spherical balloons. In 1906 they nearly succeeded in winning the Gordon Bennett Race, and actually gained second place. In 1907 the firm was appointed "Official Aeronautical Engineers to the Royal Aero Club."

The two brothers were joined by their elder brother, the late Horace L. Short, in 1908, and they added to their balloon work the design and manufacture of aeroplanes, for which purpose they established works at Shellness, near Leysdown, in the Isle of Sheppey.

In 1909, a "Short" aeroplane, fitted with a Green engine, won the "Daily Mail's" £1,000 prize for a flight over a closed circuit by an all-British aeroplane, the pilot being Mr. J. T. C. Moore-Brabazon, now Major, R.F.C. The Short Bros. were also the British agents for the Wright Bros.

In 1910 the works were transferred to Eastchurch, adjacent to the Flying Grounds of the Royal Aero Club, and there were produced a series of biplanes with two engines, which were certainly the first multiple-engined aeroplanes in the world. At Eastchurch, Messrs. Short Bros. produced also the three "Short" biplanes on which the four officers first appointed by the Admiralty to the Royal Flying Corps, Naval Wing, were taught to fly.

In 1911 the firm took up the design of seaplanes with which they achieved almost immediate success, and in 1912 a seaplane of their design, piloted by Lieut. (now Colonel) Samson, R.N., rose from the deck of H.M.S. Hibernia, this being the first "heavier-than-air" machine of any kind to achieve this feat.

By the introduction of the "Short" Patent Folding Wing device, in 1913, the firm revolutionised the use of the seaplane, making it possible for seaplanes of large dimensions to be carried in H.M. ships for operations in all parts of the world. The device also brought about an immense saving in the cost of storage of both seaplanes and aeroplanes.

In 1913, finding further development necessary, the firm erected new works at Rochester, which were placed under the charge of Mr. H. O. Short, and devoted almost entirely to the manufacture of seaplanes.

The Short seaplane was the first, and is so far the only seaplane, employed successfully in a Naval Engagement (vide the following extract from an official letter to Messrs. Short Bros.) :—

"... the flight made by Flight Lieut. Rutland, with Assistant Paymaster Trewin, as observer, which Sir David Beatty praises so highly, was carried out on a 225-h.p. 'Short Seaplane' ..."

Early in the war, a "Short" seaplane achieved the feat of carrying a torpedo into the air, and it has been officially announced that Flight Com. C. H. K. Edmonds, in a "Short" seaplane, succeeded in torpedoing a Turkish transport in the Sea of Marmora.

At the end of 1915, owing to the great development of their business, the firm found it necessary to establish an office in London, and from it the "business" side of their activities is mainly carried on. Mr. J. B. Parker, formerly Assistant-Paymaster, R.N., afterwards one of the best pilots of the R.N.A.S., was appointed to manage this office, having been previously invalided out of the Service before the war.

The firm sustained a grave loss in the death of Mr. Horace L. Short, the eldest of the three brothers, on the 6th April, 1917.

Diagram of Short "folder" Seaplane. Further improvements in detail have not in any way altered the principle involved.

SHORT BROS.—*continued*.

THE SHORT N2B FLOAT SEAPLANE.

The *Short* N 2 B bombing seaplane is the latest of the many types of float seaplanes produced by Messrs. Short Bros. before and during the war, and used by the R.N.A.S. and subsequently the R.A.F. as sea patrols, etc. The upper main plane has no dihedral and has a slight overhang over the bottom plane which has a dihedral. Two large pontoon floats are fitted to the fuselage by faired struts. The tail unit is on conventional lines except that a very large fin is used in conjunction with a balanced rudder. Wing-tip and tail floats of ample proportions are fitted, the tail float having a small water rudder. The pilot sits under the centre section wherein are carried the petrol gravity tank, and radiator. The observer sits well back and is armed with Lewis Gun carried in a Scarff mounting,

Specification.

Type of machine	Float Seaplane.
Name or type No. of machine	Short N. 2 B.
Purpose for which intended..	Bombing.
Span	55 ft.
Gap, maximum	7 ft.
Overall length	40 ft.
Maximum height	13 ft. 9 in.
Chord	7 ft. 6 in.
Span of Tail	15 ft. 6 in.
Maximum cross section of body	11.5 sq. ft.
Engine type and h.p.	Sunbeam - Coatalen "Maori," 275 h.p.
Airscrew diam.	10 ft. 6 in.
Weight of machine empty ..	3,050 lbs.
Tank capacity in hours ..	4½ hours.
Tank capacity in gallons ..	70 gallons.

Performance.

Speed low down	90 m.p.h.
Speed at 10,000 feet ..	88 m.p.h.

Climb.

To 5,000 ft.	12½ minutes.
To 10,000 ft.	40 minutes.
Disposable load apart from fuel	1,170 lbs.
Total weight of machine loaded	4,800 lbs.

General Arrangement of the Short N 2 B type Seaplane (275 h.p. Sunbeam-Coatalen "Maori" engine).

SHORT BROS.—*continued.*

Three-quarter View from the front of the modified Short "Shirl" (375 h.p. "Eagle" Rolls-Royce), prepared for an attempt on the Transatlantic Flight. Note the petrol tank under the fuselage.

THE SHORT "SHIRL" TORPEDO-CARRIER.

The *Short* "Shirl" biplane is generally similar to the N2B type seaplane except that a divided wheel and skid chassis is fitted for flying off decks and to allow the stowage of an 18 in. torpedo under the fuselage. The machine is a single-seater, the pilot being situated in rear of the main planes. which are noticeably swept back from the fuselage, and are arranged to fold for stowage on board ship.

Flotation gear in the form of air-bags are carried over the skids and small plane form hydro vanes are fitted to the front of the skids, to prevent turning over when alighting on water.

The machine entered by Messrs. Short Bros. for the trans-Atlantic flight is a modified "Shirl," fitted with somewhat larger wings and tailplane, and an immense petrol tank suspended under the fuselage.

Specification.

Type of machine	Biplane.
Name or type No. of machine ..	"Short Shirl."
Purpose for which intended ..	Torpedo carrying.
Span	52 ft.
Gap, maximum and minimum ..	6 ft.
Overall length	35 ft. 6 in.
Chord	8 ft. upper; 7 ft. lower plane.
Span of tail	15 ft.
Maximum cross section of body..	11 sq. ft.
Engine type and h.p.	Rolls Eagle 8, 400 h.p.
Airscrew, diam.	10 ft.
Weight of machine empty ..	2,850 lbs.
Tank capacity in hours	Max. 6½ hours.
Tank capacity in gallons ..	137 gallons.

Performance.

Speed low down	99 m.p.h.
Speed at 10,000 feet	97 m.p.h.

Climb.

To 5,000 feet	13 minutes.
To 10,000 feet	30 minutes.
Disposable load apart from fuel	2,500 lbs. normal
Total weight of machine loaded	5,950 lbs.

General Arrangement of the Short "Shirl" Torpedo Ship Plane (375 h.p. "Eagle" Rolls-Royce engine).

SHORT BROS.—*continued.*

THE SHORT " CROMARTY " FIGHTING FLYING-BOAT.

The *Short* " Cromarty " boat seaplane was designed as a long distance bomber and fighter.

It follows standard large flying boat practice in having a central hull and engines carried between the planes on either side of the boat. The wings are of large span, the top plane having a considerable overhang, to which are hinged unbalanced ailerons of large area.

There is accommodation for one gunner in the nose, two pilots in advance of the main planes, one gunner mid-way between the planes and tail unit, and two gunners in " crows-nests " in the top plane over the first set of struts from the power units. A biplane tail is fitted with two elevators and triple rudders.

The form of hull used on this machine is unusual. Instead of the usual V bottom, the planing surface is concave downwards. It is claimed that this form of bottom gives the gradual entry into the water and the consequent absence of shocks when alighting which is attained by the use of the Vee type, without the loss of planing efficiency which is caused by outwards spewing of water with the conventional form.

Specification.

Type of machine	Boat Seaplane.
Name or type No. of machine ..	Short Cromarty.
Purpose for which intended ..	Fighting and bombing.
Span	113 ft.
Gap, maximum and minimum ..	10 ft.
Overall length	59 ft.
Maximum height..	22 ft.
Chord	11 ft. top ; 10 ft. bottom.
Span of tail	23 ft.
Maximum cross section of body..	50 sq. ft.
Engine type and h.p.	Rolls " Condor," (two), 700 h.p. each.
Airscrew, diam. and revs.. ..	16 ft. diam. 970 r.p.m.
Weight of machine empty ..	11,000 lbs.
Tank capacity in hours	12 hours' (cruising speed).
Tank capacity in gallons ..	650 gallons.

Performance.

Speed low down	101 m.p.h.			
Disposable load apart from fuel	..	..	..	2,500 lbs.
Total weight of machine loaded	..	..	..	18,000 lbs.

General Arrangement of the Short " Cromarty " Boat Seaplane (two 700 h.p. " Condor " Rolls-Royce engines).

SHORT BROS.—*continued.*

THE "F3" FLYING BOAT.

The F3 Flying Boat designs emanate from the Seaplane Experimental Station, Felixstowe, but it has been built in quantity by Messrs. Short Bros. The boat is of the now well known Felixstowe construction with a wide Vee bottomed planing surface, fitted with two steps. The crew consists of a gunner in the nose, two pilots enclosed in a cabin in advance of the main planes, and a gunners cockpit in the rear of the planes with swivel mountings for Lewis guns firing out of the top and either side of the boat. The top plane has a considerable overhang and is fitted with ailerons of large area. Over the last set of struts are king-posts for bracing the overhang, the intervening space between the front and rear king-posts being covered in to form a fin.

Specification.

Type of machine..	Boat Seaplane.
Name or type No. of machine	Felixstowe F 3.
Purpose for which intended	Anti-submarine.
Span	102 ft.
Gap, maximum and minimum	8 ft. 6 in.
Overall length	49 ft.
Maximum height	18 ft. 9 in.
Chord	8 ft.
Total surface of wings	1,413 sq. ft.
Span of tail	22 ft.
Total area of tail	118 sq. ft.
Area of Elevators	67 sq. ft.
Area of rudder	30.3 sq. ft.
Area of fin	37.2 sq. ft.
Area of each ailerons	65 sq. ft.
Total area of ailerons	132 sq. ft.
Engine type and h.p.	Rolls-Royce Eagle 8 (two) 400 h.p. each.
Airscrew, diam.	10 ft.
Weight of machine empty	7,650 lbs.
Load per sq. ft.	842 lbs.
Weight per h.p.	17 lbs.
Tank capacity in hours	9.7 max.; 5 hours normal.
Tank capacity in gallons	212 gallons.

Performance.

Speed low down	85 m.p.h.
Disposable load apart from fuel	2,550 lbs.
Total weight of machine loaded	11,900 lbs.

— TYPE F3 BOAT — SEAPLANE —

E 23

A Projected Twin-Hulled Flying Boat designed by Short Bros.

S—*continued.*

SOPWITH. The Sopwith Aviation Co., Ltd.

Works and offices : Canbury Park Road, Kingston-on-Thames. Established by Mr. T. O. M. Sopwith, the well-known aviator, at Brooklands, Autumn of 1911, where, during 1912, a 70 h.p. tractor biplane and a 40 h.p. biplane were turned out.

The Company is now a private limited company. Directors: T. O. M. Sopwith, C.B.E., M. G. Sopwith, R. O. Cary.

General manager : R. O. Cary.

Secretary : H. P. Musgrave.

Engineering manager : F. Sigrist.

Prior to the outbreak of war the firm had produced machines of extreme interest, and amongst their outstanding performances was the winning of the " Schneider " cup, at Monaco, by Mr. Howard Pexton, on a small seaplane with a 100 h.p. Mono Gnôme engine.

This machine was the direct ancestor of the " Baby " seaplane so largely used by the R.N.A.S, during nearly the whole of the period of hostilities.

Since 1914 the firm have produced a series of machines of the very highest value.

Particularly noteworthy in their line were the famous " 1½ Shutter " produced in 1915, and the Triplane of 1916.

Sopwiths were the first to bomb Cologne and Düsseldorf, in October, 1914. (The following letter verifies the fact.)

AIR DEPT.,
ADMIRALTY, LONDON, S.W.,
28th December, 1914.

AD5062.

GENTLEMEN,

With reference to the recent attack on the German Airsheds at Cologne and Düsseldorf, carried out by Squadron Commander Spenser D. A. Grey and Flight Lieut. R. L. G. Marix, you may be interested to learn that the machines used were your " Sopwith Tabloid aeroplanes." I take the opportunity of expressing my appreciation of the excellent performance of these machines.

It is reported from Berlin that a new Zeppelin fitted with the latest silent motors, which had just been moved into the shed at Düsseldorf and a Machinery Hall alongside the Airship Shed, were destroyed by Flight Lieut. Marix. The roof of the Airship Shed has fallen in.

I am, Gentlemen,
Yours faithfully,
(Sd) MURRAY F. SUETER,
Director Air Dept.

In 1917, Captain Beaumont and Lieut. Daucourt, both on *Sopwiths*, bombed the Krupp Works, at Essen.

Later in 1917, Captain Beaumont bombed Munich and afterwards landed in Italy.

Three-quarter Rear View of the Sopwith " Pup " (80 h.p. Le Rhône engine).

SOPWITH—*continued*.

THE SOPWITH "PUP."

In point of date this machine was intermediate between the 1½ "Strutter" and the Triplane. It was a lineal descendant of the original *Sopwith* "Tabloid" of early 1914, and was largely used by the R.N.A.S. from 1915 onwards. During its existence it has maintained the reputation of being one of the most delightful machines to fly that have ever been built. In addition the performance with so low-powered an engine as the 80 Le Rhone, is astonishing.

It is extremely likely that, as a sporting single seater for the pilot owner, this type will maintain its popularity for some time to come.

Specification.

Type of machine	Single-seater Tractor Biplane.
Name or type No. of machine..	Sopwith "Pup."
Purpose for which intended ..	Fighting Scout
Span	26 ft. 6 in.
Gap, maximum and minimum..	4 ft. 4⅞ in.
Overall length	19 ft. 3¾ in.
Maximum height	9 ft. 5 in.
Chord	5 ft. 1½ in.
Engine type and h.p. ..	Le Rhone; 80 h.p.
Tank capacity in gallons ..	Petrol 18 galls.; oil 5 galls.

Performance.

Speed at 10,000 feet ..	..	99 m.p.h.

Climb.

To 5,000 feet ..	..	..	7 mins. 40 secs.
To 10,000 feet..	..	..	15 mins. 24 secs.
Total weight of machine loaded	..	.. ..	1,313 lbs.

General Arrangement of the Sopwith "Pup" (80 h.p. Le Rhône engine.)

SOPWITH—*continued.*

THE SOPWITH "CAMEL."

Is generally an enlarged and modified Pup. It was designed specially for high performances and extreme manœuvrability. To obtain these qualities some of the qualities of the "Pup" were necessarily sacrificed, and the machine has a reputation for being relatively—to the original—uncomfortable to fly.

As a single seater fighter however it was a very great success, and did an immense amount of work in 1917.

A distinctive feature of this machine is the great dihedral on the bottom plane, combined with a flat top plane.

A very slightly modified "Camel" with a folding fuselage and fitted with a 150 h.p. B.R.1 Engine was also produced as a "ship plane" fighter.

Specification.

Type of machine..	Single-seater Tractor Biplane.
Name or type No. of machine..	"Camel"—F.I.
Purpose for which intended ..	Fighting Scout.
Span	28 ft.
Gap, maximum and minimum..	5 ft. max; 4 ft. $1\frac{1}{16}$ in. min.
Overall length	18 ft. 9 in.
Maximum height..	9 ft.
Chord	4 ft. 6 in.
Engine type and h.p.	Clerget; 130 h.p.
Tank capacity in hours.. ..	Petrol $2\frac{1}{2}$ hrs.; oil $2\frac{1}{2}$ hrs.
Tank capacity in gallons ..	Petrol 26 galls.; oil $5\frac{3}{4}$ galls.

Performance.

Speed at 10,000 feet.. ..	113 m.p.h.

Climb.

To 5,000 feet..	5 minutes.
To 10,000 feet..	12 minutes.
Total weight of machine loaded	1,524 lbs.

The Sopwith "Scooter," a Monoplane "run-about" with a 130 h.p. Clerget.

Front View of the Sopwith "Camel" type Ship Plane (150 h.p. B.R.1. engine).

Three-quarter Rear View of the Sopwith "Camel."

General Arrangement of the Sopwith "Camel" (130 h.p. Clerget engine).

Side View of the Sopwith "Camel" (130 h.p. Clerget engine).

SOPWITH—*continued*

THE SOPWITH "DOLPHIN."

This is another single seater fighter, and retains many distinctively *Sopwith* features.

In appearance however it differs considerably from all previous *Sopwith* Single Seaters.

Unlike its predecessors it is fitted with a stationary water cooled engine.

It has two rows of interplane struts on each side and the top plane is staggered back. The gap is considerably less than in the previous *Sopwith* machines and the fuselage reaches nearly to the centre section.

The pilot's seat is between the rear and front spars of the upper wing, with the pilot's head protruding.

Specification.

Type of machine..	Single-seater Tractor Biplane.
Name or type No. of machine..	" Dolphin "—5 F.I.
Purpose for which intended ..	Fighting Scout.
Span	32 ft. 6 in.
Gap, maximum and minimum ..	4 ft. 3 in.
Overall length	22 ft. 3 in.
Maximum height.. ..	8 ft. 6 in.
Chord	4 ft. 6 in.
Engine type and h.p. ..	Hispano-Suiza; 200 h.p.
Tank capacity in hours.. ..	Petrol 2¼ hrs.: oil 2¼ hrs.
Tank capacity in gallons ..	Petrol 27 galls.; oil 4 galls.

Performance.

Speed at 10,000 feet	121½ m.p.h.

Climb.

To 5,000 feet	5 minutes.
To 10,000 feet..	12 minutes.
Total weight of machine loaded	1959 lbs.

THE SOPWITH "SNIPE."

A further development of the single seat fighter. The rotary type of engine has been installed again, and in general appearance the machine approaches more closely to the earlier *Sopwith* types.

The fuselage is faired out to a circular section, in conformity to the shape of the engine cowl, and the normal stagger forward of the top plane has returned.

Specification.

Type of Machine..	Single-seater Tractor Biplane.
Name or type No. of machine..	" Snipe "—7 F.I.
Purpose for which intended ..	Fighting Scout.
Span	Top plane 31 ft. 1 in.; bottom plane 30 ft.
Gap, maximum and minimum..	4 ft. 3 in.
Overall length	19 ft.
Maximum height..	9 ft. 6. in.
Chord	5 ft.
Engine type and h.p. ..	B.R.; 200 h.p.
Tank capacity in hours ..	Petrol 3 hrs.; oil 3 hrs.
Tank capacity in gallons ..	Petrol 38½ galls.; oil 7 galls.

Performance.

Speed at 10,000 feet	121 m.p.h.

Climb.

To 5,000 feet	3 mins. 45 secs.
To 10,000 feet..	9 mins. 25 secs.
Total weight of machine loaded	2,020 lbs.

Three-quarter Front View of the Sopwith "Dolphin" (200 h.p. Hispano-Suiza engine).

Three-quarter Front View of the Sopwith "Snipe" (230 h.p. B.R. 2 engine).

SOPWITH—*continued.*

5'-0"

1'50

19'-10"

31'-1"

4'3"

4'5"

30'-0"

5-0"

16"

SOPWITH   **SNIPE.**

FORD-JONES

FEET

172a

SOPWITH—*continued.*

THE SOPWITH "TRANSPORT" (Trans-Atlantic Type.)

This machine, designed for commercial transport purposes, and adapted for the special purpose of the trans-Atlantic type is quite a distinct departure from the single seat fighter type with which the *Sopwith* firm has been mainly concerned hitherto. The following table gives the particulars of the trans-Atlantic machine.

Specification.

Type of machine	Two-seater Tractor Biplane.
Name or type No. of machine ..	" Transport."
Purpose for which intended ..	Atlantic Flight.
Span	46 ft. 6 in.
Gap, maximum and minimum ..	6 ft.
Overall length	32 ft.
Maximum height	10 ft.
Chord	6 ft. 3 in.
Span of tail	11 ft. 6 in.
Engine type and h.p. ..	375 h.p. Rolls-Royce.
Airscrew, diameter and pitch and revs.	10 ft. dia.
Weight of machine empty ..	3000 lbs.
Tank capacity in hours	22 hours at 100 m.p.h.
Tank capacity in gallons ..	330 gallons.

Performance.

Speed low down .. .. Max. speed 120 m.p.h.

Climb.

Total weight of machine loaded .. .. .. 6150 lbs.

Side View of the Sopwith trans-Atlantic Machine (375 h.p. Rolls-Royce engine).

Three-quarter Front View of the Sopwith trans-Atlantic Machine.

SOPWITH—*continued.*

SIDE

FRONT

SOPWITH   TRANSPORT

SCALE

SOPWITH—continued.

THE SOPWITH SALAMANDER.

A single seater designed for use against infantry, produced late in the war. Is fitted with protective armour to the cockpit.

Type of machine	Tractor Biplane.
Name or type No. of machine ..	"Salamander."
Purpose for which intended ..	Ground Fighting.
Span	31 ft. 3 in.
Gap, maximum and minimum ..	4 ft. 3 in.
Overall length	19 ft. 6 in.
Maximum height	9 ft. 4 in.
Chord	5 ft.
Span of tail	9 ft. 2 in.
Total area of empennage ..	15 sq. ft.
Area of elevators	11 sq. ft.
Area of rudder	9 sq. ft.
Area of fin	$2\frac{3}{4}$ sq. ft.
Area of each aileron and total area	14 sq. ft. each (4 off).
Engine type and h.p. ..	200 h.p. BR.
Weight of machine empty ..	1700 lbs.
Load per sq. ft.	9.7 lbs.
Weight per h.p.	11.35 lbs.
Tank capacity in hours ..	$1\frac{1}{2}$ hours at ground level
Tank capacity in gallons ..	29 gallons.

Performance.

Speed low lown	125 m.p.h.
Speed at 10,000 feet	117 m.p.h.

Climb.

To 10,000 feet..	17 minutes.
Total weight of machine loaded	2945 lbs.

SOPWITH TF2. SALAMANDER.

FORD·JONES

SCALE OF FEET

Three-quarter View from rear of the Sopwith "Salamander" (220 h.p. "B.R.2" engine).

THE SOPWITH CUCKOO.

Produced in 1917. A very successful example of the British torpedo carrying machine.

Type of machine	Tractor Biplane.
Name or type No. of machine ..	" Cuckoo."
Purpose for which intended ..	Torpedo carrying.
Span	46 ft. 9 in.
Gap, maximum and minimum ..	6 ft.
Overall length	28 ft. 6 in.
Maximum height	11 ft.
Chord	6 ft. 3 in.
Span of tail	11 ft. 9 in.
Total area of empennage ..	$35\frac{1}{3}$ sq. ft.
Area of elevators	$18\frac{1}{2}$ sq. ft.
Area of rudder	8 sq. ft.
Area of fin	5.6 sq. ft.
Area of each aileron and total area	20 sq. ft.
Engine type and h.p.	200 h.p. Hispano-Suiza (Experimental).
	220 h.p. Sunbeam Arab (Production).
Weight of machine empty ..	2140 lbs.
Load per sq. ft.	6.7 lbs.
Weight per h.p.	17.9 lbs.
Tank capacity in hours ..	4 hours at full speed.
Tank capacity in gallons ..	56 gallons.

SOPWITH TORPEDO CARRIER

FORD JONES 19

SCALE OF FEET

Performance.

Speed low down	90 kts.
Speed at 10,000 feet	85 kts.

Climb.

To 10,000 feet..	26 minutes.
Total weight of machine loaded	3880 lbs.

Side View of the Sopwith " Cuckoo " Torpedo Carrier (200 h.p. Hispano-Suiza engine).

176a

SOPWITH—*continued*.

38'-9"

4'-6"

5°

24'-0"

21 ⅛"

5'-0"

SOPWITH   HIPPO

Ford-Jones
19

0 1 2 3 4 5 6 7 8 9 10 11 12 13 14
SCALE OF FEET.

Three-quarter Front View of the Sopwith "Hippo" (200 h.p. Clerget engine).

177a

S—*continued.*

THE SOUTH COAST AIRCRAFT WORKS,

Shoreham, Sussex.   Telephones : Day Service, 83, Shoreham ;
Night Service, 89, Shoreham.   Telegrams : " Scaw, Shoreham-
by-Sea."

Aeronautical constructional engineers and contractors to
the Admiralty and War Office.

STANDARD MOTOR CO., Ltd., Coventry.

Well-known motor manufacturing firm.   Have been making
aircraft with success for some years.

STANDARD AIRCRAFT MANUFACTUR- ING CO., Ltd. Effingham House, Arundel Street,
W.C., and at 28, Bow Common Lane, E.

Made aeroplanes and parts to official specifications.

Part of a week's output of the Standard Motor Co

S—continued.

SUPERMARINE.

The Supermarine Aviation Works, Ltd.

Registered offices and works : Southampton. Flying water and slipways : Woolston.

Designers of the *Supermarine* aeroplanes and flying boats. Founded in 1912, by Mr. Noel Pemberton Billing, then known as a pioneer of aviation, and as a motorist and yachtsman.

Before the war, he built some very interesting experimental flying-boats, some of which were ordered by Germany before the war, but were not delivered.

The Supermarine Works worked during the war on Admiralty designs, but built some experimental machines.

The name of the firm was changed during the war from Pemberton Billing, Ltd., to The Supermarine Aviation Works, Ltd., and Squadron-Commander Pemberton Billing ceased to have any connection with it.

The directors are : Capt. A. de Broughton (late R.F.C.), Mr. C. Cecil Dominy and Mr. Hubert Scott-Paine, the last-named being managing director.

The firm has of late been devoted chiefly to the construction of seaplanes of various types, all with marked success.

The following details concern the firms' experimental machines of 1916 to 1919, which it is permissible to describe.

SUPERMARINE BABY.

Type of machine	Single-seater Flying-boat.
Name or type No. of machine ..	Supermarine " Baby."
Purpose for which intended ..	Single-seater Seaplane Fighter.
Span	30.5 ft.
Gap, maximum and minimum ..	
Overall length	26.3 ft.
Maximum height	10.6 ft.
Chord	5.5 ft.
Total surface of wings	309 sq. ft.
Engine type and h.p. ..	150 h.p. Hispano-Suiza.
Weight of machine empty ..	1699 lbs.
Load per sq. ft.	7.5 lbs. per sq. ft.
Weight per h.p.	15.5 lbs. per h.p.
Tank capacity in hours	3 hours.
Performance.	
Speed low down	117 m.p.h.
Landing speed	57 m.p.h.
Disposable load apart from fuel	627 lbs.
Total weight of machine loaded	2326 lbs.

Front View of a Supermarine " Baby " Flying-Boat (150 h.p. Hispano-Suiza engine).

Side view of the Supermarine " Baby " with wings folded.

SUPERMARINE—*continued.*

The Supermarine "Baby" Flying.

Rear view of the Supermarine "Baby" Boat.

Bow view of the Supermarine "Baby" Boat.

The Supermarine "Baby" being towed in heavy weather.

Three-quarter Rear View of the Supermarine "Baby" Afloat.

Front view of the "Baby" folded.

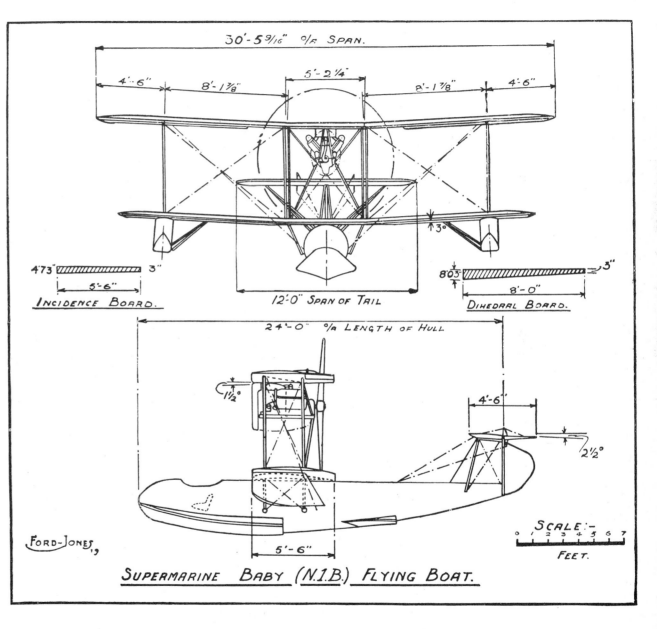

30'-5 9/16" O/E SPAN.

4'-6"   8'-1 3/8"   5'-2 1/4"   8'-1 7/8"   4'-6"

3°

4·73"   3"
5'-6"
INCIDENCE BOARD.

12'-0" SPAN OF TAIL

8·03"   3"
8'-0"
DIHEDRAL BOARD.

24'-0" O/A LENGTH OF HULL

1 1/2°   4'-6"   2 1/2°

5'-6"

FORD-JONES, 19

SCALE:-
0 1 2 3 4 5 6 7
FEET.

SUPERMARINE BABY (N.1.B.) FLYING BOAT.

SUPERMARINE—*continued.*

THE A.D. FLYING BOAT.

This machine, with the exception of the hull, was completely re-designed by the firm and fitted with Hispano-Suiza engine. It carried 4½ hours' fuel, wireless, gear, Lewis gun and ammunition, pilot and passenger, sea anchor, ground anchor, 40 fathoms of line, etc. It is believed to have put up new world's records for flying-boats in March, 1917.

In addition to these machines, the firm has the following projected designs in hand :—

Type " A." A single-seater high performance Scout flying boat which can be looped, rolled and spun and is expected to make a maximum speed of 130 m.p.h. with a climb of 10,000 feet in 8 minutes and 20,000 feet in 20½ minutes.

Three-quarter Front View of a Supermarine-built A.D. Flying Boat, with gunner in tandem in front of pilot.

Side View of an A.D. Flying-Boat (200 h.p. Hispano-Suiza), built by the Supermarine Company.

Type " B." A twin—engined training flying boat. The hull is specially strengthened and the whole machine has a very high factor of safety. Side by side dual control is fitted together with an additional seat. A maximum speed of 90 m.p.h is expected with two 100 h.p " Cosmos " radial engines. This machine is also to be fitted up as a sporting machine with slight modifications, and additions in fitting-up.

Type " C." A small passenger and mail carrier with an accommodation for one pilot and 3 passengers. It is to be fitted with a 160 h.p. Beardmore engine with which a speed of 89-90 m.p.h. is expected.

Type " D." A long distance passenger mail and commercial triplane fitted with three 500 h.p. Jupiter " Cosmos " engines. Accommodation allows for two pilots, one navigator, one engineer and wireless operator and 24 passengers, or 1½ tons of mails. A speed of 98 m.p.h is expected, together with a radius of action of 4 hours fully loaded.

SUPERMARINE—*continued.*

34'-9"

27'-6

34'-9"

7'-0"

S.S. SUPERMARINE   FLYING BOAT.

FORD-JONES 19

0 1 2 3 4 5 6 7 8 9 10 11 12 FEET
SCALE.

183a

SUPERMARINE—*continued.*

FORD-JONES/19

SUPERMARINE 3 SEATER FLYING BOAT.

0 1 2 3 4 5 6 7

SCALE

T

TARRANT, W. G.

Tarrant, W. G., Offices : Clock House, Arundel Street, W.C. 2.
Works : Byfleet.

A firm of building contractors. The close proximity of the works to Brooklands track led to frequent resort thereto by those of the early inhabitants of that place who required timber or woodwork for repairs, etc., to aeroplanes. It was therefore not unnatural that on the outbreak of War Mr. Tarrant should have turned some of his plant onto aircraft construction.

THE TARRANT "TABOR" TRIPLANE.

The most interesting point in the machine is the novel wooden girder construction, which must be considered as an attempt on the part of the adherents of wood construction to meet the growing tendency towards the use of metal construction, by adopting a distribution of material very similar to that commonly employed in metal structures.

WING STRUCTURE.

The machine is a triplane with wings of R.A.F.15 section, loaded to approximately 9 lbs. per sq. ft.

The ribs are of standard type, made of spruce, and weigh on the average 2 lbs. 3 ozs. per rib. They are spaced 15 ins. apart with two intermediate nose riblets. The leading and trailing edges are of wood.

The spar consists of two Warren girders displaced relatively to each other. The detailed construction is clearly shown in the accompanying sketch. It is evident that with this construction short lengths of timber can be used to the best advantage. The tail plane spars, fuselage longitudinals and formers are all constructed in a similar manner.

It is estimated that these spars are some 10 per cent. lighter than a corresponding box section, because for practical reasons the sides and flanges of the boxes cannot be made thinner than 5/16 in.

AILERONS.

The ailerons are fitted to the centre plane only, and are approximately 100 sq. ft. each, are of a balanced type, the balanced portion extending the whole length of the aileron, which is about 23 ft. in length. To reduce the chord of the aileron a false spar is overhung from the main spar with stout box ribs projecting to take the hinges. The chord of the ailerons is 3 ft. 9 in., and the hinge line is 9 in. inside the leading edge of the aileron.

FUSELAGE.

The fuselage is of a monocoque construction, and is attached to the wings between the middle and bottom planes, and is built up on a series of main rings made on a system similar to that used for the spars, with intermediate series of lighter

Two Views of the Tarrant "Tabor" Triplane (6—500 h.p. Napier "Lion" Engines)

TARRANT, W. G. — *continued*.

single rings or formers. Longitudinals run from the nose to the tail of the body and are constructed in such a way that neither the rings nor the longitudinals are cut away where the two intersect.

Over the parallel portion of the body the longitudinals are built up like the spars, but aft of this the inner flange of the longitudinal tapers down and forms a single member which extends to the end of the body.

The skin is made of two-ply. This is built on formers in four quarter rounds, the thickness varying from 5 mm. to 3 mm. The four sections are scarfed together and the whole skin is screwed to the longerons, formers and rings, and covered with fabric, varnished and enamelled.

CONTROLS.

The controls are duplicated throughout, with two rudder bars, and two aileron and elevator controls side by side. Immediately behind the pilots is a partition which carries all the engine controls, and at the bottom of this board are two collecting tanks for the petrol systems for the upper and lower engine systems respectively. This partition forms the front of the engineer's cabin, and in the rear of this under the floor is the main petrol collecting tank, through which all petrol from the main tanks passes on the way to the engines.

TAIL UNIT.

The tail unit is of the biplane type with an inter-elevator fitted between the planes, and immediately below the main elevators. The inter-elevator, which is a balanced surface, is connected to the lower elevator, also balanced, by means of struts. These two are connected to the control column.

For trimming the machine, the top elevator is connected to a pair of inter-connected hand wheels in the pilot's cockpit, which are situated one on the outside of each pilot's seat.

The interplane struts on the tail plane form the structure for the two fins behind which are fixed two balanced rudders.

CHASSIS.

The chassis consists of two separate units, each placed below the engines. There are three wheels on each axle, the axle being carried at the centre of a beam built up of platework and attached to another beam of similar construction, which forms the lower member of the chassis structure, by means of the shock absorber.

ENGINES.

The six engines, each a Napier "Lion" of 500 h.p., are arranged as follows :—

One set of two in tandem with tractor and pusher airscrews are mounted on each side of the fuselage between the bottom and middle planes, and two single engines driving tractor airscrews are carried vertically above the tandem engines between the middle and top planes. All engine bearers and mountings are made of spruce.

The tractor airscrews are two-bladed, 12 ft. 6 in. diameter, and the pusher airscrews are four-bladed, 10 ft. 7¼ in. diameter.

The radiators are situated under the engines, and are fitted with radiator shutters to control the temperature of the water.

Fully loaded, the machine weighs approximately 45,000 lbs. Of this 19,000 is disposable load. Tanks are fitted for 10,000 lbs. of petrol, leaving 9,000 lbs. available for passengers and cargo.

Diagram of the Tarrant Spar Construction.

TARRANT, W. G.—*continued*

A Typical Tarrant Wing Fitting, in this Case for the Bottom Central Strut.

PERFORMANCE.

With this load, and under full power, it is estimated that a speed of over 110 m.p.h. will be obtained and that a ceiling or "maximum height obtainable" of 13,000 ft. can be reached.

The estimated figures of climb are as follows :—

Climb to 5,000 feet in $10\frac{1}{2}$ minutes.
Climb to 10,000 feet in $33\frac{1}{2}$ minutes.
Climb to 13,000 feet in just over one hour.

The 10,000 lbs. of petrol is sufficient for 8 hours' flight at an average speed of $113\frac{1}{2}$ m.p.h. or a distance of 900 miles. If the engines be throttled down, or only four engines used at once, the duration can be increased to 12 hours at an average speed of $91\frac{1}{2}$ m.p.h., giving a range of 1,090 miles. By still further throttling down, and flying at the "cruising" or most economical speed, a distance of 1,200 miles can be covered.

GENERAL SPECIFICATION.

The following is a detailed list of the leading dimensions and weights :—

Engines.—Six 500 h.p. Napier "Lion."
Span.—Middle plane, 131 ft. 3 in. ; top and bottom plane, 98 ft. 5 in.
Total Surface of Wings.—4,950 sq. ft.
Overall height.—37 ft. 3 in.
Overall Length.—73 ft. 2 in.
Body—Round Streamline.—Maximum diameter, 11 ft.
Gap (Top and Middle Planes).—14 ft. 9 in.
Gap (Middle and Bottom Planes).—14 ft. 9 in.
Chord.—15 ft. 2 in.
Dihedral.—4 degs. on all planes.
Area of Ailerons—on Middle Plane only.—105 sq. ft. each = 210 sq. ft. total.
Area of Fin.—42 sq. ft. each ; total, 84 sq. ft.
Area of Rudders.—31 sq. ft. each ; total, 62 sq. ft.
Area of Tail Planes.—184 sq. ft. each ; total, 368 sq. ft.
Area of Elevators.—81 sq. ft. each ; total, 162 sq. ft.
Area of Inter Elevator.—54 sq. ft.
Span of Tail Planes.—30 ft.
Gap of Tail Planes.—10 ft.
Wings are set at 3 degs. to the body.
Top tail plane at 2 degs. to the body.
Bottom tail plane at 0 deg. to the body.

WEIGHTS.

				lbs.
Top plane	..	..	..	1903
Bottom plane	..	..	..	2691
Middle plane	..	..	..	1833
Interplane struts		..	..	2543
External bracing wires	..		..	608
	Total	..	..	9578 lbs.

				lbs.
Tail planes	..	..	..	334
Elevators	..	..	..	117
Fins	..	..	..	98
Rudders	..	..	..	40
	Total	..	..	589 lbs.

Fuselage (including bomb girders)			3590	
Chassis	..	..	..	2582
Tail skid	..	..	..	60
Controls	..	..	..	501
	Total	..	..	6733 lbs.

Engine, propellers, radiators, water, etc.	7200	,,
Engine accessories	..	650	,,
Petrol and tanks (1,600 galls.)	..	12662	,,
Oil and tanks, etc. (92 galls.)	..	1050	,,
Crew (five)	..	1080	,,
W.T.	..	100	,,
Guns and ammunition	..	380	,,
Bombs and gears	..	4650	,,
Total	..	44672	,,

Fuselage Longeron and Former Joint.

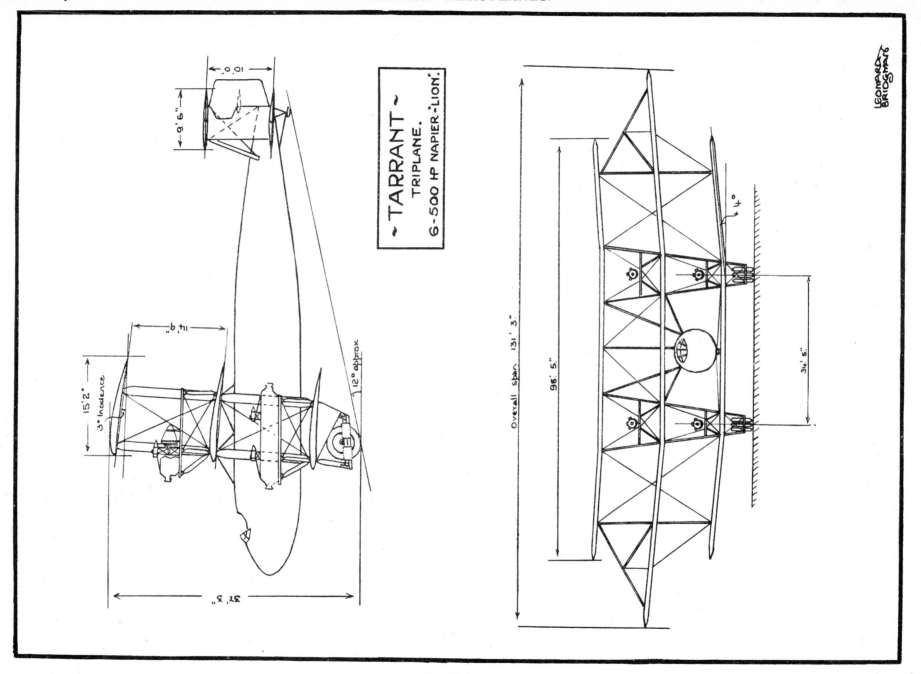

~ TARRANT ~

TRIPLANE.

6-500 H? NAPIER-"LION."

LEONARD BRIDGMAN

10' 0"

9' 6"

11' 4"

15' 2"

3° Incidence.

12° approx

37' 3"

Overall span 131' 3"

96' 5"

34' 5"

4°

V

VICKERS. Vickers, Ltd., Vickers House, Broadway, Westminster.

Aviation Department founded in 1911, under the control of the late Major H. F. Wood, 9th Lancers. Capt. P. D. Acland is now in control. The firm's Commercial Aviation Dept. is under the control of Brig.-General Caddell.

Originally the firm acquired the sole British rights in the R.E.P. machines of M. Robert Esnault Pelterie. Starting from this basis the department under Major Wood developed the series of machines with which the name of Vickers is associated.

The firm suffered a very severe loss by the death of Major Wood, early in 1919.

The Vickers "gun bus," originally produced in 1913, was the only practicable fighting machine in the possession of the R.F.C at the outbreak of war, and rendered invaluable services during the first six months of hostilities.

Details of the more recent machines produced by the firm are given hereafter.

THE VICKERS F.B. 16 H.

The Vickers F.B. 16 H. is a single-seater fighting Scout type. The planes are rather heavily staggered and fitted with two pairs of interplane struts either side of the fuselage. No centre section is fitted, the planes being fixed direct to the inverted Vee type pylons in front of the pilot's seat. The upper plane is well cut away over the pilot's cockpit to give a clear view upwards.

The tail-unit consists of a large fin and unbalanced rudder and a tail plane and divided elevator, the fin and tail plane being well braced above and below with Rafwire lacing.

The elevator controls are outside the fuselage.

The armament consists of two fixed Vickers guns which are fitted inside the fuselage synchronised to fire to the propeller.

Specification.

Type of machine..	Tractor Biplane, single-seater
Name or type No. of machine ..	F.B. 16 H.
Purpose for which intended ..	Fighter.
Span	T. 31 ft.; b. 30 ft.
Gap, maximum and minimum ..	45 ft.
Overall length	21 ft. 8 in.
Maximum height..	8 ft. 1 in.
Chord	T. 5 ft. 4 in.; b. 4 ft. 2 in.
Total surface of wings	272 sq. ft.
Span of tail	11 ft.
Total area of Tail	33.8 sq. ft.
Area of elevators..	15.3 sq. ft.

Front View of the Vickers Single-seat Fighter, type F.B. 16H. (300 h.p. Hispano-Suiza engine.)

Side View of the Vickers Single-seat Fighter, type F.B. 16H.

VICKERS—*continued.*

THE VICKERS F.B. 16 H.—*continued.*

Area of rudder .. .. .. 6.5 sq. ft.
Area of fin .. .. .. 7 sq. ft.
Area of each aileron and total area $2 \times 9.5 + 2 \times 6 = 31$ sq. ft.
Maximum cross section of body. 8 sq. ft.
Horizontal area of body .. .. 36 sq. ft.
Vertical area of body .. · .. 57 sq. ft.
Engine type and h.p. .. .. Hispano-Suiza; 300 h.p.
Airscrew, diam., pitch and revs. .. 8 ft. diam., 6 ft. pitch, 1,875 r.p.m.
Weight of machine empty .. 1,636 lbs.
Load per sq. ft.... .. 8.45 lbs.
Weight per h.p. (300 h.p.) .. 7.65 lbs.
Petrol .. .. Oil
Tank capacity in gallons.. .. Petrol 40 galls; oil 5 galls.

Performance.
Speed low down .. .. 147 m.p.h.
Speed at 10,000 feet .. .. 140 m.p.h.
Speed at 20,000 feet .. ..
Landing Speed.. .. .. 53 m.p.h.

Climb.
To 5,000 feet .. .. .. 3.3 minutes.
To 10,000 feet .. .. .. 7.8 minutes.
To 20,000 feet.. .. .. 23.5 minutes.
Disposable load apart from fuel (including crew) .. 327 lbs.
Total weight of machine loaded .. .. .. 2,300 lbs.

THE VICKER'S "VAMPIRE."

The Vickers "Vampire" is a small single-seater pusher biplane designed primarily for trench fighting.

The small nacelle is directly under the undersurface of the upper plane and is connected to the lower plane by short struts. The tail booms are fitted at the ends of each of the rear inner interplane struts and are parallel in plan view but, in elevation, converge at the fixed tail plane. The chassis is of the customary Vee–type rubber sprung.

Specification.

Type of machine .. .. .. Pusher Biplane, single-seater.
Name or type No. of machine .. "Vampire" B.R. 2.
Purpose for which intended .. Trench fighting.
Span .. .. Top 31 ft. 6 in.; bot. 27ft. 6 in.
Gap, maximum and minimum .. 52 in.
Overall length .. .. 22 ft. 11 in.
Maximum height.. .. .. 9 ft. 5 in.
Chord .. .. Top 5 ft. 6 in.; bot. 4 ft. 6 in.
Total surface of wings .. .. 267 sq. ft.
Span of tail .. .. .. 12 ft. 3 in.
Total area of tail .. .. 38 sq. ft.
Area of elevators .. .. 16 sq. ft.
Area of rudder .. .. .. 6.7 sq. ft.
Area of fin .. .. .. 6.4 sq. ft.
Area of each aileron and total area $(2 \times 12) + (2 \times 6) = 36$ sq. ft.
Maximum cross section of body. 7.6 sq. ft.
Horizontal area of body.. .. 16.6 sq. ft.

Three-quarter Front View of the Vickers' "Vampire" (200 B.R. 2 engine).

Side View of the Vickers' "Vampire" Single-seat Fighter.

VICKERS—*continued.*

THE VICKERS " VAMPIRE."—*continued.*

Vertical area of body	24.5 sq. ft.
Engine type and h.p.	B.R. 2; 200 h.p.
Airscrew, diam., pitch, and revs. .	8.75 ft., 9 ft., 1,300.
Weight of machine empty (including 500 lbs. steel armour)..	1,870 lbs.
Load per sq. ft.	9.1 lbs.
Weight per h p. (228 h.p.) ..	10.7 lbs.
Tank capacity in gallons.. ..	Petrol 29 galls.; oil 6 galls.

Performance.

Speed low down	121 m.p.h.
Speed at 10,000 feet	115 m.p.h.
Landing speed..	54 m.p.h.

Climb.

To 5,000 feet	5 minutes.
To 10,000 feet	12 minutes.
Disposable load apart from fuel (including crew) ..	568 lbs.
Total weight of machine loaded	2,438 lbs.

VICKER'S " VIMY " TWIN-ENGINED BIPLANE.

The Vickers " Vimy " biplane was designed as a long-distance bomber, and, following the usual practice in twin-engined machines, has a single fuselage, carrying the pilot and two gunners, one in the nose and the other just aft of the trailing edge of the main planes.

The engines are housed in " power-eggs," each containing one complete power unit with its respective petrol and oil tanks, carried halfway between the planes, one on either side of the fuselage.

Under each engine-housing is a separate under-carriage consisting of two vees of steel tube, between which an axle and two wheels are slung on shock-absorbers.

To prevent the machine standing on its nose after too fast a landing, a skid is fitted under the nose of the fuselage.

Four large balanced ailerons are fitted to the main planes. The empennage consists of a biplane tail unit with two unbalanced elevators, and turn rudders with no fixed fin-area.

It was on a Rolls-Royce engined Vickers " Vimy " that Capt. John Alcock, D.S.C. and Lieut. Arthur Whitten Brown made the first direct flight across the Atlantic ocean.

The following specifications give particulars of this machine fitted with various types of engine :—

THE VICKERS " VIMY."—(Fiat Engines.)

Type of machine	Twin-engine Biplane.
Name or type No. of machine ..	" Vimy " Fiat
Purpose for which intended ..	Bombing.
Span	67 ft. 2 in.
Gap	10 ft.
Overall length	43 ft. 6½ in.
Maximum height	15 ft. 3 in.
Chord	10 ft. 6 in.

Front View of a Vickers' " Vimy " Bomber. (two Fiat engines, type A. 12 Bis).

Three-quarter Front View of a Fiat-engine Vickers " Vimy " Bomber.

VICKERS—*continued.*

THE VICKERS "VIMY"—(Fiat engines)—*continued.*

Total surface of wings	1,330 sq. ft.
Span of tail	16 ft.
Total area of tail	177.5 sq. ft.
Area of elevators	63 sq. ft. (total).
Area of rudder	21.5 sq. ft. (total).
Area of fin	None.
Area of each aileron and total area	60.5 sq. ft.; 242 sq. ft.
Maximum cross section of body..	3 ft. 9in. by 3 ft. 9 in.
Horizontal area of body	125 sq. ft.
Vertical area of body	120 sq. ft.
Engine type and h.p.	Fiat A/12/Bis.
Airscrew, diam., pitch and revs...	9.4 ft. dia., 5.85 ft. pitch, 1,700 revs.
Weight of machine empty ..	6,426 lbs.
Tank capacity in gallons ..	Petrol 170 galls.; oil 17 galls.

Performance.

Speed low down	98 m.p.h.
Speed at 5,000 feet	96 m.p.h.
Landing speed..	53 m.p.h.

Climb.

To 5,000 feet	14 minutes.
To 10,000 feet..	45 minutes.
Disposable load apart from fuel	2,479 lbs. (including crew of 3)
Total weight of machine loaded.	10,300 lbs.
Load per sq. ft.	7.75 lbs.
Weight per h.p, ...	17.2 lbs.

Three-quarter view from Aft of a Vickers "Vimy" Bomber (Fiat engines).

THE VICKERS "VIMY."—(Hispano-Suiza Engines)

Type of machine..	Twin-engine Biplane.
Name or type No. of machine..	"Vimy" Hispano.
Purpose for which intended ..	Bombing.
Span	67 ft. 2 in.
Gap	10 ft.
Overall length	43 ft. 6½ in.
Maximum height	15 ft. 3 in.
Chord	10 ft. 6 in.
Total surface of wings ..	1330 sq. ft.
Span of tail	16 ft.
Total area of tail	177.5 sq. ft.
Area of elevators	63 sq. ft. (total).
Area of rudders	21.5 sq. ft. (total).
Area of fin	None.
Area of each aileron and total area	60.5 sq. ft.; 242 sq. ft.
Maximum cross section of body.	3 ft. 9 in. by 3 ft. 9 in.
Horizontal area of body ..	125 sq. ft.
Vertical area of body ..	120 sq. ft.
Engine type and h.p.	Two 200 h.p. Hispano-Suiza.
Airscrew, diam., pitch and revs. .	9.25 ft. dia. 5 ft. pitch, 2,100 revs.
Weight of machine empty ..	5,420 lbs.
Tank capacity in gallons ..	Petrol 91; oil 14

Performance.

Speed low down	90 m.p.h.
Speed at 5,000 feet	87 m.p.h,
Landing speed	51 m.p.h.

Climb.

To 5,000 feet	23.5 minutes.
Disposable load apart from fuel	2,900 lbs. (including crew of 3)
Total weight of machine ..	9,120 lbs.
Load per sq. ft.	6.85 lbs.
Weight per h.p.	22.8 lbs.

VICKERS—*continued*.

THE VICKERS "VIMY."—(Rolls-Royce Engines)

Type of machine	Twin-engine Biplane.
Name or type No. of machine ..	" Vimy " Rolls.
Purpose for which intended ..	Bombing.
Span	67 ft. 2 in.
Gap	10 ft.
Overall length	44 ft.
Maximum height	15 ft.
Chord	10 ft. 6 in.
Total surface of wings	1,330 sq. ft.
Span of tail	16 ft.
Total area of tail	177.5 sq. ft.
Area of elevators..	63 sq. ft. (total).
Area of rudder	21.5 sq. ft.
Area of fin	None.
Area of each aileron and total area	60·5 sq. ft.; 242 sq. ft.
Maximum cross section of body..	3 ft 9 in. by 3 ft. 9 in.
Horizontal area of body ..	125 sq. ft.
Vertical area of body	120 sq. ft.
Engine type and h.p.	Two 350 h.p. " Eagle Mark VIII " Rolls-Royce.
Airscrew, diam., pitch, and revs .	10.5 ft. dia., 9 ft. 11 in. pitch, 1,950 revs.
Weight of machine empty ..	7,100 lbs.
Tank capacity in gallons.. ..	Petrol 452; oil 18.
Performance.	
Speed low down	103 m.p.h.
Speed at 5,000 feet	98 m.p.h.
Landing speed..	56 m·p.h.
Climb.	
To 5,000 feet	21.9 minutes.
Disposable load apart from fuel.	2,010 lbs. (including crew of 3)
Total weight of machine loaded.	12,500 lbs.
Load per sq. ft.	9.4 lbs.
Weight per h.p.	17.8 lbs.

Side View of a Vickers " Vimy " Bomber (two 375 h.p. Rolls-Royce " Eagle " engines).

VICKERS VIMY AEROPLANE

44′-0′

6′-0″

19′-0″

67′-2″

10′-0″

SCALE

FEET

FORD-JONES '9.

Front View of the " Vimy " passenger-carrier (Rolls-Royce engines)· Note the deep streamlined body.

The Luggage Door of the " Vimy " passenger-carrier.

The Cabin unit of the " Vimy " passenger-carrier.

Side View of the " Vimy " passenger-carrier (Rolls-Royce engines).

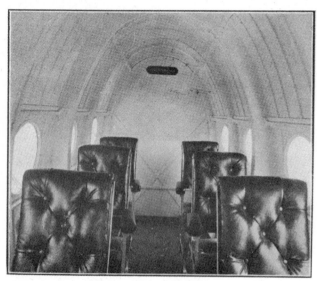

The Interior of the Cabin of the "Vimy" unfurnished.

The "Vimy" Biplane (Rolls-Royce engines) on which Captain Alcock and Lieut. Brown, R.A.F., flew the Atlantic.

The "Vimy" passenger-carrier in the air.

A section of the rings on which the Cabin structure is built.

The Interior of the Cabin furnished.

THE WESTLAND AIRCRAFT WORKS,

Yeovil, Somerset.

Branch of famous engineering firm of J. B. Petter.

Under the management of Mr. R. A. Bruce, M.I.M.E., A.M.I.C.E., M.Sc., formerly of British and Colonial Aeroplane Co., Ltd., and previously connected with the Brennan Torpedo and Brennan Gyroscopic Monorail.

During the period of hostilities the firm built numerous machines to the specifications of the Air Department, Admiralty, and have in addition produced the machines hereafter described to their own designs.

THE WESTLAND "WAGTAIL."

The Westland "Wagtail" was designed in answer to a general demand for a fast, quick-climbing, general utility single-seater fighter.

It conforms in general arrangement with most other machines of this type.

The pilot's view is very good both upward and downward, more than half the centre section being left open. Main planes of equal span are fitted, the upper plane having a dihedral of 5 degrees, whereas the lower plane is flat, i.e., no dihedral.

THE WESTLAND "WAGTAIL."

Specification.

Type of machine	Single-seater Tractor Scout. Aeroplane.	
Name and type No. of machine ..	Westland "Wagtail."	
Purpose for which intended ..	High altitude fighting.	
Span	23 ft. 2 in.	
Gap .. .. { maximum .	At outer strut 4 ft. 6 in.	
{ minimum .	Centre section 4 ft.	
Overall length	18 ft. 11 in.	
Maximum height	8 ft.	
Chord	4 ft. 6 in.	
Total surface of wings	190 sq. ft.	
Span of tail	7 ft. 10¾ in.	
Total area of tail, incldg. elevators	25 sq. ft.	
Area of elevators	9.5 sq. ft.	
Area of rudder	4.4 sq. ft.	

Area of fin.	2.1 sq. ft.	
Area of each aileron	6 sq. ft.	
Total area of ailerons	24 sq. ft.	
Maximum cross section of body ..	7.1 sq. ft.	
Horizontal area of body	29.3 sq. ft.	
Vertical area of body	36.5 sq. ft.	
Engine type and h.p.	170 b.h.p. "Wasp" Fixed Radial.	
Airscrew, diam., pitch and revs. .	Pitch 2070 m/m., diam. 2590 m/., revs. 1,900.	
Weight of machine empty ..	965 lbs. (including 219 lbs. for fuel and oil).	
Weight of machine empty (without fuel and oil).	746 lbs.	
Load per sq. ft.	Fully loaded 7 lbs.	
Weight per h.p.	7.7 lbs.	
Tank capacity in hours	2½ hours at 15,000 feet.	
Tank capacity in gallons.. ..	Petrol 26 galls.; oil 3 galls.	

Three-quarter View from rear of a Westland "Wagtail" Single-seat fighter.

Side View of the Westland "Wagtail" Single-seater fighter. (170 h.p. A.B.C. Wasp engine). 197a

Performance,
Speed at 10,000 feet	125 m.p.h.	
Landing speed..	50 m.p.h.	

Climb.
To 5,000 feet	3½ minutes.	
To 10,000 feet..	7½ minutes.	
To 17,000 feet..	17 minutes.	

Disposable load apart from fuel 365 lbs. { Pilot . . 180 lbs. Two guns, gear & 1,000 rounds . 160 „ Oxygen . 25 „

Total weight of machine loaded 1,330 lbs.

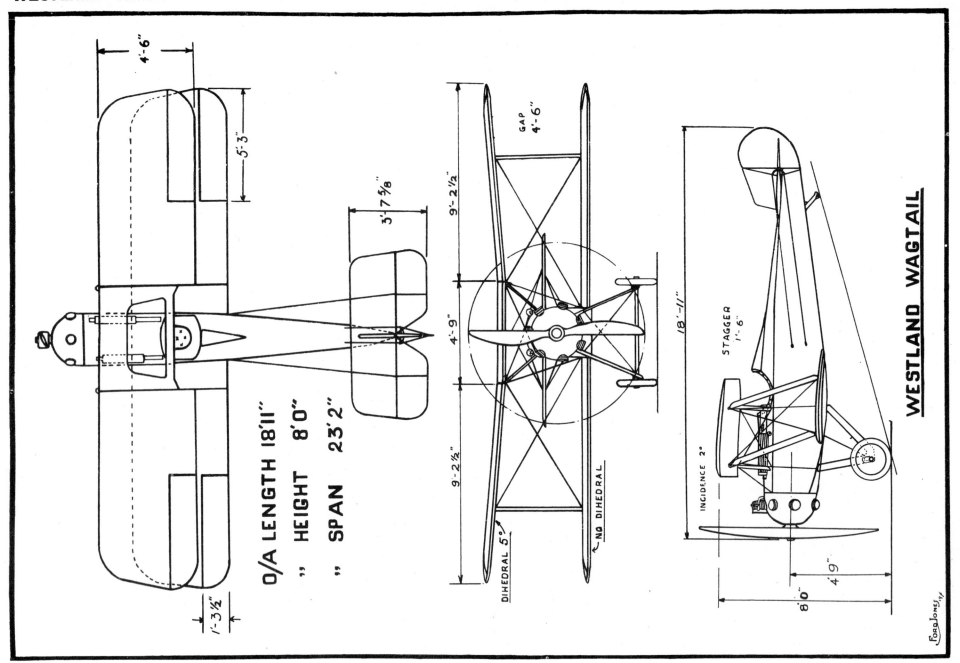

O/A LENGTH 18'11"
  ,, HEIGHT 8'0"
  ,, SPAN 23'2"

WESTLAND WAGTAIL

WESTLAND—*continued.*

WESTLAND SEAPLANE N16.

The Westland seaplane N16 is a small single-seater seaplane fitted with two pontoon floats and a large single tail float, and was designed as a fighter and light bomber for use from seaplane carrier ships.

The fuselage is of normal type, with a pronounced bump in the fairing ahead of the pilot's seat. In this bump is fitted a fixed synchronised Vickers gun.

In order to reduce the space for stowage on board ship, the main planes are made to fold. Both upper and lower planes are of equal span, and two sets of interplane struts are fitted on each side.

The wings are fitted with trailing edge flaps along the whole span, giving a variable camber, which is controlled from the pilot's seat.

Ailerons are fitted to both upper and lower wings,

The Westland N17 seaplane is exactly the same except that the main floats are increased in length, slightly turned up at he rear, and no tail float is fitted.

Specification.

Type of machine	Single-seater Tractor Seaplane Scout.
Name of type of machine ..	Westland Seaplane N.16.
Purpose for which intended ..	Fighter Scout, capable of getting off deck of ships.
Span	31 ft. 3½ in.
Overall length, fuselage horizontal	25 ft. 3½ in.
Overall length resting on tail float	26 ft. 5½ in.
Maximum height ,, ,,	11 ft. 2 in.
Chord	5 ft.
Total surface of wings, includes centre sections	278 sq. ft.
Span of tail	11 ft.
Area of tail plane..	24.5 sq. ft.
Total area of tail, incldg. elevator	42 sq. ft.
Area of elevators	17.5 sq. ft.
Area of rudder	7.5 sq. ft.
Area of fin	6.8 sq. ft.
Area of each outer aileron ..	9.9 sq. ft.
Total area of ailerons	39.6 sq. ft.
Maximum cross section of body..	10¾ sq. ft.
Horizontal area of body ..	44 sq. ft.
Vertical area of body ..	55 sq. ft.
Engine type and h.p.	Air-cooled rotary B.R.1; 150 b.h.p.; 1,240 r.p.m.
Airscrew, diam., pitch and revs. .	Diam. 2,650 m/m., pitch 2,650 m/m., 1,240 r.p.m.

Wing section	R.A.F. 14. Variable camber device.
Weight of machine empty, without fuel and oil	1,460 lbs.
Weight of machine empty, but with 268 lbs. for fuel and oil ..	1,728 lbs.
Load per sq. ft.	7.7 lbs. sq. ft. fully loaded.
Weight per h.p.	14·2 lbs.
Tank capacity in hours	2½—3 approx. ground level.
Tank capacity in gallons.. ..	Petrol 30 galls.; oil 5 galls.

Performance.

Speed low down	108 miles per hour.
Landing speed	50 m.p.h. with no flaps ; 45 m.p.h. with flaps.

Climb,	
To 5,000 feet	10 minutes.
To 10,000 feet	28 minutes.
Disposable load apart from fuel	405 lbs.

Pilot . .	180 lbs.
Bombs&Gear	150 ,,
Gun and 250 rounds.	60 ,,
Sundries	15 ,,

Total weight of machine loaded 2,133 lbs.

Three-quarter Front View of the Westland Seaplane N.16 (150 h.p. B.R.1. rotary engine).

WESTLAND—*continued*.

Three-quarter View from rear of the Westland N.17 Seaplane (150 h.p. B.R.1 engine).   Note the unusual form of the floats.

5'·0"

FRONT

31'· 3½"

2½°

STAGGER 3°

SIDE

7'·6"

25'· 5½"

11'·2" FOLDED

PLAN

WESTLAND   SCOUT

SEAPLANE

5'· 0"

150 H.P.   A.R.1.   ENGINE.

FEET

FORD JONES

Australian Commonwealth.

VICTORIA.

In January, 1913, the Australian Flying Corps was instituted, as a part of the citizen forces.

The force was then designed to consist of 4 officers, 7 warrant officers and sergeants, 32 mechanics.

The school is at Point Cook, Werribee, Victoria. Course includes— mechanics of the aeroplane, aerial motors, meteorology, aerial navigation by compass, aerial photography, signalling, etc.

The first commanding officer was Captain Henry Petre, R.F.C., lent to the Australian Commonwealth Forces. In his absence on active service, Captain Eric Harrison, late of the British and Colonial Aeroplane Co., Ltd., commanded.

An engine-Instruction Class in progress at the Commonwealth Central Flying School at Point Cook.

Early in 1916 it set about providing the personnel, including mechanics and transport drivers, for a complete squadron up to the "establishment" of a squadron of the Royal Flying Corps. Since then a number of full squadrons have been supplied to the R.F.C. and have distinguished themselves greatly on active service.

Several aeroplanes have been built by the mechanics of the School, chiefly of "box-kite" biplane type, and the first aero-engine built in Australia was produced by the Sydney Tarrant Motor Proprietary Co., in September, 1915.

The machines at the Werribee School were mostly *B.E.*'s and *Bristol* box-kites, but various *Maurice Farmans* and *F.E.*'s have been added. Major Harrison (formerly Capt. as mentioned above) was in command at the signing of the Armistice, and later came to England to acquire the latest available knowledge of aeronautical developments.

The Government policy is to encourage the production of aircraft and parts thereof by indigenous firms.

Privately owned aeroplanes have been imported by Mr. Hordern (*Maurice Farman* seaplane), Mr. Delfosse Badgery (*Caudron*), and by various foreign aviators who gave exhibitions.

NEW SOUTH WALES.

A new Military School was opened on Aug. 28th, 1916, by the New South Wales Government, at Richmond, near Sydney.

This school is equipped with American *Curtiss* biplanes.

The chief instructor is Mr. W. J. Stutt, formerly of the British & Colonial Aeroplane Co., Ltd. (Bristol), and later of the Royal Aircraft Factory, Farnborough) himself an Australian.

QUEENSLAND.

A group of aeronautical enthusiasts enrolled themselves in November, 1915, under the title of "The Queensland Volunteer Flying Civilians."

This body built a biplane, somewhat on *Caudron* lines, for training purposes, at Hemmaut, near Brisbane.

Later several of them joined the British Flying Service, four receiving commissioned rank in the R.F.C. and four becoming air mechanics, R.F.C.

CANADA.

MILITARY AVIATION.

In June, 1914, two officers of the Ottawa defence force were sent to Salisbury Plain for instruction, in connection with the proposed establishment of a flying corps, but nothing came of this beginning.

In 1915 a Flying School was started by a Canadian branch of the American Curtiss Co., under the management of the first Canadian pilot, Mr. J. A. D. McCurdy. Here a number of Canadians were trained to fly. Others were trained at Ithaca, New York, at a school founded by the Thomas Bros., two Englishmen from the Argentine, who had started an aeroplane factory there.

In 1917 the R.F.C. opened an official flying school in Canada and here a large number of Canadians were taught to fly by British instructors.

During the winter the bulk of the *personnel* of the school moved to Fort Worth, Texas, U.S.A., but those who remained achieved remarkable results by flying off the snow in standard type military machines mounted on ski instead of wheels, thus proving the possibilities of aeroplanes in winter in snow-covered country.

Canadian pilots in both the R.N.A.S and R.F.C. have done excellent work and have won many decorations, including two V.Cs. Altogether some 14,000 Canadians have become pilots in the Flying Services.

Late in the war an attempt was made to establish a Canadian Naval Air Service, but this was apparently washed out on the signing of the Armistice. The formation of a Canadian Air Force has now been undertaken.

Early in 1919 an Act was passed in the Canadian House of Commons setting up an Air Board, to control flying in Canada.

Various activities are being undertaken in Canada, but at the time of going to press they are all somewhat nebulous, and no actual Air services are being run. It is noteworthy that Canadian railways are taking Parliamentary powers to run air services as tributaries to the railway lines.

A syndicate, largely of American origin, has bought up a number of Canadian military training aeroplanes of American design and is endeavouring (May 1919) to sell them to Canadians, but as they are only elementary training vehicles they cannot be expected to be of use on regular air services.

AERIAL SOCIETIES.

The Aero Club of Canada, Toronto. Which represents the Royal Aero Club of Great Britain and Ireland, in issuing aviators' certificates, &c.

The Aeronautical Society of Canada, c/o. M. P. Logan, 99, Gloucester Street, Toronto.

McGill Aviation Club, McGill University, Montreal.

MANUFACTURE.

The Canadian Curtiss Aeroplane Co., Ltd., of Toronto was the first Canadian firm to manufacture aircraft. It was working on large contracts for the British Navy and Army, and has produced land-going aeroplanes and seaplanes (flying-boat type), with two or more engines apiece.

Later the Polson Ironworks Co., of Toronto, began to build aeroplanes, and their first production (in 1916) was a biplane with an American Sturtevant engine. The fuselage of this machine was built entirely of steel tubing. The machine was taken to the United States for test, and gave good results, but one gathers that the firm has given up aircraft work.

The only other firm of which one can learn is :—

CANADIAN AEROPLANES, Ltd.

Toronto, Ont.

President : Sir William Baillie. Chief Engineer : F. G. Ericson.

This firm was organised late in 1916 to supply a portion of the demand of the British Empire and her Allies for aeroplanes and seaplanes, particularly for training and anti-submarine defence. At the time the Armistice was signed, Canadian Aeroplanes, Ltd., were producing 350 training aeroplanes of the Canadian Avro and Curtiss types and eight F.5 L. flying boats per month. The company was then employing 2,300 workers.

The whole of the share capital of the company was vested in the Imperial Munitions Board, which advanced a million dollars to finance the initial operations of the firm.

CANADIAN TRAINING AEROPLANE (Modified Curtiss J.N.4.)

General description.

Wing area, including ailerons	358.9 sq. ft.
Wing span overall (top)	43 ft. 7$\frac{5}{16}$ in.
Wing span overall (lower)	33 ft. 11$\frac{1}{4}$ in.
Wing chord	59$\frac{1}{2}$ in.
Overall length of machine	26 ft. 10$\frac{1}{2}$ in.
Net weight machine empty	1,170 lbs.
Gross weight per sq. ft. of surface, including ailerons	5.1 lbs.
Gross weight, machine and load	1,850 lbs.
Dihedral angle	1 degree.
Sweepback	0 degree.
Stagger	9$\frac{1}{2}$ degrees.
Curtiss Model O.X Engine	**90 B.H.P.**
Weight of engine	350 lbs.
Weight per h.p.	3.88 lbs.
Bore and stroke	4 × 5.
Normal speed at full motor load	1,400 r.p.m.
Provided capacity, fuel tank	37 gallons.
Fuel consumption per hour, throttle wide open	8.37 gallons.
Fuel consumption per hour, average flight	6 gallons.
Oil consumption per hour	$\frac{1}{2}$ gallon.
Provided oil capacity, crankcase	4 gallons.

Performance.

Horse power at 1,400 r.p.m.	90 h.p. rated.
Speed, maximum	85 m.p.h.
Speed, minimum	40 m.p.h.
Climb in 10 minutes	4,000 feet.
Useful load	680 lbs.

Distribution of useful load (may be changed if desired).

Fuel	200 lbs.
Water	35 lbs.
Oil	30 lbs.
Pilot	175 lbs.
Passenger and other load	240 lbs.
	680 lbs.

Maximum tank capacity at full motor load	4.4 hours.
Tank capacity for ordinary service flight	6.2 hours.
Maximum, tank capacity for duration flight	9 hours.

NEW ZEALAND.

Little flying was done in New Zealand until the outbreak of war. One *Bleriot*, 80 h.p., was presented in 1913 to the New Zealand Government by the *Standard*, London.

Mr. Scotland imported a *Caudron* biplane and flew in 1915.

The most notable New Zealand pilot of the early days, was Capt. J. J. Hammond, who, flying on active service for a considerable time, was employed in experimentally testing new types of aircraft. He was killed in 1918 while flying an American aeroplane in the United States.

New Zealand has contributed largely by voluntary subscriptions to the purchase of aeroplanes for the R.F.C. and has supplied a relatively large number of pilots to the Flying Services during the war. These have nearly all received their initial training at either Walsh Bros. School at Auckland, or at the Canterbury School.

THE NEW ZEALAND FLYING SCHOOL

(WALSH BROS. & DEXTER, LTD.),

AUCKLAND, NEW ZEALAND.

Walsh Brothers (Leo A. and Vivian C.) having been interested in the early developments of flying, purchased sufficient materials from Howard Wright, England, in 1910, to enable the construction of a biplane to be commenced in Auckland in August of that year.

The machine was completed by January, 1911, and on Feb. 5th (1911), V.C. Walsh made a short flight. The incident was naturally of great interest to the builders, inasmuch as it was the first flight to be made in this dominion.

The machine was equipped with a 60 h.p. E.N.V. motor (British), which ran excellently.

In connection with the early experiments in learning to operate this machine, it was soon found, by hard experience, that the English design of undercarriage was quite unsuitable for the rough ground used as a flying field.

After having made good progress in gaining knowledge of the control of the machine in the air, the pilot (Vivian) had the ill-luck to capsize the 'plane when running on the ground at high speed just preparatory to taking off. The short skids caught in a depression, and the pilot fortunately crawled out of the complete wreckage unhurt.

Several months were then occupied in re-building the machine completely, and further trials were commenced. Good progress was being made when developments occurred which brought the experiments to a close.

In common with most pioneers of aviation at the period mentioned, financial assistance had been obtained from other parties, and the brothers met with the usual discouraging demands for speedy recoupment for the outlay incurred. Impossible flight and financial conditions were imposed by the financiers—a not uncommon proceeding in other parts of the world during the early days—and a breach of relations followed,

resulting in a complete loss to the brothers of all financial interests in their handiwork. The machine in other hands promptly came to grief, and was damaged beyond repair.

The difficulties surrounding the operation and construction of this first machine were accentuated by the difficulty of obtaining not only information on the art of flying, but most necessary materials to repair breakages, on account of the great distance separating the local experimenters from other centres of flying activities. With no assistance obtainable from anyone versed in flying to fall back upon, it was naturally a case of feeling the way step by step. Incidentally, it may be mentioned that the brothers' financial resources were extremely limited, and on many occasions their enthusiasm was sorely taxed in consequence.

This set-back did not have the effect of causing the brothers to lose interest in the progress of aviation. They determined to tackle it from a different angle, and in August, 1913, commenced the building of a flying boat of their own design. As the construction of a shed in which to carry out building operations, and the actual building of the machine could only be done in the brothers' spare time, progress was naturally somewhat slow, and although on the outbreak of war every effort was made to accelerate the completion of the machine, it was not until Dec., 1914, that the flying boat was ready for trials.

On Jan. 1st, 1914, a successful flight was made by V. C. Walsh—the first to be made in New Zealand—on a seaplane.

Part of the Staff and Equipment of the New Zealand Flying School at Auckland, N.Z., in 1918.

Adverse weather conditions and minor adjustments delayed progress to a certain extent, but the pilot having demonstrated the stability of the machine and the success of the design generally, commenced carrying passengers on March 14th, 1915.

Upon the outbreak of hostilities, the brothers, fully believing that aircraft would play a most important part in the war, devoted themselves entirely to the completion of the flying boat and subsequent experiments in connection with learning to operate it. Having successfully overcome the initial difficulties, and proved both machine and pilot capable of use in the training of aviators for war service, the brothers urged the New Zealand Government to recognise the importance of the work.

At the time the importance of military aviation did not appeal to the N.Z. Authorities. The brothers therefore cabled the Royal Aero Club asking for certificates to be issued to pupils in New Zealand who were able to comply with the usual conditions.

Owing to the recognition of their efforts by the Royal Aero Club, the brothers were able to inform the Imperial Government that they were in a position to train and despatch suitable candidates for the Royal Flying Corps possessed of certificates issued by the Royal Aero Club. (There being no Naval Establishment in New Zealand, the military authorities did not care for candidates leaving the dominion to enter any other than a military branch of the service, thus the apparent anomaly of men trained upon seaplanes entering the R.F.C.)

After the exchange of various communications, the Imperial Government notified the brothers that suitable candidates for the R.F.C. from New Zealand would be accepted, and that the usual Imperial grant of £75 towards the expense of qualifying would be available to accepted candidates, and that all expenses in connection with transport to England and training charges subsequently would be borne by the British Government.

It was not until October, 1915, that arrangements could be completed to enable the brothers actively to engage in the training of men destined for the Imperial Air Service.

The *Walsh* flying boat, equipped with a 70 h.p. Anzani motor, was used in the early training operations. Subsequently a *Caudron* biplane, fitted with a 60 h.p. Le Rhone motor, was purchased. Floats were built at the school and the machine converted to a hydro-aeroplane. Good progress was made with these two machines, but the difficulty of obtaining spares for the motors frequently hampered operations.

A *Curtiss* 90 h.p. flying boat was later added to the equipment, and two of the pupils trained by V. C. Walsh joined the staff in order to assist in the training work.

The initial preparation of candidates for the Imperial Air Service created interest throughout the dominion, and the school had considerable difficulty in coping with the increasing number of applicants for admission, many of whom being young men ineligible for enlistment in the N.Z. Forces on account of

their youth, but who were eager and anxious to serve their country in some capacity, and who recognised that an opening was available to serve in the R.F.C.

The difficulties and delays experienced in obtaining suitable materials and engine spares interfered very materially with the school work from time to time. Many spares and replacements had to be made in the school workshops. Notwithstanding these somewhat frequent delays and interruptions, a steady supply of certificated men were leaving for England, and the demand for tuition constantly increased.

Mr. R. A. Dexter, of Auckland, N.Z., has been associated with the brothers Walsh since 1914. The financial assistance and support given by this gentleman was of great assistance in enabling the brothers to bring the construction and operation of the flying boat built in that year to a successful issue. The efforts of the founders to establish the school were helped by the financial support of Mr. Dexter.

The continued expansion of the undertaking necessitated further capital being provided. A limited liability company was formed at the latter end of 1917, and in a short time the capital was fully subscribed by well-wishers of the school throughout the dominion.

The strengthening of the financial resources enabled the construction of further machines, provision of additional workshops, and an ample supply of engines, spares, and construction materials to be carried out. At the time of the signing of the Armistice the equipment included :—

Two twin-float hydro-aeroplanes, equipped with six-cylinder 125 h.p. A 5 Hall-Scott motors.

One *Walsh* flying boat (nearing completion) equipped with a six-cylinder 125 h.p. A 5 motor, Hall-Scott.

One *Walsh* flying boat equipped with a four-cylinder 100 h.p. A 7a motor, Hall-Scott.

One *Walsh* flying boat (the original flying boat), previously equipped with a 70 h.p. Anzani motor, and now fitted with a four-cylinder 100 h.p. A 7a motor, Hall-Scott.

One *Walsh* flying boat (for solo work) fitted with 70 h.p. Anzani motor.

One *Curtiss* flying boat equipped with 90 h.p. OX 5 Curtiss motor.

Although the school is only on a small scale, it represents a considerable expenditure of energy and unremitting work in overcoming the many handicaps that have had to be surmounted, and no little credit is due to the members of the school staff, who have loyally and enthusiastically supported the founders in their efforts to promote aviation in this dominion generally, and in particular to aid in contributing to the winning of the War in the Air.

As regards the *personnel* (members of the staff) :—Leo A. Walsh, Director of the School and Managing Director of the Company ; Vivian C. Walsh, Chief Pilot and Works Manager ;

M. Matthews, P. R. Going and G. B. Bolt, Flight Instructors ; R. Johnston, Mechanical Instructor.

Many of the ex-pupils have done excellent work at the Front. Although the school records are not complete, information has been received of the following decorations awarded to ex-pupils, details of which may, doubtless, be found in the Honours List :—

Major K. L. Caldwell, M.C., D.F.C. (succeeded to the command of the 74th Squadron after Major Bishop).

Captain C. G. Callender, Order of the Silver Crown of Italy (recently O.C. 1st School of Aerial Gunnery, Hythe).

Captain M. C. McGregor, M.C., D.F.C. (for some time in the 85th Squadron, Major Ball's).

Captain H. W. Collier, M.C. (squadron unknown).

Captain W. W. Cook, M.C. (squadron unknown).

Captain H. F. Drewitt, M.C. (squadron unknown.)

Capt. R. B. Bannerman, D.F.C. and Bar (squadron unknown).

Several other ex-pupils have made excellent fighting pilots, and may have gained distinction that we are not aware of. The foregoing honours list may be incomplete, and the men mentioned may have been awarded further decorations of which the firm have no record.

In proportion to the numbers trained at this school, the progress as military aviators of ex-pupils has been a record of achievement, and all concerned with the institution are naturally very proud of this fact.

THE CANTERBURY AVIATION CO.

The Canterbury (N.Z.) Aviation Company, Ltd., was formed in 1917 to equip and run a flying school in Canterbury. Ground was secured at Sockburn, four miles or so out of Christchurch, and a *Caudron* with 60-h.p. Anzani imported. Later other machines were also imported and much good training work was done.

Mr. Hill, who learned to fly at Hendon, was engaged as instructor and manager. He was killed in an accident in 1918, but the school instruction is being carried on by his former pupils.

Since the cessation of the war the number of pupils has fallen off considerably, but it is believed that the return of New Zealand aviators from the war will give a fresh impetus to flying.

The immediate difficulty in the way of flying in New Zealand is that all engines have to be imported, and considerable delay is, therefore, inevitable in obtaining engines and spares.

New Zealand affords great opportunities for aviators, especially for flying-boat services round the coast, which, owing to indented nature, provides excellent harbours.

INDIA.

Military Aviation.—A large number of officers belonging to the Indian Army have qualified as pilots. A flying school was started at Sitapur, but on the outbreak of war all the officers came to England and joined up with the R.F.C. These officers have all distinguished themselves by good work. Apparently the Sitapur School and one at Lahore are now in operation. Many aerodromes exist along the North-West Frontier.

A detachment of the R.F.C. came into action late in 1916 in operations against troublesome hill tribes. The aeroplanes were used largely as actual weapons of offence, with bombs and machine-guns, as well as being used for reconnaissance, and their presence had very considerable effect in subduing the trouble.

R.A.F. detachments played a highly important part in the attack by Afghan troops in May, 1919. Bomb raids were made on Kabul, Jellalabad, and other important Afghan towns, as well as on camps and on troops on the march. So great was the effect of these aerial attacks that after a few days of them the Amir of Afghanistan sued for peace.

Private Aviation.—In the past, two or three home-made machines appeared, and one or two were imported, but all are now extinct, as private flying is prohibited.

THE UNION OF SOUTH AFRICA.

Military Aviation.—Officers of the Union Defence Force were trained in England by the R.F.C. in 1914. Some of them served in Flanders early in the war, and afterwards were formed into a South African Aviation Corps, which was built up of mechanics from the Royal Naval Air Service and untrained men from South Africa. Certain R.N.A.S. officers were also lent to the S.A.A.C. The Corps did excellent work in German S.W. Africa, and afterwards came to England where most of it was absorbed into the R.F.C. At a later date a portion of it was used in East African operations, where the South African Squadron, comprising a large proportion of Boers as well as Anglo-South Africans, under Major Wallace, D.S.O., a South African pilot, has won considerable distinction. Boer officer-aviators in the R.F.C. have also distinguished themselves highly in France and elsewhere.

Private Aviation.—John Weston is a qualified pilot, and imported sundry aeroplanes to the Orange Free State, besides building some machines there. He has been on active service, at first with the S.A. Flying Corps, then with the R.N.A.S., and later as an R.A.F. officer, since the outbreak of war.

In 1912, Capt. Guy Livingston (later Brig. General R.A.F.) went to South Africa with Mr. Compton Paterson and Mr. E. F. Driver, and organised exhibition flights all over Cape Colony, the Transvaal and the Orange Free State. These exhibitions, which were later continued by Mr. Paterson alone, did much to influence the Government in forming the South African F.C. Mr. Paterson also established a school at Kimberley where he gave their first instruction to Major Wallace (mentioned above) and various other South African officers who have since distinguished themselves highly.

A number of Aeroplanes have been presented to the Royal Flying Corps by the Overseas Club as the result of subscriptions raised in British Colonies and Dependencies, such as the West Indies, the Malay States, East Africa, &c.

BULGARIAN.

In the Balkan War, 1912-13, Bulgaria hastily organised an aviation corps, the pilots being chiefly foreigners, French, Russian, Italian, and British,—but no Germans. The observers were generally Bulgarian officers. This corps, though necessarily lacking in military organisation, proved very useful on several occasions. After that war, aviation was neglected till the Great War began. The corps was then reorganised, with German assistance.

Military Aviators.—The early Bulgarian aviators were trained in France and England, and latterly a number of Bulgarians were trained in flying and observing in Germany. The Bulgarians themselves do not seem to be able to fly with any skill.

Early Military Aeroplanes.—(Monos.) *Bleriot* and *Bristol.*
(Biplanes) *Albatros*, *Farman*, and *Bristol.*
During the 1914-1918 war the aeroplanes used by the Bulgarian Army were all of German or Austrian make, and appear to have been piloted by Germans or Austrians, judging by captures made in the Balkan war area.

DANISH.

(Scandinavian pages Revised by E. Hildesheim, B.A.)

Aerial Societies :—

Det Danske Aeronautiske Selskab, 34 Amaliegade, Copenhagen.

Aerial Journals :—

Auto : 12, Rosengaarden, Copenhagen.
Motor : 42 Vimmelskaft, Copenhagen.

AVIATORS.

(The numbers are, when not otherwise stated, those issued by the Danish Aero Club).

Svendsen (1)	Lünd-Hansen (29)	O. F. Möller (55)
Thorup (2)	Foltman (30)	G. Erlind (56)
Nervö (3)	Bjarkow (31)	H. J G. S. Erlind (57)
Nielsen (4)	Buhl (32)	W. G. G. H. Watervall (58)
Severinsen (5)	Engberg (33)	C. Bohnstedt Petersen (59)
Ullidtz (6)	Larsen (34)	
Ussing (7)	Sætter-Lassen (35)	C. J. L. Jansen (60)
Christiansen (8)	Eivil (36)	
Laub (9)	Koch (37)	
Prince Axel (10)	Möller-Jörgensen (38)	Pollner (German certificate No. 657)
Grut (12)	Sörensen (39)	
Hammelev (13)	P. F. Yde (40)	Leth-Jensen (French certificate)
von der Maase (14)	A. J. Rasmussen (41)	
Kofoed-Jensen (15)	A. Andersen (42)	Kraüse-Jensen (French certificate)
Waage-Jensen (16)	J. G. Johansen (43)	
Caspersen (17)	H. I. Hansen (44)	Willing-Nielsen (killed on voluntary service in France, March, 1918)
Ekman (18)	K. U. Hansen (45)	
Gundel (19)	E. Hildesheim (46)	
Jörgensen (20)	R. Houndinghouse Jensen (47)	
Erlind (21)		Hildesheim (Swedish certificate No. 120)
Ehlers (22)	R. Ziemsen (48)	
Hansen (23)	V. A. C. Arndal (49)	Christoffersen (American certificate, killed 1916).
Stockfleth (24)	C. C. J. Förslev (50)	
Friese (25)	R. Rasmussen (51)	
Flor-Jacobsen (26)	H. R. M. Herschind (52)	Uffe (killed on voluntary service in France, 11/9/1915).
Holfelt (27)	K. R. K. Höyer (53)	
Bildsöe (28)	L. Sörensen (54)	

Killed.

1913. 10/10.	1918.
Birch	Kabell
	Larsen
1915. 27/7.	Ekmanen
Hoeck	Ubbesen
	Caroc
	Friese
1917. 27/6.	
Hammelev	1919
Stockfleth	Flohr-Jacobsen

Flying Grounds :—

Christianshaven by Copenhagen.
Lundtofte.
Avedöre.
Viborg.

Army Aeroplanes:—

Caudron, Henry and *Maurice Farman. H. Morane-Saulnier, N. & W., Scea, Vickers.*

Navy Aeroplanes:—

Flying boats, 100—200 h.p. } Danish construction.
Seaplanes   160   ,,

Naval Air Stations:—

Copenhagen, harbour and sheds.
Slipshavn, shed.

Aircraft Companies:—

NIELSEN & WINTHER A/s, Öresundsvej, Copenhagen.
VIKING AEROPLANE & MOTOR CO., 2, Toldbodgade, Copenhagen.

A DANISH SERVICE FLYING BOAT, photographed from another aeroplane.

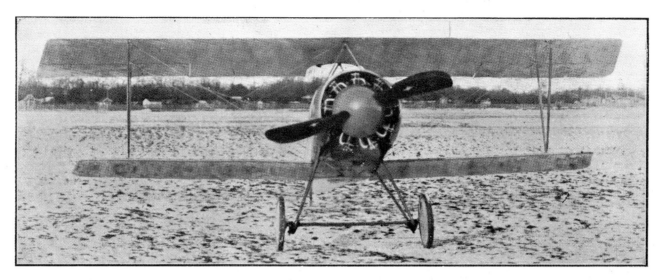

Front View of Nielsen & Winther Nieuport type Chaser Biplane.

Three-quarter Rear View of Nielsen & Winther Nieuport type Chaser Biplane.

A Nielsen & Winther Seaplane.

A Danish Government biplane, designed and built
in the Government Workshops.

210a

A Danish Flying Boat built by the Danish Navy.

A Danish seaplane, built by the Danish Navy.

FRENCH.

Aerial Societies :—

Aéro-Club de France, 35, rue François 1er, Paris VIIIe.

Académie Aéronautique de France, 17, rue de la Présentation, Paris.

Aéronautique Club de France, 58, rue Jean-Jacques Rousseau, Paris.

Ligue Aéronautique de France (Association générale aéronautique, Comité national pour l'Aviation militaire, et Ligue nationale aérienne réunis), 35, rue François 1er, Paris.

Société des Aeronautes du Siège.

Aéro Club du Nord, 11, contour Saint-Martin, Roubaix.

Aéro Club du Rhône, 4, quai des Pêcheries, Lyon.

Aéro Club du Sud-Ouest, 2, place de la Comedie, Bordeaux.

Société Française de Navigation Aérienne, 19, rue Blanche, Paris.

Société d'Encouragement a l'Aviation.

Stella (Aéro-Club Féminin), 6, rue de l'Amiral-Courbet, Paris.

Union Aéronautique des Pilotes et Observateurs de la Guerre (U.A.P.O.G.), 35, rue François 1er, Paris.

Chambre Syndicale des Industries Aéronautiques, 5, rue Denis-Poisson, Paris XVIIe.

Aerial Journals :—

L'Aerophile (Revue Technique et Pratique des Locomotions Aériennes), 35, Rue François 1er. Directour, M. Georges Besançon. Appears fortnightly.

Bulletin mensuel de la Ligue Aéronautique de France.

Principal Flying Grounds :—

Amberieu.—(Military ground.) (Ain.)

Antibes.

Avor (Camp d').—Military ground.

Belfort.—Military ground.

Betheny (près Reims).

Biscarosse (Landes).—Ecole militaire.

Bordeaux.—(Military ground.) La Croix d'Hins.

Bourget (Le), près Paris.—Military ground.

Bron (Lyon).—Military ground.

Buc (près Versailles).

Cazaux (Gironde).—Ecole de Tir Aérien.

Chalais-Meudon.—(Matériel Aérostatique Militaire.)

Chalons (Camp de).—Military ground.

Chartres.—Military school.

Chateauroux (Indre).—Military school.

Compiègne-Corbeaulieu (Oise).

Principal Flying Grounds (*continued*) :—

Crotoy (Le) (Somme).—Caudron and military school.

Douai (La Brayelle, Nord).—Military ground.

Etampes (Seine et Oise).—Farman and military school.

Fréjus (Var).—Naval Station.

Issy les Moulineaux (Paris).—Military ground.

Istres-Miramas, Bouches du Rhône.—Military school.

Juan les Pins.—Seaplane station.

Juvisy, near Paris.—Military ground.

Mailly (Camp de) (Aube).—Centre militaire.

Moisson (Seine et Oise).

Mourmelon (Marne).—Military ground.

Nancy.—Military ground.

Nanterre (Establissement central de l'Aéronautique militaire), près Paris.

Pau.—Military ground.

Reims.—Military ground.

Romorantin.—American ground.

Saint Cyr (Seine et Oise), près Versailles.—Ateliers de réparations de l'aéronautique militaire et dirigeables.

Villacoublay (Seine et Oise), près Versailles.—Military ground.

Vineuil (Chateauroux, Indre).—Military school.

Direction de l'Aéronautique Militaire (et Civile) :—
280, Boulevard Saint-Germain (Paris).

212a

FRENCH MILITARY AND NAVAL AVIATION.

(By JEAN LAGORGETTE.)

Military aviation in France dates from 1910. Up to then, outside four balloon sections organised by Colonel Hirschauer, a few soldiers—some of them officers—interested themselves personally and individually in the testing and piloting of aeroplanes.

On January 1st, 1910, the Aero Club of France instituted the regulations concerning pilots' certificates, and it is in January and February, 1910, that the birth of military aviation may be placed, by the formation of the first "phalanx" of military aviators. A number of officers who had passed for their certificates took part in various tests, such as the Circuit de l'Est, and did splendid performances, in spite of frequent disaster.

THE FIRST MILITARY USE OF AEROPLANES.

In September, 1910, there took place the first aerial manœuvres in Picardie, and as a result of the experience it was concluded that avions (military aeroplanes) could be used in war, and that it was important to develop their employment.

On October 20th, 1910, General Roques was nominated to the new post of Permanent Inspector of Military Aeronautics (Inspecteur Permanent de l'Aéronautique Militaire).

In 1911, there were numerous fine performances, the first regional schools for military aviation were formed, then came regional manœuvres, flights by escadrilles [An escadrille does not quite correspond to a British squadron.—Ed.] under Colonel Etévé, the Paris-Rome flight and the European Circuit by Naval Ensign Conneau, the Grand Manœuvres of 1911, cavalry manœuvres at the Camp de Mailly, competitions for the test of co-operation of aeroplanes and artillery, and finally the Military Competition, in which the machines had to satisfy arduous conditions.

The Department of Inspection of Military Aeronautics was created under the Minister of War, and was placed under the control of General Roques, later himself Minister of War. The flying personnel was recruited in various Arms and was not organised into a special Corps. It was without distinct organisation, but it had modified autonomy. The materiel depended at the same time on the artillery and on the engineers.

THE RECONSTRUCTION OF 1912.

On February 2nd, 1912, M. Millerand, Minister of War, co-ordinated this embryonic organisation, of which he maintained the general lines. He created a special bureau attached to the engineers to deal with materiel. He created aviation parks, central and secondary, with sheds for the machines. The first of these parks was installed in March, at Verdun, with repair shops, stores, etc.

At the end of February, the Association Générale Aéronautique took the initiative in organising a National Subscription to present to the Army aeroplanes, landing grounds with sheds, and funds for instruction. It was seconded by Le Comité National Pour L'Aviation Militaire, under the presidency of Sénateur-aviateur Reymond and by the Press generally.

At the end of March, M. Millerand, Minister of War, fixed the rules for the recruiting of personnel. Colonel Hirschauer was then nominated Permanent Inspector of Aeronautics, and on June 29th, 1912, the Women's Aero Club, known as the Stella, presented to him a flag for the aeronautic troops.

PROGRESS IN 1912.

In the second half-year of 1911, the number of pilots and pupils were 120, and between them they had covered a distance of 300,000 kilometres in that period. At the end of June, 1912, there were 250 aviators, or more than double the number, and in this first half-year they had covered 650,000 kilometres.

Commencing with June 25th, 1912, the test for military aviation certificates became more rigorous. It included a triangular voyage of 200 kilometres in two journeys or more ; two voyages of 150 kilometres in a straight line, and 45 minutes flying at a height of at least 800 m. The commissaries at the start and finish were agreed upon by the Aero Club of France.

At this time, M. Michelin, the famous tyre manufacturer, with his usual foresight, presented a handsome prize for a competition for bomb dropping.

THE AERONAUTICAL ESTABLISHMENT.

On August 28th, 1912, a decree by the President of the Republic created ten Aeronautic Sections, composing (with seven companies already existing) three Groups forming Aviation Corps—the first at Versailles, the second at Reims, and the third at Lyon.

Headquarter's Staff was composed of Lieut.-Col. Bouttieaux (1st Group) ; Lieut.-Col. Breton (2nd Group) ; and Lieut.-Col. Estienne (3rd Group). An administrative personnel was included in the scheme.

Lieut.-Col. Voyer was nominated Director of Aeronautical Matériel at Chalais-Meudon, which became ultimately the S.F.A. (Service des Fabrications de l'Aéronautique). [This corresponded almost exactly in its scheme, and in its ultimate effect with the Royal Aircraft Factory at Farnborough.—Ed.]

NAVAL AERONAUTICS.

Naval aeronautics were organised as from March, 1913, and comprised a double system of observation with airships and

A group of French officer-aviators and N.C.O. aviators, on active service.

hydro-aeroplanes—one section for the Mediterranean and the other for the Ocean.

A MODIFICATION OF 1913.

On April 22nd, 1913, a new decree was issued, modifying the organisation of military aeronautics, notably the attributes of the Permanent Inspector. He was now charged first as Inspector of technical affairs, personnel, and materiel, and secondly to direct the formation of the personnel and to command the schools.

In October, 1913, the direction of military aeronautics was confided to General Bernard, who militarised the Service, and the office of Permanent Inspector passed from Colonel Hirschauer to Colonel Romazotti.

The Permanent Inspector, theoretically powerful, could not in fact manage the aeronautic finances. The duty of the Inspector was to keep in touch with the resources and progress of aeronautics in general, but it was the Fourth Directorate (The Engineers) who managed the finance which was voted, and the Aeronautical Section, created in February, 1912, by M. Millerand in the Fourth Directorate, had not the necessary personnel to bring its task to a satisfactory issue. A central organisation was necessary, which had to be an autonomous directorate. Its rôle was to put order into the multiplicity of little institutions not organised. (See report of M. Bénazet in the Chamber of Deputies, November 17th, 1913.)

THE DEVELOPMENTS OF 1914.

In January, 1914, at the moment when Senateur Reymond (who later fell on the Field of Honour), was criticising severely the Military Aeronautical Service, a presidential decree instituted a Superior Council for military aeronautics. This was charged with co-ordinating the efforts of public services and private initiative for aeronautical progress and in the military application thereof.

On February 21st, 1914, M. Noulens, Minister of War, approved a decree separating aerostation (that is airships and balloons) from aviation (aeroplanes). He suppressed the old Directorate of Aeronautical Matériel and transformed the establishment at Chalais-Meudon. He replaced the services of the Directorate of Matériel by special autonomous establishments as follows :—

1.—The Central Establishment for Aerostation Matériel, comprising all the services of military aerostation, such as the laboratory of aerology and of telephotography.

2.—Le Service des Fabrications de l'Aviation (S.F.A.), comprising the purchases for military aviation, and the workshops for motor repairs. It controlled in a permanent fashion the construction of machines in the constructors' works, and not only the reception of finished machines.

[Incidentally, this Establishment, before it was reformed towards the end of 1917, had done serious harm to the French Service d'Aviation Militaire.—Ed.]

3.—The Aeronautical Laboratory—Chalais-Meudon.
4.—The Aviation Laboratory—Vincennes.
These last two were to carry out practical experiments.

A NEW TECHNICAL ESTABLISHMENT.

Another decree of the same date created another autonomous establishment ; La Section Technique de l'Aviation Militaire (S.T.A.), which has become during the war La Section Technique de l'Aéronautique (S.T. Aé.), now including aerostation. This was charged with theoretical studies under Commandant Dorand.

An Inspectorate of Aviation Matériel was attached for the administration of the S.T.A. [This corresponded pretty well to the British A.I.D. and operated in a very similar manner.—Ed.]

THE DUTIES OF THE INSPECTORATES.

The two Inspectorates depended upon the Minister—that is to say, on the Directorate of Aeronautics at the Ministry of War. Their attributes were, notably, consolidation of technical instruction ; the allotting of certificates ; control of aerial service ; the checking of matériel in service and in reserve ; the study on the spot of technical observations and the consideration of extension or creation of aviation centres.

The Technical Inspector of Aviation was besides charged with the higher direction of the schools.

The old Permanent Inspectorate of Aerostation matériel was transformed into a Technical Inspectorate, the two Permanent Inspectors, Col. Caron for aviation, and Col. Romazotti for aerostation, became Technical Inspectors.

The Directorate of Aeronautics at the War Ministry existed, crowning the two branches, but it could not assure unity of views, or avoid friction, complications and delays. This was at the period when, on February 25th, England handed over her seaplanes and airships to the Navy and kept the heavier-than-air machines for the Army.

FRENCH NAVAL AVIATION.

In France, Parliament having voted thirty million francs for Naval aviation, M. Monis, Minister of Marine, allotted eight and a half millions of it to the first year, 1914.

On March 13th of that year, two Naval officer aviators, Ensigns de l'Escaille and Destrem, made the sea crossing from France to Corsica on a seaplane.

For the first time, from May 15th–19th, seaplanes participated in Naval manœuvres, notably at Bizerte. (Ensigns Delage, de l'Escaille, etc.)

The Naval centre at Fréjus—St. Raphael was reserved for tests, studies, and instruction in Naval aeronautics, and two other centres were then to be created, but delays occurred, money was not voted, programmes were not realised.

According to a French communiqué, in August, 1914, Naval aviation was possessed of 8 experimental hydravions and an effective total of 200 men.

On the 1st October, 1918, French Naval Aviation comprised 1,264 avions or hydravions, of which 870 were on active service, the balance being used at the Schools for training, etc.

There were also 58 airships and 198 kite balloons and 11,000 men.

During the last year of the war only,—from November 1st, 1917, to November 1st, 1918,—the Naval avions accomplished 70,700 hours' flying and had covered 3,721,670 miles, and the airships in the same Service had done 13,152 hours' flying and had covered 523,970 miles.

These figures give an idea of the effort accomplished by the Franco-British Services in the fight against German submarines for the defence of the coasts and for the spotting of mines.

On October 1st, 1918, the distribution of French Naval Aircraft on active service was as follows :—

Station.	Aeroplanes and Seaplanes.	Airships	Kite Balloons.
Dunkirk to Cherbourg	168	21	22
Brittany	104	11	39
The Loire to the Bidassoa ..	74	7	21
French Mediterranean Coast ..	110	4	41
Corsica	38	2	—
Portugal	16	—	—
Algeria and Tunis	176	11	31
Morocco and Senegal	44	—	—
Corfu	54	3	12
Ægean Sea	86	—	32

MILITARY PROGRESS.

Always recruiting and instruction progressed well ; military pilots became experts to such an extent that the War Ministry had to forbid aerobatic flying, in the hopes of reducing breakages due to inexperience or imprudence.

THE OUTBREAK OF WAR.

Immediately on mobilisation, August 1st, 1914, aerial navigation was forbidden, except by the Military.

Alongside the Directorate of Aeronautics at the Ministry of War, where General Hirschauer had succeeded General Roques, a new organisation—which made a twelfth Directorate—was formed. This was the Directorate of Aeronautics at Army Grand Headquarters. This was confided to Commandant Barès, himself a pilot, who remained in office for three years. With him was Commandant Girod, Captains de Goys (aviator), Jaillet (airship pilot), Tulasne, etc.

Commandant Girod became ultimately a Colonel, and in 1917 Commandant Du Peuty controlled this important Service. At the moment of writing, Colonel Duval is at the head, with Commandant Dorsemaine as chief assistant.

Also there was a great development in the military aeronautical repair workshops under Commandant Duperron, which at the end of 1917 were under Commandant Laroche.

HOME DEFENCE & DEVELOPMENTS BEHIND THE FRONT.

As a result of incursions by German avions, there was created a special Aeronautical Service for the " Entrenched Camp of Paris," at first under the orders of Commandant Girod, and later under Commandant Leclerc.

For the formation of pilots, the development of schools became necessary. An Inspectorate was created under Commandant Girod, and this was ultimately transformed into a Directorate of Schools and Aviation Depots. There Lieut.-Col. Girod continues to command with his usual zeal.

Under a decree of August 21st, 1915, the pre-war organisation which existed theoretically, but greatly developed, was somewhat modified. Aerostation, which owed its pre-eminence to its age and importance of its Service more than to the complexities of its duties, had the first place, and after a period of separation, aviation and aerostation tended to re-unite. A report of the Ministry of War had shown the importance at the Front of aerostation, kite balloons, etc., the relation of the numerous studies common to aviation and aerostation, particularly those concerning armament, munitions, explosives, optical apparatus, etc., and demonstrated the extension to both services of questions concerning meteorology, photography, etc.

In consequence, La Section Technique de l'Aviation (S.T.A.) became and has remained La Section Technique de l'Aéronautique (S.T.Aé.) with extended attributes. It remained under the command of Colonel Dorand, but his personnel, reduced in 1914 to a few officers, developed till it included some hundreds of soldiers.

At the beginning of 1918, Colonel Dorand took the new post of Inspecteur-Général des Etudes et Expériences Techniques, while Commandant Caquot, the inventor of the sausage-balloons which bear his name, replaced him at the head of the S.T.Aé.

REFORM OF THE TECHNICAL BRANCH.

The same decree of August 21st, 1915, suppressed the Inspectorate of Aviation Matériel, The Aeronautic Laboratory, and the Aviation Laboratory. The General Inspectorate of Aeronautical Matériel was re-established in October, 1916, under Commandant Raymond Sée, formerly Assistant to Colonel Duperron, Director of Repair Workshops of the Aerostation branch at St. Cyr.

Also, it is known that the Aéro-technic Institution at St. Cyr, founded by M. Deutsch de la Meurthe, and presented by him to the University of Paris, has now been placed for the duration of the war at the disposition of the Military Authorities represented by the Section Téchnique.

THE POSITION AT THE END OF 1915.

Thus, at the end of August, 1915, the special establishments for Military Aeronautics comprised :—

1.—Schools and aviation depots, divided into three groups.
2.—Central Establishment for Aerostation Matériel.
3.—Le Service des Fabrications de l'Aviation Militaire (S.F.A.).

4.—La Section Technique de l'Aeronautique Militaire (S.T.Aé.).

Each of these groups were under an officer of superior rank—that of Colonel.

Commandant Dorand had, until then, commanded la Section Technique de l'Aviation, but it was Lieut.-Col. Fleuri who took over the direction of the Section Technique de l'Aeronautique, retaining under his authority Commandant Dorand so far as aviation was concerned.

[This was at the moment when the extension of naval aeronautics in England resulted in the creation of a Director of Air Services, under Admiral Vaughan Lee, while Commodore Sueter, formerly Director of the Air Department, became Superintendent of Aircraft Construction.—Ed.]

A little later, the French Government decided on the creation of an Under-Secretariat of State for the Fifth Arm. General Hirschauer, Director of Aeronautics, was placed at the disposal of the Commander-in-Chief, and took a command at the Front. A member of Parliament, M. René Besnard, a talented young lawyer, was placed at the head of the new Department, and took the title of Under Secretary of State for Aeronautics.

Specialists, those interested, the Press and public opinion had already given voice over a " crisis in aviation," and apparently were under the illusion that with the stroke of a pen one man could transform the whole situation from top to bottom. In spite of all his goodwill and his activity, M. René Besnard could not hold the superhuman role which had been thrust upon him, but nevertheless he made several happy decisions, some of which—thanks to the slowness of official methods—only bore fruit after his disappearance.

M. Besnard wished to rely upon the counsels of recognised authorities. At his proposal, the Ministry of War instituted a Consulting Committee on Military Aviation, of which the General Secretary, Lieut.-Col. Mayer, was at the same time the Chief of the Cabinet of the Under-Secretary. The first meeting took place on October 21st, 1916. Col. Bouttieaux was attached to the Under-Secretary, as formerly to General Hirschauer, and very little of the Personnel of the Directorate was changed.

M. Painlevé, as Minister of War, retained M. Besnard in the Under-Secretariat.

On November 22nd, the Service of Personnel and Matériel of the S.F.A. took the name of the Service Industriel de l'Aeronautique Militaire (S.I.A.M.) and was attached directly to the Under-Secretariat under Col. Gerard. He was replaced at the head of the S.F.A. by Lieut.-Col. of Artillery Raibaud, while at the S.T.Aé. Lieut.-Col. Fleuri was replaced by Battery Commander of Artillery Lafay, who retained Commandant Dorand for special aviation service. M. Lafay soon resigned because of illness, and Commandant Dorand, now promoted to Lieut.-Col., became again Director of the S.T.Aé., which he founded in 1914.

In turn, Colonels Stammler, Bertrand and Richard, in 1917, were appointed to Chalais-Meudon.

At the end of a few months, a new press compaign resulted in the resignation of M. Besnard and his replacement by Col.

Régnier, Director of Aeronautics at the Ministry of War, with Commandant Faure as second in command. There was less talk about " an aviation crisis " in the papers, and the task of Col. Regnier was executed in silence and without abuse—or at any rate with much less abuse than formerly.

THE 1917 ALTERATIONS.

As soon as General Lyautey was appointed Minister of War, he interested himself in obtaining the best possible Aeronautical Services, and in assuring unity of views and of control, as well as a more close linking up between the branches of the different Services and the Armies in the Field. To this praiseworthy end the decree of February 12th, 1917, created for the duration of the war a General Directorate of Aeronautical Services, which was placed under Brigadier-General Guillemin of the Artillery.

As the direct representative of the Minister, he was able to establish a complete link with the Naval Aeronautical Service and with Allied Armies. He had under his authority the Director of Aeronautics, who was still Col. Régnier. He had power on all the Fronts ; he was able to learn the needs and desires of the Armies ; to make decisions concerning construction and organisation of new units ; to dispose of troops and matériel ; to direct the research of instructors ; to intensify production and to ensure economy.

[It was at this period that Lord Cowdray became President of the Air Board in England.—Ed.]

A QUICK CHANGE PERIOD.

This Directorate only lasted for a few days. About April 1st, following on a change in the Government, the Under-Secretariat for Aviation was re-established and was given to M. Daniel Vincent, a former aeroplane observer. Col. Régnier remained for a long time as his Assistant.

There was then created an Inter-Allied Aeronautical Service, under the direction of M. P. E. Flandin, a Deputy, and a former pilot.

On June 15th, 1917, M. Daniel Vincent created an inter-ministerial Commission for civil aeronautics, under the Presidency of M. d'Aubigny, Deputy—analogous to the British Civil Aerial Transport Committee.

Following on another ministerial crisis, M. Dumesnil replaced M. Vincent, and was still in office in April, 1918.

THE IMPORTANT ALTERATION.

The principal modification of the interior organisation of Military Aeronautical Services took place in November, 1917. The Service of Aviation Construction (which was more or less the development of the original S.F.A.), with the organisations dependent thereon, was placed thenceforth under the direction of the Ministry of Armament—M. Loucheur.

Maritime Aeronautics, which up to then had been independent, was re-united with Military Aviation in the hands of the Under-Secretariat for Military Aeronautics, and this itself was joined to the Ministry of Armament to assure in concert with him the efficiency of the S.F.A.

The same ministerial decision nominated M. Gille, chief engineer of naval construction, as Chief of the Central Office of the S.F.A., at the Ministry of Armament and War Material.

A decree of the same date nominated as Director of Military Aeronautics Lieut.-Col. Paul-Francois Dhé, replacing Lieut.-Col. A. E. Greffart. Also the Under-Secretary of State nominated as Chief of his Cabinet, Col. Lalanne, a pilot aviator.

GENERAL REFLECTIONS.

Such, up to April, 1918, was the organisation of Military Aeronautics in France. This disquisition may be a trifle confused and may not seem to disclose a clear line of evolution. This is due to successive modifications in a multitude of organisations created without an inclusive plan before the war, merely as immediate needs demanded. The whole organisation is an empirical product of variable necessities, and not the result of an elaborate project. Possibly it is none the worse for that.

The attachment of Military Aeronautics to the Ministry of Armament at first excited considerable agitation, because it seemed to break up the unity of Military Aeronautics, but aviation depends on the Ministry of War as well as the Ministry of Armament, and on certain sides it concerns the Navy. Meanwhile, in practice, the system has not presented any great inconvenience. Institutions are worth what the men in them are worth.

CHANGES IN 1918.

The principal change during 1918 in the personnel of the Service d'Aviation Militaire has been the suppression of the Under-Secretariat of Aeronautics following on the resignation of M. Dumesnil in consequence of bad health. He was replaced by a Director of Aeronautics attached to the Ministry of War despite which fact he has up to the present also controlled Civil Aeronautics, the administration of which remains under military authority. The first Director of Aeronautics has been Colonel Dhé, formerly collaborating with the Under Secretary.

On the 20th April, 1919, he was replaced by General Duval.

THE CHIEFS OF 1919.

Among the Chiefs of the Aeronautical Service during 1919 have been the following :—Lieut-Col. Leclerc, Director of Civil Aeronautics, a pilot of ancient date and formerly Chief of the Aeronautical Service of the entrenched camp of Paris and of the aerial defence of the same camp against airships.

He was replaced in May, 1919, by Major Saconney, well known before the war by his experiments with kites.

The Inspector General of Research and Technical Experiments is Lieut.-Col. Dorand.

The Director of the Service of Aeronautical Construction, (Service des Fabrications de l'Aèronautique) commonly known as the S.F.A. at Nanterre, is Major Fould.

The Director of Material of Military Aerostation is Major Perrin. Colonel Girod has left the Directorate of Schools.

These changes in the high Personnel have been made so as to give an important place to the former collaborators of the General Headquarters of the Army.

At the moment of going to press the re-organisation of Civil and Military Aeronautics is almost completed.

M. Daniell-Vincent former Under Secretary of State of Aeronautics, now a Deputy, has caused to be adopted a project for a general Directorate of Civil and Military Aeronautics, which will centralise the efforts of the Service which at present insist on being concerned solely with the Ministry of War. This would have to deal also with Posts, Customs, Colonies, Public Works, the Ministry of Commerce, etc.

From 63,000,000 in 1914, the Credits for aeronautics increased in September, 1917, to 1,342,000,000 francs. It is noteworthy in passing, that in the Budget presented in 1919 to the French Chambers these Credits were £40,160,000 (roughly 2,008,000,000 francs.

At the sitting of the Chamber on March 29th, 1019, M. Flandrin, Deputy, formerly Chief of the French Inter-Allied Aviation Commission proposed a reduction of £560,000 and finally obtained a reduction of £420,000.

THE PERSONNEL OF THE SERVICE.

As regards the Personnel of the French Aviation Services, in which the conditions of test are becoming more strict, it is to be noted that up to 1915 the Aero Club of France allotted the civil certificates—that is to say, certificates of the Fédération Aeronautique Internationale (F.Aé.I.).

These certificates, for which the tests took place on a track or aerodrome, constituted a kind of first degree, nevertheless, they sufficed for more than one civilian pilot early in the war to qualify him as a military pilot. As to the military certificate, it was allotted for a series of more difficult tests across country and observation by officers, or by civilians appointed by the Aero Club. In the first instance, the certificate was delivered direct by the Military Authorities, and in the second on the proposal of the Aero Club.

Since 1915—from which time the aerodromes were crowded—there have been no civil certificates, but the Aero Club, by way of compensation, allots its pilot's certificate, when so desired, to all holding the military certificate, as the latter have to satisfy more rigorous conditions.

At the beginning of the war the Service d'Aviation Militaire was possessed of 21 escadrilles of which the total effectives including pilots, observers and mechanics was only 4,343 persons. At the signing of the Armistice the French Army included 6,000 avions, 6,417 pilots, and 1,682 observers. The total effectives of the aeronautical troops exceeded 80,000 men.

THE AERO CLUB DE FRANCE.

Meantime, the Aero Club of France has played its part. It has supplied a vast amount of information ; it has acted as an intelligence office, and has rendered many services to the Military Authorities, especially at the beginning of the war ; and it has published illustrations of Allied and enemy avions, booklets, and so forth. As a source of propaganda and education, it has been of high value.

The number of certificated pilots has grown, not in arithmetical progression, but in geometrical progression. According to L'Aérophile, of November, 1917, one sees that from 900 pilots in 1912, the number grew to 2,700 at the end of 1915, to 5,000 at the end of 1916, and to 7,700 towards October, 1917. As to the actual figures of pilots on Active Service, this of course must remain unknown to the public.

The number of Aviators' certificates delivered to the Aero Club of France has grown from 1,718 at the beginning of the war to 15,845 at the end of March, 1919.

LOSSES.

During the war 1,215 French aviators have been killed for certain.

Added to these must be 1,344 aviators reported as missing, which only signifies that it has not been possible officially to discover the cause of their death.

Thus there are 2,559 aviators killed.

Besides this there have been 2,843 wounded.

This total of 5,400 and odd killed and wounded represents a considerable proportion of the effectives of aviation.

Among the pilots, most of the distinguished civil aviators of the past have in turn disappeared, such as Gilbert, Garros, Védrines, etc. The younger " Aces " who came into being during the war have also lost many of their best, such as Guynemer, Maxime Lenoir, Chaput, etc., but France still has the " Ace of Aces " of all the belligerent Armies, Réné Fonck, and a constellation of young pilots whose sole desire is to surpass their predecessors.

It is estimated that 2,049 enemy avions have certainly been brought down by French aviators, but there is reason to believe that the official statistics are incomplete, and that this figure has been considerably surpassed without counting the doubtfuls.

AN IMPRESSION OF RESULTS.

As regards the results achieved by the French Aviation Service, according to an official communiqué, during 77 days from December 1st, 1917, to February 15th, 1918, in spite of this being the worst period of the year for weather, the French avions made 22,518 flights, either chasing, bombarding, artillery observing, infantry contact, or reconnaissance. 104 enemy avions were brought down during the same period, of which 39 fell in the French Lines, and only 38 French machines were lost, either behind the French Lines or in enemy territory. 1,400 photographic flights were made, and during these 21,328 photographs were taken. Such is a fine record for the worst period of the year, and may give some impression of what is done in the periods when weather and daylight permit greater activities.

CIVIL AVIATION.

Civil aviation in France is still in process of formation.

The greater part of the civil aviation lines organised in France have their point of departure at Paris, as for example Paris-Brussels, Paris-Bordeaux, Paris-Strasbourg. The only important exception is the line from Toulouse to Casa Blanca, in Morocco.

B

BLÉRIOT Aeroplanes. L. Blèriot, "Blériot-Aeronautique," 39, Route de la Révolte, Paris, Levallois. Flying grounds: Buc, Pau, and Brooklands (England). L. Blériot began to experiment in 1906, along Langley lines. By 1909 he was one of the leading French firms; and the first cross Channel flight was made by him on July 9th, 1909.

At the beginning of war the *Blériot* "Parasols," which afford the pilot a perfectly clear view below him, did much valuable reconnaissance work. The "tandem" type also did much good work. Later, these machines were found to be too slow for modern requirements, and the Blériot works at Buc and in Paris were turned on to produce various other types of machines required by the French Government.

No fresh information has been vouchsafed by the firm.

BRÉGUET. Soc. Anonyme des Ateliers d'Aviation, Louis Bréguet. Paris office: 25, Boulevard Jules Sandeau. Head office: Velizy per Chaville (S-et-O). Aerodrome: Villacoublay.

Owned and directed by M. Louis Bréguet, one of the great pioneers of French aviation. M. Bréguet was one of the first designers to produce a satisfactory tractor biplane.

Has always specialised on steel construction. Made the best seaplane of 1913. Built in collaboration with the Bristol Co. in 1914. One of his machines won its class in the "Concours des Avions Puissants" in 1915.

At the end of the war the types of Bréguets were as follows:

THE BRÉGUET BIPLANE, TYPE 14 A.2.

Type of machine	Bréguet Biplane.
Name or type No. of machine ..	14 A.2.
Purpose for which intended ..	Reconnaissance, photography and artillery spotting.
Span	14.364 metres.
Overall length	9 m.
Maximum height	3.3 m.
Total surface of wings	49 sq. m.
Engine type and h.p.	300 h.p. Renault.

Performance.
  Speed low down .. .. .. 190 kms. per hour.
Climb.
  To 5,000 metres in 21 minutes 45 seconds.
  Ceiling at 6,100 metres.

The Type 14 A.2 Bréguet Bomber with 300 h.p. Renault Engine.

THE THREE-MOTORED BRÉGUET—Three 250 h.p. Renault Engines. Flew for three hours at a height of 2,500 metres with a load of 1200 kilogrammes.

BRÉGUET—continued.

THE BRÉQUET TYPE 14 B.2.

(Translated by a Neutral Contributor).

In a German technical journal, the automobile and aerotechnical paper "Der Motorwagen," an extensive description of the *Bréguet* 14 *B.2* biplane, with a 300 h.p. Renault engine, is to be found in the issues of July 30th and Aug. 10th.

THE WINGS.

This biplane, characterised by two sets of struts, is produced almost exclusively of aluminium, and is intended for bombing purposes. The upper planes have a backwards stagger of 0.21 m. and a span of 14.4 m., and are mounted on a cabane frame, while the lower planes have a span of 13.77 m.

Both upper and lower planes have large cuttings at the fuselage and their arrow shape amounts to 175 deg. The angle of incidence of the upper planes is 4.5 deg. in the middle and 2.5 deg. at the ends, that of the lower ones decreasing from 3 deg. to 2 deg.

The spars of both planes are drawn aluminium tubes of rectangular section 65.6 × 34.6 mm. The thickness of the walls of these tubes amounts in the inner section of the upper plane to 2.6 mm., elsewhere to 1.6 mm. The rear spar grows thinner towards the wing tips till the thickness of the edge, where auxiliary spars with ash bands of 6 mm. thickness and 3 mm. three-ply wood glued to both sides are provided. At the points of juncture and at the end of the stampings the spars are strengthened by ash pieces, in some instances of I shape. A socket of 20 cm. length, made of welded sheet steel of a thickness of 1.5 mm. is provided at the strut ends of the upper planes and at the strut bases. These sockets and the wooden linings are held in position by iron tube rivets.

The main spar of the upper plane is strengthened in the interior section of a pine support of a thickness of 10 mm. being fixed to one side of the spar by means of small brass screws. The spars of the upper planes are equipped with compression supports at the joints of the two sets of struts and the lower planes for the outer strut set, the support being an aluminium tube of the diameters 30 and 27 mm. exterior and interior. Further there are two aluminium ribs of a width of 40 mm., one at the beginning of the ailerons and one by the bomb store in the lower plane. The interior wiring consists of single wire.

The ribs are very strong. They have a depth of 2 mm. above, of 1.9 below. A web provided with weight diminishing holes is glued between the longitudinals of three-ply wood, 3 mm. thick. On both sides of the spars as well as at five points between them the flange is strengthened by glued and nailed birch laths and wrapped bands. The ribs are arranged loosely on the spars. The ribs lie parallel to the axis of longitude, forming in relation to the spars an angle corresponding with the arrow shape. They are connected with each other by means of the veneer planking, reaching on the upper side from the leading edge from the main spar, as well as by the leading and trailing edges. Further they are connected by two bands, lying behind each other and alternately wound from above and below the ribs. The distance between them amounts to 40 mm. Forward and in front of the rear spar more 4 mm. thick auxiliary ribs of plywood are arranged. To reinforce the aerofoil, thin birch ribs reaching to the trailing edge are screwed to the rear of the ribs on the underside.

Side and Front Elevation and Plan of the Bréguet Bombing Biplane, type 14 B.2.

218a

BRÉGUET—continued.

The yellow-white coloured fabric is sewed to the ribs and secured with thin nailed strips where exposed to the airscrew draught. The provision of hooks and eyes on the under side of the planes behind the leading edge and in front of the trailing edge is to permit the draining off of moisture.

Only the upper planes are provided with ailerons, attached direct to the rear spar.

The part of the lower plane lying behind the rear spar is hinged along its total length and is pulled downwards by means of 12 rubber cords fixed on the under side of the ribs, the tension of these can be adjusted by means of screws, an automatic change of the aerofoil corresponding with the load and speed thus results with an easier control of the aeroplane with and without a load of bombs. The stampings for the hinges of the ailerons and the flexible lower plane pieces embrace the spars and are connected with them by means of bolts passing right through. The spars have no linings at these points.

The construction of the stampings of the spars is very simple. Several sheet steel pieces with corresponding angle pieces are fixed to the spars with two screws penetrating them.

The interplane struts are made of streamlined aluminium tubes with aluminium sockets in both ends. The inner struts are further strengthened by the insertion ef riveted U iron. The aluminium employed has a strength of 40 kg. per sq. mm. with a stretching of 18 per cent.

The 4.5 mm. thick load carrying cables are double, the space between them being filled by a wooden lath. In the same manner the landing wires as well as those crossing from the upper planes forward and backwards of the fuselage are arranged, being wires of a thickness of 2½ mm. that are connected with the stampings and the turnbuckles in a primitive way by means of eyes and spiral wire pushed over. To give a better support to the lower planes, being much stressed by the bomb store, the load-carrying cables are in the inner section led to the stampings on the main ribs arranged by the bomb-store, and thence downwards to the landing gear. The rear spar of the upper planes is also provided with a cable to the fuselage between the cabane and strut.

The stampings for the fixing of the wiring is constructed very simply. A bent sheet metal of U form and with drilled holes for the bolts carries the nipples of the eyebolts.

THE FUSELAGE.

The canvas-covered body consists almost exclusively of aluminium tubes that are riveted with welded steel tube sleeves and spanned with wire. Only at specially stressed points in the front part have steel tubes been employed. The upper and lower sides of the fuselage are rounded by the employment of fairings.

The engine rests on aluminium U bearers that are supported by riveted aluminium struts. Two pairs of large view traps are provided below the seats of the pilot and observer, and are operated by cable by the observer.

THE UNDERCARRIAGE.

The very strong landing gear has three pairs of struts of aluminium streamline tubes, strengthened by U irons riveted in, and resting below on horizontal steel tubes. The wheel shaft rests in an auxiliary one of steel sheet in U shape welded on. The back root points of the struts are connected by means of a second steel tube auxiliary shaft, welded on, and by a tension band lying behind. A diagonal wiring is further provided horizontally in the auxiliary shaft level. The streamlining of the shafts is cut out in the middle behind the front auxiliary shaft to improve the sight downwards. There is only a diagonal wiring to the fuselage in the level of the middle struts.

The ash tail skid hangs in rubber springs from the fuselage and is strengthened in the rear end by a covering of a rectangular aluminium tube. Its wire stay is supported in the rear stem by a spiral spring. Leaf springs are further fixed to the end of the skid.

Tail plane, rudder and elevator are of welded thin steel tubes.

The aeroplane is equipped with complete dual control. The control in the observer's cockpit can be removed,

The ailerons are interconnected. The twin control cables run behind the rear spar of the lower planes to two direction changing rollers resting on a shaft. Here they part and are led as separate wires of thickness of 2 mm. to the uuderside of the ailerons. In the upper planes the ailerons are connected by control cables, governing two levers in each side. The ailerons are balanced and welded to a common shaft.

According to a label on the aeroplane the performance of the 12-cylinder Renault engine of V type is 300 h.p. at 1500–1600 normal r.p.m. The engine is the same as the 260 h.p. model, the increase in horse-power being the result of the employment of aluminium pistons and a greater number of revolutions. The engine drives the two bladed airscrew direct. The exhaust going inwards is led above the upper planes by a collector.

The aluminium radiator forms the front part of the fuselage, and is divided in the middle, each row of cylinders having thus its own cooling system with a separate water-pump.

THE PETROL SYSTEM.

Two gravity tanks of 130 litres capacity each are positioned behind the motor. As their underside lies only little above the carburettors an auxiliary tank of 5.6 litres capacity is provided in front of each carburettor behind the engine, the petrol being led on to the tank from the carburettor. These tanks fill themselves by gravity in horizontal or descending flight from the main tanks. Whereas, if the main tank may be unable to supply any more petrol in climbing, the auxiliary ones then feed the carburettor. Check non-return valves are mounted in the piping to prevent the petrol from running back into the main tanks.

As there is by this arrangement a petrol quantity of 11.2 litres in front of the carburettors without any possibility of being cut off, grave accidents may occur by carburettor fires.

The petrol level in the main tanks is indicated electrically by pressing a contact. A hard rubber tube is mounted in each tank inside a tube and wound with a resistance wire of 0.4 m. thickness, above which a cork float with contacts moves. An oil tank of 18 litres capacity is mounted on the right side of the engine. The fuel suffices for a flight of about 2½ hours' duration under ground conditions.

THE INSTRUMENTS.

On the instrument board, protected by a large Triplex safety glass, in aluminium framing, is mounted a tachometer, a watch, altimeter, two cooling water thermometers, the pressure buttons and the indicator arrangement of the petrol height with the dry cell battery lying behind, and the compass. To right of the pilot is to be found the manipulation of the radiator-blinding arrangement, the starting magneto, the petrol start spray pump, oil and petrol stop-cocks, as well as the connections for the illumination for night flying and for wireless. To left are the levers for the gas throttle, the spark timing, the regulation of extra air supply, the magneto switch, as well as a petrol stop-cock.

The observers' cockpit is arranged in the middle of the turning and raising machine-gun ring mounted on the top of the body. The seat is hinged so that the observer may sit either high or low on the bottom of the fuselage. The mounting of Cellon windows in both sides gives him an outside view. The bottom is of steel tube girder work, the sight being thus unhindered downwards when the sight-trap is opened by means of the cables arranged to right of the seat. On the right fuselage wall the bomb-dropping mechanism is mounted; to left levers connected with gas lever and magneto switch in the pilot's cockpit. To both sides are connections for wireless.

The aeroplane is equipped with illumination for night flying and with position lights on the outer struts. Under the root points of the front struts hanging provision for the mounting of searchlights is further to be found. The current for the light and the wireless is produced by a dynamo, which is mounted on a seat below the fuselage and driven by a propeller.

To left on the outside of the body a fixed machine-gun for the pilot is mounted, being operated from the camshaft of the left row of cylinders.

The observer is armed with two machine-guns clutched together and mounted on a raising and turning ring. As the ring is mounted high, the firing range forward is good.

The bomb store is mounted in the inner section of the power planes with a capacity of 16 small bombs, arranged hanging in two rows of eight. In the dropping operation the two bombs, lying behind each other, are released, at the same time, by a camshaft lying in front of the main spar. The camshafts are

BRÉGUET—continued.

connected by chain drive with a shaft in cross position in the fuselage with a grooved pulley mounted, driven by a strong rubber cable. Another chain drive connects this shaft with a gear wheel mounted to right of the seat of the observer, on the shaft of which a locking quadrant as well as a transmission gear for the stretching of the rubber chord is keyed on. To load the bomb store the chain wheel is first by means of the crank-handle in the observers' cockpit turned till the locking engages again after revolution. When the rubber cord is thus much stretched the bombs are hung in. When the upper gear wheel is now released by pulling the locking lever for bomb-dropping, the stretched rubber cord starts turning the shaft lying across in the fuselage as well as the camshafts of the bomb stores, so that all bombs are released by one revolution. To enable a timing of the bomb dropping a glycerine brake cylinder, with adjustable throttle valve, is mount edin the chain drive leading upwards. Being connected with the inner bomb pairs and fixed to both sides of the seat, two special cables make the dropping of these four bombs possible, independently of the rest.

One aeroplane has further had a hanging provision for two large bombs mounted inside the cockpit to right of the seat of the pilot. The cables run to the observer.

The aiming arrangement is mounted inside the observer's cockpit on a swivelling arm on the left body side.

The empty weight of the aeroplane was fixed at 1,215 kg. A notice on the rudder gives the weight of the fuel at 216 kg., that of the normal useful load to 514 kg. and the maximum useful load at 614 kg. Reckoning with the normal load the total weight of the aeroplane loaded is thus 1,915 kg., corresponding with a load on the planes of 40 kg. per sq. m., as well as a performance load at 300 h.p. of 6½ kg. per h.p.

CHARACTERISTIC FEATURES.

Beside the usual backwards stagger to be found on other aeroplanes the following features should be emphasised : the high fuselage with the right-angled rudder and forward sharp rounded keel fin, the landing gear with three pairs of struts and a right-angled cutting of the streamlining of the shafts, the small arrow-shape of the trapeze-shaped planes with the sharp and large cuttings, the bomb stores projecting forwards in front of the planes, the triangular-fixed tail plane, the divided elevator, with cornered balance, as well as the dihedral upper planes and horizontal lower ones.

Specification.

Type of machine	Bréguet Biplane.
Name or type No. of machine	14 B.2.
Purpose for which intended	Day Bomber.
Span	14.364 metres.
Overall length	9 m.
Maximum height	3.3 m.
Total surface of wings	51 sq. m.
Engine type and h.p.	300 h.p. Renault.
Weight of machine empty	1,127 kilos.

Performance.

Speed low down .. .. 185 kms. per hour.

Climb.

To 5,000 m. in 47 min. 30 secs.
Ceiling at 5,750 metres.
Disposable load apart from fuel 882 kilos.

Armament : One gun in front (synchronised), 2 guns aft. 300 kilos. of bombs.

The Bréguet Biplane type 14 B.2 (300 h.p. Renault engine).

Sectional Plan and Side Elevation of the Fuselage of the Bréguet Biplane. Type 14 B.2.

BRÉGUET—continued.

Der Doppeldecker von Bréguet
Typ 14. B 2.

Holmquerschnitt, Aluminium

Wandstärke
Oberflügel Innenfeld 2,6 mm
Mitte u Außen 1,6 m—
Unterflügel 1,6 mm

An den Knotenpunkten
mit Holz gefuttert (Esche)
Einlage im Oberflügel Vorderholm.
Inners Feld (Kiefer)

Diagram showing Timber reinforcement of Aluminium Main Spar.

Sectional Plan Views of Upper and Lower Bréguet Wings, and Side Sectional Elevation of Lower Wing of a 14 B.2.

From a German Print.)

2 E 2

BRÉGUET--*continued.*

General Arrangement Drawing of the 14 B.2 as issued by the Bréguet firm.

The Bréguet Upper Wing Section (above).   Below—Section of Lower Aileron.

BRE. 16 BN. 2

SECTION TECHNIQUE DE L'AÉRONAUTIQUE MILITAIRE

SERVICE GÉNÉRAL DES AVIONS

AVION BRÉGUET
Type 16 Bn. 2

Moteur Renault FC 300 HP
et Liberty US 400 HP
Surface 72 m²

THE BRÉGUET BIPLANE, TYPE 17 C.2.

Type of machine	Bréguet Biplane.
Name or type No. of machine ..	17 C.2.
Purpose for which intended ..	Two-seat Fighter.
Span	14,280 metres.
Overall length	8.1 m.
Maximum height	3.42 m.
Total surface of wings	45.3 sq. m.
Engine type and h.p.	450 h.p. Renault.

Performance.

Speed low down	225 kms. per hour.

Climb.
To 5,000 m. in 24 mins. 51 secs.
Ceiling at 7,000 metres.

Armament : Twin synchronised guns in front ; two guns aft.
One gun firing below fuselage.

THE BRÉGUET BIPLANE, TYPE 16 B.N.2.

Type of machine	Two-seater Tractor Biplane.
Name or type No. of machine ..	16 B.N.2.
Purpose for which intended ..	Night Bomber.
Span	17 metres.
Chord	2.35 m.
Overall length	9.55 m.
Maximum height	3.42 m.
Total surface of wings	73.5 sq. m.
Span of tail	4.66 m.
Engine type and h.p.	Renault 300 h.p. or Liberty 400 h.p.
Airscrew	3.42 m. diam.
Weight of machine empty ..	1,265 kilos.

Performance.

Speed low down	160 kms. per hour.

Climb.
To 4,000 metres in 51 minutes 10 seconds.
Ceiling 4,600 metres.

Disposable load apart from fuel : machine gun aft, and 550
kilos. of bombs=1130 kilos.

The Bréguet Biplane, type 17 C.2 (Renault 450 h.p. engine).

The Caudron, Type R.II. (2—200 h.p. Hispano-Suiza engines.)

Performance.

Speed low down ..	.. 190 k.p.h. full ; 95 k.p.h. throttled.
Speed at 2,000 metres	.. 185 k.p.h.
Speed at 3,000 metres	.. 180 k.p.h.
Speed at 4,000 metres	.. 173 k.p.h.
Speed at 5,000 metres	.. 167.3 k.p.h.

Climb.

To 2,000 metres in 8·10 minutes.
To 3,000 metres in 14·3 minutes.
To 5,000 metres in 39 minutes.

Disposable load apart from fuel .. .: ..	405 kgs.
Total weight of machine loaded .. .: ..	2,167 kgs.

C

CAUDRON. René Caudron, Issy-les-Moulineaux. (Seine).

School : Le Crotoy (Aerodrome de la Baie de la Somme).

The *Caudron* has proved on active service to be one of the most useful French aeroplanes. It has been largely used for artillery control and for bomb-dropping, because of its great weight-lifting capacity, and its imperviousness to bad weather. Other firms whose own designs have not been successful have been turned on by the French Government to build *Caudrons*.

The following descriptions and illustrations give all the particulars at present available of Caudron machines not hitherto described.

THE CAUDRON R.II TWIN-ENGINED BOMBER.

Type of machine	Caudron Twin Tractor.
Name or type No. of machine	R. II.
Purpose for which intended ..	Bombing.
Span	17.92 m. top ; 16.9 m. bottom plane.
Overall length	11.25 metres.
Maximum height	2.70 metres.
Engine type and h.p.	Hispano-Suiza, two 200 h.p.
Weight of machine empty ..	1,422 kgs.
Tank capacity in litres ..	220.

The Caudron, Type C.23. Two Salmson engines.

224a

CAUDRON—continued.

THE CAUDRON C.23 TWIN-ENGINE BIPLANE.

Type of machine	Caudron Twin-engined Tractor.
Name or type No. of machine	C. 23 B.N. 2.
Purpose for which intended ..	Night Bombing.
Span	24.47 m. upper plane; 23.57 m. lower plane.
Overall length..	13 metres.
Maximum height	3.4 metres.
Total surface of wings ..	104 sq. metres.
Engine type and h.p... ..	Two Salmson C-U. Z.!9—250 h.p.
Weight of machine empty ..	2,670 kgs.
Tank capacity in litres ..	980.

Performance.

Speed at 1,000 metres ..	143.5 k.p.h. (throttled 82.2 k.p.h.)
Speed at 2,000 metres ..	140.5 k.p.h.
Speed at 3,000 metres ..	136 k.p.h.

Climb.

To 1,000 metres in 8.55 minutes.
To 1,500 metres in 14.10 minutes.
To 2,000 metres in 20.37 minutes.
To 2,500 metres in 27.5 minutes.
To 3,000 metres in 37.26 minutes.

Total weight of machine loaded	4,420 kgs.
Useful load	1.050 kgs.
Fuel load	700 kgs.

This machine has since the armistice been transformed for passenger carrying, and some illustrations of it in this guise are attached.

The Type C.23 Caudron with a load of passengers.

The Caudron, Type C.23.   (2—250 h.p. Type Z.9 Salmson engines.)

CAUDRON—*continued.*

THE CAUDRON. TYPE G.6.

Specification.

Type of machine	Twin-engined Biplane.
Name or type No. of machine ..	Caudron G6.
Span	17.21 m.
Overall length	8.6 m.
Maximum height	2.95 m.
Total surface of wings ..	39.7 sq. m.
Engine type and h.p. ..	2—80 or 110 h.p. Le Rhone.
Weight of machine empty ..	850-940 kgs.
Load per sq. m.	34-36.3 kgs.
Weight per h.p.	6-7.3 kgs.

Performance.

Speed low down	.. ..	152 km.p.h.

Climb.

To 2,000 metres	.. ..	9 mins.
To 3,000 metres	.. ..	18 mins.
Disposable load apart from fuel	.. .. ..	500 kgs.

Three-quarter View. from Rear, of the Caudron, Type C.23 Twin engined Biplane.

A Twin-engined Caudron Biplane of the tail-boom type, known as G.6. (2—110 h.p. Le Rhone engines.)

D

DE MARÇAY. Société de Marçay, Paris.

Founded by the Comte De Marçay and his brother-in-law, M. Pierre Verrier, formerly a well-known pilot at Hendon.

Recently produced a very fast single-seater biplane.

THE DE MARÇAY BIPLANE.

Type of machine	Single-seater Scout.
Span	Top plane 9 m. 25.
Overall length	6 m. 50.
Engine type and h.p.	300 h.p. Hispano-Suiza.
Performance.	
Speed low down	252 km.p.h.
Speed at 3,000 metres ..	237 km.p.h.
Speed at 4,000 metres ..	231 km.p.h.
Speed at 5,000 metres ..	220 km.p.h.
Speed at 6,000 metres ..	208 km.p.h.
Useful load	339 kgs.

The de Marcay Single-seater Fighter (300 h.p. Hispano-Suiza engine), which, on test at Villacoublay, showed a speed of 252 k.m.h (162 m.p.h.) low down; 237 k.m.h. (148 m.p.h.) at 3,000 metres; 231 k.m.h. (143 m.p.h.) at 4,000 metres; and 208 k.m.h. (139 m.p.h.) at 6,000 metres. An overall factor of safety of 14 is claimed for the machine.

D. N. P.

MM. Duperron, Niepce and Fetterer made, in 1916, a peculiar three-engined biplane of the type illustrated. No details are available beyond the fact that it was driven by three Renault engines of 200 h.p. each.

The D.N.P. Biplane (3—200 h.p. Renault engines).

D—*continued.*

DONNET.

Hydravions J. Donnet, 57, Rue de Villiers, Neuilly-sur-Seine. Works : 13a rue Levallois-Prolongé, Levallois-Perret, and at Sidi Abdallah, Ferryville, Tunis. (Manager at Ferryville : M. P. Jeltés.)

DONNET FLYING BOAT.

Type of machine	Donnet Flying Boat.
Name or type No. of machine ..	Type D.D., 200 h.p.
Purpose for which intended ..	Bombardment.
Span	16.80 m.
Gap	1.83 m.
Overall length	9 m. 50.
Maximum height	3 m.
Chord	Top plane, 2 m. ; Lower plane, 1 m. 45.
Total surface of wings	53 sq. m.
Span of tail	3 m. 20.
Total area of tail	7 sq. m.
Area of rudder	1.20 sq. m.
Area of each aileron	2 sq. m.
Maximum cross section of body	1 m. 20.
Engine type and h.p.	200 h.p. Hispano-Suiza.
Weight of machine empty ..	950 kgs.
Tank capacity in hours	4 hours.
Tank capacity in litres	140 each (two tanks).

Performance.
Speed	130 km.p.h.
Landing speed	80 km.p.h.

Climb.
To 1,000 metres	6.30 mins.
To 2,000 metres	15 mins.
Disposable load apart from fuel	650 kgs.
Total weight of machine loaded	1,800 kgs.

Three-ply wood central float or boat, so constructed that fixed tail fin forms part and whole with it. Two small three-ply floats at wing ends. Seat for pilot and observer side by side. Third seat for gunner in front. Several watertight compartments.

Three-quarter Front View of the Donnet Flying-Boat (200 h.p. Hispano-Suiza engine.)

Side View of the Donnet Flying-Boat.

D—*continued.*

DORAND.

Biplanes designed by Colonel Dorand, of the Section Technique d'Aviation, and built under his instructions, at the Government establishment at Chalais-Meudon, which corresponds to the Royal Aircraft Establishment at Farnborough.

THE DORAND RECONNAISSANCE BIPLANE.

Type of machine	Two-seater Reconnaissance Biplane.
Name or type number of machine	A.R.
Purpose for which intended	Reconnaissance.
Span	13.3 metres.
Gap, maximum and minimum	2 m. to 1.825 m.
Overall length..	8.225 m.
Total surface of wings ..	50.36 sq. meters.
Engine type and H.P. ..	8 cyl. Renault, 190 h.p.
Weight of machine empty ..	890 kgs.
Load per sq. metre	7 kgs.
Tank capacity in litres ..	170.

Disposable load apart from fuel .. .. .. 300 kgs.
Total weight of machine loaded .. .. .. 1330 kgs.

"Flugsport" for Aug. 14th describes the *Dorand* biplane, explaining that this machine is known as "A.R." or "A.L.D." according to its equipment with a Renault or a Lorraine-Dietrich engine. The machine described, naturally one captured from the French, bears the description, "A.R.," and the number 309. The letter "A" indicates that it is a Reconnaissance machine.

The empty weight of the aircraft is 890 kilos. A note on the rudder gives the weight of the fuel (poids combustible) as 140 kg. and that of useful load (poids utile) at 300 kg., the total load working thus out at 1,330 kg. As the planes have an area of

50.36 square metres, the loading of the planes is thus $\dfrac{1330}{50.36} =$

26.40 kg. per sq. m., and the engine performance $\dfrac{1330}{190.36} =$

7 kg. per h.p.

The main object of the design seems to have been the production of a light aeroplane with fairly high wing loading. The construction of component parts, such as stampings, has, therefore, been kept simple and light.

Three-quarter Front View of the Dorand Biplane, type A.R., with 200 h.p. Renault engine (running).

Side View of the Dorand Biplane, type A.R., with 200 h.p. Renault engine. The group in front include, from left to right, Commandant Maurer, Colonel Dorand, and Commandant Lepère—(all wearing caps).

DORAND—*continued*.

Weights.	Kg.
Engine	245
Cooling water	25
Airscrew	22
One main petrol tank ..	22.5
One auxiliary petrol tank	2
One oil tank	2
Engine equipment, exhaust collector body with tools	244.5
Landing gear	60
Control arrangement ..	6
Planes	234.5
Rudder and elevator ..	26.5
Empty load	890
Total weight ..1330	

Load (Approximately).	Kg.
Pilot and observer ..	150
Armament	75
4 bombs @ 12 kg. ..	48
Wireless and photography equipment	27
182 lit. petrol; 7 lit. oil	140
	440

Note painted on the rudder :
"Useful load" .. 300 kg.
Fuel .. .. .. 140 kg.
Average useful loading of the
planes : 4.65 kg. sq. m.

FRANZ. A.R. Type I

Sectional Plan and Side Elevation of the Fuselage of the Dorand Biplane. (This and the illustrations on the following page are taken from the German paper " Flugsport.")

Franz.
A. R.
Type I

Schnitt a-b

Größter Querschnitt

Inhalt
0,92 m²

Rumpf Holzdrahtboot
Rumpfholme u Skele: Esche u. Spruce
Rumpfverspannung Draht
Rumpfaußenhaut Leinen

Rippe des Ober- und Unterflügels   Rippenabstand 300–340 mm

Höhenruder

Seitenruder

Drahl   Seil

Drahl

Seil

Steuerungsschema

Verspannung

		mm ∅				mm	∅
1	vorn	Draht, doppelt 3.5	6	vorn	Draht, einfach		1.5
"	hinten		"	hinten	"		
2	vorn	" einfach	7	vorn	"		3.0
"	hinten		"	hinten	"		
3		" 2.5	8	vorn	Kabel		5.0
4	vorn	" doppelt 3.0	"	hinten	"		1.0
"	hinten			Tiefen		
5	vorn	" einfach	kreuzweise	Draht, einfach		2.5
"	hinten		spannung		

Motorachse

Flächen-Inhalt m²	Motor	Luftschraube	Kühler	Fahrgestell	
Oberflügel mit Querruder } 25,50 m²	190 PS Renault Bremsleistung:	Eclair, Holz, 2 flg. Durchm = 276 cm	Stirnkühler mit Abdeckvorrichtg.	Streben Stahlrohr ohne Füllerung	Federung. Gummischnur Federungsweg ohne Begrenzung
Unterflügel = 24,86 "	N = 190 PS	Blattbreite = 21 cm Steigung —	10 L Inhalt Gesamtes Kühlwasser	31 × 375 mm	Reifen 750 × 125
Gesamt — 50,36 m²	n = 1550 ÷ 1600	n = 1550 ÷ 1600	25 Liter		Nade. Breite 100 mm innerer Durchm. 56 mm

231a

F

FARMAN. Aeroplanes.

Henri and Maurice Farman, 167, Rue de Silly, Billancourt (Seine). *School* : Buc, près Versailles and Etampes. Depôts : Buc, Etampes (Seine and Oise). Camp de Chalons—Reims. Boulogne s/mer. Established by H. Farman in 1908. M. Farman established works a little later. In 1912 the two brothers combined. Present works were opened in January, 1912.

Various *Farman* machines did good work early in the War, notably the "short-horn" *Maurice Farman* and the Salmson-engined *Henry Farmans*.

An interesting type is a combination of the "Henri" and "Maurice" Farman characteristics, and on this account it is commonly known among British aviators as the "Horace."

The aeroplane factory of Henri and Maurice Farman, at Billancourt (Seine), is said to be able to produce machines of various types at the rate of ten every day. The factory is two miles long, and, with its extensive facilities and a force of 5,000 employees, the Farman establishments produce all parts of the aeroplane at the Billancourt factory, including all the wood-work and metal parts.

The illustrations and descriptions which follow relate to various types produced during and since the War.

THE FARMAN. TYPE F50P.

Type of machine	Twin-engine Passenger Carrier.
Span	22 m. 350.
Chord	2 m. 350.
Overall length	12 m.
Span of tail	5 m. 750.
Engine type and h.p. ..	2 Lorraine Dietrich. 275 h.p.
Weight of machine empty ..	1800 kgs.

Performance.

Speed low down	150 km.p.h.

Note.—The type *50 B.N.2*, shewn in a general arrangement drawing, is the original of the passenger carrier *F50P*. The general dimensions and arrangement are the same. One machine is fitted as a night bomber and the other as a passenger carrier.

Three-quarter Rear View of one "power egg" and the Cabin-Farman type F50 P.

Three-quarter Front View of the Farman Type F50P (2—275 h.p. Lorraine Dietrich engines).

PLAN.

~ENGINES~
2 LORRAINE 240/275 HP

WEIGHT EMPTY 1800 K.

SPEED PER HOUR 150 K

FRONT ELEVATION

SIDE ELEVATION

AVION FARMAN

TYPE F.50-P

FARMAN—*continued*.

THE FARMAN "GOLIATH."
Specification.

Type of machine	Twin-engine Passenger Carrier.
Span	28 m.
Chord	3 m. 065.
Overall length	14 m.
Maximum height	5 m.
Span of tail	5 m. 500.
Engine type and h.p.	2 Salmson. 260 h.p.

Performance.

Speed low down	70 km.p.h.

Three-quarter Front View of the Farman " Goliath ". (2—260 h.p. Salmson engines).

PLAN

SPEED 160 KM HOUR.

WEIGHT EMPTY 2000 K.

ENGINES

2 – 260 HP SALMSON.

FRONT ELEVATION

28 m

SIDE ELEVATION.

AVION FARMAN F-60 (AEROBUS TOURISTE)

FordJones

The Farman "Goliath."

FARMAN—*continued.*

THE FARMAN. TYPE 50BN2.
Specification.

Type of machine	Twin-engined Tractor. Biplane.
Name or type No. of machine ..	Farman. Type 50BN2.
Purpose for which intended	Night Bomber.
Span	Top plane, 22.85 m. ; Bottom plane, 20.4 m.
Overall length	10.92 m.
Maximum height	3.3 m.
Chord	2.35 m.
Total surface of wings	100 sq. m.
Span of tail	5.76 m.
Engine type and h.p.	2—240 or 275 h.p. Lorraine Dietrich.

FAR. 50 BN. 2

SECTION TECHNIQUE DE L'AÉRONAUTIQUE MILITAIRE

SERVICE GÉNÉRAL DES AVIONS

AVION FARMAN
Type 50 Bn. 2

2 Moteurs Lorraine 8 B 240 ou 275 HP
Surface 100 m²

Echelle 1/100e

FARMAN—*continued*.

THE FARMAN F30B. TYPE AR2.
Specification.

Type of machine	Two-seater Biplane.
Span	14 m.
Chord	1 m. 970.
Overall length	8 m. 540.
Engine type and h.p. ..	Salmson. 260 h.p.
Weight of machine empty ..	825 kgs.
Weight of fuel	200 kgs.

Disposable load apart from fuel	350 kgs.
Total weight of machine loaded	1,375 kgs.

ENGINE 260 HP SALMSON.

POIDS À VIDE 825 ᴷ

PU POIDS UTILE 350 ᴷ

PC POIDS COMBUSTIBLE 200 ᴷ

CHARGE TOTALE (550 ᴷ)

POIDS COMPLETE EN CHARGE 1375 ᴷ

AVION FARMAN

F 30 B

Type AR²

FARMAN—*continued*.

THE FARMAN F31. TYPE C2.

Type of machine	Two-seater Biplane.
Span	11 m. 760.
Overall length	7 m. 890.
Overall height	2 m. 580.
Chord	1 m. 750.
Engine type and h.p.	400 h.p. Liberty.
Weight of machine empty ..	870 kgs.
Weight of fuel	280 kgs.
Disposable load apart from fuel	320 kgs.
Total weight of machine loaded .. .. ..1,470 kgs.	

PLAN

ENGINES :—
2 - 275 H.P. LORRAINE.

SPEED 140 K PER HOUR.

WEIGHT EMPTY 2220 K.

ELEVATION.

FRONT

SIDE ELEVATION.

HYDRAVION FARMAN (TYPE F.51)

FORD JONES.

THE FARMAN FLYING BOAT.   TYPE F.51.
Specification.

Type of machine	..	..	..	Twin-engine Flying Boat.
Span	..	..	..	23 m. 350.
Chord	..	..	..	2 m. 350.
Overall length	..	..	..	14 m. 850.
Maximum height	..	..		4 m. 400.
Span of tail	..	..		6 m. 500.
Engine type and h.p.	..		2 Lorraine Dietrich. 275 h.p.
Weight of machine empty	..		2220 kgs.
Performance.				
Speed low down	..	..		140 km.p.h.

AVION FARMAN.

TYPE F.40-P.

The " Horace " Farman.

Side View of the Farman type F40P, commonly known in England as the
" Horace " (Lorraine-Dietrich Engine.)

240a

F—*continued*.

F.B.A. Franco-British Aviation (Société Anonyme), Paris.

Founded 1914, by Lieut. Jean de Conneau, of the French Navy (better known as André Beaumont, winner of the Paris-Rome, Circuit-European, and Circuit of Britain races), and M. Schraeck, of the French Wright Company, to work to patents pertaining to the *Donnet-Lévêque* and *Artois* flying boats.

Equipped with Monosoupape Gnôme, Clergêt and Hispano, Suiza engines, these boats have been proved to be very fast and suitable for high-speed coastal flying.

They were largely used by all the Allied Naval Air Services for fighting over water and did very good work.

No recent particulars have been received.

HANRIOT.

Hanriot & Cie, 84, Avenue des Moulineaux, Billancourt, Seine.

Founded during the war by M. Hanriot, who had retired from aviation before the war. Made a number of Sopwith machines for the French Government, and latterly produced the machine illustrated here.

THE HANRIOT 3C2.

Specification.

Type of machine	**Two-seater Tractor Biplane.**
Name or type No. of machine ..	**Hanriot 3C2.**
Purpose for which intended ..	**Fighting Scout.**
Span	**9 m.**
Overall length	**6.95 m.**
Maximum height	**3 m.**
Chord	**1.52 m.**
Total surface of wings	**25.5 sq. m.**
Engine type and h.p.	**230 h.p. Salmson.**
Airscrew, diam.	**3 m.**

An F.B.A. flying boat on the water. Actually in the service of Italy. *Reproduced from " La Guerra," the Italian official publication.*

SECTION TECHNIQUE DE L'AÉRONAUTIQUE MILITAIRE

SERVICE GÉNÉRAL DES AVIONS

AVION HANRIOT
Type 3 C. 2

Moteur CU. 9 Z 230 HP
Surface 25 m² 50

L

LETORD.

Société d'Aviation Letord, Paris.

A manufacturing firm founded by the aviator Letord.

Has for some time been manufacturing twin-engined biplanes, originally notable for the backward stagger of the wings. This characteristic has disappeared in a later type.

THE LETORD. TYPE 5.

Specification.

Type of machine	Twin-engined Tractor Biplane.
Name or type No. of machine ..	Letord. Type 5.
Purpose for which intended ..	Bomber.
Span	18 m.
Overall length	11.17 m.
Maximum height	3.7 m.
Total surface of wings	62.2 sq. m.
Engine type and h.p.	240 h.p. Lorraine Dietrich.
Load per sq. m.	38.96 kgs.
Weight per h.p.	5.0 kgs.
Tank capacity in hours ..	3 hours.

Performance.

Speed at 2,000 mteres ..	160 km.p.h.
Disposable load apart from fuel	548 kgs.
Total weight of machine loaded	2,423 kgs.

Side View of the Letord Twin-Engined Biplane, type V.

The Letord type V Twin-Engined Bomber.

242a

LETORD.—*continued*.

THE LETORD. TYPE 9B.N.2.
Specification.

Type of machine	Twin-engined Tractor Biplane.
Name or type No. of machine ..	Letord. Type 9B.N.2.
Purpose for which intended ..	Night Bomber.
Span	25.94 m.
Overall length	14.95 m.
Maximum height	4.26 m.
Total surface of wings	135 sq. m.
Engine type and h.p.	2—350 h.p. Liberty.
Weight of machine empty ..	40.9 kgs.
Load per sq. m.	7.88 kgs.
Tank capacity in hours	6 hours.

Performance.

Speed at 2,000 metres ..	145 km.p.h.	
Disposable load apart from fuel		1,243 kgs.
Total weight of machine loaded		5,521 kgs.

Three-quarter Front View of the Letord Type 9 Night Bomber.

Side View of the Letord Type 9 Night Bomber (2—400 h.p. Liberty engines).

LÉVY.

Hydravions George Lévy, 4, Rue de Cormeilles, Levallois, Paris.

THE GEORGES LÉVY. TYPE R FLYING BOAT.

Specification.

Type of machine	Three-seater Flying Boat. Type R.
Span	Upper plane, 18 m. 50 ; Lower plane, 12 m. 00.
Overall length	12 m. 40.
Maximum height	3 m. 85.
Total surface	68 sq. m.
Engine type and h.p.	Renault. 280 h.p.
Weight of machine empty ..	1450 kgs.
Disposable load	1,000 kgs.
Performance.	
Speed	145 km.p.h.

M

MOINEAU.

M. Louis Moineau, the famous pilot of Bréguets before the War, turned constructor in 1915.

In 1916-17 he produced the curious biplane illustrated herewith.

It is driven by a Salmson-Canton-Unné engine, placed with its shaft thwart-wise of the fuselage. Each end of the shaft drives a cross-shaft to a bevel gear at the intersection of the cross-bracing of the wings, so that the engine drives two air-screws, one on each side of the machine.

A gunner sits in front of the engine, and has a very big arc of fire. Another gunner sits behind the pilot.

The machine flew, but was never put into production.

The Salmson-Moineau Biplane of 1916.

M—continued.

MORANE-SAULNIER. Aeroplanes. Morane-Saulnier, Soc. de Constructions Aéronautiques, 205, Boulevard Pereire, Paris. School : Villacoublay.

The Morane machines, particularly the Parasol monoplanes, rendered great services during the earlier part of the War.

The firm has since turned out a number of biplanes, including certain two-engined machines.

The only information not previously published that has been received is given in the two attached drawings.

THE MORANE SAULNIER.   TYPES 27C.1 & 29C.1.

Type of machine	Single-Seater Parasol Monoplane.
Name or type No. of machine ..	Morane-Saulnier. 27C.1, single gun. 29C.1, two guns.
Purpose for which intended ..	Fighting Scout.
Span	8.72 m.
Overall length	5.7 m.
Maximum height	2.4 m.
Chord	2.013 m.
Total surface of wings ..	13.5 sq. m.
Span of tail	2.7 m.
Engine type and h.p.	160 h.p. Mono. Gnôme.

THE MORANE SAULNIER.   TYPE C.2.

Type of machine	Two-seater Tractor Biplane.
Name or type No. of machine ..	Morane Saulnier. Type C.2.
Span	11.726 m.
Gap	1.7 m.
Overall length	8.345 m.
Chord	1.9 m.
Total surface of wings ..	41 sq. m.
Span of tail	3.66 m.
Engine type and h.p.	420 h.p. Bugatti.
Airscrew, diameter	3.1 m.

SECTION TECHNIQUE DE L'AÉRONAUTIQUE MILITAIRE

SERVICE GÉNÉRAL DES AVIONS

AVION MORANE=SAULNIER

Types 27 C.1 et 29 C.1

Moteur Gnôme 9 N 160 HP
Surface 13 m² 5

Nota : Le type 27 est mononitrailleuse.
Le type 29 est bimitrailleuse.

SECTION TECHNIQUE DE L'AÉRONAUTIQUE MILITAIRE

SERVICE GÉNÉRAL DES

AVION MORANE=SAULNIER

Type C.2

Moteur Bugatti 420 HP
Surface 41 m²

N

NIEUPORT. Soc. Anonyme des Etablissements Nieuport, 46, 48 and 50, Boulevard Gallieni, and 15, Rue Camille Desmoulins, Issy-les-Moulineaux (Seine). *School :* Villacoublay (Seine and Oise). Established 1910 by the late Edouard de Nieport, commonly called Nieuport.

The *Nieuport* biplane has been one of the greatest successes of the war, owing to its high speed and quickness in manœuvre. The lower plane in this type is so small that the machine is really a "parasol," with half a plane attached to give girder formation to the wing bracing. It is frequently called the "one-and-a-half plane."

The whole of the recent information available as to Nieuport developments is supplied by the illustrations herewith.

THE NIEUPORT. TYPE 28C.1.

Type of machine	Single-seater Scout.
Name or type No. of machine ..	Nieuport. 28C.1.
Span	Top plane, 8.16 m. ; Bottom plane, 7.77 m.
Overall length	6.3 m.
Maximum height	2.3 m.
Chord	Top plane, 1.3 m. Bottom plane, 1.0 m.
Total surface of wings ..	16 sq. m.
Span of tail	2.8 m.
Engine type and h.p.	160 h.p. monosoupape Gnôme.
Airscrew, diam.	2.5 m.

Side View of the Nieuport Type 28C.1 Single-seat Fighter (160 h.p. Monosoupape Gnôme Engine).

Three-quarter Front View of the Nieuport Type 28C.1 Single-seat Fighter (160 h.p. Monosoupape Gnôme Engine).

NIEUPORT—*continued.*

SECTION TECHNIQUE DE L'AERONAUTIQUE MILITAIRE

SERVICE GÉNÉRAL DES AVIONS

AVION NIEUPORT
Type 28 C. 1

Moteur Gnôme monosoupape 9 N 160 HP
Surface 16 m²

Echelle 1 100e

An Experimental Nieuport, with Lorraine Dietrich Engine.

247a

NIEUPORT—*continued.*

An Experimental Nieuport, with 240 h.p. Renault Engine.

An Experimental Nieuport, with Renault Engine.

NIEUPORT—*continued.*

An Experimental Nieuport, with Lorraine Dietrich Engine.

An Experimental Nieuport, with Hispano-Suiza Engine.

An Experimental Nieuport, with Hispano-Suiza Engine.

A Nieuport Scout, with the Prieur Incendiary Rockets in position.

Three-quarter Front View of an Experimental Nieuport Triplane (110 h.p. Le Rhone Engine).

Side View of the Nieuport Experimental Triplane.

R

R.E.P. Cabinet á Etudes en Recherches Techniques. Robert Esnault-Pelterie, 37, Rue des Abondances, Boulogne sur Seine (Seine). *School* : Buc. One of the earliest established French firms. The first to go in for steel construction.

The *R.E.P.* "parasols" proved to have excellent climbing and weight lifting power, and so did well early in the war.

Of late, M. Esnault-Pelterie has been engaged on experimental designs, and his works have been employed on special work which cannot be described.

S

SALMSON.

Société des Moteurs Salmson, Billancourt, Seine.

Aircraft factory, allied to the famous aero-engine firm, constructors of the Salmson-Canton-Unné engines.

Have built various aeroplanes on which to demonstrate the firm's engines, and have achieved remarkable results.

M. Salmson is a great engineering employer, and has spent a fortune on experimental work with aero-engines and aircraft generally.

The following description and illustrations give the information available as to the firm's recent products.

THE SALMSON S.A.L. 2-A. 2.

Type of machine	Biplane.
Name or type No. of machine ..	S.A.L. 2-A. 2.
Span	11 m. 75.
Gap	1 m. 700.
Length overall	8 m. 500.
Maximum height	2 m. 900.
Chord	1 m. 676.
Surface of wings	37.27 sq. m.
Surface of tail	4.20 sq. m.
Surface of rudder	1.25 sq. m.
Surface of each aileron and total area	2.7 × 4 = 5.08 sq. m.
Fuselage section (maximum) ..	1 m. 25 × 1 m. 75.
Engine type and h.p.	Salmson Z9. 250 h.p.
Airscrew, diam.	2 m. 75.
Pitch	2 m. 100.
Weight of machine empty ..	834 kgs.
Weight per h.p.	5.5 kgs.
Tank capacity in litres	Petrol, 265 litres. Oil, 47 litres.

Performance.

Speed at ground level ..	187 km.p.h.
Speed at 3,000 m.	175 km.p.h.

Climb.

To 2,000 m.	11 mins.
To 3,000 m.	$17\frac{1}{4}$ mins.
To 5,000 m.	$40\frac{1}{4}$ mins.
Weight of machine in flying order	..1,380 kgs.

Three-quarter Front View of the Salmson type S.A.L. 2-A. 2. (250 h.p. Salmson engine.

SALMSON—*continued.*

THE SALMSON. TYPE 4AB.2.

Specification.

Type of machine	Two-seater Tractor Biplane.
Name or type No. of machine ..	Salmson. 4AB2.
Span	15.14 m.
Maximum height	3.12 m.
Chord	2.00 m.
Total surface of wings	49.5 sq. m.
Span of tail	5.008 m.
Engine type and h.p.	230 h.p. Salmson.

SECTION TECHNIQUE DE L'AÉRONAUTIQUE MILITAIRE

SERVICE GÉNÉRAL DES AVIONS

AVION SALMSON
Type 4 Ab. 2

Moteur 9 Z 230 HP
Surface 49 m² 5

SAL. 4 AB. 2

SALMSON—*continued.*

THE SALMSON. TYPE 5A.2.

Specification.

Type of machine	Two-seater Tractor Biplane.
Name or type No. of machine ..	Salmson. 5A2.
Span	12.2 m.
Gap, maximum and minimum ..	1.75 m.
Overall length	7.8 m.
Maximum height	2.91 m.
Chord	1.8 m.
Total surface of wings	40 sq. m.
Span of tail	4.2 m.
Engine type and h.p.	230 h.p. Salmson
Airscrew, diam.	2.8 m.

THE SALMSON. TYPE 7A.2.

Specification.

Type of machine	Two-seater Tractor Biplane.
Name or type No. of machine ..	Salmson. 7A2.
Span	12.34 m.
Gap, maximum and minimum ..	1.7 m.
Overall length	8.83 m.
Maximum height	2.86 m.
Chord	1.67 m.
Total surface of wings	39 sq. m.
Span of tail	4.36 m.
Engine type and h.p.	230 h.p. Salmson.
Airscrew, diam.	2.8 m.

254a

S—continued.

SCHMITT.

Paul Schmitt, 39, Route de la Révolte, Levallois Perret (Seine).

Constructors of the *Paul Schmitt* biplanes, in association with the Morane Saulnier firm.

The first machine produced before the outbreak of war was notable chiefly for its ability to give variable angle of incidence to the main planes.

During 1916 and 1917 the firm has built war aeroplanes of more orthodox types.

M. Paul Schmitt has experimented since 1904 with large kites and gliders, and has been concerned with flying since 1909. He has invented, constructed, and tuned up various types of aeroplanes of destructive kinds.

In 1910, he experimented with a biplane without a fuselage or tail, analogous to the *Dunne*, but of a different shape. It had variable incidence, weighed 1,000 kilos, and had a 70 h.p. engine.

In 1913, M. Schmitt exhibited at the Paris Aero Show his fuselage biplane, three-seater, with variable incidence. It was bought by the French Army.

At the beginning of 1914, his pilot, M. Garaix—since fallen on the field of honour—put up, on the *Paul Schmitt* biplane, 42 World's Records, which stand to-day in 1918, so far as single-engined machines are concerned, and barring records put up by multi-engined types such as the *Caproni* and *Handley Page*. These included height, speed, duration and distance, with four to nine passengers.

M. Schmitt was winner of the Concours Pour La Securité (Safety Competition) in 1914.

He also came out first in the French competition for high powered aeroplanes in 1915.

During the war, after serving as a bomber-machine-gunner, he built several types of aeroplanes, specially for bombing, and a hydro-aeroplane for the United States. His three-seater with two gunners was the leading machine of its class.

It is claimed that the fuselages of these machines, of steel tube, cannot get out of truth. The controls are of a special type, dating back to 1913. Comparing these machines with the *Albatros*, it is seen that both fuselages terminate in a triangle running into a T-shape for tail and rudder-post, the rudder being above the tail and in front of it, thus giving special solidity at this vital point. In both machines the rudders and elevators are balanced. In both there is a vertical surface under the fuselage. In both the elevator is a single flap, and is not in the usual two pieces. Thus it appears that the *Albatros* designer has profited by study of the *Paul Schmitt* design.

In 1917, the *P. S.* biplanes (bombers) carried two machine-guns, and carried several hundreds of kilos of bombs, with fuel for many hours' flying. With this big load, the "ceiling" of the machines was well over 4,000 m. (13,000 ft.).

The chief characteristic of all the *P. S.* machines is the variable incidence of the main planes, which permits good balance between 0° and 12°. The main cellule is a single block, solid on the four centre-section struts—of steel tube—which can rotate round a central horizontal pivot. The rotation is controlled by a wheel and chain.

This permits the pilot to adjust the angle of incidence to suit his load and speed, while keeping the fuselage always at its correct flying angle, either for climbing, fast flying, or slow landing.

The *P. S.* machines have always been fitted with fixed-cylinder engines, first a Salmson radial, and later V-type Renault.

Three-quarter Rear View of Paul Schmitt biplane. Note the wheels in the centre section for the operation of the ailerons.

S—*continued.*

S.E.A. Société d'Etudes Aéronautiques, Aubervillers, Seine

A new firm, which was moved during the bombardment of Paris to Angers, and altered its name to the "Société des Etablissements Angevins."

By now it has probably returned to Aubervillers.

THE S.E.A. TYPE 4C.2.
Specification.

Type of machine	Two-seater Tractor Biplane.
Name or type No. of machine ..	S.E.A. 4C2.
Span	12 m.
Overall length	8.5 m.
Maximum height..	3.1 m.
Chord	1.6S m.
Total surface of wings ..	537. sq. m.
Engine type and h.p.	350 h.p. Lorraine Dietrich.

SPAD. The Spad (Société Pour Aviation et ses Dérivés) is the old Deperdussin firm, founded in 1910, and revived in the first year of war by a company, at the head of which is M. Blériot.

Address :—Société SPAD, 19, Rue des Entrepreneurs, Paris ; also at Quai de l'Industrie, Juvisy, near Paris.

A *Deperdussin* monoplane, designed by M Bécherau and M. Koolhoven, covered 124·8 miles in one hour, flying round a 20 kilometre circuit, in August, 1913, and numerous others of his designs had notable success.

To preserve the organisation and collected talent of the firm, M. Blériot took it over soon after the outbreak of war, and it was then known as the Société Pour les Appareils Deperdussin, hence the initials Spad, which have since taken on a new meaning, namely, Société Pour Aviation et Dérivés.

The new *Spad* biplanes, the product of M. Bécherau's mature genius, are in the very front rank for speed and climbing power, and are recognised as among the finest "*aéroplanes de chasse*," or "destroyers," of the war.

The following illustrations and descriptions are all the information available as to *Spad* machines not previously described.

THE SPAD. TYPE 7.
Specification.

Type of machine	Single-seater Tractor Biplane.
Name or type No. of machine ..	Spad. Type 7.
Purpose for which intended ..	Fighting Scout.
Span	7.82 m.
Overall length	6.10 m.
Maximum height	2.35 m.
Total surface of wings ..	18 sq. m.
Engine type and h.p.	150 h.p. Hispano-Suiza.

SECTION TECHNIQUE DE L'AÉRONAUTIQUE MILITAIRE
SERVICE GÉNÉRAL DES AVIONS

AVION S. E. A.
Type 4 C. 2

Moteur Lorraine 350 HP
Surface 37 m²5

THE SPAD. TYPES 13 AND 17.
Specification.

Type of machine	Single-seater Tractor Biplane.
Name or type No. of machine ..	Spad. Types 13 and 17.
Purpose for which intended ..	Fighting Scout.
Span	8.20 m.
Overall length	6.30 m.
Maximum height	2.30 m.
Total surface of wings ..	20 sq. m.
Engine type and h.p.	220 h.p. Hispano-Suiza.

THE SPAD. TYPE 12.
Specification.

Type of machine	Single-seater Tractor Biplane.
Name or type No. of machine ..	Spad. Type 12.
Purpose for which intended ..	Fighting Scout.
Span	8.00 m.
Overall length	6.40 m.
Maximum height	2.30 m.
Total surface of wings ..	20 sq. m.
Engine type and h.p.	220 h.p. Hispano-Suiza.

SPAD—continued.

SECTION TECHNIQUE DE L'AÉRONAUTIQUE MILITAIRE

SERVICE GÉNÉRAL DES AVIONS

AVION SPAD
Type 18 Ca. 1-2

Moteur Hispano-Suiza 8 G 300 HP
Surface 30 m²

THE SPAD. TYPE 18CA. 1—2.

(Commonly known as the Spad-Herbemont).

Specification.

Type of machine	Tractor Biplane.
Name or type No. of machine ..	Spad. 18C.A 1—2.
Span	10 m.
Overall length	7.35 m.
Maximum height	2.75 m.
Total surface of wing	30 sq. m.
Span of tail	2.9 m.
Engine type and h.p.	300 h.p. Hispano-Suiza.
Airscrew, diam.	2.8 m.

The Spad-Herbemont Biplane (300 h.p. Hispano-Suiza Engine). A recent product of the S.P.A.D. firm with an extraordinarily high performance.

T

TELLIER.

Etablissements Tellier, Quai de Seine, Argenteuil, Seine et Oise.

Famous boat-building firm which produced many famous racing motor-boats and hydroplanes.

Built very successful monoplanes in 1910 and 1911, when M. Dubonnet, the well-known French sportsman, took an interest in the firm.

Gave up aeroplane work before the War, but took to making flying-boats soon after War broke out. Towards the end of the War, a number of these boats, of the type illustrated, and fitted with "Maori" Sunbeam engines, did remarkably good work on anti-submarine patrols.

A Tellier Flying-Boat with "Maori" Sunbeam-Coatalen Engine, 350 h.p.

The Power Plant Instalment of a "Maori" Sunbeam in a Tellier Flying-Boat.

A Tellier Flying-Boat (350 h.p. Sunbeam-Coatalen "Maori" Engine) about to take off.

V

VENDÔME.

M. Vendôme, one of the earliest of French constructors, produced in 1916 a machine somewhat after the style of the *Moineau*.

In the fuselage, one on each side, were two Monosoupape Gnôme engines, each driving a shaft to a bevel gear, which in turn drove a tractor airscrew. Thus the machine had two rotary engines turning in opposite directions, which would give it considerable lateral stiffness (though not stability), owing to their gyroscopic action.

A gunner sat in the nose of the machine and another behind the pilot.

As in the case of the *Moineau*, it was never put into production.

VOISIN.

Aeroplanes Voisin, Boulevard Gambetta, Issy-les-Moulineaux, (Seine).

Associated with the Etablissements Ch. Lefevre & Cie. Société Anonyme, with capital of 3,000,000 francs.

Paris Office : 105, Rue St. Lazare, Paris.

The oldest aeroplane firm in the world, founded by the Brothers Voisin, in 1905.

THE VOISIN 4-ENGINED BIPLANE. TYPE 13.

Specification.

Type of machine	4-engined Biplane.
Name or type No. of machine ..	Voisin. Type 13.
Purpose for which intended ..	Night Bomber.
Span	Top plane, 30 m. ;
	Bottom plane, 24.162 m.
Chord	3.00 m.
Total surface of planes ..	155.686 sq. m.
Tank capacity in kgs. ..	1,100 kgs.
Engine type and h.p. ..	4—230 h.p. Hispano-Suiza.
Airscrews, type	Lumière.
Weight per h.p.	6.19 kgs.
Weight per sq. metre ..	36.53 kgs.
Performance.	
Speed	146 km.p.h.
Climb.	
To 3,000 metres in minutes ..	30 mins.
Useful load	1,300 kgs.
Total weight of machine loaded	..5,700 kgs.

The Vendôme Biplane of 1916 (2—100 h.p. Gnome Engines.)

General arrangement of a four engined Night-Bomber slightly modified from the type B12.

VOISIN—*continued.*

THE VOISIN TWO-SEATER NIGHT BOMBER.

Type of machine	Voisin—Bombardement de Nuit.
Purpose for which intended ..	Night bombing.
Span	18 metres top; 17 metres bottom plane.
Overall length	10 metres.
Total surface of wings ..	63 sq. metres.
Engine type and h.p... ..	280 h.p. Renault.
Weight of machine empty ..	1,400 kgs.

Performance.
    Speed .. .. .. 130 k.p.h. max.

Climb.
    To 4,000 metres in 45 minutes.
Disposable load apart from fuel .. .. .. 650 kgs.

THE VOISON. TYPE 12 B.N.2.

Specification.

Type of machine	Four-engined Biplane.
Name or type No. of machine ..	Voisin. Type 12 B.N.2.
Purpose for which intended ..	Night bombing.
Span	30.6 m. Folded, 16.6 m.
Overall length	16.6 m.
Maximum height	4.3 m.
Chord	2.7 m.
Total surface of wings	145 sq. m.
Engine type and h.p.	4—220 h.p. Hispano-Suiza.

The Voisin Type 12 B.N.2 Night Bomber (4—220 h.p. Hispano-Suiza Engines).

Side View of the Voisin Type 12 B.N.2 (Night Bomber) (4—220 h.p. Hispano-Suiza Engines).

VOISIN—continued.

SECTION TECHNIQUE DE L'AÉRONAUTIQUE MILITAIRE

SERVICE GÉNÉRAL DES AVIONS

AVION VOISIN
Type 12 BN. 2

Moteur H.-S. 8 B 220 HP
Surface 145 m²

Voi. 12 BN. 2

The Voisin Twin-engined Triplane.

2 к 2

VOISIN—*continued.*

The Voisin "Aéro-Chir," a Flying Ambulance, which carries one complete operating theatre in boxes under the wings.

A Twin-engine Voisin Triplane of 1915. In its four-engined form it developed into the design shown on page 263.

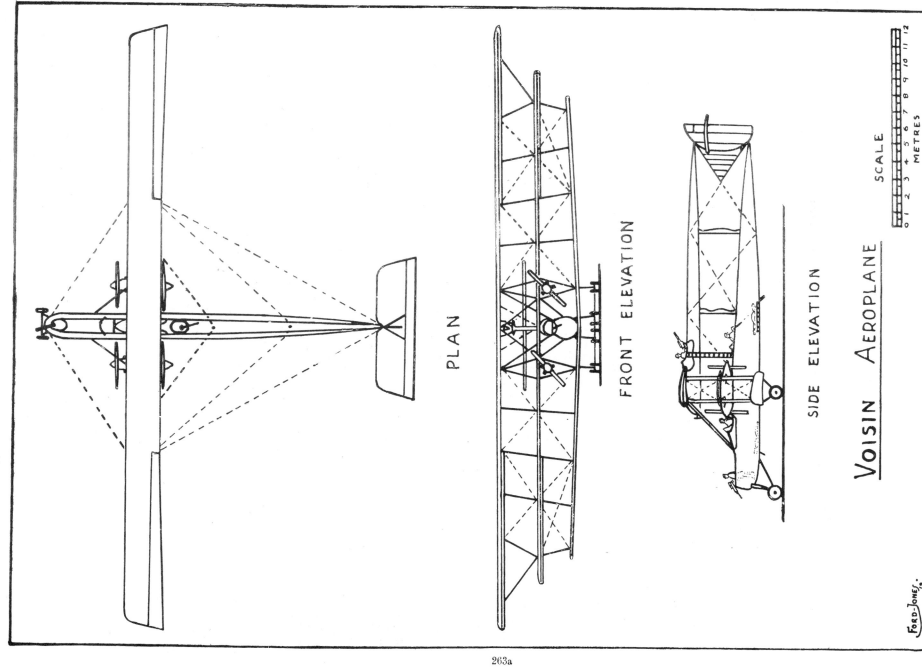

PLAN

FRONT ELEVATION

SIDE ELEVATION

VOISIN AEROPLANE

SCALE

METRES

Ford-Jones.

The Voisin Triplane, showing gun emplacements.

The Three-engined Voisin Triplane.

The Voisin Single-engined Bomber Type 10 (400 h.p. Liberty Engine).

WEYMANN.

M. Charles Weymann, winner of the Gordon-Bennet Race of 1911, and one of the earliest Franco-American pilots, produced in 1916 the small biplane illustrated herewith.

The peculiarity of the machine was that it was driven by an airscrew behind the rudder, in the manner of the *Paulhan-Tatin* monoplane of 1912.

The Weymann biplane was built by the Société de St. Chamond and the fuselage and wing construction was entirely of metal. The machine made several trial flights, but was not put into production.

The All-Metal Weymann Biplane of 1916.

GERMAN.

GERMAN MILITARY AVIATION.

Aerial Societies :—

Aero Klub (Imperial), 3, Nollenderfplatz, Berlin. Sec.: H. Von Frankenberg und Ludwigsdorf.

Automobil-und Flugtechnische-Gesellschaft (E. V.) Nurnberger Platz 5, Haupyverein Berlin, Hochster Str. 1, Bezirksverein Frankfurt a. M. Neuer Wall 44, II, Hamburg.

ARMY GENERAL.

The Army law of 1914 provided £400,000 (80 million marks) for Army aviation (including dirigibles), in addition to a considerable share of the £4,000,000 which was to be spread over a period of five years.

The Army aerial force was commanded by 2 inspector generals. The aviation force was put at 4 battalions. In 1916, the Army Aviation Service was placed under a separate "Intendantur." The officer commanding having the grading of the Commander of an Army Corps.

Headquarters: Berlin. *Stations*: Aachen, Allenstein, Cologne, Darmstadt, Doebritz, Freiburg, Graudenz, Hannover, Insterburg, Jüterbog, Koenigsberg, Metz, Posen, Strassburg, Zeithain, etc.

The scheme was complete by the end of the year 1914.

The Army Flying Schools then in operation were :—

Darmstadt (3, Kompagnie Flieger Bataillon 3).
Döberitz (1 und 2 Kompagnie Flieger Bataillon 1).
Freiburg (3 Kompagnie Flieger Bataillon 4).
Germersheim (Kgl. Bayernsche Heeresverswaltung).
Graudenz (2 Kompagnie Flieger Bataillon 2).
Hannover (2 Kompagnie Flieger Bataillon 2).
Jüterbog (Truppenkommando).
Köln (1 Kompagnie Flieger Bataillon 3).
Königsberg (3 Kompagnie Flieger Bataillon 2).
Metz (2 Kompagnie Flieger Bataillon 4).
München-Oberschleissheim (Kgl. Bayernsches Flieger Bataillon).
München-Oberwiesenfeld (Kgl. Kommandatur).
Posen (1 Kompagnie Flieger Bataillon 2).
Saarbrücken (Kgl. Preussische Herresverwaltung).
Schneidemühl (Kgl. Preussische Heereverwaltung).
Strassburg (1 Kompagnie Flieger Bataillon 4).
Zeithain (3 Kompagnie Flieger Bataillon 2).

ARMY AEROPLANES.

The early growth of the aeroplane force may be seen from the following notes :—

Bought in 1913 **120 monoplanes** (*Albatros, Aviatik, Bristol, D.F.W., Fokker, Gothaer, Jeannin, Rumpler*).

120 biplanes (*A.E.G., Albatros, Aviatik, Bristol, D.F.W., Euler, L.V.G., Otto*).

Bought in 1914-15 or ordered sufficient to replace all the 1913 machines. The scheme then was to provide 1000 machines. all of more or less standard *Taube* type (monoplanes) or *Arrow* type (biplanes). Practically all war machines were at first of the *Arrow* type. These were afterwards replaced by higher powered machines with straight planes, which were almost indistinguishable from British tractor biplanes.

Under the 1914 regulations, military machines had to comply with the following conditions :—

1. Must be of entirely German manufacture, with ample and comfortable seating accommodation for pilot and passenger.

2. Design must permit of fitting bomb droppers and photographic apparatus.

3. Speed capabilities must not be less than 90 kilometres (56 m.p.h.)

4. Dimensions must not exceed 49 feet span (14·50 m.), 39 feet long (12 m.), 13 feet high (3·50 m.), and the motor not more than 100 h.p.

5. Minimum endurance, 4 hours.

Since then, speed, climbing capacity and endurance have all increased notably.

A comparison of the German programme for each year with the British programme shows how much more clearly the German Government realised the importance of Military Aviation than did the British Government of the period.

WAR SERVICE.

From time to time, despite the calls on the German Flying Service on other fronts, the German aviators have held a limited superiority over the French and British on the West Front, owing to their rapidity in placing new types of machines in the air in quantities.

At the end of 1915, a number of picked pilots, notably Capt. Immelmann and Capt. Bölcke, mounted on *Fokker* monoplanes, were able to inflict considerable damage on the slower flying and climbing British and French reconnaissance machines of the period. They had the advantage of always flying over their own territory, being on defensive work, and so could carry light loads of petrol, thus adding defensive work.

A group of German officer aviators in front of one of their machines on Active Service.

GERMAN MILITARY AVIATION.

to both their speed and manœuvrability. When their operations were checked by superior British machines, and after the deaths of Immelmann and Bölcke the Germans lost their superior defensive power, and by the Battle of the Somme, in the Autumn of 1916 they were markedly inferior.

Soon afterwards the Germans produced the single-seater Albatros type of machine—which included besides the *Albatros*, such machines as the *Roland*, the *Pfalz*, the *Halberstadt*, and the *Fokker* biplane. The chief exponent of this type was Rittmeister (Cavalry Captain), Freiherr Manfred von Richthofen, formerly of Bölcke's *Fokker* monoplane squadron. He developed the "Circus" idea to a fine art, and himself scored 80 aerial victories before being killed on April 21st, 1918. He deserves to be remembered as the first of the really great Jagdstäffel, or "Chaser Formation" leaders.

The victorious career of the German Circuses was checked about the middle of 1917 by the advent in quantities of *Sopwith* "Camels" (single-seaters), and of *Bristol* "Fighters," big two-seaters. By the end of 1917 the British Royal Flying Corps had established a marked superiority over the Germans in the air, and by May, 1918, the British—including the Australian Flying Corps—practically held the mastery in the air. This mastery was fully maintained until the end of the war. The ingenuity of the German designers seemed to have departed and the output of their constructors did not seem to increase. Consequently in quantity and quality the German aeroplanes were utterly outclassed by the British aircraft industry.

1917 was also remarkable for the introduction of the *Gotha* twin-engined bombers. These machines were first tried on defenceless Bucharest early in 1917, and thereafter a raid was tried on Salonika—which lost the Germans two *Gothas* in a day. During the rest of the year the *Gothas* gave much of their attention to bombing London, and occasionally Paris. These machines, and their bigger descendants the "Riesenflugzeugen" —or "Giant Flying Machines"—also bombed Dunkerque, Calais, Boulogne and other towns behind the Allies' lines, but after one or two attempts at day-light raiding, they confined their operations entirely to night-flying.

During the early part of 1918 the Germans introduced armoured machines for "contour fighting," or "ground-strafing"—as it is more commonly called, but these were not very successful.

After July, 1918, the whole *moral* of the German Air Service fell to pieces, and the British, French and American aviators had matters almost entirely their own way.

THE REORGANISATION OF THE GERMAN FLYING CORPS.

The following article by "Austerlitz" (a well-known cosmo-politan writer), sets forth clearly the organisation for the German Flying Corps in 1917, which organisation was retained till the end of the war :—

The Allied offensive of the Somme, in July, 1916, proved beyond doubt the overwhelming superiority of the Royal Flying Corps and of the French *Aviation Militaire* over the aerial forces of the enemy. During the preliminary stages of that battle a powerful aeroplane barrage of the Allies effectually prevented enemy aviators from crossing our lines to discover our preparations ; in addition to this strategical blinding, the enemy's artillery was also deprived of its *eyes*, all of its kite-balloons being either destroyed or driven down by Allied aviators. German army orders, found on officers taken prisoner, acknow-

ledged with great frankness the inferiority of their air service, and directly ascribed to it the costly defeat the enemy suffered.

Since then, however, the enemy has furnished a very considerable effort, with a view of re-establishing the aerial situation in his favour, and this effort, pragmatised by an ambitious building programme, eventually resulted in a complete reorganisation of the German Flying Corps.

This reorganisation, which now appears to be completed, affected both the tactical formation and the *matériel*. There are at present four major tactical formations within the German Flying Corps ; these are :—

(1) Army squadrons (Armeeflieger-Abteilung).
(2) Army corps squadrons (Truppenflieger-Abteilung).
(3) Pursuit squadrons (Jagd-Staffeln).
(4) Battle wings (Kampf-Geschwader).

1. The *Army squadrons* are placed under the direct orders of the O.C. the aviation service of each army ; they are primarily employed for strategical reconnaissances, but may sometimes be detailed on photographic work and even bombardments.

The *machines* forming the Army squadrons all belong to a standard model in which only minor details may vary, as a certain latitude is given the contractors in this respect. The machines are two-seater tractor biplanes of from 41 to 45 feet span, and are fitted with a stationary Benz or Mercédès engine developing from 225 to 240 horse-power. Their horizontal speed is from 100 to 105 miles per hour.

The *armament* consists of (1) two machine guns, one of which is mounted on a fixed emplacement in front of the pilot, and fires through the propeller by means of a synchronising device ; the other machine gun is mounted *en barbette*, aft of the pilot, on the observer's seat ; (2) one or two bomb gears, munitioned with four or six bombs.

The firms building this type are the L.V.G., the D.F.W., the Aviatik, and the Albatros. The latter firm has, however, recently produced a more powerful model, which is fitted with a 260-h.p. Mercédès engine, and develops a horizontal speed of 115 miles per hour. The climbing speed is said to be 6,600 feet in 9 minutes, fully loaded. It is confidently expected that eventually all the machines of the Army squadron type will be fitted with the new 6-cylinder, 260-h.p. Mercédès engine, which is, though but slightly heavier, much more reliable than the 8-cylinder, 240-h.p. model. As the engine base of both models has the same width, only slight alterations would be necessary to fit the above described type of machine with the 260-h.p. model, although the wing area would probably have to be somewhat increased. It is worth noting that in 1916 the standard 150-h.p. two-seater tractor biplane was similarly modernised when it was fitted with the 175-h.p. Mercédès.

2. The *Army-Corps squadrons* are assigned to individual army corps, and are, as a rule, commanded by a captain who is placed directly under orders of the second bureau of the army corps staff. Their chief function is tactical reconnaissance, photography, gun spotting, and, during active operations, contact patrol work between the units engaged in an advance.

The army-corps squadrons are equipped with machines which are in every way similar to those forming the Army squadrons, except for a smaller power plant which endows them with lesser speed. Such are, at present, the two-seater tractor biplanes built by A.E.G., Albatros, Aviatik, L.V.G. and Rumpler, which have a span of from 39 to 43 feet, and are fitted with a 6-cylinder, 175-h.p. Mercédès engine. The horizontal speed is from 90 to 95 m.p.h.

The armament is the same as on the army squadron type. Provision is made on these machines for the quick exchange of the bomb gear against a radio installation or a photographic apparatus.

3. The *Pursuit Squadrons* are assigned to individual armies in numbers varying in accordance with needs. Although their principal function is the defence of the army corps squadrons engaged in tactical reconnaissance work, they are also employed in some instances, on convoy duty with bombers and for the destruction of Allied kite-balloons.

There appear to be, at present, on the Western front, about 40 pursuit squadrons, each of which consists of 12 machines. In some instances two or more squadrons are combined into Pursuit Wings which are placed under the leadership of particularly capable chiefs ; these units are not permanently assigned to particular sectors, but are entrusted with special missions according to needs. Such are the now celebrated "travelling circuses" of Von Bulow and Von Richthofen. These special wings generally scour the Western front for Allied machines, travelling up and down the line from Nieuport to Belfort.

A number of pursuit squadrons are detached to the local defence of important German towns, in particular at Metz, Strasbourg, Mulhouse, Friedrichshafen, Stuttgart, Essen, Cologne, and Treves.

The pursuit squadrons are equipped with one-seater biplanes of from 28 to 30 feet span which are fitted with a 175-h.p. Mercédès engine driving a tractor screw. The horizontal speed of these machines is from 110 to 125 miles per hour ; they are principally built by Albatros, Fokker, L.T.G. (Lufttorpedo-Gesellschaft), and Roland.

The armament consists of two Spandau machine-guns, mounted "fixé" in front of the pilot, which are synchronised to fire either simultaneously or alternately through the propeller. No bomb gear is provided.

The older pursuit machines, such as the Halberstadt, with a 120-h.p. Argus engine, the Rex, with a rotary 100-h.p. Rex engine, and the Fokker, with a 100-h.p. rotary Oberursel (German Gnôme), all of which are tractor biplanes, appear to be employed, at present, chiefly on the "easier" Eastern front.

4. The *Battle wings* are placed under the direct orders of General Headquarters, and are not, as a rule, permanently assigned to particular sectors.

These wings consist of from 40 to 50 machines, and are sub-divided into four or five squadrons. The machines are mostly Gotha twin-pusher biplanes, which have a span of 78 feet, and are fitted with two 260-h.p. Mercédès engines.

A certain number of bomber squadrons are, however, equipped with A.E.G. twin-tractor biplanes and a huge Rumpler bomber was to have been placed in commission. The Germans had no mean hopes of this machine, particularly as regards speed and climb.

There are, at present, three battle wings in commission. Wings No. 1 and No. 2 are mobile formations, each of which disposes of a special railway train for the transport of the *matériel* and the *personnel*. These wings are assigned by General Headquarters, from time to time, to such sectors as may require the co-operation of a powerful bombing unit.

Wing No. 3 is stationed in Belgium, and appears to be chiefly entrusted with expeditions against Great Britain. This wing consists of Squadrons No. 13, 14, 15, 16, and 17, all of which are equipped with Gotha bombers.

GERMAN NAVAL AVIATION.

NAVY GENERAL.

The 1913 expenditure on naval aviation (including airships) was £250,000 (50 million marks), plus a portion of the special expenditure.

NAVAL FLYING SCHOOLS AND STATIONS.

Kiel.   **Putzig** b. Danzig.   **Wilhelmshaven.**

Stations are also known to have existed at Heligoland, Langeoog, and Cuxhaven, and at numerous points along the North Sea and Baltic Coasts. Antwerp, Ostend, and Zeebrugge in Belgium also contain German Naval Air Stations.

NAVY AEROPLANES.

Early in 1914 the total effective force was 36 seaplanes as follows :—

1912 {
4 monoplanes (*Rumpler*).
10 biplanes (4 *Albatros*, 2 *Curtiss*, 4 *Euler*).

1913 {
2 monoplanes (*Rumpler*).
30 biplanes (*A.G.O.*, *Albatros*, *Avro*, *Curtiss*, *Wright*).

Total **14** old and **32** new machines.

In 1914, a *Wight* seaplane and a *Sopwith* "bat-boat" were bought in England, and a large number of German seaplanes were built.

1914-1915 {
Since war broke out it is known that a very large number of seaplanes have been added for patrol work, and for co-operation with fast ships at sea.

1915-16-17 {
The German Naval Air Service has increased consistently. German seaplanes are constantly met and fought over the coast of Flanders, and have made frequent raids on the Kentish coast. Seaplanes have also been reported along the Baltic coast, and from Denmark and Holland. Seaplanes have been picked up far out in the North Sea, and have been reported as taking part in Naval actions far from the coast. Seaplane stations are known to exist at Ostend, Zeebrugge, on the Frisian Islands, on Helgoland and on the Island of Sylt, as well as on the Baltic.

The most notable exploit by a German seaplane during 1917-18 was in connection with the cruise of the "Wolf," the famous commerce-destroyer which did so much damage in the Indian Ocean. This ship carried a seaplane, known as the "Wölfchen," or "Little Wolf," and on many occasions this machine discovered victims for her mother-ship. She was brought home safely.

During 1917 and early 1918 seaplane patrols were frequently met in the North Sea by British seaplanes, and a number of actions were fought, in which several German machines were brought down. German seaplanes also took part in all Naval actions during the year, except at night.

During the summer of 1918 the German seaplanes, chiefly Brandenburgers and Rumplers (*q.v.*), obtained a distinct superiority over British seaplanes in the North Sea, owing to the fact that they were small, very fast, and quick in manœuvring, and were opposed to big slow flying-boats carrying heavy loads of petrol for long patrols. The British Authorities had discouraged the production of fast fighting seaplanes, and consequently none were available to counter the German Navy's attacks.

The British losses in big boats and also in airships became so heavy that ultimately the Navy was forced to move in the matter, and when the Armistice was signed the balance of fighting power was on the point of being redressed.

Types of German Naval pupils at the Lübeck Naval Flying School. It will be noted that these pupil-pilots are of non-commissioned rank, contrary to British custom, where almost all pilots are officers.

German information is naturally hard to come by, but it has been possible to obtain a considerable amount from various sources. This information will, it is hoped, be of considerable interest to all students of aviation.

GERMAN FLYING GROUNDS.

ADLERSHOF (School and Depot). Albatros, Ago.

ALTENBURG. Drill ground at the outskirt of the wood to East of Altenburg. Size: About 800 metres × 800 metres.

ALTENBURG (Depot).

AUGSBURG. The large drill ground of the garrison, 200 metres off the railway station Oberhausen. Size: 750,000 m². grass surface.

BERLIN-JOHANNISTHAL AERODROME, JOHANNISTHAL. Proprietors: Flying and Sport Ground Berlin-Johannisthal, Ltd., Berlin W. 35, Potsdamer Str. 112. Manager: Major out of service von Tschudi. Size of the aerodrome: About 830 morgen, and thus 2,120 metres' length by a beam of 1,240 metres. The total ground is surrounded by a 3 metres to 4 metres high enclosure of planks. In 1914 there were located on the aerodrome: 29 aircraft firms, 4 works, and 24 sheds (holding) for more than 100 aeroplanes, further several buildings of the "German Experimental Institute of Aviation," as well as an assembling shed of the aviation school of the "German Air Fleet Association," a shed as motor test stand of the N.A.G. (New or National Automobil Gesellschaft) and conduits, Abessiniers-an Deep wells in sufficient quantities. Electric current for light, and power too, for the total buildings.

BERLIN-SCHULZENDORF. Flying field of the "Berlin Flying Sport Club." Size of the free ground for alighting: 1,500 metres by 800 metres. Flying course: 300 metres × 450 metres. Compact sand, short grass surface. Two sheds of the size: 14 metres × 18 metres, and one 14 metres × 56 metres. Partly marking of the ground by wire fence.

BERLIN-TELTOW AERODROME. City office: Berlin 62, New Friedrich Str. 1. Three-cornered course of about 1,500 metres' base line and 1,000 metres side. Hard grass surface, interior flying course rolled. Starting track cemented. 8 sheds. Restaurant, grand stand. Partly fixed wooden enclosure. Proprietors: Flying Training Field, Teltow, Ltd. Several schools of flying.

BONN BY RHINE. Hangers around heath, with some sheds of the Werntgen Aircraft Works.

BORK IN MARK. **AERODROME MARS,** by the Bork railway station. Berlin office: Martin Luther Str. 91, W. 30. Size of the ground: About 1,000 metres × 500 metres. Distance from the railway station: 400 metres. 9 heatable sheds. The surface is coarse-grained sand with grass, complete level without any obstructions for landing, surrounded by a low pine wood.

BRAUNSCHWEIG. Large drill ground of the garrison. Size: 1,000 metres × 800 metres, compact grass surface.

BREMEN. Drill ground to South West of Bremen-New City, hired by the Bremen Aero Club of the military authorities. Size: 600 metres × 700 metres, grass surface. About 5 kilometres off the railway station Bremen. 3 sheds, 14 × 15 m.

BRESLAU. Drill ground, **GANDAU BY BRESLAU.** Size: 1,300 metres × 600 metres. 2 sheds: 18 × 13 m. Medical rooms, workshops and stores.

BRESLAU (School and Depot). Albatros.

BROMBERG. Race ground: **BLEICHFELDER PLACE.** Grass level, with much mould. Fixed enclosure only partly, else railway embankment and wood.

BURG. Ordnance drill ground. Size: 1,400 metres × 800 metres. Grass surface. 2 sheds of the Schulze Aircraft Works.

CASSEL-WALDAUER. Drill ground. Size: 133 ha. 1 shed of the dimensions: 24 m. × 10 m.

CHEMNITZ. Garrison drill ground. Size: 150 ha. 3 kilometres off the main railway station of Chemnitz. Grass surface. 2 sheds of 225 m². area each.

COLOGNE. 1. **DRILL GROUND, MERHEIM,** with 2 sheds, belonging to the Cologne Club of Aeronautique, and holding 3 areoplanes each. 2. **DRILL GROUND, KALK-HÖHENBERG,** to east of the suburb Kalk.

COLOGNE. Army flying station on the **BUTZWEILERHOF,** with sheds for 20 aeroplanes.

COLOGNE (Köln) (School and Depot).

DANZIG. Naval flying station in **PUTZIG.**

DARMSTADT. Troops' training ground, **GRIESHEIM BY DARMSTADT,** mostly compact sand start track.

DARMSTADT (School and Depot). Aviatik, L.V.G.

DÖBERITZ. Army aerodrome of the flying troops.

DÖBERITZ (Depot). Appareils divers.

DRESDEN. Vogelwiese, 400 metres × 600 metres. Compact grass surface.

DÜSSELDORF. Drill ground, **LOHAUSER.** Size: 1,800 metres × 1,500 metres. Grass surface. 5 sheds of 15 metres × 15 metres area each, belonging to the Dusseldorf Flying Sport Club.

ERFURT. Flying field, belonging to the military fiscus, with 1 shed for 2 aeroplanes of the firm O. Schwade & Co.

ESSEN-GELSENKIRCHEN. Aerodrome in size of 1,100 metres × 600 metres, with sheds for about 20 aeroplanes, workshops, medical rooms, and covered visitors' stands. Surrounded by fixed enclosure.

FLENSBURG. Flying field of The Airship Landing Ground, with 2 sheds of 15 metres × 15 metres × 4 metres each.

FRANKFURT A M. 1. Aerodrome by the airship shed by **REBSTOCK.** Size: 400,000 m². Surface conditions: Level grass, without trees or shrubbery, smooth starting track of 60 metres' length. 6 sheds. Lasting outer wire and interior wooden enclosure. 2. Aerodrome of the firm August **Euler** in **FRANKFURT-NIEDERRAD.**

FRANKFURT-AM-MEIN (School and Depot). Euler.

FREIBURG IN BREISGAU. Drill ground of the garrison. Size: About 1 km²., Dry grass surface. About ten minutes off the railway station. Sheds for 2 or 3 aeroplanes by size 28 metres × 17 metres × 42 metres.

FREIBURG-IM-BRISGAU (School, transferred to Leipzig). Aviatik.

FÜHLSBÜTTEL (School). Hansa et Brandenburg.

GOERRIS (Schwerin) (School). Fokker.

GOTHA (School and Depot). Albatros, Aviatik, Gotha.

GRAUDENZ (School and Depot). Albatros.

GROSSENHEIM (School and Depot). Albatros, L.V.G.

HANNOVER. 1. **BULT RACEGROUND.** 600 metres × 450 metres. Very level starting track of 300 metres' length. Constant enclosure, barriers between the visitors' ground and the flying track. 2. **DRILL GROUND VAHRENWALDER HEATH.** 2000 metres × 800 metres. Small starting track, queer running trenches, private sheds.

HANNOVER (School and Depot). Albatros, L.V.G.

HAMBURG. 1. **AERODROME GROSS-BORSTEL-FUHLSBÜTTEL.** Size: About 45 ha. Constant enclosed. The large airship shed is situated on the ground. Good surface conditions. Public loan in 30 years for air traffic purpose to the Hamburger Airship Shed Co., Ltd. 2. **DRILL GROUND GROSS-BORSTEL.** 3. **DRILL GROUND LURUP.** 4. **DRILL GROUND WANDSBECK.** 2 sheds.

HOLTEN ON LOWER RHINE. Flying field with own aircraft works.

JOHANNISTHAL (School and Depot) (near Berlin). L.V.G., A.E.G., Rumpler.

KARLSRUHE. 1. Large **DRILL GROUND BY FORCHEIM.** 5 kilometres to 6 kilometres off the goods railway station of the city. 2. **DRILL GROUND BY THE GRENADIER BARRACKS.** 1,100 × 700 metres. Sand ground, partly overgrown with grass. The use of the ground with the reservation of the sanction of the military authorities.

KIEL. Aerodrome Kiel (The City Sport and Playing Ground). 28 ha. Flying track : 700 metres by length, 50 metres to 300 metres' beam. Complete level, drained, compact grass surface. Constant enclosure over all. 2 sheds of 15 metres × 15 metres' area each.

KIEL-KRONSHAGEN. Aerodrome **KRONSHAGEN.** Size : 260,000 m², length 950 metres. 7 sheds. Enlargement planned.

KŒSLIN (School) (Pomerania). L.V.G.

KÖLN (School and Depot), and Waune, Herten, near Köln.

KONSTANZ. Drill ground. Rail of the station **PETERSHAUSEN** adjoining the ground. Size : 700 × 600 metres. Level grass surface. Size of the flying track itself : 500 × 50 metres. Tents for holding of aeroplanes are always to hire from the firm Strohmeyer.

LEIPZIG. Flying field **LINDENTHAL-LEIPZIG.** Five minutes off the railway station Wahren-Leipzig railway station. Size of the ground itself : 1,000 metres × 300 metres. The total free ground useable for landing : 15,000 metres × 1,300 metres. The surface level with short grass stretch. Enclosure by 250 metres high planks, partly by railway embankment. 1 double aeroplane shed, 11 single, and 1 shed for 6 aeroplanes. Stands, medical rooms, fire guard, offices, judges' stand tower, petrol stores.

LEIPZIG. Aerodrome **MOCKAU.** Length : 1,800 metres. Breadth : 1,200 metres. Enclosure by planks, 2·75 metres high. Iron airship shed taking 2 Zeppelins. Length : 180 metres. Beam : 63 metres. 12 aeroplane sheds, restaurant with hotel, rails, siding to the Royal Saxon public railways, works, factory sites for hire. Proprietors : Leipziger Aerodrome, Ltd.

LEIPZIG-LINDENTHAL (School). D.F.W.

LEIPZIG-MOCKAU (School). Aviatik.

LÜBECK. Flying field of the airship landing ground by **CARLSHOF.** Complete level ground. The surrounding country suitable to a far extent too for the landing of aeroplanes.

MAGDEBURG. Flying field. 1. On the **BIG ANGER, BURG.** Size : 1,200 metres × 900 metres. Sand, scarce grass surface. Several sheds of the Schulze Aircraft Works. 2. On the **RACE GROUND.** Size : 700 metres × 600 metres. Level meadow, few trees and shrubbery groups.

MAINZ. Drill ground. **BIG SAND.** Size : 2,200 metres × 1,500 metres. Sand ground with compact starting track. Length : 400 metres. Breadth : 300 metres. 3 sheds, two of them belonging to the Goedecker Aircraft Firm, the Mainz Aerial Association being the proprietors of one, holding 4 aeroplanes, with club's house and additional workshop building.

MANNHEIM. 1. **FLYING FIELD ON THE RACE GROUND.** Size : 600 metres × 300 metres. Grass surface. The ground is completely enclosed. 2. **DRILL GROUND BY THE BARRACKS.** 1,000 metres × 800 metres. Sand, partly grass surface, 2 sheds holding 3 aeroplanes.

MANNHEIM (School). Fokker.

MARBURG. Flying ground on the **LAHN** meadows, by the northern outskirt of Marburg. Size : 1,000 metres × 500 metres. 1 shed by the side of the gas work, with the ground area of 18 metres × 20 metres.

METZ. Drill ground **FRESCATY** 3 kilometres to southwest of Metz. Meadow ground, aeroplane sheds of the military authorities.

MÜLHAUSEN IN ALSACE. Flying field on the drill ground **HABSHEIM,** close east to the railway station Rixheim. Circumference of the ground : 5,200 metres. Flying course : 4,000 metres. Meadow ground. Several sheds of the Aviatik Co.

MUNCHEBERG (School). Rumpler.

MÜNCHEN. 1. **AERODROME PUCHHEIM.** Flying course : length 120 metres, breadth 20 metres. Ground conditions : Meadow, no trees, shrubbery, etc. within the aerodrome, only pylons, judges' stand. 9 sheds. Iron beton fence round the total ground, 2·20 metres high. Aerodrome serving only aerial sport purposes. Proprietors : Academy of Aviatik. 2. **DRILL GROUND OBERWIESENFELD.** Size of the whole flying ground : Length about 3 kilometres, breadth 2 kilometres. Extension of the real flying course : two parts about 2 kilometres by length, one 1 kilometre to all three, 1 kilometre broad. Ground conditions : Meadow. Military Flying School and that of the Gustav Otto Aircraft Works. 3. **FLYING GROUND BY SCHLEISSHEIM,** 1 kilometre to south of the railway station Schleissheim. Size : About 700 × 500 metres. Heath ground.

MÜNSTER. Drill ground **LODDENHEIDE.** Size : 1,180 × 750 respective 615 metres. Partly sand ground, partly heath surface. Starting track on the sand field : 325 metres × 750 metres, in the north-western corner on the heath. Surface : 400 metres × 300 metres. One club shed for 2 or 3 aeroplanes, 2 sheds of the inventor Knubel for own-designed monoplanes.

NÜRNBERG. 1. **DRILL GROUND HAINBERG.** Size : 4 km²., suitable as landing ground ; 800 metres × 500 metres, grass and sand. 2. **DRILL GROUND OF THE GARRISON.** Size : 900 metres × 600 metres. Grass surface. Starting track of 400 metres' length.

OBERSCHLEISSHEIM, near Münich. (School and Depot).

OLDENBURG. Flying fields. 1. **DRILL GROUND OF THE GARRISON.** 2. **RACE GROUND BY OHMSTEDE.**

OSNABRÜCK. Flying ground. The Netter Heath. 1 shed.

PLAUEN IN V. 1. **DRILL GROUND KOBITZWALDE.** Size : 900 metres × 800 metres. Surface : Hard, short grass. Small flat trench from north-east to south-west (visible from afar by three single small trees), otherwise no hindrances. Good start track. 2. **AERODROME PLAUEN-REISSIG.** Size : 400 × 400 metres. Sheds. Level surface, solid fence in west.

POSEN. 1. Flying ground on the **RACE-GROUND OF THE POSENER RACE ASSOCIATION.** 2. **DRILL GROUND BY LAWICA,** with compact grass surface.

POSEN (School and Depot). Albatros.

RENDSBURG. Flying field on the there landing ground of airships. 1 shed.

SAARBURG. Drill ground by **BÜHL,** 2 kilometres to south-west of Saarburg, 3 kilometres off the railway station. 1 shed of the south-west section of the German Aerial Touring Association.

SCHNEIDEMÜHL (School and Depot).

SCHNEVERDINGEN. Aerodrome by size : 2,000,000 m². Aircraft works with 2 sheds of the firm Oertzin Hamburg.

SCHWERIN (Depot).

SENNELAGER. Troops' training ground, with sheds.

SPEIER (School). Eversbuch.

STETTIN. Drill ground by **PASSENDORF.**

STRASSBURG IN ALSACE. STRASSBURGER POLYGON. Size : 1,500 × 1,200 metres. Compact, level meadow surface. 1 kilometre to south-east of the railway station Strassburg-Neudorf. Aeroplane sheds of the military authorities.

STUTTGART. CANNSTATTER DRILL GROUND. Size : 1·3 km². 5 private-owned sheds, the one of the Würtemberg Flying Sport Club. Ground area : 2,034 × 1,534 metres. With workshops and forge adjoining.

TOGEL, près Berlin (School). A.E.G., Wangen, près Stuttgart (Ecole).

ULM ON B. 1. **FRIEDRICHSAU,** 4 kilometres off the railway station Ulm. Size : Three corner with side lengths of metres 900, 750 and 1,200. Sand, some grass. 2. **DRILL GROUND LERCHENFELD,** 7 kilometres off the railway station Ulm. Grass surface. Size : Four corners with side lengths of metres, 1,800, 1,300 1,100 and 900. 3. **DRILL GROUND LUD-WIGSFELD.** Size : 1,000 metres × 800 metres.

WANNE-HERTEN. Aerodrome with constant enclosure. Size : 1,100 metres × 750 metres. Cleared and levelled wood surface. Sheds, with workshops, for at least 12 aeroplanes.

WEIMAR. Small drill ground. Flying course : 230 × 500 metres. Surrounding country completely unobstacled. Compact grass surface. 4 sheds, club house with sleeping accommodation, workshops, restaurant, stands, partly wire enclosure.

WIESBADEN. Drill ground by **DOTZHEIM.** Size : 1,600 metres × 1,400 metres. 1 shed of the Mainzer Automobile Teknic School.

WARNEMÜNDE (School). D.F.W.

WÜRZBURG. Garrison drill ground, **GALGENBERG.** 1 shed.

ZWICKAU. Flying field. Drill ground of the garrison.

A

A.E.G. Allgemeine Elektricitäts Gesellschaft.

This big electric company, which also owns and runs the N.A.G. motor works, building up to 1914 Wright and own design aero engines, formed an aircraft branch at Henningsdorf by Berlin, in 1913, the position of which may be compared with the aircraft works of British firms like Vickers and Armstrong-Whitworth, in that they strengthened by their influential financial backing behind them the whole aircraft trade at a time when the latter was looked upon as very problematic by the financial world, and thus not worth investing into.

The activities of the A.E.G. aircraft works have always been confined to military aviation, its flying being open only to and supplied by army pupils, and its aeroplanes never being entered for civil flying competitions.

Steel-built aircraft was always specialised in, the first biplane turned out being of general tractor outlines, the folding of the planes along the fuselage being similar to the British *Short* device.

The well-known former Wright pilot, Schauenberg, was employed, and an A.E.G. biplane entered for the 1914 Prince Henry flight under his pilotage. Schauenberg has been accidentally killed in the firm's service during the war.

The A.E.G. also turned out what was, up to its time, the only successful monoplane flying boat.

During the war the A.E.G. double-engined battleplane has been turned out. One of these is illustrated hereafter.

THE A.E.G. BOMBER.

PERFORMANCE.

(a) CLIMB, 5,000 FT. IN 10.3 MINS.
Rate of climb at 5,000 ft.—390 ft. per min.
Climb, 9,000 ft. in 23.4 mins.
Rate of climb at 9,000 ft.—235 ft. per min.

(b) SPEED AT HEIGHTS.
Level to 5,000 ft.—90 miles per hour approximately.
At 9,000 ft.—86 „ „ „ „

(c) LANDING SPEED.
The aeroplane is best landed at a speed between 75 and 80 miles an hour ; after flattening out it sinks to the ground quickly and pulls up rapidly.

(d) CONTROL.
1. Lateral—Good.
2. Elevators—Bad, especially when landing.

NOTE.—It is stated that it is not advisable to fly this machine without a passenger in the front seat.

Three-quarter Front View of the A.E.G. Bomber, 1918 type.

Front View of the A.E.G. Bomber. 1918 type.

A.E.G. BOMBER—*continued.*

The leading particulars of this machine are as follows :—

Weight empty : 5,258 lbs.
Total weight : 7,130 lbs.
Area of upper wings : 395.2 sq. ft.
Area of lower wings : 335.2 sq. ft.
Total area of wings : 730.4 sq. ft.
Loading per square foot of wing surface : 9.77 lbs. per sq. ft.
Area of ailerons, each : 17.9 sq. ft.
Area of balance of aileron : 1.8 sq. ft.
Area of tail plane : 34.0 sq. ft.
Area of fin : 11.5 sq. ft.
Area of rudder : 20.8 sq. ft.
Balanced area of rudder : 2.6 sq. ft.
Area of elevators : 31.2 sq. ft.
Balanced area of elevators : 3.6 sq. ft.
Horizontal area of body : 206.4 sq. ft.
Vertical area of body : 209.2 sq. ft.
Total weight per horse power : 13.7 lbs. approx.
Crew—pilot and two passengers : 540 lbs.
Armament : 2 guns.
Engines : 2—260 h.p. Mercédès.
Petrol capacity : 123 gallons=861 lbs.
Oil capacity : 11 gallons=110 lbs.
Water capacity : 13 gallons=130 lbs.

THE A.E.G.

THE A.E.G. ARMOURED BIPLANE.

[*The following Report on the A.E.G. Armoured Biplane is published by kind permission of the Technical Department of the Air Ministry, to whom the thanks of the Editor are due.*]

This machine was brought down by an R.E.8. of the 21st Squadron, near Hinges, on May 16th, 1918.

It bears the date February 3rd, 1918, stamped on the main planes, and also on portions of the fuselage, and is the first of its type to have been secured.

This aeroplane is designed for the purpose of carrying out offensive patrols against infantry, and is furnished with armour, which affords protection for its personnel. This armour appears, however, to be more or less experimental.

In general construction it closely follows the lines of the A.E.G. Twin engined Bomber G.105, reported on in I.C. 607, though the arrangement of the power plant is, of course, entirely different.

A steel tubular construction is used practically throughout. The machine was badly crashed, and some details are, therefore, not available ; but the General Arrangement Drawings at the end of this report may be regarded as substantially accurate.

Side View of the **A.E.G. Bomber. 1918 type.**

FIG. 1. **Wing-Spar Butt and innermost Ribs of the A.E.G.**

FIG. 2. **Centre-Section Strut and Fuselage Junction of the A.E.G.**

THE A.E.G.—*continued*.

Gravity Tank

Radiator

Steel Struts

Oil Tank

Armour Plates

Petrol Tanks

Steel Struts

Oil Tank

Gravity Tank

Radiator

Petrol Tanks

Armour Plates

Steel Struts

Steel Tubes

Fabric

Steel Tubes

Steel Tubes

Radiator

— A.E.G.—ARMOURED—AEROPLANE —

SPAN	42' 6"
CHORD	5' 4"
GAP	6' 6"
TAIL PLANE SPAN	9' 0"
OVERALL LENGTH	23' 7"
ENGINE ("BENZ")	200 H.P.
PROPELLER	10' 3" DIA
THICKNESS OF ARMOUR	5 m/m
TRACK	6' 10½"

THE A.E.G.—*continued.*

The leading particulars of the machine are as follows :—

Area of upper wings	.. .. ..	190.4 sq. ft.
Area of lower wings	.. .. ..	168 sq. ft.
Total area of wings	.. ..	358.4 sq. ft.
Area of upper aileron	.. ..	11.2 sq. ft.
Area of lower aileron	.. ..	10 sq. ft.
Area of tail plane	.. ..	9.4 sq. ft.
Area of fin..	.. .. ..	7.6 sq. ft.
Area of rudder	.. .. ..	6 sq. ft.
Horizontal area of body..	..	48.6 sq. ft.
Side area of body..	.. ..	54.8 sq. ft.
Cross sectional area of body	..	14.4 sq. ft.
Area of side armour	..	33 sq. ft.
Area of bottom armour ..	..	29.4 sq. ft.
Area of armour bulkhead	..	10.4 sq. ft.
Engine, 200 h.p. " Benz."		
Crew—pilot and gunner ..	..	360 lbs.
Armament—three guns.		
Petrol capacity	.. ..	38 gallons.
Oil capacity	.. .. ..	3 gallons.

CONSTRUCTION.

WINGS.

The manner in which the wings are constructed is exactly as shown in the report of the A.E.G. Bomber—*i.e.*, the spars consist of two steel tubes 40 mm. in diameter by 0·75 mm. thick. At their ends the upper and lower surfaces of the spars are chamfered away, and flat plates welded in position, so as to provide a taper within the washed-out portion of the wing tips. The wings were, unfortunately, so badly damaged that no accurate drawing of their section can be taken, but there is evidence that this very closely follows the section of the bomber, which has already been published. The ribs are of wood, and between each main rib is placed a half-rib joining the front spar to the semicircular section wooden strip which forms the leading edge. The wing construction is strengthened by two light steel tubes passing through the ribs close behind and parallel to the leading spar, which are used for housing the aileron control wires. The bracing against drag consists of wires and transverse steel tubes welded in position. At the inner end of the wings special reinforced ribs of light gauge steel tube are provided. The method of construction at this point is clearly shown in Fig. 1, which also indicates the manner in which the bracing tube is welded to a socket driven on the main spar. The spars are attached to the fuselage by plain pin joints.

CENTRE SECTION.

The centre section of the upper surface is constructed in a similar manner to that of the wings, except that it is considerably reinforced, and the spars are larger in diameter. The leading spar has a diameter of 51 mm. and the rear spar 45 mm. The centre section is secured to the fuselage by a system of stream-lined steel struts, the feet of which terminate in ball-ends dropped into sockets and there bolted in position.

FIG. 3. **Tail-plane Adjustment.**

FIG. 4. **Tail-stay Adjustment.**

FIG. 5. **Rudder-post Arrangement.**

FIG. 6. **Tail-skid Arrangement.**

FIG. 7. **Method of Attaching Armour.**

FIG. 8. **Method of fixing guns to fire through floor.**

FIG. 9. **Triggers for fixed guns.**

THE A.E.G.—continued.

The centre section contains an auxiliary gravity petrol tank, and also the radiator, and is, therefore, substantially braced with steel tube transverse members.

The wings are set with a dihedral angle of approximately 6 deg.

AILERONS.

The aileron framework is of light steel tube throughout, the tube forming the trailing edge being flattened into an eliptical section. The ribs are fixed by welding. The framework of the ailerons on the upper wing is reinforced by diagonal bracing of light tube.

STRUTS.

These are of light steel tube streamline in section, tapered at each end, and terminating in a socket which abuts against a ball-headed pedestal carried on the wing spars; through the socket and the ball is passed a small bolt. The manner in which this attachment is carried out is exactly similar to that described in the report on the A.E.G. Bomber.

FUSELAGE.

The whole of the fuselage is built up of steel tubes welded together, and having affixed at their junctions sheet steel lugs, which serve as the anchorage for the bracing wires. The diameter of the longerons and of the frame verticals is 20 mm., except the last three members adjacent to the tail, of which the diameter is 16 mm. The welding throughout the fuselage appears to be of very high quality. In Fig. 2 is illustrated a joint which occurs in the fuselage immediately in front of the pilot's cockpit. The longeron is, from this point to the rear of the gunner's cockpit, fitted with a wooden strip taped in position. This joint shows the method in which the cross bracing wires are furnished with an anchorage. In one or two points in the frame construction the bracing wire lies in the some plane as the transverse tube, and to allow for this a diagonal hole is drilled through the tube, and filled in with a small steel tube welded in place.

ENGINE MOUNTING.

This consists of a triangulated arrangement of steel tubes carrying hollow rectangular section steel bearers, on which the crank chamber is slung. The bearers are well trussed both in the vertical and horizontal planes, and are shown in dotted lines in the General Arrangement of Drawings. The engine bearers themselves are 2 mm. in thickness, and have an approximate section of $2\frac{1}{16}$ ins. by $1\frac{1}{2}$ in.

TAIL.

The empennage possesses no particular points of interest, the frames having the usual tubular framework. The tail plane is not fitted with any trimming gear, but a method of adjustment is provided. This is shown in Fig. 3, which is self-explanatory. The diagonal struts which proceed from the base of the fuselage

to the tail plane spar are fitted at each end with a method of adjustment (shown in Fig. 4), allowing them to be extended as required according to the particular socket, which is used to carry the leading edge of the tail plane. Neither the elevators nor the rudder are balanced. The rudder post is mounted on the end of the fuselage (as shown by Fig. 5), in which it will be seen that the vertical frame tube of the fin is very stoutly attached to the frame by a triangulated foot.

LANDING GEAR.

This is of the usual A.E.G. type, and is furnished with shock absorbers consisting of metal coil springs in direct tension, as is clearly shown in the General Arrangement Drawing.

The landing carriage axle has a diameter of 55 mm. The landing carriage struts, which are of similar section to those used between the planes, measures 70 mm. by 37 mm. At their upper ends they are furnished with ball and socket attachments similar to those of the interplane struts.

FIG. 10.   **Cradle for Movable Gun.**

274a

The wheels are fitted with 810 by 125 mm. tyres, and the track is 6 ft. $10\frac{1}{2}$ ins.

The tail skid is unusually heavy, and it is a built-up construction of welded sheet steel. It is mounted on a stout tail post, which is reinforced by four stream-line steel diagonals. The forward end of the tail skid projects inside the fuselage, and is there provided with four steel springs in direct tension. A sketch of the tail skid is given in Fig. 6.

CONTROL.

This consists of the usual double-handled lever mounted on a transverse rocking shaft, which carries the elevator control cranks at each end. The upper ailerons are worked positively by wires which pass over pulleys on the wings spars at the outer struts, the outer and lower ailerons being connected by a stream-line steel tubular strut.

ENGINE.

The 200 h.p. Benz engine possesses no new features, and has already been made the subject of an exhaustive report.

PETROL SYSTEM.

Underneath the pilot's seat are the two main petrol tanks, each of which contains 80 litres (equals 16 gallons). These tanks are of brass, and are fitted with Maximall level indicators. The gravity tank, containing 27 litres (equals $5\frac{1}{2}$ gallons), is embedded in the centre section of the upper plane, where it forms the leading edge on the left-hand side. The tank is made of lead-covered

FIG. 11.   **Locking device for Movable Gun.**

FIG 12.   **Method of Fuselage Bracing.**

THE A.E.G.—*continued*.

steel. Cocks are provided, so that either the gravity tank or the pressure tanks, separately or together, can feed the carburettor.

It is of interest to note that the chamber which is used in connection with the Benz petrol supply system is not, as is usually the case, contained in the main tank, but is a separate fitting mounted on the side of the engine.

RADIATOR.

The radiator is of the Daimler-Mercédès type, measuring $32\frac{1}{2}$ ins. long by $11\frac{1}{2}$ ins. high and 6 ins. deep. This is fitted with imitation honeycomb tubes, of which there are 118 running vertically, each being fitted with 48 gills. The radiator is carried in a steel cradle, into which it is easily inserted from above, and this in turn is supported on specially built-up steel ribs. It is placed so that the tank, which forms the upper part of the radiator, lies about flush with the centre section of the top plane. The shutter or flap for controlling the water temperature is made of 3-ply-wood stiffened with a light steel framework, and is mounted immediately behind the radiator, being worked by a handle within reach of the pilot. This handle is provided with a rack and pawl device. The shutter is $3\frac{3}{4}$ ins. deep, and is capable, therefore, of covering up about one-third of the total radiator surface. It will be noted that the position of the shutter behind the radiator is unusual.

ARMOUR.

Protection for the pilot and gunner is afforded by armour, which is shown in the General Arrangement Drawing in thick lines. There are three panels at each side and three panels at the bottom of the fuselage, an armour bulkhead being placed at the rear of the gunner's cockpit to protect him from behind. The armour is 5.1 mm. thick, and its total area is 105.8 sq. ft. The weight of the armour is thus approximately 860 lbs.

Careful tests have been made to ascertain the effectiveness of this armour, and the following table gives the ranges at which these plates are safe or unsafe against penetration by bullets of various types. These figures may be taken as correct within the limit of a practical firing test.

Ammunition,	Angle to Normal Degrees.	Safe Range. Yards.	Unsafe Range. Yards.
German A.P.	0	—	600
	15	500	400
	30	400	300
Mark VII. P. Armour piercing	0 probably	700	600
	15	400	300
	30	300	200
German Spitze	0	150	100
	15	100	50
	30	50	
Mark VII.	0	50	
	15	50	
	30	50	

The armour is undoubtedly too light to afford protection against British armour-piercing bullets fired from the ground at a lower height than 500 feet, while a machine armoured with it would have to fly at, at least, 1,000 feet to be safe from all but a very low percentage of hits.

The armour does not appear to have been employed, as it might well have been, in a structural capacity—*i.e.*, it is simply an attachment to the framework, to which it adds no material strength. Its appearance seems to point to the fact that it had been added by way of experiment, and that it was of a more or less makeshift character. It had, for instance, evidently been necessary to open out existing holes and cut new holes in the course of erection. The armour is attached by setscrews to clips clamped on the fuselage members, as shown in Fig. 7.

In this machine the pilot is not provided with a gun, but the observer has to control three, of which two (Spandau) are fixed on the flooring of his cockpit, whilst the other (Parabellum) is carried on a rotable mounting.

With regard to the fixed guns, these are secured to a couple of tubular steel brackets, mounted as shown in Fig. 8. The oval-section steel tubes, of which these brackets are composed, are welded to a light steel base, which forms a sort of tray, and is in turn bolted to the armour forming the cockpit floor.

Adjacent to these two guns, which fire forward at an angle of 45 deg., is a bracket carrying the belts of ammunition, which are fed from a large rotating drum.

In the right-hand front corner of the pilot's cockpit floor is a circular hole which he would appear to use for sight purposes.

The fixed guns are controlled by Bowden wires and triggers mounted on a diagonal frame member, convenient to the gunner's right hand, as shown in Fig 9.

The movable gun is of the Parabellum type, and the mounting is of the usual built-up wood variety. The gun-cradle is, however, novel, the fixture for this purpose being illustrated in Fig.10. It appears to be rather more handy than the usual German device, but is by no means lacking in weight. The vertical carrier is swivelled at its base, and is secured in position by sliding bolts engaging with teeth cut in the turned-up base plate. These sliding bolts are worked by a direct acting thumb lever. The turn-table is made of a single hoop of wood reinforced at the point where the gun is mounted by glued-on strips of plywood. The locking device is as shown in Fig. 11.

The transverse bracing in the immediate rear of the gunner's cockpit, at which point is mounted the armour bulkhead, suggests that it was the original intention for this aeroplane to carry a gun or guns firing downwards and backwards through a hole in the fuselage. The transverse arrangement of steel tubes and bracing wires is shown in Fig. 12.

The machine is fitted with the usual wireless leads and apparatus for heating, the dynamo being carried on a bracket attached to the fuselage immediately in front of the pilot's seat, where it is directly driven from the engine through a hand-controlled clutch. No wireless fittings, other than the dynamo leads, were found.

The instruments fitted to this machine possess no new features of interest.

The fabric throughout is of good quality, but the dope appears to have been badly applied, as in many points it had completely peeled off the fabric.

The colours used are dark purple and dark green, and in contradistinction to the usual method by which they are arranged in well-defined polygons, are applied so as to give a cloudy effect and appear to have been sprayed on.

The wing spar yields the following analysis :—

Carbon	..	..	.098 per cent.
Silicon	..	..	.011 per cent.
Sulphur	..	..	.017 per cent.
Phosphor.	..	..	.014 per cent.
Manganese	..	..	.461 per cent.
Chromium	..	..	.036 per cent.

GERMAN AEROPLANES.

A—*continued*.

AGO. Flugzeugwerke G.m.b.H. Johannisthal by Berlin.
Works just outside the main entrance to the flying ground.
Said to be financed by the A.E.G.

Being originally a branch of the Otto Company in Munich
(taking its name *Ago* from the initials of Aerowerke Gustav
Otto). Managed by Germany's fourth certificated aviator,
Baron Ellery von Gorrissen, winner of the Emperor's first
aviation prize for an altitude flight, and an early holder on
Ago of the world's record with six passengers. Rejoices also
in a feminine director, Frau Wörner, who before the war did
much flying as a passenger.

In later years, various fine flights, including records, were put
up by Schüler, who flew alternatively the *Ago* and *D.F.W.*
biplanes.

Even when the mother firm abandoned the pusher type, the
Ago Company devoted still to it among a few others, employing
the Swiss designer Haefeli, formerly of Farman Bros.

On the outbreak of war, the Ago Company was largely
engaged on experimental work with land and sea aircraft.
A small biplane "chaser" was turned out early in the war.

Aeroplanes built by the Aktien Gesellschaft Otto are not seen
at the front in large numbers. In addition to the large twin
fuselage machine, which has not been very successful, the firm
constructs general purpose two-seater machines of medium size,
with two pairs of interplane struts on either side of the fuselage,
and small single-seat biplanes, with one pair of struts on either
side.

These last machines differed from the *Nieuport* in that they
had a dihedral to the upper plane, but the wings were not swept
back. The chord of the lower wings was small, and, therefore,
they appeared to be narrow. The struts were parallel and not
V-shaped as in the *Nieuport*. The type is now extinct.

Some time ago German aero papers illustrated the twin-
fuselage *Ago* in the illustrations of *Ago* battleplanes rendered
here.

They represent two different models, varying chiefly in wing
spread. Both biplanes are twin-bodied pushers with Farman
type nacelles. The smaller one does apparently not exceed the
wing span of a normal-sized tractor biplane, and has but one
set of struts to each side beyond the two oval ones, carrying the
bodies, the chief object of which seem to yield that pusher type
a better longitudinal stability than afford the general Farman
tail-booms, for they carry no engines or passengers, and are
apparently made of two parts, with a longitudinal vertical
division.

The struts are combined by single wire crosses, the nacelle is
supported by two inclined struts from the leading edge of the
upper plane to the middle of the nacelle, between the two seats,
and the tail skids end with the metal scoops, first applied to the
middle skid of the Nieuport monoplane.

The second *Ago* twin-bodied battleplane is identical in design
and construction, and apparently in the size of the various parts
even, but for the larger wings, are almost doubled in span, with
three sets of struts to each side, and the four-wheel landing
chassis of *Voisin* type.

One imagines that the real reason for the two so-called
"bodies" is the theory that two good stout streamlined built-up
tubes will be less vulnerable, and will offer less head-resistance
than four thin tailbooms with the usual network of wires. The
idea seems quite sound, and, properly carried out, it might
produce the much-desired high-speed "pusher" biplane,
especially in large sizes, where one could fit an enormous engine.

Three-quarter Front View of an Ago Biplane of 1917. Note the tapered wing and the single strut between the outer pair and the fuselage.

Side View of the Ago Biplane, with tapered wings and single intermediate strut. 276a

An Ago Flying Boat of 1918 type.   Note the various wing-struts.

An Ago Seaplane of 1918 type.

ALBATROS WERKE. G.m.b.H. Johannisthal by Berlin.

Works and civil flying school at the aerodrome. Military flying, aerodrome and repair works plant at Schneidemühl.

Austrian Branch, The Oesterreichische Albatros werke, G.m.b.H. (see AUSTRIA).

One of Germany's most important aircraft works, established 1910 by building *Farman* type box kites (later with nacelle) and Gnôme engined Antoinette monoplanes by license. One of the first exponents of Albatros aircraft was Brunhüber, who put up a rather astonishing record with three passengers on a 50 h.p. Gnôme engined *Albatros* box kite (with combined lever and wheel control), disappearing soon afterwards from civil aviation, being put in charge of the Doeberitz Army Flying School.

In 1911 a biplane of "Taube" outlines was produced, a graceful machine, being exhibited at the French aero show of the year. It was one of the first examples of employing inclined struts, but did not prove successful.

Germany's then most successful pilot, Hellmuth Hirth, joined the Albatros Company as a director, end of 1912, which resulted in a "Taube" monoplane being turned out.

In one of these the Benz aero engine, which went just from the design room to the Kaiser prize, was tried out, first in school work, then in a non-stop three hours' passenger's flight by Hirth from Johannisthal to the entrance of the Benz motor works in Mannheim.

A star pilot of quick rise and fall, Alfred Pietschker, piloted the *Albatros* box kite to victory in the Johannisthal autumn flying week, 1912, and carried out a three hours' round Berlin flight, but with his death the following day on a self-designed monoplane, the type disappeared.

Hirth gained considerable success with a "Taube" waterplane (combined wheel and two-float chassis) at the Boden See, and first place in the Italian seaplane circuit 1913, while Thelen, whose performances on a huge-spanned, two-float *Albatros* box kite were considerable at the first German seaplane competition (Heiligendamm, 1912), later achieved equal results with *Albatros* tractor seaplanes and further competed with the French passenger record specialist, Garaix, in performing various altitude world record flights with three and four passengers.

Late in 1913, the new *Albatros* tractor biplane was produced, the lamp in the underside of the fuselage of which was prophetic of the 1914 duration performances of Landmann and Boehm in 21 hours' and 24 hours' flights.

Hirth put up a fine flight in the Monaco rally, 1913, on this machine too by his Gotha-Marseille flight, and a remark in a report of this flight by the former monoplane pilot is interesting, saying "Most astonished I was by the surplus power (of the 150 h.p. Benz engine) and the climbing capacity, compared with the heavy-loaded "Taube" monoplanes."

In the 1914 Vienna meeting, Hirth and Von Loessl, again on 150 h.p. Benz-engined *Albatros* biplanes captured the altitude records with two and three passengers.

Albatros biplanes have been largely used in the war, at first as rather slow two-seater fighting machines, and reconnaissance types.

At the end of 1916 there came a very small *Albatros* single-seater with an engine (Benz or Mercédès) of some 175 h.p., and with this little "destroyer" much damage was done to the Allies' aeroplanes, until it was met and defeated by still faster British and French machines.

The speed of this little *Albatros* was computed to be between 120 and 130 miles per hour at its best height.

Front View of the D III Type Albatros Chaser.

Three-quarter rear view of the D III Type Albatros Chaser.

278a

ALBATROS—*continued.*

THE ALBATROS D III.

Enverg. : 9 ᵐ. 03

THE D III ALBATROS.

Span.—Upper Wing 9.03 m. (30 ft.).

Span.—Lower Wing 8.75 m. (29 ft.).

Chord.—Upper Wing 1.5 m. (4 ft. 11 in.).

Gap.—1.5 metres (4 ft. 11 in.).

Stagger.—0.22 metre (9 in.).

POINTS TO BE NOTED.—Upper and Lower Span almost equal. Projecting Ailerons. Dihedral to Lower Plane only. Rudder and Fin entirely above Fuselage. Tiny Fin below Fuselage. Solid Elevator with balanced projections, Rounded Fuselage, with pot on Propeller.

Motor.—Fixed Mercédès, 175 h.p.

**THE ALBATROS B.F.W. 225-h.p.
BIPLANE, TYPE C.V.**

Span : Upper Wing, 41 ft. 6 in.

Span : Lower Wing, 40 ft. 4 in.

Length : 28 ft.

POINTS TO BE NOTED :

General resemblance to single-seater
Albatros D.I. Curiously balanced
ailerons.

THE ALBATROS 225-H.P. TWO-SEATER BIPLANE.

THE ALBATROS "GROSSFLUGZEUG," a twin-engined type which has not become familiar on active service.

LBATROS—*continued.*

Side View of the Latest Type D.V. Albatros (photographed in April, 1918).

An Albatros " C " Type Two-seater Biplane, with arrow-shaped wings and curious strutting arrangements.

THE ALBATROS D.XI SCOUT.

The single streamlined and outwards inclined strut idea has been carried out with the clear object of minimising the interplane connection head resistance, and in conjunction with the inclined struts from the interplane strut bottom joint to the upper fuselage longitudinals doing altogether away with wiring. The *Albatros* strut form was first seen in the fashion of the 1916-17 L.F.G. Roland whale effort, while the two inwards inclined struts appear to be of usual streamline shape.

The body nose and the fairly forward position of the *Albatros* gives the impression of a rotary engine installation.

One fails to see immediately the object of advancing the fin and balanced rudder on the *Albatros*.

The tail fin and undivided balanced elevator is similar to the one of the biplane scout of the same firm.

The Albatros D.XI.

A—continued.

AVIATIK.   Automobil & Aviatik A.G.

Formed 1910, by Georg Chatel and Germany's most successful pilot of that date, Emil Jeannin, to sell Peugeot motor cars and build *Farman* box-kite type biplanes and *Hanriot* monoplanes by license. Works at Mülhausen in Alsace. Aerodrome : Habsheim.

While the box-kite type nacelled biplane was still used, Faller put up a number of duration records with four, five, six and seven passengers. The early monoplanes were very clumsy, but when the 1913 tractor arrow biplane was produced, fine performances were achieved by Ingold with a 16 hours' flight, and by Stoeffler in various distance flights across Germany, foremost his record of 2,100 km. in 24 hours, in September, 1913.

The fate of the Aviatik aircraft works since the outbreak of war has been tossed about. As an instance of German thoroughness it is worth quoting the preparation for this munition factory that it was moved in the days of mobilizing by rail to prearranged works at Breisgau, not to be exposed to likely French attacks on Alsace, as wise was, Châtel being killed with his wife, in his villa at Mülhausen, by a long range shell in the early fights there (Jeannin having long ago left the Aviatik Co. to form his own firm).

Allied raids found the Breisgau works, and the next move to Freiburg was still within the range of French aviators. Yet finances do not seem to have suffered for the income of 1914-15 was 800,000 marks, by a joint stock capital of 1,000,000 marks.

At present the Aviatik plant is installed at the Leipzig-Heiterblick aerodrome of the Leipziger Luftschiffhaten und Flugplatz Gesellschaft at Mockau, where it is managed by Ernest Stoeffler, the famous pre-war long-distance flier.

AVIATIK (Late 1916 Type).

Span: Top Plane, 40 ft. 8 ins.
Span: Bottom Plane, 35 ft. 5 ins.
Chord: 6 ft. 1 in.
Gap: 6 ft. 4 ins.
Total Surface: 430.5 sq. ft.
Ailerons (Top Planes only): 7 ft. 4 ins. × 2. ft 5 ins. (17.2 sq. ft.)
Tail Plane (semi-circular): 4 ft. 10 ins. × 9 ft. 2 ins.
Elevators (two semi-oval): 4 ft. 3 ins. × 2 ft. 2 ins.
Fixed vertical fin (triangular: 5 ft. 1 in. × 2 ft. 5.5 ins.
Rudder: 3 ft. × 2 ft. 3 ins.
Surface of elevator: 12.1 sq. ft.
Surface of fixed tail plane: 35.3 sq. ft.
Surface of rudder: 6.45 sq. ft.
Angle of incidence of main planes: 4.38°.
Length of fuselage: 21 ft.
Total length of machine: 26 ft.

The fore part of the 1916 type Aviatik.
Reproduced from "L'Aérophile," from a French military photograph.

IMPORTANT FIGURES.

The total weight of the *Aviatik* of 1916 is the same as that of the *L.V.G.*, and about the same as that of the *Rumpler.*

Weight of the body (including radiator, tanks, and pipe lines) ..	757 lbs.
Weight of the wings..	308 lbs.
,, struts..	28 lbs.
,, propeller	42 lbs.
,, engine	673 lbs.
,, cooling water	55 lbs.
Total weight empty ..	1,863 lbs.
Weight of fuel ..	418 lbs.
Useful weight—pilot, passenger, armament, accessories, etc.	550 lbs.
Total load ..	968 lbs.
Total load ..	2,831 lbs.
Weight per sq. ft. of sustaining surface ..	6.81 lbs.

Speeds.	Test in France.	From German source.
Maximum speed at sea-level ..	82 m.p.h.	
Minimum speed at sea-level ..	49 m.p.h.	
Speed at 1,000 m. ..	79 m.p.h.	83 m.p.h.
Speed at 2,000 m. ..	74.5 m.p.h.	80.7 m.p.h.
Speed at 3,000 m. ..	66 m.p.h.	
Climb to height of 500 m. ..		4 min. 30 sec.
Climb to height of 1,000 m. ..		9 min. 30 sec.
Climb to height of 2,000 m. ..		21 min. 30 sec.
Climb to height of 3,000 m. ..		47 min. 30 sec.

Supplies carried for 4 hours and 30 minutes' flight.

The "ceiling" of the machine is at 3,500 m., or nearly 11,500 ft., with a useful load of 720 lbs. German pilots have, however, affirmed that they have climbed as high as 15,750 ft. with their observer and 18.5 gallons of gasolene.

Aviatiks with Benz and Mercédès motors of 220 h.p., differing from the 170 h.p. in cylinder bore only, were said to be in building, in 1917, with two machine-guns, one of which was to fire through the propeller. They were expected to have a speed of 93 miles per hour at a height of 2,000 m.

AVIATIK—*continued.*

An Aviatik Single-seater Biplane, Type D11.

An Aviatik D VI Single-seater Scout (1918). (195 h.p. geared Benz engine).

An Aviatik Twin-engined Biplane, Type G1. (2—230 h.p. Benz engines.)

AVIATIK—*continued.*

An Aviatik, Type C VIII Biplane, of late 1918 design.

An Aviatik Biplane (1917), Type CVI, embodying Vee-strut Warren Type wing-bracing and a curiously-shaped top plane.

An Aviatik CIX Biplane of late 1918 design.   Evidently an attempt to use the characteristics of the "Bristol Fighter."

B

BAVARIAN RUMPLER WORKS, Munich. (Branch of the Johannisthal firm.)

B.F.W. Bayerische Flugzeug Werke, Fürth.

One of the newcomers to the German aircraft trade during the war. The Gothaer Waggon Fabrik partook in the formation of the new company, so it may be assumed that the aeroplanes of the latter's aircraft department are produced by license.

It is also known that the Bayerische Company has been making *Albatroses (see Albatros.*).

The city of Fürth gratis supplied an area of 300,000 square metres for works site and testing ground.

BLEICHERODER AEROPLANE TRADE Co., Ltd. Near Harz.

Contractors to the German and Austrian War Offices and Admiralties.

BRANDENBURGISCHE FLUGZEUGWERKE.

See Hansa und Brandenburgische Flugzeugwerke.

D

DEUTSCHE BRISTOL-WERKE FLUGZEUG.

Ges.m.b.H., see Halberstadter Flugzeugwerke.

D.F.W. Deutsche Flugzeug Werke, formerly "Mars, G.m.b.H.," Lindenthal by Leipzig.

Formed in 1910, by Commercial Counsellor Bernhard Meyer, who died during the war, after having, like the late Sir George White, of Bristol, established an important factor in his country's war needs by his keen faith in the future of aviation. Other concerns of Herr Meyer were the seaplane works at Lubeck-Travemünde, the Jeannin Company, and sundry motor firms.

Austrian branch "Lloyd Flugzeugwerke G.m.b.H.," Budapest.

At one time turned out *Maurice Farman* biplanes, later a *Jeannin* copied "Steel dove," and producing a characteristic bodied aircraft, winning, as monoplane, the 1913 Prince Henry trophy, and flying much in the first Balkan War, on Turkish side, as biplane. This machine was constructed under the direction of Ober-Lieutenant Bier, the famous Austrian pilot, and was known as the "Mars." With the design was associated Mr. Cecil Kny, who was well-known in the British Aircraft Industry, and who has been interned—being an Austrian subject—during the war.

In 1914, the D.F.W. company was busy turning out a number of successful types, one of their biplanes, with a 150 h.p. Benz motor winning the "three-cornered flight," and the standard 100 h.p. Mercédès-engined type putting up the world's altitude record of 25,750 feet shortly before outbreak of war, piloted by Oelerich.

On the outbreak of war the performance of the 150 h.p. aircraft (Benz, Mercédès or Rapp motors) were : 110 kms. per hr. max. and 57½ min., fully loaded for 300 miles, flying with pilot and passenger

FRONT VIEW OF THE CAPTURED D.F.W. AVIATIK IN PARIS.—The shape of the nose shows clearly how the Germans obtained better propeller efficiency than we did, and also how, by fitting their radiators directly in the slip stream, they managed to run big engines with small radiators. These points contrasted favourably with our own contemporary methods.

D. F. W.—continued.

THE D.F.W. AVIATIK, TYPE CV.

The Deutsche Flegzeug Werke Gesellschaft was well-known in peace-time for its somewhat ungraceful aeroplanes, some of them with crescent-shaped wings, and others with arrow-shaped wings similar to those of the Austrian Lohner biplanes.

This firm has since produced a somewhat different machine, which, according to M. Lagorgette of "L'Aerophile," was in favour in Germany, and was not only constructed in the firm's own works, but also in those of the Aviatik und Automobil Aktien Gesellschaft, at Leipzig-Heiterblick.

The wings have a dihedral, but are not swept back. The span of the lower wings (12.85 m. or 42 ft. 5 in.) is nearly equal to that of the upper wings (13.25 m. or 43 ft. 8 in.).

The ends of the upper planes are oblique, those of the lower planes retreating and rounded.

Their maximum chord is 1.75 m. (5 ft. 9 in.). The total lifting surface is about 42.5 sq. m. (421 sq. ft.). The gap is considerable, namely, 1 7 m. (5 ft. 7 in.), which gives the machine a tall appearance.

The wings progressively wash out from root to tip. The lower wings have an incidence of 6 deg. near the fuselage as far as the third rib. This decreases to 4.3 deg. at the 13th rib, which is placed 0.4 m. beyond the external struts.

The incidence of the upper plane is 5 deg. from the cabane to the sixth rib, and 3.3 deg. at the 13th rib, where the aileron commences. The incidence on the right and left wings is uniform.

The cabane is of traditional D.F.W. type, trestled-shaped, and constructed of four struts 1.25 m. long.

Above the cabane is a central wing section, 13 centimetres wide, to which the upper main planes are attached, and which contains a small reservoir holding about 3 litres.

There are two pairs of struts on each side of the fuselage.

The distance between the front and rear spars, and consequently between front and rear interplane struts, is 0.76 m., considerably less than half the chord of the wing. The spars taper considerably towards the ends, and are lapped with fabric.

In addition to the four cables which connect the wing attachments on the cabane and the fuselage to the summits and bases of the inner struts, there is a cable which runs between the top of the front chassis strut and the top of the rear inner interplane strut.

The rectangular ailerons are 2.45 m. by 0.5 m., with rounded ends. Their frame is metallic, as are the frames of the fixed tail planes.

The control planes preserve the appearance of the early models. The fixed stabilising plane is 1.72 m. long and is supported by two tubes, and together with the elevator flaps has a heart-shaped appearance, with a span of 3 m. The rudder, fixed vertical fin, and the end of the fuselage together present the contour of a spatula, a trifle elevated.

The controls differ, however, from earlier models, in that the elevator flaps and the rudder are balanced by triangular extensions which conform to segments cut from the fixed planes.

The fuselage terminates in a vertical knife-edge, rather shallow in depth. The section is rectangular with rounded edges.

As in earlier models, it is entirely covered with three-ply, which is painted with green and brown camouflage streaks. The underneath of the wings is a bright yellow. The rest of the machine is green and brown.

The nose of the machine, and its propeller pot, are somewhat pointed, thus avoiding blanketing the centre part of the propeller.

The landing-carriage is standard, the wheelbase being 2 metres wide. The suspension is rubber cord. The cross-axle is streamlined. There is cable cross-bracing between the front chassis struts. There is a claw brake.

The motor is a fixed Benz, giving 228 h.p. at 1,410 r.p.m. The cylinders are almost entirely enclosed in a special cowl.

The propeller, a 3-metre "Wotan," is made of ash and walnut in alternate layers.

The radiators are placed on the sides of the fuselage, where they form rather deep projections (14 cm.), and are 75 cm. high and 21 cm. from front to back. Their base is found between the front chassis strut and the leading edge of the lower wing. They are made by Hans Windhoff.

The water reservoir on top of the engine is triangular like that in the Albatros D.I.

The pilot sits upon the petrol tank, which also forms a back and arm-rest. He has a machine-gun placed to the right of the motor.

The passenger sits behind, surrounded by a gun-ring.

There is only one bomb-release for six bombs, placed one above another.

The full load is 950 kgs. (2,100 lbs.), of which, 300 kgs. (660 lbs.) is useful load.

13ᵐ25
12ᵐ87

THE D.F.W. AVIATIK, TYPE C.V.

Span.—Upper, 13.25 m. (43 ft. 8 in.).

Span.—Lower, 12.85 m. (42 ft. 5 in.).

Chord.—1.75 m. (5 ft. 9 in.).

Surface.—42.5 sq. m. (421 sq. ft.).

Gap.—1.7 m. (5 ft. 7 in.).

Engine.—228-h.p. Benz.

POINTS TO NOTE :

Wings of almost equal span. Two pairs of struts per side. Rounded lower plane. Fin to end of fuselage, with rudder-balance above it. Heart-shaped tail, with elevator balance on each side. Round-backed fuselage with pot on propeller.

D.F.W.—*continued.*

THE LATEST D. F. W. BIPLANE—TYPE C. 37 III.

Specification.

Span	Upper plane, 13.27 m. ; Lower plane, 12.8 m.
Chord	1.75 m.
Maximum height	3.252 m.
Overall length	7.825 m.
Weight of machine empty ..	970 kgs.
Useful load	460 kgs.
Engine type and h.p.	200 h.p. Benz.

Performance.

Speed	155 k.p.h.

Climb.

To 1,000 metres	4 mins.
To 2,000 metres	9½ mins.
To 3,000 metres	16½ mins.
To 5,000 metres	49 mins.
Useful load	460 kgs.
Total weight of machine loaded	1,430 kgs.

A D.F.W. type C.37 iii.

A D.F.W. " D " Class Single-seater Biplane.

E

EULER. August Euler, Niederrad bei Frankfurt a.M.

Germany's first certificated aviator. Acquired the German license for *Voisin* biplanes, and long stuck, alone in Germany, faithfully to the Gnôme engine.

On a modified pusher biplane, Prince Henry of Prussia took his certificate and carried out a 50 km. flight.

The newer *Euler* tractor biplanes were copies of the *L.V.G.*, and no special aircraft or activities of the Euler company has been heard of during the war. Since the Armistice the photograph shown below has been obtained but without any specification.

The plant of the Euler firm at Frankfurt is a fine one, in white appearance, with five sheds (one letter of the word Euler on each of them), a picturesque flower bed produced in the form of a 7-cylinder Gnôme, and a white propeller, and the level flying ground is fenced.

An Euler " D " class Single-seater Scout.

F

FRIEDRICHSHAFEN. F.F. Flugzeugbau Friedrichshafen, Bodensee. Branch of the Zeppelin Airship Building Company, formed in 1912.

Up to the outbreak of war, devoted solely to the construction of seaplanes, built in few numbers and many forms under Curtiss influence, as single or twin-float seaplanes and flying boats, all pushers.

Performed well (putting up a passenger's duration world's record under the Swiss Gsell's pilotage) at Bodensee, and in long cross-river flights—up the Elbe and Rhine.

During the war the German aviation writer and engineer, Roland Eisenlohr, joined the F.F. Company as designer and both land and sea-going aircraft were produced.

During 1917, the firm concentrated on the production of twin-engined " pusher " bombers, one of which is illustrated herewith, and described in detail on the next page.

A Friedrichshafen Single-seater Fighter.

The Friedrichshafen Seaplane, Type FF67, used extensively in the North Sea ; operating from land stations and also seaplane carriers.

288a

FRIEDRICHSHAFEN—continued.

THE 450-h.p. FRIEDRICHSHAFEN BIPLANE.

The French technical journal, "L'Aérophile," has published an interesting description by M. Jean Lagorgette of a three-seater Friedrichshafen biplane, captured in 1917 by the French, near Verdun. Other specimens have been captured on the Macedonian front.

M. Lagorgette points out that the Flugzeugbau Friedrichshafen Gesellschaft, m.b.H.—a branch of the Zeppelin Company—has for a long time specialised in the construction of single and twin-engined seaplanes, the location of their works on Lake Constance making this very natural.

One of the principal changes is the use of arrow-shaped wings, a return to an early German principle.

The machine is of what is sometimes called the "general purpose type."

The dimensions are considerably less than those of the Gotha:—

Length, 11 metres (36 ft.). Height, 3.6 m. (11.7 ft.). Span, top plane, 20.3 m. (66 ft.); lower plane, 18.85 m. (61.2 ft.). Chord of planes, 1.8 m. to 2.3 m. (5.9 ft. to 7.5 ft.).

The gap is 1.95 m. (6.2 ft.). The total surface of the wings is 70 sq. metres (695 sq. ft.).

The wings are set at a dihedral and are slightly swept back, with the exception of the fixed centre section; the top and bottom members of which are slightly unequal, because of the arrangement of the "V" supports of the motors. There is a very slight stagger to the planes, which are oblique at their extremities.

The ailerons are set into the planes, and project outwards at the tips. They have also a slight "balanced" projection into the plane.

A considerable portion of the trailing edge in the centre of both planes is cut away to allow clearance for the airscrews.

The distance between the two main spars, and consequently between the front and back interplane struts, is 1 metre (3.25 ft.).

The spars in the centre section are constructed of steel tube. Those in the outer sections are made of wood. The cabane consists of four vertical struts.

Contrary to Gotha practice, the ribs are parallel with the axis of the machine.

Each aileron has at its extremity a balanced part in front of its hinge. The span of each aileron is 3.8 m. (13.3 ft.), the surface being about 2.3 sq. m. (22 sq. ft.).

The horizontal tail members are 3.95 m. span, and 3.65 m. in length, and have an irregular polygonal shape like that of certain 1914 Albatros machines.

As in nearly all German machines, the tail controls are balanced, and are constructed of tube work. The balance portion of the rudder is 1 m. × 0.25 m.

The fuselage is of the ordinary rectangular type, the upper surface being horizontal when in flight. The maximum height is 1.27 m., the width being 1.2 m.

THE 450-h.p. FRIEDRICHSHAFEN THREE-SEATER.

PLAN AND FRONT ELEVATION.

Span.—Upper Plane, 66 ft.

Span.—Lower Plane, 61.2 ft.

Chord.—5 ft. 9 in. to 7 ft. 5 in.

Gap.—6.2 ft.

Total Surface.—695 sq. ft.

Length.—36 ft.

Height.—11.7 ft.

Engines.—Two 225-h.p. Benz.

FRIEDRICHSHAFEN—*continued.*

The fuselage is constructed in two portions for ease of transport, the joint being in line with the trailing edge of the planes, so that the rear gun-ring comes away with the tail end of the fuselage, leaving a compact central section.

The landing-carriage is not characteristic of German aeroplanes generally. Underneath each motor is a pair of 965 mm. wheels, mounted on a common axle, giving a track of 0.8 metres. sprung by elastic cord from a large streamlined horizontal skid.

The motors are mounted between two pairs of " V " struts at a distance of 2.1 metres from the centre of the machine, and are linked to the fuselage by three nearly horizontal tubes. The Benz engines have six cylinders each. One, numbered 22799, gave 226 h.p. at 1,410 r.p.m. No. 25344 gave 221 h.p. at 1,400 r.p.m.

The airscrews, trade-mark " Imperial," are 2.9 m. in diameter.

The petrol tank and the two independent gravity tanks in the upper plane have a capacity of about 550 litres.

	kgs.		lbs.
Weight of machine, empty......	2,200	=	4,840
Useful load	520	=	1,180
Fuel load	432	=	940
Total	3,152	=	6,960

This represents 45 kgs. per sq. metre or 10 lbs. per sq. ft., and 7 kgs. (15.4 lbs.) per horse-power.

Three-quarter Front View of a Friedrichshafen Bomber.

The Friedrichshafen Twin-engined Tractor Biplane, Type FF62. of 1918. (2—260 h.p. Mercedes engines.) It will be noticed that the projecting bow for the gunner has disappeared and that this machine is a Twin Tractor instead of a pusher.

F—*continued*.

FOKKER. Fokker Flugzeugwerke, Schwerin-Gorries in Mecklenburg.

Fokker, a skilful Dutch pilot, had a monoplane built by Goedecker, of inherent stable **V** shape, without warping, which he then manufactured at the Johannisthal aerodrome by the Fokker Aeroplanbau, G.m.b.H.

This monoplane was difficult to handle, even by clever pilots, and Fokker himself had a narrow escape during one of the early flying weeks at Johannisthal, when, during an altitude flight, he had a nosedive, and his passenger, a German flying officer was killed. Credit must, however, be given for the feminine altitude record of 6,600 feet by the Russian aviatrice Miss Galanchikoff, with a lady passenger.

The military authorities ordered Fokker to abandon this model, when he left the Johannisthal aerodrome, where his daring bankings were admired, for a private aerodrome at Schwerin-Gorries with a slipway to the sea. Here he produced his flying boat, as he intended, according to his advertising, to cater for water flying, " the noblest sport."

Yet matters turned out different. Early in 1914 a modified *Morane* type of machine was produced, on which Fokker himself gave looping exhibitions during the three-cornered and Prince Henry flights, when its climbing capability was admired.

This feature led to quantity manufacture early in the war, when the Allies had not too plenty of aircraft, so that the Fokker campaign cost for some months, starting October, 1915, some loss of "*Fokker* Fodder," most of the German star turns, who manned the *Fokkers*, going however out in the end, like Boelcke, Immelmann, Wintgens, etc.

Fokker has not only taken over the large Schwerin piano works, but has formed a company for the manufacture of machine guns.

Below are given some details of *Fokker* war aircraft, samples of which have been captured as biplane and monoplane and triplane.

At the end of the war the *Fokker* biplane (Type D.7) was the best single-seat fighter in the German Air Service.

THE FOKKER SINGLE-SEATER BIPLANE—TYPE D.7.

The British No. of the machine illustrated is B/2B 14 and the German No. is Type D.7 F.N. 1,450 ; maker's No. 2,455.

It was brought down north of Hazebrouck on June 6th, 1918, by a British S.E.5a, and is a single-seater fighter.

The principal dimensions are as follows :—

Span	..	..	..	..	29 ft. 3½ ins.
Chord (upper wing)	..	..	..	..	5 „ 2½ „
Chord (lower wing)	..	..	..	..	3 „ 11¼ „
Overall length	..	..	..	..	22 „ 11½ „
Gap	..	..	..	..	4 „ 2 „
Area of Upper Wings (with Ailerons)	..	140.7 sq. ft.
„ „ Lower Wings	..	..	..	78.3 „ „
„ „ Aileron (one only)	..	..	..	5.7 „ „
„ „ Balance of Aileron	..	..	.5 „ „
„ „ Horizontal Tail Plane	..	..	21.1 „ „
„ „ Elevators	..	..	..	15.2 „ „
„ „ Balance of Elevator	..	..	1.1 „ „

The Family Tree of the Fokker Firm.

FOKKER—*continued.*

Area of Fin ..	..	..	..	..	2.8 sq. ft.		
,, ,, Rudder	..	..	..	..	5.9 ,, ,,		
,, ,, Horizontal Area of Body..		..	35.6 ,, ,,			
,, ,, Vertical Area of Body	..	..	58.6 ,, ,,			
,, ,, Plane between Wheels	..	..	12.4 ,, ,,			

This aeroplane presents features of very great interest, whether viewed from the standpoint of aerodynamic design or of actual construction. The machine which has been the subject of investigation was, unfortunately, rather extensively damaged, thus making absolute accuracy of description difficult, and trials of performance impossible.

A similar machine has, however, being tested for performance by the French authorities, who have issued the following report :

Altitudes.		Time of climb.		Speed at this height.
1,000 metres (3,281 ft.)	4 mins. 15 secs.			116.6 m.p.h.
2,000 ,, (6,562 ,,)	8 ,, 18 ,,			114.1 ,,
3,000 ,, (9,843 ,,)	13 ,, 49 ,,			109.7 ,,
4,000 ,, (13,124 ,,)	22 ,, 48 ,,			103.5 ,,
5,000 ,, (16,405 ,,)	38 ,, 5 ,,			94.9 ,,

There are many points in which there is distinct divergence from accepted German, and tendency towards British, practice. The undercarriage, position of radiator, and aileron control levers, or kingposts, are examples.

This fact is some indication that the designer of this machine has approached the various problems and compromises which confront one who sets out to create such a machine, with a quite open mind, and, if this be allowed, there is a very strong case for a thorough investigation of those features which are in contradiction to contemporary British practice. These points include the wing design, which is without any external bracing, but of especially deep section ; the steel-tubular fuselage, and the peculiar bracing of this member.

There is nothing to prevent the adoption of the first and last features ; but it should be pointed out with regard to the steel work that experienced welders have expressed the opinion that this art has been developed by the enemy to a high degree of efficiency. Indeed, the welding is sufficiently good to give rise to the belief that new methods, involving radical changes, have been adopted.

*The following data regarding weights is taken from a French source :—

Weight of fuselage, complete with engine, etc...			1322.2 lbs.
,, ,, upper wing with ailerons	..	..	167.2 ,,
,, ,, lower wing ..	..	..	99.0 ,,
,, ,, fin and rudder..	..	..	6.6 ,,
,, ,, fixed tail plane	..	..	17.6 ,,
,, ,, elevators	..	..	9.9 ,,
			1622.5 lbs.

A different French report gives the following figures, which are taken from inscriptions found on one of the Spandau guns on a captured *Fokker* of the same type :—

Weight (empty) ..	..	..	..	1,540 lbs.
Permissible load (useful load and fuel) ..	..	396 lbs.

* The schedule of principal weights given on page 294 is the result of weighing the actual components mentioned, which were taken from the aeroplane allotted G/2B/14.

A side view of the Fokker Biplane, showing the curious strut arrangement.

Front view of the Fokker Biplane.

292a

FOKKER—*continued.*

WINGS.

As in the *Fokker* triplane, the extreme depth of wing section and the absence of external bracing are distinctive features. Both upper and lower wings are without dihedral, and are in one piece. The way in which the lower wings are fitted into their place is described in detail under the heading " Fuselage." Both upper and lower chords are set parallel to the crankshaft, *i.e.*, at no angle of incidence, and the inscription " Angle of incidence, ₀°" is painted on the upper plane.

WING CONSTRUCTION.

In sharp contradistinction to the fuselage, which is constructed of steel, even including members where wood is almost universally used, the wings contain no metal parts, if we exclude strut fittings and other extraneous features. There are no steel compression members, but where the internal wiring lugs occur, special box-form compressed ribs are fixed. The leading edge is of very thin three-ply, which has a deeply serrated edge finishing on the main spar (Fig. 2). The ribs are of three-ply, and are not lightened, although holes are, of course, cut where necessary, to accommodate the control and bracing wires. A rib from the top centre section, and one from the root of the lower wings, are both drawn to scale in Fig. 1.

The extreme thinness of the three-ply has given rise to a new method of fixing the flanges on the ribs. Instead of grooved flanges tacked on so that the tacks run down the length of the three-ply, two half flanges of approximately square section are tacked together horizontally with the ply sandwiched between (see Fig. 2).

SPARS.

As may be seen from the various sections drawn to scale in Figs. 3 and 4, the spars are made up of fairly narrow flanges at top and bottom, joined on either side by thin three-ply webs. They are placed approximately 30 cms. apart. The flanges are made of Scots pine and consist of two laminations. The three-ply has the two outer layers of birch and an inner ply, which is probably of birch also.

The three-ply webs are tacked on to the flanges, and fabric is glued over the joint. The cement is an ordinary gelatine glue.

The spar webs are glued to the flanges by a waterproof casein cement which is proved to contain gelatine, while the plywood adhesive—also a casein cement—is waterproof and of sufficiently good quality to withstand four hours' immersion in boiling water.

The trailing edge is of wire, and tape crosses from the top of one rib to the bottom of the next in the usual way. This tape lattice occurs about half-way between the trailing edge and the rear spar.

Fig. 3 shows the sections of the front and rear upper plane spars, taken in the centre section and at the interplane struts, while Fig. 4 gives the corresponding lower spar sections.

The ribs are stiffened between the spars by vertical pieces of wood of triangular section. There are two such pieces on each rib in the upper plane, and one in the lower plane.

Rear view of the Fokker Biplane.

Three-quarter rear view of the Fokker Biplane

THE FOKKER SINGLE-SEATER BIPLANE.—
Type D.7.

Span	29′ 3½″	app.
Chord Top Plane	5′ 2½″	,,
Chord Bottom Plane	3′ 11¼″	,.
Overall Length	22′ 11½″	,,
Tail Plane Span	6′ 0″	,,
Height	9′ 2½″	,.
Airscrew		
Gap	4′ 2″	,,
Stagger	1′ 11½″	,,
Engine	Mercédès 160 h.p.	

FOKKER—*continued.*

All the woodwork of the wings is varnished, and fabric is bound round the flanges of the ribs and glued to the top and bottom of the spars.

The workmanship is decidedly good, and the finish neat and careful.

SCHEDULE OF PRINCIPAL WEIGHTS.

	lbs.	oz.
Upper wing, complete with ailerons, pulleys, bracing wires, fabric and strut fittings	156	0
Lower wing (no ailerons fitted), complete with strut fittings and fabric	97	0
N strut between wings	6	9
Straight strut, between fuselage and trailing spar of upper wing	2	8
Aileron frame, with hinge clips, without fabric ..	4	8
Rudder frame, with hinge clips, without fabric ..	4	11
Fin frame, without fabric	1	14
Tail planes (complete in one piece), without fabric.	12	6
Elevators (complete in one piece), without fabric ..	11	2
Radiator, empty	48	0
Undercarriage strut, each	2	10
Undercarriage axle, with shock absorber bobbins..	18	2
Bobbin, each	0	7
Shock absorber, each	3	9
Undercarriage (complete), without wheels and tyres, and without plane, but including struts ..	29	4
Aluminium tube, forming rear spar of undercarriage plane	1	8
Wheel, without tyre and tube	11	8
Tyre and tube	9	4
Tail strut	1	15
Fabric, per square foot, with dope	0	1
Bottom plane compression rib	0	15
Bottom plane ordinary rib	0	11
Top plane, ordinary rib, at centre of plane ..	1	0
Bracket, with bolts, attaching top plane to fuselage struts	1	11
Main spar, top plane, including fillet for ribs, per foot run in centre	1	12

Owing to tapering ends the average weight per foot of the spars will be slightly less than this figure.

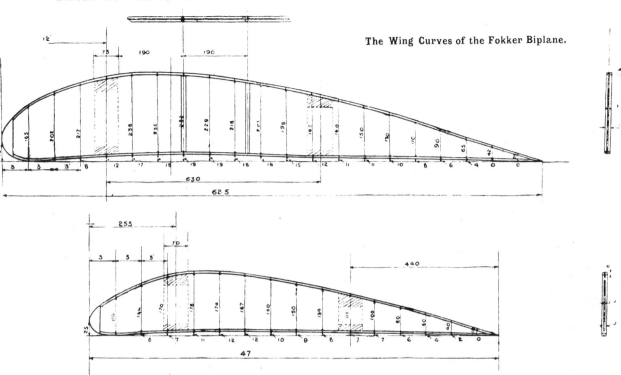

The Wing Curves of the Fokker Biplane.

FIG. 1.   Rib sections, top centre section (top), and bottom wing roots (below).

FIG. 2.   Leading edge, shewing serrated three-ply nose.

FIG. 3.   Sections of upper wing spars.

FOKKER—*continued.*

Radiator and Method of Fixing.

FIG. 4. Sections of Lower Wing Spars.

Control Column.

Fuselage Construction.

Tail Arrangement, showing off-set Fin.

Lower Front Spar and
Interplane Strut Fixing.

Fuselage Joint at Junction
of Lower Wing Spar.

Rudder Bar.

Engine-Bearer Tubes.

Side-elevation of Cabane and Engine-bearer Tubes.

Arrangement of Axle Springs.

THE FOKKER "PARASOL" MONOPLANE.

This aircraft is stated to be powered by a 110 h.p. rotary motor, and appears to include the usual *Fokker* components, like landing gear, body, rudder of comma shape, tail plane and balanced elevator as known from the *Fokker* triplane and biplane editions. Both the absence of any wiring and the thickness of the undivided parasol plane induces, together with the known business connections of the Fokker aircraft concern and the Junker's newcomer one, the impression that the plane of this *Fokker* parasol monoplane had been made of metal.

The Fokker "Wireless" Parasol Monoplane, with 200 h.p. Goebel rotary engine. The ailerons, contrary to usual practice, do not extend to the wing-tips.

Instrument Board of Fokker Monoplane.

G

GERMANISCHE FLUGZEUGWERKE.

Leipzig.

Formed during the war, producing aircraft of general German tractor type. Has taken over the sheds left at the aerodrome of that city, and runs a flying school, open to private pupils.

GOEDECKER. Goedecker Aircraft Works, Niederwallauf-on-Rhine.

Produced an early interesting, steel-built "Taube" (named *The Storm Bird.*)

Of small importance, being rather a flying school, building its own machines. Reported, without proof, to manufacture during the war a copy of the *Avro* biplane, shot down at Friedrichshafen during the British attack on the Zeppelin Works there.

GOETZE. Commandit Gesellschaft Richard Goetze.

Running four works : I and II at Treptow, Elsenstrasse 106-7 ; III in Berlin, Schlesische Strasse 26 ; and IV at the Johannisthal aerodrome, entrance VI.

A firm of new date, which has apparently turned out no design of its own. From the papers it appears that the Goetze Company turn out aeroplanes as sub-contractors.

GRADE. Hans Grade Flieger Werke, Bork, Flugplatz Mars.

Post : Bruck in der Mark.

Hans Grade was the first German to fly in a self-designed triplane with an engine (two-cycle) of his own design. Won the Lanz prize of 40,000 marks. (*See Historical Section.*)

The position of the Grade Aircraft Works is unique, having been run on a commercial scale by private support alone.

In spite of all efforts—Grade flew voluntary in the Sachsen manœuvres and designed a nacelled and military control model—the military authorities would never accept his parasol monoplane with hanging warp control.

The highest percentage of pupils trained on one type stands to the credit of the *Grade* monoplane, many of the present German pilots having had their first experience on it. The general development of later years in military direction and some fatal accidents, after long avoidance of same, have restricted the importance of the Grade works.

In 1914, a looping model monoplane was turned out with double chassis, on which the first German looping flights were made.

A Germania Biplane.

A Germania Single-Strut Biplane of the "C" Class, with a curious circular-shaped radiator.

GOTHA. Gothaer Waggonfabrik A.G. Aircraft department.
Running the Duke Carl Edward flying school at own aerodrome by Gotha.

The Gotha Company did not go through the early days of aviation, but as a capital potential firm secured success by manufacturing large quantities of proved sound aeroplane models and by engaging first-class pilots for them—Ernst Schlegel winning 1st prize of 60,000 marks in the National-flugspende competition.

During the war the Gotha Company has partly floated other aircraft firms.

Gotha seaplanes were developed early. An early war product was the small rotary-engined and Morane-bodied *Falke* (Falcon) single-seater biplane, influenced by and an answer to the Allies' scouts. A big twin-engined " pusher " bombing biplane has since been produced, and has been largely used in raids on England.

THE TWIN-ENGINED GOTHA.

The standard type of two-engined *Gotha* is a pusher, the appearance of which is characterised by the backward sweep of the main planes, which are also set at a lateral dihedral angle.

The set back of the planes is 4 deg., and the dihedral approximately 2 deg.

The following are the principal dimensions of the aeroplane.

Maximum span	77 ft.
Span of lower plane	71 ft. 9 ins.
Gap	7 ft.
Maximum chord	7 ft. 6 ins.
Minimum chord	7 ft. 2½ ins.
Over-all length	41 ft.
Area of top plane	521.6 sq. ft.
Area of bottom plane ..	464 sq. ft.
Total area	985 sq. ft.
Area of upper aileron ..	32 sq. ft.
Area of balance of aileron..	3.2 sq. ft.
Area of bottom aileron ..	22.4 sq. ft.
Span of tail planes.. ..	13 ft. 6 ins.
Area of tail planes	45 sq. ft.
Area of rudder	16 sq. ft.
Area of rudder balance ..	3.2 sq. ft.
Area of elevators	19.2 sq. ft.
Area of fin	11.2 sq. ft.
Area of body in horizontal plane..	96 sq. ft.
Area of body in vertical plane	107 sq. ft.
Weight empty	2,740 kg.=6,039 lbs.
Useful load	1,235 kg.=2,722 lbs.
Total weight fully loaded ..	3,975 kg.=8,763 lbs.
Loading per sq. ft... ..	8.9 lbs.

ENGINES.

Two 260 h.p. Mercédès.

Engine centres	14 ft.
Airscrew diameter	10 ft. 2 ins.
Track of main landing wheels	3 ft. 2½ ins.
Track of auxiliary landing wheels	2 ft. 7½ ins.

The speed of this machine at 12,000 ft. is estimated at 72 miles per hour.

THE GOTHA BOMB DROPPER.—Outline views of the twin-engine three-seater biplane used largely for raiding purposes by the Germans. The sketches are reproduced from the French technical paper 'L'Aérophile.'

GOTHA—*continued*.

GOTHA BROUGHT DOWN BY FRENCH A.A. FIRE NEAR CROCHTE ON JULY 4th-5th, 1918.

The general construction of this machine appears to be similar to that described above in most respects, except for three modifications, which are worthy of note :—

1. A biplane tail unit. It is similar in design to that of the *Handley-Page*, and embodies two fins on either side of the fuselage between the planes of the tail. The rudders are hinged to the trailing edges of these fins. The measurements of the tail unit are as follows :—

Top elevator span	5 ft. 7 ins.
Top elevator chord	2 ft. 7 ins.
Bottom elevator span	5 ft. 3 ins.
Bottom elevator chord	1 ft. 6½ ins.
Balance piece	11½ ins. by 10¾ ins.
Gap	2 ft. 9½ ins.
Bottom tail planes each average fore and aft measurement ..	2 ft. 5 ins.
Span along trailing edge, each ..	4 ft. 2 ins.
Top tail plane, average fore and aft measurement.. ..	2 ft. 5 ins.
Span along trailing edge	8 ft. 10 ins.

This tail unit would appear to have been adapted in order to give the after gunner a better chance of attacking chasing aeroplanes, as the span is considerably smaller than that of the monoplane tail. It is constructed throughout of steel tubing.

2. Extensions are fitted to the top ailerons as shown in Fig. 35. It would appear from these that the lateral control of the *Gotha* has been found insufficient.

3. The undercarriages are arranged in a similar manner to those of the *Friedrichshafen*, that is to say, there is a two-wheeled undercarriage underneath each engine, and a third two-wheeled axle mounted on to the fore part of the fuselage ; the wheels throughout are of equal size, carrying 810 by 125 mm. tyres.

FIG. 1.　Wing Section.
FIG. 2.　Rear Spar.
FIG. 3.　Front Spar.
FIG. 4.　Joint between upper wings and centre section.
FIG. 5.　Joint between lower wing and centre section.
FIG. 5a. Another view of same joint.
FIG. 6.　Interplane strut junctions.
FIG. 7.　After cock-pit and machine-gun mounting, showing gun-tunnel.
FIG. 8.　Fuselage, with gun-tunnel. (The illustration shows it lying on one side.)
FIG. 9.　Ball-socket fitting for bracing.

Fig. 1.

Fig. 2.
TRAILING SPAR

Fig. 3.
LEADING SPAR

Fig. 4.

Fig. 5.

Fig. 5a.

Fig. 6.

Fig. 7.

Fig. 8.

Fig. 9.

Three-quarter Front and Rear Views of a 1918 type Gotha Bomber.

THE GERMAN BOMBER.—A twin-engined Gotha biplane. The balanced ailerons and rudder are noteworthy.

A Gotha Twin-engined Tractor Biplane of late 1918 design, showing the abolition of the front gunner-observer's cockpit.

GOTHA—*continued*.

FIG. 10. Axle and spring gear.
FIG. 11. Tail-skid and fuselage fittings.
FIG. 12. Tail-skid springs.
FIG 13. Arrangement of Engine-bearers.
FIG. 14. Section of Engine-bearers.
FIG. 15. Ball-socket joints of Engine-bearer struts.
FIG. 16. Rear ties across Engine-bearers.
FIG. 17. Fitting of diagonal struts to Engine-bearers.

Fig. 10.

Fig. 11.

Fig. 12.

Fig. 13.

Fig. 14.

Fig. 3.

Fig. 16.

Fig. 17.

GOTHA—*continued.*

FIG. 18   Radiator and shutters.
FIG. 19.   Alternative shutter arrangement.
FIG. 20:   Shutter Control.
FIG. 21.   Exhaust pipe.
FIG. 22.   Alternative type of exhaust pipe and flame-
           damper.
FIG. 23.   Control Pillar.
FIG. 24.   Elevator quadrant-lever.
FIG. 25.   Twin Rudder-levers.
FIG. 26.   Engine Controls.
FIG. 27.   Instrument Board.
FIG. 28.   Petrol-pressure control-tap.

Fig. 18.   Fig. 19.   Fig. 20.   Fig. 21.   Fig. 22.   Fig. 23.   Fig. 24.   Fig. 25.   Fig. 26.   Fig. 27.   Fig. 28.

GOTHA—*continued.*

FIG. 29.   Forward Gun-Ring.
FIG. 30.   Gun Mounting for same.
FIG. 31.   Gun-Ring Hinge to allow passage between
           Cock-pits.
FIGS. 32 & 33.   Detectors to show that bombs have left
           carriers.
FIG. 34.   Bomber's Cockpit showing Bomb-release
           levers, folding seat, etc.
FIG. 35.   Aileron arrangement.
FIG. 36.   Rudder-bar.
FIG. 37.   Rudder operating lever.

Fig. 29.

Fig. 30.

Fig. 34.

Fig. 37.

Fig. 32.

Fig. 31

Fig. 35

Fig. 33.

Fig. 36.

A Twin-engined Gotha Seaplane of the Pusher Type.

An Early Gotha Twin-float Seaplane built for the Turkish Navy.

A Twin-engined Gotha Seaplane of the Tractor Type.

305a

H

HALBERSTADT. Halberstädter Flugzeugwerke G.m.b.H. Works and aerodrome at Halberstadt by Harz.

Formerly known as Deutsche Bristol Werke manufacturing for 1914 a "Taube" with the Rover patent tube-shaped wooden body.

Changed during the war into above name, the *Halberstadt* 1915 biplane being, as most of the German aeroplanes, under English and French influence, and in reality a compound of *Bristol*, *Avro* and *Morane*, with either rotary or stationary motor.

During 1917 and 1918 the Halberstadt firm produced one of the best two-seater fighters of the war.

THE HALBERSTADT TWO-SEATER FIGHTER.

This machine is a two-seater fighter. It was brought down at Villers Bocage, by Lts. Armstrong and Mert on an *R.E.8* on 9/6/18. The machine is marked "Type H.S. C.L.2," and bears the military number C.L.2, 15,342/17. The date of construction 14/4/18, is stamped on various parts. On the side of the fuselage is the following inscription :—

> Leergewicht (weight unladen), 796 k.g.
> Nochstbelastung (useful weight), 370 k.g.
> Einschl Vollen Tank. (Including full tanks).

There is also a red line about 30 inches long drawn at both sides of the fuselage, showing the horizontal in the normal flying position.

GENERAL DETAILS.

The *Halberstadt* represents, in all probability, the high water mark of a two-seater German aeroplane construction, as it is not only well and strongly constructed, but its general behaviour in the air is good according to modern fighting standards.

Its general design will be gathered from the drawings at the end of this report and also from the photographs. Constructional details are dealt with by sketches.

Span of upper plane	35 ft. 3¼ in.
Span of lower plane	34 ft. 11 in.
Chord of upper plane	5 ft. 3¼ in.
Chord of lower plane	4 ft. 3½ in.
Gap, maximum	4 ft.
Gap, minimum	3 ft. 8½ in.
Dihedral angle of lower plane	2°
Horizontal dihedral of main planes	4°
Total area of main planes	310 sq. ft.
Area of each aileron	11.6 sq. ft.
Area of aileron balance	2.0 sq. ft.
Load per square foot	8.2 lbs.

A general view of the Two-seater Halberstadt Fighter.

A rear view of the Halberstadt Fighter showing tail plane arrangement.

306a

HALBERSTADT—*continued.*

Area of tail planes	.. ..	13.6 sq. ft.
Area of elevator	.. ..	12.4 sq. ft.
Area of fin	.. ..	6.4 sq. ft.
Area of rudder	.. ..	7.9 sq. ft.
Area of rudder balance	.. ..	1.0 sq. ft.
Maximum cross section of body	..	8.8 sq. ft.
Horizontal area of body	.. ..	44.0 sq. ft.
Vertical area of body	.. ..	52.8 sq. ft.
Length over all	.. ..	24 ft.
Engine	.. ..	180 h.p. Mercédès.
Weight per h.p. (180)	..	14.07 lbs.
Capacity of petrol tanks	..	34 gallons.
Capacity of oil tanks	..	4 gallons.
Crew	.. .. ..	Two.
Guns	.. .. ..	1 fixed and 1 moveable.
Military load on test	..	545 lbs.
Total load on test	.. ..	2,532 lbs.

PERFORMANCE.

Speed at 10,000 ft., 97 m.p.h., 1,385 r.p.m.

	Mins.	Sec.	Rate of Climb in Ft. Min.	Indicated Air Speed.
Climb to 5,000 ft.	9	25	440	69
Climb to 10,000 ft.	24	30	240	64
Climb to 14,000 ft.	51	55	80	58

Service ceiling (height at which climb is 100 feet per minute), 13,500 feet.

Estimated absolute ceiling, 16,000 feet.

Greatest height reached, 14,800 feet in 64 minutes 40 seconds.

Rate of climb at this height, 50 feet per minute.

STABILITY AND CONTROLLABILITY.

This machine cannot be considered stable. There is a tendency to stall with the engine on, and to dive with the engine off. Directionally, owing to the propeller swirl, the machine swings to the left, but with the engine off is neutral.

Pilots report the machine light and comfortable to fly. The manœuvrability is good, and this feature, taken in conjunction with the exceptionally fine view of the pilot and observer and the field of fire of the latter, makes the machine one to be reckoned with as a "two-seater fighter," although the climb and speed performances are poor judged by contemporary British standards.

PRINCIPAL POINTS OF THE DESIGN.

Single bay arrangements of wings.

Conspicuous set back of the main planes.

Empennage free from wires.

Fuselage tapers to a horizontal line at the rear in direct contradistinction to the usual German practice.

Pilot's and observer's cock-pit constructed as one.

Construction.

WINGS.

The upper wings are supported by a large centre section having a span of 6 ft. 3 in. This centre section is at right angles to the centre line of machine, but at each side of it; the wings are thrown back with a horizontal dihedral of 4 degrees. The lower wings are smaller in chord and very slightly smaller in the span than the upper, and are fixed direct to the lower surface of the fuselage, and it is to be noted that where the trailing edge joins on to the fuselage it is shaped so as to avoid a surface of discontinuity at the root of the wing. This is done by smoothly turning upwards the trailing edge.

The actual construction of the wings is of considerable interest, especially on account of the novel type of spar which is employed. This applies to both the upper and the lower planes. The front spar measures $2\frac{3}{4}$ inches by 1 inch and at the butt is placed about 4 inches from the leading edge. It is of "I" section, but is left full at such points as those at which internal bracing wires are fixed. This spar is connected to the leading edge by means of ply-wood, both top and bottom.

It will be seen that on the upper surface the ply-wood is extended rearwards for a distance of some $4\frac{3}{4}$ inches from the centre of the spar, and terminates in a small transverse flange about $\frac{1}{2}$-inch deep. This construction furnishes a leading edge

Gunner-observer on a Halberstadt, equipped for Contour-fighting, with hand-grenades.

HALBERSTADT—*continued.*

of great rigidity and strength, and at the same time it would also appear to be light in weight.

In the case of the rear main spar, the main member is of "O" or box section, and is built up of two pieces let into one another in a rather unusual manner. This is clearly shown in the drawing. Both at the top and bottom of the spar, thin strips of wood are used to cover the glued joint, and on this is tacked, both above and below, a flat length of ply-wood 7 inches wide which overhangs the main member of the spar an equal distance at each side.

This ply-wood web is flanged at each end with strips of wood glued in position, and on these strips are fitted small corner pieces which serve to support the ribs. The latter are also of ply-wood, to which are glued and tacked rails of solid wood, top and bottom.

A notable point of the wing construction is the fact that steel tubes are not used as the compression members of the internal bracing, as is the common practice. These members are made of box form ribs which occur at intervals along the spars. Adjacent to the root of the wing a very large reinforced box rib occurs.

The absence of steel tubes considerably simplifies the attachment of the bracing lugs to the spar. It will be noticed that it is of a very simple form, and in this respect it is characteristic of the design of the aeroplane on the whole, which, from this point of view, is far less elaborate than the majority of German designs and appears to be in many ways more practical, especially having regard to quantity production.

Schedule of Principal Weights.

	lbs.	ozs.
Total weight .. ..2532 lbs.		
Upper wing, complete with aileron, aileron rod, drag bracing, and strut attachments, but without lift bracing wires and fabric	62	6
Lower wing, as above (no aileron fixed)	52	8
Aileron complete, without fabric	7	12
Aileron bar, with flange	4	0
Interplane strut, front, without bolts.. ..	3	3
,, ,, rear ,, ,, ...	3	14
Centre section, complete, with radiator and gravity tank, aileron control crank, and bracing wires ..	101	0
Fixed tail plane (each), with fabric	7	8
Rudder, complete, with fabric	7	8
Elevator, complete, with hinge clips and fabric ..	12	0
Fin, complete, with fabric	9	6
V centre section strut	2	7
Straight centre section strut	3	7½
Undercarriage, complete, with struts and bracing, wheels, tyres, and shock absorbers	102	0
Shock absorber (multiple coil spring type), each ..	4	6
Axle, with shock absorber bobbins and caps ..	14	8

A front view of the Halberstadt Fighter.

Radiator in Upper Plane.

Passenger's Gun-ring.

HALBERSTADT—*continued*.

	lbs.	ozs.
Wheel, with tyre	20	4
Tyre and Tube	8	12
Wings, leading spar, per foot run	1	4
Wings, trailing spar, per foot run	0	14½

HISTORICAL NOTE.

The present *Halberstadt* fighter is a development of the earlier single-seater, an example of which was brought down on 29/10/17. In the latter case ash was used to a fairly large extent, both in the fuselage and wings, but in the more modern design spruce is exclusively adopted. The rear spar was of the ordinary " I " Section type without three-ply reinforcement. The fuselage, of somewhat similar shape, was fabric covered. Balanced elevators and rudder were fitted, but no fixed tail-plane or fin. The arrangement of the centre section, with tank and radiator, was substantially the same. Double bays of interplane struts were adopted, but the struts themselves were of the welded-up tapered pattern. The ailerons were controlled by wires and not, as in the present example, positively. Both planes had the same chord and the upper wings had an overhang. The weight of the complete machine, without pilot, was 1,778 lbs.

HALBERSTADT TWO-SEATER, TYPE C.L.IV.

This machine, which is allotted G/5Bde./22, landed near Chipilly on Aug. 23rd, 1918. Dates stamped on the main planes give the date of construction as July, 1918.

It is very similar in design and construction to the *C.L.II* type, which has already been fully reported upon (I.C.642), but many detail differences are incorporated.

Below is a comparative list of the principal dimensions of both *C.L.II* and *C.L.IV* types.

	C.L.IV	C.L.II
Span of upper plane	35 ft. 2¼ ins.	35 ft. 3¼ ins.
Span of lower plane	34 ft. 9¼ ins.	34 ft. 11 ins.
Chord of upper plane ' ..	5 ft. 2⅝ ins.	5 ft. 3¼ ins.
Chord of lower plane ..	4 ft. 3¼ ins.	4 ft. 3½ ins.
Gap, maximum	4 ft. 4 ins.	4 ft. 0 ins.
Gap, minimum	4 ft. 0 ins.	3 ft. 8½ ins.
Dihedral angle of lower plane ..	2 degs.	2 degs.
Horizontal dihedral of main planes	4 degs.	4 degs.
Total area of main planes ..	308 sq. ft.	310 sq. ft.
Area of each aileron	12 sq. ft.	12 sq. ft.
Area of aileron balances	2.0 sq. ft.	2.0 sq. ft.
Area of tail planes	16 sq. ft.	13.6 sq. ft.
Area of elevator	13.6 sq. ft.	12.4 sq. ft.
Area of fin	11.4 sq. ft.	6.4 sq. ft.
Area of rudder	7.9 sq. ft.	7.9 sq. ft.
Area of rudder balance ..	1.0 sq. ft.	1.0 sq. ft.
Horizontal area of body	36 sq. ft.	44 sq. ft.
Vertical area of body ..	41 sq. ft.	52.8 sq. ft.
Length overall	20 ft. 11½ ins.	24 ft. 0 ins.

Rear view of tail of Halberstadt.

TWO-SEATER. TYPE C.L. IV. **Rear end of fuselage.**

Control Pillar of C.L.2 type.

Quick detachment fittings for lower wing of C.L.2 type.

HALBERSTADT—*continued.*

	C.L. IV.	C.L. II.
Engine	180 Merc.	180 Merc.
Capacity of petrol tanks	34 galls.	34 galls.
Capacity of oil system	4 galls.	4 galls.
Crew	Two.	Two.
Guns	1 fixed and 1 moveable.	

WINGS.

The wings, both in disposition and construction, are substantially the same as in the former machine. The characteristic wash-out at the root of the lower planes is even more pronounced than was the case in the *C.L.II* machine. It will be seen from the photograph that the rear spar is bent and twisted by this wash-out. The exact shape of the trailing edge of one of the lower planes is shown in the scale drawings.

Fig. 1 gives a section of the upper wing drawn to scale, and Fig. 2 a comparison of the upper aerofoil of the *C.L. IV.* with the *R.A.F.* 14 section, which is dotted. From Fig. 1 it will be noticed that the three-ply surrounds to the spars are still employed. They are drawn to scale in Fig. 3.

The ailerons remain unaltered in the *C.L.IV* machine, and this is also true of the interplane and centre section struts.

The attachment of upper wings to centre section and of lower wings to fuselage are unaltered, except that the tube which, in the earlier machine, passed right across the fuselage and connected the spars of the port and starboard lower wings is no longer found.

SCHEDULE OF WEIGHTS, HALBERSTADT, C.L.IV.

	lbs.	ozs.
Body, with undercarriage, engine, Spandau gun, petrol tank, gauges and controls	1,220	0
Engine (dry), 180 Mercédès	635	0
Upper wing, complete (no bracing wires)	70	8
Lower wing, complete (with bracing wires).. ..	64	0
Centre section, complete (with struts and wiring)..	108	8
Gravity petrol tank	11	4
Radiator	36	0
Centre section strut (Vee)	5	3
Centre section strut (straight)	2	4
Interplane strut (front), with cable	4	8
Interplane strut (rear), with cable	4	0
Undercarriage, complete, approximately	112	0
Shock absorber (one)	4	6
Axle, with bobbins and caps	14	8
Wheel, complete with tyre	20	4
Tyre and tube	8	12
Leading spar of wings (per foot run)	1	4
Trailing spar of wings (per foot run)		14½
Tail plane and elevator (covered)	25	0

Fig. 1.   Wing Rib of C.L.IV type.

Fig. 2.   Wing Section of C.L.IV with " Raf 14 " section shown dotted.

UPPER WING - FRONT SPAR

UPPER WING - REAR SPAR

Fig. 3.   Three-ply reinforcements of C.L.IV type wing spars.

Rear Spar of C.L.2 type.

Front Spar of C.L.2 type.

General Arrangement Drawings of Halberstadt C.L.2.

Wing Attachment of Upper Planes
of C.L.2 type.

HALBERSTADT C4

SCALE.

INCHES |12 6 0 1 2 3 4 5 6 7 8 9 10| FEET

GENERAL DETAILS

SPAN UPPER PLANE   35'-2¼"

SPAN LOWER PLANE   34'-9¼"

CHORD UPPER PLANE   5'-2⅝"

CHORD LOWER PLANE   4'-3½"

LENGTH OVERALL   20'-11½"

SPAN TAIL PLANE   10'-1½"

GAP   4'-4" TO 4'-0"

SET BACK OF TOP PLANE - 4°

STAGGER   2'-0" TO 1'-2"

HANNOVER. Hannover Waggonfabrik Aktien Gesellschaft. Hannover-Linden.

Formed during the war for the manufacture of waggons and aircraft. Made a two-seater fighter of the type shown in the following illustrations, which is peculiar in having a biplane tail, the idea being apparently to give plenty of tail control, while at the same time keeping the tail narrow so that the after gunner is not "blinded" by a big tail-plane.

THE HANNOVERANER BIPLANE.

The machine illustrated was brought down by anti-aircraft fire, near Lestrem, on March 29th, 1918. As will be seen from the photographs, it is of highly characteristic design, and possesses numerous features of interest.

On labels protected by celluloid, and on the upper surfaces of the wings and fuselage, are identification marks with the date 15/2/18, showing that this machine is of recent construction.

Generally speaking, the construction is of wood throughout, steel being used sparingly, except in the interplane struts, landing chassis struts, centre section and some details of the tail.

Judging by contemporary British standards of design, the *Hannoveraner* biplane reaches a fairly high level, the construction throughout being sound, and the finish quite good.

The performance of the machine is not by any means bad.

The leading particulars of the machine are as follows :—

Weight empty	1,732 lbs.
Total weight	2,572 lbs.
Area of upper wings	217.6 sq. ft.
Area of lower wings	142.4 sq. ft.
Total area of wings	360.0 sq. ft.
Loading per sq. ft. of wing surface	7.29 lbs.
Area of aileron, each	16.4 sq. ft.
Area of balance of aileron ..	1.6 sq. ft
Area of top plane of tail ..	10.0 sq. ft.
Area of bottom plane of tail ..	19.2 sq. ft.
Total Area of tail plane ..	29.2 sq. ft.
Area of fin	6.5 sq. ft. approx.
Area of rudder	6.4 sq. ft.
Area of elevators	22.0 sq. ft.
Horizontal area of body ..	53.2 sq. ft.
Vertical area of body	91.6 sq. ft.
Total weight per h.p.	14.3 lbs. per h.p.
Crew	Pilot and Observer.
Armament	1 Spandau firing through propeller. 1 Parabellum on ring mounting.
Engine	Opel Argus, 180 h.p.
Petrol capacity	37¼ gallons.
Oil capacity..	3 gallons.

Side view of the Hannoveraner Biplane.

Front view of the Hannoveraner Biplane.

HANNOVER—*continued.*

PERFORMANCE.

(*a*) Climb to 5,000 ft. .. .. 7 mins.
    Rate of climb in ft. per min.. 590.
    Indicated air speed .. 68.
    Revolutions of engine.. .. 1,495.
(*b*) Climb to 10,000 ft. .. .. 18 mins.
    Rate of climb in ft. per min... 340.
    Indicated air speed .. 65.
    Revolutions of engine.. .. 1,475.
(*c*) Climb to 13,000 ft. .. .. 29 mins. 45 secs.
    Rate of climb in ft. per min.. 190.
    Indicated air speed .. 62.
    Revolutions of engine.. .. 1,445.

SPEED.

At 10,000 ft. 96 miles an hour; Revolutions, 1,565.
At 13,000, 89½ miles an hour; Revolutions, 1,520.
Service ceiling at which rate of climb is 100 ft. per
    min. 15,000.

Estimated absolute ceiling .. 16,500.
Greatest height reached .. .. 14,400 in 39 mins. 10
                          secs.
Rate of climb at this height .. 120 ft. per min.
Air endurance .. .. .. About 2½ hours at full
                       speed at 10,000 ft.,
                       including climb to
                       this height.
Military load .. .. .. 545 lbs.

STABILITY.

The machine is nose-heavy with the engine off, and slightly tail-heavy with the engine on. It tends to turn to the left with the engine on.

CONTROLLABILITY.

The machine is generally light on controls, except that the elevator seems rather insufficient at slow speeds. It is not very tiring to fly, and pulls up very quickly on landing.

VIEW.

The view is particularly good for both pilot and observer. The former sits with his eyes on a level with the top plane, and also enjoys a good view below him on account of the narrow chord of the lower plane.

HANNOVERANER AEROFOIL SECTION
WITH R.A.F. 4 SECTION SUPERIMPOSED THEREON

Three-quarter rear view of the Hannoveraner Biplane.

Hannoveraner Wing-Rib.

Tail of the Hannoveraner.

Undercarriage of the Hannoveraner.

HANNOVER—*continued*.

Construction.

WINGS.

The general arrangement of the *Hannoveraner* wings is somewhat reminiscent of the R.E.8, except of course, that the bottom planes have no ailerons. The upper wings are practically flat in end elevation, but the lower have pronounced dihedral angles of 2.7 deg., and are set with a positive stagger of 2 ft. 7½ ins. The chord of the upper plane is 5 ft. 10¾ ins., and that of the lower plane 4 ft. 3 ins. In flying position, therefore, the trailing edge of the lower plane is slightly in advance of that of the upper plane. The angles of incidence marked on the manufacturer's rigging diagram, which is fixed to the side of the fuselage, and stamped on the fabric of the wing, are as follows :—

Lower wings   ..   ..   ..   5½ deg. at fuselage.
                                         5 deg. at struts.
Top wings ..   ..   5 deg. throughout.

The lower wings are carried direct from the bottom edge of the fuselage, the roots of the upper planes being carried on a rigidly constructed centre section, which embraces the radiator and the gravity feed petrol tank. The rearward portion of the centre section is cut away immediately over the pilot's seat, and at this point the wing is about 1 ft. above the upper surface of the fuselage. The lower plane has no very pronounced wash-out, but this feature is more noticeable in the upper plane, and is enhanced by the design of the ailerons, the tips of which are set at a slightly negative angle. This gives the characteristic German appearance to the aeroplane when seen in flight. In contrast with that of the majority of German aeroplanes, the wing section is rather flatter than usual.

The Pilot's Office in the Hannoveraner Biplane.

A Hannover Biplane, Type C.L.V., with large single wooden streamline struts and a monoplane tail.

A Hannover Biplane, Type C.L.IV, with curious strutting arrangement. (300 h.p. Maybach engine.)

Radiator and Gun-Emplacement.

Rear Gun Attachment and Ring.

Interior of Fuselage, looking aft.

Rudder-Bar Arrangement.

Centre-Section Strut Arrangement.

Method of Attaching Struts.

HANOVERANER BIPLANE.

Span		39′ 2¼″
Span, Lower Plane		36′ 8½″
Chord		5′ 10¾″
Gap	(about)	5′ 3″
Tailplane Span	(Upper)	6′ 9″
Tailplane Span	(Lower)	8′ 0″
Overall Length		25′ 5¼″
Engine (Opel-Argus)		180 h.p.
Propeller..		9′ 4″
Track		6′ 0″

H—continued.

HANSA. Hansa & Brandenburgische Flugzeugwerke A.G., Brandenburg on Havel, Berlin-Rummelsburg and Hamburg-Wandsbech.

With a capital of 1,500,000 marks, and a staff of 1,000 workmen in Autumn, 1915, these works were then the biggest concern in the German aircraft industry. Manufacturing at Brandenburg, repair works at Rummelsburg and Fuhlsbüttel. Military flying schools for German and Austrian pupils, at Briestly, by Brandenburg and at Fuhlsbüttel aerodrome, near Hamburg.

The German Aero Company, Ltd. was formed in March, 1915, with a capital of 450,000 marks, chiefly by the Austrian Commercial Councillor Castiglioni, the first director of the concern, and also founder cf and controlling the Hungarian Aircraft Works, and by the German aircraft manufacturer Trinks, for the building of *Lohner* biplanes in Germany under license.

On the 7th September, 1915, the stocks were raised to one million and a half marks, and the above name taken by the amalgamation of the Hansa Aircraft Works, Karl Caspar, Hamburg (a former branch of the Gothaer Waggonfabrik), and of the Brandenburgische Aircraft Works, into which the Etrich Works at Libau, and the branch company, the Sports Flieger Flying School at Johannisthal had been transformed.

The chief designer of Hansa & Brandenburgische Flugzeugwerke was Engineer Director Hunkel, formerly of the Albatros firm, who brought out the 160 h.p. Mercédès engined tractor biplane, on which the Austrian chief pilot of the company, Reiterer, put up various passenger altitude record flights, but was killed.

The Hansa-Brandenburg Aircraft Co. was one of the three main suppliers of German seaplanes.

THE BRANDENBURG SEA MONOPLANE.

The later *Brandenburg* seaplane to land in a Danish harbour, as illustrated, bore evidence of the development in the German seaplane line, and the sea monoplane, dealt with here, is the last word in German naval war aviation.

This craft was known for some time to be in existence and at the disposal of Captain Lieut. Christiansen, for North Sea service of the Zeebrugge squadron under his command. It is easily seen that the object strived at has been to obtain a seaplane mount approaching land scouts in controllability, which end, however, renders the aircraft apparently difficult to handle, and thus confines its pilotage to skilled hands.

A comparison shows the biplane and monoplane seaplanes to have the fuselage with the features of raised body curve and tail plane fixing, and rudder form and the floats-cum-strut chassis as identical components. Too, the lower planes of the biplane appear to be in the same position as the wings of the monoplane with its aileron and exterior control cables, and the lower wing strut support of the monoplane is another instance proving the requirements of skilled handling not to have plane damage as the result of a hard descent.

An excellent view and fire range of both pilot and observer will clearly be seen to be attained, besides a live craft, and the weight of the floats may to some extent bring the centre of pressure in approach of the point of gravity.

A front view of the Brandenburg Sea Monoplane of late 1918.

Side view of the Brandenburg Sea Monoplane.

A Brandenburg Sea Biplane of 1913.

HANSEATIC AEROPLANE WORKS, CARL CASPAR.

An early German pilot of pluck, Carl Caspar, in spite of a heavy fall by entangling in cables on an overland flight in mist, consistently partook in the various German competitions, such as the Prince Henry, Johannisthal, Round Berlin, East German meetings, and others, with various success.

With headquarters in Hamburg, he founded a flying school at the Fuhlsbüttel drill ground there.

In the last years before the war, he piloted a *Gotha* "dove" and won the £2,500 prize as third best flight in the "National-spende" overland competition as best achievement. He himself started the manufacture of similar "Hansa" tauben.

During the war, Caspar has himself been on active service, and is said to have been the first German aviator to pay the British islands an air visit, by route of Dover as the usual port of call.

His aircraft works was, in 1915, combined with the Brandenburg company, but separated again later. The Hanseatic Aeroplane Works, Carl Caspar, were then run on a successful scale with a capital of £150,000, no news being to hand of the aircraft turned out.

HANUSCHKE. Hanuschke, Bruno, Flugzeugbau, Johannisthal bei Berlin.

A young and early designer and skilled pilot of parasol monoplanes. His last machine before the war was a *Morane* imitation, and later activity has not been heard of.

J

JATHO. Hannoverische Flugzeugwerke, G.m.b.H., Carl Jatho, Hannover, Vahrenwalderstrasse.

Carl Jatho was one of the German aviation pioneers, and for many years has produced experimental aeroplanes. Since the formation of the above company has concentrated on steel monoplanes, the last dove-designed being fitted with zanonia and arrow-shaped wings, but nothing was reported of business activity before or during the war.

JEANNIN. Jeannin, Emil, Flugzeugbau, G.m.b.H., *Steeldove* and *Race* monoplane manufacturing works, and flying school at Johannisthal, bei Berlin.

Formed by the early successful German aviator Jeannin, on his leaving the Aviatik Company.

The racing monoplanes of *Nieuport* outlines first produced brought the German pilots to fatal accidents, a steel "Taube" being then built, in a rather original edition, which was one of the fastest German aircraft on account of its flat wing section.

During the war the firm has been turned into the Nationale Flugzeug Werke (see latter), under new management, Jeannin leaving.

J—*continued*.

JUNKERS-FOKKERS WORKS, Ltd.

Dessau.

One of the most interesting new formations of 1917. Has a capital of £75,000. Founded by the co-operation of the well-known concerns of the aeroplane manufacturer, Fokker, and the Diesel engine manufacturer, Junkers.

The subtitle of "metal aeroplane building" indicates, possibly, the field of activity.

THE JUNKER ALL-METAL (ALUMINIUM) MONOPLANE.

The same comments as applied to the *Brandenburg* sea mono plane scout, may be employed on this monoplane version of the foregoing biplane of the *Junker* company, the more, as in this instance there are no heavy floats to bring the point of gravity within approach of the centre of pressure. The body is of monocoque appearance with pronounced streamlining behind the pilots and looks as are the planes, provided with large trailing curved ailerons, the divided triangular tail fin and the undivided balanced elevator to be made of corrugated aluminium.

The fuselage ends with a point of sheet metal, and the rudder, of sharp-cornered shape, is attached unsupported to the stern post. What looks like a wire post is to be seen on top of the right plane, but not on the left. A car type radiator is employed, as is a stationary engine and an old-time backwards led exhaust pipe collector. Besides the usual V-shaft rest, the landing gear comprises a forward converted, narrow and stream-lined V strut set and two inclined ones of circular tubes, meeting in the middle below the fuselage.

[NOTE.—There is no recent information concerning the Hanuschke, Jatho, Jeannin or Krieger firms, which in any case are of little note. The accompanying information is retained merely for purposes of record.—Ed.]

Side view of the Junker All-Metal Biplane.

The Junker All-Metal Monoplane.

A rear view of the Junker Monoplane.

Three-quarter front view of the Junker All-Metal Biplane.

Front view of the Junker All-Metal Biplane.

The All-Metal Wireless Junker-Fokker Monoplane, Type **C LI** (160 h.p. Mercédès engine.)

K

K.K. Karl Krieger, Berlin-Johannisthal.

The Emperor's former car driver, pilot designer of speedy German monoplanes. Has during the war produced the first modern type parasol aircraft in Germany.

KONDOR. Flugzeugwerke, G.m.b.H.

Works at the Gelsenkirchen-Rotthausen aerodrome.

Formed by the aviator Joseph Suvelack, who has brought out various monoplanes, biplanes and seaplanes.

Killed on active service on an *Albatros* biplane in combat with British aircraft.

The designer Westphael has apparently during the war joined the firm, producing now a tractor biplane, 160 h.p. Mercédès motor, on which an altitude record with four passengers was established at Johannisthal.

No particulars of this biplane are available.

The Kondor E 111 Wireless Parasol Monoplane. (140 h.p. Oberursel rotary engine), which is said to give a speed of 195 kms. per hour and a climb of 5.000 metres in 16 minutes.

The Kondor E 111a " Wireless " Parasol Monoplane (200 h.p. Goebel rotary engine) which gives a speed of 200 kms. per hour and a climb of 5,000 metres in 11 minutes.

Three-quarter Rear View of the Kondor D VI Biplane. (200 h.p. Goebel rotary engine.) The elimination of the centre section, in an endeavour to improve the pilot's vision, should be noted.

Front View of the Kondor D VI Biplane. (200 h.p. Goebel rotary engine).

L

L.F.G. ROLAND. Luft Fahrzeug Gesellschaft m.b.H.
City office : Berlin W. 62, Kleiststrasse.

Builds *Parseval* airships at Bitterfeld, aircraft works at Adlershof, the latter were almost completely burned down on September 6th, 1916.

The early type aeroplanes were a "Taube" monoplane with elevator tail and an "Arrow" biplane, on which Bruno Langer put up the first German duration record of 14 hours in 1914.

A tractor biplane of general type was manufactured during 1914-15, while the 1916-17 model possess the features given below.

As the pre-war and early war monoplanes of Germany were generally nomenclatured "Tauben" (doves), owing to their zanonia back-swept shaped planes, the latest German fighting biplanes (like *Roland, Halberstadt,* and so on) are likely to be named "Walfische" (whales), as their aspect comes to them from the big front part of the body, which houses the 160 h.p. or 220 h.p. motor.

The *Roland* is the name of aircraft manufactured by the Luft Fahrzeug Gesellschaft (L.F.G. by initials), at Adlershof, successors of the old German Wright Aeroplane Co., and thus not to be confused with the L.V.G. Co. at Johannisthal (Luft Verkehrs Gesellschaft, or Air Traffic Co.).

THE ROLAND SINGLE-SEATER FIGHTER.

L'Aérophile for May, 1918, gives the following particulars of the *Roland* single-seater fighter. For this information and the accompanying drawings one is indebted to the editor of that excellent paper.

The single-seater *Roland Biplane D II.,* which first made its appearance in March, 1917, is once more frequently encountered by French pilots, chiefly in the Eastern sectors.

The dimensions of the machine are as follows :—

Span, upper plane	8.90 m.
„ lower „	8.50 m.
Total length	6.95 m.
Height	2.95 m.

Its weight, 827 kgms., is slightly greater than that of the *Albatros D III.* The lifting surface being 23 sq. m., the load carried per square metre of surface being 36 kgs. (about 7.3 lbs. per square foot).

THE FUSELAGE.

The construction of the fuselage is worthy of special notice. It is built entirely of plywood, covered with fabric, monocoque fashion, and has an oval section finishing up with a vertical knife edge at the stern-post.

Longueur totale 6ᵐ95

Side Elevation of the Roland Single-Seater.

L.F.G. ROLAND—*continued.*

The construction is of the lightest, the framework consisting merely of extremely thin longerons extending the whole length of the fuselage.

Rigidity is due only to two plywood partitions uniting the middle of the top half with the middle of the bottom half. The total thickness of the six layers of the plywood is only 1½ millimetres. At the rear of the pilot's seat one can count only four thin layers.

Between the pilot's seat and the engine there is a superstructure to the fuselage which thins itself at the top to a fin 11 m. thick, to which is attached the radiator and the upper plane.

The centre section of the upper plane is hollowed out to provide space for the radiator. This arrangement replaces the cabane.

One finds on the lower part of the fuselage two shoulders, one on either side, to which are fixed the lower planes.

At the rear the tail skid, built of timber and shod with metal, penetrates the fuselage through a kind of swelling, reminiscent of Nieuport practice.

The pilot is seated high up, his view being assured by two wind-screens placed one on each side of the central ridge. The field of view ahead is very obstructed, and visibility is not so good as in other machines.

THE UPPER PLANES.

The planes are trapezoidal in plan, unequal in span, without stagger or dihedral, but swept back 1½°. Their chord is uniformly 1.45 m., and their gap 1.34 m.

The ribs are perpendicular with the leading edge, and, as each strut of a pair is attached to a common rib and the wings are swept back, the struts are not exactly one behind the other.

The upper planes are formed on two spruce spars placed .83 m. apart, the front one being .13 m. from the leading edge.

There are twelve ribs which are placed .37 m. apart and are interspaced with laths 10 mm. wide, running from the leading edge to the rear spar.

The distance between the main spars is maintained by four compression members of steel tube. These tubes are 25 mm. diameter and are placed at equal intervals of 1.30 m. ; and are cross-braced by piano-wire 3mm. thick. Two fabric strips between the leading edge and the front spar, and two others between the front and rear spars alternately pass from one rib to another, over and under.

Certain angles in the wing frame are kept very rigid by plywood angle pieces.

The ailerons, which are fitted to the upper planes, do not project and are unbalanced. A strip of plywood placed over the fabric protects the aileron hinge at its attachment to the rear spar.

Along this line the aileron measures 1.82 m. It is .42 wide. Its axis is a 30 mm. tube. The aileron cranks are operated by two vertical tubes, Nieuport fashion.

In the upper left hand wing is found a gravity feed petrol tank.

The upper planes are attached directly to the highest part of the fuselage with the help of a special bolt which recalls the system of attachment described on the *L.V.G. C.IV.* type.

THE LOWER PLANES.

The structure of the lower wings is like that of the upper wings. The spars are disposed in the same way, and consequently maintain the same distance between one another. There are ten ribs to each wing, of which nine are .01 of a metre and the last .025 of a metre thick. Between each of them there is also a light lath 10 mm. thick. The bracing is the same as in the upper wings, except that the struts, made of four steel tubes, are slightly different, the first being of 20 mm. and the three others of 25 mm. From the first to the second is 1.17 ms., from the second to the third 1.13 ms., and from the third to the fourth 1.11 ms.

The lower wings are fixed up against the rudimentary planes on each side of the base of the fuselage.

Roland type D.2 _monoplace

Envergure superieure 8ᵐ90
_____ inferieure 8ᵐ50

L.F.G. ROLAND—*continued*.

In rigging one notices an incidence of 4 degrees at the second rib and 3 degrees at the seventh. The interplane struts are of tube of .025 ms. diameter, placed inside a streamline of wood, which gives them a depth of .09 ms.

TAIL.

The whole tail unit has the aspect of a trapezium with at the base a large triangular piece of small depth cut out.

The fixed tail plane is of wood, and the two balanced members forming the elevator are entirely of metallic construction.

The leading edge of the fixed tail plane is of wood hollowed on the inside. A piece of wood, which traverses the fuselage and sticks out .5 m. on each side of it, is embedded in the hollowed part of this leading edge, and thus ensures absolute rigidity.

Two struts of streamline tube running from the top of the fin to the angle of the elevator assist still further this rigidity.

The rudder is almost rectangular in form, with rounded angles. It is balanced by a triangular part prolonging the fin, of which the leading edge is similarly oblique.

The rudder is built of tubing and the fin is of 3-plywood, forming part of the fuselage.

The control cables of the elevator are concealed inside the fuselage, and the control cables of the rudder only come out of the fuselage about 1 metre from the end.

MOTOR.

The single-seater *Roland D.II* is fitted with a Mercédès engine of 160 h.p. of a type already described. As well as the supplementary tank placed in the upper left plane, it has a tank 70 by 70 by 25 placed under the rudder bar.

ARMAMENT.

There are two Spandau machine-guns operated by the motor. They are placed one on each side of the engine inside the fuselage, from which they only protrude at the front.

UNDERCARRIAGE.

This is formed of two tubular V's held together by two cross cables. Their point of attachment corresponds exactly to the base of a partition of the fuselage. The axle is placed between two tubes and is enclosed in a streamline casing. The wheel track is 1.75 m. The wheels are 760 by 100 and the springing is of rubber cords.

It has been said that the *D.II Roland*, owing to its light construction, often suffers from a deformation of its fuselage and is very apt to spin. No test of this machine having yet been possible, this opinion cannot be based on the evidence of our own aviators. It is, however, certain that this machine, which was quite a new idea at the time of its creation, has been among the best of the German chaser machines, and was still in use in May, 1918, in certain of the enemy escadrilles.

Rib Section.

Wing Attachment bolt.

Upper Wing of the Roland, showing radiators.

General Scheme of the raised portion of the Fuselage in front of the pilot.

A Roland Single-seater Biplane, Type D VIa. (160 h.p. Mercédès engine.)

L. F. G. ROLAND—*continued*.

An Early (1917) Roland Triplane, Type D IV. (160 h.p. Mercédès engine.)

An Experimental Roland " D " Type Single-seater Biplane. (160 h.p. Mercédès engine.) This machine was the 2,000th war aircraft turned out by the Roland factory.

A Roland Single-seater " Wireless " Biplane, Type D VIII. (190 h.p. B.M.W. engine.)

A Roland Single-seater Fighter, Type D XIV. (160 h.p. Goebel engine.)

L. F. G. ROLAND — *continued.*

A Roland Single-seater "Wireless" Monoplane. (190 h.p. B.M.W. engine.)

An Early (1915) Type, Twin-propeller and Single-engined Roland Biplane, Class G I. (260 h.p. Maybach engine.)

A Roland Parasol Monoplane, Type D XVI. (200 h.p. eleven-cylinder Siemens engine.)

A Roland Single-seater Biplane, Type D VIb. (190 h.p. Benz engine.)

L—*continued*.

LINKE-HOFFMAN.   Werke, Breslau.

Little is known of this firm, which was not much heard of till the Armistice, when certain illustrations of its products appeared in the German Press.

It is stated that none of its products have been used in any war area.

A Four-engined, Single Airscrew Linke-Hoffman Tractor Biplane.

An early type Linke-Hoffman Multiple-engined Biplane, with the engines inside the fuselage.

328a

L—continued.

L. T. G. The Luft Torpedo-Gesellschaft, Johannisthal, bei Berlin.

The Luft Torpedo-Gesellschaft, of Johannisthal, a company which has recently been established, manufactures a fighting aeroplane, nearly similar in appearance to the Albatros fighter.

The wings have no dihedral nor are they swept back, and the chord of the lower planes is slightly less than that of the upper.

The upper wings meet the top of the fuselage.

On either side there is one pair of interplane struts; placed closely one behind the other (the rear spar has behind it more than half of the wing), and the struts approach one another slightly towards their bases.

The ailerons do not project, and are compensated by a forward projection, as in other new German machines.

The tail planes are like those of the Albatros fighter. The rudder and fixed fin are similarly placed above the fuselage, but are slightly more oval.

The landing-carriage, especially its rear members, is placed somewhat farther forward than usual. The propeller has a revolving pot. The motor is of the fixed variety and gives 175-h.p.

L.V.G. Luft Verkehrs Gesellschaft m.b.H. Works and civil flying school at Johannisthal aerodrome. Military flying school at private aerodrome in Koslin, in Pommern.

One of Germany's largest aircraft works, if not the largest one. It is situated at the Johannisthal aerodrome, by the *Zeppelin* and *Parseval* airship sheds, of which the latter serves as its giant erecting shop, as the firm ran in its early days an air traffic service with *Parseval* airships, from which the name of Air Traffic Co. Ltd. was taken.

Having hitherto chiefly produced *Farman* box kite types, the company acquired in 1912 the service of the Swiss engineer, Franz Schneider, who had helped to design the various *Nieuport* monoplanes.

On being appointed a director of the L.V.G. firm, Schneider brought out, first, a monoplane following closely on the lines of *Nieuport* practice, which, however, proved unsuccessful, so long as only stationary motors were manufactured in Germany, but with an 80 h.p. German Gnôme motor won second prize in the three-cornered flight, 1914, and first prize in an attached competition classified by horsepower, and then a biplane which has set the standard to the general German military tractor type. It secured the three first places in the 1914 Prince Henry flight, and has been built under license by Otto, in Munich, for the Bavarian army and has been copied by Euler (see both).

Herr Schneider has now left the firm, and has started a factory of his own.

The L.V.G. Two-seater Biplane. Type C.V.

Aileron Lever, C.V. type.

Aileron Lever, C.VI type.

AILERON

Aileron Hinge.

WING

Interplane Strut, C.V. type.

Strut Sockets, C.VI type.

L.V.G.—*continued.*

THE L.V.G. TWO-SEATER BIPLANES.

The following illustrations and notes are concerned with two *L.V.G.* biplanes, of which one is of the *C.V.* type, while the other, a *C.VI.* type machine, is of later design, embodying certain alterations and improvements. The *C.V.* machine is allotted G/3BDE/5, and the *C.VI.*, which was brought down near Proven, on Aug. 2nd, by two *S.E.* 5's, piloted by Lieuts. Gordon and Gould, is allotted G/2Bde/21.

Any description which follows and is not definitely stated to apply to either model, must be read as appertaining to the *C.VI.* type.

The *C.V.* machine was only slightly damaged and has been put into flying order, but the *C.VI.* has suffered severely, and it must be stated that on this account the G.A. drawings at the end of this report are not guaranteed to be of absolute accuracy in every respect. The greatest care has, however, been taken in their preparation, and only features of rigging such as dihedral and stagger (besides the tail planes, which are in a very fragmentary condition) are at all doubtful. In matters of detail the drawings are accurate.

Some leading particulars of both machines are given below :—

	C.V. Type.	C.VI. Type.
Weight empty	2,188 lbs.	2,090 lbs.
Total weight	3,141 lbs.	3,036 lbs.
Area of upper wings (with ailerons)	238.4 sq. ft.	196.0 sq. ft.
Area of lower wings	190.4 sq. ft.	160.0 sq. ft.
Total area of wings	428.8 sq. ft.	356.0 sq. ft.
Loading per sq. ft. of wing surface	7.3 lbs.	8.5 lbs.
Area of ailerons, each	13.6 sq. ft.	11.2 sq. ft.
Area of balance of aileron ..	.4 sq. ft.	0.6 sq. ft.
Area of tail plane	21.6 sq. ft.	28.0 sq. ft.
Area of fin	5.2 sq. ft.	*5.2 sq. ft.
Area of rudder	6.8 sq. ft.	*6.8 sq. ft.
Area of balance of rudder ..	·6 sq. ft.	*.6 sq. ft.
Area of elevators	20.8 sq. ft.	16.0 sq. ft.
Area of balance of elevator (one)	1.2 sq. ft.	.8 sq. ft.
Total Weight per h.p.	13.7 lbs.	13.2 lbs.
Crew	2—Pilot and Observer.	
Armament	1 Spandau & Parabellum gun	
Engine	230 h.p. Benz.	
Petrol capacity	52½ gals.	52½ gals.

* Assumed same as C.V. Type.

WINGS.

There are several important differences between the arrangement of main planes of the two models, as will be seen by referring to the General Arrangement Drawings.

The wings of the *C.V. L.V.G.* are without stagger, and are not swept back, and both upper and lower planes are set at a dihedral

Rear and front views of the L.V.G. Biplane. Type C.V.

GERMAN AEROPLANES.

L.V.G.—*continued.*

angle, this being 1 deg. for the upper and 2 deg. for the lower wings. The lower planes are smaller all round than the upper, and have rounded tips. The upper planes only have ailerons, which are of equal chord throughout their length, and are balanced. These planes also follow what was, until recently, the usual enemy practice, by being joined at their roots to a central cabane. There is, therefore, no horizontal centre section in this aeroplane, except for the 3-ply box (about 4 in. wide), which surrounds the horizontal tube of the cabane. For improving the view, the upper plane is cut away over the pilot's cockpit. Relative to the crankshaft the upper wing has a constant angle of incidence of 5 deg. That of the lower wing is the same, except at the tip, where the angle is washed out to 4 deg., and at the root to $4\frac{1}{2}$ deg.

Both upper and lower wings are attached to the body by the same general means, this being adapted to the particular positions and conditions of each joint. In the case of the upper planes, the cabane has lugs welded to its upper side at both ends. The same type of hinge pin is used for all wing joints, and for the aileron hinges also. It consists of a short length of steel tube, carrying at one end some form of stop, and at its other end a slot in which a short rectangular piece of steel is free to rotate, the steel piece being pivoted at its centre. Thus, when the steel piece is placed parallel to the tube, the whole fitting can be passed through any hole which accommodates the tube, but when the piece is placed at right angles to the tube axis, the tube cannot be withdrawn through a small hole. A helical spring ensures that the steel piece shall be pressed against the hole, and not be free to slip into the parallel position.

The lower wing attachments are very similar. Figures show respectively the front and rear joints, and this plan has not been changed on the *C.VI.* type of *L.V.G.*

In the later model—The *C.VI.*—the planes are of the same general shape, but important changes are remarked. The radiator has been removed from the position it occupied on the *C.V.* (see G.A. Drawings), and is now built into the horizontal centre section. It is, of course, common German practice to build the radiator into the upper plane, and such a position is not incompatible with the cabane type of centre section strutting. This is particularly true when—as is the case in the *L.V.G.*—a service petrol tank is supported by the upper plane, and can be made to balance the radiator. It is clear, therefore, that the alteration in design from the cabane system to the centre section system has not been made solely to accommodate the radiator.

So far as may be judged from the machine in its present condition, the *C.VI.* has a positive stagger of 10 in., and both upper and lower planes have a similar dihedral angle, viz., 1 deg. Ailerons are still fitted to the upper plane only, but are not balanced in this model. The upper and lower wing sections of the *C.VI.* model are shown in a figure, and another gives the *C.VI.* upper wing section with the R.A.F. 14 section superimposed. The *R.A.F.* 14 section is dotted.

Front and three-quarter front views of the L.V.G. Biplane. Type. C.VI. Note the absence of balanced extension on the ailerons and the different nose-piece.

Fuselage Formers and Tail Post of C.V. type.

L.V.G.—*continued*.

Schedule of Principal Weights (C.VI Type).

	lbs.	ozs.
Fuselage, without undercarriage, engine or centre section	440	0
Lower wing, covered complete (no ailerons)	76	12
Upper wing, covered complete (with ailerons)	85	4
Centre section without struts or cable	64	0
Centre section N strut	5	8
Interplane strut, each	3	11
Aileron, covered, each	8	4
Balanced elevator, covered, complete in one piece	14	8
Undercarriage, comprising :—		
2 Vees, bare	29	1
2 Wheels, with tyres	55	8
2 Axle caps, with pins	0	6
2 Shock absorber bobbins	1	4
2 Shock absorbers	17	6
Axle and fairing	23	2½
Compression tube in front of Axle	3	0
2 Bracing wires, with strainers	2	0
4 Ferrules	0	10
Undercarriage, complete	132	5½
Tail skid, bare	4	6
Brass oil tank, with 20 ins. copper pipe	9	7
Ammunition magazine (aluminium)	5	0
Exhaust pipe	16	4
Spinner	2	9
Dynamo, without airscrew	23	12

L. V. G. SCOUT. D.V. TYPE.

In this *L.V.G.* the streamlining embraces both the interplane and plane-cum-fuselage connecting twin struts, of more or less V structure. The inner set is provided with a round cutting in the streamlining. The steepness, though not markedly whale type, camouflaged body of the *L.V.G.* may be the result of the employment of a powerful stationary motor. The chord of the lower plane of the *L.V.G.* looks large for a scout ; the rudder asks for comment. Considering the large impulses on a scout rudder from hard work the unsupported position seems daring. The hinged fixed plane and elevator position of the *L.V.G. Scout* is that of the *Brandenburg* seaplane fashion.

The L.V.G. D.V.

Three-quarter rear view of the L.V.G. Biplane. Type C.VI.

An L.V.G. Single-seater Scout produced towards the end of the War, presumably of the D.VI class.

332a

Axle Springing.

Aileron Control Pulleys.

Construction of Fuselage
End with Tail-Skid
Attachment of L.V.Gs.

Under-Carriage
Attachment.

Tail Skids

Protective Corner of Elevator.

Control Column C.V.

Control Column C.VI.

Rudder Bars.

Engine-Mounting Bulk-heads with
Aluminium Strip to protect three-
ply against dripping oil.

Section

Lower Wing Spar Attachment.   C.VI type.

333a

2 т 2

L.V.G. Biplane.　Type C.V.

Span of Top Plane (over flaps)	44'-8½"
Span of Lower Plane	42'-2½"
Length Overall	26'-7½"
Gap of Inner Struts	5'-8¼"
Gap of Outer Struts	5'-6½"
Chord of Top Plane	5'-8¾"
Chord of Lower Plane	5'-3"
Angle of Incidence	3°
Dihedral Angle (Top Plane)	1°
Dihedral Angle (Lower Plane)	2°

L.V.G
CV Type Biplane

L.V.G. Biplane.   Type VI.

L. V. G.
C VI TYPE.

Span Top Plane	42·9
Span Bottom Plane	40·8
Length overall (approx)	24·8
Gap	4·3
Chord Top Plane	5·3
Chord Bottom Plane	4·7
Angle of Incidence	
Top Plane	6½°
Bottom Plane	5°
Dihedral Angle	
both planes	1°

An L.V.G. " D " Type Single-seater Scout.

Upper Wing Ribs of C.VI type L.V.G.

Lower Wing Ribs of C.VI type L.V.G.

C.VI type Wing Section with "Raf 14" shown dotted.

An L.V.G. Twin-engined Tractor Triplane. Note, as in the Friedrichshafen and the Gotha the "sawed-off" nose.

M

"M.B." Melli Beese. This female aviator, with her husband, Charles Boutard, ran a flying school as a limited company at Johannisthal.

They manufacture a two seater *M.B.* "Taube" with 100 h.p. Mercédès for their own school work, a *M.B.* single-seater "Taube" as a sporting mount, equipped with a 50 h.p. Gnôme or Anzani, yet both types only on a small scale, and produced just prior to the war for Warnemünde seaplane meeting a flying boat with a 200 h.p. Mercédès engine mounted in the main float, with a reducing bevel drive of the propeller.

No fresh information.

MERCÉDÈS-DAIMLER.

Mercédès-Daimler Motorcar Gesellschaft. Aeroplane Works : Singelfingen.

The famous builders of aero-engines. During the War, extended their activities to the building of aircraft. No other information is available beyond the illustrations attached and the inscriptions thereto.

MERCUR. Flugzeugbau G.m.b.H., Berlin. Joint stock : 60,000 mark. Not known to produce a model of its own. Likely sub-contractors.

A Mercédès-Daimler " C " Type Two-seater Fighter No. 8.

A Mercédès-Daimler Single-seater " Wireless " Parasol Monoplane, Type L II, with curiously-shaped wing-tips.

A Mercédès-Daimler Single-seater Biplane, No. 9.

337a

N

NAGLO.

Naglo Yard, Wein [Meisterhorn, Pickelsdorf-Spandau, nr. Berlin.

As far as can be ascertained, this firm's activities have been purely experimental, and the quadruplane illustrated is their only known product.

N.F.W. National Flugzeug Werke, G.m.b.H. Works and a military flying school at the Johannisthal aerodrome, bei Berlin.

Into this the former Jeannin Company was transformed on June 15th, 1915, being taken over by Counsellor Bernhard Meyer (see D.F.W.)

A tractor biplane of the general German army type is being manufactured, and the military school of flying is run on large lines with a staff of 120 men at that date.

O

OTTO Werke, München 46, Gustav Otto, Aircraft Works, Neulercherfeld-strasse 76.

Flying schools at Oberwiesenfeld and Puchheim. 600 workmen.

As the biggest South-German aircraft works, the Otto Company has always been the chief contractors of the Bavarian army, alone to have own flying service within the Imperial German air service.

The early German pilot, Gustav Otto, manufactured first a *Henry Farman* shorthorn type, on which the Emperor's first aviation prize was won in an altitude flight by Baron von Gorrissen in the Johannisthal Spring Meeting, 1911, later one of Germany's first tractor biplanes, on which a four passengers' duration world's record was put up, then the characteristic nose-nacelled pusher biplane, which, when abandoned, was still manufactured by the Johannisthal branch, the Ago Company.

The license for building *L.V.G.* biplanes to the Bavarian army was obtained in 1914.

During the war, tractor biplanes of own and conventional type have been produced, and, as in the case of the early aircraft, Otto engines have been employed now of 200 h.p., 8-cylinder vertical type.

In 1916 the Otto Works were taken over by the big German engineering firm, Maschinenbau Augsburg-Nürnberg (building the M.A.W. Diesel engines of the German submarines), and the name being changed into Bavarian Works, light cars being now even manufactured beside aeroplanes and aero engines.

An Experimental Naglo Quadruplane.

P

PIPPART-NOLL. Flugzeugbau-Mannheim.

Of small importance. Building in 1914, on a small scale, the *P.N.* 1913 steel "Taube," had steel cables instead of the usual bridge building below the planes, with a U chassis and a drop-like body.

No fresh information.

PFALZ. Flugzeugwerke G.m.b.H., Speyer on Rhine.

(Founded by the brothers Everbusch, one of whom has fallen on active service.)

Building, prior to the war, a military model, similar to the *Ago* pusher biplane, doing 120 km. with a 100 h.p. Rapp motor.

Little was heard of this aeroplane from Germany, but Bruno Büchner carried out the African flight Swakopmund-Karibib with a passenger, and the post for the latter city on a *Pfalz* biplane, which was together with Truck's *Aviatik* biplane used on the German side in the South-West African campaign.

During the war, a *Pfalz* fighter monoplane has been produced, similar in appearance to the *Fokker*, but with two machine guns fixed for firing through the propeller instead of the latter's one.

Scout biplanes constructed by this firm have recently been captured.

THE PFALZ SINGLE-SEATER (G. 141).

This machine landed in the British lines near Bonnieul, on Feb. 26th, 1918. It is a single-seater scout of interesting design. The number D.3, 4184/17 is painted on the fuselage. From its light construction and clean design, and from the great amount of care that has been taken to keep the fuselage of very good streamline shape and so free from irregularities, it appears to be the result of a serious attempt to produce a scout machine with good performance.

In this connection the actual performance of the aeroplane as given below is especially interesting and instructive. Some leading particulars follow :—

Weight empty	..	..	..	1,532 lbs.
Total weight	..	..	..	2,056 lbs.
Area of upper wings		..	..	151.6 sq. ft.
Area of lower wings		..	..	88.4 sq. ft.
Total area of wings		..	..	240 sq. ft
Loading per sq. ft. of wing surface			8.56 lbs.
Area of aileron, each		..	..	10.25 sq. ft.

Front view of the Pfalz Single-seater D.III Type.

Three-quarter rear view of the Pfalz Chaser. D.III Type.

PFALZ—*continued*.

Area of balance of aileron..	..	0.6 sq. ft.
Area of tail plane ..	.. ..	12.1 sq. ft.
Area of fin ..	.. ..	2.8 sq. ft.
Area of rudder ..	.. ..	6.0 sq. ft.
Area of elevators ..	..	12.7 sq. ft.
Total weight per h.p.	.. ..	12.84 lbs.
Crew ..	.. .. ..	1.
Armament ..	.. ..	2 Spandau guns firing through propeller.
Engine	.. ..	160 h.p. Mercédès.
Petrol capacity	.. ..	21½ gallons.
Oil capacity..	.. ..	4 gallons.

PERFORMANCE.

(a) Climb to 5,000 ft.	.. ..	6 min. 55 secs.
Rate of climb in ft. per min...		605.
Indicated air speed	..	73 m.p.h.
Revolutions of engine..	..	1,330.
(b) Climb to 10,000 ft.	..	17 min. 30 sec.
Rate of climb in ft. per min...		360.
Indicated air speed	..	67 m.p.h.
Revolutions of engine..	..	1,310.
(c) Climb to 15,000 ft.	..	41 min. 20 sec.
Rate of climb in ft. per min...		110.
Indicated air speed	..	50 m.p.h.
Revolutions of engine ..	..	1,280.

SPEED.

At 10,000 ft.	.. .. ..	102½ m.p.h.
At 15,000 ft.	.. .. ..	91½ m.p.h.
Service ceiling at which rate of climb is 100 ft. per min..	..	15,800
Estimated absolute ceiling	..	17,000.
Greatest height reached	..	15,000 ft
Rate of climb at this height	..	110 ft. per min.
Air endurance	.. ..	About 2½ hours.
Military load	.. ..	281 lbs.

STABILITY AND MANŒUVREABILITY.

This machine is reported to be stable laterally and unstable directionally and longitudinally. It answers well to all controls, much better than does the *Albatros D.5*, but tends to turn to the left in flight. It is not tiring to fly, and is normally easy to land. Though the tail skid is of the non-steering type, no difficulty is found in directing the machine on the ground.

VIEW.

As may be expected from the shape and disposition of the wings, the view is excellent in all directions—except, perhaps, on a downward glide, when the top plane interferes to some extent.

Rear view of the Pfalz Chaser, D.III type.

Fuselage Construction, D.III.

Method of Covering Fuselage, D.III.

PFALZ—*continued.*

WINGS

The wings and wing bracing are a copy of the *Nieuport* practice. The top plane is in one piece, and has no dihedral angle. The smaller type lower planes have a dihedral angle of 1 deg.

In flying position the leading edge of the upper plane is 15 inches in front of the leading edge of the lower plane.

Ailerons are fitted to the upper wings only, and both upper and lower planes have the characteristic wash-out at the tips.

WING CONSTRUCTION.

The spars of this machine are well worthy of attention. The webs are made of a thick central core of good straight grained wood, covered on each side with one layer of extremely thin 3-ply. The 3-ply stiffens up the webs against buckling inwards, thus enabling thinner webs to be used than if not reinforced. The flanges are spindled to give good glueing area and fillet, and diaphragms are fixed at each rib to transmit the sheer stress across the spar. This is a good feature, and might with advantage be incorporated in all box spars.

The ribs are built up in the usual way of 3-ply and flanges, and are of light construction.

Undercarriage Arrangement, D.III.

Rear End of Fuselage showing method of building the Fin and of attaching the Tail-Skid, D.III.

Front Spar Construction, D.III.

Construction of Tail Unit, showing Rudder, part of Elevator and Fin, D.III.

Interplane Strut and Mounting, D.III.

2 z 2

PFALZ—*continued.*

D.III Wing Section, with " Raf 14 " section shown shaded.

D.III type Wing Rib.

Control Column, D.III.

Rear End of Fuselage, D.III.

Rudder Bar, D.III.

PFALZ SCOUT

SCALE ¾ = 1 FOOT

THE D.III TYPE PFALZ

Span of Top Plane	30' 10½"
Span of Lower Plane	26' 7⅜"
Length Overall	23' 2"
Gap at Inner Struts	4' 9⅝"
Gap at Outer Struts	4' 6⅞"
Chord of Top Plane	5' 5⅜"
Chord of Lower Plane	3' 11"
Angle of Incidence	6° 20'
Dihedral Angle (Lower Plane)	1°

PFALZ—*continued.*

THE PFALZ (D. XII) SINGLE-SEATER FIGHTER.

This aeroplane, which was allotted G/H.Q/6, was brought down near Dury, on 15/9/18 ; by Lt. Cameron (No.1 Squadron) and Capt. Staton (No. 62 Squadron).

Although in construction it is strongly reminiscent of the Nieuport-like type of *Pfalz* the design of this machine is entirely new, and is of considerable interest.

GENERAL DESIGN.

As will be seen from the General Arrangement drawings on page 2190 the *D.XII Pfalz* has a car-type radiator in front of the engine, and wings which have two bays a side. The lower planes are faired off into the body in the characteristic *Pfalz* way, but the fin, which in the earlier model was built of 3-ply as an integral part of the body, is now a separate fitting.

Area of upper wings (without ailerons)	104.8 sq. ft.
Area of lower wings (both) ..	117.6 sq. ft.
Area of aileron (one only) ..	8.4 sq. ft.
Area of balance of aileron ..	0.8 sq. ft.
Area of elevators (each)	8.4 sq. ft.
Area of balance of elevator (one)	0.6 sq. ft.
Area of rudder	8.8 sq. ft.
Area of balance of rudder ..	0.4 sq. ft.
Area of tail plane (both sides) ..	16.0 sq. ft.
Area of fin	4.4 sq. ft.
Area of body (horizontal).. ..	32.8 sq. ft.
Area of body (vertical)	53.6 sq. ft.
Engine	180 h.p. Mercédès.
Petrol capacity	18¾ gallons.
Guns	Two Spandau (fixed).

The portion of body 3-ply which bears an inscription regarding weight and permissible load is missing.

WINGS.

The flat upper plane is built in one piece as before, but the centre section contains neither gravity tank nor radiator, and the tips are no longer heavily raked. The two ailerons of high aspect ratio, are very similar to those of the *D.VII Fokker*, as are the placing of the radiator and the form of the interplane struts.

The lower planes, which are attached to a kind of centre section that may be said to grow out of the body, are of the same chord as the upper plane, and only slightly shorter in span. The lower planes possess a dihedral angle, in this case of 1½ deg., and the two pairs of interplane struts on each side slope outwards.

The attachments of the lower plane to the body are unchanged.

The latest type Pfalz Biplane in use at the end of the war.

Side and three-quarter front views of a wrecked Pfalz D.XII Single-seater Fighter.

344a

PFALZ—*continued.*

A lug on the fuselage has a circular-section base round which the open end of the tube on the spar fits, while the lug itself is pinned into the fork on the spar in the usual manner. Both front and rear spars are attached in this way.

A figure shows the upper aerofoil section compared with that of the *R.A.F.* 14, which is shown dotted. It will be noticed that the two sections approximate more closely than was previously the case.

The wing construction of upper and lower planes is similar. Each lower wing contains 11 ribs, spaced at equal intervals of approximately 13½ ins. The wood leading edge of the plane is not of the usual " C " section, but is more solid. The spars retain the former *Pfalz* design, but the section is of a squarer shape than formerly, and the flanges are not spindled. The upper and lower plane spars are exactly similar. As those points where the strut attachments occur, the spars are solidified by the insertion of small blocks of wood. The various components of the spars are very strongly glued together with a casein cement, and fabric is glued round the whole.

The tape lattice work that was found in the old-type *Pfalz* between the spars, and between the rear spar and trailing edge is no longer present, but a vertical-section strip of wood lies parallel to the rear spar between that member and the trailing edge, and strips of wood are tacked on to the leading edge, and on to the two spars, and finish just behind this strip. These false ribs are placed midway between the true ribs, and the space between each false and true rib is again bisected by another strip. These pieces simply pass from the leading edge to just behind the front spar, and are built up with a vertical strip so that the whole is of T section. The ribs are of a 2 mm. 3-ply, with flanges tacked on in the usual way, and are lightened. The trailing edge is of wire and each rib has fabric sewn over it. There are 12 steel compression tubes in the upper plane, and five in each of the lower planes. The bracing varies from steel tie rods of 5 mm. diameter to 12-guage piano wire.

Propeller.

This is of Heine make, No. 26,206 ; diameter 2.780 m., pitch 2.000 m. It has eight laminations of mahogany and walnut.

Schedule of Principal Weights. (*D.XII* Type.)

	lbs.	ozs.
Fuselage, without engines, guns, auxiliary tank or oil tank, but with main tank and tail skid ..	257	0
Starboard lower wing, with control cables but no bracing wires. Only one side fabric covered ..	46	0
Upper wing, with bracing wires, but only one side fabric covered	127	0
One centre section M strut	7	4
Radiator	44	8
Brass oil tank	5	1
Auxiliary petrol tank	7	8
One outer N strut	8	9
Fin (covered)	3	2

	lbs.	ozs.
One inner N strut	10	6
Aileron (covered)	7	12
Aileron hinge rod	0	8
3-ply tail plane (partly estimated)..	19	0
Aluminium rose cowl	3	14
Cockpit cowl and padding	2	6
One aluminium side cowl	2	12
Ammunition magazine	7	12
Two clutches for synchronising gear	5	13
Two gun channels	5	5

The weights of the various components of the earlier *Pfalz*—the *D. III* type—make an interesting comparison, and are given below :—

	lbs.	ozs.
Fuselage, without engine, guns, or empennage, but with tanks and all fittings	295	0

	lbs.	ozs.
One lower plane, covered, but without bracing wires..	49	0
Complete upper plane, covered, with ailerons, bracing wires, radiator, and gravity tank ..	225	0
One centre section strut	9	6
Radiator	37	3
Brass oil tank	3	2
One U interplane strut	8	13
Aileron, covered	10	14
Fixed tail planes, without fabric	14	9
Aluminium spinner	1	7
Cowl behind spinner	2	13
Exhaust pipes..	11	8
Tail skid, bare	5	0
Elevator, without fabric	9	0
Rudder, with fabric	6	13

Wing Section of the D.XII Pfalz, with " Raf 14 " section shown dotted.

Wing Structure of the D.XII Pfalz.

A Pfalz 1917 Type Rotary-engined Triplane.

345a

LENGTH OVERALL 21'·5"

LENGTH OF FUSELAGE 17'·6½"

180 H.P. MERCEDES.

GRAVITY PETROL TANK

RADIATOR.

PETROL TANK

STAGGER.
← 1'·4" →

SPAN OVERALL 29'·6"

SPAN OF UPPER PLANE 27'·7"

SPAN OF LOWER PLANE 26'·4"

MACHINE GUNS

CENTRE LINE

9'·0"
7'·3"

1'·11½"
⅝

11¾"

2'·9½"

7'·9" AILERON

PILOTS SEAT

4'·7½"

4'·7½"

11¾"

11¾"

DRIFT WIRE

CENTRE LINE

PFALZ SCOUT

TYPE D XII

SCALE

INCHES ▮▮▮▮▮▮▮▮▮▮▮▮▮▮ FEET

OVERALL SPAN	29'·6"
SPAN OF UPPER PLANE	27'·7"
SPAN OF LOWER PLANE	26'·4"
LENGTH OVERALL	21'·5"
GAP AT INNER STRUTS	4'·6"
GAP AT OUTER STRUTS	4'·3½"
CHORD OF BOTH PLANES	4'·7½"
ANGLE OF INCIDENCE	3¾°
DIHEDRAL ANGLE (LOWER PLANE)	1½°
STAGGER	1'·4"
SPAN OF TAIL PLANE	7'·3"

R

REX. Flugmaschine Rex Gesellschaft m.b.H., Cologne on Rhine. Aircraft works at 1, Antwerpener Street, flying school at the Wanne-Herten aerodrome.

Formed during the war by Dr. Friedrich Hansen, formerly of the Statax Engine Co., London, for the building of light destroyer aeroplanes of English-French features (*Bristol* and *Morane*).

THE REX FIGHTING BIPLANE.

The chaser-biplane, constructed by the Rex Company of Cologne is not definitely known to have been used on active service on the Western Front.

The information available shows it to be a single-seater fighter of the D.II type.

The machine offers a striking resemblance to the Nieuport, the more especially because the lower wings have a span slightly less than that of the upper wings (about 9 metres), and a much smaller chord. In fact, the lower plane is smaller and lighter in all its aspects.

Contrary to Nieuport practice, the lower wings have no dihedral, and it is almost certain that they are not swept back. The upper wings are trapezoidal in plan view.

There is only one pair of interplane struts on either side of the fuselage, which are arranged " V " fashion as in the Albatros D.III.

The upper wings are placed very close to the fuselage, and are attached to a central section, which is supported by short splayed-out struts reinforced with wire bracing.

The elevating planes are placed in line with the axis of the motor, and have no incidence.

The rudder is very tall, and is believed to be placed entirely above the fuselage, as in the Albatros fighter.

The fuselage is a three-ply monocoque, with projecting flats for the attachment of the lower wings.

The landing-carriage is ordinary " V " type, with cable cross bracing.

The Rex is apparently always fitted with a rotating monosoupape Rex engine (Gnôme type), and carries a machine-gun placed to the right and synchronised with the motor.

This machine may be distinguished from the Albatros D.III by the absence of a dihedral to the lower plane.

R—continued.

RUMPLER. Werke G.m.b.H. Formerly E. Rumpler, Luftfahrzeugbau. Works and flying school at Johannisthal aerodrome by Berlin. Military flying school at Moncheberg.

The start of the first aircraft works in Germany is characteristic of German business procedure. The former engineer of the Daimler Motoren Gesellschaft, E. Rumpler, was charged by the German Aero Club with issuing a book of aviation—somewhere in 1908—for the material of which he wrote to and was supplied by trade and inventors of all countries. Acquired the German license for building the *Etrich* "Taube," on which Hirth attained his early successes, winning the Upper Rhine, Prince Henry, the München-Berlin and Berlin-Vienna flights, the latter on a special race dove.

Controversies arising between Rumpler and Etrich, the latter dropped the German patent rights, which led to the general adoption of the "Taube" type by almost every aircraft works in Germany.

Hirth left, and Rumpler lost much in influence. Linnekogel put up further altitude records on the new *Rumpler* monoplane, of modified "Taube" design, in that the plane underbridge was abandoned and the back-swept elastic wing tips replaced by usual ailerons of same shape.

The same body, canvas covered over steel tubes, was employed in the first *Rumpler* biplane, on which Basser performed his 18 hours' duration record and the passenger overland flight Berlin-Budapest-Sofia-Constantinople non-stop, excepting the three capitals.

During the war this biplane has been produced as a seaplane, earlier efforts in this field being the *Rumpler* flying boat, an intermediate between the *Curtiss* and *F.B.A.* types and the ordinary "Taube" design, only with a two-floats landing gear.

THE TWO-SEATER RUMPLER BIPLANE (Type C.V.).

(260 h.p. Mercédès Engine).

This machine, which was used by the enemy at the commencement of 1918, is of the C.V. type, but differs only in detail from the earlier C.IV. type of 1917.

The general shape and disposition of the wings is maintained, including the characteristic sweep-back of the main planes, and

Front view of the Rumpler, C.V. type, biplane.

Three-quarter rear view of the Rumpler (C.V. type).

RUMPLER—*continued.*

the fitting of ailerons to the upper planes only. Some important particulars follow :—

Weight empty (but with water) ..	2439 lbs.
Weight, fully loaded	3439 lbs.
Total Military load	545 lbs.
Span (upper)	41 ft. 6 ins.
Span (lower)	40 ft.
Chord (Upper)	5 ft. 8 ins.
Chord (lower)	4 ft 4 ins.
Sweep back	3 degrees.
Dihedral	$2\frac{1}{2}$ degrees.
Area of upper wings (with ailerons)..	217.6 sq. ft.
Area of lower wings	146 sq. ft.
Area of ailerons (each)..	15.3 sq. ft.
Total area of main planes	363.6 sq. ft.
Loading per sq. ft. of wing surface ..	9.5 lbs.
Area of tail plane	22 sq. ft.
Area of fin	4 sq. ft.
Area of elevators	20.8 sq. ft.
Area of rudder	6 sq. ft.
Total weight per h.p.	13.2 lbs.
Petrol capacity..	59 gallons.
Oil capacity	3 gallons.
Water capacity	10 gallons.
Endurance	About 4 hours.

PERFORMANCE.

			ft.	m.p.h	revs.
Speed at	..	..	10,000	100.5	1510
Speed at	..	..	15,000	87	1390

Rate of climb in ft. per

	ft.	m. s.	min.	revs.
Climb to ..	10,000	16 0	400	1375

Service ceiling, 15,500 ft. (estimated).
Estimated absolute ceiling, 17,500 ft.
Greatest height reached 15,300 ft. in 38 min. 25 secs.
Rate of climb at this height is 125 ft. per min.

CONTROL.

Longitudinal (elevators), good.
Lateral (ailerons), very heavy and very ineffective.
Directional (rudder), moderately light and quite effective.
It is reported that the machine is tiring to fly owing to the very poor lateral control; that it is nose-heavy, and rather liable to get into a spin.

AIRSCREW.

The airscrew is an "Axial," No. 6987, diameter 3,150 mm., pitch 1,830 mm. It is secured to the crankshaft by eight bolts, an extra pair being fitted between two of the pairs of the usual six.

Rear view of the C.V. type Rumpler.

SECTION OF AEROFOIL – RUMPLER C.V.

"Raf 14" Wing Section shown shaded.

2 x 2

RUMPLER—*continued.*

Tail and Fin Bracing of the Rumpler. Note the saw-
teeth on the low tail stay tube to prevent mechanics
from lifting the machine by this tube.

Radiator and Shutter of the Rumpler C.V.

Engine Emplacement in the C.V. Rumpler.

Front Spar of C.V.

Cup and ball coupling of
Upper Wing, C.V.

Coupling of Lower Wing, C.V.

RUMPLER—continued.

SECTION

Well for Compass.

Piano-stool Seat for Gunner.

Strut and Bracing-Wire Attachment.

Cabane and Radiator Attachment.

ELEVATOR WIRES
TO UPPER LEVERS
TO LOWER LEVERS

AILERON WIRES

Control Cross-Bar.

Axle Attachment.

Under-Carriage Strut Junction.

Tail-Skid Arrangement.

Rudder-Bar.

DETAILS OF RUMPLER C V. TYPE.

351a

Control Column, showing Handles and Machine-Gun Control Lever.

Radiator and Shutters.

Throttle Controls.

Well for Second Camera.

Fitting for Large Camera.

The Latest Rumpler "C" Type Biplane. (260-300 h.p. Basse and Selve engine). Note the crossed interplane struts—a fashion now becoming prevalent in Germany.

Span Upper Plane		41'·6⅛"
" Lower Plane		40'·0"
Chord Upper Plane (inner struts)		5'·7"
" Lower Plane		4'·3⅝"
Length overall		26'·11½"
Incidence of Top Plane		2°·40'
" Lower		3°
Gap at Inner Struts		6'·0½"
" Outer		6'·0½"

Scale :- ¼" to 1'·0"

RUMPLER C5 TYPE.

S

SCHÜTTE-LANZ, LUFTSCHIFFBAU.

Aeroplane works : Zeesen, nr. Konigswusterhausen.

The well-known airship building firm. Commenced to build aeroplanes early in the War. It seems probable that no Schütte-Lanz aeroplanes passed far beyond the experimental stage—as they have not been heard of at the front.

The accompanying photographs are given because, although some of them are of type of 1914-15, they have never yet been illustrated in Great Britain.

An early (1914–15) Schütte-Lanz " G " Type Twin-engined Biplane, possessing many features betraying its relationship to lighter-than-air craft.

A 1918 Type Schütte-Lanz " C " Type Biplane.

354a

SCHÜTTE-LANZ—*continued.*

A Schütte-Lanz Single-seater Triplane Scout.

A Schütte-Lanz Single-seater Fighter of the " D " Class.

An Early (1914-15) Type Schütte-Lanz Pusher Biplane.

S—continued.

SIEMENS-SCHUCKERT. Berlin.

One of the many branches of the great Siemens electrical firm, which had world-wide ramifications before the war.

The Siemens "Grossflugzeug," or "Big Aeroplane," which is illustrated herewith, is said to have been succeeded by the Siemens "Riesenflugzeug," or "Giant Aeroplane," a species of Super-Gotha, with four or six engines.

The firm built an experimental airship some years before the war, but never built aeroplanes until recently.

THE SIEMENS-SCHUCKERT AND SIEMENS-STEFFEN GIANTS.

(A Description by a Neutral Correspondent).

The efforts of the Siemens-Schuckert Company, confined, like the aircraft branch of its great competitor the A.E.G. concern, apparently to military requirements with a determination of staying with the aircraft department in the business line by catering for the requirements of commercial aviation to come, appear in two editions resulting, both of which appear more workmanlike than the Staaken biplane, which is to the air traffic aeroplane as the pre-war Sikorsky was to the Handley Page.

The one Siemens-Schuckert giant illustration looks as having suffered from the retoucher's hand. Judging from the right side of the view, the aircraft appears to be equipped with four engines, two motors, apparently of V types, may be Körting model, driving tractor screws to each side. Though the motor mounting is not visible, one motor looks as if installed on the fuselage with the screw in an impossible position for revolving. The skid rudiments act probably as mudguards and so as to prevent the wheels of the weighty aircraft from sinking into muddy ground.

The name of Steffen combined with Siemens in the other product may be that of the flying officer, known as a pre-war daring lieutenant pilot. The idea of the designers with the split body relates undoubtedly to the stability; the other feature is the nose stepping, looking almost too prominent to be radiators, so one may have a guess at some blinding armourment for engine or engines and crew. The nearest struts to the body are carried out as double V rests for the shafts of the two screws, being driven by transmission from inside the fuselage. The landing gear is like those found in the various models in the German G class.

A further feature is the appendicitis (presumably the writer means "attachment") combined with two struts to the ailerons and recalling the Curtiss interplane ailerons from the days of the Wright patent flights.

A Four-engined Siemens Schuckert Biplane, with 110 h.p. Mercédès engines. The first multiple-engined machine built by this firm.

An early type of Siemens-Steffen Giant Aeroplane. This is the machine illustrated on following page, but with 2-220 h.p. Mercédès engines substituted for the two inner 110 h.p. engines originally used.

SIEMENS-SCHUCKERT—*continued*.

THE SIEMENS-SCHUCKERT BIPLANES.

To judge from general appearance, the D4 model looks the older, with its numerous interplane cross wiring. The form of the cabane struts here and of the interplane ones of the other scout edition are similar to the familiar construction from the Pfalz biplane. So far as can be seen, both Siemens biplanes are provided with balanced ailerons at both planes, as well as with balanced rudders and elevators. The D4 machine is equipped with a four-bladed screw, being, in fact, the result of an attachment of two, and rotary motors being employed the broad form from the body nose is given, the other model looking, with its monocoque fuselage and striking streamlining aft the pilot's head, altogether the more finished. In this connection due attention may be paid to the news in the book on rotary aero engines of the Swedish aircraft manufacturer, Dr. Thulin, as source that the associated Siemens and Halske concerns have for some time manufactured a rotary motor with cylinder and crankshaft rotating in opposite directions, with the same r.p.m. of 900. The airscrew is mounted on the crankshaft, and the advantage to be obtained is that the screw gives by a fairly low number of revolutions a better effect without the employment of reduction gear, all while the chargings and accordingly the power development is the effect of the relative low number of revolutions. Yet at the same time the low number of r.p.m. has a bad influence on the air-cooling of the motor.

An early type of Siemens-Schuckert Giant Aeroplane. The engines are within the fuselage and drive both airscrews through clutches and a gear box.

The Siemens-Schuckert D.IV.

Rear view of Siemens-Schuckert of another Type.

A Siemens-Schuckert Monoplane, with a rotary engine.

GERMAN AEROPLANES.

S—continued.

SABLATNIG. Aircraft works.

Being of the first batch of pilots to be trained in Germany on the *Wright* biplane, the Austrian *Sablatnig* achieved special results in passenger altitude records on the peculiar arrow biplane of the Union Works.

His own aircraft works were formed during 1917 with a capital of £25,000.

SCHNEIDER. Franz. Aircraftworks. Siegefeld in Spandau.

The Swiss engineer, Schneider, was the chief collaborator of Nieuport, and on being engaged in 1912 by the German L.V.G. Company, his first effort was to produce a monoplane of those characteristic lines.

Later he produced the 100 h.p. *L.V.G.* tractor biplane, which was the originator of that German class which has played an important part before and during the war.

Though no informing news is available, one is apt to believe the designer to continue his activities in his own work in the line started.

SCHWADE. Schwade & Co., Erfurt.

Before the war built *Henry Farman* type biplanes. Reports of later activities not to hand.

SCHULZE. Gustav, Aircraft Works, Burg by Magdeburg.

Run on similar, but smaller lines to the Grade Co. of pupil training. Not heard of during the war years.

SIGISMUND. Friedrich Prince Sigismund of Prussia, Danzig.

Forbidden by his father to fly either as pilot or passenger, he turned his interest in aviation to the design of various monoplanes, which he built at his own small works in Danzig, where he also ran a flying school for gentlemen aviators. His racing type monoplane, 100 h.p. Mercédès, named *Bull Dog*, was flown with some success in various competitions during 1914 by Stiefvater, who was killed early in the war in a test flight near Berlin, though no news is to hand of his mount, nor of further activities of the principal aircraft during the war.

During the war, both Prince Friedrich Sigismund and his brother Carl Friedrich, received permission to go on active service in the air force, where, shortly after a flight of the two brothers from Doeberitz to Hannover and return, the latter was wounded and shot down in the British lines during a fighting trip on an *Albatros* scout, and died shortly afterwards.

A Sablatnig Two-seater Tractor Biplane C II. (230 h.p. Benz engine.)

A Sablatnig Two-seater Tractor Biplane, Type C I. (180 h.p. Argus engine and later a 230 h.p. Benz engine.)

An 160 h.p. Benz-engined Sablatnig Seaplane, largely used by the German Navy.

A Sablatnig Single-seater Triplane Scout Seaplane.

U

UNION. Flugzeugwerke G.m.b.H., Berlin, S.W., 48, Friedrichstrasse 235.

Flying school at Teltow aerodrome. On the *Union-Arrow* biplane, system Bombard, with the lower planes swept upwards, various passenger records were set up with a 120 h.p. Austro-Daimler engine, and looping demonstrations carried out in 1914 by one of the present German star turns, Höhndorff, with a biplane, equipped with a rotary Oberursel motor.

URSINUS.

The *Ursinus* is said to have been built to the designs of Oskar Ursinus the Editor of the German paper, " Flugsport."

The German idea was to have the twin-engine drive concentrated as much centrally as possible, raising the fuselage and having the tractor screw tips almost touching, with the object of improving the control of large aircraft.

The experimental biplane was built at the Barmstadt Air Station, and the type was next put into production at the Gotha Works, both as a land and seagoing model.

THE URSINUS HYDRO-AEROPLANE at rest.

An early Ursinus twin engined biplane. It was produced at Darmstadt in 1914. Later it was built under licence by the Gotha company first as a land machine and later as a seaplane with 2-100 h.p. motors, which were subsequently replaced by more powerful power units.

359a

Z

ZEPPELIN.

Zeppelin Works : Lindau, v Staaken.

The famous Zeppelin airship firm very early in the War took up the development of aeroplanes and seaplanes through the medium of the F.F. Friedrichshafen Flugzeugbau, under whose name will be found a description of the Friedrichshafen product.

At a later stage the parent company itself, at its Lindau and Staaken works, devoted itself to the building of aeroplanes, particularly those of the " Giant " type, and certain of their products are described and illustrated hereafter.

THE FOUR-ENGINED ZEPPELIN BIPLANE.

The following description of a four-engine Zeppelin is due to M. Jean Lagorgette, and is based on an examination of the *debris* of a machine which was captured, in a badly damaged condition, on the French front on June 4th, 1918 :—

Overall Dimensions.

In reality the total height is 6.4 ms. of which 1.5 m. is under the fuselage and 4.4 m. between the wings in the centre section. Total length, 22 ms. Total span, 41 ms.

Sketch of the Method of Fastening the Bracing Wires on the Wing-spars of the Zeppelin Four-engined Biplane.

The Wing Form.

FORM.—The span of the lower wings is equal to that of the upper wings and the chord is the same except for a difference of some centimetres in the centre section. There is no stagger.

The upper wings have no dihedral, the lower wings only being so provided, and they also only have a dihedral outside the base of the cabanes which carry the engines, but what there is is accentuated. From 4.4 ms. at this point the gap decreases to 3.6 ms. at the tips, or .8 ms. decrease in a little less than 16 ms., or almost 5 centimetres per metre.

The two planes indubitably are arrow-shaped only as to the leading edge, and in a somewhat marked manner. The whole recalls the form of the L.V.G. of 1913-17, and not that of the earliest Morane-Saulniers, of which the L.V.G. was the inverse.

From 4.5 ms. at the axis of the machine and as far as the summits and bases of the engine cabanes, the chord decreases to 3.5 ms. at the tips, or 1 m. of arrow in about 17 ms.— that is to say, about 6 cms. per metre. As to this arrow of the two planes, it is no less certain than as regards the V of the lower wings that it begins only at 110 mms. from the exterior bases of the cabanes and at 100 mm. from the summits. Beyond these points the gap of the wings is then at each point a little greater or a little less than their chord, and the average gap is equal to the average chord.

All these dimensions are, besides, confirmed by the height of the interplane struts as to the dihedral, and by the length of the compression tubes between the spars as to the arrow—that is to say, in plan and front elevation.

The trailing edge of the wings seen in plan is, as distinct from the leading edge, a straight line. The wing tips are slightly oblique and rounded.

INCIDENCE AND WING SECTION.—The incidence of the wings from the axis of the machine to the engine cabanes is determined by the two following points. The lower longerons of the fuselage being horizontal in front, the lower side of the front spar of the lower wing rests directly on their upper surface, while the upper side of the rear spar only comes flush with the upper surface of the fuselage longeron. This is to say, the angle of the under surface of the wings between the spars is fixed by the depth of the rear spar—that is to say, about 160 mms.

The incidence is thus approximately 0.45 ms. in the 4.5 ms. of the total chord, or about 1 in 10.

Even if with the idea of simplification, and, contrary to the rule of nearly all German biplanes, the angle of incidence does not diminish from the middle of the machine to its extremities, the difference in level between the leading edge and the trailing edge would decrease progressively in the same direction, since the wings narrow towards the tips. But as it seems certain that the curves of the wings are more accentuated towards the centre of the machine than at 15 ms. from the centre, I have

A Zeppelin " C " Class Two-seater Biplane.

A Zeppelin " D " Class All-metal Wireless Scout.

ZEPPELIN.—*continued.*

taken the curve illustrated, it is possible that the angle of incidence decreases correspondingly with the concavity of the wings.

Wing Structure.

WING SPARS.—There are two principal spars which are true girders, a third spar, the shape of a gutter placed on its side, holds the ribs .75 ms. from their ends. In the upper planes this only runs as far as the beginning of the ailerons. The aileron spar, also of a gutter section, supports the aileron hinge and is placed about a metre from the trailing edge.

Both of the true wing spars cross the fuselage at their different levels. The front spar on top of the lower fuselage longeron to which it is held by eight bolts. The rear spar comes flush with the longerons to each of which it is united by a heavy spar-box of a T shape, which spar-box also serves for the fixing of the rigging cables.

By this continuity across the fuselage it is possible to dispense with special compression tubes, and the position of the leading spar of the wing permits the existence below it of the metal cross-bracing of the fuselage, while the rear spar itself fulfils the purpose of a similar cross member.

Each of the spars is composed in the course of its length of three pieces, each in a straight line. The rear spars are assembled all three in a straight line, but the front spars, outside the engine cabanes, are set back in the arrow shape, and as regards the lower wings, both spars are assembled to give a dihedral.

Thus the centre part of the spars which traverse the fuselage are a single piece in a straight line without either arrow or dihedral as far as the outside of the engine cabanes.

As may be seen in a Fig., each spar forms a double box composed of seven grooved pieces assembled, glued and reinforced on the two sides by one or two layers of ply-wood, then wrapped with fabric in a spiral before placing the ribs in position. At the points of attachment and at the centre they are left solid. The upper spars, as well as being larger, especially the rear spar, are made of ash, and the lower ones of spruce.

RIBS.—Outside the central fixed part where they are perpendicular to both edges, the ribs form with the leading edge and with the front spar an angle clearly obtuse on the side of the fuselage and acute on the opposite side, while they are perpendicular to the rear spar and trailing edge. The same is true of the compression tubes situated between the bases of the interplane struts.

The construction of the ribs recalls that of the Handley Page, also of certain Albatroses, and specially that of the framework of the Zeppelin airships, as may be seen by comparing the sketches.

There are top and bottom flanges glued and nailed to a central web, also in spruce, which is bedded into the flange. Webs in

the form of double laths unite the opposite flanges, and in the case of those in compression are made into boxes by the addition of three-ply strips (Fig. 3). They are disposed in zig-zags and fixed to the web of the rib by duralumin rivets.

All these wooden elements are glued. The ribs are nailed to the spars. Everything except the ply-wood is made of spruce. The trailing tip of the rib is sheathed in a sort of square thimble of thin brass. The trailing edge of the wing is held by a simple piano wire which goes through this thimble.

The distance between the ribs, which is enormous, varies from .565 m. to .43 m. It is less in the vicinity of the airscrews.

Between two neighbouring ribs a flat lath, 15 by 10 mm., extends to the leading edge above the front spar to maintain the shape of the fabric.

On top of each rib the fabric carries a strip of braid glued outside. It is fixed to the ribs by a thread which passes over this tape and on top of the lot is glued a strip of fabric 3 to 4 cm. in width.

Between the spars two series of bands pass alternatively over and under the ribs of the flanges to which they are nailed, maintaining the position of the ribs laterally. Exactly in the middle between the interplane struts two ordinary ribs are much closer together than the others, being .15 m. apart. They maintain the distance between the longerons against the compression which is exercised by the secondary cross-bracing in the vicinity of these ribs.

BRACING.—The wings have a double system of cross-bracing, one between the bases of the struts, which is very long and consists of thick cables, and the other is in simple 3 mm. piano-wire joined to the ends of the twin ribs which are placed halfway between the struts.

These wires, by a curious disposition in crossing the spars, penetrate through them obliquely, and they are connected to a simple nut and bolt arrangement. In the spruce block situated in the exterior angle between the rib and spar they are fixed solely by the pull of the turnbuckle.

Details of Ribs and Spars. Wings of Four-engined Zeppelin Biplane.

AVION GÉANT ALLEMAND

Reconstitution par Jean Lagorgette

Envergure totale 41ᵐ00

Scale Drawings of the Zeppelin Four-engined Biplane.

ZEPPELIN.—continued.

The long cable bracing is fixed to the extremities of the compression tubes. This extremity is fixed to the spar by two lateral lugs, pierced with holes, to which are attached the cables and wires of the cross-bracing.

COMPRESSION TUBES.—These are situated between the extremities of the interplane struts, and between the engine cabanes. They serve at the same time to maintain the distance against the incidence bracing. Given that there are two for the base of each cabane, and a single one for the single summit, there are altogether ten in the lower plane, and eight in the upper plane, a number which is frequently surpassed in the small German aeroplanes.

The tubes are round, 50 mms. in diameter, for those at the summit of the cabane, 45 mms. at the base of the cabane and decreasing, as they get away from the centre of the machine, from 40 mms. down to 12 mms. between the external masts.

Interplane Bracing.

CABANES.—Each of the three cabanes is composed of two A's, of which the bases and summits are fixed by sheaths to the wing spars, or to the fuselage in the case of the base of the central cabane, and they are inter-connected by compression tubes inside the wing and bolted to the sheath.

The width of the engine cabane at the base is 1.2 ms., both front and rear, and the distance between the A's longitudinally is 2.48 ms. Each of the A's is of round tube, 55 × 60 ms., except the rear tubes of the engine cabanes, of which internal and external diameter are 60 × 65 mms. The cross-piece is of 32 mm. tube.

INTERPLANE STRUTS.—These are parallel to one another and vertical; of round steel tube with conical ends stuck inside and welded. They are bolted into lugs on the bottoms of which they press, which lugs are themselves raised on a large steel sheath surrounding the longerons.

Their diameter and thickness diminish from the internal pair (55 × 60 mm.) to the intermediate pair (44 × 48), and the external pair (35 × 38 mm.). These dimensions in each pair are the same for the front and rear struts, contrary to what would have seemed natural and to what exists in the legs of the engine cabanes, and for the front and rear cable bracing.

They are surrounded by fairings of 3-ply with little interior ribs, as on the Bréguet, open at the top and bottom to enclose all attachments.

BRACING.—The cables are disposed in transverse and longitudinal X's. As regards the longitudinal cables, there are two cables from the top of the front strut to the bottom of the rear strut, and one from the top of the rear strut to the bottom of the front strut.

By a disposition peculiar to this machine, and general in the bracing in other directions (except transverse) of its fuselage, each transverse cable of the wings as well as in the stabilising planes is formed of an endless cable. Or, more exactly, after it has been passed diagonally round three faces of the wing spar, without having been linked to a fixed point, but passing simply in a groove or gutter welded on to the sheath of the spar, one of the extremities of the cable returns from the opposite side towards the other extremity with which it is linked by the turnbuckle. It is thus, in a sort of way, doubled, but although weighing double, it does not offer double strength or double security.

Undoubtedly this procedure ensures a certain elasticity from which the avion and the cable itself profits, but if a rupture occurs the entire cable ceases to fulfil its functions, because, having no point of attachment, instead of having four, it slacks off and offers no resistance to strain. One can only see in it inconvenience in compensation for very slight and problematic advantages.

An analogous system was applied on the Zeppelin airships in which it was impossible to have absolute rigidity, and if the

FRONT VIEW OF THE FOUR-ENGINED ZEPPELIN BIPLANE. The right wing is partly cut away so as to make the drawing as large as possible. M. Lagorgette has indicated in a most pains-taking manner the sizes of tubes, cables, and fairings, "t" stands for tube, "g" for "gaine" or fairing, "c" for corde or cable. "Nourr," on the side of the starboard engine stands for "nourrice," or "nurse-tank." The word "longeron" written along the starboard leg of the fuselage cabane refers to the upper plane spar, and not to the fuselage longeron. The symmetrical arrangement of the engine-cabanes and their continuation to the under-carriage struts is noteworthy. The front elevation of the tail is shown in dotted lines behind the fuselage and engine-cabanes.

ZEPPELIN.—*continued.*

engineers of this firm have adapted it to avions in the same way as the employment of aluminium, it is undoubtedly because of the psychological influence of tradition not less than for the doubtful technical reason of suppleness.

To avoid distortion of the struts an almost horizontal tube links at mid-height each front strut with the strut behind in the same pair.

Moreover a set of cables of which one extremity is fixed at the intersection of the wing spars with the bases of the engine cabanes runs transversely at half their height from the internal struts to the external struts, and thence terminates .08 or .1 ms. from the extremity of the spars, thus linking up by cable the ends of the horizontal steel tubes already mentioned.

At the crossing of these cables with the transverse bracing cables, the cables are enclosed in a little fairing of poplar profiled in the form of a hollow olive. Over and above this, all the cables, including the double transverse cables, are enveloped in a fairing of light ply wood surrounded by glued fabric.

AILERONS.—As in all German biplanes, except the Albatros, C. type, and the Friedrichshafen, ailerons are only fitted to the upper wings. In spite of the gutter shape form of the third spar it is fairly certain that this would not serve as a hinge fixing ; and that no ailerons exist for the lower wings.

The ailerons are rectangular and do not project. The outer angle is rounded, as are the tips of the lower wings, and is slightly raised towards the rear tip, according to the German habit. They are not balanced, contrary to another habit, and this characteristic seems singular when one recalls the effort necessary to manœuvre the machine even if there were two pilots. And what is more strange the elevators are not balanced either, although there is no servo-motor.

The maximum span of the ailerons is 7.16 ms. and chord 1.02 m., measured from the middle of the 60 mms. tube, which acts as a hinge, and which is imbedded up to that point in the gutter-shaped false spar which supports the ailerons.

Their structure is entirely metallic, being made of steel tubes like those of the ailerons and rudders of all German aeroplanes, though the rudders of the Zeppelin itself are of aluminium. The idea in this is doubtless to give enough strength with slight thickness, and to avoid the warping of the wood.

The ribs, spaced .5 ms. apart, corresponding to those of the wing, are composed of two steel tubes in an elongated V surrounded at half their length by a little band of sheet steel welded to them which maintains their distance. The two rear extremities, to decrease the thickness, are welded one alongside the other, and not one on top of the other, to the trailing edge of the aileron, which is also of steel tube, 25 by 14 mms. Other tubes of 15 mms. are disposed crosswise as bracing. All these

tubes are wrapt with light fabric, on which is stuck that of the ailerons.

The Tail.

CONTROLS.—The tail of the Zeppelin is the least banal part of the machine, on account of its structure, no less than on account of its dimensions. It is remarkable for the turning of its curvature upside-down, and for the large and almost exclusive use of aluminium. Enormous and heavy, each of its planes

would have a surface sufficient to build a monoplane, and, as a whole, they would form a small two-seater biplane, or a large single-seater.

TAIL PLANES.—The tail planes, or longitudinal stabilisers, partly fixed and partly mobile, are biplanes. Not only are they of a surface equal to that of a biplane, but they are a complete biplane in general structure, internal constitution, cabane, struts, bracing, etc. This cellular character permits one to fix the tail

Various Details of the Four-engined Zeppelin.

ZEPPELIN.—continued.

at suitable horizontal points on the fuselage, which is flattened and raised and built as high as possible to avoid accidents on landing. The directional controls, or rudders, are included between the altitude controls.

The tail planes are of a rounded arrow shape very much accentuated, and their aspect in plan is exactly that of a Taube. The analogy is striking and complete and cannot remain unnoticed.

In spite of the difference in the centre, due to the fact that the lower tail planes are fixed on the sides of the fuselage, they are equal in span (9 ms.) and in chord; 1.6 m. at the centre tapering to 1.5 m. towards the struts, for the fixed tail planes, and .44 ms. to .72 ms. for the mobile flap.

The gap is 2.15 ms. much greater than that of an ordinary biplane, and greater than the chord.

FIXED PORTIONS.—The incidence of the upper surface which is adjustable is sufficiently great (.17 ms.) in a chord of 1.57 ms., or about 1 in 10, which is about the same as that of the wings. That of the lower face is still more marked.

This is made necessary by the weight of the tail, but comparison with ordinary planes would necessitate a special examination, for one characteristic which is peculiar and worthy of remark, is that the curve of the tail planes, which is very much like that of current types, is completely reversed. That is to say, the upper surface is absolutely flat, while the lower surface has a curve similar to that of the upper surface of the wings. That is to say, it is convex instead of concave to the extent of having 112 ms. thickness.

The section of the elevator flap proper is triangular with a slight curve on both faces.

RUDDERS.—The rudders, which are three in number, are connected to fixed fins, one of them fixed on the axis of the machine, and the others 3.5 ms. out on each side. They are all entirely comprised inside the level of the two-tail planes, even to the extent of leaving a slight margin of 8 to 10 cms.

The rudders have a similar form, but the central fixed fin differs from the other two. Mounted on a vertical duralumin tube between the front struts of the cabane, this central fin is prolonged as far as the fifth transverse member of the fuselage, in the middle of which it is fixed at its leading point, while the two other fins mounted on the front struts of the tail are only prolonged forward a little way. At the trailing edge all three of the fins are limited partly by the longitudinal bracing to which they are fixed by their duralumin edges. The rudders are mounted on the rear struts or on the vertical tube (which is a shade shorter)—also of duralumin—which is situated between the rear struts of the cabane. In front of these pivots is a balanced portion which extends to the vicinity of the cross-bracing to which the fixed fins also extend from the other direction.

The fixed fins and the rudders are entirely constructed of aluminium. Their ribs consist of little aluminium girders, analogous to those of the elevators and very similar to the girder work of the Zeppelin airships.

For the rudders the control cables, after passing over horizontal pulleys near the fifth transverse member of the fuselage, set out obliquely, and one cable passes through a window in each of the external fixed fins to a single transverse lever on the outer rudder. It seems then the more necessary that the three rudders should be linked up so as to be movable in both directions.

The Body.

FUSELAGE.—As on the smallest aeroplanes, there is a single fuselage. Its general characteristics are those of the old German fuselages built in the form of a lattice girder and not, as in the newer types, as a plywood monocoque as in the chaser machines, or in plywood with wooden frames without bracing. The length is 21.35 metres.

The two upper longerons are in a horizontal plane on a level with the axis of the airscrews for practically the whole length, and from 1.8 metres, cross measurement, they approach one another progressively in a straight line from the front of the gun-turret to the rear extremity, where the width is 1.08 metres.

The two lower longerons are horizontal from the front of the machine to the back of the gun-turret, whence they rise in a straight line to the last cross-strut but one, and then rise in a curve, so that the fuselage thins down in a horizontal line as in the Albatros and the early Fokkers. Thus, the maximum section of the fuselage, from behind the pilots to the gun-turret, is 1.8 metres wide by 1.68 metres in height, and thence it flattens out progressively.

These dimensions are concerned with the naked woodwork, but on each angle, so as to fix the fabric on the whole surface and to hold it clear of the cables, turnbuckles and ferrules, which might damage it, there has been added a wooden edging which consists of a strip of poplar, 30 by 40 mm. This strip is cut away frequently to allow for the numerous and somewhat thick ferrules and it forms on each side of the fuselage, a projection of 25 mm. or about 50 mm. to be added to the total width and height of the fuselage.

At 3 metres from the front of the machine, above the leading under-carriage, the longerons are interrupted, and the whole of the front part can, if necessary, be removed. From this point the true upper longerons, which are of ash, 65 × 65 mm. in this vicinity, descend to the summit of two 55 mm. tubes, which come to a point at the leading extremity of the fuselage. The part above these is super-added, and is composed of wood and round light tubing, which is not part of the actual construction.

CROSS-BRACING.—As differentiated from the transverse cross-bracing, but in the same way as the cable bracing of the wings, the bracing of the four faces of the fuselage is composed of endless cables.

The Zeppelin Four-engined Biplane in Flight. (4—250 h.p. Maybach engines.)

GERMAN AEROPLANES.

ZEPPELIN.—continued.

Internal Arrangements.

Right in the nose of the machine, which is rounded and little raised is a place for at least one gunner-observer who is provided with a handle, probably for the bomb-dropping apparatus.

Behind him and somewhat more elevated so that there is a view behind the "habitacle" (a delightful French word for a cockpit), and protected by a transparent windscreen (partition B general arrangement) are installed the two pilots whose controls will be described later.

Behind them there seems to be a wireless operator. Then on a level with the front of the wings are two mechanics who are certainly not too many for the surveillance of the four engines with their various controls, pumps, and so forth.

From the level of the front spar to the trailing edge the multiple tanks are suspended by girths to the girder frames which have already been mentioned, and the bombs are hung under the fuselage.

Between the tanks a passage is arranged through the partitions B to I, from the front to the cabin behind the gun-turret.

Finally, in the turret there are at least two machine-gunners who can fire not only above but under the fuselage from a sort of cabin which is situated behind, and to which they have access by crawling under the partition I.

There are thus a total crew of eight or nine persons. Underneath the gun-turret is a long trap door with the hinges set longitudinally. An external ladder on the left, made of welded tubes, permits the crew to mount into the turret, and another one seems to have been fitted to the front part of the fuselage. The fuselage is covered almost entirely with fabric. The front is three-ply and sundry sheets of aluminium close the roof of the machine towards the front.

The Under-carriages.

In spite of its 18 wheels, the landing system is of the most simple, but not of the most diminished. As on the Friedrichshafen and on the majority of big two-engine machines, it is composed of three parts. One is merely an accessory under the front of the fuselage.

THE FRONT UNDER-CARRIAGE.—This is composed of two widely opened V's, each practically in a longitudinal plane. The after legs, which are 2.6 ms. long, are of 55 mm. tube. They are 1.6 ms. apart and are fixed by bolts under partition C to the lower fuselage longerons at the point where the true longerons are prolonged by false longerons. This entirely detachable part is undoubtedly susceptible to frequent breakage in landing.

The summits of the leading legs, which are short, being 1.1 m. in length, and almost vertical, and made of 40 mm. tube, are joined to the leading extremity of the fuselage by a single bolt in such a fashion that in plan they form a V. The lower ends of these tubes telescope into an elbow of an intermediate diameter, which itself telescopes into a rear tube of 55 mm., the whole being welded together.

Between the elbows of the two V's for a space of about .35 ms. are welded 30 mm. tubes, to which are fixed the rubber shock-absorbers. The two wheels which are .9 ms. apart, have rims of .48 m. diameter by .11 m. wide.

THE MAIN UNDER-CARRIAGE.—This is situated at the level of the motors, under the wings, which particularly, for this reason, have neither a V nor an arrow.

Being subjected always to considerable strains, it is possible that the original under-carriage was miscalculated, which seems to be indicated by the inscription "Verstarkt" ("re-inforced") on each, from which one judges that several modifications have been made in the original arrangements.

Each of them is composed of two longitudinal V's resting under the spars on two 65 mm. bolts, held in a clip which is bolted to another, under the steel sheath which links the engine-cabane to the wing-spar exactly at the level of the foot of the cabane, and not in the prolongation of the leg of the cabane. Thence, where they are 1.2 m. apart, the two V's divide from one another to 1.55 mms. at the base.

The two legs of each V are united by a large hollow steel elbow with rounded angles to avoid cutting the rubber shock-absorbers, and, to hold these "sandows," carry a projection in front and two at the back.

The distance between these bases is maintained by an horizontal tube, one in front and one behind the wheel-axle, and by double-bracing of 8 mm. wire. The axle is held in these V's by sandows in the ordinary manner of an under-carriage, between two bobbins made of several pieces of pressed and welded steel.

This axle, enormous, and fatter than those of railway waggons, is of 110 by 120 mm. tube, and carries at each end two pairs of twin wheels. That is to say, eight wheels for each under-carriage.

The rims are 700 mm. diameter by 120 mm. wide. The tyres appear to be about 1,000 mm. (1 metre) in diameter.

Almost all the pieces of the under-carriage are autogenously welded. The whole thing appears to be strong, but the wheels alone form a cylindrical surface, of which the section is about 2.8 sq. ms., and this must offer considerable resistance to progress.

THE TAIL SKID.—This is single and of the usual type, pivoted under the middle to a lower fuselage cross-strut.

This tail skid is a single piece of ash, 1.2 ms. long, 70 mm. diameter at its upper part, 110 mm. diameter at the pivot and

then square with a side of 110 mm. enlarged at the lower end by a steel sole.

Controls.

For transverse and longitudinal control there are two vertical levers of aluminium tubing, plugged with wood at the base only, permanently mounted on a single transverse axle and each furnished with a wheel.

The levers operate in the ordinary manner for longitudinal control.

The three rudders are controlled by means of two horizontal rudder-bars, and sectors and pulleys guiding the cables along the side of the fuselage as on old L.V.G's and almost all German aeroplanes.

After passing over a horizontal pulley on a level with the fifth partition from the end of the fuselage, the cables divide out horizontally and very obliquely, traverse the outer fixed fins by an opening in their base and thus to the rudder lever.

Armament.

The armament consists of at least four machine-guns, and possibly six. One at least is placed in front of everything.

A huge gun-turret of 1.4 m. internal diameter is situated behind the wings.

On each side, a little behind the middle, a gun-mounting is permanently fixed between the turret and the longeron, to which it is clipped by a collar. The gun-mounting is in the form of a "Z," which can turn on itself, and allows the gun to point downwards outside the fuselage without circulating round the turret. These two mountings make it possible to fire over the sides and upwards, as well as towards the rear.

It is possible that other machine-guns have been installed at the back of the turret to fire backwards and upwards; also the compartment behind the turret makes it possible to fire below the fuselage.

There exists, it seems, only two bomb-carriers, but each is for a bomb of 1,000 kilos. (about 1 ton). They are suspended longitudinally under the fuselage between the wing-spars, to which they are fixed by two collars at each end.

Each bomb-carrier is composed of two triangular girders of steel tubes, braced by crossed tubes, all welded together and cross-braced by piano wire.

This frame, measuring 2 m. in height by .35 m. in width, projects above the longerons into the interior of the fuselage. It carries two longitudinal tubes and two transverse arcs, 1.1 metres apart, under which the bombs would be held by a releasable girth.

It goes without saying that such bombs are not suitable for all sorts of objectives, even if their ratio of action compensates for their small number.

366a

ZEPPELIN.—continued.

Engines.

The four independent engines are placed on the same level, two by two in opposite directions, one being a prolongation of the other with an interval between. Being of the same model they thus turn in opposite directions. The same disposition of engines was tried in France in 1916.

Each of them is held in a rocker between the two legs of a cabane front and rear, half of their length being in front and half behind. Each of their bearers, to which they are bolted direct, is a girder composed of two pieces of ash with a layer of plywood vertically between them.

The whole is held up by a complex wooden frame—uprights of wood and sheet steel 50 mm. wide by 300 mm. high and 450 mm. apart—which on one part butt up against the cabane and on the other part hold up by the intermediary of a cross-strut, the gearbox and the airscrews.

Each cross-strut rests on two tubular sockets of 55 mm., which are adjustable at the base, and rest against the base of the cabane on the wing spar. Cable cross-bracing of a complex nature completes the edifice.

These cabanes are built of two tubular "A's," 55 × 60 mm. in the front, and 60 × 65 mm. on the rear, and not of two "V's," as on the Friedrichshafen. This composition seems quite favourable against smashing, and gives four points of union at the summits of the under-carriage.

Each of the "A's" carries, besides a bracing of 32 mm. under the radiator, a bar of "U" section sheet steel, 100 mm. deep, and .88 to .9 m. in length. At the two extremities of this bar, each front "A" is linked to the rear "A" by two wooden longerons, .9 of a m. apart.

Each base and summit of the cabane is united to the corresponding wing-spar by a clip of 3 mm. sheet steel, 230 mm. wide.

A bonnet of aluminium, at any rate in front, encloses the engines.

These motors are 6-cylinder vertical Maybachs, but their power, which is ordinarily about 250 h.p. in this type, seems to have been forced up to 300 h.p., or 1,200 h.p. in all.

It is worthy of note that the German authorities impose on the engine constructors limited dimensions, lengths of base and other characteristics, which permit the interchangeability of different makes of engines.

Two of the motors are provided with a species of gear, almost destroyed, probably a starting-gear.

AIRSCREW GEARING.—Instead of the airscrew being mounted directly on the shaft, the following arrangement is interposed :—

1. A fly-wheel of cast iron of .4 metres diameter, unlike anything which exists in any other German aeroplane.

2. A connection in aluminium with plates of leather in notches, .36 metres diameter, of which the female part is half engaged in the fly-wheel.

3. A transmission tube, very short indeed for the front engines, but .75 metres long in the rear engines.

4. A gear-box containing two toothed pinions in an aluminium case, made in two parts and bolted together horizontally.

By this gearing the axis of the airscrew is placed 170 mm. above the axis of the motors, and its level corresponds thus with the upper longeron of the fuselage.

Under this one finds an oil reservoir-radiator, semi-cylindrical in shape, .35 by .1 m. thick, with 20 mm. tubes running through it. This has a pump at the base and two electric thermometers.

Airscrews.

The axes of the airscrews are 6.8 metres apart, laterally, and the bosses of the screws are 5.8 m. apart fore and aft. The screws are two-bladed, of 4.3 metres diameter.

From .185 m. towards the boss the thickness changes quickly to .3 m. The maximum width of the blade is .4 m. There are about a dozen laminations, mostly in badly chosen spruce with knots in it, except one which is in mahogany, and the whole length is covered by a thin layer of plywood.

Accessories.

As we have seen, the tanks are suspended to the upper part of the fuselage level with the wings. By each motor there is a gravity tank suspended by two little tubes to the inside leg at the bottom of the cabane at a level with the cylinders. A pump is placed in the fuselage on a level with the front wing spar.

The radiators, of N.I.G. type, and .2 m. thick, .4 m. high and .85 m. wide. Of this width .23 m. consists of a supplementary section, which can be added or taken away as required. The radiators are placed in front and at the top of each "A" of the cabane. They are suspended by two vertical cables.

Electric lighting is installed. Six fire extinguishers were found among the wreckage.

All the fabric is of poor quality, and is camouflaged with dark coloured hexagons, dark blue or violet, on which the black cross does not stand out. The paint used offers little resistance to oil and petrol.

If one reckons on a total weight of 12,600 kilograms, the upper spars of ash must work at a pretty high stress. The most fatigued part, situated immediately outside the engine cabanes, works at 1.7 kilograms per sq. mm. On the same reckoning the spars on the lower plane work at 1.3 kilograms per sq. mm.

The figures for the work of the interplane struts of steel tubes vary from 1.1 kilos to 3.8 kilos per square mm.

Some of the cables vary from 10 kilos. to 25 kilos. per square mm. The cables are flexible and of quite good quality.

If the weight is 12,600 kilograms, the surface 314 square metres and the horse power 1,200 the load would be 40 kilograms per square metre—which is not enormous—and 10.5 kilos. per horse power.

It seems unlikely that the speed of this machine is more than 120-125 kilometres per hour.

THE ZEPPELIN BIPLANE.

Specification.

Type of machine	Four-engined Biplane.
Name or type No. of machine	Zeppelin " Giant " Biplane
Purpose for which intended	Bombing.
Span	41 m.
Gap, maximum and minimum	4.4 m. ; 3.6 m.
Overall length	22 m.
Maximum height	6.4 m.
Chord, maximum and minimum	4.5 m. ; 3.5 m.
Total surface of wings	314.5 sq. m.
Span of tail	9 m.
Total area of tail	20 sq. m.
Area of elevators	5 sq. m.
Area of rudders (3)	4.2 sq. m.
Area of each aileron and total area	7.25 sq. m. ; 14.55 m.
Engine type and h.p.	4—300 h.p. Maybach.
Airscrew diameter	5.2 m. dia.
Load per sq. metre	40 kgs.
Weight per h.p.	10.5 kgs. per h.p.

Performance.

Speed low down	120-125 kms. per hr.
Total weight of machine loaded	12,600 kgs.

ZEPPELIN.—*continued.*

THE ZEPPELIN FIVE-ENGINED GIANT.

A 5-engined bomber was brought down near Talmas on Aug. 10th, but unfortunately, owing to the explosion of one of its bombs, the machine was damaged beyond hope of reconstruction.

Some of its components have been recovered.

The principal item of interest is the gear box, which is used for all five engines, each of which is a 300-h.p. Maybach of the standard 6-cylinder vertical type.

The power plants are arranged as follows :—In the nose of the machine is one engine driving a tractor screw. On each side of the fuselage, supported by the wings, is a long pair of engine bearers carrying two engines apiece, which drive tractor and pusher screws.

The use of the gear box and driving shafts necessitates the employment of a fly-wheel on the engine, to which is added the female portion of a flexible coupling of the type already described.

Whereas the gear box in the 4-engined Giant, of which notes have already been given in this report, is of a somewhat crude type employing external driving shafts between the gear box and the engine, in the 5-engined machine the gear-box design is considerably improved. The casing consists, as shown in the photograph, of a massive aluminium casting provided with four feet which are bolted to the engine bearers.

Two kinds of gear boxes are employed. These differ only in over-all dimensions and the length of the propeller shaft.

The larger type is used for the pusher screw in order to obviate the necessity of cutting a slice out of the trailing edge of the main planes.

All the gear boxes were very badly damaged except one. This is the longer type, but it would appear that the shorter design is very similar in appearance.

In each case the gear reduction is 21—41.

The over-all dimensions of the gear box is as follows :—
Length, 1,025 mm.
Breadth, 675 mm.
Height, 535 mm.

The weights of the gear box and its attachments are as follows :—

Gear box, long type, 280 lbs.
Fly wheel and female clutch, 44 lbs.
Male clutch, 5 lbs.
Oil radiator, 12½ lbs.

This it will be seen represents an additional weight of considerably more than 1 lb. per h.p.

The oil radiator in conjunction with each gear box is of a roughly semi-circular shape, and is slung underneath the main transverse members of the engine bearers so that it comes immediately beneath the large feet of the gear box, as shown. The radiator is entirely of steel construction, and embraces 65 tubes of approximately 20 mm. internal diameter. These are expanded and sweated into the end plates, to one of which is fitted a stout flange, against which is bolted a small gear pump which constantly circulates the oil from the gear box case through the radiator.

View Shewing the Pusher Airscrew of the Zeppelin
Five-engined Giant.

A Zeppelin Giant Biplane Seaplane. (4—250 h.p. Maybach engines.)

ZEPPELIN.—*continued.*

This gear pump is driven by a flexible shaft from the small pinion, the shaft and its casing being in all respects similar to those employed for engine revolution counters. As shown in the photograph illustrating the complete gear box upside down, this flexible drive is taken off a small worm gear.

It will also be seen that underneath the oil sump of the gear box proper an electrical thermometer is fitted, which communicates with a dial on the dashboard.

Fitted on each gear box and working in connection with the oil circulation is a filter. This is provided with an aluminium case and a detachable gauze cylinder through which the oil passes.

The arrangement of the gear box is such that the axis of the airscrew is raised about 220 mm. above that of the engine crankshaft.

The construction of the long engine bearers is not without interest, as amongst other things, it indicates that German manufacturers are finding themselves short of suitable timber. Each bearer consists of a spruce or pine central portion, to which are applied, top and bottom, five laminations of ash. On each side are glued panels of 3-ply, about $\frac{1}{8}$ in. thick.

The engine bearers taper sharply at each end, and are strengthened by massive steel girders under each gear box.

The screws revolve at approximately half the speed of the engine, and having therefore a moderately light centrifugal load to carry, are made of a common wood that would scarcely be safe for direct driving screws.

Although fitted to 300 h.p. Maybach engines, they are marked 260 p.s. (h.p.) Mercédès. The diameter is 4.30 metres, and the pitch 3.30, for the pusher screw, but unfortunately, owing to the airscrews being badly damaged, not only by the crash, but by fire, it is not possible to state whether the tractor screws are of the same dimensions and pitch.

The construction is very interesting; each screw is made of seventeen laminations of what appears to be soft pine, and these laminations are themselves in pieces, and do not run continuously from tip to tip. They are, of course, staggered, so that the joints in successive layers do not coincide. Two plies of very thin birch veneer are wrapped round the blades. The grain of this veneer runs across the blade instead of along it.

It is difficult to say from the appearance of the screw whether this veneer has been put on in the form of two-ply or as two separate layers, one after the other.

Among other details salved from the wreckage is the engine control. This is a very massive affair. It consists of five stout steel tubular levers, two of which have become unbrazed in the fire which broke out when the machine crashed.

Three-quarter Front View of a Zeppelin Five-engined "Giant."

The Zeppelin Five-engined "Giant."

ZEPPELIN.—*continued*.

The levers are fitted with rachets so that each one can be operated individually, but the presence of a large single-diameter toothed wheel in the centre of the lever shaft would seem to indicate that all five levers could, when desired, be controlled simultaneously. This fitting had, however, been very badly fused, and it is impossible to give details with certainty.

A smaller fitting recovered from the wreckage consists of a windmill of a type similar to that used on the D.H.9 aeroplane. It is mounted at the top of an aluminium tube, but it is not possible to say for what purpose this mill is employed.

A small and very heavy rotary pump was found in the wreckage. This is possibly the hand-driven petrol pump, though it would appear unusually massive for this purpose.

The Douglas type of engine, carried for the purpose of driving the dynamo of the wireless and heating installation, is a very close copy of the 2¾ h.p. Douglas, and is made by Bosch. The fly-wheel is furnished with radial vanes which induce a draught through a sheet-iron casing, and direct it past cowls on to the cylinder heads and valve chests.

The generator is direct-driven through the medium of a pack of flat leaf springs, which act as dogs, and engage with the slots on the fly-wheel boss.

What appears to be a transformer, used in conjunction with the wireless set, was found.

THE FIVE-ENGINED GIANT.

Specification.

Span	42 m.
Total surface	330 sq. m.
Weight of machine empty	10 tons.
Useful load	4.5 tons.

Rear View of the Zeppelin " Giant " Biplane. (5—250 h.p. Maybach engines.)

GREEK.

Aerial Societies:—

None.

Aerial Journals:—

None.

Military Aeroplanes:—

Towards the end of 1914, Greece possessed a few dilapidated *Farman* land-going machines and several very workmanlike *Sopwith* seaplanes, these latter being imported by and handled by the British Naval Mission which was then in Greece endeavouring to reform the Greek Navy.

This mission was under the command of Rear-Admiral Mark Kerr, M.V.O., R.N., the late Acting Squadron-Commander Collyns Pizey, R.N., being in command of the Air Service section, with the rank of *Capitaine de Frégate.*

The latter officer died in Athens in 1915, and the whole Mission later left Greece.

Since a part of Greece came into the war on the side of the Allies, a number of Greek officers and men have been trained for aviation service by British and French instructors. Several of them have done good work in the war since then.

Captain H. C. J. A. R. West, late R.N., and late Wing-Commander R.A.F., was until recently in command of the Royal Hellenic Naval Air Service.

Military Aviators:—

Adamis (824 Ae. C.F.)
Kamberos (744 Ae. C.F.)
Montoussis (839 Ae. C.F.)
Mutassas, Sub-lt., naval.
Savoff, Lt.
And others.

A Sopwith " Pusher " Seaplane (100 h.p. Anzani engine), in use by the Greek Naval Air Service.

HOLLAND.

Aeronautical Journal :—

Periodical (Monthly). *Het Vliegveld*, official organ of the Royal Dutch Aero Club.

Editorial Staff :

J. G. C. Duinker, 1st Flight Lieutenant.

B. Stephan, Engineer L.A.

Dr. H. Wolff, Director of the Government Study Service for aerial locomotion.

A. C. Perk, 1st Lieutenant L.A. (in command of the photo technical service.)

Names of the chief Aviation Centres in the Netherlands :

Soesterberg (near Utrecht) : Chief army flying ground, 21 hangars. Flying school.

Schiphol (near Amsterdam) : Army flying ground. Flying school.

Gilze Ryen (near Breda) : Army flying station. 2 Hangars.

Oldebroek : Artillery camp. 2 Hangars.

De Mok (on Tessel) : Naval flying station for hydroaeroplanes.

De Kooi (near den Helder) : Naval flying ground for land machines. 6 Hangars. Flying school.

Schellingwoude (near Amsterdam) : Naval flying station for hydroplanes.

Veere (Zeeland) : Naval flying station for hydroplanes.

Ede : Private aerodrome.

In Command of the Flying Corps : Major H. Walaardt Sacré.

In Command of the School for Observers : Captain J. C. M. Simon Thomas.

In Command of the Photo-technical service : 1st Lieutenant A. C. Perk.

In Command of the Wireless service : 1st Lieutenant G. M. Claus.

Engineers belonging to the Flying Corps : Ir. H. A. Vreeburg, Ir. H. C. Olivier, Ir. B. Stephan.

Instructors at the flying schools : Capt. F. A. van Heyst. 1st Lieut. W. C. J. Versteegh, 1st Lieut. A. K. Steup, 1st Lieut. C. Land, 1st Lieut. J. G. C. Duinker, 1st Lieut. G. A. Koppen.

Flying Officers in active service : Capt. F. A. van Heyst, 1st Lieut. W. C. J. Versteegh, 1st Lieut. L. J. Roeper Bosch, 1st Lieut. L. F. E. Coblyn, 1st Lieut. A. N. S. W. L. Coblyn, 1st Lieut. M. L. J. Hofstee, A.D.C. to the Commander, 1st Lieut. A. K. Steup, 1st Lieut. G. A. Koppen, 1st Lieut. C. Land, 1st Lieut. J. G. C. Duinker, 1st Lieut. H. Schlimmer, 1st Lieut. A. Plesman, 1st Lieut. H. G. van Voorthuysen, 1st Lieut. W. P. van den Abeelen, 1st Lieut. H. van Weerden Poelman, 1st Lieut. G. P. van Hecking Colenbrander, 1st Lieut. M. C. van Dijk, 1st Lieut. W. L. Bisschoff, 1st Lieut. E. J. Hofman, 1st Lieut. W. E. Hoogenboom, 1st Lieut. F. Raland, 2nd Lieut. I. A. Aler.

Flying Officers in reserve now engaged on active service :

1st Lieut. in the Reserve, P. M. van Wulfften Palthe.

,,	,,	,,	J. N. Wallast.
2nd Lieut.	,,	,,	R. Drost.
	,,	,,	J. Jongbloed.
1st. Lieut.	,,	,,	P. ten Zeldam.
2nd. Lieut.	,,	,,	J. Balder.
,,	,,	,,	N. T. van der Stok.
,,	,,	,,	A. C. Kamerman.
,,	,,	,,	H. G. B. de Kruyff van Dorssen.
,,	,,	,,	U. F. M. Dellaert.

2nd Lieut. in the Reserve, W. B. van Doorninck.

,,	,,	,,	F. M. Copes van Hasselt.
1st Lieut.	,,	,,	Ch. J. Graaf Schimmelpenninck.
2nd Lieut.	,,	,,	H. J. F. Nab.
,,	,,	,,	K. Soutendyk.
,,	,,	,,	C. van Vliet.

Flying Officers of the Naval Flying Service : Lieut.-Comm. D. Vreede, Lieut. A. S. Thomson, Lieut. H. Nieuwenhuis, Lieut. K. W. F. M. Doorman, Lieut. K. Muller, Lieut. Buenink, Lieut. van Hengel, Lieut. Backer, Lieut. Bakker, Lieut. Gauw, Lieut. Scheffelaar, Lieut. Hekman, Lieut. Huese, Lieut. Weemhof, Sub.-Lieut. Anwerda, Sub.-Lieut. Akveld, Sub.-Lieut. van der Maesen de Sombreff, Sub.-Lieut. Schmidt Craus, Sub.-Lieut. Verploegh Chassé.

Personal Notes on the Chief Men concerned with the Development of Aviation in the Netherlands.

Major H. Walaardt Sacré, Commandant of the Dutch Flying Corps (Luchtvaartafdeeling), born in 1873. He commenced ballooning in 1909, in Germany, to which country he was commanded several times for instruction, as also to France, where he was trained as airship pilot. He organised the Flying Corps and became commander of the corps in July, 1913, which position he still holds.

F. A. van Heyst, Flight Captain, is the oldest Dutch flying officer. He gained his certificate in 1911, and became an instructor in 1914. Several of the present flying officers were his pupils.

W. C. J. Versteegh, 1st Flight Lieut., also got his brevet in 1911, and is a well-known instructor. Several times he was sent out to buy aeroplanes for the Dutch Government.

Henri Wynmalen, born in 1889, started flying in 1909, first on a *Bleriot-Anzani* Channel type monoplane. Went over to *Farman* biplanes, summer, 1910. Height record, 2,800 metres, 1st October, 1910, on a 50 h.p. *Farman*, at Mourmelon. He won the Grand Prix (100,000 francs) of the Automobile Club de France for the aero race from Paris to Brussels and back, 16th-17th October, 1910. Took part in the European circuit organised by "Le Journal." Established the first aeroplane manufactory in Holland (March, 1914). Took over the Spyker Works in 1915, since when the name of the factory has been changed into "The Netherlands Automobile and Aeroplane Manufacturing Co., Trompenburg," which, besides the construction of aeroplanes and aircraft motors, continued to build the well-known Spyker motor cars.

Some Officers of the Dutch Flying Corps at Soesterberg. H.R.H. Prince Hendrick centre. On his left is Commandant-Major Walaardt Sacré, and on his right Senior-Instructor Capt. F. Van Heyst.

The N.C.O.'s of the Dutch Flying Corps.

DUTCH AEROPLANES.

SPYKER.

Netherlands Automobile and Aeroplane Co., Trompenburg, Amsterdam.

Manager, Mr. Henri Wynmalen.

Build for the Dutch Government the following types :—

SPYKER TWO-SEATER SCOUT.

Type of machine	Spyker two-seater Scout.
Name or type No. of machine ..	V.4.
Purpose for which intended ..	Reconnaissance.
Span	10.190 m.
Overall length	6.825 m.
Maximum height	3 m.
Engine type and h.p.	Spyker 130 h.p. Rotary.
Load per sq. m.	34 kg.
Petrol tank capacity in gallons ..	53½ gallons.
Oil tank capacity in gallons ..	8 gallons.

Performance.

Speed .. .. 160 km. per hour.

Climb.

To 1,000 ms. in minutes .. 5½ minutes.

Armament : 2 machine guns and 6 bombs.

SPYKER SINGLE-SEATER FIGHTER.

Type of machine	Spyker single-seater Fighter.
Name or type No. of machine ..	V.3.
Purpose for which intended ..	Air Fighting.
Span	8.190 m.
Overall length	6.100 m.
Maximum height	2.6 m.
Engine type and h.p.	Spyker 130 h.p. Rotary.
Load per sq. m.	25 kg.
Petrol tank capacity in gallons ..	28 gallons.
Oil tank capacity in gallons ..	4 gallons.

Performance.

Speed .. .. 180 km. per hour.

Climb.

To 1,000 ms. in minutes .. 3 minutes with full load

Armament : 2 machine guns.

SPYKER SCHOOL BIPLANE.

Type of machine	Spyker dual control School Biplane.
Name or type No. of machine ..	V.2.
Purpose for which intended ..	Training.
Span	10.850 m.
Overall length	6.640 m.
Maximum height	3 m.
Engine type and h.p.	Spyker 80 h.p. Rotary.
Load per sq. m.	23 kg.
Petrol tank capacity in gallons ..	25 gallons.
Oil tank capacity in gallons ..	5½ gallons.

Performance.

Speed, maximum .. .. 135 km. per hour.

Speed, minimum .. .. 70 km. per hour.

Climb.

To 1,000 ms. in minutes .. 8 minutes with full load.

VAN BERKEL'S PATENT Ldt.

Offices :—Boezemsingel, 33, Rotterdam.

Directors :—W. A. van Berkel, C. F. M. Van Berkel.

Aviation Department :—Keilweg, 9, Rotterdam.

Motor Section :—Chief Manager, John Kerner.

Aeroplane Section :—Chief Manager, C. J. Castendijk.

The manufactory is building hydro-aeroplanes for the Dutch Government (Royal Naval and Colonial Service).

The machines are biplanes, two seater, with two floats and with an engine of 200 h.p.

The speed will be about 160 r.m.p.h.

Further particulars about the machines are :—

Length	9.425 m.
Span	11.20 m.
Height	3.34 m.
Stagger	0.09 m.
Depth of Planes	1.80 m.
Length of Floats	5.65 m.
Breadth	0.71 m.

The type is called " W.A."

A Fokker Biplane used by the Dutch Flying Corps.

A Spyker School Machine used by the Dutch Flying Corps.

SPYKER—*continued.*

SIDE

FRONT.

PLAN.

O/A SPAN 10850.

" LENGTH 6640.

SCHOOLVLIEGTUIG V 2.

The Spyker-Trompenburg Two-Seater Fighter.

Half front view of a Spyker-Trompenburg Two-Seater
School Machine, type V.2.

374a

O/A LENGTH 6825
" HEIGHT 2825
" SPAN 10!46

VERKENNINGSVLIEGTUIG
TYPE V 4.

The Spyker-Trompenburg Two-Seater Training Machine.

The latest type Spyker-Trompenburg Scout,
Holland's leading aeroplane.

ITALIAN.

Aerial Societies :—

Ae. C. d'Italia (Ae.C.I.), 52 via Colonna, Rome.
Ae. Club di Roma (Ae.C.I.), 183, via del Tritone, Rome.
Lega Aerea Nazionale (L.A.N.), 6 via della Signora, Milan.
Societa Aeronautica Italiana (S.A.I.), 4 via Boccaccio, Milan.
     ,,   ,,   ,,   6, via Cernaia, Turin.
Societa Aviazone, di Torino (S.A.T.), Galla. Naz^e Scala B., Turin.
Societa Ital. di Aviazone, (S.I.A.), 14 v. Monte Napoleone, Milan.
La Sezione Aeronautica del Comitato Nazionale Scientifico Tecnico.
    President : D. Lorenzo Santoni.
Associazione Aeronautica Partenopea, 424 via Roma, Naples.

Aerial Journals :—

Alì d' Italia (L.A.N.), 6 via Signore, Milan. 20 cti. Fortnightly.
Nel Cielo, Corso P. Nuova 19, Milan. 30 cti. Fortnightly.
L'Aeronauta, organ of It. Aero Club, via Colonne 52, Rome. Lire—2. Monthly.
La Rivista dell'Aviazione, via Petrarca 4, Milan. Lire—1·20. Monthly.
La Via Azzurra, via S. Carlo 6, Naples. Lire—1·50. Monthly.
La Rivista dei Trasporti Aerei, via Volturno 40, Rome. Lire—3. Monthly.

Publications dealing regularly, but not *exclusively*, with Aviation :

Il Secolo Illustrato, C. Porta Nuova 19, Milan. 1 lire. Monthly.
T.C.I. (Rivista del), Corso Italia 10, Milan. Gratis to members. Monthly.
M.a.C.S., via Manzoni 31, Milan. 50 cti. Fortnightly.
La Stampa Sportiva, via Bertolotti 5, Turin. 10 cti. Weekly.
    And others.

Flying Grounds (before Italy's entry into the war) :—

Cameri.—About 10 kms. from Novara. Circular in form, about $2\frac{1}{2}$ kms. in diameter. This was the first introduced in Italy. One of the first, and a famous flying ground and training school. Since 1913, the home of the Gabardini concern, on the monoplane of which name hundreds of pilots have been trained, with excellent results, since the war started. Landini is Chief Pilot-Instructor.

Mirafiori.—Close to Turin. Founded in 1911. Has a total area of 900,000 sq. metres, and which is being extended to 1,500,000 sq. metres.

Taliedo.—A short distance from Milan. Founded in 1900. Has a total area of about 1,000,000 sq. metres.

Vizzola Ticino.—About 10 kms. from Gallarate and 6 kms. from the military flying school of Somma Lombardo. Founded in 1909, by Ing. Caproni. In July, 1913, the Battaglione Aviatori took over the school and workshops of Ing. Caproni, who continues to act as technical director. The workshops are now employed in making spare parts for the machines in use by the battalion, and the construction of propellers.

Pisa S. Giusta.—Padua-Centocelle (Rome).

Aerodrome "Savoia."—Sezione Lombarda, Cascina Costa (Malpensa). Inaugurated 1st July, 1914. Barracks and workshop. Savoia-Farman school.

Airship Headquarters :—

    Milan.
    Bracciano (Rome).
    Venice.
    Verona.
    Iesi.
    Ciampino (Rome).

ITALIAN NAVAL AND MILITARY AERONAUTICS.

CHIEFS OF THE ITALIAN MILITARY AVIATION SERVICE.

General Officer Commanding :—Lt. General Morris.
Officer Commanding Personnel :—Maj. General Vincengo Craniello.
Officer Commanding Organisation (The Under Secretary for
Officer Commanding Supplies \ War.
Chief of Air Staff, Attached G.H.Q. Staff :—Major-General Leone Andrea Maggiorotti.
Director-General of Aeronautical Services :—General M. Rieni.

CHIEFS OF ITALIAN MARINE AVIATION.

General Officer Commanding :—Admiral Orsini.
Second in Command :—Commander Marsiglia.
Officer Commanding Supplies :—Commander Roberti.
Officer Commanding Personnel :—Commander Calderara.
Officer Commanding Dirigible Section :—Commander Valle.

MILITARY AND NAVAL FLYING SERVICES.

Dating from the time of the first Wright flying machine on which Lt. Calderara learnt from the "Master" at Centocelle,—where later Lieuts. Savoia and Ginocchio first left the earth,—Service aviation as in England was for a long time a private but countenanced Military sport which luckily drew its recruits from the more wealthy and scientifically-minded officers.

When flying first became—some little time after the first Brescia meeting in 1909—a recognized Military sideline, these and the other pioneers were classed as a "Specialist" Engineer Brigade, with the balloonists, electrical, and wireless folk.

In the progress of things, the heavier-than-air "specialists" were detached and grew into the Aviation Battalion, with the late Col. Piazza, Capt. Moizo, Lieuts. Falchi and Gavotti in leading parts.

Thus the Tripoli campaign found them mounted on Blériots, Farmans, a few Caproni and Nieuport monoplanes, perhaps even two Bréguets and certainly an Etrich. Even thus, the experience gained opened all Military eyes to possibilities, and things began to move. In spite of ceaseless winds and moving sands, a great deal of flying was done, and albeit the enemy defence was only from below. Captain (as he then was) Moizo was captured and various casualties had to be deplored, though as a whole the Aerial Force was considered to have done all, if not more, than was required of it, and the New Arm was established on the throne to reign.

So in 1914 we find an Aeronautical Corps composed of all things Aerial, learning the lessons as taught in Flanders and other places where men were flying and fighting.

THE NAVAL SECTION.

Meanwhile, the Naval section had some good time before drifted apart and settled to its own element. The Monaco epoch of 1913 was probably the corner stone, or rather the turning point, here as elsewhere.

From then onwards one heard of Lieuts. Calderara, Savoia, Guidoni, Ginocchio and Miraglia, designing and testing their own "seaplanes" while flying foreign types at Venice, Spezia, and other coastal places where seamen are mostly found, and entering into combined manœuvres with airships, what time the Guidoni palette and other national features were on trial.

AIRSHIPS.

It was among the Airship Section (for that period a powerful one) that the Navy's influence was especially felt. The seaworthy boat-bodies, useful repeatedly on the Tripoli coast,— a feature of the vessels from the very beginning,—and the prominent number of the seamen from among whom the first L. T. A. pilots were recruited, point conclusively to this influence —so natural too and evident when one considers the affinity between the elements and their navigation.

Even were it permitted, it would seem among so many brave pilots invidious to say of anyone that his name stands out. It can not be forgotten that the whole crew of one new vessel perished in flames rather than surrender their secrets to the enemy !

Italian Aviators and Civilian Aviators with an Italian Service machine.

377a

FLYING BOATS.

Curtiss, Italian-built Lohners and later a variety of F.B.A's. constructed by the Savoia firm, Messrs. Macchi, and others, were the first craft to be much used by the Italian Marine Aviation in the Great War.

The variety of types still in use may be explained by the extent of fresh water to be patrolled. The inland water boundary on Lake Garda and elsewhere entails large depôts and stations all over Italy, as well as along the coast line, as he who reads maps may see. However, for some time now the use of land-going machines by the Navy has been discontinued, this Service being thus able to confine itself to its element and better co-operation between it and the Army fliers is the result.

EARLY TRAINING.

Though not then much mentioned, a vast amount of squadron flying and cross-country work was being done in 1914. This, and the policy of allowing Military pilots to take part in competitions, is probably one of the causes of the brilliant results obtained from the very first day of Italy's entry into the war.

PERSONNEL.

About six months is about the period normally occupied by a pilot's technical and practical training, during which time, as afterwards, he wears the uniform of the regiment to which he belongs.

Aspirants commence with instruction in the theory of heavier-than-air machines, resistance of material and particular instruction in the various type of aero motors in use. They are taken for flights as passengers.

All then go to the training camp about 80% for monoplane work, the remainder for biplanes.

For the *military brevet* the examination is most comprehensive, special attention is paid to flying in high winds, manœuvring, climbing, good landings without inconvenience to passengers, cross-country flights, etc. The course is generally modelled on war experiences.

FLYING SCHOOLS.

Aviano.—Central school. Size about 5 × 2 kilometres. Sheltered from all winds except westerly, by banks of trees. Workshops capable of any type of repairs. Numerous hangars, both of iron and of wood, as also one of the hexagon type.

Centocelle.—Military school for advanced training. Caudrons and Farmans mostly used.

Mirafiori (Turin).—Mixed military and civil school. Repairing shop. Testing shop for motors, chemical laboratory. Arranged for testing all necessary apparatus, motors, lubricants, etc. Acceptance tests of aeroplanes are made here and examinations for pilots' certificates. The whole ground is completely enclosed and admission is only obtained by special permission.

An Italian Seaplane Mother Ship, with her brood of Flying Boats.

378a

Rome.—Aerial acrobatics advanced school.

Varese)
Bolsena }- Seaplane schools.
Taranto)

Pordenone.—School for superior brevets. Five .kilometres from Aviano. Treeless plain about 1½ × 1 kilometre, but open in all directions to the wind. Small repairing shop, many spacious hangars, with barracks for both officers and men.

S. Francesco al Campo.—Has two hangars, each suitable for seven *Farman* machines, small repairing shop and carpenters' shop. In July, 1913, it ceased to be a flying school and is now headquarters of the Farman squadron.

Somma Lombardo.—School for *Nieuport* and *Caproni* machines. Large flying grounds, fairly flat with low vegetation only. Buildings adjoining the ground for accommodating the staff and students and with shops capable of every type of repairs and also of constructing machines. Capacious hangars.

Marine Flying School (Venice).—Constituted by Royal Decree. 25th August, 1913.

S. Giusto (Pisa).

Coltano.—(The Vickers-Terni School.)

Padua.—S. Pelagio (Sva H.Q.)

THE ITALIAN AIRCRAFT INDUSTRY.

In spite of restrictions and the difficulty of obtaining raw material, the intense Government demand for aeroplanes in Italy is more than met by the supply.

When the difficulty of getting seasoned wood and tubing before 1915 is remembered, one is at a loss to understand whence now comes all that is needed, and it follows that many bless the war for its revival of those cardinal trade virtues, " push " and goodwill.

Again, when one recollects the conditions under which our pioneers got a machine built—even maybe a copy of an aeroplane which had lowered a world's record—one, after four years of war, is left breathless when he has learnt with what facility aeroplanes in series are turned out nowadays. No one who knew Italy in 1914 would have believed that she could have been in a position to export two or three types of machines after a period of two years of war-régime, as was the case.

ITALIA REDENTA.

The partial explanation of this may be attributed to the fact that formerly chained down by foreign trade oppression, Italy was yet ready for the imprescindable necessity, " the mother, etc.," which hás released her. Another reason is that she holds up her head with lawful pride because before the rest of Europe

and the world she had used aeroplanes in a first barbaric warfare, and so had learnt what possibilities might be expected before the end of the present one. She therefore started her preparations with a larger and clearer vision than the politicians who ruled in other countries and thought to do here would have voted ample.

Aviation, however, seems to have gone through similar processes in various lands, near and far. So, as in England, Italy's builders had a fight infernal to be recognized as of any good by the authorities.

Luckily, few were felled quite to the ground—the rest propagandered or laid low and were still alive to show when Europe fell on war that Italy could do without Germans, and that she could build war-aeroplanes without the foreign help which had constantly been contracted for by her emissaries afflicted with that mistaken modesty which habitually kept this great people from its place in the hemisphere.

What use was an Italian aeroplane, people asked, when everywhere abroad people were flying foreign machines ? This quite regardless of the fact that " people abroad " had never been encouraged to believe that there were Italian flying machines.

GOVERNMENT APATHY.

When the *Asteria* biplane or the *Antoni* monoplane or the *Chiribiri* or any of the *Caproni* early types put up an excellent performance, well ahead of the time, and in spite of untold difficulties, did any financial help or subsidy from the Government henceforward assist that successful firm ?

Yet the Dirigible question was tackled thus by the authorities, and these vessels were built under control of Military engineers on Italian lines, with the greatest success. The brains behind the designs were in both cases Italian.

So one is led to conclude the absence of faith in the Heavier-than-Air theory in those days which occasioned scepticism towards even practical manifestations of the principle. Somewhat as England thought to do safely in respect of airships. " Let foreigners do the experimenting, then we can reap the results." She had almost done so !

EARLY DAYS.

This purporting to deal with business, there is unfortunately no room for the most interesting part of flying, to wit, the pioneering days. It was, however, always upheld that the first Italian aeroplane to be sold abroad—I think to a Russian Maecenas—was a *Faccioli* biplane. Now the family of this name built and flew biplanes, etc., at Turin and elsewhere in the remote ages round about 1909. So there the trade began and stopped till the Capronis began to sell to patriotic associations for presentation hints to the State about the time that the pioneer firms were at their last financial gasps and were induced to contemplate agency work, or, in a few rare cases, even the reproduction of foreign types.

Capital for this was found *cela va sans dire*, and we find in 1913 or thereabouts, the leading foreign firms, English and French of course, for the Teutons were not out to let their rather uncertain vassals know the tricks of their trade, disposing themselves to plant their patents in fertile Italian soil. Thus the Bristol, the Blériot, and the Farman—the Voisin Bros.' patents had been under the care of Ing. Thouvenot at Cameri before anything did much serious flying here—were spoken of as the future mounts for Italians.

In reality, shortly the S.I.T. at Turin and the Savoia at Milan, did begin to trade seriously with foreign push and business propensities, the former holding in concession the Blériot and the latter the Farman manufacturing rights.

THE SPUR OF WAR.

It was not till 1914, however, when foreign consignments became no longer hopeful, that the blinded turned to their nearest of kin—for blood is stronger than the strongest foreign water—for wings and more wings for Italy. They were forthcoming, because the designs had been tried and not found wrong, and because the men had faith in themselves, though they might all have taken themselves abroad, as some had done, or to the motor trade, to which some hopeless of the future had returned.

So the war caused an Italian trade renaissance, for the Government, by treaties or entreaties or by mere money, got the materials, and with these two essentials behind it we see the *Caproni* (illustrated in last year's edition) taking the world by storm, the *Gabardinis* finally recognized and ordered to multiply, and an Italian *Voisin*, exhibited ages before, built in series. It is " an ill wind," etc., and by its war blast the fine Italian power producers, the Isotta-Fraschini motor and the F.I.A.T.'s aero-engine, long talked-of hopefully, became live necessities, and flying boats over which laudable enterprise had eaten its heart out were marked " v. urgent," and the goods were delivered.

THE ENTRY OF THE BIG FIRMS.

Big firms like the Ansaldo, the F.I.A.T. mentioned above, and the fast-growing Pomilio, produced types of their own creating, while other companies, such as the Aer and the S.A.M.L. were constituted for definite objects, the reproducing of good Allied or the best enemy aircraft. And so the pre-war firms Caproni, Gabardini, Savoia, Sit, Macchi, Chiribiri, Bossi and others, have seen the rise of many new lights in the firmament.

THE CENTRE OF THE INDUSTRY.

As could be expected, Turin has never been ousted from the place it has held from the earliest days as the centre of things aviatic, as it is that of mechanical traction, but Milan, with its extra facilities, its more central position, and its very character as the Commercial Capital of Italy, has crept up rather close to it. And especially if one includes the big aircraft concerns in the province of Milan and the neighbouring towns.

Now, however, the movement for various and obvious reasons, is towards the south, *via* Genoa and the west coast, as hydro-aero and aero-hydroplanes become of greater importance.

For the big shipping firms are coming in and one might safely prophesy the Spezia-Leghorn district a future Paradise for waterplane builders. When, that is to say, transatlantic liners, aero or marine, will carry flying boats instead of lifeboats—their collapsible wings perhaps spread by engine power in the twinkling of an eye.

Trials of these will be of interest to the shipbuilders, and let us say the insurance agencies, in the early years of peace when stray mines may be met with on the high seas and other floating obstacles be drifting about. Hulls may even have to be converted into flying-boat bodies, a la hydroplanes, if there is a boom in aerial transport. At any rate, large companies have been floated among the sea-going folk down south to be ready to meet these needs, and it is sure that large gun-founders must have foreseen the time when orders will be less brisk, nor will the making of plough-shares occupy their whole output.

FINANCE.

The question of the financial amount that this nation has invested in aviatory enterprises is so vast and complicated owing to war reserve, that even an approximate guess has no chance of getting near the figure. Add the unknown amounts that big engineering works have allocated to experiment—and possibly to adaptation of shops and factories—to the sums dropped by the earliest builders, and the capital of the new expressly-founded companies dealing in commercial aviation, and we get an enormous total. Judging merely by the excess-profits taxes paid in Piedmont alone, of which province Turin is the chief town, one could easily come to a very wrong solution of the matter, even if one did so in strict conjunction with the figures of the various Aero-companies' Share-Price List.

OUTPUT.

In conclusion, one should congratulate the Trade here on the fact that no one has ever heard of a dearth of machines for the front. Everything, not only the carrying out of big flights at home, abroad and across the seas for trade or war propaganda, but the exportation to the Allies advertised by more than one of the big firms, points to the contrary.

It is true that certain types of *Avions* were not used in the numbers thought by some to be necessary or advisable, but the reasons for this are held to be sentential, not commercial. As far as the Trade is concerned, one can rely on Italy's share in international progress in 1919, being up to the standard and warranted efficient and effective.

T. S. HARVEY.

AERIAL COMMERICAL COMPANIES.

The following firms have been formed for commercial purposes, either as traders in parts, or with a view to aerial transport. Some are manufacturers of aircraft in the ordinary :—

SOCIETA TRASPORTI AEREI INTERNAZIONALI. Milan. An international carrier and forwarding agency. Capital : £1,000,000. President : Senator Don Prospero Colonna. Bankers : Banca Commerciale.

SINDACATO INDUSTRIALE AERONAUTICO ITALIANO. Milan. Society of Aeronautical Traders. President : Avv. Goria Gatti. Developed in 1919, into "Locomozione Meccanica."

AGENZIA GENERALE FORNITURE AERONAUTICHE. Via P. Amedeo II. Milan. General Aviation Supply Contractors. A Savoia offshoot.

SOCIETA LAVORAZIONE D'AVIAZIONE. Milan. Capital : £3,000,000.

ING. NICOLO ROMEO e CO. Via Paleocapa, 6, Milan. Nominal capital, 50,000,000 lire. Paid up capital, 30,000,000 lire.

A

ANTONI. Soc. di aviazione Antoni, via Vitt. Emanuele, 46, Pisa. School : S. Guisto, Pisa. Made a name by means of a curious type of monoplane of his own design. No warp to wings. Nearly one-fourth of surface nearest body, and along the trailing edge of wing was left flexibly. A variable camber substituted for warp. Large horizontal empennages, plus usual monoplane rudder and elevators formed tail. Of interest as the first aeroplane to fly from Italy (Pisa) to Corsica. Of late constructing more normal designs. No fresh information available.

"A.E.R." Orbassano, Turin. Offices at Via Governolo No. 4. Turin.

This large new firm dates from practically the beginning of the European war.

Its products have been perhaps the most useful machines turned out in this country, both in the fighting zones and at the home-camps, where they are said to have helped upwards many records, and to have greatly speeded up the perfecting of new pilots.

Commonly credited with building *Caudrons*, used for artillery spotting, and training pilots at Centocelle. No fresh information available.

C

CAPRONI. Società Per Lo Sviluppo Dell'Aviazione in Italia. Taliedo and Vizzola.

Designer : Comm. Gianni Caproni, the Apostle of big planes.

Technical Manager—at Taliedo : Ing. Aldredo Fioroili.

The city address of the firm is Corso Venezia 82, Milan.

Commendatore Ing. Gianni Caproni is to the Italian mind all that is rarest in patriotism and aviation.

He was born at Massone, in the Trentino, in 1886, and is thus of that region the release of which, from foreign bondage, Italy ever aspired.

Caproni at 17 was deep in his studies for the diploma of civil engineer at Munich, having obtained which the following years saw him first at Liege studying electrical engineering, then at Paris devoting himself to aeronautics with his contemporary and friend, Coanda.

It was in France that the first of his biplanes was designed ; but the first failure was that met in an attempt to get financial backing to build it somewhere in the early part of 1909, when on a visit to his native country.

So he returned to Belgium and theory, and only in the following year was it found possible to build the machine—which flew at the first trial.

From then onwards, he took up his quarters at Malpensa (Vizzola), on that lonely heath, not unfrequently then used as a manœuvring ground in the summer for cavalry, which was lent him by the War Office.

Little was heard of the brothers Caproni—he had been joined by an elder brother, Dr. Fred. Caproni—by the public, but a quiet and great work was carried through in the following years, culminating in the unavoidable publicity caused by the record-breaking monoplane's performance abroad. (Vienna, 25/6/12.) This was the machine which was used for military purposes by the Italian Government just before the monoplane ban.

Several widely differing types of biplanes had been evolved during 1910 and 1911 ; the last (tractor) with doubly cambered wings and tail-incidence variable during flight, an instructive but not effective machine.

Aero-dynamic experiments of all sorts were tried, e.g., the effects of flexible surfaces, dihedral supporting and control surfaces, side areas, body length, but especially in elicology, a real pleasure to Signor Caproni this last.

Twin engines, a machine with two engines to be used alternately, dual propeller action, skin friction and indeed every problem that was only to be resolved by experiment on full-sized machines, was gone into in practice, and reliable theory extracted from the results. It is worthy of note, however, that the forward position of the engine was from the beginning the only one for Ing. Caproni.

From these data the first 300 h.p. three-engined biplane rose to conquer in 1914, met, as one might have expected, with some scepticism by the country at first. Now this machine's doings are in everyones' mind, and its potentiality has paled before the prodigious size and perfect controllability of the 1,000 h.p. triplane here illustrated.

The principle of cellular construction, so early propounded by the designer as the only way of guaranteeing the rigidity of large span machines, is the rock of the " CA " triplane's strength.

As it has carried up to 30 passengers, we may take its strength as proved, and the " limit of size " theory held by some to be exploded.

A Caproni 450 h.p. Triplane. Speed: 200 km.

Three-quarter Front View of the Caproni Single-engined Triplane.

CAPRONI—*continued*.

THE CAPRONI TRIPLANE.

Specification.

Type of machine	Five-seater Triplane.
Name or type No. of machine ..	Caproni, Model " 1915."
Purpose for which intended ..	Bomber.
Span	130 ft.
Overall length	48 ft.
Maximum height	19 ft.
Engine type and h.p.	3—400 h.p. Liberty.
Weight of machine empty ..	11,000 lbs.
Weight per h.p.	13.3 lbs. per h.p.
Tank capacity in gallons ..	300 gallons.
Performance.	
Speed low down	100 m.p.h.
Landing speed	40 m.p.h.
Climb.	
To 5,000 ft. in minutes ..	15 mins.
Disposable load apart from fuel ..	3,300 lbs. (bombs).
Total weight of machine loaded	16,000 lbs.

A Caproni 600 h.p. Seaplane. 150 km.p.h. Carrying capacity, 2 tons.

THE CAPRONI THREE-ENGINED TRIPLANE. TYPE C.A.4.

(American Edition.)

Specification.

Type of machine	Triplane.
Name or type No. of machine ..	Caproni C.A.4.
Purpose for which intended ..	Bombing.
Span	96 ft. 6 in.
Gap	8 ft.
Overall length	42 ft. 11 in.
Maximum height	20 ft. 8 in.
Chord	7 ft.
Total surface of wings ..	2,223 sq. ft.
Engine type and h.p. ..	Three Liberty. 400 h.p.
Weight of machine empty ..	11,100 lbs.
Load per sq. ft.	7.95 lbs.
Weight per h.p.	14.7 lbs.
Performance.	
Speed at 6,500 feet	98 m.p.h.
Climb.	
To 6,500 feet in minutes ..	14 mins.
Ceiling	16,000 ft.
Disposable load apart from fuel	3,800 lbs.
Total weight of machine loaded	17,700 lbs

A Caproni Triplane for Passenger Transport. 2000 h.p.

CAPRONI—*continued*.

The Pensuti-Caproni in the air.

The Pensuti-Caproni Triplane in the air.

PENSUTI Triplane.

Designed to do what bicycle does for the man on the road, the little vehicle was ready for its trial flight when its builder, the late Emilio Pensuti, was killed in attempting to save a very valuable life for the country.

After the lapse of some months the machine was taken into the air by Lt. L. Montegani and did all that its lamented designer hoped of it.

The Pensuti 2, as it is named, leaves the ground after a run of 20 metres and pulls up in the same distance.

With an Anzani Y, 35 h.p. engine, a speed of 95 kilometres has been attained and a minimum speed of 40 is possible.

Rate of climb : 1000 metres in 1/4 hr.

Span : 4 metres.

Total length : 3.80 metres.

Over all height : 2.40 metres.

Weight in flying trim including pilot : 230 kilos.

Petrol consumption per flying hr. : 2 gallons.

Oil   ,,   ,,   ,,   ,, : $\frac{1}{2}$,,

The Pensuti-Caproni on the ground.

THE 1,000 H.P. CAPRONI TRIPLANE.   A 300 h.p. 6-cylinder engine in each fuselage, and a 400 h.p. 8-cylinder in the centre.

C—continued.

CHIRIBIRI. A. Chiribiri e C, Borgo S. Paolo, Via Caraglio, and Via Montenegro, Turin, and Stabilimenti già Nazarro; Borgata Cenisia, Corso Peschiera No. 250, Turin.

Made many interesting experimental monoplanes, on which several Italian Records were broken. Now engaged on motor work exclusively.

G

GABARDINI. Società Incremento Aviazione, Cameri, Novara.

The *Garbardini* type of monoplane took the competent by storm when it first appeared in 1913 to the public.

With two adult passengers and an 80 h.p. rotary engine, the late Philip Cevasco made a non-stop flight from Milan to Venice, and otherwise proved the powers of the machine to be quite exceptional and unusually well suited for all sorts of general conditions.

With a smaller engine, the *Gabardini* was found to be ideal for training pilots, and so a large school and works were opened at Cameri, in 1914, and were got into swing in time for the work of preparation for war.

Squat and inelegant and built largely of metal, the monoplanes are distinctive, not freakish nor reminiscent of any other aeroplane.

Signor Gabardini, who at one time dedicated himself to art of another sort, is a Piemontese by birth, and cruelly crippled, mental energy alone being in his power of recent years. He has, however, the satisfaction of having produced one of the very few monoplanes which has survived the ban and disfavour into which single-deckers have fallen, and his joy therein is shewn by the pride with which he claims it the best, after trial, in all the world.

The type has had a long testing during four war years of gruelling, with barely a modification, and that in the cockpit, in all that time.

So responsive to control is the *Gabardini* that its designer states that " they answer the intangible helm of the pilot's intention before the material leverage has come into action."

In flight, the *Gabardini* reminded one of the *Antoinettes*, curiously, since the design of the two is so entirely opposite. Up till now radial motors are fitted, with rotaries for school machines.

With a motor less costly in upkeep, the *Gabardini* monoplane is a machine which may, one hopes, become a useful means of commercial transport, being a good lander, a weight-carrier and stable. A commercial traveller's vehicle possibly ?

The work of training some 300 pilots carried on at Cameri has kept Signor Gabardini's designing energy rather in the background necessarily.

A biplane of characteristic design has been produced.

The school claims to have turned out as many pilots as all the others together, and it is to the praise of Machine and Masters that the casualties only average six yearly.

The first aerodrome in Italy to erect a permanent signal-tower for passing air traffic, Cameri may be the first to get its post-war commercial value recognized and realized.

A Garbardini captive monoplane used to teach the use of controls.

GARBARDINI—*continued.*

THE GARBARDINI BIPLANE.

Type of machine	Single-seater Tractor Biplane.
Name or type No. of machine ..	Garbardini.
Purpose for which intended ..	Advanced Training.
Span	7.20 m.
Maximum height	2.2 m.
Total surface of wings ..	14.81 sq. m.
Engine type and h.p.	80 h.p. Le Rhône.
Load per sq. m.	32.07 kgs.
Weight per h.p.	5.9 kgs.

Performance.
   Speed low down .. .. 180 kms.

Total weight of machine loaded .. .. .. 175 kgs.

A Garbardini Advanced Training Machine (80 h.p. Le Rhône engine).

THE GARBARDINI BIPLANE.

Type of machine	Single-seater Tractor Biplane.
Name or type No. of machine ..	Garbardini.
Purpose for which intended ..	Advanced Training.
Span	7.2 m.
Maximum height	2.25 m.
Total surface of wings ..	15.85 sq. m.
Engine type and h.p.	110 h.p. Le Rhône.
Load per sq. m.	33.7 kgs.
Weight per h.p.	4.87 kgs.

Performance.
   Speed low down .. .. 190 km.p.h.

Total weight of machine loaded. .. .. .. 535 kgs.

A Garbardini biplane with 110 Le Rhône engine.

GARBARDINI—*continued.*

THE GARBARDINI MONOPLANE.

Type of machine	Tractor Monoplane.
Name or type No. of machine ..	Gabardini.
Purpose for which intended ..	Training Machine.
Span	10 m.
Total surface of wings ..	18 sq. m.
Engine type and h.p.	50 h.p. Gnôme.
Performance.	
Speed low down	100 km.p.h.

A Garbardini School Machine (50 h.p. Gnôme engine).

Garbardini Monoplane with 50 h.p. Gnôme engine.

Garbardini Monoplane for elementary instruction (35 h.p. Anzani).

A Garbardini Monoplone with 80 h.p. Le Rhône engine.

388a

M

MACCHI. Società Anonima Nieuport-Macchi. Varese.

Well-known as an old coach-building concern, this Company, passing through the motor-body building stage, took up the constructing of *Nieuport* monoplanes some considerable time before the European conflict began.

It had by then produced certain "parasol" types with great success, creating records for Italian aviation about the time other nations were mobilizing.

Naturally, since then enormous strides must have been made, and it seems probable that the Macchi Works could more than meet any demands for machines from their own Government.

But for the preparedness of Ing. Giulio Macchi, and the organization which allowed this firm to construct even more Nieuports than the Italian Army called for, this country's position in the air at the beginning of the war might have been very serious. For one understands that the Allied Forces owe individually a considerable debt to the Macchi concern.

The latter part of the war saw the firnis flying boats in very general use both on active service and on home waters for training purposes. Ing. Macchi is turning his attention to trade on the south American rivers, as soon as the mapping of those immense waterways is completed. In this work his faster boats are, one learns, to take an active part.

MACCHI "5."

Type of machine	Single-seater Waterplane.
Name or type No. of machine	M5.
Purpose for which intended	Hunter.
Span	11.90 m.
Gap	1.90 m.
Overall length	8 m.
Maximum height	2.85 m.
Chord	Upper plane, 1.60 m. ; Lower plane, 1.10 m.
Total surface of wings	29 sq. m.
Span of tail	2.87 m.
Total area of tail	3.95 sq. m.
Elevator, maximum	2.87 × 0.55 m.
Rudder, maximum	1.20 × 0.55 m.
Fin, maximum	2.50 × 0.65 m.
Ailerons, total area	3.75 sq. m.
Fuselage dimensions	1.00 × 0.85 sq. m.
Engine type and h.p.	Isotta Fraschini V4 b., 160 h.p.
Airscrew, diam., pitch and revs.	2.55 m., 15,00.
Weight of machine empty	700 kilos.
Load per sq. m.	35.5 kilos.
Weight per h.p.	6.45 kilos.
Tank capacity in hours	3.15 hours.

Performance.

Speed low down	189 k.p.h.

Climb.

To 4,000 metres in minutes	20 mins.
Total useful load	270 kgs.
Total weight of machine fully loaded	970 kgs.

MACCHI "7"

Type of machine	Single-seater Waterplane.
Name or type No. of machine	M7.
Purpose for which intended	Hunter.
Span	9.95 m.
Gap	1.96 m.
Overall length	8.10 m.
Maximum height	2.95 m.
Chord	Upper wing, 1.670 m. ; Lower wing, 1.31 m.
Total surface of wings	26.6 sq. m.
Span of tail	2.84 m.
Total area of tail	2.65 sq. m.
Elevator, maximum	2.84 × 0.6 m.
Rudder, maximum	1.12 × 0.6 m.
Fin, maximum	2.50 × 0.55. m
Ailerons	2.70 sq. m.
Fuselage dimensions, horizontal	1.15 m.
Fuselage dimensions, vertical	0.90 m.
Engine type and h.p.	Isotta Fraschini V6. 260 h.p.
Airscrew, diam. and revs.	2.55 m., 1800.

Weight of machine empty		775 kgs.
Load per sq. m.		41.5 kilos.
Weight per h.p.		4.325 kilos.
Tank capacity in hours		4 hours.

Performance.

Speed low down	210 k.p.h.

Climb.

To 5,000 metres in minutes	21 mins.	
Total useful load		305 kilos.
Total weight of machine fully loaded		1,080 kgs.

MACCHI "8."

Type of machine	Two-seater Seaplane.
Name or type No. of machine	M8.
Purpose for which intended	Scouting.
Span	13.8 m.
Gap	2 m.
Length	9 m.
Maximum height	3.25 m.
Chord	Upper plane, 1.75 m. ; lower plane, 1.59 m.
Total surface of wings	40 sq. m.
Span of tail	3.270 m.
Area of tail	3 sq. m.
Elevator	3.27 × 0.7 m., 1.70 × 0.7 m.
Fin	3 × 0.58.
Area of ailerons	4.50 sq. m.
Fuselage	1.23 × 1.08.

A Single-seater Macchi-Nieuport Flying Boat.

3 c 2

MACCHI—*continued*.

MACCHI "8." —*continued*.

Engine type and h.p. .. .. Isotta Fraschini V4 B. 160 h.p.
Airscrew, diam. and revs. .. 2.7 m. 1500 revs.
Weight of machine empty .. 900 kgs.
Load .. .. 35 kgs. per sq. m.
Weight per h.p. .. .. .. 8.75 kgs.
Tank capacity in hours .. .. 4 hours.

Performance.
   Speed low down .. .. 167 k.p.h.

Climb.
   To 5,000 metres in minutes .. 55 mins.
Total useful load .. .. 500 kgs.
Total weight of machine fully loaded .. .. .. 1,400 kgs.

MACCHI "9."

Type of machine .. .. .. Two-seater Seaplane.
Name or type No. of machine .. M9.
Purpose for which intended .. Scouting and Bombing.
Span .. .. 15.4 m.
Gap .. .. 2 m.
Maximum length .. .. 9.4 m.
Maximum height .. .. 3.25 m.
Chord .. .. Upper wing, 1.8 m. ;
                     lower wing, 1.6 m.
Total surface of wings .. .. 48.5 sq. m.
Elevator .. .. .. 3.50 × 0.65 m.
Rudder .. .. .. 1.75 × 0.70 m.
Fin .. .. 3.10 × 0.75 m.
Area of ailerons and total area .. 4.10 × 0.75 m. 6.15 sq. m.
Fuselage, horizontal and vertical 4.10 × 0.75 m.
Engine type and h.p. .. .. Fiat. A 12 bis. 280 h.p.
Airscrew, diam. and revs. .. 2.65 m. 1600 revs.
Weight of machine empty .. 1,250 kgs.
Load per sq. m. .. .. .. 37 kgs.
Weight per h.p. .. .. .. 6.4 kgs.
Tank capacity in hours .. .. 4 hours

Performance.
   Speed low down .. .. 187.5 km.p.h.

Climb.
   To 5,000 m. in minutes .. 40 mins.
Total useful load .. .. 550 kgs.
Total weight of machine fully loaded .. .. .. 1800 kgs.

The Macchi-Nieuport Boat, with single rudder.

The Macchi-Nieuport Boat, with double rudder.

390a

MACCHI "9 BIS."

Type of machine	Four-Seater seaplane.
Name or type No. of machine	M9 bis.
Purpose for which intended	Transporting Persons and Post.
Span	15.4 m.
Gap	2 m.
Overall length	9.4 m.
Maximum height	3.3 m.
Chord	Upper wing, 1.8 m. ; Lower wing, 1.5 m.
Total surface of wings	44.57 sq. m.
Span of tail	3.5 m.
Total area of tail	3.37 sq. m.
Elevator	3.50 × 0.65 m.
Rudder	1.75 × 0.70 m.
Fin	3.10 × 0.75 m.
Area of each aileron and total area	4.10 × 0.75 × 2.6. Area 15 sq. m.
Fuselage, section	1.29 m. × 1.17 m.
Engine type and h.p.	I.F V6 250 h.p.
Airscrew, diam. and revs.	2.65 m. 1800 revs.
Weight of machine empty	1,100 kgs.
Load per sq. m.	36.5 kgs.
Weight per h.p.	6.5 kgs.
Tank capacity in hours	3 hours.
Tank capacity in gallons	170 litres motor fuel, 10 litres of oil.

Performance.

Speed low down	180 k.p.h.
Useful load	520 kls.
Total weight of machine fully loaded	1.620 kls.

MACCHI "12."

Type of machine	Three-seater Seaplane.
Name or type No. of machine	M12.
Purpose for which intended	Scouting and Bombing.
Span	17 m.
Gap	2.10 m.
Maximum length	10.765 m.
Maximum height	3.665 m.
Chord	Upper plane, 2.34 m. ; lower plane, 2.08 m.
Supporting surface of wings	61 sq. m.
Span of tail	3.6 m.
Area of tail	4.90 sq. m.
Area of elevator	2.90 sq. m.
Area of rudder	2 sq. m.
Area of fin	2.10 sq. m.
Area of ailerons	4.16 sq. m.
Fuselage, horizontal and vertical	1.69 m. 1.25 m.
Engine type and h.p.	Ansaldo S. Giorgio. 4.E.28. 450 h.p.

Airscrew, diam. and revs.	3 m. 1600 revs.
Weight of machine empty	1,750 kgs.
Load per sq. m.	41.300 kgs.
Weight per h.p.	5.600 kgs.
Tank capacity in hours	4 hours.

Performance.

Speed low down	190 k.p.h.
Total useful load	770 kgs.
Total weight of machine fully loaded	2,520 kgs.

MACCHI "12 BIS."

Type of machine	Five-seater Seaplane.
Name or type No. of machine	M12 bis.
Purpose for which intended	Transporting Persons and Post.
Span	18 m.
Gap	2.20 m.
Maximum length	11 m.
Maximum height	3.65 m.
Chord	Upper wing, 2.34 m. ; Lower wing, 2.08 m.

Total surface of wings	66 sq. m.
Span of tail	4.50 m.
Area of tail	6.6 sq. m.
Area of elevator	3.84 sq. m.
Area of rudder	970 × 1,250 and 750 × 750 at widest points.
Area of fin	4.10 × 0.65 at widest part.
Area of ailerons	5.6 sq. m.
Fuselage, section	1.69 m. × 1.60 m.
Engine type and h.p.	Ansaldo S. Giorgio. 4.E.28. 450 h.p.
Airscrew, diam. and revs.	3 m. 1600 revs.
Weight of machine empty	1,715 kgs.
Load per sq. m. of supporting surface	38.5 kgs.
Weight per h.p.	5.6 kgs.
Tank capacity in hours	3 hours.

Performance.

Speed low down	180 k.p.h.
Total useful load	810 kgs.
Total weight of machine fully loaded	2525 kgs.

Another Variant of the Macchi-Nieuport Boat.

MACCHI "14."

Type of machine	Single-seater Land Biplane.
Name or type No. of machine ..	M 14.
Purpose for which intended ..	Hunter.
Span	8.1 m.
Gap	1.15 m.
Maximum length	5.65 m.
Maximum height	2.30 m.
Chord	Upper plane, 1.32 m. ; Lower plane, 1.20 m.
Supporting surface of wings ..	16.6 sq. m.
Span of tail	2.8 m.
Total area of tail	2.4 sq. m.
Area of elevators	1.4 sq. m.
Area of rudder	0.49 sq. m.
Area of fin	0.98 sq. m.
Area of ailerons	1.68 sq. m.
Fuselage, section	0.70 m. × 0.75 m.
Engine type and h.p. ..	Le Rhône. 110 h.p.
Airscrew, diam. and revs. ..	2.45 m. 1200 revs.
Weight of machine empty ..	405 kgs.
Load per sq. m. of lifting surface	36.5 kgs.
Weight per h.p.	5.5 kgs.
Tank capacity in hours ..	5 hours.

Performance.

Speed low down	182 k.p.h.

Climb.

To 5,000 metres in minutes ..	21 mins.
Total useful load	200 kgs.
Total weight of machine fully loaded	605 kgs.

MACCHI "15."

Type of machine	Five-seater Land Biplane.
Name or type No. of machine ..	M15.
Purpose for which intended ..	Scouting.
Span	13.47 m.
Gap	1.95 m.
Length	8.57 m.
Height	3.365 m.
Chord	Upper plane, 2.10 m. ; Lower plane, 1.90 m.
Total surface of wings ..	42 sq. m.
Span of tail	3.27 m.
Total area of tail	4 sq. m.
Area of elevator ..	3.20 × 0.7 m.
Area of rudder ..	1.49 × 0.70 m.
Area of fin ..	2.79 × 0.94 m.
Area of ailerons ..	5.10 sq. m.
Fuselage, section	0.900 m. × 1.400 m.
Engine type and h.p. ..	Fiat 12 A bis. 280 h.p.
Airscrew, diam. and revs. ..	2.85 m. 1600 revs.
Weight of machine empty ..	1,125 kgs.
Load per sq. m.	38.750 kgs.
Weight per h.p.	5.800 kgs.
Tank capacity in hours ..	3 hours.

Performance.

Speed low down	200 k.p.h.

Climb.

To 5,000 metres in minutes ..	40 mins.
Total useful load	500 kgs.
Total weight of machine fully loaded	1625 kgs.

MACCHI "15 BIS."

Type of machine	Three-seater Land Biplane.
Name or type No. of machine ..	M15 bis.
Purpose for which intended ..	Passenger Transport.
Span	13.47 m.
Gap	1.95 m.
Maximum length	8.57 m.
Maximum height	3.36 m.
Chord	Upper plane, 2.10 m. ; Lower plane, 1.90 m.
Total surface of wings	42 sq. m.
Span of tail	3.27 m.
Total area of tail	4 sq. m.
Area of elevators	3.20 × 0.70 m.
Area of rudder	1.49 × 0.70 m.
Area of fin	2.79 × 0.94 m.
Area of ailerons	5.10 sq. m.
Fuselage, section	0.9000 m. × 1.260 m.
Engine type and h.p. ..	Fiat A12 bis. 280 h.p.
Airscrew, diam. and revs. ..	2.85 m. 1,600 revs.
Weight of machine empty ..	1,150 kgs.
Load per sq. m. of lifting surface	38.750 kgs.
Weight per h.p.	5.800 kgs.
Tank capacity in hours ..	3 hours.

Performance.

Speed low down	190 k.p.h.

Climb.

Total useful load	475 kgs.
Total weight of machine fully loaded	1,625 kgs.

A Macchi Single-seat Fighter. Type M.14.

O

OFFICINE DI SAVIGLIANO.

Head offices at 23 via Genoyo, Turin.

One of the largest electrical engineering works in Italy, and also general constructive engineers. Undertook building of dirigible hangars and big aeroplane parts during the war. Among others, *Caproni* biplanes were constructed.

P

POMILIO. Ing. O. Pomilio & Co. Società per Costruzioni Aeronautiche, Corso Francia 366, Turin.

This was a powerful company with a capital of 5,000,000 lire.

Metal biplanes with F.I.A.T. engines were its chief concern.

Capital : Lire 5,000,000. President : Dr. Arnaldo Gussi. Manager : Sig. A. Ricordi.

The firm took a place among the foremost aeroplane builders in the country and constructed two types of pusher biplanes with F.I.A.T. engines and largely of metal. Both speed and weight-carrying powers had been attained, and a big business in war machines had been built up. A large bi-motored craft of this name was illustrated at the Military Exhibit of the Milan Aeroshow (1917). It carried some 75 sq. metres of lifting surface, and I.F. motors were fitted.

The concern is now in the hands of Gia. Ansaldo and Co., of Genova.

The Bros. Pomilio left the country during 1918 to assist the American Trade to create the enormous airfleet which was to have put the fear of the air into the heart of Germany had time permitted.

Side View of a Pomilio Tractor Biplane.

S

SAVOIA. Societa Anonima Costruzioni Aeronautiche

City Offices : 5 via Manzoni, Milan.

Works : Bovisio, Milan.

Aerodrome : Mombello, Milan.

School : Cascina Costa, Milan.

This firm claimed, before Italy joined in the war, to have the largest plant in the world, and to produce some 1,000 aeroplanes annually.

The Savoia Co. was founded sometime before the war by Signor Lorenzo Santoni, of the General Aviation Contractors Ltd., London, and has since the war developed enormously.

Farman land and seaplanes are specialised in, by exclusive concession from the inventors of these types, but other machines can be and are built when needed.

The first of the big foreign firms to turn over its drawings to a properly organized Italian company was the Farman Bros., and the " Savoia " was the concern to which they were entrusted, in 1913. How the work of preparing for the wholesale construction of these machines was accomplished is to be learnt from the intimate history of the last five years of Signor Lorenzo Santoni's business life, he being the mainspring of the " Savoia " as of the several satellite companies allied with it.

It is considered that the general public first awoke to the capabilities of the Farman machines when Bille came over the Alps to Milan to do acrobatics on some of the Savoias build of the type. By that time the company was on the point of leaving its first small works at Turro and about to install itself at Bovisio, where it could expand as requirements should arise. That moment, when it came, thus found the Savoia prepared.

The name of its productions tells its technical history from then till now ; for all the world knows what may be told of recent Farman progress. Nor can one say more as to proportionate number of the various types of the machines constructed by the firm in these war years. Surely if 1,000 aeroplanes were built in the year before the war, this figure may have been at least tripled since then, year by year ? What has been the extent of the help afforded it by the Zari Bros.—an old-established wood-working company who were called to co-operate in the Savoian progress when Bovisio became the company's home—can be imagined more perhaps than judged by those who have handled the delicate egg-shell-in-wood parts turned by Messrs. Zari ; things so strong yet so delicate as to seem transparency French-polished.

Signor D. Lorenzo Santoni has had the advantage of a long experience of life abroad, in England and elsewhere, and in the early days when flying was as incredible as miracles his name was in all the newsprints.

It will be remembered that he was the first Italian to fly the Channel—from Paris too—the aeroplane being a Deperdussin with a 70 h.p. Gnôme, the year 1912.

The power of foreseeing the only right moment is undoubtedly his. He is the founder of the following list of thriving trading concerns, and of various societies and institutions for the furthering of aerial aims :—

Societa Generale Imprese Aeronautiche.

Agenzia Generale Forniture Aeronautiche.   (Propellers.)

Societa Italo-Orientale Emaillite.

Societa Idrovolanti Alta Italia.

No fresh information is to hand.

SOCIETA ADRIATICA COSTRUZIONI AERONAUTICHE. At Ortona a Mare.

S.A.M.L. Societa Anonima Meccanica Lombarda, Monza, (via Cavalieri) ; Milan, via Broggi, No. 4.

This highly important firm of Military Contractors with its 4,500,000 lire of fully-paid up capital, and employing some 3,000 workmen, decided in 1913 to enter the aeroplane trade, and constructed as almost its first effort that "Amfiplane" which did as well as any of its competitors at the Military Trials of that year.

This machine was a tractor biplane with a S.C.A.T. fixed 4-cylinder motor with automatic starter.

The S.A.M.L., after the entry of Italy into the European war, devoted most of its labour to supplying aeroplanes of its own special type with complete satisfaction to those most competent to judge.

The S. A. M. L. builds a good school machine in large numbers and an *Aviatic* type, which, with Salmson motor, was at one time esteemed a very fast mount.

No fresh information is to hand.

S.I.A. (Societa Italiano Aviazione).

Works at via Nizza 15, Turin.

Flying ground at Lingotto, Turin.

Capital paid-up : Lire 5,000,000.

This title, with its Italian-Latin word-play, must not be confounded with the pre-war firm of the same initials—which produced an excellent monoplane—nor with the S.I.A., an Aero-Club much less with the S.I.A.I. (Societa Idrovolanti Alta Italia) a Savoia offshoot (vide page 397)

This, the Turin S.I.A., builds a large tractor-biplane for the F.I.A.T. engine, with which excellent heart the machine has created many records and places its ceiling some distance farther from the earth's crust than most others.

The firm's growth was abnormal—its machines were flying before the Company was constituted it is claimed—and it is now able to supply aircraft to foreign powers.

The S.I.A. biplane is a tractor type.

The upper and lower wings are united by four pairs of vertical steel struts of oval section. The upper wings are fitted with ailerons.

The fuselage is completely streamlined and consists of four longitudinal wood members with diagonal bracing and canvas covered.

The motor is a F.I.A.T. 300 h.p. 6 cylinders vertical with direct-mounted propeller, carried behind a honeycomb radiator and under a bonnet, as in automobile practice.

It has been officially announced that Lieut. Brach-Papa, Chief Pilot of the S.I.A., has created a new world's altitude record with passenger on a S.I.A. machine of the type illustrated.

This was the third height world's record won by this pilot in 1917. Lieut. Brach-Papa is one of the oldest Italian aeroplane testers. To his credit stands the flying test of more than a thousand machines of twenty different types.

The figures concerning this last record are the following, as issued in all the Italian daily papers :—

Machine : S.I.A. 7.B.   No. 5966.

Load (Passengers and fuel) : 350 kgs. (775 lbs.).

1,000 m. in 2 mins. 30 secs.

2,000 m. „   5 mins.

3,000 m. „   9 mins.

4,000 m. „ 18 mins.

5,000 m. „ 24 mins.

6,500 m. „ 37 mins. 30 secs.

6,750 m. „ 1 hour 3 mins.

Ground level was .275 metres above the sea.

Height above the sea level reached : 7.025 m. (23,000 ft.).

Military Control Commission at a flying ground near Turin.

Date : 14 Dec., 1917, in the afternoon.

It may be of interest to technical readers to know that the machine was tuned before starting with the " Vibration " method recently adopted by Ingegnere Lerici (See " The Aeroplane," Nov. 7th, page 1342) in order to ensure the highest safety factor to the whole structure under such abnormal conditions of flight.

S.I.A.—*continued.*

THE SIA " F.B." AEROPLANE.

The S.I.A. type F.B. biplane, which Captain Laureati flew, in less than seven hours, from Turin to London, is associated with the following officially recorded performance :—

August 26th.—The height of 20,000 ft. (6,165 m.) is reached in 34 minutes with a load of 660 lb. (comprising a pilot and a passenger).

June 28th.—The height of 24,000 ft. (7,310 m.) is reached in 55 minutes, with a load of 600 lb. (pilot alone).

August 26th.—Capt. Laureati flies from Turin to Naples and back without descending, covering in 10 hours a distance of 1,000 miles (1,400 km.).

The world's height records above-mentioned were beaten by the chief pilot of the Societá Sia, Lieut. Brach-Papa.

The motor of the " Sia FB " biplane is the 250-300-h.p. Fiat " A12 " motor, of the standard type widely employed in all the Italian machines.

The aeroplane was designed for being a " jack of all trades " type. Indeed, its carrying capacity, as well as its speed and climbing powers, enable it to be employed as a bomb-dropper as well as a racer.

The machine was built in the workshops for aeronautical construction of the Societá Italiana Aviazione, commonly known as the " Sia," a sister company to the famous motor-car firm, F.I.A.T., of Turin.

The designers are the engineers, Torretta and Carlo Maurilio Lerici, of the technical staff of F.I.A.T. Co.

The initials F.I.A.T. stand for Fabbrica Italiana Automobili Torino, and the word " Fiat " in pure Latin, means " Let it Be," or " So Be it "—which, freely translated, indicates that the F.I.A.T. is undoubtedly " It." The word " Sia " in modern Italian also means " Let it be so," with a precisely similar connotation to the word " Fiat." The play on initials is ingenious.

FIAT-SIA.

Specification.

Type of machine	Biplane.
Name or type No. of machine ..	R2.
Purpose for which intended ..	Scouting and Bombing.
Span	12.32 m.
Gap	1.95 m.
Overall length	8.75 m.
Maximum height	3.30 m.
Chord	1.95 m.
Total surface of wings	45.60 sq. m.
Span of tail	3.40 m.
Total area of tail	3.05 sq. m.
Area of elevator	2.00 sq. m.
Area of rudder	1.05 sq. m.
Area of fin	2.08 sq. m.
Maximum cross section of body	0.835 m.
Fuselage, vertical and horizontal	1.425 m. 0.835 m.
Engine type and h.p.	Fiat A12 bis. 300 h.p.
Airscrew, diam., pitch and revs...	2.80 m. 1.85 m. 1,500 revs.
Load per sq. m.	36.7 kgs.
Weight per h.p.	5.56 kgs.
Tank capacity in hours	4 hours.
Tank capacity in kilograms ..	Petrol, 215 kg. ; Oil, 40 kg.

Performance.

Speed at 200 metres	180 k.p.h.
Speed at 2,000 metres ..	165 k.p.h.
Landing speed	75 k.p.h.

Climb.

To 1,000 metres in minutes ..	6 mins.
To 2,000 metres in minutes ..	14 mins.
To 3,000 metres in minutes ..	23 mins.
To 4,000 metres in minutes ..	38 mins.
Total useful load	450 kgs.
Total weight of machine loaded	1,670 kgs.

The S.I.A. Type 9B Two-Seater Fighter (700 h.p. Fiat Engine.)

S.I.A.—*continued.*

THE (1916) SIA BIPLANE.
Specification.

Type of machine	Biplane.
Name or type No. of machine ..	S.I.A.
Purpose for which intended ..	Bombing.
Span	108 ft.
Overall length	57 ft.
Chord	11 ft. 6 in.
Engine type and h.p.	Two 700 h.p. Fiat.
Weight of machine empty ..	5½ tons.
Useful load	3 tons.
Fuselage	Twin.

FIAT-SIA.
Specification.

Type of machine	Biplane.
Name or type No. of machine ..	B.R.
Purpose for which intended ..	Scouting and Bombing.
Span	15.500 m.
Gap	2.150 m.
Maximum length	9.820 m.
Maximum height	3.800 m.
Chord	2.350 m.
Total surface of wings ..	72.00 sq. m.
Total area of ailerons ..	5.50 sq. m.
Span of tail	3.90 m.
Total area of tail	7.00 sq. m.
Total area of elevators ..	3.03 sq. m.
Total area of rudder ..	1.37 sq. m.
Total area of fin	2.10 sq. m.
Maximum cross section of body	1.032 m.
Fuselage, vertical and horizontal	1.575 m. 1.032 m.
Engine type and and h.p. ..	F.I.A.T. A14. 650 h.p.
Airscrew, diam., pitch and revs..	3.45 m. 45 m. 1,650 revs.
Load per sq. m. of surface ..	45 kgs.
Weight per h.p.	5 kgs.
Tank capacity in hours ..	4½ hours.
Tank capacity in kilograms ..	Petrol, 450 kilos ; Oil, 80 kilos.

Performance.

Speed at 200 metres	262 km.p.h.
Speed at 2,000 metres ..	265 km.p.h.
Landing speed	90 km.p.h.

Climb.

To 1,000 metres in minutes ..	3.45 mins. 45 secs.
To 2,000 metres in minutes ..	7 mins. 30 secs.
To 3,000 metres in minutes ..	12 mins. 30 secs.
To 4,000 metres in minutes ..	16 mins.
To 5,000 metres in minutes ..	25 mins. 30 secs.
Total useful load	1,000 kgs.
Total weight of machine loaded	3,250 kgs.

Three-quarter front view of a twin engined S.I.A. Biplane (2-700 h.p. Fiat engines).

The type B.R. two seater (700 h.p. Fiat engine) S.I.A.

S—*continued.*

S.I.A.I. Societa Idrovolanti Alta Italia.

Works at Sesto Calende. Offices : 12 via Silvio Pellico, Milan. Flying Water, for testing, etc., at S. Anna, Lago Maggiore. Repair Shops at Castelletto.

Exclusive F.B.A. concessionaires for Italy, and a twin firm to the Savoia.

Joining up with Cape, an old house of wood-workers on Lago Maggiore, in an incredibly short time the S.I.A.I. was able to provide F.B.As. for the defence of Venice, Lago di Garda, and elsewhere, and also to run the regular twice-daily Postal Service to Sardinia. This machine is well-known and has been amply illustrated in "La Guerra."

The Colombo Hispano Suiza and various motors have been fitted to the Company's flying-boats.

Some idea as to the size of this business is provided by the statement that fifty machines can be assembled at the same time at the S. Anna establishment.

The largest hydro-aeroplane factory in Italy, founded also by Signor Lorenzo Santoni. Has been, like the Savoia hydro-aeroplanes, largely used by the Italian Navy for the defence of the Adriatic.

SOCIETÀ INDUSTRIE AEROMARITTIME "GALLINARI." Livorno.

An old-established shipbuilding concern. During the War the firm extended its activities in various ways, and started to construct seaplanes of standard types. A site for testing these was acquired at Marina di Pisa.

S. I. A. M. (Società Industrie Alto Mediterraneo.) Posillipo (Naples). Testing shops at Lucerne. Nom. capital : 10,000,000 lire. Paid up capital : 6,000,000 lire. Managing Director : Dr. Bruno Canzio.

Government contractors, Now going in for large seaplanes chiefly. Has in a short time become one of the most important firms in S. Italy.

A S.I.A.I. FLYING BOAT. Bombing Type. Three-quarter Front View.

3 D 2

S—continued.

SOCIETÀ PER'INCREMENTO BELL'VIAZIONE IN ITALIANA.

Via MARCO BRUTO TALIEDO.

Nom. Cap. 10,000,000 lire.

Paid up Cap. 5,000,000 lire.

SOCIETÀ ITALIANA. Ernest Breda: Sesto-S. Giovanni, Milan. Nom. capital : 50,000,000 lire. Paid-up capital : 37,000,000 lire.

Building *Capronis* and dealing in motors, oxygen, etc. Also at Rome and Naples. Has own flying camp.

A Ricci flying boat of 700 h-p. built by S.I.A.M., Naples.

A Twin engine flying boat built by S.I.A.M. of Naples.

S—*continued*.

S.I.T. Società Italiana Transaerea, Corso Peschiera 251. Turin.

This firm was founded in July, 1912, with a capital of 700,000 lire, under the Directorate of MM. Louis Blériot, Alberto Triaca, Manissero père et fils and Goria-Gatti for the construction of aircraft.

The exclusive manufacturing rights in Italy of the Blériot patents were secured, and these machines formed the greater part of the S.I.T.'s output up to the summer of 1914.

Since then the manufacture of two-deckers of the well-known type (*Voisin*) has been undertaken, and the firm's activities have been enormously extended.

Manager.—Ing. C. Momo.

Late in 1917 the business was incorporated with Gio. Ansaldo & Co., Genoa & Borzoli, ecc. ecc., and so will reap the benefit of that house's firm position in metallurgy and supplies.

The S.I.T. *Voisins* were well tried out in the early war, but then little was heard of even the greatest things. Now the habitual gets no comment.

A certain number of waterplanes issued from this company's works at one time.

Front View of the S.V.A. Biplane.

S.V.A. Gio. Ansaldo & Co. Borzoli, Bolzaneto, Genoa; and Turin.

Owned by the sons of the late Comm. F. M. Perrone.

This huge engineering firm, with 100,000,000 lire of capital, has recently leapt into the aeroplane business with a record-breaking biplane and other aircraft.

Some 30,000 workpeople are employed.

Ing. G. Brezzi is in charge of the aviation department of the Perrone family's immense business, of which, too, the S.I.T. Co., of Turin, who hold the manufacturing rights of the Blériot and Voisin machines for Italy, is now a part.

The great ramifications of Gio. Ansaldo & Co. entitle the firm to be called the most important of the Allied European Nations handling aircraft.

The rapid reproduction of two types of biplanes, both very speedy, is the Company's chief concern. In this it has the support of such well-known banks as "Pogliani," "Quartieri," and "Agnelli."

Spa motors are used on the S.V.A. machines, as the products of the Ansaldo works are named. The name Sva is apparently derived from Spa, Verduzio, Ansaldo, Spa being the engine, Verduzio the designer, and Ansaldo the manufacturers.

The firm advertise their seaplanes extensively, the features of which type are shewn in the illustration herewith.

An S.V.A. Seaplane.

S.V.A.—*continued.*

THE S.V.A. BIPLANE.

The famous engineering and shipbuilding concern, the Societa Gio Ansaldo of Genoa, is now making aircraft upon a very large scale. This firm, which is comparable in this country only with Vickers', Armstrong's, or Beardmore's, or in Germany with Krupps', is governed by the brothers Pio and Mario Perrone. These enterprising men, both of whom are but slightly past forty years of age, have shown enterprise in every department of engineering, and it is not surprising, therefore that their aeronautical products are equally original and successful.

The Ansaldo firm has incorporated the S.I.T. (Societa Italiana Transaerea, Turin) business, which holds the Blèriot and Voisin licenses for Italy, and the F.I.A.T. Saint-Georgio business for the manufacture of aero-engines at Muggiano. In addition an important aircraft works has been established at Borzoli, near Genoa, the whole establishment being raised upon green fields within eight months.

An aerodrome site was purchased about six miles from the works, the surrounding terrain being unsuited to this purpose. A number of houses were pulled down to clear the ground, and a first-class testing depot established.

Owing to the difficulty of procuring steel tube suitable for aircraft work, the firm laid down tube mills to work to make its own. And as first-class wing fabric was scarce, they installed a silk-weaving plant to make special fabric for themselves.

They then commenced to build S.V.A. (Savoia-Verduzio-Ansaldo) aeroplanes, successful examples being single-seater land machines and seaplanes, whose most noteworthy feature is the use of triangularly arranged tubular interplane struts, much after the practice prevailing before the war in certain German biplanes and in the French Clement-Bayard biplane, the object in view being the elimination of unnecessary bracing cables.

On a land machine of this description the military aviator Stoppani flew from Turin to Rome in 2 hr. 50 min. This machine is regarded as a long-distance fighter, and can carry fuel for eight hours, in the course of which it will fly between 1,600 and 1,700 kilometres, which represents the distance from Rome to Paris. When some of the fuel carrying capacity is utilised for bomb loads the machine becomes a formidable raiding unit. The seaplane is a similar machine fitted with long, narrow twin floats of Howard Wright type.

Some idea of the extent of the activities of the Perrone Bros. may be judged from the fact that they employ over 60,000 workmen in their various factories, an important proportion of whom are engaged upon aircraft construction.

During 1918, the firm absorbed the O. Pomilio Aircraft Company, of Turin, mentioned elsewhere in this work.

The principal outstanding work done by S.V.A. in the war was the pacific raid of 7 machines on Vienna, a 700 mile flight done in under 7 hrs. The firm are exclusively fitting the 220 S.P.A. 6-cylinder engines. During the early part of this year most of Italy's crack pilots were flying or in expectation of flying S.V.A. machines. The famous Baracca and Serenissima escadrilles are using them exclusively.

THE S.V.A. BIPLANE.

Type of machine	Single-seater Biplane.
Name or type No. of machine	S.V.A. (Savoia-Verduzio-Ansaldo).
Purpose for which intended ..	Single-seater Fighter.
Span	29 ft. 10 in.
Overall length	22 ft. 11 in.
Maximum height	11 ft. 6 in.
Engine type and (h.p. ..	220 h.p. S.P.A. (Ansaldo).
Weight of machine empty ..	1,900 lbs.
Weight per h.p.	13.2 lbs.
Tank capacity in gallons. ..	75 gallons.

Performance.

Speed low down	140 m.p.h.
Landing speed	45 m.p.h.

Climb.

To 20,000 feet in minutes ..	30 mins.

Total weight of machine loaded .. .. .. 2,900 lbs.

THE S.V.A. AEROPLANE.

Type of machine	Single-seater.
Name or type No. of machine ..	S.V.A.
Purpose for which intended ..	Daylight Bomber.
Span	29 ft. 10 in.
Length	26 ft. 7 in.
Height	10 ft. 6 in.
Total lifting surface ..	261 sq. ft.
Engine type and h.p. ..	S.P.A., 200 h.p., 6 cyl., vertical. 225 h.p. at 1700 r.p.m.
Tractor screw	Two-bladed.
Weight empty	1450 lbs.
Tank capacity in hours ..	6-7 hours.

Performance.

Speed at sea level	136 m.p.h.
Landing speed	45 m.p.h.

Climb.

To 10,000 feet in minutes ..	10 mins.
To 20,000 feet in minutes ..	28 mins.
Useful load with tanks full ..	About 450 lbs. Has been flown with 650 lbs.

Total weight with tanks full and full load of bombs 2,200 lbs.

Front View of another type of S.V.A. Biplane.

S.V.A.—*continued*.

THE ANSALDO BIPLANE.

Type of machine	Single-seater Biplane.
Name or type No. of machine ..	Ansaldo " Primo."
Purpose for which intended ..	Single-seater Fighter.
Span	22 ft. 11 in.
Overall length	19 ft. 8 in.
Maximum height	11 ft. 6 in.
Engine type and h.p. ..	220 h.p. S.P.A. (Ansaldo).
Weight of machine empty ..	1600 lbs.
Weight per h.p.	10 lbs. per h.p.
Tank capacity in gallons ..	40 gals.

Performance.
    Speed low down .. .. 145 m.p.h.
    Landing speed .. .. 45 m.p.h.

Climb.
    To 20,000 feet in minutes .. 25 mins.

Total weight of machine loaded .. .. .. 2,200 lbs.

ANSALDO 1, called also the " BALILLA."

Type of machine	Single-seater Biplane.
Name or type No. of machine ..	Ansaldo 1—nicknamed the " Balilla."
Purpose for which intended ..	Hunter.
Span	25 ft.
Length	21 ft. 8 in.
Height	10 ft. 6 in.
Engine type and h.p. ..	S.P.A., 200 h.p., 6 cyl., Vertical. 225 h.p. at 1700 r.p.m.
Tank capacity in hours	About 2½ hours.

Performance.
    Speed .. .. .. 140 m.p.h.

Climb.
    To 16,000 feet in minutes .. 16 minutes.

Guns fire through propeller.

THE ITALIAN S.V.A
210 HP SPA MOTORED
FIGHTING SCOUT
CENTIMETERS

V

VICKERS. *(TERNI).*

This firm has made recently, a very fast small biplane, known as the *M.V.T.* (*Marchetti-Vickers-Terni*), from the names of the designer, makers and place of production.

The machine is illustrated herewith.

W

WOLSIT-JACCHIA. *(LEGNANO)..*

This firm built a monoplane in two types and was of interest on account of the long, slender, streamlined metal body and absence of nearly all external bracing cables. The machine was also tried as a seaplane with floats, but nothing much was heard of it.

The Wolsit firm, which is allied to the British Wolseley firm, built a bigger model at a later date.

However, such being merely a side line, the war thrust all the firm's activities back into the main stream of its business, and one gathers that many machines have been caused to fly brilliantly by means of the motors flowing from Legnano.

Nothing new, in the way of immformation is available.

The Marchetti-Vickers-Terni (M.V.T.) biplane.

402a

JAPANESE.

[The first section of this information, and all the photographs have been kindly provided by the Japanese Authorities.–C.G.G.]

Aerial Societies at outbreak of war :—

Teikoku Hiko Kyokai (Hibia Buildings, Kojimochikn, Tokyio).

Kikyu Kenkyu Kai (connected with War Office).

Flying Grounds :—

Oihama. (Naval.)

Tokorozawa. (Army.) Airship shed.

GENERAL MILITARY AVIATION.

This was originally formed as one body without distinction between army and navy. It was subsequently re-modelled on lines somewhat similar to the British Royal Flying Corps with naval and military wings.

NAVY.

The naval section is superintended by Capt. K. Yamaji, I.J.N.

The naval headquarters are at Oihama (near Yokosuka).

The naval force in March, 1914, consisted of 10 hydro-aeroplanes (3 *Curtiss*, 2 *Deperdussin* and 5 *Farman*). The available total of qualified naval aviators was 20.

FINANCE.

The total amount granted for aviation of the navy in 1912 (fiscal year) was 100,000 yen (£10,000).

For the year 1914 the estimates amounted was 100,000 yen.

ARMY.

The army wing is responsible for the airships. It has also many aeroplanes (*M. Farman, Nieuport, Jokugawa* (Japanese Military type). *Curtiss, Grade, Bleriot, H. Farman, Rumpler*).

Japanese aeroplanes, chiefly of European make, were used extensively in the siege of Kiau-Chiau early in the war.

Since then it is known that the training of pilots has been carried on vigorously and both naval and military aviators have been produced in fair numbers.

AVIATORS.

The following have been killed :—

1912.
Aibat, Lieut. (balloon in Germany)
Kondo (*Curtiss*, in U.S.A.).
1913.
Kimura, Lieut. ⎱ *Bleriot.*
Tokuda, Lieut. ⎰
Takeishi.
Shigematsu, Lieut. (*M. Farman*).
Ogita (*Morane-Saulnier*).

PRIVATE AVIATION.

There are some private aeroplanes being regularly flown in Japan. A number of aeroplanes have from time to time been invented by naval and military officers and private individuals, and some of them are in use. Inventors include Major Hino, naval constructors Narahara and Ushioku, Baron Iga, Baron Shigeno (who was one of the French *Spad* pilots on the Western Front) and Mr. Tsuzuki.

Mr. Yamada's non-rigid type airship was not used in the fighting off Port Arthur, as was formerly reported.

THE AIR SERVICE OF THE IMPERIAL JAPANESE NAVY.

The names of officers controlling Naval Aviation are :—

Rear-Admiral J. Matsumura, I.J.N.

Captain S. Yamanouchi, I.J.N.

Captain S. Harada, I.J.N.

Names of Flying Officers :—

Commanders :—Y. Kaneko and S. Fukuoka.

Lieut.-Commanders :—S. Kono, K. Hiramatsu, C. Yamada, and H. Wada.

A Group of Japanese Naval Air Service Officers.

JAPANESE AEROPLANES.

Lieutenants :—M. Fujise, T. Nanba, N. Osaki, T. Iigura, K. Magoshi, J. Yamamoto, S. Nagamine, T. Kuwabara, M. Kaiya, N. Mikami, A. Beppu, M. Wada, N. Goto, T. Yashima, M Asada, T. Muroi, T. Onishi, T. Shokji, M. Sakamoto, O. Imamura, T. Shirase, M Niwa, and S. Kato.

Sub-Lieutenants :—T. Araki, M. Kani, M. Miki, S. Kira, S. Senda, T. Komaki, M. Sakamaki, Y. Kato, R. Ichimaru, J. Miyake, S. Kadowaki, K. Shirai, K. Uwano, I. Yonesawa, S. Ogura and T. Shimizu.

Engineer-Commander :—S. Yamashita.

Engineer-Lieut.-Commander :—N. Tada.

Engineer-Lieutenants :—K. Hanashima, R. Kuriuo, Y. Takeda, R. Sagisaka, J. Shoda, M. Kido, R Takahashi, K. Sasaki and T. Mogi.

Engineer-Sub-Lieutenants :—S. Kato and Y. Tajiri.

Naval Engineer :—K. Takeuchi

The Japanese Naval Flying School is the Yokosuka Flying School, Yokosuka.

The chief Naval aviation centres in Japan are Yokosuka and Sasebo.

The manufacturers of aircraft are :—

The Imperial Naval Dockyard, Yokosuka.

The Aircraft Engine Factory of the Mitsubishi Shipyard, Kobe.

The Aircraft Factory of the Kawasaki Shipyard, Kobe.

The Japanese Aircraft Factory, Ootamachi.

[The following information is taken from "The Japan Year Book." The Japanese themselves are not anxious to provide detailed information concerning their aviation work.—Ed.]

MILITARY AVIATION.

First airmen, two officers, trained in France, who returned home in 1911. There were two others in 1912 and three more in 1915 (names not given). Since then military training courses have been instituted at Tokorozawa (near Tokyo) and Kagamigahara (in Gifuken), and every year a number of young flight officers are turned out.

Decided to create new course in Fukuoka prefecture, Kyushu. Army now has 30 machines and one airship. The fleet (*i.e.*, Air Force) will receive an expansion to make it more "decent and up-to-date."

Gen. Oshima (War Minister) explained in Diet, 1918, that 240 training machines would be built by fiscal year 1923–24. Tokyo Arsenal will be equipped with aircraft plant capable of turning out 120 machines per month (type not specified).

Seven military aviators killed, 1913 to May, 1918. Six civilian aviators killed, 1913–18. (Names not given.)

Machines in Japan mostly *Morris-Farman* and *Newbolt* monoplanes, now out of date and toys compared with Allied and U.S. type.

[Note :—"Newbolt monoplanes" are a novelty. Query *Nieuport*. *Morris-Farman* is obviously *Maurice Farman*.]

Motors are very poor, and best power output is 75 h.p. Two U.S. aviators gave exhibitions in 1916, and stunts by Art Smith showed up the ridiculous development of Japanese military types.

In 1917, Army bought five 125 h.p. biplanes in Europe (type not specified).

In 1915–16 the vote was Y400,000, and in 1916–17, Y600,000. (1916–17 programme was for construction of 30–40 machines.)

In 1918, Diet voted Y1,540,000 for Military Aviation Corps, including establishment of two new "flying battalions."

War Department projects construction of large Y7,000,000 aviation station ; Lake Riva will be the probable site.

The airship is a poor craft of 300 h.p., with maximum speed of 20 m.p.h., but for lack of money construction of modern airships has been deferred for one or two years.

A Sopwith Schneider type Seaplane (110 h.p. Rotary engine) in the Japanese Naval Air Service.

A Tellier Flying Boat (200 h.p. engine) in the Japanese Naval Air Service.

A Maurice Farman Seaplane coming alongside a Seaplane Carrier.

Military flight officers now number about 40, which compose an Aviation Battalion (organised Dec., 1915). In Feb., 1916, Army conducted experimental flights in Manchuria "in a freezing sky."

NAVAL AVIATION.

Naval aviation dates from 1912, when officers trained in France and America came home. Shortly afterwards training ground set up at Oppama, near Yokosuka (Yokosuka is a big, fortified naval base, with navy yard, docks, shipbuilding berths, &c.—M.P.), and experiments were started in real earnest.

Naval Aviation Corps established in 1916 with a first vote of Y35,000. At the same time Y630,000 was granted as an equipment and construction Fund, to be spread over five years.

In 1918–19 fiscal year, Y1,580,000 is voted for Naval Aviation, including cost of creating two more Naval Aviation Corps at the big fleet bases at Sasebo and Kure.

The necessary equipment for Kure and Sasebo aerodromes is to be finished by end of 1819–20 fiscal year.

About 50 flight officers now.

Aviation Corps has built *Farman* machines, with " Runoux " (Renault ?) type motors.

Replying to questions in the Diet, 1918, Admiral Kato (Minister of Marine) said Naval Aviation Repletion Fund included 140 machines, to be finished by end of 1922–23 fiscal year. Five officers and one sailor have been killed up to present.

Mr. K. Yamashita, a new "ship millionaire" (query : ship-building or shipowning ?—Ed.), of Tokyo, contributed in 1918 a million yen towards aviation funds of Army *and* Navy.

CIVILIAN AVIATION.

Practically undeveloped. About 20 qualified men, mostly trained abroad, and eight which have been allowed to join French Military Aviation Service. "As for the rest, they can be said to be leading the lives of martyrs. With no regular income or support, they cannot maintain themselves as aviators, for they have no machines good enough for public flights.

"Their machines, with motors of 50 to 60 h.p., have become a byword from repeated failures. Many of them have been compelled to become chauffeurs to earn a living." Mr. Osaki, Dr. Kishi (oculist), Major Isobe and Baron Shigeno (both in France), Mr. M. Goto and Mr. Y. Sato are prominent civilian aviators, Mr. S. Tamai, opened a flying School in Tokyo, killed 1917.

A Short Seaplane (320 h.p. Sunbeam engine) in the Japanese Naval Air Service.

AVIATION ASSOCIATIONS.

Imperial Aviation Association.—Incorporated 1914, and is the first such society. Business has been pushed by the active committee, and membership is now over 5,000.

Funds are scarce and no experimental work or prizes of any value can be set up. Two donations given by an American gentleman who hopes for great things in Japanese aviation. (Considering the little love lost between the Yanks and the Japs this is rather extraordinary !—Ed.).

Just before war, Association bought two monoplanes from Germany, which were actively used by the Army in scouting work over Tsingtao for the Japanese. (The War Department bought these two machines).

In May, 1917, Barons Shibusawa and Kondo decided to collect a million yen to purchase land for an aviation station and to help civilian aviators. In 1918 land was bought at Itchujima, Tokyo, where an aerodrome is now being erected.

Mr. Masao Goto, an aviator belonging to the association, succeeded, in April, 1918, in a non-stop flight from Tokorozawa to Osaka, and set up a long-distance flight record in Japan, covering 300 miles in 6.20 hours.

Association presided over by H.H. Prince Kuni (Patron), while Marquis Okuma and Baron Sakatani are Pres. and Vice-Pres. respectively. Association has not yet joined International Aerial Convention, and therefore is not qualified to issue licenses. Civilians who have trained abroad by regular courses number about 30 (20 ?).

National Aviation Society.—Created December, 1915, chiefly by Lieut.-Gen. Gaisha Nagaoka (retired), who is reputed as a Japanese Zeppelin ; was helped by 40 public men and scientists interested in aviation. Society intends to issue appeal for public support. Publishes its own journal. Pres., Lieut.-Gen. Nagaoka. Office, Yoban-cho, Kojimachi, Tokyo.

Dr. Kishi's Aviation School.—Most reliable of all private establishments. Left profession as oculist and devoted himself to flying and development of aircraft. School on River Arakawa, Tokyo Prefecture, and covers area of 50,000 tsubo. (1 tsubo = 3.95 sq. yds.), including workshop and various equipment. School opened April, 1918. Lieut. Inouye is the chief instructor.

Aviation at University.—In 1916, Chair of Aviation created at Tokyo University, Y60,000 being appropriated for it

The following is evidently a stop press note :—

Expansion programme of military aviation for 1918–19 fiscal year has resulted in creation of Aviation Bureau. At the same time the establishment is announced of one flying battalion each at Yokka-ichi, Tachi-arai, Fuknoka-ken, while force is to receive gradual additions. Military Aviation School to be established.

The Japanese-built Yokosuka Dockyard type Seaplane (140 h.p.)

JAPANESE AEROPLANES.

PROGRESS TO AUGUST, 1919.

[The following information was received from Japan just before this volume went to press, and is published as an addition to the foregoing matter.—C. G. G.]

Aerial Societies :—

1. **Kiku-Kenkyu-Kai.** (Connected with War Office.) Tokorozawa, Saitama-Ken.

2. **Imperial Aero Club.** (Teikoku Hiko Kiyokai). 1 Chome, Yurakucho, Marunouchi, Tokio.

H.I.M. The Emperor of Japan has donated Y500,000 to the encouraging civilian aviation, and a large sum of money has been contributed to the club, also for the same purpose, by a great many people throughout the country.

The officers of the Imperial Aero Club, the only official club of its kind in Japan, are as follows :—Prince Kuni, Hon. Pres. ; Marquis Okuma, Ex Premier, Pres. ; Baron Sakatani and Gen. Nagaoka, First and Second Vice-Pres. respectively.

The club announced that cash prizes will be awarded to the winners of various contests and competitions.

Aero Journals, &c. :—

1. *Hiko Kai.* (The Aeronautical World.) Founded 1913. 2 Chome, Honhachobori, Kiyobashi-Ku, Tokio. A monthly magazine devoted to the general interests of aviation. Subscription (foreign) : Y5.10 per annum.

2. *Teikoku Hiko.* (Issued by Imperial Aero Club.) 1 Chome, Yurakucho, Marunouchi, Tokio. Monthly. Subscription (foreign) : Y4.00 per annum.

3. *Motor.* (Aviation and Motor Car, &c.). Tameike, Akasaka-Ku, Tokio. Monthly. Subscription (foreign) : Y4.00 per annum.

4. *Speed.* (Aviation and Motor Car, &c.) 667, Haneda-Machi, Tokio-Fu. Monthly. Subscription (foreign) : Y4.00 per annum.

Finance :—

The total amount granted for aviation of Army and Navy in this year (1919) was Y12,000,000.00.

Mr. K. Yamashita has donated Y1,000,000.00 to the Army and Navy Air Force a few months ago for the purpose of purchasing new machines from America and Europe.

Flying Ground :—

Tokorozawa. Army and Imperial Aero Club.
Kagamigahara. Army.
Mikatagahara. Army.
Yokkaichi. Army.
Near **Fukuoka.** Army.
Oihama. Navy. (Near Yokosuka.)

Kure. Navy.
Akabane. Civilian. (Near Tokio.)
Oota. Civilian.
Inage. Civilian.
Haneda. Civilian.
Naruo. Civilian. (Near Osaka.)

ARMY AVIATION.

The Japanese Army has bought a few hundred latest type aeroplanes direct from the French Government recently, and now selected members of the French Aviation Mission, headed by a French Colonel, who are now in Japan, instructing Japanese Army officers. These French flyers were in the battle front, each having brought down a number of Germans, and are among the best flyers (The French Mission consists of 20 Pilots, 20 Mechanics and 5 Observation Officers).

Quite recently the Imperial Air Service has become independent, which is now under direct control of Japanese Government, and a regular aviation school has also been established at Tokorozawa, and number of others are established at different places. Maj.-General Inouye is the head of the Imperial Army Air Service and Maj.-General Arikawa is the chief commanding officer.

AVIATION SCHOOLS.

The Army flyers are first trained in Maurice Farman (Pusher Type) machines and put on Sopwiths for advance training. After finishing their full course, all acrobatic and stunt flying will be taught by expert French flyers. At present, cross-country and formation flights are made almost every day as long as weather permits.

NAVY AVIATION.

The Navy has also bought a considerable number of seaplanes from France recently and is increasing her air force very rapidly.

CIVILIAN AVIATION.

The civilian aviation is progressing very rapidly day after day, and in the near future, possibly by next year, there will be more than enough of skilful aerial pilots, as the Army flying school announced that any civilian who wishes to receive actual flying instruction in the said school may be allowed to enter upon making an application to the Imperial Army Air Service. Besides this, there are a few civilian flying schools just lately established, and a few aeroplane companies are now being promoted, and some already organised, that these manufactures will need test flyers in the near future.

AERIAL MAIL SERVICE.

There will be an aerial mail service between Tokio and Osaka, the distance being about 300 miles to be operated by a private concern, under the supervision of the Imperial Aero Club. Negotiations are now being made with the post office authorities, the details of this service will be announced later.

NUMBER AND TYPE OF MACHINES.

1. ARMY.

	Machines.
Nieuport biplane, one or two seat Le Rhône 120 h.p.	30
Spad biplane, one or two seat Hispano Suiza 200 or 150 h.p.	25
Sopwith biplane, one or two seat Clerget 130 h.p. ..	50
Salmson biplane, two or three seat Salmson 300 h.p.	5
Grahame White biplane, five seat Sunbeam 350 h.p.	2
Grahame White biplane, two seat Salmson 110 h.p.	3
Farman biplane, two or three seat Renault 70 h.p. or Curtiss 100 h.p. and Mercédès Daimler 100 h.p. (Japan make)	200
Seishiki biplane, two seat Mercédès Daimler 100 h.p.	20
Nakajima biplane, two seat Hall Scott 150 or 200 h.p.	20
Another various type	10
Total ..	365

2. NAVY.

	Machines
Farman biplane, two or three seat Renault 70 h.p. or Curtiss 100 h.p. and Salmson 120 h.p., Benz 100 h.p.	150
Short biplane, two seat Sunbeam 150 or 225 h.p. ..	50
Sopwith biplane, one or two seat Gnôme 100 h.p. and 160 h.p. ..	40
Curtiss Flying Boat and Biplane, Curtiss 100 h.p. ..	10
Another various type	15
Total ..	265

3. CIVILIAN.

	Machines
Various type machines	30

MODERN AEROPLANES.

ITOH.

Itoh Aeroplane Works. Inage, Chiba-Ken.

This machine, Sopwith "Baby" type machine, and designed fighting, and fitted with Gnôme Engine (80 or 50 h.p.).

This machine is remarkable for its small size, and range speed. It was made to loop the loop successfully under the pilotage of Mr. Yamagata, at Tokio and Inage.

Details.

Span, upper plane	.. ..	23 ft. 8 in.
Span, lower plane	.. ..	21 ft. 10 in.
Chord	.. ..	3 ft. 9 in.
Gap	.. ..	4 ft.
Length	.. ..	19 ft.
Height	.. ..	7 ft. 9 in.
Area (Main Wings)	..	157 sq. ft.
Weight (full load)	..	750 lbs.
Engine	.. ..	Gnôme, 80 or 50 h.p.
Speed	.. ..	90-100 m.p.h.

NAKAJIMA.

Japan Aeroplane Works Co., Ltd., Oota, Gunma-Ken.

One of the most successful machines made in Japan, and designed for fighting and reconnaissance, and built by Capt. Nakajima, at Japan Aeroplane Works, Oota.

This machine, two-seater biplane and fitted with Hall Scott engine (150 or 200 h.p.), and many of these machines have been supplied to the Army Air Force.

It was made to loop the loop very successfully under the pilotage of Lieut. Mizuta, at Oota Aerodrome.

SEISHIKI. (Army Standard Type.)

Japan Aircraft Factory, Tokorozawa, Saitama-Ken.

SEISHIKI No. 1. (1 Go.)

This machine is a two-seater biplane, designed for reconnaissance and fitted with Mercédès Daimler engine (Japanese make), 100 h.p., and built by Lieut. Sawada, who was a famous skilful aviator in Army Air Force.

SEISHIKI No. 2. (2 Go.)

This machine was built by Lieut. Nakazawa and was fitted with Mercédès Daimler engine (Japanese make), 100 h.p. This machine's specification is as follows :—

Span, upper and lower planes	..	9.700 m.
Length	.. ..	6.700 m.
Chord	.. ..	1.500 m.
Weight (full load)	.. ..	850 kg.
Speed	.. ..	85 m.p.h.

SOGA GO.

Imperial Aero Club, Tokoroazwa, Saitama-Ken.

This machine is a two-seater biplane, designed for reconnaissance, fitted with Austro-Daimler engine, 90 h.p., and built by Mr. Ozaki, who was the most famous civilian aviator in Japan.

TSURUGI GO.

Kishi Aeroplane Works, Akabane, near Tokio.

This manufactory made two types of machines, one of Farman type, two-seater machine; and another, tractor biplane, both fitted with 100 or 150 h.p. Kishi engine (self-made).

AVIATORS :—

ARMY.

Tokugawa, Capt.	Katoh, Lieut.	Fujisaki, Sub-Lieut.
Satoh, ,,	Kozawa, ,,	Mori ,,
Oka, ,,	Abe ,,	Oshiba, ,,
Nagasawa, ,,	Sugada ,,	Satoh ,,
Nakazawa, Lieut.	Hishimura, ,,	Otsuka, ,,
Inoue ,,	Watanabe, ,,	Kihaya, ,,
Itoh ,,	Hattori, ,,	Konishi ,,
Sakamoto ,,	Kawabata ,,	Hideshima ,,
Naitoh ,,	Matsuoka ,,	Inoda, ,,
Kozeki, ,,	Nagafuchi, ,,	Yoshida, ,,
Makabe, ,,	Teramoto ,,	Takahashi, ,,
Nomi, ,,	Noguchi, ,,	Kondoh ,,
Mizuta ,,	Tanaka ,,	Kojima ,,
Takeda ,,	Tatematsu ,,	Yamamoto ,,
Nakada, ,,	Tani, ,,	Imamura ,,
Nakamura ,,	Kondoh ,,	Onozaki ,,
Katoh, ,,	Miyazato ,,	Sakeda, ,,
Iba, ,,	Nakaori, ,,	Kondoh ,,
Ashidate ,,	Watanabe ,,	Kawaida, ,,
Seto, ,,	Zintsu, ,,	Totsuka, ,,
Nagao ,,	Tsukikawa, Sub-Lieut.	Ooi, ,,
Tatetomi, ,,	Kawakami, ,,	Tedeshima, ,,
Kinoshita ,,	Shimoda, ,,	Aoki, ,,
Sakaguchi, ,,	Nakayama, ,,	Higuchi, ,,
Niijima, ,,	Noda, ,,	Katsumi, ,,
Saitoh, ,,	Wada, ,,	Kasai, ,,
Sone ,,	Kamiya, ,,	
Mitsumura, ,,	Nagada, ,,	

Note :—Other aviators :—

	Officers	80
	Men	55
In School (during training) ..	Officers	150
	Men	80

Total .. 447 persons.

NAVY.

Yamanouchi, Capt.	Nagamine, Lieut.	Kooji, Sub-Lieut.
Kaneko, Commander	Mikami, ,,	Araki, ,,
Umekita, ,,	Asada, ,,	Sakamoto, ,,
Yamada, Lieut-Comdr.	Kuwabara, ,,	Imamura, ,,
Wada, ,,	Yashima, ,,	Kani, ,,
Tada, ,,	Tsuda, ,,	Yamarmua, ..
Kono, ,,	Shirase, ,,	Miki, ,,
Hanashima, Lieut.	Wada, ,,	Takata, ,,
Nanba, ,,	Umitani, ,,	Mukai, ,,
Umakoshi ,,	Masuda, ,,	Shiose, ,,
Iikura, ,,	Goto, Sub-Lieut.	Katoh, ,,
Fuziki ,,	Yamaguchi ,,	Kira, ,,
Yamamoto, ,,	Muroi, ,,	Chida, ,,
Bepu, ,,	Asada, ,,	Takeda, ,,
	Onishi, ,,	Mukai, ,,

Shimiza, Sub-Lieut.	Shirato, Sub-Lieut.	Kogami, Sub-Lieut.
Sakami, ,,	Sakakibara, ,,	Katoh, ,,
Tomioka, ,,	Ichimura, ,,	Kadowaki, ,,
Shirai, ,,	Ueno, ,,	Yonezawa, ,,

Note :—Other aviators :—

	Officers	65
	Men	50
In School (during training) ..	Officers	100
	Men	60

Total .. 331 persons.

CIVILIAN.

Baron Shigeno	Moro	Isobe	Goto
Ozaki	Satoh	Itoh	Shirato
Yamagata	Nakajima	Mazume	Unno
Sakamoto	Tachibana	Oguri	Nakazawa
Nojima	Toteishi	Tamai	Hoshi
Inoue	Kondoh	Iimura	Fujimoto
Yoneda	Takaso	Kawakami	Fujiwara

Other aviators, 20 persons.

KILLED.

The following have been killed up to the end of August, 1919 :—

1913	Kimura, Lieut.	1919	Inouye, Capt.
	Tokuda, Lieut.		Yamanouchi, Lieut.
	Takeishi		Mitsui, Lieut.
1914	Shigematsu, Lieut.		Nishide
			Masumi, Lieut.
1915	Aoki, Lieut.		Sasakibara, Lieut.
	Adachi, Capt.		Suga, Lieut. (in Italy)
	Takebe, Capt.		Iwatomi, Lieut. (in Italy)
	Yanase		Miyake, Lieut.
	Ogita		Okada, Lieut.
	Ohashi		Suho
1916	Abe, Lieut.		
	Tongu, Capt.		
	Higuchi, Lieut.		
1917	Tamai		
	Yugawa		
	Yugawa		
	Sugino, Lieut.		
	Sawada, Capt.		
	Yamamura, Lieut.		
1918	M. Sakamoto, Lieut.		
	Takahashi, Lieut.		
	Tobimatsu, Lieut.		
	Sakamoto, Lieut.		
	Yonezawa, Lieut.		
	Tomeoka, Lieut.		
	Sasaki		

MEXICAN.

Aerial Societies :—

None.

Aerial Journals :—

Tohtli. Organ of the Military Aviation School.
Editor : R. Avila de la Vega. Offices : Avenida Francisco Madero, 1, Mexico City. (Subscription : $3 per annum.) Appears monthly.

Aerodromes :—

Valbuena, near Mexico City. (Military Flying School.) A dozen thoroughly modern sheds.

San Benito, near Hermosillo. (Military Air Station.)

Up to February 1st, 1919, twenty-nine cadets were awarded the certificate of military aviator by the Department of Military Aeronautics.

Aviation Works :—

Military Aviation Factory, Valbuena. Director : Sr. Francisco Santarini. Founded, November, 1915.

The factory is equipped with thoroughly modern machinery and produces training and fighting aeroplanes of its own design.

The engine shop produces a Mexican Anzani type engine, called Aztatl, which is used on the later training machines.

The fighting machines are equipped with Hispano-Suiza engines, production of which will begin in 1918 at Valbuena. Machinery for this purpose appears to have been imported from Spain.

The factory also builds a national type of airscrew, called Anàhuac.

The Government Aircraft Factory is constructing a new monoplane, fitted with the 80 h.p. Aztatl engine. A new engine, called S.S. Mexico, and rated 130 h.p. is also being developed.

AVIATORS.

1912. Salinas, Alberto (Ae. C. A., 170).
        Salinas, Gustavo (Ae. C. A., 172).
        Ruiz, Horacio (Ae. C. A., 182).
        Aldasoro, Juan Pablo (Ae. C. A., 217).
        Aldasoro, Eduardo (Ae. C. A., 218).
1918. Rojas, Samuel C. (Mex. Mil. Cert. No. 1.)

MILITARY AVIATION.

Mexico enjoys the distinction of being the first country to have employed aeroplanes in actual warfare. During the Constitucionalista campaigns against the Diaz *régime*, and, later, against the Villista uprising, a motley assortment of aeroplanes was purchased in the United States and American aviators were engaged to fly them. Four Mexican officers and one civilian were also sent to the United States for training as aviators.

In spite of the questionable quality of the flying *matériel* thus gathered, and the not less doubtful military value of aerial mercenaries, the small Constitucionalista Flying Corps proved quite useful in sundry patrol and reconnaissance work, particularly in the suppression of the Villista guerilla forces.

A group of Mexican Army Pilots, together with Capt. Guillermo Villasana, the Chief of the Technical Department of the Military Aircraft Factory.

A group of Mexican Military Pilots,

409a

With the stabilisation of the Constitucionalista regime, the American aviators were discharged and steps were taken to establish a regular Flying Corps.

In 1915, at the instance of Major Alberto Salinas, Mexico's first military aviator and a nephew of President Carranza, an Aviation Department was created in the Mexican War Office, and a military aerodrome and flying school were organised at Valbuena, near Mexico City.

Owing to the difficulty of obtaining a satisfactory type of training machine from Europe, owing also to the then strained relations with the United States, it was at the same time decided to begin the construction of national aeroplanes and thus create an indigenous source of supply.

Capt. Guillermo Villasana, Technical Director of the Mexican Government's Aircraft Factory.

Colonel Alberto Salinas, the founder of Mexican Military Aviation.

The Superintendent of the Government Aircraft Factory, Senor Santarini, with a Mexican pilot and one of the Mexican-built Anzani engines, known as the Aztatl.

Two Views of a Mexican-built Twin-fuselage Biplane.

MEXICAN AEROPLANES.

An aeroplane factory was organised at Valbuena, and there Blériot and Morane-Saulnier type machines were built and fitted with such aero-engines as had survived the revolutionary campaigns or could be obtained elsewhere.

A number of tractor biplanes were also built, and eventually the factory produced a satisfactory type of airscrew, the Anahuac, and an Anzani type engine, called Aztatl.

In 1917 an arrangement was made with the Hispano-Suiza Co., of Barcelona, whereby the manufacturing rights of their engines were acquired, and the equipment and organisation of a Mexican aero-engine factory was apparently entrusted to Spanish engineers.

In February, 1918, the Military Aviation Factory produced to the designs of its director, Senor Francisco Santarini, and Captain Guillermo Villasana, Chief of the Technical Department, a one-seater fighting-scout fitted with a 150 h.p. Hispano-Suiza engine. The characteristics of this machine, which is officially termed a *Microplano*, are the following :—

Specification.

Type of machine	Mexican Scout Biplane
Name or type No. of Machine .	Microplano Veloz.
Purpose for which intended ..	Single-seater Fighter.
Overall span, upper plane ..	8.00 metres.
Span of lower plane ..	6.88 metres.
Surface area	18 sq. metres.
Interplane gap	1,5 metres.
Overall length	6.60 metres.
Maximum height..	2.55 metres.
Speed, horizontal..	190-220 km.p.h.
Area of elevators	1.73 sq. metres.
Area of rudder	.76 sq. metres.
Gross weight	650 kgs.
Net weight	460 kgs.
Useful load	190 kgs.
Engine type and h.p.	Hispano-Suiza; 150-160 h.p.
Airscrew, revs.	Anahuac

The Government-built " Microplano."

The Mexican " Microplano Veloz."

The " Microplano " in skeleton form before being covered.

411a

3 F

MEXICAN AEROPLANES.

Various other types have been constructed, including the training machine described in the following specification :—

MEXICAN GOVERNMENT TWO-SEATER BIPLANE.

(Constructed in the Mexican National Aeronautical Workshops.)

Type of machine..	Mexican Two-seater Biplane.
Name or type No. of machine..	Series A.
Purpose for which intended ..	General purposes.
Span	10.15 metres.
Total surface of wings ..	35.2 sq. metres.
Engine type and h.p. ..	"Aztatl" 6-cyl. Radial ; 80 h.p.
Load per sq. metre ..	18.76 kgs.
Weight per h.p...	8.2 kgs.
Tank capacity in hours..	40 litres petrol; 20 litres oil.
Performance.	
Speed low down	90 k.p.h.
Disposable load apart from fuel	140 kgs.
Total weight of machine loaded	520 kgs.

A Mexican-built Monoplane.

PERUVIAN.

MILITARY AEROPLANES.

The Peruvian Government has made a special grant for aviation students, and war machines are projected. Actual order to end of 1912 was one *Avro* aeroplane, which was not delivered.

MILITARY AVIATION.

The creation of a fifth arm of the Army is seriously contemplated, and although no flying material is presently available, two Peruvian Army officers, 2nd Lieut. Henrique Ruiz and Aspirant Guillerme Proetgel, were sent in 1917 to El Palomar, the Argentine military flying school, wherefrom they successfully graduated.

412a   Group of Mexican Service Machines.

NORWEGIAN.

Aeronautical Journals :—
Aeroplanet, 6, Kongensgaten, Christiania.

THE NORWEGIAN ARMY FLYING CORPS.

Inspector General :—Colonel G. Grüner.

Staff officer :—Captain H. Norby.

Director of the army aeroplane factory :—Captain E. Sem-Jacobsen.

Assistant officers :—Pr. lieutnant Th. Gulliksen and O· Seippel.

Engine-engineer :—Captain T. Klingenberg.

Chief of the central flying schools :—Pr. Lieut. A. Tellefsen.

Chief pilot :—Pr. lieutnant H. Crawfurd-Jensen.

Chief of Sonnenfjellske squadron :—Captain T. Vetlesen.

Flight commanders :—Pr. lieutnants G. Gottenborg and T. Ibsen.

Chief of Nordenfjellske squadron :—Pr. lieutnant G. Bull.

Chief of Nord-Norges squadron :—Pr. lieutnant E. Haganæs.

Flying officers :—Pr. lieutnants A. Berghoff, E. Boe, K, Sundby, L. Feiring, Chr. Hellesen, Sec. lieutnants E. Herseth. E. D. Meyer, and I. A. Brandt.

AVIATION CENTRES.

Kjeller aerodrome.

Værnes flying ground.

Ovrevand flying ground.

Kjeller aerodrome is situated near Lillestrom (20 km. from the capital, Christiania). This place is the centre of all flying with aeroplanes. Here are the Flying Schools, Sennenfjellske Squadron, and the Army Aeroplane Factory.

Værnes, the flying ground of Nordenfjellske, is situated 20 km. from Trondhjem, near the railway station, Stjordalen.

Ovrevand, the flying ground of Nord-Norges Squadron is situated in Salangen, near the town Harstad.

MANUFACTURERS OF AIRCRAFT.

1. The Army Aeroplane Factory (hærens flyvemaskinfabrik), Kjeller pr. Lillestrom.

2. The Navy Seaplane Factory (marinens flyvebaatfabrik), Horten.

3. A/S. Norsk Aeroplanfabrik, Chr. Hellesen, Tansberg.

FLYING SCHOOLS.

The Army Flying School (hærens flyvevesens skoler), Kjeller pr. Lillestrom.

The Navy Flying School, (marinens flyveskoler), Horten.

✺ The latest organisation of the Army Flying Corps is dated from February, 1917.

COMMERCIAL AVIATION.

1918 saw the formation of the first three Norwegian aircraft enterprises—first, the Nordisk Luftkraft A/S, which arranged the first Scandinavian aero exhibition in Christiania, 1918, and an emergency aerial mail by Lieut. Riiser-Larsen on a Thulin-built Morane monoplane, when the railway service was interrupted by embankment slip.

Secondly, the Norwegian Air Shipping Co., to which the public has been asked to subscribe in small shares, and of which Capt. Dehli, of the Navy, is technical director. So far nothing has been done, but the company will make its chief aim the establishment of national aerial lines, owing to the limits placed upon railway lines on account of the mountainous character of the country ; and, further, will run a North Sea line to Great Britain, and, together with Swedish and Danish firms, a line to Gothenburg and Copenhagen.

The third enterprise is the Norwegian Aeroplane Works, Ltd., in Orsnes per Tonsberg, formed on June 4th, 1918, with a stock capital of towards £30,000. No aircraft have been turned out yet, but scale drawings are shown of a number of contemplated designs. Repairs of automobiles, motors, and boats are undertaken.

MILITARY AND NAVAL AVIATION.

Being the last of the three Scandinavian countries to enter upon aviation activities, Norway leads at present, which fact it owes chiefly to its good connections with England, wherefrom it has during the years of war been successful in drawing equipment, even if not of the very latest active service mounts.

As has been the case, too, in Sweden and Norway, like even the Allied warfaring countries, Henry and Maurice Farman biplanes made the chief composition of both the Army and the Naval Flying Services, both before and while expanding early in the war.

The chief naval air station is by the Royal Dock yard in Horten, and other stations are along the coasts of the North Sea and Skager Rak, like Christiansand, while the main Army flying ground is at Lillestrom, near Christiania.

The respective Government factories are at each of the two centres, under the command of Captain Dehli (Navy), and Captain Sem-Jacobsen (Army), the same officers commanding formerly the flying services. Colonel Grüner is now chief of the Army Corps.

The Army factory has built both Henry and Maurice Farman Longhorn and " Horace " Farman models, for which the Frederiksstad Mechanical Works produced 130 h.p. Renault motors. While of advanced types monocoque scouts with snow-skates for winter flying, equipped with 150 h.p. Hispano-Suiza engines, that were fetched early from Spain, and a two-seater patrol biplane of British influenced outlines and powered by a R.A.F. motor, have been produced. B.E. and Avro biplanes have further been acquired in England.

The Navy long stuck to a twin-float Farman type pusher biplane with F.E. tail fin fashion, equipped first with Curtiss motors, and next with some 170 h.p. Sunbeam engines, obtained from England. Various Naval flying officers, like Lieuts. Lützow-Holm and Rüser-Lassen were allowed to undergo a war instruction course at a British Naval flying school, and some 130 h.p. Clerget-engined Sopwith " Baby " seaplanes were acquired.

Nielsen and Winther, in Copenhagen, built a tractor school seaplane for the Norwegian Naval Air Service, equipped with a 100 h.p. Swedish-built Scania-Vabis Mercédès motor.

Monocoque-bodied Biplane (150 h.p. Hispano-Suiza engine). Built at the Norwegian Army Aircraft Factory, and fitted with ski for use on snow.

PORTUGUESE.

Aerial Societies :—
Ae C. de Portugal (Praça dos Restoradores, 16, Lisbon.

Aerial Journals :—
Rivista Aeronautica (Ae. C. Journal).

Flying Grounds :—
Campo do Seigcal. (Military School, 6 hangars.)
Mounchavo de Pavoa. (Private, 5 hangars.)

The Portuguese flying service has its earliest roots in 1912, when an agitation in favour of providing the Army with aeroplanes resulted in the subscription by the public of fairly large sums for the purchase of aeroplanes, and a *Maurice Farman*, a *Voisin*, and an *Avro* were actually purchased during that year. Either because the particular political crisis which the agitation for aircraft was intended to conceal was successfully tided over—or for some other reason of State —nothing beyond these purchases and the drawing up of various schemes for a national flying school occurred at that time.

From information contained in " Revista Aeronautica," the official organ of the Aero Club of Portugal, it appears that early in 1916 the proposed flying school was actually inaugurated.

Apparently, the proposals which were drawn up in 1912 by Mr. H. V. Roe, on his visit with the *Avro* biplane, delivered to the Portuguese Government after tests by the late Mr. Copland Perry, have been to a large extent followed, and the school has started operations on the site recommended by him.

The position—if this is indeed the case—is very nearly ideal, considering the mountainous nature of the country, providing a very large natural aerodrome—a long frontage on to an excellent stretch of water for seaplanes' work. In addition, there is direct railway and water communication with Lisbon.

Previous to the inauguration of the school, a number of officers were sent to France and England to learn to fly.

Of these, Lieut. José Barbosa de Santos Leite, of the Army, and Lieut. Artur de Sacadura Freire Cabral, of the Navy, and Senor Antonio Joaquin Caseiro, a non-executive Naval officer, proceeded to Chartres, in November, 1915.

All these obtained their pilot's certificates by March of 1916, and then proceeded to qualify for their military brevet at various French Army Schools.

Three Army officers, Senors A. Torres, A. Maia, and A. Portela, qualified for their civil brevets at the Ruffy-Baumann School, at Hendon, during June and July, 1916, and qualified as military pilots at one of the R.F.C. schools.

It may be presumed that these officers now form the instructional staff at the Portuguese flying school.

As to the actual organisation of the school, very little can be discovered. " Revista Aeronautica " contains pages of regulations for the conduct of the school, but they are all of the nature of " King's Regulations " of very considerable importance actually, but of very little general interest.

Provision is made in these regulations for training aeroplane pilots, airship pilots, and free balloon pilots, and their appropriate observers, and also for mechanics of all grades.

A commission has been sent to the Higher School of Aeronautics at Lausanne—which may be considered as an aeronautical university—and it may be assumed that this commission has as its object the institution of a fairly thorough course of theoretical training, and it may be fairly safely expected that the technical side of the instruction will be so extremely complete.

At the same time, considering the large number of extremely good horsemen to be found among Portuguese officers, it may be expected that at least a fair proportion of excellent pilots should be turned out.

The Chief Portuguese Flying School at Villa Nuova della Reinha.

" Revista Aeronautica," of Lisbon, states further :—

Four officers in training for military pilots were sent to the United States in 1915, to attend the Signal Corps Aviation School in S. Diego, California, but when Portugal declared war, they could no longer be trained in the States, so returned to Europe, finishing their instruction at the Chartres School. All of them obtained their certificates between September and December, 1916, and went on to the Caudron School, at Juvisy, where three of them obtained the School certificate in February, 1917, the fourth having been recalled to the Lisbon War Ministry for organisation work.

A fifth officer took the Caudron courses, which included training in artillery reconnaissance, chasing, fighting, and aerial acrobatics. These officers were from artillery, cavalry, and infantry units.

SPANISH.

(By Captain Don Emilio Herrera Linares.)

Aerial Societies:—

Real Aëro Club de España (Carrera de San Jeronimo, 8, Madrid).
Asociacion de Locomocion Aérea (20, Cataluna Sq., Barcelona).
Real Aero Club de Barcelona.
    „   „   de San Sebastian.
    „   „   de Santander.
    „   „   de Granada.

Aerial Journals:—

Boletin Oficial de la Asociacion de Locomocion Aérea, 20, Cataluna Sq., Barcelona (monthly).

España Automovil, 5, Isabel II Sq., Madrid. Official Organ, Spanish R. Ae. C.

Revista de Locomocion Aerea, 20, Cataluna Sq., Barcelona (monthly).

Heraldo Deportivo, Villalar, 1, Madrid.

The Spanish Royal Flying Service.—A group of the chief aviation officers at a Spanish aerodrome, with a number of " Flécha " type Spanish-built biplanes lined up ready to start.

THE SPANISH AERONAUTICAL SERVICES.

By courtesy of Colonel Señor Don Julio Rodrigeuz Mourelo, formerly Director of Air Services, it is possible to publish the following particulars of the development of the Spanish Flying Services, and the Editor expresses his indebtedness to Captain Don Emilio Herrera Linares, Officer Commanding the Aerodrome of Cuatro Vientos, for sending the information by permission of Colonel Rodriguery.

The Servicio de Aeronautica Militar is commanded by a Colonel-Director and a Second Chief, and has two wings; the Aerostacion Wing, which is concerned with captive and free balloons and airships, and the Aviacion Wing, which is concerned with aeroplanes and hydro-aeroplanes. Both wings are commanded by Comandantes (Majors).

The Parque de Aerostacion (Balloon Yard) is at Guadalajara, and the Aerodromo Central de Aviacion (Main Military Aerodrome) is at Cuatro Vientos (Madrid).

There are five squadrons of land machines in Spain (Madrid, Alcalà, Sevilla, Guadalajara and Cartagena), and one of seaplanes at Cartagena.

In the Spanish part of Morocco are three squadrons (Melilla, Tetouan and Arcila).

SPANISH AEROPLANES.

SPANISH PILOTS.

The following are military pilots of the First Category, or Class, according to priority of date in qualifying :—

Captain of Engineers, Don Alfredo Kindelan Duany.
Captain of Engineers, Don Emilio Herrera Linares.
Staff-Major, Don Alfonso Bayo Lucia.
Major of Infantry, Don Carlos Alonso Ilera.
Captain of Infantry, Don Julio Rios.
Lieut. of Cavalry, Don Angel Martinez de Baños.
Capt. of Engineers, Don Eduardo Barron Ramos.
Med. 1°, Don Antonio Perez Nuñez.
Captain of Infantry, His Royal Highness el Infante Don Alfonso de Orleans.
Capt. of Infantry, Don Luis Moreno Abella.
Capt. of Infantry, Don Antonio Zubia Casas.
Capt. of Artillery, Don Angel Pastor Velasco.
Lieut. of Cavalry, Don Roberto White Santiago.
Lieut. of Engineers, Don Luis Sousa Peco.
Capt. of Artillery, Don Carlos Cifuentes Rodrigueez.
Capt. of Engineers, Don José Ortiz Echagüe.
Capt. of Infantry, Don José Valencia Fernandez.
Capt. of Engineers, Don Genaro Olivié Hermida.
Lieut. in the Navy, Don Juan Viniegra Aréjula.
Capt. of Engineers, Don Fernando Balseiro Flore.
Lieut. in the Navy, Don Francisco Gil de Sola.
Comm. in the Navy, Don Enrique Navarro Margati
Comm. in the Navy, Don Felix Cheregine Buitrago.
Capt. of Infantry, Don José Espinosa Arias.
Lieut. in the Navy, Don Pablo Mateo Sagasta.
Lieut. of Infantry, Don Felipe Matanza Vazquez.
Capt. of Cavalry, Don José Gonzalez Camo.
Capt. of Engineers, Don Emilio Vaqueras Ruiz.
Lieut. of Infantry, Don Apolinar Saenz de Buruaga.
Capt. of Infantry, Don Juan Vallespin Zayas.
Lieut. of Artillery, Don Luis Lopez de Ayala.
Lieut. of Cavalry, Don Jesus Varela Castro.
Major of Engineers, Don Gonzalo Zamora Andreu.
Capt. of Infantry, Don Julio Balseiro Flore.
Capt. of Infantry, Don Manuel Loma Arce.
Capt. of Cavalry, Don José Romeo Sigler.
Capt. of Engineers, Don José Maria Laviña.
Lieut. of Artillery, Don Pedro Cubillo Avila.
Capt. of Artillery, Don José Gonzalez Estéfani.
Capt. of Engineers, Don Francisco Leon Trejo.
Capt. of Infantry, Don Alfonso Fanjul Goñi.
Capt. of Engineers, Don Alberto Alvarez Rementeria.
Capt. of Cavalry, Don Angel Riaño Herrero.
Capt. of Infantry, Don Joaquin Gonzalez Gallarza.
Lieut. of Artillery, Don César Gomez Lucia.
Staff-Capt., Don Luis Gonzalez Victoria.
Lieut. of Infantry, Don Francisco Martin Prats.
Com. in the Navy, Don Fernando Sartorius y Diaz de Mendoza.
Lieut. of Cavalry, Don Francisco Bustamante de la Rocha.
Staff-Capt., Don José Aymaz Mareca.

Capt. of Infantry, Don Antonio Dominguez Olarte.
Lieut. of Artillery, Don Manuel Montero Echeverria.
Lieut. of Cavalry, Don Fernando de la Macorra.
Lieut. in the Navy, Don Pedro Pablo Fernandez.
Capt. of Artillery, Don Manuel Perez Seoane y Diaz de Baldés.
Lieut. of Infantry, Don Felipe Diaz Sandino.
Lieut. of Infantry, Don José Navarro Marbati.

First Category Military Pilots of 1917.

Lieut. of Infantry, Don Alberto Moreno Abella.
Lieut. of Artillery, Don Carlos Espana.
Capt. of Engineers, Don José Fernandez Checa.
Capt. of Cavalry, Don José Rojas Rojas.
Lieut. of Artillery, Don Fernando Cifuentes.
Lieut. of Infantry, Don Tomas Barron y Ramos de Sotomayor.
Capt. of Cavalry, Don José Legorburo.
Lieut. of Cavalry, Don Francisco Javier Enrile.
Lieut. of Engineers, Don Luis Manzanaque.
Lieut. of Cavalry, Don Domingo Martinez Pison.
Lieut. of Engineers, Don Miguel Ramirez.
Lieut. of Infantry, Don Juan Valverde.
Lieut. of Infantry, Don Alberto Bayo.
Sub-Lieut. in the Navy, Don José Maria Tamayo.
Lieut. of Cavalry, Don Angel Riaño.

Capt. of Engineers, Don Antonio Peñalver.
Lieut. of Infantry, Don Arsenio Rios Angueso.
Lieut. of Infantry, Don Julio Garcia de Càceres.
Lieut. of Engineers, Don José Martinez de Aragon.
Capt. of Engineers, Don Pio Fernandez Mulero.
Lieut. of Engineers, Don Manuel Bada Vasallo.
Sub-Lieut. in the Navy, Don Enrique Navarro Marbati.
Lieut. of Engineers, Don Vicente Ros Miranda.
Major of Infantry, Don Tàrsilo Ugarte.
Capt. of Infantry, Don Antonio de la Rocha.
Capt. of Engineers, Don Antonio Navarro.
Capt. of Nav. Infantry, Don Carlos del Corral.
Capt. of Nav. Infantry, Don Serafin de la Piñera.
Lieut. of Infantry, Don Antonio Perdomo Benitez.
Lieut. of Infantry, Don Carmelo de las Morenas.
Lieut. of Infantry, Don Francisco Martorell.
Lieut. of Cavalry, Don Carlos Morenes Carvajal.
Lieut. of Cavalry, Don Francisco Riera Peña.
Lieut. of Artillery, Don José Martin Montalvo.

Killed in 1917.

Capt. Don Emilio Gimenez Millas (Engineers).
Capt. Don Juan Vallespin Zayas (Infantry).
Civilian Pilot, Don Salvador Hedilla.

A view from an aeroplane of the great Spanish Aerodrome and the quarters and workshops of the Spanish Royal Flying Service at Cuatro-Vientos, near Madrid.

SPANISH AEROPLANES.

THE CHIEFS OF SERVICES.

The following are the Chiefs of the various Aeronautical Services :—

Director of the Air Service : Colonel Senor Don Rafael Moreno y Gil de Borja (Engineers).

Second Chief of the Service : Lieut.-Col. Don Vicente Garcia Del Campo (Engineers).

Chief of Detail of Aerostacion : Lieut.-Col. Don Francisco de Paula Rojas y Rubio (Engineers).

Chief of Aerostacion : Major Don Celestino Garcia Antunez (Engineers).

Chief of Aviacion : Major Don Alfonso Bayo Lucia (Staff).

Chief of Detail of Aviacion : Major Don Carlos Alonso Ilera (Infantry).

Inspector of Aviation Works : Major Don Aristides Fernandez Mathews (Engineers).

Instructor of Observers' School : Staff Major Don Luis Gonzalo Victoria.

CHIEF INSTRUCTORS.

Captain of Engineers, Don Emilio Herrera Linares (Commanding at Cuatro Vientos).

Captain of Infantry, Don Julio Rios Angueso.

Captain of Cavalry, Don Luis Riaño Herrero.

Doctor on Staff, Don Antonio Perez Nuñez.

Lieutenant of Cavalry, Don Angel Martinez de Baños.

Lieutenant of Cavalry, Don Jésus Varela Castro.

THE SPANISH AERODROME.

The following is a list of the Chief Spanish Aerodromes, together with the rank and names of the officers commanding :—

Cuatro Vientos.—Captain of Engineers, Don Emilio Herrera Linares.

Guadalajara.—Major of Engineers, Don Gonzalo Zamora Andreu.

Jetafe (New).—Captain of Infantry, Don Julio Rios Angueso.

Los Alcaceres (Cartagena).—Captain of Infantry, Don José Valencia Fernandez.

Sevilla (New).—Captain of Engineers, Don Alberto Alvarez Rementeria.

The following are the aerodromes in Africa, with their Commanding Officers :

Arcila.—Naval Lieut., Don Pedro Pablo Hernandez.

Tetuan.—Captain of Engineers, Don Emilio Baquera Ruiz.

Zeluan.—Staff Captain, Don José Aymaz.

SPANISH FLYING SCHOOLS

Military School of Aviation.—Cuatro Venitos (Madrid).

National School of Aviation.—Getafe (Madrid).

The Director of the National School of Aviation is Don Alfredo Kindelan Duany.

Civil School of Barcelona.—Pujol y Comabella y Co.

Civilian School also at Santander and Jetafe.

There is also the Aerodrome of the Sociedad Ispañola de Construcciones Aeronauticas at Santander.

MILITARY AEROPLANE.

Various types of Spanish military aeroplanes were published last year. Two of them are retained herewith. No important change has taken place in the types used.

A new fighting machine, called the "Espana," has been evolved. It is not yet permissible to illustrate it.

THE SPANISH AERONAUTICAL INDUSTRY.

The chief manufacturers of aircraft are : Garde y Escoriaza, at Zaragoza ; Pujol y Comabella, at Barcelona ; Sociedad Española de construcciones Aeronauticas, at Santander ; La Hispano-Suiza, at Barcelona (motors) ; Elizalde, at Barcelona (motors) ; Baradal y Ereter, at Barcelona (motors) ; and Amalio Diaz, at Getafe (propellers).

A Spanish-built Biplane, apparently a combination of the " Flécha " type with Curtiss influence. Built by the Spanish Flying Service.

SWEDISH.

Aerial Societies :—

Svenska Aeronautiska Sallskapet. Nybrogaten 3, Stockholm.
Kungl. Automobil Klubben, Stockholm.

Aerial Journals :—

Svensk Motortidning, Stockholm.

Motor, Vasagatan 38, Stockholm. (Subscription : 10 kroner per annum, Sweden ; 16 kroner, foreign.) Monthly.

CHIEF AVIATION CENTRES IN SWEDEN.

Malmslatt : Military aviation grounds, sheds, works, etc.

Ljungbyhed : Civil aviation grounds, sheds, works, etc.

Furusund : Civil aviation school in the winter, sheds, etc.

SWEDISH FLYING SCHOOLS.

Thulins flying school, **Ljungbyhed.**

Northern Aviatic Company's flying school, **Furusund** by Stockholm.

MANUFACTURERS OF AIRCRAFT.

Thulin Aeroplane Manufacturing Company, Ltd., **Landskrona.**

Northern Aviatic Company, Ltd., Tellusborg, **Midsommarkransen** by Stockholm.

Palsons' Aeroplane Manufacturing Company, Ltd., **Malmö.**

Aviators.

(The number against any name is, unless otherwise stated, the Ae. C. Swedish pilot certificate.)

Cederström (1)	Beckmann (38)	Brynolf (75)
†Hamilton (2)*	Norrman (39)	Flory (76)
Dahlbeck (3)	Birger (40)	†Pfuff (77)
Fjellbeck (4)	Egnell (41)	Kreli (78)
Ångström (5)	Sandberg (42)	Lindberg (79)
†Jungner (6)*	Cronhielm (43)	Hedenmarck (80)
von Porat (7)	†de Maré (44)	Sjöberg (81)
Werner (8)	Högberg (45)	†Culström (82)
Sundstedt (9)	Eguström (46)	Kellberg (83)
Thulin (10)	Velin (47)	Soderström (84)
†Silon (11)	Elliot (48)	Harggström (85)
Bjornberg (12)	Svensson (49)	Unander-Scharin
Rudberg (13)	Vorberg (50)	(86)

Krokstedt (14)	Rosencrantz (51)	Seton (87)
Lindin (15)	Borggren-Franck	Eric-Ericsson (88)
von Segebaden(16)	(52)	Florman (89)
Hygerth (17)	Clavius (53)	Janse (90)
Björklund (18)	Petre (54)	Letterlund (91)
Bergquist (19)	von Johnstone(55)	Cederström (92)
Germundson (20)	Ligner (56)	Tparre (93)
Winbladh (21)	Gyllenberg (57)	Hamilton (94)
Netzler (22)	Schjölin (58)	Thulin (95)
†von Blixen	Boström (59)	Svanbeck (96)
Finecke (23)	Eckerström (60)	Holmström (97)
†Malmquist (27)	Hiernspetz (61)	Hierta (98)
Kindberg (25)	Rönström (62)	Böckström (99)
de la Gardie (26)	Peyron (63)	Agnell (100)

Haquinius (27)	Buggren (64)	Warvrinsky (101)
†Mannstrom (28)	Söderström (65)	Gullberg (102)
Nordensvan (29)	†Tvislaw (66)	Dickson (103)
†Sandstrom (30)	Sturnström (67)	Westman (104)
Nordquist (31)	Carlson (68)	Lind (105)
von Mantzer (32)	Rodehn (69)	Forsbeck (106)
Holmer (33)	Hullström (70)	Driefaldt (107)
Lundquist (34)	Falke (71)	Gyllenberg (108)
Florman (35)	Mörling (72)	Braathen (109)
Bergman (36)	Hedenstierna (73)	Bergström (110)
Herrström (37)	Lindberg (74)	Hildesheim (111)

*Dead, but not from flying accident.   †Killed.

Swedish Flying Officers taken immediately after a long-distance flight to Stockholm.

SWEDISH AEROPLANES.

MILITARY AND NAVAL AEROPLANES.

The Army possesses an unknown number of *Albatros*, *Morane* and *Thulin* aeroplanes.

The Navy possesses an unknown number of *Morane* and *Thulin* seaplanes.

The Committee for the Air Defence of Stockholm has six original *Albatros* scouts, which are in case of need to be flown by voluntary civil aviators of yearly training.

Further private aeroplanes are in the possession of the Thulin Flying School at Ljungby Heath (a dozen *Bleriot* and *Morane*, ordinary type, and *Parasol* monoplanes) and of the school of the Northern Aircraft Co., by Stockholm (two *Albatros* biplanes with snowskates for training on ice during the winter, and converted to seaplanes for summer training.)

PERSONAL NOTES ON THE CHIEF MEN CONCERNED WITH THE DEVELOPMENT OF AVIATION IN SWEDEN.

The first aviator in Sweden was Baron Carl Cederström, who took his certificate at the Blériot school at Pau in 1910. When coming back to Sweden, he made a lot of show and exhibition flights at nearly every great place in the country, as well as in certain places in Norway, and did a lot of work to wake the people up to understanding the possibilities of aviation. Being a director of a large automobile concern, he also at once grasped the commercial and business side of the aeroplane movement.

For a long time he was the manager of the aeroplane department of Södertelge Verkstäder, a concern which has now ceased to make aeroplanes.

In 1916 he started a concern for the making of aeroplanes, the Northern Aviatic Company, Ltd., the works of which are situated at Tellusborg, near Stockholm. He was the managing director of this company. The concern has made a great number of machines, both for the Swedish government and civilian persons in Sweden, as well as for the governments of the other neutral states in the North, especially for Finlandia.

In July, 1918, when he was out for a flight from Stockholm to Finland as passenger in an aeroplane, piloted by Captain Krokstedt, one of the best Swedish naval aviators, he met his death. The aeroplane got lost at sea in a thick fog, and both pilot and passenger were drowned.

Another person, who has contributed largely to the development of aviation matters in Sweden, is Mr. Lars Fjällbäck, M.E. Mr. Fjällbäck took his brêvet in France in 1911. However, he soon left actual flying and went over to the manufacturing of aeroplanes.

He was the leader of a company which made the first Swedish-built aeroplane for the Swedish army in 1913.

Later he was appointed to the Northern Aviatic Company as chief constructor, and after the death of Baron Cederström he was promoted to managing director of the concern, and is still working as such.

Three-quarter Front View of Swedish Triplane, used for training.

Side View of a Swedish-built Triplane with Rotary engine.

The pilot Phil. Dr. Enoch Thulin's name is also closely connected to the history of the Swedish aviation. Like the foregoing, he also took his brêvet at a French flying school. After coming back to Sweden, he made many meritorious long distance flights, and also a great number of exhibition flights.

One of his best known flights was made from Paris to Landskrona, Sweden, in a *Morane* monoplane. On this trip, his friend and constant helper, Lieutenant Ask, accompanied him as passenger.

He also started the Thulins Aeroplane Manufacturing Co., Ltd., in Landskrona, in 1915. These works have developed from a very small scale to one of the biggest industrial concerns in Sweden. They are exclusively intended for the manufacturing of aeroplanes and aero engines, but will after the war also turn their attention to other products.

The concern has sold most of its production to the Swedish and other neutral governments, especially to Holland.

Dr. Thulin has been the managing director of these works from the beginning, but has now left his place to Mr. Hakansson, M.E.

Captain in the Royal Engineers G. von Porat is also one of the more noteworthy persons in the Swedish aviation world. In 1912 he was one of the first three Swedish military aviators, and was sent to the Nieuport school in France, took his brêvet and did later a lot of successful flying on *Nieuport* monoplanes.

In 1914 he had a severe accident, and was in hospital for a long time. After that he was appointed as constructor at the Södertelge Verkstäder aeroplane department, and has constructed and built several successful types of aeroplanes.

Meritorious flights made during 1918 by Swedish aviators:— Owing to regulations now in force, no details can be given about flights done in service by military aviators. And owing to well-known causes civil flying has been prohibited, with a very few exceptions. In May, however, Dr. Thulin with a monoplane flew from Christiania, Norway, to Landskrona (near Malmö), Sweden. The distance was 500 km. and was covered in 4 hours. Strong headwind prevailed throughout the trip.

On April 27th, Flight-Lieutenant Kindberg on a private hydro-aeroplane, with a passenger, flew from Stockholm to Abo, Finland and back right across the Baltic Sea. The distance is about 300 kilometres each way, the shortest journey was accomplished in 2 hours and 20 minutes. This flight is noteworthy on account of its being the first flight for a commercial purpose from Sweden to a foreign country.

Swedish Flying Officers and an Aeroplane North of the Arctic Circle.

Front View of Swedish-built Esant Monoplane (with ailerons).

THE NORTHERN AVIATIC COMPANY.

N.A.B.

1. **Type 9.**

TWO-SEATED RECONNAISSANCE BIPLANE.

Total length	8·0 metres.
Total width	13·7 metres.
Total height	3·5 metres.
Engine	110 h.p. Mercédès fixed.
Load carried	400 kg.
Speed	120 kil. an hour.

2. **Type 11.**

TWO-SEATED DOUBLE ENGINED RECONNAISSANCE BIPLANE.

Total length	8·55 metres.
Total width	16·16 metres.
Total height	3·6 metres.
Engines..	Two 110 or 160 h.p. Mercédès, Benz or Scania-Vabis fixed.
Load carried	800 kg.
Speed for the 160 h.p. ..	140 kil. an hour.

3. **Type 12.**

TWO-SEATED DOUBLE ENGINED RECONNAISSANCE BIPLANE.

Same as above type, but equipped as hydro.

4. **Type 14.**

TWO-SEATED FLYING-BOAT.

Total length	8·6 metres.
Total width	15·0 metres.
Total height	3·55 metres.
Engine	160 h.p. Benz, Mercédès or Scania-Vabis fixed.
Load carried	500 kg.
Speed	130 kil. an hour.

Three-quarter Front View of Northern Aviatic Co.'s Biplane. Type 9.

Three-quarter Rear View of Northern Aviatic Co.'s Twin-engined Seaplane. Type 12.

423a

THE NORTHERN AVIATIC CO.—*continued.*

5. **Type 17.**

ONE-SEATED SCOUTING BIPLANE.

Total length	6·7 metres.
Total width	10·0 metres.
Total height	3·0 metres.
Engine	110 h.p. Mercédès.
Load carried	300 kg.
Speed	155 kil. an hour.

The Pålson Single-seater Sporting Biplane.

Three-quarter Front View of Northern Aviatic Co's Biplane. Type 17.

PÅLSON Aeroplanes. Malmö.

These aeroplanes are of rather unconventional design, the chief idea of the constructor being a device for altering the position and angle of the top planes.

The aeroplanes are built from three-ply wood, fuselage, wings and rudders.

The concern is a new one, machines are under construction, but the value of the special arrangements seems rather doubtful. No tests are yet made.

1. **Type 1.**

ONE-SEATED SPORTING BIPLANE.

Total length	5·7 metres.
Total width	8 metres.
Total height	2·3 metres.
Engine	50 h.p. Gnôme or Palson rotary.

2. **Type 2.**

PASSENGER-CARRYING BIPLANE.

Total length	11·7 metres.
Total width	22·3 metres.
Total height	5·3 metres.
Engine	300 h.p. fixed.
Load carried	Six passengers and fuel for six hours.

Shaded Sketch of the Pålson Single-seater.

Side View of the Palson Passenger Biplane.

SWEDISH AEROPLANES.

THULIN *Aeroplanes.* Landskrona.

Since America's entry into the war it is safe to state that the aircraft works of Enoch Thulin in Landskrona, Sweden, are the largest neutral aviation concern left.

When the war broke out there were two small Swedish aeroplane factories, one a department of the well-known Södertelje works, under the management of the Swedish pioneer aviator, Baron Cederström, and holding rights and patterns from the Farman Brothers and the Gnôme engine company, the other one being that of Dr. E. Thulin.

Sundry accidents with the *Henry Farman* biplanes led the Södertelje Works to adopt the *Albatros* model, and to equip the biplanes with original German engines, till the whole Södertelje establishment was taken over by the Government for their important work, when the aircraft department passed into the possession of Dr. Thulin.

His efforts have during the war developed into a concern of imposing Scandinavian dimensions, with a staff of 800 workmen, by the combination of three factors,—personal enterprise, a favourable time and the presence of raw materials in Sweden itself.

The Thulin Aircraft Works have furnished both the Swedish and foreign neutral governments, including Denmark, these being supplied with *Morane-Saulnier* monoplanes and 80/90 h.p. Le Rhône type motors ; and Holland getting *Thulin* scout monoplanes and 100/120 h.p. Thulin rotary engines.

The Thulin Aircraft Works run both a flying school with a number of *Bleriot* and *Morane* monoplanes, where more than half of Sweden's aviators have taken their certificates, and an aerodynamical laboratory.

The chief, Dr. Thulin, looks behind on a successful career as an aviator. Among his notable flights were one from Paris to Landskrona in 1914 ; one from Malmö to Stockholm with photos of the Baltic Exhibition, just opened then, for a

newspaper in the Swedish capital ; and two days later a flight from Gothenberg to Copenhagen with Baron Blixen-Finecke as passenger that the latter might participate in horse races in both cities, the second time this great feat was done in history, the first being by a German sportsman.

E. H.

Unfortunately, since these notes were written, Dr. Thulin has been killed in an aeroplane accident on May 14th, 1919.—C G.G.

1. Type K.
ONE-SEATED SCOUT MONOPLANE.

Total length	6·5 metres.
Total width	9·1 metres.
Total height	2·55 metres.
Engine	90 h.p. rotary Thulin.
Load carried	185 kg.
Speed	130—145 kiloms. an hour.

2. Type L.A.
TWO-SEATED RECONNAISSANCE BIPLANE.

Total length	7·5 metres.
Total width	10·4 metres.
Total height	3·52 metres.
Engine	90 or 125 h.p. rotary Thulin.
Load carried	265 kg.
Speed	125 to 140 kil. an hour.

3. Type G.A.
TWO-SEATED RECONNAISSANCE BIPLANE.

Total length	9·48 metres.
Total width	17·2 metres.

Total height	3·54 metres.
Engine	160 h.p. Benz, Mercédès or Thulin fixed.
Load carried	400 kg.
Speed	118 kil. an hour.

4. Type F.A.
TWO-SEATED RECONNAISSANCE BIPLANE.

Total length	7·9 metres.
Total width	11·7 metres.
Total height	3·39 metres.
Engine	160 h.p. Benz, Mercédès or Thulin fixed.
Load carried	550 kg.
Speed	135 kil. an hour.

5. Type N.A.
ONE-SEATED SCOUTING BIPLANE.

Total length	5·85 metres.
Total width	7·9 metres.
Total height	2·45 metres.
Engine	125 h.p. Thulin rotary.
Load carried	300 kg.
Speed	165 kil. an hour.

Three-quarter Rear View of Thulin Monoplane.

Front View of Thulin Monoplane.

Three-quarter Front View of Thulin Biplane.

SWISS.

Aerial Societies :—

Aero Club Suisse (3, Hirschengraben, Berne).   Sec. : F. Filliot.

Aerial Journals :—

Bulletin de l'Aero Club Suisse (Berne).   Monthly.

Flying Grounds :—

Avenches.
Collex-Versoix (Club Suisse d'Aviation)
Lucerne.—60 acre park.   Sheds.
Petit Lancy, Geneva (Geneva Club).
Dübendorf bei Zurich.

Airship Station (with hangars) :—

Lucerne.

MILITARY AERONAUTICS IN SWITZERLAND.

The Swiss General Staff's Press Bureau published in 1916 a memorandum dealing with the development of aeronautics in the belligerent countries, and referring also to the present status of aeronautics in Switzerland.   Regarding the latter it says :—

" The war-born evolution of aircraft cannot but force us greatly to increase our aerial establishment if we want to remain efficient in this field, too.   Here it is necessary to consider that, unlike the Great Powers, who can keep large aircraft factories working even in time of peace, Switzerland does not possess a real aircraft industry.

" Therefore, if we have succeeded in building during the war aircraft of our own, it is chiefly due to the fact that our mobilisation recalled a number of engineers who were previously working in foreign countries.   The construction of aero-engines, which is of a more exacting nature than that of ordinary petrol engines, has also been successfully undertaken ; likewise, the training of pilots, which formerly was entirely dependent on foreign schools, is now satisfactorily done at home.

" Such is, then, briefly the development of national military aeronautics.   If some think that the progress realised was not rapid enough, one should keep in mind the great technical difficulties and the corresponding expense of creating and developing this new arm.   The Swiss people have—like their neighbours—generously contributed to the national subscription for military aeronautics in order to enable the Army to increase their aerial establishment."

This report permitted one to assume that the fund of the national subscription was then nearly exhausted, as a consequence of which the Confederacy undoubtedly authorised a considerable expenditure for military aviation.   It was also proposed to enlarge the kite-balloon branch of the Army, since those craft have proven highly valuable in the great war as fire-control stations.

* * *

Thanks to the successful construction of national aeroplanes, the Swiss Flying Corps had then become a reality.   Some time ago a squadron of 10 aeroplanes was seen over Zurich, whither it had flown from the Confederate Air Station of Dübendorf.   The first of a series of air bases (*points d'appui aérien*), which will be established in the future, had been created at Aarau, and Lt. Bider, the famous cross-Alps aviator, has been made the first Army Aviation Instructor. In order to prevent accidental violations of neutrality, Swiss aviators are under orders not to trespass on the following zone :—Yverdon—Lake of Neufchàtel—Bienne (Biel)—Soleure (Solothurn) —Aar—Lägern—Rorbas—Winterthur—St. Gall—Reichenau—Tödi—St. Gotthard—Berne Alps— Rochers de Nay.

* * *

The war has influenced the situation of Swiss aviators in various ways.   The Aero Club had certificated by October, 1916, 61 pilot-aviators ; 12 of these lost their lives accidentally, and about as many gave up their profession before the war.   Of the latter are Bianchi, Bucher, Gsell, Maffei, Salvioni, Schumacher, and Taddeoli.   Nine aviators, namely : Audemars, Bider, Burri, Comte, Cuendet, Durafour, Grandjean, Lugrin, and Parmelin, offered their services to the Army, and are, though mobilised, kept on the reserve list.   This enables them to look after their business ; thus it was that Audemars broke the world's height record in 1915 in France.   Durafour was engaged at Buc, and Burri is with the Franco-British Aviation Cie.

Among the Swiss who are not Service-bound, Domenjoz was on an exhibition tour in South America, and afterwards went to the United States.   Favre is chief-pilot of the Levasseur Works, and E. Baumann runs an aviation school at Acton.   The youngest Swiss aviator, the 19-year old Pasche, was then testing, apparently with little success, an aeroplane of his own design, at Lavaux.   Parmelin was in Geneva, and had to refuse advantageous offers from Russia and England, because the military authorities would not let him leave the country.

Among the Swiss aviators serving with the French *Aviation Militaire*, Blancpain fell on the field of honour.

To his name should be added that of Sergeant Théophile Ingold, of Escadrille N. 23, who died of injuries received during a reconnaissance.   He was recipient of a *citation à l'ordre de l'armée* and was proposed for the *Médaille militaire ;* he was a cousin of Karl Ingold, serving with the German Flying Corps.

Since the publication of these notes no further information is available.   The Swiss Authorities refuse to give any information of any kind.   However, as there are no original Swiss aeroplanes or engines of any note little is lost by the refusal.

TURKISH.

Having been without aircraft, as employed by the Italian opponent in the Tripolis war, Turkey had passed through the two Balkan wars with a stock of odd machines left, including the German *Harlan* and *Mars* makes, and the French *Rep*, *Nieuport*, and others.

When Turkey entered the late war, Germany had to supply both the equipment and organisation beside personnel for the nucleus of the Turkish Air Services, and very seldom did the name of any Osmanian pilot attain publicity, so that one can take it for granted that German pilots almost exclusively manned the Turkish aircraft, though they had Turkish officer observers on the main fronts of activities, namely, with land machines in the operations against Egypt and the Suez Canal, and employing seaplanes in the Dardanelles campaign.

The German officer who distinguished himself most on this front was Lieut. Buddecke, who fell later, after 12 victories, in the French theatre of war. The officer in command of the naval air station in Constantinople was Captain-Lieut. Langfeld, one of his most active pilots being Captain-Lieut. Liebmann, who has published a book of his experiences under the title " Dardanelles Pilots."

The land aeroplanes to be employed on the Turkish theatres of war included most German types, including modern scouts, contrary to the practice of the opponent in the far-off places, while the Gotha works were the main contractors for seaplanes.

Their first model supplied to Turkey was a re-modelled twin-float two-seater (brought out for the 1914 Warnemünde naval aircraft competition), equipped either with a 150 h.p. motor (Benz or Rapp) better known under its ultimate trade mark, B.M.W. or Bayern (Bavaria) engine, with the gunner observer in front of the pilot, serving the gun, mounted on the top plane in a standing position, as in the early *Nieuport* scouts.

This seaplane was equipped with a float-cum-wheel under-carriage, the shaft with the four wheels, one on each side of each float being mounted below them, and the floats serving as landing brakes by means of an aft extended added skid, as the biplanes had to be sent to Turkey by land, owing to Roumania refusing to grant a transit permit.

So the seaplanes were sent by rail to Herkulesbad, in Hungary, where they were erected and then flew across Roumania and Servia loaded with spares to Lom Polanka, in Bulgaria, whence transport facilities to Constantinople were again available.

That the Turks benefited later from the German experiences of improving speed and performance by paying attention to reducing head resistance from stream-line effect is evident from the later type, supplied in the repeat orders.

URUGUAY.

Aerial Societies :—

Aero Club Uruguayo, Montevideo.

Aerial Journals :—

None.

Flying Grounds :—

San Fernando, Montevideo. (Military Flying School) Director : Captain Juan Boiso Lanza.

MILITARY AVIATION.

The government is making a serious effort at creating an aerial arm. For this purpose a number of officers are being trained at the San Fernando Aerodrome, and eight aero-engines have been imported from the Argentine during 1917 for the equipment of training aeroplanes.

No further information is obtainable.

MILITARY AEROPLANES.

Lt. Frigierio was despatched about May, 1914, to Europe to purchase the nucleus of a small aerial fleet. Nothing worth mention has apparently occurred since. One aeroplane was bought for experimental purposes, and was afterwards smashed.

No fresh information is available.

U. S. A.

Aerial Societies :—

Aero Club of America. (Governing Body of Aerial Sports).– 297, Madison Avenue, New York. Founded 1905.

The Aeronautical Society of America. (Technical Body).— 29, West 39th Street, New York. Founded 1910.

Society of Automotive Engineers. (Body devoted to the development of all vehicles driven by internal combustion engines ; instrumental in the standardisation of aircraft parts and accessories).—29, West 39th Street, New York City.

Manufacturers' Aircraft Association. (The Trade Organisation).—501, Fifth Avenue, New York.

International Air Service Club. (Residential Club for officers of the Air Service and Naval Flying Corps, and qualified civilians).—9 and 11, East 38th Street, New York.

Aerial League of America. (Propagandist Body).—297, Madison Avenue, New York.

Note.—The Aero Club of America lists thirty local aero clubs as its affiliations : these clubs are however of little importance, and often exist merely in name.

Aerial Journals :—

Aerial Age. (Semi-technical trade weekly, 10 cents. Subscription per annum, 4 doll. U.S.A. ; 6 doll. foreign).— 280, Madison Avenue, New York. London Office, Thanet House, 231, Strand, W.C.

Aircraft Journal. (Popular weekly, 10 cents. Subscription per annum, 2 doll. U.S.A. ; 2.50 doll. Canada ; 3 doll. abroad).—22, East 17th Street, New York.

Aviation and Aeronautical Engineering. (Technical fortnightly, 25 cents. Subscription per annum 3 doll. U S.A. ; 3.50 doll. Canada ; 4 doll. abroad).—22, East 17th Street, New York,

Flying. (Popular monthly, 25 cents. Official organ of the Aero Club of America and the Aerial League of America. Subscription per annum, 3 doll. ; 4 doll. abroad).—280, Madison Avenue, New York.

Journal of the Society of Automotive Engineers. (Technical monthly, 50 cents. Subscription per annum, 5 doll. U.S.A. ; 6 doll. abroad. Members of the S.A.E. have 50 per cent. reduction.)—29, West 39th Street, New York.

U.S. Air Service Journal. Official Publication of the Army and Navy Air Service Association. 25 cents a copy. Subscription, $3.00 per annum. Editorial offices : Munsey Building, Washington, D.C.

U.S.A. MILITARY AERONAUTICS.

By THE BARON LADISLAS DORCY.

THE EARLY BEGINNINGS.

The early development of the American Flying Service rested entirely with the Signal Corps, which had, on December 23rd, 1907, issued specifications for a man-carrying aeroplane that would be capable of remaining in the air for one hour without landing. These conditions were fulfilled the following summer by a *Wright* biplane fitted with a 35 h.p. engine, and the machine was duly purchased; but in spite of this early start the development of American military aeronautics lagged far behind the other Great Powers until the entry of the States into the war. During the eight years that elapsed in the meanwhile less than one million dollars was appropriated by Congress for military aeronautics, and the Flying Service remained a subsidiary branch of the Signal Corps, known as the Aviation Section, which had been established by Act of Congress on July 18th, 1914.

On April 6th, 1917, when the United States declared war on Germany, the establishment of the Aviation Section comprised 65 officers, 1,120 enlisted men, two small flying fields (Mineola and San Diego), and less than 300 very second-rate training aeroplanes.

Manufacturing facilities were comparatively insignificant and experienced aeroplane designers were lacking, and the latter explains why up to that date no modern service machine had been produced in the States, and why most of the American service aeroplanes produced during the war were of British or French design, with the minor alterations the fitting of the Liberty engine necessitated, if such was fitted.

WAR PROGRAMME OF THE AIRCRAFT PRODUCTION BOARD.

The original American War Programme, based on an army of a million men, made of the air service but a relatively insignificant portion of the military forces, and this was to be met by two appropriations—$10,800,000 on May 21st, 1917, and $43,450,000 on June 5th, 1917. However, after the arrival in the States of a British and a French aviation mission, the General Staff revised their views, and concurred with the recommendations made by the Aircraft Production Board, calling for the construction of 22,500 aeroplanes and as many aero engines. For this purpose Congress was asked to appropriate a sum of $640,000,000—the largest ever asked for one specific item—and this was granted in record time, taking only one week till it became law. From this date—July 24th, 1917—the big American aircraft programme was really launched, largely in response to Allied appeals.

As speed was justly deemed the essential of success, it was decided to concentrate at first upon the production of a few types for which specifications and engines were available; thus it came that during 1917, the American aircraft industry produced almost exclusively training aeroplanes. Among these were the *Curtiss* J.N 4 (B., C. and D.) and the *Standard* J. 1 for primary training, and the *Curtiss* J.N. H. (Hispano-Suiza) two-seater, and the *Thomas-Morse* S. 4 (B. and C.) and the *Standard* E. 1 single-seaters for advanced training. Some thirty flying fields were created for the training of aviators, and large numbers of Allied (specially French) specialists in military aeronautics were drawn upon for establishing the Flying Service on a thoroughly up-to-date foundation.

After a lengthy controversy as to whether or not the States should entirely concentrate on training, and have their service machines built to the best available Allied designs in France and Great Britain, a decision was arrived at whereby the United States were to standardize three types of service machines (D.H. 4, *Bristol* F. 2 B. and *Spad de chasse*), and modify them so as to allow the fitting of a standardized aero engine, which was to be built in 4, 6, 8, and 12-cyl. models.

This engine, which was to embody the best features of all existing engines, was designed and constructed with a mixed display of secrecy and advertising within a month, in the summer of 1917, and the initial tests having proven, on the surface, successful, orders were placed in August, 1917, for the construction of this so-called Liberty engine with the following firms, for the quantities stated:—Packard Motor Car Co. and Lincoln Motors Co., 6,000 each; Ford Motor Co., 5,000; Nordyke and Marmon, 3,000; General Motors Corporation, 2,000; Trego Motors Corporation, 500—A total of 22,500 engines. All these were to be of the 12-cyl., 400 h.p. model, for use in the D.H. 4 and the *Bristol* F. 2B.: an 8-cyl. model, rated 225 h.p., was to be developed for use in the modified *Spad*.

A Characteristic Group of U.S. Army Aviators in France.

After some modifications, the Liberty 12 emerged from the experimental stage, and production increased with great rapidity, so that by the time Armistice was signed 13,396 of these engines had been delivered, the output for October, 1918, alone having reached 4,200. The adaptation of the Liberty 12 to the D.H. 4 proved a success, and orders were placed for 9,500 of these machines, of which one-half was delivered during the war; the modification of the *Bristol* F. 2B. and the *Spad* for the fitting of the Liberty 12 and the Liberty 8 respectively was, however, a failure, and the orders had therefore to be cancelled, As a consequence the D.H. 4A. was the only American-built aeroplane that saw service with the American Expeditionary Force, for the war came to an end before the second American aircraft programme could be carried out.

THE ERA OF REORGANISATIONS.

The Aircraft Production Board, which was responsible for the first aircraft programme, was a purely advisory body, which had been appointed after the declaration of war by Howard Coffin, Advisory Commissioner of the Council of National Defence, at the request of the National Advisory Committee for Aeronautics. It consisted of Mr. Coffin, chairman; Brig.-Gen. George O. Squier, Chief Signal Officer, U.S.A.; Rear-Admiral David W. Taylor, Chief Constructor, U.S.N., and Messrs. S. D. Waldon, E. A. Deeds, and R. L. Montgomery.

As the A.P.B. could only make recommendations and had no executive power, there was no assurance that the construction programme it had suggested would be carried out in the most effectual manner. To overcome this drawback, Congress passed, on Sept. 27th, 1917, a bill authorising the creation of an Aircraft Board, consisting of a civilian chairman, the Chief Signal Officer of the Army, the Chief Constructor of the Navy, and two members each taken from the Army, the Navy, and civilian life. This board was empowered, under the direction of the Secretaries of War and the Navy, to supervise and direct the purchase and manufacture of military and naval aircraft. The members, appointed on December 7th, 1917, were:—Howard E. Coffin, chairman; Maj.-Gen. George O. Squier, Rear-Admiral David W. Taylor; Col. E. A. Deeds and Col. R. L. Montgomery, for the Army; Captain H. E. Irwin and Lieut-Comdr. A. Atkins, for the Navy; and Richard F. Howe.

While the Aircraft Production Board had thus been given, with a new name, a legal status, its usefulness was greatly hampered by the fact that the Flying Service of the Army had remained, in spite of its extraordinary expansion, still a branch of the Signal Corps, which it greatly exceeded in

numbers and importance—the tail was actually wagging the dog. This anomaly was responsible for many of the errors and delays which hampered the progress of America's aircraft programme, and eventually the Committee on Military Affairs of the Senate started an investigation with a view to determining responsibilities. This investigation, as well as one conducted independently by Mr. Gutzon Borglum, a sculptor, on behalf of President Wilson, resulted in a total re-organisation of the aeronautical establishment. On April 24th, 1918, the Aviation Section was separated from the Signal Corps and re-named Air Service, which was divided into a Division of Military Aeronautics and a Bureau of Aircraft Production. Brig.-Gen. William L. Kenly was appointed Director of Military Aeronautics, in charge of training operations, and Mr. John D. Ryan became Chief of the Bureau of Aircraft Production, and at the same time, Chairman of the Aircraft Board, Mr. Coffin having resigned in the meanwhile. From then on, the Aircraft Board faded into oblivion, and its existence has become purely nominal; but the Act of Congress which created it fortunately made provision for its automatic deletion six months after the ending of war.

THE SECOND AIRCRAFT PROGRAMME.

Under the energetic leadership of Mr. Ryan the aircraft construction programme was pushed to the limit and a new programme was elaborated, calling for the production, beginning early in 1919, of the following standardised types of Air Service machines:—The *Lepère*, or L.U.A.S.C 11, the U.S.D. 9A., the *Martin* bomber, the *Loening* monoplane, the S.E. 5A. the *Handley-Page* and the *Caproni*. When Armistice was signed production was not under way yet, and so the orders were deleted; all of the above machines were to be fitted with Liberty 12 engines, except the *Loening* and the S.E. 5A., for which Hispano-Suiza's were provided.

In August, 1918, a new reorganisation was effected in the Air Service with the view to bringing it under one head, whereas previously dual control had existed in the matter of production and operations. Consequently the Division of Military Aeronautics and the Bureau of Aircraft Production were placed under the Director of Air Service, to which new post Mr. John D. Ryan was appointed, while Mr. William C. Potter became Chief of the Bureau of Aircraft Production.

AEROPLANE PRODUCTION JANUARY 1st, 1919.

The aeroplane production of the Air Service on January 1st, 1919, was, according to figures made public by the Production Division of the Bureau of Aircraft Production, the following:—

Type.	Manufacturer.	Total quantity ordered to Nov. 11th, 1918	Quantity left on order after Armistice cancellations.	Total shipped to Dec. 27th, 1918.
J.1—Dayton Wright Aeroplane Co.		400	400	400
	Fischer Body Corp.	400	400	400
	Standard Aircraft Corp.	750	750	750
	Wright-Martin Aircraft Corp.	50	50	50
	Total	1600	1600	1600
J.N. 4D.—Liberty Iron Works		300	200	200
	Canadian Aeroplane Co.	680	680	680
	U.S. Aircraft Corp.	50	50	50
	Curtiss Aeroplane & Motor Corp.	2401	2002	2002
	Fowler, Howell & Lesser Co.	225	125	125
	Springfield Aircraft Corp.	975	625	536
	St. Louis Aircraft Corp.	650	450	450
	Total	5281	4132	4043
J.N. H. :—				
Training—Curtiss Aerop. & Motor Corp.		402	402	402
Gunnery—Curtiss Aerop. & Motor Corp.		427	427	427
Bombing—Curtiss Aerop. & Motor Corp.		100	100	100
	Total	929	929	929
G. 1	—Curtiss Aerop. & Motor Corp.	560	560	471
G. 2	—Curtiss Aerop. & Motor Corp.	90	90	90
J.N, 6H. :—				
Observat'n	—Curtiss Aerop. & Motor Corp.	106	106	100
Pursuit	—Curtiss Aerop. & Motor Corp.	125	125	125
Bombing	—Curtiss Aerop. & Motor Corp.	154	154	154
	Total	1035	1035	940
B.	—Thomas-Morse Aircraft Corp.	100	100	100
S. 4	—Thomas-Morse Aircraft Corp.	50	50	50
C. Le Rhone—Thomas-Morse Aircraft Corp.		1000	447	447
	Total	1150	597	597
"Penguin"—Breese Aircraft Co.		300	300	300
E. 1 (M. Defense)—Standard Aircraft Corp.		30	30	30
	Standard Aircraft Corp.	430	98	96
	Total	460	128	126
D.H. 4—Dayton-Wright Airplane Co.		5000	3104	2899
	Fischer Body Corp.	4000	1600	1599
	Standard Aircraft Corp.	500	140	89
	Total	9500	4844	4587

Type.	Manufacturer.	Total quantity ordered to Nov. 11th, 1918	Quantity left on order after Armistice cancellations.	Total shipped to Dec. 27th, 1918.
Handley-Page—Standard Aircraft Corp...		500	107	102
S.E. 5A.—Curtiss Aerop. & Motor Corp.	..	54	54	9
	Curtiss Aerop. & Motor Corp. ..	1000	1	1
	Total	1054	55	10
L.U.A.S. CII.—Packard Motor Car Co.	..	1025	25	7
(Le Père)—Brewster & Co...	..	500	0	0
	Fischer Body Corp...	2000	0	0
	Total	3525	25	7
Martin Bomber—Glenn L. Martin Co.	..	50	4	0
U.S.D. 9A.—Curtiss Aerop. & Motor Corp.		4000	0	0
Caproni—Fischer Body Corp.	..	500	0	0
	Curtiss Aeroplane & Motor Corp.	500	0	0
	Total	1000	0	0
U.S.B. 1—Curtiss Aeroplane & Motor Corp.		2000	0	0
V.E. 7.—Sturtevant Co.	..	500	0	0
	Springfield Aircraft Corp.	500	0	0
	Total	1000	0	0

THE AIR SERVICE IN FRANCE.

At the date Armistice was signed, the Air Service forces at the front included 2,161 officers and 22,351 soldiers, and those in the supply service in France, 4,643 officers and 28,353 soldiers. With the French armies there were detailed 8 officers, and with the British Expeditionary Force, 49 officers and 525 soldiers. The total personnel in France consisted of 6,861 officers and 51,229 soldiers.

There were in operation on the front 39 aero squadrons, distributed as follows : 20 pursuit, 1 night bombardment, 6 day bombardment, 5 army observation, twelve corps observation, and one night observation squadrons.

Enemy aeroplanes brought down by American aviators included 491 confirmed and 354 unconfirmed, a total of 845, while 82 enemy observation balloons were reported as destroyed, of which 57 were confirmed. The Air Service lost, on the other hand, only 271 aeroplanes and 45 observation balloons, thus showing its marked superiority over the enemy.

The number of aeroplanes, by type, received from all sources by the American Expeditionary Force between September 12th, 1917, and November 16th, 1918, was as follows :

U.S.A. MILITARY AERONAUTICS.

Pursuit for service, 3,337 ; pursuit for schools, 90.
Observation for service, 3,421 ; observation for schools. 664.
Day bombing for service, 421 ; day bombing for schools, 85.
Night reconnaissance, 31.
Other planes received included 2,285 training planes, 30 experimental planes and 108 miscellaneous, making a total of 10,472.

Eight different schools under American control were established in France and designed for training 3,800 officers and 11,700 men, as follows :—

Tours—Observers : 916 officers and 2,121 soldiers.
Issoudun—General flying : 2,175 officers and 6,100 soldiers.
Clermont-Ferrand—Bombardment : 120 officers and 660 soldiers.
St. Jean de Monte—Aerial gunners : 92 officers and 1,500 soldiers.
Souse—Artillery firing point : 256 officers and 750 soldiers.
Coetquidan—Artillery firing point : 25 officers and 120 soldiers.
Meucon—Artillery firing point : 29 officers and 110 soldiers.
Chatillon sur Seine—Observers : 204 officers and 373 soldiers.
A total of 159 officers and soldiers were killed in training.

Casualties at the front included 109 killed, 103 wounded, 200 missing, 27 prisoners and 3 interned, making a total of 442.

The total strength of the Division of Military Aeronautics, Air Service, on November 11th, 1918, was 18,688 officers, 5,775 cadets, and 133,644 soldiers. At that date the Air Service had trained 8,933 reserve military aviators at home, and about 2,300 had been trained in France, Great Britain and Italy.

The personnel of the Bureau of Aircraft Production, Air Service, comprised 32,520 officers and soldiers.

The ground establishments of the Air Service in the United States comprised 40 flying fields, 8 balloon fields, 3 radio schools, 3 photography schools, 5 schools of military aeronautics, and 14 aircraft depots.

THE NEW ORGANISATION SCHEME.

With the return to peace time conditions the Air Service has been greatly reduced and is being wholly reorganised. Mr. Ryan having resigned from the post of Director of Air Service after the signing of Armistice, Major-Gen. Charles T. Menoher was appointed in his place, while Brig.-Gen. William Mitchell was appointed Director of Military Aeronautics in lieu of Gen. Kenly. Since the latter appointment, however, the Division of Military Aeronautics as well as the Bureau of Aircraft Production have disappeared as independent organisations, and have been merged in the general arrangement of the new organisation plan, so that their directors become assistants to the Director of Air Service.

The office of the Director of Air Service will consist of :—

An Executive Staff, composed of an Executive Officer and four assistants, known as First, Second, Third and Fourth Assistant Executives, respectively.

EXECUTIVE STAFF.

Executive Officer, Col. Milton F. Davis, A.S., A.
First Assistant Executive, Col. William E. Gillmore, A.S., A.
Second Assistant Executive, Maj. Horace M. Hickam, A.S., A.
Third Assistant Executive, Brig.-Gen. William Mitchell, U.S.A.
Fourth Assistant Executive, Lieut.-Col. William F. Pearson, A.S., A.

A Technical Advisory Staff, consisting of the following :—
Supply Group (co-ordinated by and under the direction of the First Assistant Executive).

TECHNICAL ADVISORY STAFF—SUPPLY.

Chief, Air Service Property, Lieut.-Col. Augustine W. Robins, A.S., A.
Chief, Air Service Procurements, In-Col. Chalmers G. Hall, A.S., A.
Chief, Air Service Materials Inspection, Lieut.-Col. George W. Mixter, A.S., A.P.
Chief, Air Service Finance, Lieut.-Col. Alex. C. Downey, A.S., A.P.
Chief, Air Service Aeronautical Engineering, Col. Thurman H. Bane, A,S., A.

Training and Operations Group (co-ordinated by and under the direction of the Third Assistant Executive).

TRAINING AND OPERATIONS.

Chief, Air Service Training (detail to be announced later).
Chief, Air Service Operations, Lieut.-Col. Lewis H. Brereton, A.S., A.
Chief, Air Service Gunnery, Lieut.-Col. Harold E. Hartney, A.S., A.
Chief, Air Service Communications, Col. Clarence C. Culver, A.S., A.
Chief, Air Service Balloons and Airships, Col. Charles De F. Chandler, A.S., A.

An Administrative Staff (co-ordinated by and under the direction of the Fourth Assistant Executive).

ADMINISTRATIVE STAFF.

Chief, Air Service Personnel, Lieut.-Col. Rush B. Lincoln, A.S., A.
Chief, Air Service Inspector, Lieut.-Col. Frank M. Andrews, A.S., A.
Chief Surgeon, Air Service, Col. Albert E. Truby, M.C.

U.S.A. MILITARY AERONAUTICS.

The following named officers have been designated as an Advisory Board, Air Service :—

Col. Walter G. Kilner, M.A., A.S., A.
Col. Arthur L. Fuller, A.S., A.
Col. Henry C. Pratt, A.S., A.
Lieut.-Col. George B. Hunter, A.S., A.
Lieut.-Col. Henry W. Harms, J.M.A., A.S., A.
Major Charles R. Cameron, A.S., A., Secretary

The Executive Officer is the direct representative of the Director of Air Service in the co-ordination, control and direction of the activities of the Air Service, and in the temporary absence of the Director of Air Service issues orders in the latter's name.

The Second Assistant Executive is specifically charged with matters of information, statistics and publicity.

The Fourth Assistant Executive, in addition to the duties outlined above, is specifically charged with all routine executive Air Service functions, such as mail, cable and telegraph service, correspondence, central records and files, office administration and confidential records.

AIR SERVICE STRENGTH ON PEACE FOOTING.

The 1919 organisation plan of the Air Service provides for a personnel strength of 1,923 officers and 21,853 soldiers and for a *materiel* strength of 5,100 aeroplanes of all types, 1,700 of which will be in active commission and 3,400 in reserve.

The Air Service will comprise 87 service aeroplane squadrons, distributed as follows :—42 coast defence (continental and insular), 20 pursuit, and 25 mixed observation and bombing squadrons. The normal squadron comprises 18 aeroplanes and their personnel. Provision is also made for the maintenance of 42 balloon squadrons (some equipped with small airships), which will be divided among three wings of 18 companies each.

In the general plan of the Army reorganisation each army corps will have attached to it five observation and bombing squadrons and four pursuit squadrons, representing a wing formation for each type of machine.

The greater part of the Air Service flying and balloon fields organised during the war will be retained on peace footing ; in addition to six fields already owned by the U.S. Government fourteen have been purchased in March, 1919, and leases were extended on eleven others. The status of the remainder has not yet been definitely decided upon at the date of writing.

Air Service Flying Fields.

Barron Field	.. Fort Worth, Texas.
*Bolling Field	.. Anacostia, District of Columbia.
*Brindley Field	.. Commack, Long Island, N.Y.
Brooks Field	.. San Antonio, Texas.
Call Field ..	.. Wichita Falls, Texas.

Carlstrom Field	.. Arcadia, Florida.
Carruthers Field	.. Benbrook, Fort Worth, Texas.
Chanute Field	.. Rantoul, Illinois.
*Chapman Field	.. Miami, Florida.
Dick (Camp)	.. Dallas, Texas.—Cadet Gunnery School.
Dorr Field ..	.. Arcadia, Florida.
Eberts Field	.. Lonoke, Arkansas.
Ellington Field	.. Houston, Texas.—Bombing School.
*Emerson Field	.. Jackson, South Carolina.—Gun Spotting School.
Gerstner Field	.. Lake Charles, Louisiana. — Fighting School.
*Hazelhurst Field	.. Mineola, Long Island, N.Y.
*H. J. Damm Field	. Babylon, Long Island, N.Y.
*Hiestand Field	.. Fort Myers, Florida.—Landing Station.
Kelly Field ..	.. San Antonio, Texas.
Langley Field	.. Hampton, Virginia.—Experimental.
Love Field ..	.. Dallas, Texas.
*Lufbery Field	.. Wantaugh, Long Island, N.Y.
March Field..	.. Riverside, California.
Mather Field	.. Sacramento, California.
*McCook Field	.. Dayton, Ohio.—Experimental.
*Mitchel Field	.. Mineola, L. I.
Park Field ..	.. Millington, Virginia.
Payne Field..	.. West Point, Mississippi.
*Post Field ..	.. Fort Sill, Oklahoma-Observers' School.
Rich Field ..	.. Waco, Texas.
*Rockwell Field	.. San Diego, California.
*Roosevelt Field	.. —————, Long Island, N.Y.
*San Leon Field	.. Houston, Texas.—Landing Station.

Scott Field ..	.. Belleville, Illinois.
Selfridge Field	.. Mount Clemens, Michigan.
Souther Field	.. Americus, Georgia.
Taliaferro Field	.. Fort Worth, Texas.
Taylor Field	.. Montgomery, Alabama.
*Westwood Field	.. —————, Oklahoma.
Wilbur Wright Field	Fairfield, Dayton, Ohio.

All the above fields will be retained by the Air Service, except those marked with an asterisk (*), on which decision is still pending.

Air Service Balloon Schools.

Fort Omaha, Nebraska.
Langley Field, Hampton, Virginia.
Camp John Wise, San Antonio, Texas.—To be abandoned, 1919.
Arcadia, Florida.
Lee Hall, Virginia.
Fort Sill, Oklahoma.

Schools of Military Aeronautics.

University of California, Berkeley, California.
Cornell University, Ithaca, New York.
Princeton University, Princeton, New Jersey.
University of Illinois, Urbana, Illinois.
University of Texas, Austin, Texas.

Postal Air Stations.

Belmont Park, New York.
South Philadelphia.
Bolling Field, Washington.—Air Service patrol base.

The U.S. Navy's Experimental Seaplane, built by the Naval Aircraft Factory.

432a

U.S.A. NAVAL AERONAUTICS.

By THE BARON LADISLAS DORCY.

HISTORICAL.

The U.S. Naval Flying Corps was established in 1911, when Congress appropriated the sum of $25,000 for this purpose. With this sum three naval officers (Lieuts. T. G. Ellyson, John Rodgers and J. T. Towers) were trained as aviators, three shore-going machines (two Curtiss and one Wright biplane) were purchased, and an air station was constructed at Greenbury Point, Md. The latter was removed during the same year to Annapolis, Md., where it remained in operation as a flying school till 1913, when the Pensacola air station and flying school was established, except during the winter months, when the training was conducted at the Curtiss School at San Diego, Cal.

During 1912, a considerable volume of research work was done, under the direction of Capt. W I. Chambers, U.S.N., with regard to seaplane floats, flying boat hulls, and general flotation problems, and a catapult launching apparatus, operated by compressed air was developed. Toward the end of this year a temporary air station was established at Guantanamo, Cuba, but this was broken up the following spring. The development of the N.F.C. was greatly hampered by the inadequate funds available.

In 1913, the Office of Naval Aeronautics was created in the Bureau of Operations, with Captain Mark L. Bristol, U.S.N., as Director of Naval Aeronautics, and naval flying school was established at Pensacola, Fla., whither the U.S.S. *Mississippi* was assigned as an "aeronautic station ship." At the end of this year the N.F.C. had 7 flying boats and 2 float seaplanes in commission, and 3 flying boats on order.

In the spring of 1914, the Atlantic Fleet having been mobilised in Mexican waters, an "aeroplane division" (4 machines) was embarked on the U.S.S. *Mississippi* and *Birmingham*, and sent to Vera Cruz and Tampico, respectively. A number of reconnaissance flights were made in this connection over Vera Cruz. In the summer the U.S.S. *Mississippi* was sold to Greece, and her place was taken by the U.S.S. *North Carolina*.

In February, 1915, specifications were issued and bids asked for one small training airship of the non-rigid type and 6 seaplanes, and in August for 3, 6, 9, and 12 seaplanes, respectively. The specifications asked for a high speed of 60-70 m.p.h., a low speed of 40 m.p.h., a climb of 2,500 ft. in 10 minutes, an endurance of 4 hours at full power, and ability to fly in a wind of 35 m.p.h., and to take off, alight, and drift (afloat) in a wind of 25 m.p.h.

During the summer of this year, Naval Constructor H. C. Richardson, U.S.N., who had previously been identified with extensive research work on flying boat hulls, built an experimental twin-engine seaplane of the float type. Experiments were also continued with the Chambers catapult, and apparently

gave satisfactory results, for it was suggested at about this time to equip all the capital ships of the Atlantic Fleet with one or two flying boats and launching devices. As a matter of fact, the first U.S. warship to be so equipped was the *North Carolina*, and this took place in 1916.

The real expansion of the N.F.C. dates from the passage of Naval Act, 1916, the provisions of which are referred to elsewhere. On December 1st, 1916, the N.F.C. had in commission 29 seaplanes and 4 kite balloons—the latter having been

developed for the U.S. Navy by the Goodyear Tyre and Rubber Co.—and the flying personnel consisted of 9 officer-aviators, 16 student-aviators, while 24 officers and 120 enlisted men of the Navy, Marine Corps and Naval Militia were about to be sent for a course of training to Pensacola, Fla.

At the time the United States entered the great war (April, 1917), 21 seaplanes of float and boat types were in commission (out of total of 93 delivered to the N.F.C. since its formation), and 135 seaplanes, mostly of the N-9 and R-6 types, were on

A Characteristic Group of U.S. Naval Aviators on Service in France.

433a

order. Air stations were in operation at Pensacola, Fla., Bay Shore, N.Y., and Squantum, Mass; the two latter were later removed to Chatham, Mass., and Rockaway, N.Y., respectively. The training airship ordered in 1915 had also been commissioned. The personnel of the N.F.C. consisted of 30 officers and 300 men.

With the granting of a large appropriation for the fiscal year 1917-18, a comprehensive construction programme was begun, and the Naval Aircraft Factory was established at the Navy Yard of Philadelphia at a cost of $3,750,000 for the manufacture of seaplanes as well as the assembly of parts produced by trade firms and concerns not engaged in other war work. This system gave most excellent results, and the Navy aircraft programme was as a rule well ahead of schedule—an achievement much at variance with the progress of the Army aircraft programme, and for which much praise is due to Naval Constructor F. G. Coburn, U.S.N., under whose direction the factory was built and is operated. In October, 1918, the Naval Aircraft Factory employed 3,700 workers, one-fourth of whom were women, and over 7,000 people were employed by various contractors.

During the war the Naval Flying Corps extensively co-operated with the air forces of the Allies. For this purpose air stations were established in Ireland; in France (Le Havre, Brest, La Pallice, Bordeaux), and in Canada (Halifax), from which stations incoming and outgoing merchant vessels were convoyed for considerable distances in addition to patrol flights and bombing raids made for the purpose of combating the submarine menace. With the ending of the war these stations will be turned over to the respective countries in which they were established—if this has not already been done.

On October 2, 1918, the total strength of the Naval Flying Corps was 40,383 officers and men.

ORGANISATION.

The present organisation of the Naval Flying Corps was laid down in Naval Act, 1916, which fixed the personnel strength at 150 officer-aviators and 350 enlisted airmen, and provided for the creation of the Naval Reserve Flying Corps for qualified civilians, and the yearly appointment, from civil life, of fifteen probationary ensigns, for air duty only, and for a duration of three years.

The Naval Appropriation Bill, of March, 1918, increased the strength of the enlisted personnel of the N.F.C. to 10,000 men.

The Naval Flying Corps sub-divides, as to organisation, into four branches, which are attached to four Bureaux of the Navy Department, respectively. The Director of Naval Aviation, in the Bureau of Operations, is in charge of administration, inspection, training, materiel, personnel, and operations. The

Aircraft Division of the Bureau of Construction and Repair is responsible for design, specifications, construction and supply of aircraft, minus their motive apparatus, and research work. The Aviation Division of the Bureau of Steam Engineering is in charge of the production of engines and their parts, airscrews, radiators, and station and school equipment, instruments, and balloon gas. The Aviation Section of the Bureau of Ordnance supplies aircraft armament.

NAVAL AIR EXPENDITURES.

1912-13 :	$24,532·79.
1913-14 :	$56,032·90.
1914-15 :	$194,492·46.
1915-16 :	$219,429·20.
1916-17 :	$684,679·28.
1917-18 :	$61,133,000 (appropriation).
1918-19 :	$220,383,119 (appropriation).
1919-20 :	$35,000,000 (appropriation).

THE 1919-20 PROGRAMME.

The amount originally asked for aeronautics in the Naval Appropriation Bill, 1919, was $225,000,000, but after Armistice Day this was reduced to $85,000,000, and later to $35,000,000.

The reduced programme provides for the construction of 108 fighting escorts, 54 twin-engine patrol machines, 54 single-engine patrol machines, 108 three-engine fleet seaplanes, and 300 school machines, a total of $8,162,000; and 31 airships, 57 kite-balloons, and 10 free balloons, a total of $19,615,000 for lighter-than-air craft.

It is proposed to have two squadrons of fighting escorts of 18 each, one replacement squadron, and one training squadron; two squadrons and a replacement squadron of large and small patrol machines each; two squadrons of fleet machines, one replacement squadron, one training squadron. Full replacement is provided for the fleet machines and the fighting escorts.

The fighting escorts are to be of the Dunkirk type; experiments are now under way with a Curtiss float triplane, which has developed a speed of 140 m.p.h. The large patrol machines are of the F-5-L and F-6 types; the small patrol machines of the HS-2-L type; the fleet machines of the NC-1 type; the school machines of the Curtiss N-9 (100 h.p.) and R-6 (200 h.p.) float-types, the Curtiss F boat type, beside Curtiss JN-4 and Thomas M.I. types for operating from the land and the decks of ships, respectively.

The Curtiss-built N.C.1 Flying Boat, designed by the U.S. Naval Aviation Department.

U.S.A. NAVAL AERONAUTICS.

n the airship programme, provision is made for 4 rigid hips, 12 large non-rigid airships, and 64 twin-engine coastal hips ; it is not, however, expected to build all these craft ing the fiscal year 1919-20.

NAVAL AIRCRAFT STRENGTH.

On Dec. 31, 1918, the following numbers of aircraft were in mission in the United States Navy :

    34 twin-engine service seaplanes ;
    337 single-engine service seaplanes ;
    100 land aeroplanes (Marines, training) ;

    401 training seaplanes ;
    12 experimental seaplanes ;

a total of 884, in addition to which there were shipped abroad, for the war emergency, the following :

    159 twin-engine seaplanes ;
    229 single-engine seaplanes ;
    140 land aeroplanes ;

that is, a total of 528 machines. The grand total of naval seaplanes and aeroplanes commissioned was therefore 1,412, to which must be added 17 airships and 116 kite-balloons, of which latter 42 were shipped to Europe.

SERVICE FLYING BOATS OF THE U.S.N.F.C.

Type	NC. 1.	F. 5 L.	H. 16.	HS. 2 L.
Span, overall	126 ft. (38.43 m.)	103 ft. 9 in. (31.92 m.)	95 ft. (29 m.)	74 ft. (22.60. m.)
Length, overall	68 ft. 2½ in. (20.75 m.)	49 ft 3½ in. (15.00 m.)	46 ft. 1½ in. (14 00 m.)	38 ft. 6 in. (11.75 m.)
Height, overall	24 ft. 6 in. (7.47 m.)	18 ft. 9 in. (5.78 m.)	17 ft. 8 in. (5.40 m.)	14 ft. 7 in. (3.45 m.)
Chord	12 ft. (3.66 m.)	8 ft. (2.44 m.)	7 ft.. ¾ in. (2·15 m.)	6 ft. 3 in. (1.91 m.)
Wing area	2,380 sq. ft. (2,114.2 sq. m.)	1,397 sq. ft. (125.7 sq. m.)	1,164 sq. ft. (104.8 sq. m.)	803 sq. ft. (72.3 sq. m.)
H.P.	1,200	800	800	400
Engines	3 Liberty 12	2 Liberty 12	2 Liberty 12	1 Liberty 12
Airscrews	3 Tractors.	2 Tractors	2 Tractors	1 Pusher
Weight, fully loaded.. ..	22,000 lbs. (9,900 kgs.)	13,000 lbs. (5,850 kgs.).	10,900 lbs. (4,900 kgs.)	6,432 lbs. (2,894 kgs.)
Useful load	7,750 lbs. (3,490 kgs.)	4,750 lbs. (2,140 kgs.)	3,500 lbs. (1,575 kgs.)	2,132 lbs. (960 kgs.)
High speed	81 m.p.h.* (129.6 km.p.h.)	87 m.p.h. (139 km.p.h.)	95 m.p.h. (152 km.p.h.)	91 m.p.h. (145.6 km.p.h.)
Low speed	61 m.p.h.* (97.6 k.m.p.h)	57 m.p.h. (91 km.p.h.)	56 m.p.h. (90 km.p.h.)	55 m.p.h. (88 km.p.h.)
Initial climb	1,050 ft. 320 m. in 5 mins.	2,625 ft. (800 m.) in 10 mins.	3,000 ft. (915 m.) in 10 mins.	2,500—3,000 ft. (760—915 m.) in 10 mins.
Full speed endurance. ..	13 hours	10 hours.	hours	hours
Armament	8 M.G.	1 Q.F., 4 M.G. 2—500 lb., or 4—230 lb. bombs	6 M.G.	1 M.G.
Complement	5	5	4	3
Builder	Curtiss	Naval Aircraft Factory	Curtiss	Standard

* Carrying a load of 21,560 lbs. (9,700 kgs).

THE NC-1
1,050 H P
FLYING BOAT

Scale of feet

435a

3 1

NAVAL AIR STATIONS.

Atlantic Coast :

Chatham, Mass.—2 airships, 24 seaplanes, 6 K.B.
Montauk, L.I., N.Y.—4 airships.
Rockaway, N.Y.—24 seaplanes, 6 K.B.
Cape May, Del.—4 airships, 18 seaplanes, 6 K.B.
Hampton, Va.—4 airships, 24 seaplanes, 6 K.B.
Yorktown, Va.—6 K.B.
Moorehead City, N.C.—12 seaplanes.
Charleston, S.C.—4 airships, 6 K.B.
Brunswick, Ga.—18 seaplanes, 6 K.B.
Miami, Fla.—2 airships, 12 seaplanes.

(The General Board of the U.S. Navy recommended the construction of an air station between Rockland and Portland, Me., for 4 airships, and an air station at Narraganset Bay., R.I., for 24 seaplanes and 6 K.B. This item was struck out after the armistice.)

Gulf Coast :

Key West, Fla.—2 airships, 24 seaplanes, 6 K.B.
Pensacola, Fla.—6 K.B.
Galveston, Tex.—24 seaplanes, 6 K.B.

(An air station at Port Arthur, Tex., for 2 airships, was recommended by the General Board.)

Canal Zone :

Coco Solo (Colon).—2 airships, 24 seaplanes.

West Indies :

(The General Board recommended the construction of an air station at St. Thomas, Virgin Islands, for 4 airships, 18 seaplanes, and 6 K.B., and one each at Guantanamo and Samana, Cuba.)

Pacific Coast :

San Diego, Cal.—2 airships, 24 seaplanes, 6 K.B.

(The General Board recommended the construction of air stations at San Francisco, Cal., for 4 airships, 24 seaplanes, and 6 K.B. ; at the mouth of the Columbia River, for 4 airships and 6 K.B. ; at Port Angeles, Wash., for 4 airships and 6 K.B., and at Seward, Alaska, for 4 airships, 6 seaplanes and 4 K.B.)

Hawaian Islands :

(The General Board recommended the construction of air stations at Pearl Harbor, for 4 airships, 24 seaplanes, 6 K.B., and at Hilo, for 24 seaplanes and 6 K.B.)

Guam :

(The General Board recommended the construction of an air station at Port Apra, for 4 airships, 24 seaplanes and 6 K.B.)

Phillippine Islands :

(The General Board recommended the construction of an air station at Cavite, for 4 airships, 12 seaplanes and 6 K.B.)

FACTORIES AND SCHOOLS,

Naval Aircraft Factory, Philadelphia, Pa.—Builds seaplanes of all types, and airship cars ; normal output, 50 twin-engine machines per year. Also engaged in research and experimental work.

Helium Production Plant, Fort Worth, Tex.—Owned by the Linde Air Products Co., but operated for the Navy.

Naval Ground School, Massachussetts Institute of Technology, Cambridge, Mass.

Naval Flying School, Pensacola, Fla.

Naval Balloon School, Arcadia, Fla.

Naval Airship School, Akron, Ohio.

Marine Corps Flying School, Miami, Fla.

Coast Guard Flying School (proposed.)—The U.S. Coast Guard is the result of an amalgamation of the Revenue Cutter and Life Saving Services ; it is proposed to use aircraft for life saving whenever it cannot be done by other means.

Side View of the U.S. Navy's N.C.1 Flying Boat.

U.S.A. POSTAL AVIATION.

The Aerial Mail Service of the Post Office Department was established with an appropriation of $300,000 dollars, on May 15th, 1918, between Washington and New York, with the co-operation of the War Department, which furnished the aeroplanes and the aviators, and conducted the flying and maintenance operations until August 12th, 1918, when the entire service was taken over by the postal authorities.

The Washington-New York route has been in continuous operation ever since, and has functioned quite satisfactorily, even throughout the winter months. It is true the winter of 1918-19 was exceptionally mild and devoid of storms. One round trip daily, except Sunday, is being made without fail. The trip from Washington to New York is performed on an average of 2 hrs. and 30 mins., and from New York to Washington in 2 hrs. and 50 mins., the difference in time being due to the prevailing winds, which are usually from a westerly direction. A stop for the exchange of mail on each trip is made at Philadelphia. An average of 7¾ tons of letter mail is being carried each month.

The cost of the operation of the service since it began, including developments of new routes, is at the rate of 74 cents per mile operated. The cost per ton-mile of mail carried is $5 35. By this service mail between New York and Washington is advanced from 2½ to 3 hours over the train service.

The postage charged on mail carried by aeroplane was originally 24 cents (1s.) for each ounce, but it was soon found that this charge exceeded the cost of the service, and on July 15th, 1918, the aeroplane postage was reduced to 16 cents for the first ounce and six cents for each additional ounce, ten cents of the initial charge being for special-delivery service.

The after-the-war programme of the Post Office Department contemplates the establishment of an aerial mail service which will connect the principal commercial centres of the States by a system of trunk lines and feeders, which in their turn will connect with the West Indies, Central and South America. The trunk and feeder lines decided upon under this programme, for which an appropriation of $860,000 is available in the fiscal year 1918-19, are :—

1. New York to San Francisco, with feeders from—
   (a) Chicago to St. Louis and Kansas City.
   (b) Chicago to St. Paul and Minneapolis.
   (c) Cleveland to Pittsburg.
2. Boston to Key West, with feeders from—
   (a) Philadelphia to Pittsburg.
   (b) Washington to Cincinnati.
   (c) Atlanta to New Orleans.
3. Key West, via Habana, to Panama.
4. Key West, via the West Indies, to South America.

The present American postal fleet consists of six *Standard* E. 4 biplanes (150 h.p. Hispano-Suiza), Six *Curtiss* J.N. 4H. biplanes (150 h.p. Hispano-Suiza), and six *Curtiss* R. 4L.M. biplanes (400 h.p. Liberty).

U.S.A. NAVAL AERONAUTICS.

The U.S. Navy's F.5.L. type Flying Boat ashore.

The U.S. Navy's F.5.L. Flying Boat afloat.

THE U.S. NAVY'S TRANS-ATLANTIC FLIGHT.

THE honour of being the first machine to cross the Atlantic Ocean by air was won by the American Naval Flying Boat *N.C.4*, commanded by Lieut.-Commander Read, U.S.N.

On May 8th, 1919, three *N.C.* (Navy-Curtiss) Flying Boats, *N.C.1*, *N.C.3*, and *N.C.4*, left Rockaway Beach, U.S., and flew to Trepassey, Newfoundland, a distance of 950 miles. Owing to slight defects at the start, *N.C.4* did not arrive till May 10th.

On May 16th, after adjustments and repairs, the three boats left Trepassey and flew towards the Azores. *N.C.4* reached Horta, the first port of the Azores, 1,381 miles from Trepassey, in 15 hours 18 minutes.

N.C.1 (Lieut.-Commander Bellinger) was obliged to descend, owing to fog, and sank before she could be got on board one of the salvage ships which were stationed along the course.

N.C.3 (Commander Towers) was also brought down by fog, but, although badly damaged by the sea, she was brought into Horta under her own power, after navigating for 200 miles on the surface. She was then too badly damaged to fly any further.

The Senior Naval Officer, U.S.N., at the Azores, suggested that Commander Towers, as the organiser of the flight, and as Senior Naval Aviator, should take command of *N.C.4*. Commander Towers very properly objected to being called upon to supplant one of his own officers in the honour of being the first to cross the Atlantic by air. The Senior Naval Officer telegraphed to the Navy Department at Washington for permission to appoint Commander Towers to *N.C.4*. This permission was promptly refused, so Lieut.-Commander Read remained in command, as Commander Towers wished.

Unfortunately the telegram of the S.N.O. was widely published, and still more unfortunately the position adopted by Commander Towers was not made equally well-known.

On May 20th, *N.C.4* flew from Horta to Porta Delgada— the port in the Azores nearest to Europe—169 miles in 1 hour 45 minutes.

On May 27th, *N.C.4* flew from Porta Delgada to Lisbon, 925 miles in 9 hours 44 minutes, and thus achieved the crossing of the Atlantic by air for the first time.

At a later date—May 30th—*N.C.4* started for England, but, owing to adverse winds, came down near Ferrol. And on May 31st she flew over Brest and alighted at Plymouth.

The flight was carried out officially by the U.S. Navy, which stationed salvage ships at intervals of 50 miles along the course over which the *N.C.* boats were to fly. The flying arrangements were made and the organisation was carried out by Commander Towers.—*C.G.G.*

The Start of the Three N.C. Boats from Rockaway Beach, U.S.A., on May 8th.

THE AMERICAN OCEAN-GOING FLYING-BOATS.

BY "AUSTERLITZ."

The ocean-going flying-boats which the U.S. Naval Air Service fitted out for the crossing of the Atlantic *via* the Azores belong to the so-called "N.C." class of machines, which has been developed by the Curtiss Engineering Corporation at their Garden City works to the designs of the Aircraft Division, Bureau of Construction and Repair, Navy Department. Hence the official designation N.C., which stands for Navy-Curtiss, and not for Nonpareil Colossus—as an ingenious-minded individual suggested.

The officers chiefly responsible for the design of the *N.C.* boats are Comdr. G. C. Westervelt, Lieut.-Comdr. H. C. Richardson, and Lieut.-Comdr. J. C. Hunsaker, of the Construction Corps, U.S.N.

These boats were built by Mr. Glenn Curtiss, whose "Engineering Corporation" is quite independent of the Curtiss Aeroplane and Motors Corporation.

THE TRIALS OF THE N.C.1.

The first of these boats, the *N.C.1*, made her initial trial flight on November 8th of last year, when she carried a complement of fifteen from Rockaway Naval Air Station to Washington, D.C., and later in the day flew from the national capital to Hampton Naval Air Station. All those concerned with the construction and operation of the boat were highly elated over these flights, for, despite a certain sluggishness experienced in the take-off, the huge boat proved quite manageable in other respects—not a mean achievement, if one considers that the *N.C.1* (as she was then) weighed, fully loaded, a matter of 11 tons. A high speed of 81 m.p.h. was developed during the trials, and an altitude of 2,000 feet was reached in about 10 minutes.

TO BE OR NOT TO BE A FLYING-BOAT.

As may be seen from the accompanying illustrations, the *N.C.* boats divert from customary practice in that the tail surfaces, instead of being fitted to the stern of the hull, are carried on three outriggers, with consequent short-hull construction, which bring us back to the venerable days of the Voisin "Icare," the Sopwith "Batboat," and the Colliex-Janson tandem seaplane.

The object of this construction is to reduce the frictional resistance which a flying-boat develops on the under-side of the hull while taxying to take off, with a consequent slowing down of the starting speed. Now in a rough sea the take-off is in general accompanied by "porpoising"—that is, by striking the crest of each succeeding wave as the boat gathers speed and is already partly supported by the air. This is not only exceedingly uncomfortable for the crew, but also puts the hull to often dangerous strains. Any shortening of the get-away distance is therefore exceedingly desirable for the safe operation of seaplanes, and the short-hull construction appears to answer well this requirement.

Unfortunately, owing to its smaller excess of flotation, it introduces a certain longitudinal instability when afloat, and affords less protection to the tail group than a long-hull flying-

THE NON-STARTER.—N.C.2, which differed from the rest of the series and was not used—for reasons given below.

Stern View of N.C.4 Ashore at Rockaway.

439a

boat. This explains why on small flying-boats the short-hull construction has not found great favour thus far.

Owing to their type of construction, the *N.C.* boats are often referred to as a compromise between the boat and float type seaplanes, although, were a precise definition wanted, a flying-boat may be described as a sea-going aeroplane which affords accommodation to the crew in a hull ensuring flotation.

Consequently, long and short hull seaplanes may both be considered as flying-boats "pure and simple."

PHYSIOGNOMY AND ANATOMY.

The hull of the *N.C.1* has an overall length of 44 ft. 8¾ in., a beam of 10 ft., and an overall height of 7 ft. 5½ in. It is of the straight V-bottom type, with a single step located 18 ft. 2 in. from the stem. Unlike the Felixtowe and the American *F* boats, the *N.C.1* has no fins flaring out on either board, but is nearly semi-circular in cross section.

The hull is built up around a keel and four longerons of white ash, with veneer bulkheads; keelson and stringers are of basswood. The planking is composed of an inner skin of Port Orford cedar, placed at right angles to the keel so as to act as a strength member, and an outer skin of Spanish cedar, with Courtrai fabric laid in marine glue in between, and secured to one another by brass nails. The step is reinforced by mahogany veneer.

The wings are composed of a centre section of 25 ft. 4 in. span and outer sections of 44 ft. 4 in. (upper) and 35 ft. 4 in. (lower) span, with a uniform chord of 12 ft. Including the balanced portion of the ailerons, the span of the upper wings is 126 ft., and that of the lower wings 96 ft.; the interplane gap is 13 ft. 6 in. at the centre section, whence it decreases towards the tips to 12 ft. because the lower outer sections are set at a dihedral of 3 deg. The angle of incidence of both wings is 3 deg.; there is no stagger or sweep-back.

Ten bays of interplane struts secure the wings to one another; six of these occur in the centre section, where they serve in pairs as engine supports. Where the outermost interplane bays abut against the *cellule*, a vertical drift plane is fitted to the upper wing, and a streamline balancing float is secured to the lower wing. The *cellule* is extensively trussed by swaged wires.

The power plant consists of three Liberty-12 engines of the low-compression Navy type, which develop each 330 h.p. at 1,590 r.p.m., and actuate a four-bladed tractor airscrew of 10 ft. 10 in. diameter by direct drive. The engines are mounted in streamline *nacelles,* which are secured to the inter-bays of the centre section; the centre engine *nacelle* is fitted with a cockpit for a mechanic, to which access is had from the boat by means of a scaling ladder.

The outriggers which carry the tail unit are of hollow spruce and form a pyramid-like structure, the base of which is attached to the upper rear wing spars and the stern of the hull, while the truncated apex affords the points of attachment of the biplane tail. The latter is composed of an upper tail plane of 47 ft. 11 in. span, and a lower tail plane of 26 ft. span, set at a gap of 9 ft. 3 in., to which are hinged balanced elevators. Three rudders are fitted in the tail *cellule*; the central is balanced, but the outer rudders are hinged to a vertical fin.

THE CREWS.

The normal complement of the *N.C.1* consists of five officers and sailors, two of the officers being pilots; these are seated side-by-side in a cockpit fitted amidships and provided with dual control and the necessary instruments. A gunner's nest is fitted in the bows, and another was originally provided for in the middle of the upper wings, with access through the centre engine nacelle; the wing gun emplacement has, however, been removed, in view of the attempt to cross the Atlantic.

The fuel tanks contain about 300 American gallons of petrol, which is sufficient for a continuous flight of 13 hours. The disposable load is 7,750 lbs., and the full flying weight 21,560 lbs.

A MORE POWERFUL SISTER.

When, to quote a Presidential proclamation, "the war came to an end" with the signing of the Armistice, the Navy people at once made extensive plans to carry off the palm of the first crossing of the Atlantic. With the experience gained in the operation of the *N.C.1*, three more boats of this class, but of an improved type, were laid down at the Curtiss works in Garden City, L.I., and Comdr. John H. Towers, U.S.N., the veteran American naval flyer, was ordered by the Navy Department to take charge of the organisation of the ocean flight. At the same time Rockaway Naval Air Station was designated as the American starting-place of the flight.

The second of the *N.C.* boats, *N.C.2*, made her maiden flight on April 12th, at Rockaway. Except for her power plant, which consists of four Liberty-12 engines arranged in tandem sets, with each set driving tractor and pusher airscrews, and the fitting of a pilot nacelle in the place where the *N.C.1* had her central engine, the new boat is identical with her older sister.

N.C.4.—Lieut.-Commander Read, U.S.N.—on her arrival at Plymouth, from Portugal.

The wing area is the same in the two boats—2,380 sq. ft.—but the N.C.2 has shown in trials to have a loading efficiency of 47 per cent. as against 36.4 per cent. for the N.C.1 although, owing to her fourth engine, the power loading of the N.C.2 is only 17.9 lbs./h.p. as compared with the 22·2 lbs./h.p. of the N.C.1.

It is true that as a consequence of the greater load carried— 28,500 lbs. in flying trim—the wing loading has jumped from 9.1 to 12 lbs./sq. ft., an unusually high figure, judged by contemporary standards.

During her initial trials the N.C.2 took off after a 35 seconds' run (7 seconds better than the best performance of the N.C.1), and developed a high speed of 95 m.p.h., but both tests were made in "light" condition.

Since then the boat has lifted a total weight of 28,500 lbs., of which, it was believed, about 11,500 would be available in fuel for the trans-Atlantic flight.

However, the N.C.2 was not destined to participate in the grand adventure. Among the reasons given for this decision of those in power is the belief that the tandem arrangement of the engines is not conducive to best efficiency, because the pushers work in the slipstream of the tractors, while the operation of machine with both engines of either board cut out also appears a somewhat questionable proposition. Finally it was realised that the pilot nacelle unnecessarily increases head resistance, while certain misgivings are felt with regard to the advisability of having a worn-out pilot climb down the scaling ladder with a wind of 90 m.p.h. doing its utmost to blow him off.

THE REBUILT N.C.1.

Consequently it was decided that the N.C.2 should shed her wings, or rather the outer sections, so they might be fitted to the N.C.1, which had her wings damaged by a storm, and that the power plant of the latter boat should be modified to conform to the practice followed in the N.C.3.

The latter, which made her maiden flight on April 23rd, was fitted with three tractor airscrews, with engines arranged as in the N.C.1, but had besides a fourth engine, actuating a pusher, mounted tandem fashion with the central engine. This arrangement is believed to permit a much more efficient utilisation of the power plant, as airscrew interference can in the worse case extend to only one of the power units, while the possibility of an offsided pull is reduced from one-half to one-third.

This was well brought out during the initial flight of the N.C.3, marked by the antics of the starboard engine, which balked, despite the most strenuous efforts of the crew.

In spite of this handicap, the N.C.3 displayed great stability (in light condition it is true) during her trials, and great satisfaction was felt by the Navy people over this vindication of their views. Afterwards the N.C.3 was given a 2-hour sea trial, with a total weight of 29,500 lbs., for the purpose of testing her seaworthiness; this appears to have come off quite satisfactorily.

OTHER PREPARATIONS.

Shore parties of mechanics and sailors were sent to Trepassey Harbour, N.F., Horta (Azores), and Lisbon, to establish air stations. N.C. Seaplane Division 1 flew the so-called Southern course—that is, by way of Newfoundland, the Azores, and Portugal. There was 940 land miles from Rockaway to Trepassey Harbour, thence 1,230 miles to Horta, and 950 miles from there to Lisbon. The American boats did not follow the Northern or direct route, because their fuel tanks had insufficient reserve capacity for this purpose.

All three boats were equipped with radio direction finders and wireless sending and receiving instruments as well as with flame and smoke flares, which were to be dropped en route to ascertain the drift and permit due correction in the course.

The Arrival of N.C.4 at the R.A.F. Air Station at Cattewater, Plymouth, on May 31st, after her flight from Portugal.

THE WINNER.—N.C.4 at her moorings off Cattewater, Plymouth.

[For the following information the Editor is indebted largely to the Baron Ladislas D'Orcy, and to the two American Journals "Aviation" and "Aeria Age."]

A

AEROMARINE PLANE AND MOTOR COMPANY.

Offices: 1511 Times Building, New York. Factory: Keyport, N.J. President, I. M. Uppercu; Chief Engineer, Charles M. Willard.

Build aeroplanes and seaplanes for naval and sport use. Contractors to the U.S. Navy.

AEROMARINE, SPORT SEAPLANE.

Type of machine	Flying Boat.
Name or type No. of machine ..	Model 40-T.
Span, upper wing..	48 ft. 4 in.
Span, lower wing..	37 ft. 4 in.
Stagger	8 in.
Chord	75 in.
Gap	78 in.
Dihedral	2 degrees.
Area, upper panel (with ailerons)	304 sq. ft.
Area, lower panel	200 sq. ft.
Ailerons, each	29 sq. ft.
Elevators, each	12.8 sq. ft.
Stabilizer	39.5 sq. ft.
Vertical stabilizer fin	15 sq. ft.
Rudder	17.5 sq. ft.
Skid fin	5.5 sq. ft.
Length overall	28 ft. 11 in.
Weight, light	1,925 lbs.
Weight, loaded	2,485 lbs.
Gasoline	35 gallons.

Seating Arrangement. Model 40-T is arranged for one operator and one passenger, and is an ideal machine for instruction or sporting purposes.

Performance.

Aeromarine 125-130 h.p. motor:

High speed	80 m.p.h.
Landing speed..	38 m.p.h.
Climb	2,500 feet in 10 minutes.

100 h.p. motor:

High speed	70 m.p.h.
Landing speed..	38 m.p.h.
Climb	2,100 feet in 10 minutes.

Hull.—The hulls of these boats are constructed in the most modern and durable fashion.

The bottoms are constructed of two-ply, placed diagonally with cloth between and fastened with brass fastenings.

The sides and decks are of three-ply waterproof veneer.

The Aeromarine Sport Seaplane (Curtiss 100 h.p. O.X. 5 engine.

The Aeromarine Central Float Seaplane.

The decks forward of the cockpit and after the rear beam may be removed, as well as the floors in the passenger compartment, and as it is possible to enter the hull between the wing beams through the hatch, the entire bottom and inside of the boat may be inspected and repaired more easily.

50 of these machines have been delivered to the U.S. Navy. Price : $9,000.

Specifications of Model 50 Flying Boat.

The Aeromarine Plane and Motor Company's Model 50 is of the same general dimensions as that of Model 40-T.

The seating arrangement, however, is for three persons—two passengers side by side and a pilot sitting in a separate cockpit forward of the passengers.

This model will be supplied either with the passenger space enclosed or open, with movable windshield to protect the passengers.

Price : $9,500.

AEROMARINE, PRIMARY TRAINING (ARMY).

Type of machine	Land machine.
Name or type No. of machine ..	Model M.L.
Span	37 ft. 3 in.
Overall length	25 ft. 11 in.
Overall height	12 ft. 4 in.
Total wing area	430 sq. ft.
Weight, loaded	2,050 lbs.
Dihedral (top and bottom) ..	1 degree.
Sweep back	None.
Stagger	12 in.
Decalage	1 degree.
Gap	6 ft. 6 in.
Chord	6 ft. 3 in.
Aileron area (two ailerons) ..	56 sq. ft.
Rudder area	13 ft.
Elevator area (two elevators) ..	21 sq. ft.
Stabilizer area	33 sq. ft.
Upper plane—span	37 ft. 3 in.
Chord	6 ft. 3 in.
Area (not including ailerons)..	194 sq. ft.
Lower plane—span	32 ft. 10 in.
Chord	6 ft. 3 in.
Area	180 sq. ft.

The Aeromarine Model M.L. is a two-place land machine, equipped with the Aeromarine Model L. (6-cylinder) motor.

Seating Arrangement. The seats are arranged in tandem, and controls can be had in either or both cockpits.

Performance.

High speed	90 miles per hour.
Landing speed..	42 miles per hour.
Climb	6,000 feet in 10 minutes.

Price : $8,250.

Aeromarine Central Float Seaplane.

A--*continued*.

AIRCRAFT ENGINEERING CORPORA-TION, 2, East End Avenue, New York. Sales Offices: 220, West 42nd Street, New York. Factory A: 37, East 79th Street; factory B: 19, East 93rd Street, New York.

Build a small single-seater sporting aeroplane, the *Ace*, to the designs of N. W. Dalton, chief engineer of the firm.

Specification.

Span	..	..	..	28 ft. 4 in.
Length overall	..	..	..	16 ft. 1 in.
Chord	..	..	..	4 ft 6 in.
Engine	..	..	..	4-cylinder 40 h.p. B.W.W. (air-cooled).
Tractor airscrew	..	..	..	Direct driven.
High speed	..	..	..	60 m.p.h.
Low speed	..	..	..	30 m.p.h.
Weight, light	..	..	..	600 lbs.
Useful load	..	..	..	225 lbs.

The Aircraft Engineering Corporation's " Ace " (40 h.p B.W.W. engine).

B

BOEING AIRPLANE COMPANY.

Seattle, Wash.

The only seaplane constructors of the Pacific coast. Contractors to the U.S. Navy.

General Description of Model C.L. 4 S.

The model C.L. 4 S. is a modification of the model "C" seaplane. Although the general appearance and characteristics remain the same, the new engine installation together with a few minor changes have added to the performance of this machine.

The wing structure with its center cabane of steel simplifies assembly and clears the approach to, and vision from, the cockpits.

The tail unit, consisting of balanced elevators, rudder and fin, is independently complete, readily assembled and firmly fixed in place by steel tubing, forming a compact structure in keeping with the wind surfaces.

The body, although short in appearance, is wholly in keeping with the aero and hydro conditions met with in this type of seaplane.

Specification.

Power Plant.

(Hall-Scott Liberty Four) ..	125 h.p.

Wing and Control Surface Areas.

Main planes (including ailerons)	475 sq. ft.
Upper planes (including ailerons)	246 sq. ft.
Lower planes	229 sq. ft.
Ailerons	36.0 sq. ft.
Number of ailerons	2.
Elevators	30.0 sq. ft.
Rudder	12.0 sq. ft.
Vertical fin	6.0 sq. ft.

Overall Dimensions.

Span, upper	43 ft. 6 in.
Span, lower	43 ft. 2 in.
Chord, upper and lower ..	69 in.
Gap	72 in.
Length overall..	27 ft.

Incidence of Wings with Propeller Axis.

Upper	6½ degrees.
Lower	4 degrees.
Dihedral	2¾ degrees.
Stagger	29½ in.

Performance.

Get away	11 sec.
Climb in 10 min. (full load) ..	3,600 ft.
High speed	75 m.p.h.
Landing speed	38 m.p.h.
Endurance at full speed ..	3 hours.
Gasoline consumption (during altitude climb)	10.5 gallons per hour.
Oil consumption (during altitude climb)	1.0 gallon per hour.

Weight.

Fully loaded	2,430 lbs.

BREESE AIRCRAFT COMPANY.

New York.

Built "Penguin" training machine for the U.S. Army, and an experimental seaplane.

No details available.

THE BURGESS COMPANY.

Marblehead, Mass.

Subsidiary company of the Curtiss Aeroplane and Motor Corporation; specialised in the construction of seaplanes to Curtiss designs.

Built *Wright* types under license, also machines of their own. Later adopted the patents of Mr. J. W. Dunne, the British experimenter in inherent stability, and have had considerable success.

An Experimental Breese Seaplane.

The Boeing Seaplane, type C.L. 4 S. (124 h.p. 4-cylinder Liberty engine.)

3 K 2

C

CANTILEVER AERO COMPANY.

1269 Broadway, New York.

Constructors of the *Christmas* "Bullet," a high-speed single-seater biplane without external wing truss.

THE CHRISTMAS "BULLET."

A single-seater tractor biplane of quaint appearance was tested at the U.S.A. Government Experimental Field No. 1 on Dec. 3rd and 7th.

The machine is named the *Christmas* "Bullet" after its designer, Dr. W. W. Christmas, and is driven by a Liberty "6" engine, which develops 185 h.p. at 1,400 r.p.m. The "Bullet" was reported to have attained a speed of 175 m.p.h. at three-quarter throttle.

The "Bullet" has what is termed one-and-a-half planes, as used in the *Nieuport* biplanes, the upper plane having a span of 28ft, and a chord of 5 ft., the lower plane being 12 ft. in span with a chord of 2½ ft. External bracings and struts do not exist, the upper wing being fitted to the top of the fuselage and the lower wing to the bottom.

The wing curve is one developed by Dr. Christmas, and is of fairly deep section between the main wing spars, but tapers off sharply aft of the rear spar, merging into a flat and thin flexible trailing edge. The wing thus maintains a high angle of incidence and a fair camber at low speeds, and a lower angle and a flatter camber at higher speeds. This system of wing construction is reminiscent in a measure of the earlier *Bréguet* and *Caudron* machines.

Another View of the Christmas "Bullet."

Both upper and lower planes have the same aspect ratio. The upper plane has a maximum thickness of 5 ins. Fuller details of the wing construction cannot at the moment be given, as patents were still pending when the last was heard of the machine.

The car-type radiator and engine are placed in the front part of the fuselage, which is very deep. The two-bladed airscrew has a projecting bullet-shaped hub. The landing carriage struts are of deep section, such as is used in the *Curtiss* land machines and *Burgess* seaplanes. The pilot's cockpit is located behind the upper plane, affording a fairly good view in most directions.

The elevator is not divided, as the rudder is fitted to the vertical fin in such a manner as not to interfere with free elevator movement. This method is similar to that employed in the *Pfalz* single-seater scout. The tail-skid is fixed to the stern-post.

The principal details of the *Christmas* "Bullet" are as follows:

Span, upper plane	..	..	28 ft.
Span, lower plane	..	..	12 ft.
Chord, upper plane	..	..	5 ft.
Chord, lower plane	..	..	2 ft. 6 in.
Area, upper plane	..	..	140 sq. ft.
Area, lower plane	..	..	30 sq. ft.
Length overall	..	..	21 ft.
Weight, machine empty	..	..	1,820 lbs.
Weight, fully loaded	..	..	2,100 lbs.
Minimum speed	..	..	50-60 m.p.h.
Maximum speed	..	..	175 m p.h.
Cruising radius	..	..	550 miles.
Ceiling	..	..	14,700 ft.

The Christmas "Bullet" (185 h.p. 6-cylinder Liberty engine).

C—continued.

THE CONTINENTAL AIRCRAFT COR-PORATION.

Office : 120, Liberty Street, New York City. Factory : Amityville, Long Island, New York. Demonstrating ground : Central Park, Long Island.

THE CONTINENTAL KB-3T TRAINING TRACTOR.

The Continental Aircraft Corporation's new training tractor KB-3T recently tested at Amityville, has come up to all expectations of the designer Vincent J. Buranelli. The short " over-all " length of this machine, 23 feet 4 inches, is noteworthy and characteristic of Continental machines.

Mr. Buranelli's chief object in designing the KB-3T was to produce a training machine that could be cheaply constructed. This has been accomplished by an extensive use of one-piece standardized fittings. A very complete list of measurements and weights are given which should prove useful in checking up with other machines.

General Specifications.

Span upper plane	.. ..	40 ft. 3in.
Span lower plane	.. ..	34 ft.
Chord both planes	.. .. ..	5 ft. 6 in.
Sap	.. ..	5 ft. 4 in.
Stagger	.. .. ..	6 in.
Length over all	.. .. ..	23 ft. 4 in.
Height	.. .. ..	9 ft. 3 in.
Net weight ..	.. .. ..	1,340 lb.
Useful load ..	.. .. ..	540 lb.
Gross weight ..	.. .. ..	1,880 lb.
Motor, Curtiss..	.. .. ..	OX 100 h.p.
Speed range ..	.. .. ..	45-75 m.p.h.
Climb in ten minutes..	.. ..	3,200 ft.

Weights.

Upper planes	.. ..	118 lb.
Lower planes	.. .. ..	102 lb.
Struts ..	.. .. ..	30 lb.
Wires and turnbuckles	.. ..	20 lb.
Fittings and bolts	.. ..	18 lb.
Total ..	.. .. ..	288 lb.
Fuselage	.. .. ..	310 lb.
Seats upholstered	.. ..	12 lb.
Stick controls and mountings	..	17 lb.
Dash with instruments	..	13 lb.
Total ..	.. .. ..	352 lb.

Ailerons	.. ..	24 lb
Elevators	.. ..	16 lb.
Rudder ..	.. .. ..	10 lb.
Vertical stabilizer	.. .. ..	3 lb.
Horizontal stabilizer	.. .. ..	19 lb.
Control cables ..	.. .. ..	16 lb.
Total ..	.. .. ..	88 lb.
Motor complete	.. .. ..	390 lb.
Propeller	.. .. ..	22 lb.
Radiator and piping ..	.. ..	53 lb.
Gas tank and gauges ..	.. ..	22 lb
Exhaust pipe ..	.. .. ..	16 lb.
Total ..	.. .. ..	503 lb.

Landing chassis and incidentals = 109 lb.

Planes.

The wing curve is Eiffel 36. The planes are set with an angle of incidence of $2\frac{1}{2}$ degrees. Top and bottom are the same. The tips of planes are slightly rounded as is in general use on Continental machines. There is no sweepback, but a dihedral of 1 degree and a stagger of 6 in. The upper planes are made in two main sections with a three-foot panel over the body. The lower plane is in two sections and attaching to the body. Wing beams are of " I " section and made of Douglas fir. The overhang is braced by a steel strut made of $\frac{7}{8}$ in. seamless tubing with a fairing of spruce.

The struts are of streamline section, the maximum $3\frac{3}{4}$ in. $\times$ $1\frac{1}{2}$ in. occurring at the centre, and tapering in proportion to each end where it sets into a special strut socket. Flying cables are double $\frac{5}{32}$ in. in inner panel, $\frac{1}{8}$ in. outer panel, landing wires are single of the same sizes. Double drift and single trueing wires are used. All control wires are internal.

Ailerons on top plane only. and are 11 ft. $\times$ 1 ft. 6 in. Where ailerons are attached, a bevel on the aileron permits the surface to be moved without a space occurring between aileron and wing.

R. A. F. stitching is employed in attaching the fabric to the ribs. To finish four coats of " dope " and two coats of Valspar are used. A factor of safety of 7 is employed. The lift to drag ratio is 12.

THE CONTINENTAL
MODEL KB-3T 100 H.P.
TRAINING TRACTOR

C—continued.

CURTISS AEROPLANE AND MOTORS CORPORATION. 52, Vanderbilt Avenue, New York.

Factories at Buffalo and Hammondsport, N.Y. Flying fields at Buffalo, Hammondsport, Newport News, Va., and Miami, Fla.

The largest American aeronautical construction firm; their activity ranges from the smallest to the largest aeroplanes and seaplanes, and from aero engines to airship cars. Contractors to the U.S. Army and Navy.

Glenn H. Curtiss in 1907 and 1908 was a member of the Aerial Experiment Association, formed by Dr. and Mrs. Alexander Graham Bell. This Association built four machines, each along the lines of one of the four engineers belonging to the Association, F. W. Baldwin, Lieut. T. E. Selfridge, G. H. Curtiss and J. A. D. McCurdy. The last built was the *June Bug*, designed by Curtiss and was the most successful. In the spring of 1908, the Association was disbanded and The Aeronautical Society gave Curtiss an order for an aeroplane with *carte blanche* as to design. He produced a 4-cyl. machine, with a Curtiss engine, and flew it.

A duplicate was hurriedly built, an 8-cyl. engine installed, and taken to Europe for the first Gordon Bennett, which he won. Returning, the same type was continued with minor improvements. Later the front elevator was brought closer in, finally discarded, and the fan tail adopted. In April, 1913, a military tractor was built and flown.

On January 26th, 1911, first successful flights were made with a hydro-aeroplane, at the Winter camp at San Diego, California. This had two floats tandem. One was finally adopted and great success was achieved. With this machine various experiments were made.

In 1912 he brought out his present type of flying boat. This is being rapidly developed and minor changes in details are made in practically every machine put out.

In May, 1913, he produced a special 4-passenger flying boat for a customer to special order.

In 1914, much attention was paid to flying boats, and a huge two-engined machine was built to the order of Mr. Wanamaker and designed by Lieut. John Porte, R.N., the intention being that it should fly the Atlantic.

Just before the war this machine was fitted with three engines. Later on a big triplane with four 250 h.p. Curtiss engines was built, and was taken over by the British Navy. It was, however, not a success.

Many school biplanes of the "J.N." type were supplied to the belligerent powers, and did remarkably well for their purpose. Late in 1916, a remarkably good flight was made on an "R. 7" type, from Chicago to New York, with one stop, by the late Victor Carlstrom.

CURTISS TYPE 18T. TRIPLANE.

Specification.

General Dimensions.

Wing span, upper plane..	31 ft. 11 in.
Wing span, middle plane	31 ft. 11 in.
Wing span, lower plane ..	31 ft. 11 in.
Depth of wing chord (upper, middle and lower)	42 in.
Gap between wings (between upper and middle)	42 in.
Gap between wings (between middle and lower)	$35\frac{9}{16}$ in.
Stagger	None.
Length of machine overall	23 ft. $3\frac{3}{16}$ in.
Height of machine overall	9 ft. $10\frac{3}{8}$ in.
Angle of incidence	$2\frac{1}{2}$ degrees.
Dihedral angle	None.
Sweepback	5 degrees.
Wing curve	Sloane.
Horizontal stabilizer—angle of incidence	0.5 degrees.

Areas.

Wings, upper	112.0 sq. ft.
Wings, middle	87.71 sq. ft.
Wings, lower	87.71 sq. ft.
Ailerons (middle 10.79, lower 10.79)	21.58 sq. ft.
Horizontal stabilizer	14.3 sq. ft.
Vertical stabilizer	5·2 sq. ft.
Elevators (each 6.51)	13.02 sq. ft.
Rudder	8.66 sq. ft.
Total supporting surface	309.0 sq. ft.
Loading (weight carried per sq. ft. of supporting surface)..	9.4 lbs.
Loading (per r.h.p.)	7.25 lbs.

Weights.

Net weight, machine empty	1,825 lbs.
Gross weight, machine and load..	2,901 lbs.
Useful load	1,076 lbs.
Fuel	400 lbs.
Oil	45 lbs.
Pilot and passenger	330 lbs.
Useful load	301 lbs.
Total	1076 lbs.

The Curtiss Triplane, type 18T., Single-seater Fighter (Curtiss K. 12 400 h.p. engine).

CURTISS—*continued*.

CURTISS TYPE 18T. TRIPLANE—*continued*.

Performance.

Speed, max. (horizontal flight) ..	163 m.p.h.
Speed, min. (horizontal flight) ..	58 m.p.h.
Climbing speed	15,000 ft. in 10 mins.

Motor.

Model K. 12, 12-cylinder, Vee, four-stroke cycle	Water cooled.
Horse power (rated) at 2500 r.p.m.	400.
Weight per rated h.p.	1.70
Bore and stroke	$4\frac{1}{2} \times 6$.
Fuel consumption per hour ..	36.7 galls.
Fuel tank capacity	67 galls.
Oil capacity provided, crankcase	6 galls.
Fuel consumption per b.h.p. ..	.55 lbs. per hour.
Oil consumption per b.h.p. ..	.030 lbs. per hour.

Propeller.

Material.—Wood.
Pitch.—According to requirements of performance.
Diameter.—According to requirements of performance.
Direction of rotation, as viewed from pilot's seat.—Clockwise.

Details.

One pressure and one gravity gasoline tank located in fuselage.
Tail skid independent of tail post ; landing gear wheel, size 26 in. × 4 in.
Standard Equipment.—Tachometer, oil gauge, gasoline gauge, complete set of tools ; other equipment on special order.

Maximum Range.

At economic speed, about 550 miles.

CURTISS MODEL J.N. 4D. 2 TRACTOR.
Specification.

General Dimensions.

Wing span, upper plane.. ..	43 ft. $7\frac{3}{8}$ in.
Wing span, lower plane	33 ft. $11\frac{1}{4}$ in.
Depth of wing chord	$59\frac{1}{2}$ in.
Gap between wings	$61\frac{1}{4}$ in.
Stagger	.16 in.
Length of machine overall ..	27 ft. 4 in.
Height of machine overall ..	9 ft. $10\frac{5}{8}$ in.
Angle of incidence	2 degrees.
Dihedral angle	1 degree.
Sweepback	0 degrees.
Wing curve	Eiffel No. 6.
Horizontal stabilizer—angle of incidence	0 degrees.

Areas.

Wings, upper	167.94 sq. ft.
Wings, lower	149.42 sq. ft.
Ailerons, upper	35.2 sq. ft.
Horizontal stabilizer	28.7 sq .ft.
Vertical stabilizer	3.8 sq. ft.
Elevators (each 11 sq. ft.) ..	22 sq. ft.
Rudder	12 sq. ft.
Total supporting surface ..	352.56 sq. ft.
Loading (weight carried per sq. ft. of supporting surface) ..	6.04 lbs.
Loading (per r.h.p.)	23·65 lbs.

Weights.

Net weight, machine empty	1,580 lbs.
Gross weight, machine and load	2,130 lbs.
Useful load	550 lbs.
Fuel	130 lbs.
Oil	38 lbs.
Pilot..	165 lbs.
Passenger and other load.. ..	217 lbs.
Total	550 lbs.

The Standard type Curtiss J.N. Training Tractor. The type most used by the U.S. Army.

CURTISS—*continued.*

CURTISS MODEL J.N. TRACTOR—*continued*

Performance.

Speed, max. (horizontal flight) ..	75 m.p.h.
Speed, min. (horizontal flight) ..	45 m.p.h.
Climbing speed	3,000 ft. in 10 mins.

Motor.

Model O.X. 8-cylinder, Vee, four-stroke cycle	Water cooled.
Horse power (rated) at 1400 r.p.m.	90.
Weight per rated h.p.	4.33 lbs.
Bore and stroke	4 in. × 5 in.
Fuel consumption per hour ..	9 galls.
Fuel tank capacity	21 galls.
Oil capacity provided (crankcase)	4 galls.
Fuel consumption per b.h.p ..	0.60 lbs. per hour.
Oil consumption per b.h.p. ..	0.030 lbs. per hour.

Propeller.

Material.—Wood.
Pitch.—According to requirements of performance.
Diameter.—According to requirements of performance.
Direction of rotation, viewed from pilot's seat.—Clockwise.

Details.

One gasoline tank located in fuselage.
Tail skid independent of tail post.
Landing gear wheel, size 26 in. × 4 in.
Standard Equipment.—Tachometer, oil gauge, gasoline gauge, complete set of tools.
Other equipment on special order.

Maximum Range.

At economic speed, about 250 miles.

Shipping Data.

Fuselage Box.—Dimensions : 24 ft. 6 in. × 5 ft. 3 in. × 3 ft. 1 in.; gross weight, 2,380 lbs.
Panel Box.—Dimensions : 20 ft. 9 in. × 5 ft. 8 in. × 3 ft.; gross weight, 1,450 lbs.

CURTISS MODEL H. 16A. FLYING BOAT.
Specification.

General Dimensions.

Wing span, upper plane..	..	96 ft. 6$\frac{5}{8}$ in.
Wing span, lower plane ..	..	68 ft. 11$\frac{3}{8}$ in.
Depth of wing chord ..	..	84$\frac{49}{64}$ in.
Gap between wings ..	..	96$\frac{9}{16}$ in.
Stagger	..	None.
Length of machine overall ..	46 ft. 1$\frac{15}{32}$ in.
Height of machine overall ..	17 ft. 8$\frac{5}{8}$ in.
Angle of incidence ..	..	4 degrees.
Dihedral angle	..	1 degree.
Sweepback	..	None.
Wing curve	..	R.A.F. No. 6.
Horizontal stabilizer—angle of incidence	..	2 degrees pos.

A Curtiss Single-Seat Fighter (400 h.p. K. 12 Curtiss engine). A very high speed single-seat fighter.

The Curtiss Model 18 B. Two-seater Fighter (400 h.p. K. 12 Curtiss engine).

CURTISS—*continued.*

CURTISS MODEL H. 16A. FLYING BOAT—*continued.*

Areas.

Wings, upper (without ailerons)	616.2 sq. ft.
Wings, lower	443.1 sq. ft.
Ailerons	131 sq. ft.
Horizontal stabilizer	108 sq. ft.
Vertical stabilizer	31.1 sq. ft.
Elevators	58.4 sq. ft.
Rudder	27.9 sq. ft.
Non-skids	24 sq. ft.
Total supporting surface ..	119.3 sq. ft.
Loading (weight carried per sq. ft. of supporting surface) ..	8.54 lbs.
Loading (per r.h.p.)	15.42 lbs.

Weights.

Net weight, machine empty	6,956 lbs.
Gross weight, machine and load	10,172 lbs.
Useful load	3,216 lbs.
Fuel and oil	1,527 lbs.
Crew	660 lbs.
Useful load	1,029 lbs.
Total	3,216 lbs.

Performance.

Speed, max. (horizontal flight) ..	95 m.p.h.
Speed, min. (horizontal flight) ..	55 m.p.h.
Climbing speed	4,000 ft. in 10 mins.

Motor.

Two Liberty 12-cylinder, Vee, four-stroke cycle	Water cooled.
Horse power (each motor 330) ..	660
Weight per rated h.p.	2.55
Bore and stroke	5 in. × 7 in.
Fuel consumption (both motors)	62.8 galls. per hour.
Fuel tank capacity	300 galls.
Oil capacity provided	10 galls.
Fuel consumption per b.h.p. ..	0.57 lbs. per hour.
Oil consumption per b.h.p. ..	0.03 lbs. per hour.

Propeller.

Material.—Wood.
Diameter.—According to requirements of performance.
Pitch.—According to requirements of performance.

Maximum Range.

At economic speed, about 675 miles.

Shipping Data.

Hull Box.—Dimensions : 44 ft. 9 in. × 11 ft. × 9 ft. 4 in. ; gross weight, 1,300 lbs.
Panel Box.—Dimensions : 30 ft. 4 in. × 7 ft. 7 in. × 6 ft. 6 in. ; gross weight, 4,850 lbs.
Panel Box.—Dimensions : 21 ft. 2 in. × 7 ft. 5 in. × 3 ft. 6 in. ; gross weight, 2,170 lbs.
Engine Box.—Dimensions : 6 ft. 2 in. × 4 ft. 4 in. × 2 ft. 9 in. : gross weight, 1,645 lbs.

The Curtiss type R. 8 Bomber (160 h.p. Curtiss engines).

The Curtiss H. 12 Boat (two 160 h.p Curtiss engines).

CURTISS MODEL H.S. 2L. FLYING BOAT.
Specification.

General Dimensions.

Wing span, upper plane	74 ft. $0\frac{19}{32}$ in.
Wing span, lower plane	64 ft. $1\frac{21}{32}$ in.
Depth of wing chord . .	6 ft. $3\frac{5}{32}$ in.
Gap between wings (front) . .	7 ft. $7\frac{1}{8}$ in.
Gap between wings (rear) . .	7 ft. $5\frac{19}{32}$ in.
Stagger	None.
Length of machine overall . .	40 ft.
Height of machine overall . .	14 ft. $7\frac{1}{4}$ in.
Angle of incidence, upper plane .	$5\frac{1}{2}$ degrees.
Angle of incidence, lower plane .	4 degrees.
Dihedral angle	2 degrees.
Sweepback	0 degrees.
Wing curve	R.A.F. No. 6.
Horizontal stabilizer—angle of incidence	0 degrees.

Areas.

Wings, upper	380.32 sq. ft.
Wings, lower	314.92 sq. ft.
Ailerons (upper 62.88, lower 42.48)	105.36 sq. ft.
Horizontal stabilizer . .	54.8 sq. ft.
Vertical stabilizer . .	19.6 sq. ft.
Elevators (each 22.8 sq. ft.) . .	45.6 sq. ft.
Rudder	26.5 sq. ft.
Total supporting surface . .	800.6 sq. ft.
Loading (weight carried per sq. ft. of supporting surface) . .	7.77 lbs.
Loading (per r.h.p.)	18.85 lbs.

Weights.

Net weight, machine empty	4,359 lbs.
Gross weight, machine and load	6,223 lbs.
Useful load	1,864 lbs
Fuel	977 lbs.
Crew	360 lbs.
Useful load	527 lbs.
Total	1,864 lbs.

Performance.

Speed, max. (horizontal flight) . .	91 m.p.h.
Speed, min. (horizontal flight) . .	55 m.p.h.
Climbing speed	1,800 ft. in 10 mins.

Motor.

Liberty 12-cylinder, Vee, four-stroke cycle	Water cooled.
Horse power (rated)	330.
Weight per rated h.p.	2.55 lbs.
Bore and stroke	5 in. × 7 in.
Fuel consumption	32 galls per hour.
Fuel tank capacity	152·8 galls.
Oil tank capacity . .	8 galls.
Fuel consumption per b.h.p. . .	0.57 lbs. per hour.
Oil consumption per b.h.p. . .	0.03 lbs. per hour.

The Curtiss Central Float Seaplane (Curtiss K. 12 400 h.p. engine).

A Curtiss Training Seaplane.

CURTISS MODEL H.S.2 L. FLYING BOAT—*continued.*

Propeller.
Material.—Wood.
Pitch.—According to requirements of performance.
Diameter.—According to requirements of performance.
Direction of rotation, viewed from pilot's seat.—Clockwise.

Maximum Range.
At economic speed, about 575 miles.

Shipping Data.
Hull Box.—Dimensions : 35 ft. 5 in. × 8 ft. 6 in × 6 ft. 4 in. ;
  gross weight, 8,525 lbs.
Panel Box.—Dimensions : 23 ft. 6 in. × 6 ft. 9 in. × 3 ft. 5 in. ;
  gross weight, 2,900 lbs.
Engine Box.—Dimensions : 6 ft. 2 in. × 4 ft. 4 in. × 2 ft. 9 in. ;
  gross weight, 1,645 lbs.

CURTISS MODEL M.F. FLYING BOAT.
Specification.

General Dimensions.

Wing span, upper plane.. ..	49 ft. $9\frac{3}{8}$ in.
Wing span, lower plane	38 ft. $7\frac{5}{32}$ in.
Depth of wing chord	60 in.
Gap between wings at engine section	6 ft. $4\frac{5}{54}$ in.
Stagger	None.
Length of machine overall ..	28 ft. $10\frac{3}{16}$ in.
Height of machine overall ..	11 ft. $9\frac{3}{8}$ in.
Angle of incidence	6 degrees.
Dihedral angle, lower panels only	2 degrees.
Sweepback	None.
Wing curve	U.S.A. No. 1.
Horizontal stabilizer—angle of incidence	0 degrees.

Areas.

Wings, upper	187.54 sq. ft.
Wings, lower	169.10 sq. ft.
Ailerons (each 22.43 sq. ft.) ..	44.86 sq. ft.
Horizontal stabilizer	33.36 sq. ft.
Vertical stabilizer	15.74 sq. ft.
Elevators (each 15.165 sq. ft.) ..	30.33 sq. ft.
Rudder	20.42 sq. ft.
Total supporting surface ..	401.50 sq. ft.
Loading (weight carried per sq. ft. of supporting surface) ..	6·05 lbs.
Loading (per r.h.p.)	24.32 lbs.

Weights.

Net weight, machine empty		1,796 lbs.
Gross weight, machine and load		2,432 lbs.
Useful Load		636 lbs.
Fuel	240 lbs.	
Oil	22.5 lbs.	
Water	36 lbs.	
Pilot	165 lbs.	
Passenger	165 lbs.	
Miscellaneous accessories ..	7·5 lbs.	
Total		636.0 lbs.

Performance.

Speed, max. (horizontal flight) ..	69 m.p.h.
Speed, min. (horizontal flight) ..	45 m.p.h.
Climbing speed	5,000 ft. in 27 mins.

Motor.

Model O.X.X. 8-cylinder, Vee, four-stroke cycle	Water cooled.
Horse power (rated) at 1400 r.p.m.	100.
Weight per r.h.p...	4.01 lbs.
Bore and stroke	$4\frac{1}{2}$ in. × 5 in.
Fuel consumption	10 galls. per hour.
Fuel tank capacity	40 galls.
Oil capacity provided (crankcase)	5 galls.
Fuel consumption per b.h.p. ..	0.60 lbs. per hour.
Oil consumption per b.h.p. ..	0.030 lbs. per hour.

Propeller.
Material.—Wood.
Pitch.—According to requirements of performance.
Diameter.—According to requirements of performance.
Direction of rotation, as viewed from pilot's seat.—Clockwise.

Details.
Dual control.
Standard Equipment.—Tachometer, oil gauge, gasoline gauge,
  complete set of tools.
Other equipment on special order.

Maximum Range.
At economic speed, about 325 miles.

Shipping Data—Foreign Shipment.
Hull Box.—Dimensions : 26 ft. 6 in. × 6 ft 3 in. × 4 ft. 11 in. ;
  gross weight, 2,390 lbs.
Panel Box.—Dimensions : 22 ft. 3 in. × 5 ft. 11 in. × 3 ft. 9 in. ;
  gross weight, 730 lbs.
Engine Box.—Dimensions : 5 ft. 4 in. × 3 ft. 3 in. × 2 ft. 9 in. ;
  gross weight, 680 lbs.
For domestic shipment, sidewalks and engine section are
  crated with hull ; gross weight, 2,680 lbs.

CURTISS ENGINEERING CORPORATION. Garden City, Long Island, New York.

A company was founded by Mr. Glenn Curtiss and quite distinct from the Curtiss Aeroplane and Motors Corporation. Mainly engaged in experimental work. For this purpose a complete aerodynamical laboratory and a large flying field is available.

The *Curtiss* 18-2 triplane, the 18-B biplane and the N.C-1 flying boat are the most notable achievements of this organisation.

The Curtiss M.F, Sporting type Flying Boat (100 h.p. Curtiss O.X.X. engine).

453a

D

THE DAYTON-WRIGHT AIRPLANE COMPANY. Dayton, Ohio.

President, C. F. Kettering; General Manager, G. M. Williams.
Factory: Dayton, Ohio.

This company was organised during the war for the quantity production of aeroplanes to government specifications. On February 1st, 1919, the total number of machines constructed comprised 400 Standard J.1 training aeroplanes and 3,100 D.H. 4 A "battle-planes."

THE AMERICAN D.H. 4 BIPLANE.
(Built by Dayton Wright Aeroplane Co.)

Specification.

Type of machine	Two-seater Biplane.
Name or type No. of machine ..	American D.H. 4.
Purpose for which intended. ..	Reconnaissance.
Span	42 ft. 5¾ in.
Overall length	30 ft. 5⁶¹⁄₆₄ in.
Maximum height	10 ft. 3²⁹⁄₃₂ in.
Chord..	5 ft. 6 in.
Span of tail	13 ft. 7 in.
Engine type and h.p. ..	Liberty 12; 400 h.p.
Weight of machine empty ..	2,391 lbs.
Tank capacity in gallons ..	88 gallons.

Performance.

Speed low down	124.7 m.p.h.
Speed at 6,500 feet	120 m.p.h.
Speed at 10,000 feet	117 m.p.h.
Speed at 15,000 feet	113 m.p.h.
Landing speed	58 m.p.h.

Climb

To 10,000 feet in minutes ..	14 minutes.
Ceiling	19,500 feet.
Endurance at 6,500 feet (full throttle).. ..	2 hrs. 13 mins.
Endurance at 6,500 feet (half throttle) ..	3 hrs. 3 mins.
Track	6 feet.
Total weight of machine loaded	3,582 lbs.

THE DAYTON-WRIGHT LIMOUSINE.

This machine is a D.H. 4, modified for civilian passenger-carrying.

Specification.

Type of machine	Three-seater " Limousine " Biplane.
Name or type No. of machine ..	D. 4K.—The Honeymoon.
Purpose for which intended ..	Civilian Flying.
Span	42 ft. 5½ in.
Overall length	31 ft. 1½ in.
Maximum height	11 ft. 9 in.
Engine type and h.p.	400 h.p. Liberty.
Weight of machine empty.. ..	2,400 lbs.
Petrol tank capacity in gallons ..	88 gallons.

Performance.

Speed low down	115 m.p.h.
Landing speed	53 m.p.h.

Climb.

To 10,000 feet	10 minutes.
Total weight of machine loaded	3,410 lbs.

The Dayton-Wright " Honeymoon Express " (400 h.p. Liberty engine). A converted American De H. 4.

DAYTON-WRIGHT—*continued*.

Since the signing of the Armistice this company have turned their attention toward producing a small single-seater sport aeroplane, the "Messenger."

THE DAYTON-WRIGHT "MESSENGER."

Biplane tractor, equipped with a 2-cycle, 4-cylinder air-cooled "V" type De Palma engine, weighing 3.7 lb./h.p., with a fuel consumption of 4 gal. per hour.

Specification.

Total area..	106 sq. ft.
Fully loaded weight	636 lbs.
Speed range (as given by manufacturer)	37-85 m.p.h.
Engine develops ..	37 h.p. at 2,000 r.p.m.
Weight empty	476 lbs., with a gasoline supply of 12 gallons.
Overall length	17 ft. 6 in.
Span	19 ft. 3 in.
Height	6 ft. 1 in.

It has a certain family resemblance to the DeHavilland machines, in landing gear, attachment of wings to center, section, etc. One or two interesting features are present. Single cables are used for both flying and landing wires, streamlined with rubber fairing. The fuselage consists of longerons, veneer sides and wood strips in lieu of wires.

The Dayton-Wright "Messenger" Single-seat Sporting Model (35 h.p. De Palma engine).

G

GALLAUDET AIRCRAFT CORPORATION

East Greenwich, Conn.

New York Office : 15 West 40th Street.

Seaplane and aeroplane constructors : contractors to the U.S. Navy. In addition to a Liberty-motored single pontoon sea-plane, which is notable for its fuselage-propeller, this firm have recently produced a small sport aeroplane, the "Chummy Flyabout," which is driven by two motorcycle engines and twin screws.

THE GALLAUDET D.4 LIGHT BOMBER SEAPLANE.

Specification.

Type of machine	Two-seater Seaplane.
Name or type No. of machine	D. 4.
Purpose for which intended	Bombing.
Span	46 ft. 6 in.
Overall length	33 ft.
Maximum height	11 ft. 6 in.
Single central float.	
Engine type and h.p.	Liberty (power unstated).
Weight of machine empty	3,800 lbs.
Petrol tank capacity in gallons	64 gallons.

Performance.

Speed (maximum)	130 m.p.h.
Landing speed	45 m.p.h.

Climb.

To 8,100 feet in minutes	15 minutes.
Total weight of machine loaded	5,430 lbs.

THE GALLAUDET "CHUMMY FLYABOUT," or E.L.2 MONOPLANE.

Weight fully loaded	1,080 lbs.
Wing area	130 sq. ft.
Wing loading	8.3 lb./sq. ft.

Two engines, Indian motorcycle, with no important departures from usual form, developing between 18 and 20 h.p. each and giving a power loading of 27 lb./h.p.

Fuel capacity, 8 gal., giving an endurance at full power of, 2 hours.

Span	33 ft.
Chord	4 ft. 6 in.
R.A.F. 15 wing section modified.	
Dihedral	2 degrees.
Overall length	18 ft. 7 in.

Tail areas as follows : Stabilizer, 12 sq. ft. ; elevators, 8.5 sq. ft.; vertical fin, 2 sq. ft. ; rudder, 4 sq. ft.

The pilot and passenger side by side, and vision good.

The propeller drive for the two pushers is intended to minimize the danger of engine breakdown by employing a twin drive. The single transverse shaft is driven by a chain from each engine, and by means of two disc clutches, either of the two engines can drive both propellers.

In the case of one engine stalling, there is, under these conditions no tendency for a spin, as in the case of twin engines with two separately driven propellers. As an offset to these advantages there is the additional weight and complication of long shafting, two bevel gear systems, etc.

An interesting point in this design is the extremely low landing gear. This permits the wheels to be half enclosed within the boat-like body, with a corresponding decrease in resistance. On rough landings, however, the low landing gear entails somewhat the risk of the wing tips striking the ground.

No news has been received of the machine having flown.

GENERAL AEROPLANE COMPANY.

Detroit, Mich.

Constructed three types of *Verville* aeroplanes, a flying boat, seaplane and land machine. Also run a flying school.

Building to official specifications.

The Gallaudet "Chummy Flyabout" (two Indian motor cycle engines).

K

THE KYLE-SMITH AIRCRAFT
COMPANY. Wheeling, West Virginia, U.S.A

Manufactured a two-seater tractor biplane intended for sporting and training purposes, with six cylinder radial engine.

Building to official specifications.

L

LANZIUS AIRCRAFT COMPANY.

149, Broadway, New York, U.S.A.

Manufactured tractor biplanes with incidence varying from 0° to 15°.

Building to official specifications.

LAWRENCE-LEWIS AEROPLANE
COMPANY. Peoples' Gas Building, Chicago, Ill.

Manufactured two types of tractor biplanes, inherently stable and without ailerons, one a curious flying boat (See Historical Section, 1916).

Building to official specifications.

LAWSON AIRCRAFT CORPORATION.

Green Bay, Wisconsin. President : Alfred W. Lawson.

Manufacturers of a two-seater tractor biplane destined for training and civil flying.

Specifications.

Span, upper plane	39 ft.
Span, lower plane	36 ft.
Chord	5 ft. 2 in.
Gap	5 ft. 1 in.
Stagger	8 in.
Incidence	3 degrees.
Dihedral	1 degree.
Area, upper plane (including ailerons	200 sq. ft.
Area, lower plane	150 sq. ft.
Length, overall	25 ft.
Height, overall	8 ft.
Weight, empty	12,000 lbs.
Weight, loaded	1,900 lbs.
Speed range	40-90 m.p.h.
Climb in 10 minutes	6,000 ft.
Gliding angle, full load	1 in 9.
Engine, Hall-Scott	100 h.p.

The Lawson Aircraft Corporation's Two-seater (100 h.p. Hall-Scott engine).

L—*continued*.

LOENING ENGINEERING CORPORATION. 351 West 52nd Street, New York.

President: Grover C. Loening.

Aeronautical constructional engineers, engaged during the war in experimental work for the U.S. Army and Navy, as the result of which they produced a fighting monoplane of highly original design and a ship-plane of very small dimensions.

THE LOENING MONOPLANE.

It is stated that in its actual performance the *Loening* monoplane has, with the full two-seater fighter load, not only exceeded all the performances of other machines, but has with this same load equalled, if not exceeded, all of the performances of the very best European single-seaters with the same engine.

In the tests made by the manufacturer at Mineola, the machine showed a high speed of 146 m.p.h., and on one occasion climbed to 24,000 ft. in 43 min. with pilot, passenger, two hours fuel and considerable gun equipment, thus establishing an unofficial height record for two-seaters.

The new monoplane of the same type tested at Dayton by the U.S. Army showed practically the same high speed, and climbed—with a live load almost equal to the weight of the aeroplane—16,000 ft. in 18 min.

The outstanding feature of the machine is the manner in which the wings fasten to the upper body longitudinals, and are braced by two enormous braces to the bottom of the body. This method of wing bracing has so much simplified the construction of the machine, that it has permitted to cut in halves the structure weight.

A very interesting feature of the design proven by the tests made is the slow speed on landing and general buoyancy of the machine, despite the fact that the wing loading has gradually been stepped up to almost 12 lb. per sq. ft.

Construction.

The wings, body, tail surfaces, landing gear, etc., are all built of most approved spruce and metal fitting airplane construction. All metal fittings are of stamped sheet metal, with practically no brazed or welded parts; all joints are pin connected, particularly the joints of the main wing braces to the wings and body, which are free to move in any direction, so that vibration will not fatigue these members. In addition to which, all parts are readily adjustable for alignment.

Safety Factor.

Sand load tests that have been carried on exhaustively to prove the strength of the machine show a safety factor of 14 on drift stresses, and a safety factory of 8 on lift stresses.

All tail surfaces and fin surfaces, stabilizers, rudders, etc., withstand on actual sand test a load of 35 lbs. per sq. ft. area.

Military Features.

It is claimed that the visibility afforded to the pilot is so complete that he has practically no blind spots at all. He can see either above or below the wings or to either side, and in addition to that can see quite well in the front, due to the narrowness of the body.

The Gun Range.

The gun range is also very good, particularly as the gunner can shoot forward, the only obstruction being the arc of the airscrew.

The deep body offers ample room for all kinds of military equipment, oxygen tanks, wireless apparatus, cameras, etc., and in addition to that the arrangement of the cowls is such as to give the occupants ample protection against the wind without interfering with the view.

The construction has everywhere been studied so as to give maximum strength to all of the parts that are vital due to damage from bullets. This is particularly true of the main braces supporting the wings which can be half shot away before they will lose the safety factor of 8 provided.

Performance.

It has been found that the machine lands very slowly, gets off the ground in 4 seconds from a dead start, and that in flight the machine is very easy to handle on all its controls in spirals, loops, barrel rolls, etc.

The performances of the machine with full load are as follows :

Slow speed	48 m.p.h.
High speed	146 m.p.h.
Indicated ceiling, light load	26,000 ft.
heavy load	22,000 ft.

The principal characteristics of the *Loening* monoplane are as follows :—

Areas.

Main planes, total	238.9 sq. ft.
Upper planes, including ailerons	214.9 sq. ft.
Strut planes	24.0 sq. ft.
Ailerons (2)	24.0 sq. ft.
Fins (2)	8.8 sq. ft.
Stabilizer	14.9 sq. ft.
Rudders (2)	9.0 sq. ft.
Elevator	15.0 sq. ft.

Weights.

Weight, empty	..	1,328 lbs.
Fuel and oil	..	360 lbs.
Military load	..	680 lbs.
Total weight	..	2,368 lbs.

Power Plant.

Engine, Hispano-Suiza, model H, developing 340 h.p. at 1,800 r.p.m. Weight, including airscrew, 618 lbs. Fuel consumption per h.p.-hr., 0.53 lbs.

Performances.

Altitude.	Speed.	Climb.
Sealevel	146 m.p.h.	0 min.
20,000 ft.	..	20 min.

THE LOENING "KITTEN" SEA-MONOPLANE.

Type of machine	Single-seater Monoplane.
Name or type No. of machine	Loening "Kitten."
Purpose for which intended	Sporting.
Span	18 ft.
Overall length	13 ft.
Maximum height	5 ft.
Engine type and h.p.	60 h.p. 3-cyl. Lawrence air-cooled engine.
Weight of machine empty	300 lbs.
Petrol tank capacity in gallons	10 gallons.

Performance.

Speed (maximum)	105 m.p.h.
Landing speed	50 m.p.h.

Climb.

To 1,500 feet in minutes	1 minute.
Total weight of machine loaded	530 lbs.

The Loening Monoplane (300 h.p. Hispano-Suiza engine).

L—*continued*.

LOUGHEAD AIRCRAFT.

The machine illustrated herewith was built by the brothers Malcolm and Allan H. Loughead, at Santa Barbara, Cal. Originally built as a seaplane, it flew from Santa Barbara to San Diego with four passengers, and was there fitted with a land chassis in preparation for a flight across America to Washington.

No particulars or specification of this machine are available.

Loughead Model F.I. Seaplane (two 160 h.p. Hall-Scott engines).

The Loughead F.I.A. Machine.   This is the Seaplane F.I. fitted with a land chassis.

LOUGHEAD AIRCRAFT—*continued.*

Loughead Model F.I.A.

Loughead Model F.I.A.

L—continued.

THE L.W.F. ENGINEERING COMPANY.

College Point, N.Y.

Constructors of tractor biplanes for training and fighting purposes and of seaplanes and flying boats.

THE L.W.F. MODEL G, FIGHTING AEROPLANE.

Among the most successful of the all-American designs is the L.W.F. machine, the first experimental model of which was in the air early in January, 1918. This first machine, known as Model G., was powered with a Liberty 12 motor and was taken off with the wind, looped and tailspun the first time it was in the air.

Specification.

General.

Type	Two-seater land tractor biplane.
Use	Military reconnaissance, advanced training, or commercial

Dimensions.

Length overall	29 ft. 2 in.
Height overall	10 ft. 7 in.
Width overall	46 ft. 6 in.

Wings.

Wing curve	L.W.F. No. 1.
Chord	80 in.
Gap	80 in.
Stagger	8 in.
Span : Upper wing ..	46 ft. 6 in.
Lower wing ..	38 ft. 4 in.

Areas.

Total supporting area	555 sq. ft.
Area of ailerons	42 sq. ft.
Area of elevators.	22 sq. ft.
Area of horizontal stabilizer ..	29 sq. ft.
Area of vertical stabilizer ..	5.5 sq. ft.
Area of rudder	11.5 sq. ft.

Control.

Deperdussin control centre column single or dual. Stick control can be furnished if preferred.

Power Plant.

Liberty 12-cylinder engine ..	350 b.h.p.
Gasoline consumption per b.h.p.	.54 lbs. per hour.
Oil consumption per b.h.p. ..	.03 lbs. per hour.
Propeller	Two blade, 1,650 r.p.m

Weights.

Gross weight, fully loaded	3,522 lbs.
Light weight, empty	2,498 lbs.
Useful load	1,024 lbs.
Water (11 gallons)	92 lbs.
Gasoline capacity (86 gallons)	532 lbs.
Oil capacity (6 gallons)	42 lbs.
Two men or equivalent	330 lbs.
Accessories	28 lbs.

Performance (fully loaded).

High speed	125 m.p.h.
Low speed (landing)	47 m.p.h.
Climbing speed	10,000 ft. in 7½ mins.
Ceiling	24,000 ft.
Endurance at full speed ..	2¾ hours.

This machine is capable of carrying a cargo of about 1,200 lbs.. in addition to the above load.

Model G. 1, an improvement over Model G., was built and flown successfully during the summer of 1918, demonstrating before various government officials its speed, climb and carrying capacity. This machine, loaded as a fighter, with full tanks, seven machine guns, ammunition, pilot and gunner, made 128 m.p.h. and climbed 10,000 feet in ten minutes.

Later in the summer, Model G. 1 was radically changed into Model G. 2 by cutting off the overhang, balancing all control surfaces, doubling the number of wing ribs and later installing a wing curve radiator. The following description refers to the later machine, Model G. 2, which, as before stated, is a modification of Models G. and G. 1.

The L.W.F. "Model G" Two-seater (350 h.p. Liberty engine).

L.W.F.—continued.

General Description.—Model G. 2 is a general service, 425–450 h.p., two man biplane of the land tractor, military type, armoured, and carries an armament of seven machine guns. In addition it can also be equipped with four large bombs. As will be noted, a wing nose radiator was used at the time the photos for the accompanying figures were made. All parts of the machine seen from above are finished in earth brown, while from below it is sky blue. The general specifications follow :—

THE L.W.F. MODEL G. 2 FIGHTING AIRPLANE.
Specification.

Dimensions.

Overall width	41 ft. 7½ in.
Overall length	29 ft. 1¼ in.
Overall height	9 ft. 4⅜ in.
Tread of wheels	5 ft. 6 in.
Wheels	26 in. × 4 in.

Wings.

Wing curve L.W.F. No. 1 (modified R.A.F. 6) upper and lower wings.

Incidence : lower wing	0 degrees.
upper wing	+ 1 degree.
Decalage	1 degree.
Chord	80 in., upper and lower.
Dihedral	0 degrees.
Gap	72 in., nose to nose on vertical line with body horizontal.
Backsweep	0 degrees.
Stagger	7⅛ in. (positive).
Span : upper wing, inc. ailerons	41 ft. 7½ in.
lower wing	38 ft. 5¾ in.
Aspect ratio : Upper wing, inc. ailerons	6.3
Lower wing ..	4.78, average 5.54.

Areas.

Total supporting area, including ailerons)	515.54 sq. ft.
Net area of main wings, not inc. ailerons	465·46 sq. ft.
Net area of upper wings, including ailerons	268.78 sq. ft.
Net area of upper wings, not inc. ailerons	218.70 sq. ft.
Net area of lower wings.. ..	246.76 sq. ft.
Total area of one aileron ..	25·04 sq. ft. balanced area, 1.95 sq. ft.
Total area of both ailerons ..	50.08 sq. ft.
Total area of one elevator ..	13.85 sq. ft. balanced area, 1.5 sq. ft.
Total area of both elevators ..	27.70 sq. ft.
Total area of rudder ..	12·65 sq. ft. balanced area, 1.31 sq. ft.
Total area of horizontal stabilizer (both sides)	29.15 sq. ft.
Total area of vertical stabilizer..	5.21 sq. ft.

Controls and Control Surfaces.

Dual stick control. Aileron wires enclosed in wings.
Horizontal stabilizer double camber with centre line set at 0 degrees to thrust line.
Elevator curve included in stabilizer curve.
Aileron curve included in wing curve extended.
Rudder and vertical stabilizer flat.

Power Plant.

Liberty 12-cyl. engine, direct connected	435 hp. at 1,700 r.p.m.
Airscrew, 2 blade, tractor, diam..	9 ft. 7 in ; av. pitch 7.38 ft.
Propeller turned	1,800 r.p.m.

Weights.

Case 1. Weight of complete machine empty, with gun mounts, but no guns	2,675	lbs.
Case 2. Equipped as a fighter.		
Weight, light	2,675.5	lbs.
90 galls. gas	553.5	lbs.
14 galls. water	118	lbs.
6 galls. oil	44	lbs.
Ammunition	150	lbs.
7 machine guns	152	lbs.
2 men	330	lbs.
Total full load	4,023	lbs.
Case 3. Equipped as a bomber.		
Weight, light	2,675.5	lbs.
120 galls. gasoline..	752	lbs.
6 galls. oil	44	lbs.

14 galls. water	118	lbs.
Ammunition	150	lbs.
7 machine guns	152	lbs.
Armour	66	lbs.
4 bombs, rack and release ..	592	lbs.
2 men	330	lbs.
Total full load..	4,879.5	lbs.

Loadings (based on 515.54 sq. ft. area and 435 h.p.

Case 1. Loading per sq. ft. ..	5.185	lbs.
Loading per h.p. ..	6.15	lbs.
Case 2. Loading per sq. ft. ..	7.82	lbs.
Loading per h.p. ..	9.25	lbs.
Case 3. Loading per sq. ft. ..	9.47	lbs.
Loading per h.p. ..	11.22	lbs.

Performance.

High speed at 10,000 ft.	=	130 m.p.h. (loaded as in Case 2).
High speed at low altitude	=	138 m.p.h. (loaded as in Case 2).
Low speed (landing)	=	50 m.p.h (loaded as in Case 2).

Climb.

Case 1. 10,000 feet in	7 mins. 28 secs.
Case 2. 10,000 feet in	9 mins. 18 secs.
Case 3. 10,000 feet in ..	14 mins. 45 secs.

Endurance.

Four hours at full speed.

The L.W.F. Model " G. 2 " Two-seater (350 Liberty engine).

Angle of fire of lower guns in horizontal plane.

Angle of fire in horizontal plane 192°

Lines of fire of fixed guns

Angle of fire in vertical plane perpendicular to line of flight 360°

Angle of fire in vertical plane parallel to line of flight 280°

Rear angle of vision 130°

Datum Line

Angle of fire in vertical plane parallel to line of flight 85°

Front angle of vision at side of radiator 75°

Front angle of vision beneath radiator 65°

Line of fire of fixed guns

Line of fire of fixed guns

C.L.

Screw

74" Gap

General arrangement of the L.W.F. type G. 2 Two-seater Fighter, showing the arcs of gun fire available.

M

THE GLENN L. MARTIN COMPANY.

Cleveland, Ohio.

This company, which was organised during the war, produced the first successful twin-engined aeroplane of American design. Intended to serve as a night bomber. The *Martin* " Twin " is now being converted into a passenger aeroplane. Four of these machines will be put in operation in California by the Apache Aerial Transportation Company, of Phœnix, Arizona.

THE MARTIN TWIN-ENGINED BOMBER.

The *Martin* twin-engined bomber constitutes one of the most important developments in bombing airplanes of original American design. In its official test, at Wilbur Wright Field, the all-round performance of this machine, considering the load carried, has easily excelled any other record from a similar bomber, either here or abroad. The machine shows excellent workmanship and such thoroughness of engineering that the organization is to be complimented upon the talent of their personnel. Mr. Martin is proud of the ability of his assistants, Mr. Lawrence D. Bell, factory manager ; Mr. Eric Springer, pilot ; and Mr. Donald W. Douglas, aeronautical engineer ; and he prophesies important futures in their respective specialties. Lawrence D. Bell, has been with Mr. Martin for seven years, and is noted for his production management. Eric Springer learned to fly at the Martin School five years ago. He is an unusually capable tester and flyer, having made an enviable record in five years of piloting for the Martin Company without an accident. Donald W. Douglas came from the Boston Tech., joining the Martin plant in Los Angeles four years ago, and in that short length of time has grown to be recognised as one of the foremost aeronautical engineers.

The all-round efficiency of the Martin bomber has been proven in its official performance trials. An official high speed at the ground of 118.5 m.p.h. was made on the first trials, with full bombing load on board. This speed has been bettered since, due to the better propeller efficiency arrived at by expensive experiments. With full bomb load, the climbing time to 10,000 feet was 15 minutes, and a service ceiling of between 16,000 and 17,000 feet was attained.

General Description.

As a military machine, the *Martin* " Twin " is built to fulfil the requirements of the four following classes:—(1) Night bomber, (2) day bomber, (3) long-distance photography, (4) gun machine.

(1) As a night bomber it is armed with three flexible Lewis machine guns, one mounted on the front turret, one on the rear, below and to the sides, under the concave lower surface of the body. It carries 1,500 lbs. of bombs and 1,000 rounds

The Glenn L. Martin Twin-engined Bomber (two 400 h.p. Liberty engines).

The Glenn L. Martin Twin Bomber.

THE GLENN L. MARTIN Co.—*continued*

of ammunition. A radio-telephone set and the necessary instruments are carried on all four types. The fuel capacity in all four types is sufficient for four and a half hours' full power at the ground and six hours' full power at 15,000 feet. This gives the machine gasoline for the climb to 15,000 feet, and enough more for about six hundred miles.

(2) As a day bomber two more Lewis guns are carried, one more on each turret. The bomb capacity is cut to 1,000 lbs. to give the higher ceiling necessary for day work.

(3) When equipped as a photography machine, the same number of guns as in the case of the day bomber are carried ; but in place of the bombs two cameras are mounted in the rear gunner's cockpit. One camera is a short focal length semi-automatic, and the other is a long focal length hand-operated type.

(4) The gun machine is equipped for the purpose of breaking up enemy formations. In addition to the five machine guns and their ammunition as carried on the photographic machine, a semi-flexible 37 mm. cannon is mounted in the front gun cockpit, firing forward, and with a fairly wide range in elevation and azimuth. This cannon fires either shell or shot, and is a formidable weapon.

The *Martin* " Twin " is easily adaptable to the commercial uses that are now practical. They are :—(1) Mail and express carrying, (2) transportation of passengers, (3) aerial map and survey work.

(1) As a mail or express machine a ton may be carried with comfort, not only because of the ability of the machine to efficiently handle this load, but because generous bulk stowage room is available.

(2) Twelve passengers, in addition to the pilot and mechanic, can be carried for non-stop runs up to six hundred miles.

(3) The photographic machine, as developed for war purposes, is at once adaptable to the aerial mapping of what will become the main flying routes throughout the country. The accuracy that is being obtained in aerial photography should be of vast value in survey and topographical map work. The *Martin* airplane, with its great cruising radius and complete camera installation, presents itself as the logical machine in this field.

General Dimensions and Data.

1,—Power Plant,
    Two 12-cyl. Liberty engines.

2,—Wing and Control Surface Areas.

Main planes, total	1,070 sq. ft.
Upper planes, including ailerons	550 sq. ft.
Lower planes, including ailerons	520 sq. ft.
Ailerons, each	32.5 sq. ft.
No. af ailerons	4
Vertical fins. each	8.8 sq. ft.
No. of fins	2
Stabilizer	62.25 sq. ft.
Elevator	43.20 sq. ft.
Rudders, each	16.50 sq. ft.
No. of rudders	2

3, Overall Dimensions,

Span, upper and lower	71 ft. 5 in.
Chord, upper and lower	7 ft. 10 in.
Gap	8 ft. 6 in.
Length overall	46 ft.
Height overall	14 ft. 7 in.
Incidence of wings with propeller axis	2 degrees.
Dihedral	None.
Sweep back	None.
Decalage, wings	None.
Stabilizer, setting with wing chord	÷ 1 degree.
adjustable between	− 5 degrees.
normal setting	− 2 degrees.

Side View of the Glenn L. Martin Bomber (two 400 h.p. Liberty engines).

M—continued.

MARTIN.   The J. V. Martin Aeroplane Factory, Elyria, Ohio.

Office : 299, Maddison Avenue, New York.

Many of the old-timers in British aviation will remember the flying exploits of Mr. J. V. Martin and his wife at the Grahame-White Aviation Company's School at Hendon, notably on the *Grahame-White* "Baby" biplane.   Thereafter Mr. Martin returned to the United States, where from time to time he produced various types of aeroplanes, some of which displayed considerable ingenuity.

He has developed a number of novel features, such as the K bar truss for interplane struts, the retractable chassis, the Martin type of wing end ailerons, and a very promising form of lateral stabilizer, in which the side wind due to side-slipping acts on a pivoted vertical plane interconnected to the ailerons.

THE MARTIN K III SINGLE-SEATER.

His latest production, known as the *K* 3, is a single-seater, which displays much originality of thought, and constitutes a distinct contribution to the problem of producing a cheap and small machine for peace-time flying.

Among other features, the machine includes a two-cylinder horizontally-opposed engine of 45 h.p., of what has been called in this country the "pop-bottle" type, which, as a matter of fact, has much to recommend it when a low-power aero-engine is required.

The fuselage construction is also worthy of note, which consists almost entirely of 3-ply timber. The system of wing bracing also is unusual, as is the arrangement of the undercarriage, which makes it possible for the wheels and their struts to be folded into the fuselage during flight, with a resultant reduction of head resistance.

Originally the *K* 3 was designed as an altitude fighter, provision being made for oxygen tanks and electrically heated clothing.

The dimensions of the machine are exceedingly small, the total span being under 18 ft., and it is claimed that the machine can therefore comfortably start from any country road. The overall length of the machine is 13 ft. 4 ins. and its height 7 ft. 4 ins. The total area of the wings is 100 ft. and the total weight 350 lbs., including engine.

No figures are yet available concerning the actual performance of the machine, but the estimate prepared by the designer suggests a speed of 135 miles per hour at ground level—of 112 miles per hour at 10,000 ft.—and 97 miles per hour at 25,000 ft.   In his opinion, when fitted with a 60 h.p. motor, the speed at 10,000 ft. would be 145 miles per hour. It will be interesting to compare these with the figures shown by actual test.

The Jas. V. Martin K III Scout (45 A.B.C. Gnat engine.)   Showing undercarriage retracted, the K-bar strut. and the wing-tip ailerons.

MARTIN—continued.

The main planes have neither stagger nor dihedral.   The wing section is known as Ofenstein 1, which at 40 miles per hour has a lift-drag ratio of 22 to 1.   This fact, though, is not very informative, as the machine is intended for high speeds.

The upper plane is a single continuous structure, and the principal main spar is 14½ ins. from the leading edge.   The front of this spar is coincident with the greatest forward travel of the centre of pressure.   The lower plane is constructed in two sections, attached one on either side of the fuselage.

The interplane struts are of the " K-bar " construction similar to that found in some of the *Curtiss* aeroplanes, the actual wing bracing consisting of the minimum possible number of wires— namely, a flying and landing wire in each bay.

The ailerons are a new departure so far as modern practice is concerned, being placed at the ends of the top planes with their leading edges somewhere in the neighbourhood of the centre of pressure of the machine.   They have a symmetrical double convex surface, and are so balanced that their operation requires very little effort, and naturally such a disposition gives them a considerable degree of effectiveness. M. Louis Blériot used somewhat similar ailerons on some of his earliest monoplanes.

The overall length of the fuselage from the engine plate to the stern post is 10 ft. 10½ ins., and its comparatively great depth— namely, 3 ft., is largely responsible for the squat appearance of the machine.

The fixed tail plane has a span of 7 ft. 6 ins. and a chord of 2 ft. 6 ins., and is placed in line with the centre of thrust at such an angle as to exert no lift.   Behind this is a pair of elevator flaps, the junction of which, with the tail plane, is screened by rubber fabric, giving a smooth, unbroken outline.

The rudder, which is substantially constructed, has balanced portions above and below the fuselage.   An interesting feature is the enclosure of the tail skid in the thickness of the rudder, its pivot being fixed through the bottom of the rudder post.   The combination of rudder post and tail skid effects a considerable saving of weight, and also presumably assists steering on the ground.

The engine is an air-cooled 2-cylinder opposed " Gnat " A.B.C. engine, which develops 45 h.p. at 1,915 r.p.m.   The fuel consumption is said to be 0.56 lbs. per h.p. per hour, the total weight of the engine being 50.4 lbs.   The fuel tank is placed in the upper main plane above the fuselage, and has a capacity of 9 gallons, sufficient for a flight of two hours.

THE MARTIN
45 H P   A B C   ENGINE
K III   SCOUT

Scale of Feet

McLaughlin

MARTIN—*continued.*

The undercarriage is simple in the extreme, consisting of a pair of " Vee " struts connected by a cross-stay and a rigid cross axle, which carries a pair of Ackerman wheels. These " Vee " struts are hinged and can be drawn up into the fuselage, thus bringing the wheels also partially within the fuselage and reducing head resistance.

The mounting of the horizontally opposed engine in the nose of the machine and the hemispherical pot on the airscrew boss gives the machine a very neat appearance, and, although it cannot claim to possess the beautiful lines found in many modern aeroplanes, it is full of useful and original ideas.

Specification of Martin K III.

Type of machine	Sporting Single-seater.
Name or type No. of machine ..	Martin K3.
Span	17 ft. 11¼ in.
Gap, maximum and minimum ..	4 ft. 6 in.
Overall length	13 ft. 3½ in.
Maximum height	7 ft. 4¾ in.
Chord	3 ft. 6 in.
Total surface of wings ..	100.3 sq. ft.
Total area of tail	9.5 sq. ft.
Area of elevators	6.6 sq. ft.
Area of rudder	4.8 sq. ft.
Area of each aileron and total area	5 sq. ft., 10 sq. ft. total.
Engine type and h.p.	45 h.p. A.B.C. Gnat.
Weight of machine empty ..	350 lbs.
Load per sq. ft.	560 lbs.
Weight per h.p.	12.5 lbs.
Tank capacity	2 hours.
Tank capacity	9.5 gallons.

Performance (Estimated).

Speed low down	135 m.p.h.
Speed at 10,000 feet	112 m.p.h.
Speed at 20,000 feet ..	108 m.p.h.

Disposable load apart from fuel .. .. .. 160 lbs.

In addition to this machine, Capt. Martin is responsible for the large twin-engine bomber illustrated.

The photograph shews clearly the K bar interplane struts and the vertical plane of the Martin stabilizer.

In this machine both engines are in the fuselage and the airscrews are gear driven.

The Jas. V. Martin Twin-engined Bomber (2—400 h.p. Liberty engine), showing K-bar struts, Martin automatic stabilisers, and gear-driven airscrews.

M—continued.

MARYLAND PRESSED STEEL COMPANY. (Aircraft Department,) Hagerstown, Maryland.

New York Sales Manager, Harry E. Tudor, 299, Madison Avenue.

Constructors of small sport aeroplanes to the designs of Mr. Joseph Bellanca, Chief Engineer of the Aircraft Department.

THE BELLANCA 35 H.P. BIPLANE.

The light passenger-carrying *Bellanca* biplane has been designed to answer the requisites of quick get-away, fast climb, and high speed, and to have at the same time light weight, the ability to glide at a flat angle, and low flying speed to insure a great degree of safety in landing. To these qualities are added the item of moderate cost and ease of maintenance, high-grade construction and the possibility of rapidly assembling and dissembling.

The machine was tested out at Central Park, Long Island, just about a year ago by Pilot Arthur Heinrich. On his first flight he released the controls when an altitude of 1,000 feet was reached. The throttle was full open. Without touching the controls, the throttle was retarded to diminish the power about 50 per cent. and the machine proceeded in straight horizontal flight. With the engine shut off the machine quietly disposed itself to a flat glide.

Other tests of the machine's speed show that with full power, it is capable of 85 m.p.h., and by throttling the engine the speed can be reduced to 34 m.p.h.

In climb tests the *Bellanca* biplane ascended to 3300 feet in 10 minutes and 4600 feet in 14 minutes, with the engine throttled down to 1080 r.p.m., equal to 18 h.p.

With the engine turning at 1080 r.p.m. the machine made a speed of 69½ m.p.h. in three consecutive half-mile flights at a height of 15 feet from the ground. The speed mentioned was the average for the three flights. With the engine increased to 1,200 r.p.m. equal to 24 h.p., the climb of the machine increased to 530 feet per minute and the horizontal speed was 76 m.p.h. The climb was measured by means of a barograph and aneroid.

In testing the gliding quality, the pilot began a glide from an altitude of 4,600 feet at a distance of about ten miles from the starting point. With the engine shut off the field was reached and passed, and it was necessary to turn back and glide against the wind toward the field, adding two miles to the distance traversed. In this manœuvre a time of 8 minutes and 5 seconds elapsed before the ground was touched. In this glide the machine was favored by a wind of 6 to 7 m.p.h. The incidence angle indicator showed that the machine was gliding at an angle of 5 degrees, which is equal to a ratio of 1 to 11.5.

The above test shows that in case of a forced landing from an altitude of 4,600 feet, the pilot will have ample time to select a landing place within a diameter of 24 miles.

General Specifications.

Span, upper plane	.. ..	26 ft. 0 in.
Span, lower plane	.. ..	20 ft. 6 in.
Chord, upper plane	.. ..	4 ft. 0 in.
Chord, lower plane	.. ..	2 ft. 4 in.
Total area.. ..	..	150 sq. ft.
Length overall ..	..	17 ft. 7 in.
Weight, machine empty..	..	400 lbs.
Useful load	.. ..	375 lbs.

Performances.

Maximum speed, light, 35 h.p...	85 m.p.h
Maximum speed, light, 24 h.p...	76 m.p.h.
Maximum speed, light, 18 h.p...	70 m.p.h.
Minimum speed	34 m.p.h.
Maximum climbing speed, 35 h.p.	820 ft. per min
Maximum climbing speed, 24 h.p.	530 ft. per min
Maximum climbing speed, 18 h.p.	330 ft. per min.
Gliding angle	1 to 11.5
Min. h.p. required for horizontal flight	6

The Bellanca Single-seat Sporting Model (35 h.p. Anzani engine).

MARYLAND— *continued.*

THE BELLANCA C. E. BIPLANE.

The *Bellanca C. E.* two-seater biplane, with a 55 h.p. Anzani engine, has been designed to meet the requirements of quick get-away, fast climb, and very high speed, and—at the same time—a very low landing speed, such as insures the greatest degree of safety. Consistent with these qualities, the design and construction embrace light weight and economic upkeep to the most satisfactory degree. An acceptable feature lies in the rapidity and ease with which the machine can be dissembled and re-assembled.

General Specifications.

Span, upper plane	28 ft.
Span, lower plane	21 ft. 5 in.
Chord, upper plane	4 ft 6 in.
Chord, lower plane	2 ft. 9 in.
Total area..	184 sq. ft.
Length overall	18 ft. 6 in.
Weight, machine empty .	470 lb.
Useful load	510 lb.

Performances with useful load of 250 lbs.

Useful load of 250 lb. :

Pilot	150 lb.
Fuel for 3–4 hours' flight	100 lb.
Maximum speed	101 m.p.h.
Minimum speed	34 m.p.h.
Rate of climb, first minute, ft. per min.	1,020

Performances with full useful load of 500 lb.

Full load of 510 lb. :

2 passengers	300 lb.
Fuel for about 3 hr. flight at full power or about 4 hr. throttling the motor to 40 h.p.	110 lb.
Other load which can be sufficient for nearly as much fuel as above, or other load	100 lb.
Maximum speed	97 m.p h.
Minimum speed	41 m.p.h.
Minimum horse-power required for horizontal flight	14
Rate of climb, first minute	600 ft. per min.

Performances with useful load of 400 lb.

Useful load of 400 lb. :

2 passengers	300 lb.
Fuel for 3–4 hr.	100 lb.
Maximum speed	99 m.p.h.
Minimum speed	38 m.p.h.
Minimum horse-power required for horizontal flight	11
Rate of climb, first minute	780 ft. per min.
Climb in 10 minutes	6,000 ft.
Climb in 15 minutes	7,500 ft.
Climb in 27 minutes	10,000 ft.

Performances with very light load.

Useful load, pilot and one hour of fuel	185 lb.
Maximum speed	102 m.p.h.
Minimum speed	32 m.p.h.
Minimum horse-power required for horizontal flight	7
Rate of climb, first minute	1,180 ft. per min.
Climb in 10 minutes	9,000 ft. per min.
Climb in 12 minutes	10,000 ft.
Climb in 25 minutes	15,000 ft.

Engine Group.

An air-cooled 6–cyl. Anzani 6-C type, 55 h.p. is used. Its weight is 154 lb. Airscrew is 7 ft. in diameter. The engine is so attached as to form, with the rest of the body, a perfect streamline form with low head resistance.

O

ORDNANCE ENGINEERING COR-
PORATION. 120, Broadway, New York. Factory:
Baldwin, Long Island. Chief Aeronautical Engineer: Walter
H. Phipps.

Aeronautical constructional engineers, engaged in experimental
work for the U.S. Army.

THE ORDNANCE SCOUT BIPLANE.
Specification.

Type of machine	Single-seater Biplane
Name or type No. of machine ..	Ordnance Scout.
Purpose for which intended ..	Advanced training.
Span	26 ft.
Gap	3 ft. 10 in.
Overall length	18 ft. 9 in.
Chord..	4 ft. 5 in.
Maximum cross section of body ..	41½ ins.
Engine type and h.p.	80 h.p. Le Rhône.
Airscrew, diameter	8 ft. 3 in.
Weight of machine empty ..	335 lbs.

Performance.

Speed low down	98 m.p.h.
Speed at 6,500 feet	94 m.p.h.
Speed at 10,000 feet	84 m.p.h.
Speed at 15,000 feet	70 m.p.h.

Climb.

To 6,500 feet in minutes ..	9 minutes.
To 10,000 feet in minutes ..	17 mins. 30 secs.
To 15,000 feet in minutes ..	55 minutes.
Service ceiling	13,500 feet.
Total weight of machine loaded	1,117 lbs

Two Views of the Ordnance Engineering Corporation's Single-seat Scout.

ORDNANCE
continued.

The Ordnance Engineering Corporation's Single-seat Scout (80 h.p. Le Rhône engine.

FRONT VIEW

SIDE VIEW

ORDNANCE SCOUT WITH LE RHONE 80 ENGINE

TECHNICAL DATA BRANCH
TECHNICAL SECTION
DIVISION OF MILITARY AERONAUTICS

TOP VIEW

ORDNANCE SCOUT WITH LE RHONE 80 ENGINE

TECHNICAL DATA BRANCH
TECHNICAL SECTION
DIVISION OF MILITARY AERONAUTICS

472a

PACKARD MOTOR CAR COMPANY.

Detroit, Michigan.

These well-known motor car builders had been experimenting with aero engines for several years when the War Department requested their chief engineer, Mr. J. G. Vincent to collaborate with Mr. E. J. Hall, chief engineer of the Hall-Scott Motor Car Company, of San Francisco, Cal., for the purpose of creating a standardized aero engine of high power. The Liberty engine, which resulted from this collaboration, thus derived at least part of its inspiration from experiments made at the Packard Works.

After the Armistice, this firm produced an 8-cyl. V-type engine, developing 160 h.p., around which a luxuriously-fitted sport aeroplane has been built. This machine was, however, still in the experimental stage when these notes were written.

In the late fall of 1918 a two-seater fighter and day-bomber was also developed to the designs of Captain G. Lepère, of the French Air Service, and was being put into production when the war came to an end.

THE LE PÈRE FIGHTER.

Captain G. Lepère, an aeronautical engineer in the French Air service, designed the *Lepère* " Fighter " with a Liberty engine for production in the United States. It was intended for use as a fighter or reconnaissance machine, and carried two fixed guns firing forward, synchronized with the engine, and two Lewis guns attached to a movable Scarff ring surrounding the rear cockpit.

General Dimensions.

Span, upper plane	.. ..	39 ft. $0\frac{1}{4}$ in
Span, lower plane	.. ..	39 ft. $0\frac{1}{4}$ in.
Chord, both planes	.. ..	5 ft. 6 in.
Gap between planes	.. ..	5 ft. $0\frac{5}{8}$ in.
Stagger	.. ..	2 ft. $0\frac{15}{16}$ in.
Length over all ..	.. ..	25 ft. $4\frac{5}{8}$ in.
Height over all ..	.. ..	9 ft. $10\frac{7}{8}$ in.

Weights.

Machine empty	2,468 lbs.
Pilot and gunner	360 lbs.
Fuel and oil	475 lbs.
Armament..	352 lbs.
Total	3,655 lbs.

Performances.

Height.	Speed.	Time of Climb.
0 ft. ..	136 m.p.h. ..	0 mins. 0 secs.
6,000 ft. ..	132 m.p.h. ..	5 mins. 35 secs.
10,000 ft. ..	127 m.p.h. ..	10 mins. 35 secs.
15,000 ft. ..	118 m.p.h. ..	19 mins. 15 secs.
20,000 ft. ..	102 m.p.h. ..	41 mins. 0 secs.

Service ceiling, or height beyond which the machine will not climb 100 feet per minute, 20,800 feet.

Side View of the Le Père Fighter (400 h.p. Liberty engine).

Three-quarter View from rear. (The Le Père Fighter.)

PACKARD—*continued*.

Main Planes.

Planes are flat in span and have no sweepback. Top plane is in three sections—a centre section over the body and two outer panels. Lower plane in two sections attached at lower sides of fuselage in the usual manner.

Upper and lower planes are similar in shape, and with ailerons $21\frac{3}{4}$ ins. wide by $94\frac{1}{4}$ ins. long attached to both. An interconnecting streamlined rod is used between each pair of ailerons, located between the outer wing struts.

Leading edge of outer plane is located $49\frac{9}{16}$ ins. from front of propeller hub. Middle struts located $94\frac{5}{8}$ ins. from centre of machine; outer struts $98\frac{1}{2}$ ins. from middle struts; overhang, 41 ins. Interplane strut design is unique, inasmuch as it eliminates the usual incidence wires.

Fuselage.

Veneer is used for exterior finish. Overall length of fuselage, 22 ft. $0\frac{1}{8}$ in Maximum section at the gunner's cockpit, $32\frac{1}{2}$ ins. wide, $45\frac{1}{2}$ ins. deep.

Front View of the Le Père Fighter.

The Le Père Fighter. (400 h.p. Liberty engine.)

474a

PACKARD—continued.

Centre of gravity occurs at a point 6 ft. 3 ins. from nose of fuselage.

Axle of landing gear 22¾ ins. forward of centre of gravity. The landing gear wheels have a 65$\frac{9}{16}$ ins. track and are 28 ins. in diameter.

Tail Group.

Overall plan of stabilizer, 98¾ ins. ; chord, 35½ ins. It is fixed at a non-lifting angle, and attached to upper fuselage longerons.

Tail flaps or elevators measure 158½ ins. from tip to tip. Their chord is 31¾ ins., and in addition to this there are small balancing portions extending beyond the tail plane.

Rudder is 30 in. wide and has a balancing portion above the fin, 25 in. wide.

Engine Group.

A Liberty " 12 " 400 h.p. engine is used. It develops 400 h.p. at 1,750 r.p.m. Bore, 5 ins. ; stroke, 7 ins. ; weight, without propeller and water, 858 pounds. Two Zenith Duplex carburetters are used.

The radiator is located in the upper plane centre section, and its location has necessitated some slight modifications in the engine to increase the water circulation.

Propeller, 9 ft. 4 ins. in diameter. Front propeller plate projects 11¾ ins. forward of fuselage nose.

Propeller axis 15$\frac{7}{16}$ ins. below top of upper longerons. In flying position the propeller hub is 5 ft. 2⅞ ins. above the ground line ; when at rest on the ground the propeller hub is 6 ft. 1⅝ ins. above ground.

THE PACKARD BIPLANE.

Type of machine	**Two-seater Biplane.**
Name or type No. of machine ..	**1 A. Packard.**
Span	**37 ft.**
Overall length	**25 ft.**
Maximum height	**8 ft. 11 in.**

Wing and Control Surface Areas.

Main planes, total	387.6 sq. ft.
Ailerons, total	48.3 sq. ft.
Vertical fin	7·0 sq. ft.
Rudder	12·0 sq. ft.
Tail plane	35.7 sq. ft.
Elevator, total	21.9 sq. ft.
Engine type..	**8-cyl. 1 A. Packard ; 160 h.p. at 1,525 r.p.m.**
Petrol tank capacity in galls. ..	**34 galls.**
Fuel consumption per h.p. ..	**.50 to .54 lbs. per h.p. at sea level.**

Weight.

Machine empty	1,520 lbs.
Gasoline	210 lbs.
Oil	30 lbs.
Water	52 lbs.
Tools and extras	25 lbs.
Pilot	165 lbs.
Passenger	465 lbs.
Normal flying weight	2,167 lbs.
Weight, lbs. per h.p.	13.5 lbs.
Wing loading per sq. ft...	5.6 lbs.
Permissible extra luggage	100 lbs.

Performance.

High speed near sea level ..	102 m.p.h.
High speed at 5,000 feet ..	100.5 m.p.h
High speed at 10,000 feet ..	98 m.p.h.
High speed at 15,000 feet ..	90.5 m.p.h.

Climb.

To 5,000 feet	7.5 minutes.
To 10,000 feet	18.1 minutes.
To 15,000 feet	34.5 minutes.
Absolute ceiling	19,500 ft.
Fuel range, wide open, near sea level	**2.5 hours.**
Fuel range, wide open, at 5,000 ft.	**3 hours.**
Fuel range, wide open, at 10,000 ft.	**3.5 hours.**
Fuel range, wide open, at 15,000 ft.	**4 hours.**

The Packard Two-seater. (160 h.p. Packard engine.)

S

SPERRY.

The Lawrence Sperry Aircraft Company, Farmingdale, Long Island, N.Y.

This company was organised since the signing of the armistice by Mr. Lawrence Sperry, co-inventor with his father, Mr. Elmer A. Sperry, of the gyroscopic aeroplane stabiliser, the synchronised drift set, the turn indicator, etc. Mr. Sperry, Jr. has developed a two-seater sport aeroplane of small dimensions, which is notable for being fitted with two 2-cycle, 4-cylinder, B.W.W. air-cooled engines, each of which drives a tractor airscrews. Folding wings are incorporated in this machine.

SPERRY SPORTPLANE.
Specifications.—Twin Motor, Two Passenger.

Span	.. .. ..	27 ft.
Span, wings folded	..	13 ft. 4 in.
Length	.. ..	21 ft.
Chord mainplanes	.. ..	4 ft. 6 in.
Angle of incidence	.. ..	40
Gap	.. .. ..	4 ft. 8 in
Stagger	.. ..	0°
Dihedral	.. .. ..	3°
Wing curve	.. ..	U.S.A. 3
Wing area..	.. ..	234 sq. ft.
Rudder area	.. ..	12 sq. ft.
Elevator area	.. ..	17 sq. ft.
Vertical Stabiliser	..	10 sq. ft.
Horizontal Stabiliser	..	25 sq. ft.
Height, ground to propeller hub	5 ft.
Diameter propeller	.. ..	5 ft. 6 in.
Wheel track	.. ..	7 ft. 10 in.
Weight empty	.. ..	576 lbs.
Weight loaded	.. ..	1050 lbs.
Horse power	.. ..	76
Loading sq. ft. wing area	..	4½ lbs.
Loading per h.p. ..	..	14 lbs.
Low speed	.. ..	36 m.p.h.
High speed.	.. ..	88 m.p.h.

2–38 h.p. B.W.W 2-cycle, 4-cyl., V type engines, air-cooled ; (weight complete 130 lbs. each engine).

STANDARD AIRCRAFT CORPORATION.

Elizabeth, N.J.

President, Mr. Harry Bowers Mingle. Chief Engineer, Charles E. Day. Factories at Elizabeth and Plainfield, N.J.

This, the second largest American aeronautical construction firm, has produced during the war a great variety of machines. Among these is the first postal aeroplane distinctly designed for this purpose, and various numbers of standard J-1 training machines, *Caproni* and *Handley-Page* night bombers fitted with Liberty engines, *DH-4a* two-seater fighters, and *HS* class (Navy) flying boats.

THE STANDARD AIRCRAFT CORPORATION SINGLE-SEATER MAILPLANE.

The *Standard* single seater mailplane is a tractor biplane of 31 ft. 4 in. span and 26 ft. 7 in. overall length, and is fitted with a model I Hispano-Suiza engine, which develops 170 h.p. at 1,700 r.p.m. The machine has a horizontal speed, near the ground, of 100 m.p.h., and climbs 5,300 ft. in 10 min., and 10,000 ft. in 24 min. Its best gliding angle is 1 in 8, and its maximum endurance, 3 hours at 5,000 ft. at full speed, that is, approximately 280 miles.

The fuel tanks have a capacity of 60 gal., the oil tanks contain 4 gal. The radiator, Livingston nose type, holds 9 gal. of water. The mail compartment is situated in front of pilot's cockpit.

The machine weighs fully loaded 2,450 lb. with overhang, and has a normal mail carrying capacity of 180 lb. The wing loading is 7.12 lb. per sq. ft., and the power loading, 14.1 lb. per h.p.

A detailed itemization of the general characteristics follows.

Main Dimensions.

Overall length	.. .. ..	26 ft. 7 in.
Overall height	.. ..	10 ft. 10⅜ in.
Wing action employed	..	R.A.F. 15.
Area of upper wing	..	150.9 sq. ft.
Area of lower wing	..	138.1 sq. ft.
Total wing area including ailerons	337 sq. ft.
Span, upper wing	..	31 ft. 4 in.
Chord, upper wing	..	6 ft.
Aspect ratio, upper wing	..	5.2
Span, lower wing..	..	31 ft. 4 in
Chord, lower wing	..	6 ft.
Aspect ratio, lower wing	..	5.2
Gap	.. .. ..	5 ft. 6 in.

The Standard Aircraft Corporation's Mail Carrier (170 h.p. Hispano-Suiza engine).

STANDARD AIRCRAFT—continued.

SINGLE-SEATER MAILPLANE—continued.

Stagger	5 inches.
Sweepback in degrees	5 deg.
Dihedral	3 per cent.
Angle of lower wing chord to propeller axis	$2\frac{1}{2}$ deg.
Height of axis of propeller above ground with :	
1. Machine resting on ground	6 ft.
2. Propeller axis in line of flight	5 ft.
Angle between line from base of wheel to C. G. with a vertical line when machine is horizontal	14 deg.
Angle between line joining wheel base and skid to a horizontal line	11 deg., 30 min.
Stabilizer setting to lower wing chord	0 deg.

Areas of Control System.

Aileron area, lower wing . ..	24 sq. ft., unbalanced.
Aileron area, upper wing ..	24 sq. ft., unbalanced.
Aileron of Stabilizer	23.7 sq. ft.
Area of elevators	22 sq. ft., unbalanced.
Area of fixed fin	4.6 sq. ft.
Area of rudder	10.1 sq. ft., unbalanced.

Weight Schedule: (a) Power Plant.

	Pounds.
Engine complete with carburetter and ignition system	455
Radiator	74.5
Radiator and engine water ..	75
Fuel tank empty ⎱ Oil tank empty . ⎰	50
Propeller and propeller hubs ..	27.5
Cowling	61.5
Pipes, etc...	35
Total	778.5

(b) Fuel and Oil.

Fuel (60 gallons)	360
Oil (4 gallons)	30
Total	390

(c) Passenger and Miscellaneous Equipment.

Pilot and Clothing	170
Dashboard Instruments.. ..	32.25
Miscellaneous	62
Total	264.31

(d) Mail.

Total	180

(e) Body.

Body frame	219
Engine bed	14
Seats and floor	31.3
Front and rear control	23.75
Total	288.1

(f) Tail Surfaces with Bracing.

Stabilizer	24
Elevators	17.5
Fin..	3.
Rudder	9.5
T. B. fittings, wires, etc. ..	21.5
Total	75.5

(g) Wing Structure.

Upper wing with fittings and aileron	143.5
Lower wing with fittings and aileron	129.5
Interplane struts and cables ..	51
Total	324

(h) Chassis.

Weight of wheels complete .. ⎫	
Weight of axle .. .. .. ⎬ 96	
Weight of shock absorber ..	
Weight of miscellaneous parts.. ⎭	
Total	96
Three wheel type landing gear..	25 extra
Total	121

Summation of Weights.

Group	Weight	Percentage of Gross Weight
(a) Power Plant	778.5 lb.	32.4
(b) Fuel and Oil	390 lb.	16.2
(c) Passengers and Miscellaneous Equipment	264.3 lb.	11.0
(d) Mail	180. lb.	7.5
(e) Body Structure	288.1 lb.	12.
(f) Tail Surfaces with Bracing ..	75.5 lb.	3.2
(g) Wing Structure	324. lb.	13.5
(h) Chassis	100.0 lb.	4.2
	2400. lb.	100

Equipped with Overhang Section.

Area, main planes	382.4 sq. ft.
Area, upper plain with aileron	220.3 ,,
Area, lower plane with aileron..	162.1 ,,
Area, upper aileron (2)	28 ,,
Area, lower aileron (2)	24 ,,

Another View of the Standard Mail Carrier.

THE STANDARD E 1 OR M DEFENCE BIPLANE.

Specification.

Type of machine	Single-seater Biplane.
Name or type No. of machine ..	E. 1. (M. Defence)
Purpose for which intended ..	Reconnaissance & fighting.
Span	24 ft.
Gap	4 ft.
Overall length	18 ft. 10$\frac{11}{16}$ in.
Maximum height	9 ft. 1in.
Chord	42 ins.
Area of elevators	10.3 sq. ft.
Area of rudder	6.8 sq. ft.
Area of fin	2.5 sq. ft.
Total area of ailerons ..	23.2 sq. ft.
Engine type and h.p. ..	80 h.p. Le Rhône,
Airscrew, diameter ..	8 ft.
Weight of machine empty ..	828 lbs.
Load per sq. ft.	7.5 lbs.
Weight per h.p.	14.3 lbs.
Tank capacity in hours ..	2 hours.

Performance.

Speed low down	99.8 m.p.h.
Speed at 6,400 feet ..	94 m.p.h.
Speed at 10,000 feet ..	85 m.p.h.
Landing speed	48 m.p.h.

Climb.

To 6,000 feet in minutes ..	10 minutes.
To 10 000 feet in minutes ..	22 mins. 20 secs.
Theoretical ceiling ..	14,800 ft.
Disposable load apart from fuel	201 lbs.
Total weight of machine loaded	1,144 lbs.
Dihedral	3%.
Stagger	13$\frac{1}{4}$ in.
Track	5 ft.

STANDARD E-1 WITH 80 H.P. LE RHONE ENGINE

FRONT VIEW

SIDE VIEW
STANDARD E-1 WITH
80 H.P. LE RHONE ENGINE

Front View of the Standard Aircraft Corporation's type E.1 Single-seater (80 h.p. Le Rhône engine.)   478a

STANDARD AIRCRAFT—*continued.*

THE STANDARD J. R. 1 BIPLANE.

(Built by the Standard Aircraft Corporation.)

Specification.

Type of machine	Single-seater Biplane.
Name or type No. of machine ..	J. R. 1.
Span	31 ft. 4¾ in.
Overall length	26 ft. 2 in.
Maximum height	10 ft. 10³⁄₁₆ in.
Engine type and h.p.	170 h.p. Hispano-Suiza engine.
Weight of machine empty ..	1,566 lbs.
Petrol tank capacity in gallons ..	60 gallons.

Performance.

Speed low down	100 m.p.h.
Landing speed..	48 m.p.h.

Climb.

To 5,300 feet in minutes ..	10 mins.
Total weight of machine loaded..	2,400 lbs.

THE AMERICAN HANDLEY PAGE TYPE 0-400 BOMBER.

Both in Great Britain and in the United States, the Handley Page has been the principal machine to be put into quantity production for bombing purposes. The American design is similar to the British, except that Liberty "12" 400 h.p. engines are employed in the former, and the Rolls-Royce or Sunbeam in the latter. The Handley Page machines described here were built by the Standard Aero Corporation, Elizabeth, N. J. The scale drawings of this type will be found along with the illustrations of the British Handley Pages in the BRITISH section of this book.

Accommodations are made for one pilot and two or three gunners, and an observer who operates the bomb-dropping devices. Their placing is as follows : At the forward end of the fuselage is the gunner who operates a pair of flexible Lewis machine guns. Bowden cables at one side of the cockpit permit the release of bombs. Behind the gunner is the pilot's cockpit from which the gunner's cockpit is reached through an opening in the bulkhead separating the two compartments. The pilot is seated at the right side of the cockpit. Beside him is the observer's seat, hinged so that it may be raised to permit access. Bomb-releasing controls are placed on the left side of the observer extending to the forward gunner's compartment and running back to the bomb racks located in the fuselage just between the wings.

Forward compartments are reached via a triangular door on the under side of the fuselage.

Aft of the bomb rack compartment, the rear gunners are placed. Two guns are located at the top of the fuselage and a third is arranged to fire through an opening in the under side of the fuselage. One gunner may have charge of all the rear guns, although usually two gunners man them. A platform is situated half way between upper and lower longerons of the fuselage, upon which the gunner stands when operating the upper guns.

Side View of The Standard E. 1 Single-seater.

The Standard type E. 1 Single-seater.

STANDARD AIRCRAFT—*continued.*

AMERICAN HANDLEY-PAGE TYPE 0-400—*continued.*

General Dimensions.

Span, upper plane	100 ft. 0 in.
Span, lower plane	70 ft. 0 in.
Chord, both planes	10 ft. 0 in.
Gap between planes	11 ft. 0 in.
Length over all	62 ft. 10 in.
Height over all at overhang cabane..	22 ft. 0 in.
Height over all at center panel ..	17 ft 6 in.
Width, wings folded	31 ft. 0 in.

Areas.

	Square Feet
Upper plane with ailerons	1018
Ailerons (2) each	172
Lower plane	630
Total wing area with ailerons	1648
Upper stabilizer	64
Lower stabilizer	47·6
Elevators (4)	63·0
Fin	14·7
Rudders (2)	46

Weights, General.

	Pounds.
Machine empty	7894
Fuel and Oil	2496
Bombs	3000
Military load	910
Total weight loaded	14300
Weight per square foot	8·7
Weight per horse power	17·9

Summation of Weights.

Power Plant	3044
Fuel and Oil	2496
Passengers and miscellaneous equipment ..	610
Armament	300
Bombing equipment	3000
Body structure..	1210
Tail surfaces	187
Wing structure..	2738·5
Chassis	710
Total	14300

WEIGHT SCHEDULE.

Power Plant.

	Pounds
Engine complete with carburetter and ignition system 2 × 835 = ...	1688
Radiator 2 × 112 = ...	224
Radiator and engine water 2 × 150 = ..	300
Fuel tank empty and pipes	350
Oil tank empty and pipes 16 × 2 = ..	32
Exhaust manifolds 2 × 75 = ...	150
Propeller and propeller hubs 2 × 60 = ..	120
Cowling 2 × 100 = ...	200
Total	3044

Fuel and Oil.

Fuel (280 gallons)	2280
Oil (2 × 15·3 gallons 2 × 108 lbs.)..	216
Total	2496

Passengers and Equipment.

Pilot and clothing	170
Gunners and clothing..	340
Dashboard instruments, fire extinguisher, tools and maps	100
Total	610

Armament.

Two forward machine guns, mounting and ejection ammunition and sights	120
Three rear machine guns, mounting and ejection ammunition and sights	180
Total	300

Bombing Equipment.

Bombs	2500
Bomb releases and sights	500
Total	3000

Body.

Body frame 953 + 97 = ...	1050
Seats	60
Front control and rear control	100
Total	1210

Tail Surfaces with Bracing.

Stabilizers (no covering) 3	57·2
Elevators (no covering) 4	34·4
Fin (no covering) 1	6·4
Rudder (no covering) 2	28·8
Covering	35·4
Struts and wires	24·4
Total	187·

Wing Structure.

Upper wing with fittings, aileron and fuel tank in center section ; lower wing with fittings..	2032
Interplane struts	235·5
Interplane cables	261
Nacelle supports 2 × 105 = ...	210
Total	2738·5

Under Carriage.

Wheels complete, 2 × 170 = ...	340
Shock absorber, 4 × 50 = ...	200
Miscellaneous parts, 4 × 30 = ..	120
Tail skid	50
Total	710

Volumes.

	Cu. Ft.
Bomb section, 3 ft. 5¾ in. × 5 ft. 2 in. 15/16 in. × 4 ft. 5 in...	80·6
Rear gunner's platform (upper) 3 ft. 3⅞ in. × 5ft. 1⅛ in. × 4 ft. 2¼ in.	71·45
Rear gunner's platform (lower) 2 ft. 4 in. × 5 ft. 1⅞ in. × 4 ft. 2¼ in.	54·2
Total volume	206·25

Performances.

Height (Feet)	Speed (M.P.H.)	Time of Climb (Minutes)
0 ..	92	0
5,000 ..	90	12
7,000 ..	—	18
10,000 ..	85	32

Service ceiling 10,000 feet.

STANDARD AIRCRAFT—*continued.*

AMERICAN HANDLEY-PAGE TYPE O-400—*continued.*

Main Planes.

Planes are not swept back and have no stagger nor decalage. Beyond the engine nacelles, both upper and lower planes have a dihedral angle of 4 degrees.

Wing section employed, R. A. F. No. 6. Angle of lower wing chord to propeller axis, 3 degrees,

Aspect ratio of upper wing, 10 ; lower wing, 7.

Planes are in nine sections. Upper plane center section 16 ft. wide. Intermediate sections 22 ft. wide ; overhang sections 16 ft. 10 in. wide. Beyond this, the ailerons project for a distance of 3 ft. 2 in.

Lower plane in four sections ; two between fuselage and engine nacelles and two outer sections.

Interplane struts spaced as follows ; nacelle struts 8 ft. from center of body ; intermediate struts 10 ft. from nacelle struts ; outer struts 12 ft. from intermediate struts. Overhang rods anchored 14 ft. from outer struts. Overhang beyond bracing 6 ft., including ailerons.

Ailerons are 20 ft. 7⅛ in. long ; 3 ft. 9 in. in chord. Overhang portion 3 ft. 1¼ in. wide.

The accompanying drawing illustrates the manner in which the main planes are hinged aft of the engine nacelles, permitting the wings to be folded back so as to facilitate housing in a comparatively narrow hangar. In folded position the measurement from leading edge of wing to centerline of fuselage is 15 ft. 6 in.

For bracing between planes, oval section steel rods are used exclusively. Ends are formed to a solid section which is threaded and fitted with a trunnion barrel and forked terminals.

Fuselage.

The fuselage is built up with the usual longerons and cross members. Bracing is with solid wires with swaged or forked ends.

Total length of fuselage, 62 ft. 10¼ in. ; maximum width at the wings, 4 ft. 9 in., tapering in straight lines to 2 ft. 11 in. wide at the stern ; maximum height, 6 ft. 10 in. In flying position the top longerons are horizontal to the propeller axes ; top longerons 12 ft. 3 in. above ground.

Leading edge of planes 12 ft. 2 in. aft of fuselage nose.

Tail Group.

The tail is of the biplane type with a gap of 6 ft. Average chord, 3 ft. 6 in. 17/32 in. Chord, above body, 5 ft. 6 in. Span of stabilizers, 16 ft. 7½ in.

There are two pairs of elevators 1 ft. 10 in. 15/32 in. wide and 8 ft. 5½ in. long.

Struts from body to top tail plane spaced 2 ft. 9¼ in. from center to center. From these, the outer forward struts and rudders are spaced 6 ft. 3⅞ in.

Central vertical fin 4 ft. wide.

Rudders are balanced.

STURTEVANT. The B. F. Sturtevant Company, Hyde Park, Boston, Massachusetts.

Big engineering firm. Turned out some time ago a " battle " aeroplane of naval type, to designs of Mr. Grover C. Loening, B.Sc., M.A.C.E., former Aeronautic Engineer to U S. Army.

No fresh information. Presumably building to official specifications.

A U.S. Naval Flying Boat of the H.S. 2 L. type, built by the Standard Aircraft Corporation.

T

THOMAS-MORSE AIRCRAFT CORPORATION. (Late Thomas Bros.,) Ithaca, New York.

The brothers Thomas began experimenting and flying in 1908 with a machine on the lines of a *Curtiss*. In the winter of 1909-10, a type of their own was produced and was flown during 1911 by Walter Johnson in exhibitions. In 1912 they continued the same type, with refinements. In 1913 they adopted the overhanging top plane type, but of the same general order of construction.

In 1915 the firm supplied various Tractor biplanes to the Allied Governments. In 1916, the firm was reconstructed, and became the Thomas-Morse Aircraft Corporation. It has since supplied numerous machines to the U.S. Government.

THE THOMAS-MORSE SINGLE-SEATER M.B. 3.

Type of machine	Single-seater Biplane.
Name or type No. of machine	M.B. 3.
Purpose for which intended	Fighting.
Span	26 ft.
Overall length	19 ft.
Maximum height	8 ft.
Chord	5 ft. 3 in.
Total surface of wings	250 sq. ft.
Engine type and h.p.	300 h.p. Hispano-Suiza.
Weight of machine empty	1,360 lbs.
Load per sq. ft.	8 lbs.
Petrol tank capacity in gallons	65 gallons.

Performance.

Speed low down	164 m.p.h.
Landing speed	55 m.ph.

Climb.

To 1,000 feet	20 secs.
To 10,000 feet in minutes	4 mins. 52 secs.
Total weight of machine loaded	2,000 lbs.
Two Browning machine guns.	
Useful load (with water)	800 lbs.

The Thomas-Morse type M.B. 3 (300 h.p. Hispano-Suiza).

A Thomas-Morse Single-seater.

THOMAS-MORSE—*continued.*

THE THOMAS-MORSE SINGLE-SEATER SCOUT BIPLANE.

Type of machine	Single-seater Scout Biplane
Name or type No. of machine ..	S. 4C.
Purpose for which intended ..	Fighting.
Span	26 ft. 6 in.
Overall length	19 ft. 10 in.
Maximum height	8 ft. 1 in.
Engine type and h.p. .. '..	80 h.p. Le Rhône.
Weight of machine empty	940 lbs.
Petrol tank capacity in gallons ..	30 gallons.

Performance.
Speed (maximum)	97 m.p.h.
Landing speed	45 m.p.h.

Climb.
To 7,500 feet in minutes ..	10 minutes.
Total weight of machine loaded	1,330 lbs.

THE THOMAS MORSE S.4E.

Type of machine	Thomas Morse.
Name or type No. of machine ..	S.4E. Scout.
Purpose for which intended ..	Advanced training.
Span	Top 22 ft. 6 in.; bottom 20 ft.
Overall length	19 ft. 4 in.
Chord	Tapered.
Total surface of wings ..	145 sq. ft.
Total area of tail	12 sq. ft.
Area of elevators	$16\frac{4}{5}$ sq. ft.
Area of rudder	$8\frac{1}{2}$ sq. ft.
Area of fin	$3\frac{1}{2}$ sq. ft.
Area of each aileron and total area	$8\frac{1}{4}$ sq. ft.; $16\frac{1}{2}$ sq. ft.
Engine type and h.p.	Le Rhône; 80 h.p.
Weight of machine empty ..	1,150 lbs.
Weight of machine loaded ..	1,150 lbs.

Performance.
Speed low down	55—105 m.p.h.

Climb.
To 7,500 feet in 10 minutes.
Ceiling 17,000 feet.

Three-quarter Rear View, of the Thomas-Morse type S.4C. (80 h.p. Le Rhône engine).

Front View of the Thomas-Morse type S.4E. Single-seater (80 h.p. Le Rhône engine).

THOMAS-MORSE—*continued.*

THE THOMAS-MORSE SINGLE SEATER SEAPLANE.

Type of machine	Single-seater Seaplane.
Name or type No. of machine ..	S. 5.
Purpose for which intended.. ..	Training.
Span	26 ft. 6 in.
Overall length	22 ft. 9 in.
Maximum height	9 ft. 7 in.
Total surface of wings (inc. ailerons)	240 sq. ft.
Total area of fixed tail plane ..	16.8 sq. ft.
Area of elevators	22 sq. ft.
Area of rudder	8.5 sq. ft.
Area of fin	3.5 sq. ft.
Total area of ailerons	30 sq. ft.
Engine type and h.p.	100 h.p. Monosoupape Gnôme.
Airscrew, diameter and revs. ..	8 ft., 1250 r.p.m.
Load per sq. ft.	6.25 lbs.
Weight per h.p.	14·3 lbs.
Tank capacity in hours.	3 hours.
Tank capacity in gallons	30 galls.

Performance.

Speed low down	95 m.p.h.
Landing speed	50 m.p.h.

Climb.

To 5,200 feet in minutes ..	10 minutes.
Total weight of machine loaded	1,500 lbs.

THE THOMAS-MORSE SIDE-BY-SIDE TWO-SEATER.

Type of machine	Side-by-side Two-seater.
Name or type No. of machine ..	S. 7.
Purpose for which intended ..	Civilian use.
Span	32 ft.
Overall length	21 ft. 6 in.
Maximum height	9 ft.
Total surface of wings (inc. ailerons)	322 sq. ft.
Total area of fixed tail plane ..	14.5 sq. ft.
Area of elevators	16.8 sq. ft.
Area of rudder	8.5 sq. ft.
Area of fin	3.6 sq. ft.
Total area of ailerons	40 sq. ft.
Engine type and h.p.	80 h.p. Le Rhône.
Airscrew, diameter and revs. ..	8 ft., 1,250 r.p.m.
Load per sq. ft.	4.6 lbs.
Weight per h.p.	16.5 lbs.
Tank capacity in gallons	20 galls.

Performance.

Speed low down	90 m.p.h.
Landing speed	40 m.p.h.

Climb.

To 6,700 feet in minutes ..	10 minutes.
Total weight of machine loaded.	1,480 lbs.

Three-quarter Rear View of the Thomas-Morse type S. 4 E.

The Thomas-Morse S. 4 E. Single-Seater.

THOMAS-MORSE—*continued*.

THE THOMAS-MORSE TWO-SEATER BIPLANE.

Type of machine	Two-seater Biplane (dual control).
Name or type No. of machine ..	S. 6.
Purpose for which intended ..	Training and civilian use.
Span	29 ft.
Overall length	20 ft. 8 in.
Maximum height	8 ft. 10 in.
Total surface of wings (inc. ailerons)	296 sq. ft.
Total area of fixed tail plane ..	14.5 sq. ft.
Area of elevators	16.8 sq. ft.
Area of rudder	8.5 sq. ft.
Area of fin	3.5 sq. ft.
Total area of ailerons	31.5 sq. ft.
Engine type and h.p.	80 h.p. Le Rhône.
Airscrew, diameter and revs. ..	7 ft. 10 in., 1,250 r.p.m.
Load per sq. ft.	4.68 lbs.
Weight per h.p.	15.4 lbs.
Tank capacity in gallons	20 galls.

Performance.
Speed low down	105 m p.h.
Landing speed	40 m.p h.

Climb.
To 8.000 feet in minutes.. ..	10 minutes.
Total weight of machine loaded	1,385 lbs.

The Thomas-Morse Two-seater type S. 6 (80 h.p. Le Rhône engine).

THE THOMAS-MORSE SEAPLANE.

Type of machine	Two-seater Seaplane.
Name or type No. of machine ..	S.H. 4.
Purpose for which intended ..	Training.
Span	44 ft.
Overall length	29 ft. 9 in.
Chord..	5 ft. 9 in.
Engine type and h.p.	100 h.p. (type unstated).

The Thomas-Morse S.H. 4 Seaplane.

U

UNITED AIRCRAFT ENGINEERING CORPORATION. 52, Vanderbilt Avenue, New York.

President, F. G. Diffin ; Chief Engineer, M. B. Stout.

This firm was organised early in 1919 for the purpose of promoting commercial aeronautics through the development of aircraft engineering and the construction of aeroplanes to their own designs.

Shortly after their organisation this firm purchased from the Canadian Government a great stock of flying material, valued at $10,000,000, in which were comprised 350 Canadian *Curtiss* J.N. two-seaters, 1,000 Curtiss O.X. engines, hundreds of airscrews and spare parts in proportion. It is intended to sell this material to American sportsmen and others interested in civil aviation.

A number of elementary training machines of various types and conditions were also bought from the British Aircraft Disposal Board.

Single and two-seater monoplanes are being developed to the designs of Mr. Stout.

THE UNITED EASTERN AEROPLANE CORPORATION. 1251, De Kalb Avenue, Brooklyn, New York.

Build three types of tractor biplane.   Factor of safety of 10 claimed for all parts.

Wing curve throughout " Eiffel 36."

Capital recently increased from $30,000 to $1,000,000.

Owns the Eastern School of Aviation.

Were engaged on Military machines for the U. S. Government.

V

VOUGHT. Lewis & Vought Corporation, Long Island City, N.Y.

This firm constructs to the designs of Mr. Chance M. Vought, president and chief engineer, a two-seater biplane fitted with a 180 h.p. Hispano-Suiza engine, which is used by the U.S. Army as an advanced training machine.   This aeroplane won, in 1918, the Army competition for advanced training machines.

THE V.E.7 " BLUEBIRD " TRAINING MACHINE,

Type of machine	Two-seater Biplane.
Name or type No. of machine ..	V.E. 7 " Bluebird."
Purpose for which intended.. ..	Training.
Span	34 ft. 4 in.
Gap	4 ft. 8 in.
Overall length	24 ft. 5⅜ in.
Maximum height	8 ft. 7½ in.
Chord	4 ft. 7½ in.
Span of tail	10 ft.
Engine type and h.p.	150 or 180 h.p. Hispano-Suiza.
Airscrew, diameter	8 ft. 8 in.
Weight of machine empty	1,392 lbs.

Performance.

Speed low down..	106 m.p h.
Speed at 6,500 feet	103 m.p.h.
Speed at 10,000 feet	97 m.p.h.
Speed at 15,000 feet	86 m.p.h.
Landing speed	48 m.p.h.

Climb.

To 6,500 feet in minutes.. ..	8 mins. 50 secs.
To 10,000 feet in minutes ..	15 mins. 15 secs.
To 15,000 feet in minutes ..	29 minutes.

Total weight of machine loaded   ..   ..   .. 1,937 lbs.

Side View of the Lewis & Vought V.E.7 Training Machine (Hispano-Suiza engine).

Three-quarter Rear View of the Lewis & Vought V.E.7 150 h.p. Hispano-Suiza).

FRONT VIEW

SIDE VIEW

V-E-7 PLANE WITH 150 H.P. HISPANO-SUIZA ENGINE

PLAN VIEW

V.E.7 PLANE WITH 150 H.P. HISPANO-SUIZA ENGINE

W

WITTEMAN - LEWIS AIRCRAFT COR- PORATION. Newark, N.J.

Aeronautical constructional engineers, manufacturing to private specifications. Have produced the *Sundstedt* seaplane, which was intended for the trans-Atlantic flight, but crashed in the course of its trials.

Have also produced a tractor biplane of their own design.

THE SUNDSTEDT-HANNEVIG SEAPLANE.

At the plant of the Wittemann-Lewis Aircraft Co., probably one of the largest seaplanes in the United States has been constructed by the prominent Swedish aviator, Captain Hugo Sundstedt, and the well-known Norwegian financier, shipbuilder and shipowner, Mr. Christoffer Hannevig.

Captain Sundstedt is one of the pioneers in aviation, having flown since 1910. In July, 1914, just before the war broke out, he made a non-stop flight from Buc, near Paris, France, to Stockholm, of about 1,200 miles, in a *Henry Farman* biplane, in 13 hours and 20 minutes. During the war Capt. Sundstedt has been about two years in France, and received several decorations. About three years ago he left France for the United States for the purpose of building an aeroplane for a trans-Atlantic flight.

The *Sundstedt-Hannevig* seaplane has been designed for the specific purpose of long-distance flying over the sea. In general, it has been designed with an extra heavy substantial construction, particularly on those parts subjected to the greatest amount of strain during flight and at landings, such as pontoons, wings, and the entire rigging.

In the design, however, only proved aero-dynamical principles have been embodied, assuring a positively efficient machine, and Captain Sundstedt has made a large number of improvements in structural details, affording the utmost strength and lightness of construction.

The seaplane is equipped for two pilots and two passengers in the cabin of the fuselage.

General Dimensions.

Span, upper plane	..	100 ft.
Span, lower plane	..	71 ft. 6 in.
Wing chord, lower plane	..	8 ft.
Wing chord, upper plane	..	8 ft.
Gap between wings	..	8 ft. 72 in.
Length of machine overall	..	50 ft. 6 in.
Height of machine overall	..	17 ft. 7 in.
Dihedral angle, lower plane	..	2 degrees.
Wing curve	..	U.S.A. No. 5.
Total lifting surface	..	1,587 sq. ft.
Rudder area	..	22 sq. ft.
Elevator area	..	54 sq. ft.
Weight	..	10,000 lbs.
Loading per h.p.	..	25 lbs.
Loading per sq. ft.	..	6 lbs.
Speed, estimated, full load	..	80 m.p h.
Climbing speed, estimated	..	3,000 ft. in 10 mins.
Horse power, total	..	440.

The Sunstedt-Hannevig Transatlantic Seaplane before complete erection.

488a   **A View of the Sunstedt-Hannevig Seaplane without wings.**

WITTEMAN-LEWIS—*continued.*

Pontoons.

The pontoons are of special Sundstedt design, embodying the highest developed features of streamline, and follow the most accepted construction practice. They are made of Capt. A. P. Lundin's special three-ply Balsa wood veneer, covered with linen, and are each divided into eight watertight compartments, painted and varnished with torpedo grey enamel. They are 32 ft. long, spaced 16 ft. apart from centres, and are light in weight, being 400 pounds apiece including fittings.

Each pontoon is equipped with an emergency food locker accessible from the deck by means of a handhole.

The pontoons are braced to the fuselage and wings by a series of steel tubing struts with Balsa wood streamline fairing. These tubes are of large diameter and fit into sockets mounted on the pontoons and wing spars. The entire assembly is amply braced by steel cables and tubing connecting struts.

Fuselage.

The fuselage is of streamline design, and is flat sided in order to provide sufficient vertical surface necessary for good directional stability. It has a curved streamline bottom and hood running fore and aft. The construction is of white ash and spruce, consisting of four longerons and ash and spruce compression struts fastened thereto with light universal steel fittings, to which are also fastened and connected diagonally the solid steel brace wires and turnbuckles.

The front end of the fuselage is fitted up much after the style of a closed motor car, with comfortable upholstered seats for the pilots and passengers. This cabin is accessible by a door on each side at the rear end of the cabin. A very complete field of vision is obtained through a series of glass windows around the front of the pilots' seats, forming a recess in the upper deck forward of the windows.

Directly behind this cabin and balancing with the centre of pressure is the main gasoline tank, with a capacity of 750 gallons, sufficient for 22 hours of full speed flying, and to the rearward of this is the adjustable open trussing, with a detachable hood and covering for access and inspection.

The forward section is covered with a thin three-ply mahogany veneer up to the rear of the cabin doors, and aft of these it is covered with linen, doped, painted and varnished.

Control.

The control system operates on the standard wheel and rudder bar method, and is of special Sundstedt design, whereby all cables are located beneath the floor, leaving a clean control column and rudder bar without any wires in the way of passengers or pilots. Dual control is fitted, side by side, directly connected, so that the machine can be controlled by either pilot at will.

All engine controls and switches are located on the dashboard, operative from both seats.

Instruments.

A substantial dashboard is fitted in front of the pilot's seat in a plainly visible position, and is equipped with tachometers for both motors, clock, altimeter, speedometer, radiator thermometers, oil pressure gauges, shut off valves, ignition switches, and so forth, which are located in within easy reach of the pilot.

Power Equipment.

The power plant consists of two Hall-Scott Model "L. 6" 220 h.p. engines, directly connected to two bladed pusher airscrews. Each are mounted on a specially constructed bed by the Vee method of interplane struts, with the engine beds, housings and radiators all securely braced to the wings, pontoons and fuselage.

SUNDSTEDT-HANNEVIG
TWIN MOTORED
SEAPLANE

Scale of feet

The engines are supplied with gasoline by turbine-driven Miller gasoline pumps, which maintain a pressure of 3 lbs. in a special reservoir of the pump itself, under automatic adjustment, and eliminating all of the difficulties and dangers of the gravity and pressure feed systems. These pumps are regulated from the cabin and within easy reach of the pilots.

WITTEMAN-LEWIS—continued.

THE WITTEMANN-LEWIS TRACTOR BIPLANE.

Type of machine	Wittemann-Lewis.
Name or type No. of machine ..	" T. T."
Purpose for which intended ..	Military training.
Span	42 ft. top; 34 ft. bottom plane.
Gap	5 ft. 6 in.
Overall length	27 ft. 2 in.
Maximum height.. ..	11 ft. 6½ in.
Chord	5 ft. 6 in.
Total surface of wings ..	400 sq. ft.
Total area of tail	28.8 sq. ft.
Area of elevators	21.6 sq. ft.
Area of rudder	12 sq. ft.
Area of fin	5.37 sq. ft.
Area of each aileron & total area	17.44; 38.88 sq. ft.
Engine type and h.p. ..	Hall-Scott, 100 h.p.
Weight of machine empty ..	1,560 lbs.
Load per sq. ft.	5.41 lbs.
Weight per h.p.	21.6 lbs.
Tank capacity in hours ..	3.6 hours.
Tank capacity in gallons ..	36 gallons.

Performance.
  Speed .. .. .. 74 m.p.h. max.; 38 m.p.h. min.
Climb.
  To 3,000 feet in 10 minutes.
Disposable load apart from fuel .. .. .. 605 lbs.
Total weight of machine loaded .. .. .. 2,165 lbs.

The Witteman-Lewis Biplane, type T.T. (100 h.p. Hall-Scott engine).

THE WRIGHT-MARTIN AIRCRAFT CORPORATION. 60, Broadway, New York City.

Western office: 937, S. Los Angelos St. Los Angelos St., Cal.
Foreign office: 35, bis Rue d'Anjou, Paris.

The original type of *Wright* machine was mounted on skids only, and started along a rail. Its special features were a biplane elevator forward, main planes with warpable tips to trailing edge, small keel in gap, two propellers, chain driven in rear of planes, double rudder in rear, and no tail. Orville Wright made the first flight worthy of the name on this machine on December 17th, 1903. He flew a machine of this type for 2h. 20m. 23⅕s. in 1908. (For details of early *Wrights* see previous editions of this book.)

During 1916, the Wright Co., represented by Mr. Orville Wright, the surviving brother, formed a " merger " with the Glenn L. Martin Co., the Simplex Automobile Co., the Wright Flying Field Inc., and the General Aeronautic Co., of America.

Mr· Orville Wright continued to work as a private experimenter at the experimental factory at Dayton, Ohio.

The firm has factories at Los Angelos, (Cal.), at New York, at Simplex Works, New Brunswick, New Jersey.

The aerodromes are at Los Angelos (Cal.) and at Hempstead Plains, Long Island.

There is a seaplane station at Port Washington, Long Island. 2,400 men were employed in 1916.

The president of the firm is Edward M. Hagar; vice-presidents, Glenn L. Martin and C. S. Jennison; secretary, J. G. Dudley.

Capital, 5,000,000 dollars.

Before the war this firm built biplanes to their own designs, but during the war this work was entirely dropped and all activity centred on the production of Hispano-Suiza engines and on the production of aeroplanes to official designs.

Mr. Glenn L. Martin also started a new concern of his own.

THE WORLD'S AERO-ENGINES.

ARRANGED IN THE ALPHABETICAL ORDER OF THEIR NAMES.

WITH A PREFACE BY

CAPTAIN W. H. SAYERS (LATE) R.A.F.

A

THE DEVELOPMENT OF THE AERO-ENGINE, 1903-1919.

By CAPTAIN W. H. SAYERS (Late) R.A.F.

THE development of the aeroplane has always waited upon the development of its source of motive power. Had there been in existence 50 years ago any prime mover capable of developing 1 h.p. for even 10 mins. for a total weight, including fuel, of 5 lbs., it is more than likely that mechanical flight would have been an accomplished fact 45 years ago.

In actual fact it became possible only in 1903, when Mr. Thomas Manley designed and built for Samuel Pierpont Langley a 5-cylinder radial petrol engine which actually developed 50 h.p. for under 200 lbs. weight. By a series of misadventures this engine never took the air till in 1914 Glenn H. Curtiss flew the Langley machine for which it was built with the original engine.

A little later the Wright brothers, having practically solved the whole of the basic aerodynamic problems of flight, and practised the art by gliding downhill, had to develop their own engine before the power-propelled Wright biplane could be made to fly.

From those days to the present is but a very short time, as time goes, but in the development of dynamic flight it has covered a phenomenal advance.

The rate of this advance has been determined almost entirely by the progress of aero-engine design, and it has been entirely an advance in the direction of increased maximum performance on the part of the aeroplane and engine combined.

To take the matter back no farther than 1912, at which date the general trend of aeroplane design had settled down to lines from which it has yet to depart, it will be found that the best available aero-engine, considering possible performance alone, was the Gnôme of 50, 70, or 80 nominal h.p., whose bare weight varied from 4 to 3½ lbs. per b.h.p. These engines were extravagant as to fuel and oil consumption, but, as long-duration flights were in small demand, they almost invariably beat their more economical but initially heavier competitors.

At that date a machine with a top speed of 85 m.p.h. and a climb to 5,000 ft. in 15 mins. would have been phenomenal.

ENGINES TO-DAY.

To-day, air-cooled engines up to 500 h.p. each, at 1.7 lbs. per h.p., with quite low fuel and oil consumptions, are available for high-performance machines for moderate durations of flight, and, for cases where longer ranges are required, there are water-cooled engines of anything up to 700 h.p., weighing, with water and radiators, less than 3 lbs. per b.h.p., which regain some, at least, of the handicap of their initially greater weight through their lower fuel consumption, and which have a reputation for reliability superior to that of the air-cooled type.

Whether this reputation for superior reliability will be long retained is at present open to doubt.

With this increase in the size of power units, and the decrease in the specific weight per h.p. of the power unit, the performance of the aeroplane has advanced, and to-day 130 m.p.h. and a climb to 15,000 ft. in 15 mins. will cause less astonishment than would the 85 m.p.h. and 5,000 ft. in a quarter of an hour seven years ago.

Notwithstanding the great reduction of the weight per h.p. which has been attained in the modern engine, reliability and economy have distinctly improved.

An examination of the underlying causes for the particular lines of development which have led to the present aero-engine will show that the main impulse to progress has been the need for higher and still higher performance on the part of the aeroplane, and therefore to lower weight per h.p. on the part of the engine.

In the earlier days, up to 1911 or thereabouts, it was a question of obtaining an engine sufficiently light and powerful to fly a machine at all.

Between this period and August, 1914, better and better performance was needed simply to make the aeroplane reasonably independent of the normal vagaries of the wind, and from the outbreak of war till almost the present time the military necessities of aerial warfare have intensified the demand for performance.

WAR DEMANDS.

It is true that with the war demand for performance there has been coupled a demand for reliability, but this has always been, within certain limits, a secondary matter.

A one in ten risk of engine failure, on a machine which can outdistance and outclimb any enemy machine one is likely to meet, is better worth taking than a one in three chance of being shot down by a superior adversary, even if the risk of engine failure be nil.

Roughly speaking, the actual evolution of the aero-engine under the influence of this crying call for better performance, or in the terms of the engine itself, for lower weight per h.p. has been confined to two main lines.

Probably most important has been a better use and distribution of the materials of which the engine is constructed, together with the development of materials possessing better physical qualities for their particular purpose.

This has led to a very considerable decrease in the weight of engines of given dimensions.

Almost equally important has been the increase in the mean effective pressure developed within the cylinders.

DISGUISED DEVELOPMENT.

This second line of development has in many cases been disguised. There has been a noticeable increase in the actual developed pressure which has led directly to an increased h.p. from a given sized cylinder at a given speed of rotation.

This increase, it must be noted, cannot be extended indefinitely, without increasing the structural weight, unless there is either a better use of materials or the use of better materials in the working parts. Thus this line of development is dependent upon the first to a certain extent.

Over and above the increase in the effective working pressure there has been an increase in the rotatory speed, or more accurately the piston speed, at which such pressures have been maintained.

This is really the same line of development in a less obvious form. The air and petrol mixture flowing through carburetter, induction pipes, and inlet valves encounters a certain resistance, which increases as the square of the speed at which the gas flows through any given part of the induction system.

This resistance is manifested by a reduction in the pressure, and therefore in the density, of the gas entering the cylinders, and the faster any given engine is made to run the lower the density of the incoming charge.

The lower the density of the charge the lower become both the compression and the mean explosion pressure.

Hence increasing the speed of rotation of any engine, other conditions remaining unchanged, must decrease the mean effective pressure developed.

For any given engine there will be a range of speed over which this effect is negligible, but it eventually shows itself by a marked falling off of the m.e.p. and the torque developed as the speed rises.

Therefore the problem of efficiently increasing the speed of rotation of any given engine beyond a certain limit becomes one of increasing the mean effective pressure at the higher speed.

Very largely this problem reduces to one of the design of inlet pipes, valves, and valve gearing which will offer the minimum of air resistance to the inflowing charge.

Both main lines of development, and both the forms of the second line mentioned lead to higher intensity of stress in the working parts of the engine.

The use of material better adapted for its purpose leads to a reduction in size of a member carrying a given load.

INCREASED STRESSES.

Increase in the developed mean effective pressure obviously leads to increased stress intensity ultimately, since such items as bearing surfaces and so forth cannot be enlarged beyond definite limits imposed by the general layout and leading dimensions of the engine, except at the cost of excessive weight in other parts.

Increase in the speed of the engine increases all *inertia* loads throughout the engine.

Thus the whole development of the aero-engine must be regarded as merely one huge conspiracy to load every working part to as near its ultimate strength as possible.

This process has been extended to all, or nearly all, the accessories of the engine proper.

Increased output from a cylinder of given size means that a greater amount of heat must be transferred through the cylinder walls.

In the water-cooled engine this calls for an increased speed of water circulation through the jackets. The process of loading up thus extends to the circulating pump.

Increased bearing pressures call for increased oil supply, therefore the oil pump shares the fate of the water pump.

Even the magneto, always a source of amaze and wonder, on account of the unexpected reliability of this piece of high-tension electrical apparatus most brutally ill-treated, is forced to do its share of the extra work.

THE TWO CLASSES.

And in consequence it is possible to divide the modern aero-engine roughly into two classes.

One, and it is by no means the least effective class at the moment, is in the main just a decently designed engine based in all its main features upon its motor-car ancestor, run up to what is, for the original design, a violent overload, and covered with what can only be described as " gadgets " applied to fortify those parts which practice has shown most to need it.

The second class, which will almost certainly outlive the first, consists of those types of engine which have actually been designed without reference to the conventions of the ancestral car engine, but with an eye to so disposing their parts that they shall best withstand the heavy stress intensities under which they will have to work.

These two classifications are very general, and it would be impossible to affirm that any known aero-engine was either entirely devoid of any trace of car-engine influence or shewed no sign of special design to meet the conditions under which it has to work.

Most aero-engines are hybrids between these two classes, but most of them definitely incline toward one or the other type.

Broadly, one might fairly classify all the vertical and " Vee " type engines as amongst those predominantly influenced by the conventions of car practice, and all the radials and rotaries as belonging to the type which has broken away from this tradition.

Considering that line of the development of aero-engines which has depended on improved use of the materials of construction, it will be found to be mainly concerned with the transformation of the " car-type " engine into its modern derivatives.

The specially designed type of engine, particularly the rotary type, were forced to use constructional materials with widely different qualities to those used in the car type of engine.

CYLINDER MATERIAL.

Cast iron, which is an ideal material for cylinders both because of the ease of moulding and machining this metal, and because of its excellent wearing qualities when used as a cylinder wall, is intrinsically weak and must therefore be heavy.

Heavy cylinders in a rotary engine mean great loads due to centrifugal force imposed upon both cylinders and crankcase. The designers of rotaries therefore had to use a stronger material —steel—for their cylinders, and discover ways and means of overcoming the disadvantages of this material from the wearing point of view.

Having solved the problem more or less satisfactorily, the designers of stationary engines followed in their footsteps—at first to the half-way house of using Steel Castings—a material not markedly inferior to Cast Iron in its wearing qualities—and later still, when suitable alloy steels became available, to the full extent of machining cylinders from forgings or solid billets.

Thus to-day Cast Iron is obsolete as a cylinder material for aero-engines.

A CURIOUS DEVELOPMENT.

One most curious development in cylinder construction is due to M. Birkight, the designer of the Hispano-Suiza engines.

In this type the cylinder, cylinder heads and water-jackets are aluminium castings, into which steel cylinder liners are screwed.

From the strength-weight point of view this would seem to be a retrograde step, but it has in fact certain important advantages.

Aluminium has a very high heat conductivity, so high that an aluminium alloy cylinder wall will allow the transfer of heat through it to the surrounding jacket water—or air in the case of an air-cooled engine—more readily than will the much thinner steel wall of equal strength. Thus it is easier to cool cylinders built in this manner than those of either Steel or Cast Iron.

Weight for weight, aluminium is probably stronger than any steel or semi-steel from which a satisfactory mono-block cylinder casting, with integral water-jackets could be made, and the monobloc cylinder arrangement has the advantage of being inherently stiff, and therefore does not need so stiff nor so heavy a crankcase as does the separate cylinder arrangement.

The Birkight system has been further extended by Mr. Kirkham, who in the " K " type engines designed by him for the Curtiss Co. has made both the cylinders and the upper crankcase half in one aluminium alloy casting.

In this case the stationary type engine led the way and the rotary has followed. The B. R. (Bentley Rotary) engines have aluminium alloy cylinders, steel liners and steel heads, and the centrifugal and explosion loads are taken to the crankcase *via* the steel head by steel holding-down bolts.

PISTON MATERIAL.

As with cylinders, so with pistons. Cast Iron has disappeared in favour of either Steel or Aluminium. On the whole, aluminium seems to be in favour for this purpose, though steel pistons are not without their advocates.

Aluminium owes its popularity largely to its high heat conductivity, which greatly assists in keeping cool the piston-head.

As a contributory factor, the very great tendency of steel rubbing on steel to seize up has doubtless had its effects since steel cylinders have become universal.

Apart from cylinders and pistons, there has been little change of a revolutionary nature in the class of material used in the construction of aero-engines. There have been very great improvements in the physical qualities of the materials throughout the whole structure.

These improvements generally have been greatly accelerated by war conditions, which not only increased the volume of the demand for steel, but called for steels of higher quality than had been needed before.

The immensely increased demand for aircraft and their engines was partly responsible for this, but, in the main, engine designers merely took advantage of the better materials available, and the fact that—thanks to their increased output and the relative unimportance of cost—they could afford to employ expensive materials to their heart's content.

INCREASING OUTPUT.

Taking the second line of development, that of increasing the output of a given cylinder volume—the general effect on the design of engines of the stationary type has been much more a matter of detail design than of anything else.

More noticeable than any other effect probably has been the almost universal adoption of overhead valves.

This is largely a direct effect of increased compression ratios and the consequent decrease in clearance volume. In a low compression engine, small variations in the clearance volume have no noticeable ill effect, and cast pockets at the cylinder sides to house the valves and their seating are possible.

Such pockets cannot be accurately machined, and the small variations in their volume may lead to a variation in compression and in explosion pressure of considerable magnitude in an engine with a high compression ratio.

Apart from this, the design of a valve pocket which shall give a free flow of gas from the valves to the cylinder without unduly increasing the clearance volume is in itself a difficult problem.

With the universal use of overhead valves, the overhead camshaft has become prevalent. This not only saves the weight of long tappet rods, but tends to secure the quicker opening and closing of valves—because in opening valves quickly a long tappet rod always springs more or less, and the valve fails to follow the cam accurately, and in closing, since the valve spring has to move the tappet as well as the valve itself, the *inertia* of the tappet rod retards the movement.

Quick opening and closing of valves means less resistance to the flow of gas past those valves, because the less time spent in opening and closing, the longer the time fully open.

DETAIL IMPROVEMENT.

Beyond these two items, development has been mainly devoted to detail improvement tending to secure easy gas passages, particularly between the carburettor and the cylinders, and the methods adopted have been many and diverse, and it is impossible to recognise any uniformity of tendency except perhaps in the provision of multiple carburettors for multi-cylinder engines.

With a large number of cylinders it is practically impossible to keep equal induction pipe resistances between a single carburettor and each cylinder, or to avoid abrupt changes in the direction of gas flow as successive inlet valves open.

As a result, different cylinders receive varying changes, and irregular running occurs.

It is found easier to obtain even running from a number of carburettors, each supplying a few cylinders, than to arrange an induction system giving the same result from a single carburettor.

SPECIALISED TYPES.

The development of special types of engine designed solely with a view to their use in aircraft has so far been limited to two main lines of procedure, neither of them entirely novel—but both carried to much greater lengths in certain aircraft engines than in any previous type.

Firstly, there has been the development of air-cooling already largely employed in motor cycle and other small internal combustion engines.

The saving in weight of water and radiators which can be effected thus is obvious.

The difficulty encountered with air-cooling is due to the low heat conductivity, and the low specific heat, of air. Small cylinders, adequately finned, can be satisfactorily air-cooled without difficulty.

Because the volume of a cylinder increases as the square of the bore, and the wall surface increases only directly with the bore, the cooling surface of any cylinder, air or water-cooled, becomes less and less in proportion to the power capacity of that cylinder as the bore becomes larger, and large air-cooled cylinders cannot be satisfactorily cooled unless special precautions are taken.

METHODS OF AIR-COOLING.

The designers of rotary engines overcame the difficulty, because the rotation of the engine enormously increased the air flow past the cylinders.

In the Renault engine and some others, the same effect was produced by using forced draught from a fan. Both these methods absorb a considerable amount of the power developed by the engine.

The total surface in contact with the air may be increased indefinitely by increasing the number and the depth of the fins on the cylinder. This is not a solution of the problem—because it increases the resistance of the heat path from the inside of the cylinder to the outer surface, and ultimately defeats the object aimed at.

In the case of the B.R. engines, the high thermal conductivity of aluminium is used to overcome this trouble—apparently very successfully—and the method of coating steel cylinders with electrically deposited copper, used by Mr. Granville Bradshaw, in the A.B.C. engines, owes its effect to the increased cooling surface obtained by increasing the effective outside diameter of the cylinder, and to the low heat resistance of the copper.

The A.B.C. copper deposition method probably gains slightly because the surface of electrically deposited copper is unpolished, and polished surfaces are invariably bad radiators of heat—but this effect must be relatively small.

Careful design, and the use of expedients such as those mentioned above, has made it possible to build successful air-cooled engines of large power, but the air-cooled engine has not yet been able to operate at such high explosion pressures and temperatures as its water-cooled competitors, and it has in consequence never reached quite so high a thermal efficiency, or so low a fuel consumption.

The actual difference in this respect is, however, now quite small—somewhere about 0.03 lbs. of fuel per h.p., or roughly 6% of the total consumption—and is unimportant compared with the saving of engine weight which can be obtained.

THE RADIAL ENGINE.

The second line upon which the specialised types have advanced has been in the use of a common crank by more than one cylinder.

The twin-cylinder Vee-type motor-cycle engine is probably the best known example of this practice, but the Manley engine of 1903 to which reference has already been made, was probably the earliest internal combustion engine of the type. The Brotherhood 3-cylinder radial compressed air engine for torpedoes is considerably older than either, and probably even earlier examples could be found.

Obviously weight can be saved in both crankshaft and crankcase by this method, because the overall length needed for a given number of cylinders is reduced.

The most obvious step in this direction was to take two rows of cylinders similar to those of a normal vertical stationary engine and inclining their axis to make both rows drive a common crankshaft.

AN INTERMEDIATE PHASE.

The Antoinette of 1907, or thereabouts, and the E.N.V. (literally " En Vee ") engine of 1909, are early—if not the earliest—examples of this practice applied to the normal " car type " engine, and the Vee arrangement is now practically standard for all large stationary aero-engines.

The method has been extended in the Green 450 h.p. engine, and the Napier "Lion" of the same power, and in the 'Sunbeam' of 1917, to three rows in the form of a " broad arrow," and in the pages to follow there will be found at least one case of an engine designed with four rows each of four cylinders arranged as a cross.

In the radial and the rotary types the method has been carried to its logical conclusion.

Three, five, seven, or nine cylinders are equally spaced round a common crankshaft, and all drive the same crank. Occasionally, two such radials are coupled together one behind the other through a two-throw crankshaft to form one unit.

Thus the maximum use is made of both crankshaft and crankcase, both of which are subjected to a nearly continuous series of impulses from the cylinders around them, thus securing an even turning movement and a well balanced engine.

In the pages which follow, the particular manifestations of the various design tendencies which have been briefly commented upon above can be traced fairly clearly, and to the succeeding illustrations and descriptions of engines the reader is referred for illustrations of their more particular details.

A.B.C. (British).

A.B.C. MOTORS, LTD., Walton-on-Thames, formerly the All British Engine Co., Ltd., Hersham, Surrey.

Founded early in 1912 by Mr. Ronald Charteris—later Capt., R.F.C.—with Mr. Granville Bradshaw as chief designer. Built many experimental engines in succeeding years.

One of the earliest makers of aero engines. An A.B.C. engine (40 h.p. four-cylinder, vertical, water-cooled) on a *Sopwith* biplane, piloted by Mr. Hawker, beat the British Duration Record, and won the Michelin Cup, in 1912.

Since then the firm has developed air-cooled stationary-cylinder engines, known as the "Gnat," the "Mosquito," the "Wasp," and the "Dragon-fly" respectively, with 2, 6, 7, and 9 cylinders.

Front and Back View of A.B.C. "Gnat" (45 h.p.)

THE A.B.C. GNAT II.

Type of engine	2-cylinder horizontally opposed.
Type of cylinder	Steel, fins A.B.C. copper coated.
Bore	4.75 ins.
Stroke	5½ ins.
Normal b.h.p.	45. Max. 50.
Rotation	Anti-clockwise facing propellor.
Normal speed	1800 r.p.m. Max. 2000.
Lubrication	One rotary plunger pump from tank to crankcase and then splash to cylinders.
Oil recommended	Wakefield Castrol "R."
Oil consumption	1.7 pints.
Oil consumption per b.h.p. hour ..	.037 pints.
Carburetters	1 A.B.C. 48 mm.
Petrol consumption	56 pints per b.h.p. hour.
Magnetos	1 M.L. Magneto. Type K2.
Speed of Magnetos	½ engine speed.
Mag. rotates	Anti-clockwise facing driving end of armature.
Weight of engine, including prop. boss, but without oil or fuel	115 lbs.
Weight of engine per b.h.p. ..	2.3 lbs.

THE A.B.C. DRAGON-FLY I.A.

Type of engine	9-cylinder stationary radial
Type of cylinder	Steel, fins A.B.C. copper coated. 3 overhead valves, 2 exhaust and 1 inlet.

Cam-ring, Tappets and Big-end Bearing of A.B.C. "Dragon-fly."

A.B.C.—*continued.*

THE A.B.C. "DRAGON-FLY" I.A.—*continued.*

Bore	5½ ins. = 139.7 mm.
Stroke	6½ ins. = 165.1 mm.
Normal b.h.p.	340.
Rotation	Anti-clock facing pro-pellor.
Normal speed	1650 r.p.m.

Lubrication	2 rotary plunger pumps. 1 feeding through hollow crankshaft to crankpin, centrifugal feed to big end and thence splash. 1 feeding to nose, dropping into cam and forming a permanent sump for gears in bottom of nose
Oil recommended	Wakefield Castrol "R."
Oil consumption	7 pints per hour.
Oil consumption per b.h.p. hour ..	.021 pints.

Carburetters	2 A.B.C. carburetters.
Petrol consumption	.56 pints per b.h.p. hour.
Magnetos	2 A.K. 9 magnetos, 4 spark.
Speed of magneto	1⅛ engine speed.
Mag. rotates	Clockwise, facing driving end of armature.
Rev. counter rotates	Anti-clock, facing driving shaft.
Speed of rev. counter drive	¼ engine speed.
Weight of engine, including prop. boss, but without oil or fuel	600 lbs.
Weight of engine per b.h.p. ..	1.765 lbs.

A.B.C. "Dragon-fly," 330 h.p. (Front View).

A.B.C. "Dragon-fly," 330 h.p. (Back View).

A.B.C.—continued.

Connecting Rod and Piston Assembly of A.B.C. " Dragon-fly."

Cylinder of " Dragon-fly."

Three-quarter Rear View of A.B.C. " Dragon-fly."

.B.C.—*continued.*

THE A.B.C. WASP II.

Type of engine	7-cylinder stationary radial.
Type of cylinder	Steel, fins A.B.C. copper coated, 3 overhead valves, 2 exhaust and 1 inlet.
Bore	4¾ ins.
Stroke	6¼ ins.
Normal b.h.p.	200.
Rotation	Anti-clock facing propeller.
Normal speed	1800 r.p.m.
Lubrication	2 rotary plunger pumps, 1 feeding through hollow crankshaft to crankpin, centrifugal feed to big end and thence splash. 1 feeding to nose, dropping into cam and forming a permanent sump for gears in bottom of nose.
Oil recommended	Wakefield Castrol " R."
Oil consumption	4 pints per hour.
Oil consumption per b.h.p. hour ..	.02 pints.
Carburetters	2 A.B.C. 48 mm.
Petrol consumption	.56 pints per b.h.p. hour.
Magnetos	2 P.L. 7 type. 2 spark.
Speed of magnetos	1¾ engine speed.
Mag. rotates	Clockwise facing driving end of armature
Rev. counter rotates	Anti-clock facing driving shaft.
Speed of rev. counter drive	¼ engine speed.
Weight of engine, including prop. boss, but without oil or fuel	320 lbs.
Weight of engine per b.h.p.	1.6 lbs.

A.B.C. " Wasp " (Mark II.), 200 h.p.

Cam-ring and Tappets of A.B.C. " Wasp."

Crankcase Components (two views) of A.B.C. " Wasp."

AERO-MARINE (American).

THE AERO MARINE Co., Times Building, New York.

Mr. J. F. Willard, Engineer.

This firm made in 1917 the following engines.

90 h.p. Model.

    Type : Water-cooled vertical.
    No. of cylinders : 6.
    Bore : $4\frac{5}{16}$ in. $5\frac{1}{8}$ in.
    R.P.M. :
    Cylinders : Domed heads, cast head jackets, copper
        side jackets
    Valves : Overhead, push rods from crankcase.
    Carburetters : 2, each feeding three cylinders.
    Lubrication : Forced feed.
    Weight : 420 lbs.

150 h.p. Model.

    Type : Water-cooled " V "
    No. of cylinders : 12.
    Bore : $4\frac{5}{16}''$.
    Stroke : $5\frac{1}{8}''$.
    R.P.M. : 1400.
    Cylinders : Separate castings.
    Valves : Overhead, push rods.
    Carburetters : 2 Zenith.
    Ignition : 2—12-spark Dixie.

In 1918 made the 6-cylinder vertical engine illustrated herewith　No details have been vouchsafed by the makers.

The Aero-Marine engine, 125—130 h.p.

ANZANI (British & French).

ANZANI MOTEURS d'AVIATION, 112, Boulevard de Courbevoie, Courbevoie (Seine).

BRITISH ANZANI ENGINE Co., Ltd., 32, Scrubbs Lane, Willesden, London, N.W.

100 h.p. Model.
Type : Radial, air-cooled.
No. of cylinders : 10.
Bore : 105 m/m.   Stroke : 140 m/m.
R.P.M. : 1,100.
Cylinders : Cast iron.
Valves : Inlet and exhaust on cylinder head.
Carburetter : Zenith.
Ignition : Magneto.
Lubrication : Splash and pump.

150 h.p. Model, as above, but :—
No. of cylinders : 14.

60 h.p. Model, as above, but :—
No. of cylinders : 6.
Bore : 105 m/m.   Stroke : 120 m/m.

45 h.p. Model, as above, but :—
Bore : 90 m/m.   Stroke : 120 m/m.

35 h.p. Model, as above, but :—
No. of cylinders : 3.
Bore : 105 m/m.   Stroke : 120 m/m.

Most of the above engines still exist, but no fresh particulars are available.

The 200 h.p. Anzani air-cooled engine.

The 35 h.p. Y type Anzani engine.
3 cylinders.

The 100-110 h.p. Anzani engine.   10 cylinders.

Front view of the 45 h.p. Anzani engine,
6 cylinders.

Diagram of interior of 45 h.p. Anzani engine.

Back view of the 45 h.p. Anzani engine.
6 cylinders.

Side view of the 100-110 h.p. Anzani engine.

ARGUS (German).

ARGUS MOTOREN G.m.b.H., Flottenstrasse 39 and 40, Reinickendorf bei Berlin.

Established 1900 and supplying in the early days axles and other components for the automobile trade. Turned out on strict motor car engine lines, the first German water-cooled aero engine, first rather unreliable, but soon improving so that by 1912 the "Argus" motor was almost exclusively used on German aircraft.

Did, however, not stand the competition of the Mercédès engine, being in 1913 and 1914 employed only on *Jeannin* and *Ago* aircraft. Used to a fair extent during the war.

It is rumoured that the Argus Company has lately turned out an aero turbine of ¾ kilo weight per h.p., which has, however, not yet proven its existence by public appearance.

115 h.p. Model.
Type : Water-cooled vertical.
No. of cylinders : 6.
Bore : 130 m/m.   Stroke : 130 m/m.
R.P.M.: 1350.
Cylinders : Variously cast in pairs of gray iron or turned from chrome nickel steel.
Valves : Overhead, operated by push rods from crankcase.
Carburetters : Duplex.
Ignition : 2 six-spark Bosch magnetos.
Lubrication : Forced feed.

130 h.p. Model, as above :—
Bore : 130 m/m.   Stroke : 130 m/m.

145 h.p. Model, as above :—
Bore : 140 m/m.   Stroke : 140 m/m.

190 h.p. Model, as above :—
Bore : 150 m/m.   Stroke : 145 m/m.

No fresh particulars are available concerning 1918 type engines.

End View of the 190 h.p. Argus engine.

Side View of 190 h.p. Argus engine.

ARMSTRONG-WHITWORTH (British).

Sir W. G. ARMSTRONG, WHITWORTH & Co., Ltd., Newcastle-on-Tyne.

An experimental Vee-type engine. No specification has been supplied.

Front View of the Armstrong-Whitworth Engine.

Side View of the Armstrong-Whitworth Engine.

ASHMUSEN (American).

ASHMUSEN MANUFACTURING Co., 266, Pearl Street, Rhode Island.

Made in 1917 the following model:

105 h.p. Model.

> Type: "Self-cooled" (Air-cooled).
> No. of cylinders: 12 double-opposed horizontal.
> Bore: 3.75 ins.
> Stroke: 4.5 ins.
> R.P.M.: 1800.
> Propeller speed: 900 r.p.m.
> Overall length: 42¼ in.
> Overall width: 34 in.

No fresh information available since America entered into the war.

AUSTRO-DAIMLER MOTOREN GESELL-SCHAFT (Austrian). Wiener Neustadt.

THE 200 H.P. AUSTRO-DAIMLER.

INTRODUCTORY NOTE.

The following report on the design, construction, and general performance of the latest type of Austro-Daimler engine is based on an examination and tests carried out at the R.A.E. on the engine (No. 19,218) taken from a captured Austrian *Berg* scout (R.A.F. No. A.G.6).

This machine, a single-seater biplane brought down on the Italian Front in April, 1918, was captured in very good condition; the engine had apparently only been in use for a few hours.

With the exception of its high stroke: bore ratio and the construction of a detachable inlet valve seating in each cylinder, the design of this engine shows no great resemblance to the earlier types of Austro-Daimler engines; generally speaking, the new 200 h.p. Austro-Daimler possesses more than the usual amount of originality in design found in enemy aero engines.

The general construction of the 200 h.p. Austro-Daimler is shown in the two photographs of the complete engine,

Airscrew End of the 200 h.p. Austro-Daimler Engine, 1917-18 type.

AUSTRO-DAIMLER—*continued*.

and also in the accompanying cross sectional and general arrangement drawings.

Following the usual German practice, the engine is of the six-cylinder, vertical, water-cooled type with separate built-up steel cylinders. The principal characteristics of the design and its general performance are given in the following leading particulars of the engine :—

Number of cylinders	Six, vertical.
Bore	135 mm.
Stroke	175 mm.
Normal b.m.e.ph. ..	123.3 lbs. per sq. in.
Average b.h.p. and speed ..	200 b.h.p. at 1,400 r.p.m.
Compression ratio ..	5.02 : 1
Petrol consumption per hour..	111.0 pints.
Petrol consumption per b.h.p. hour	0.555 pints.
Oil consumption per hour ..	7 pints.
Oil consumption per b.h.p. hour	0.035 pints.
Total weight of engine, dry ..	728.5 lbs.
Weight per b.h.p. (normal) ..	3.64 lbs.

The compression ratio is considerably higher than that of any of the enemy engines except the Maybach, and from the complete data published at the end of this report it will be seen that the general efficiency of the engine is good, the h.p. per cu. ft. of stroke volume being 377.3 and the h.p. per sq. ft. of piston area being 216.6.

During calibration and endurance tests carried out at the R.A.E., the running of the engine was very good, being very steady between 700 and 1,700 r.p.m. The engine was remarkably clean, having no trace of oil or water leakages during tests.

Compared with the usual high weight standard of enemy engine design, the weight per b.h.p. of 3.64 is quite normal. From our own standard of weights, however, the weight per b.h.p. is disproportionately high. This is chiefly due to the heavy construction of the crank-chamber and oil base, rather than to the design of the cylinders and reciprocating parts, which are well designed and are of light construction compared with other enemy engines.

GENERAL DESCRIPTION.

As a preliminary survey of the general design of the 200 h.p. Austro-Daimler engine, the principal features of the engine are briefly described in the following summary :—

The six separate cylinders are of the usual built-up steel construction with pressed steel water jackets, and are fitted with twin inlet and exhaust valves in the cylinder heads, which are integral with the cylinder barrels. The valve pockets are

Exhaust side of the Austro-Daimler engine.

15b

AUSTRO-DAIMLER—*continued*.

welded into position, with the exception of one inlet valve pocket in each cylinder, which is constructed so as to be easily detachable with its valve seating and guide, as in previous Austro-Daimler engines, so that all the valves can be removed without dismounting the cylinder.

Aluminium pistons are adopted, and with the exception of those recently fitted to the 230 h.p. Benz engines, were at the time of capture apparently the only aluminium pistons in use in enemy engines, although since this engine was captured a Rumpler biplane has been brought down fitted with a 270 h.p. Bassé-Selve engine using aluminium pistons. A detailed report of this engine is in course of preparation and will be published very shortly.

The H section connecting rods are of normal design, and the crankshaft runs in seven white metal bearings, which are carried by the top half of the crankcase. The bottom halves of the journal bearing housings are steel forgings and are very deep in cross section, being similar in design to the journal bearings fitted to the Maybach engines.

The design of the valve gear and camshaft drive presents several interesting details. As shown in the illustrations of the engine, the overhead camshaft is driven by a vertical shaft off the front end of the crankshaft. The camshaft runs in four phosphor bronze bearings in the centre of an aluminium camshaft case.

A compression release gear, very similar to the Mercédès type, is provided. The water circulation passage from the cylinders to the top of the radiator is taken through to the front end of the cast aluminium camshaft-casing, just behind the driving bevel gear.

A reciprocating plunger type oil pump is fitted in the front end of the oil base. This pump is driven by bevel and worm gearing directly off the crankshaft and is unusually heavy, but of interesting design.

The lubrication is on normal principles and embodies a large air-cooled oil sump at the bottom of each base chamber, which is supplemented by an auxiliary fresh oil reservoir cast in the front end of the top half of the crank chamber. The fresh oil is delivered by a small auxiliary plunger, working in conjunction with the main oil pump, to the front end of the camshaft, the lubrication of which is well carried out.

A "V" type honeycomb radiator is fitted directly behind the airscrew, and the centrifugal water pump, which is driven obliquely off the rear end of the camshaft, is of ordinary design.

Two Bosch Z.H.6 magnetos are driven diagonally at 52 degs. off the vertical camshaft driving shaft at the front of the engine, and two plugs are provided in each cylinder. The magneto controls are interconnected with throttle control, so that the ignition is automatically retarded when throttling down.

Cross Sectional Arrangement of Engine.

16b

Sectional View of Cylinder.

USTRO-DAIMLER—*continued.*

heavy duplex carburetter feeds the cylinders through separate steel induction manifolds, which are galvanised, lagged with asbestos ; each manifold feeds three cylinders.

he carburetters are water-jacketed and heated by the nder water circulation system in the usual way.

Main and slow running jets are fitted, the two annular ts being housed in chambers surrounding the choke tubes. e main air intake is taken through a passage cast in the halves of the crankcase leading to the chamber below false bottom of the oil sump.

An air pump of the spring plunger type is driven off the mshaft and is mounted on the top of the camshaft casing wards the rear end of the engine. A transverse shaft driven the rear end of the crankshaft carries two cams for the nchronised gun interrupter gear.

No exhaust manifold is provided, each cylinder being fitted th a short streamline section exhaust pipe about 12 ins. ng, as shown in the illustrations of the engine.

DETAILS OF CRANKSHAFT.

Number and type of main bearings	Seven, bronze cage, lined white metal.
ylinder centres	166.0 mm. (6.53 in.)
JOURNALS.	
utside diameter	58.0 mm. (2.28 in.)
nside diameter (front two) ..	21.0 mm. (0.82 in.)
,, ,, (others) ..	30.0 mm. (1.18 in.)
ength airscrew end	56.0 mm. (2.20 in.)
,, rear end	43.5 mm. (1.71 in.)
,, centre	50.0 mm. (1.97 in.)
,, intermediate	50.0 mm. (1.97 in.)
CRANKPINS.	
utside diameter	56.0 mm. (2.20 in.)
nside diameter	30.0 mm. (1.18 in.)
ength	68.0 mm. (2.67 in.)
CRANK WEBS.	
Width	74.0 mm. (2.91 in.)
Thickness (front two)	24.5 mm. (0.96 in.)
,, (others)	24.0 mm. (0.94 in.)
Radius at ends of journals and crank pins	4.5 mm. (0.17 in.)
Weight of complete shaft	96.5 lbs.

R.A.E. CALIBRATION AND ENDURANCE TEST REPORT.

The 200 h.p. Austro-Daimler engine was coupled to a Heenan and Foude dynamometer, and run for the usual calibration and one-hour endurance tests. Power, throttle, and consumption curves are given.

Details of Connecting Rod.

CALIBRATION RESULTS.

R.P.M.	1300	1400	1500	1600
B.H.P.	186	200	212	222
Brake M.E.P.	125.5	123.3	122	119.7
Petrol consump. in pts./B.H.P./ hour	.55	.545	.546	.548

ENDURANCE TEST.

The engine was submitted to an endurance test of one hour's duration at normal revs., *i.e.*, 1400 r.p.m., with the following results :—

Average output	202 B.H.P.
Average speed	1,400 r.p.m.
Petrol consumption per hour ..	14 gallons.
Petrol consumption B.H.P. hour ..	0.555 pints/b.h.p./hour
Oil consumption per hour	7 pints.
Oil pressure	5 lbs./sq./inch.
Oil temperature	50° C.

View of Valve Gear.

AUSTRO-DAIMLER—continued.

ENDURANCE TEST—continued.

Water temperature (inlet)	54.5° C.
Water temperature (outlet) ..	60° C.
Total duration of tests ..	10 hours 25 mins.
Complete weight of engine.. ..	728.5 lbs. dry.

WEIGHT PER B.H.P.

At 1,300 r.p.m. = 3.81 lbs. per B.H.P.
1,400 ,, = 3.64 ,, ,, ,,
1,500 ,, = 3.43 ,, ,, ,,
1,600 ,, = 3.28 ,, ,, ,,

RUNNING DURING ONE HOUR ENDURANCE TEST.

Very steady between 700 and 1,700 r.p.m.
At 500 r.p.m. vibration was bad, and below this speed running was generally unsteady.

DISTRIBUTION.

Very good.

CLEANLINESS.

Throughout the test the engine kept remarkably clean. No trace of oil or water leakage was observed.

TROUBLES EXPERIENCED ON TEST.

The K.L.G. spark plugs fitted for the test gave trouble by shorting internally.

The valve tappets required to be re-adjusted during the test.

TEST OF WATER PUMP.

Speed of the water pump spindle = 1.894 : 1 crankshaft revolution.

The delivery of the water pump under varying pressures has been made the subject of a separate test, the results of which are given in the following test report and delivery curves.

The pump was coupled to an electric motor and run with the following results :—

R.P.M.	Pressure.	Delivery.
1800 ..	2 lbs. sq. in. ..	42 galls. per. min
1800 ..	4 ,, ,, ,, ..	35 ,, ,, ,,
1800 ..	6 ,, ,, ,, ..	28.5 ,, ,, ,,

The weight of the complete water pump = 7.6 lbs.

R.A.E. METALLURGICAL TEST REPORT.

The chemical compositions and the relative material strengths of the principal parts of the engine are given in the following chemical analysis and mechanical test reports :—

(1) CHEMICAL ANALYSIS.

Per Cent.:	C.	Si.	Mn.	S.	P.	Cr.	Ni.
Crankshaft ..	.14	.27	.43	.030	.006	1.34	3.45
Cylinder ..	.47	.19	.67	.037	.046	Nil.	Nil.
Connecting Rod	.40	.16	.73	.043	.023	.36	1.50
Camshaft (case-hardened) ..	—	.21	.43	.035	.012	.57	3.15
Inlet Valve ..	.46	.24	.42	.023	.022	.47	2.28
Exhaust Valve .	.44	.24	.41	.025	.022	.47	2.36
Valve Rocker ..	.46	.09	.63	.051	.028	.42	1.57
Gudgeon Pin (case-hardened) ..	—	.12	.49	.028	.011	1.5	3.70

(2) CHEMICAL ANALYSIS.

	Crankcase. Per Cent.	Piston. Per Cent.
Copper	2.79	7.67
Zinc	6.61	1.33
Tin	Nil.	2.21
Silicon	0.76	0.52
Iron	2.06	1.32
Manganese	0.02	Trace
Nickel	—	Nil.
Magnesium	—	0.29
Aluminium (by difference) ..	87.76	86.66

(3) BEARINGS.

Per Cent. :	Journal Bearings.	Big-End Bearings.	Camshaft Bearings.	Valve Rocker Bearings.
Copper	6.70	5.10	87.51	96.29
Zinc	—	—	0.28	Trace.
Tin	81.13	81.42	11.34	2.52
Lead	0.71	1.64	0.17	0.28
Antimony ..	12.00	12.00	—	—
Manganese ..	—	—	Nil.	0.21
Nickel	—	—	0.35	0.07
Iron	—	—	0.17	0.13
Phosphorus ..	—	—	0.05	—

(4) MECHANICAL TESTS.

	Mark.	No.	Area sq.in.	Y.S T/sq.in.	M.S T/sq.in.	Elong: p.c.	Red: of Area p/c.	Impact ft.lbs.
Journal ..	A.	1.	.002	66.7	75.1	13.33	57.4	
,,	B.	2.						30.5
Pin	C.	3.	.005	62.7	72.5	15.55	59.8	
,, ...	D.	4.						33.5
Web, Longitude	E.	5.	.005	71.6	75.8	10.0	35.0	
,, ...	F.	6.						7.5
,, Transverse	G.	7.	.005	72.9	74.5	7.78	25.1	
,, ,,	H.	8.						(1) 5.0
								(2) 7.0

Aluminium Piston.

Details of Piston and Gudgeon Pin.

AUSTRO-DAIMLER—*continued.*

GENERAL DATA.

Make of engine and rated h.p.	Austro-Daimler 200 h.p.
No. of cylinders	Six.
Type number	8,597
Bore	135.0 mm. (5.31 ins.)
Stroke	175.0 mm. (6.89 ins.)
Stroke/bore ratio	1.29 : 1
Area of one piston	143.1 sq. cm. (22.2 sq. ins.)
Total piston area of engine	858.6 sq. cm. (133.1 sq. ins.)
Swept volume of one cylinder	2504.9 cu. cm. (152.8 cu. ins.)
Total swept volume of engine	15029.7 cu. cm. (916.8 cu. ins.)
Clearance volume of one cylinder	623.1 cu. cm. (38.0 cu.ins.)
Compression ratio	5.02 : 1
Normal b.h.p. and speed	200 b.h.p. at 1400 r.p.m.
Maximum ditto.	222 b.h.p. at 1600 r.p.m.
Normal b.m.e.p.	123.3 lbs. per sq. in. at 1400 r.p.m.
Maximum ditto.	123.5 lbs. per sq. in. at 1300 r.p.m.
Piston speed	1607 ft. per min.
Mechanical efficiency (calculated)	89.7 per cent.
Indicated mean pressure (calculated)	137.5 lbs. sq. in.
Fuel consumption per b.h.p. hour	0.555 pint = 0.499 lb.
Brake thermal efficiency	27.4 per cent.
Indicated thermal efficiency	30.6 per cent.
Air standard efficiency	47.5 per cent.
Relative efficiency	64.4 per cent.
Cub. in. of swept volume per b.h.p.	4.58 cu. ins.
Sq. in. of piston area per b.h.p.	0.665 sq. in.
H.p. per cub. ft. of stroke volume	377.3 b.h.p.
H.p. per sq. ft. of piston area	216.6 b.h.p.
Direction of rotation of crankshaft	Anti-clockwise.
Direction of rotation of airscrew	Ditto.
Type of gear reduction to airscrew	None.
Ratio crankshaft speed/airscrew speed	1 : 1
Type of valve gear	Overhead camshaft.
Type of starting gear	Compression release.

CARBURETTERS.

Number and type of carburetters	One dual Austro-Daimler.
Diameter of choke tube	24.0 mm. (0.945 in.)
Bore of main jets	35.0 c.c. through per min.
Bore of pilot jets	5.8 c.c. through per min
Fuel consumption per hour	111.0 pints = 100.0 lbs.
Fuel consumption per b.h.p. hour	0.555 pint = 0.499 lb.

Camshaft and Air Pump.

Details of Crankshaft.

AUSTRO-DAIMLER—*continued*.

GAS VELOCITIES, VALVE AREA, ETC.
Diameters.

Induction pipe	59.0 mm. (2.32 ins.)
Inlet and exhaust effective valve ports (each)	44.0 mm. (1.73 ins.)
Inlet and exhaust cylinder ports (each)	42.0 mm. (1.65 ins.)

CROSS SECTIONAL AREAS.

Induction pipe	27.33 sq. cm. (4.22 sq. ins.)
Inlet valve (π dh) .. }each ..	13.69 sq. cm. (2.12 sq. ins.)
Exhaust valve (π dh) ..	14.05 sq. cm. (2.18 sq. ins.)
Exhaust branch pipes	38.25 sq. cm. (5.92 sq.ins.)

MEAN GAS VELOCITIES (1400 R.P.M.)

Induction pipe	141.0 ft. per sec.
Inlet valves	140.0 ft. per sec
Exhaust valves	136.0 ft. per sec.
Exhaust branch pipe	100.5 ft. per sec.

INLET VALVES.

Number per cylinder	Two.
Largest diameter	48.0 mm. (1.89 in.)
Effective port valve diameter	44.0 mm. (1.73 in.)
Width of seating	2.5 mm. (0.09 in.)
Angle of seating	45 degs.
Lift of valve	9.9 mm. (0.39 in.)
Diameter of stem	10.0 mm. (0.39 in.)
Length of valve guide ..	68.0 mm. (2.67 ins.)
Overall length of valve ..	135.0 mm. (5.135 ins.)
Number of springs per valve ..	One.
Free length of spring ..	60.0 mm. (2.36 ins.)
Length of spring in position (no lift)	46.0 mm. (1.81 in.)
Mean diameter of coils ..	34.0 mm. (1.34 in.)
Diameter of wire	4.0 mm. (0.157 in.)
Ratio length of spring/lift of valve	4.61: 1.
Weight of valve complete with spring	0.50 lb.
Weight of spring bare ..	0.16 lb.
Inlet valve opens	10 degs. early.
Inlet valve closes	30 degs. late.
Period of induction	220 degs.
Inlet valve tappet clearance	0.25 mm. (0.01 in.)

EXHAUST VALVES.

Number per cylinder	Two.
Largest diameter	48.0 mm. (1.89 ins.)
Effective valve port diameter	44.0 mm. = 1.73 in.
Width of seating	2.5 mm. (0.09 in.)
Angle of seating	45 degs.
Lift of valve	10.16 mm. (0.40 in.)
Diameter of stem	10.0 mm. (0.39 in.)
Length of valve guide ..	68.0 mm. (2.67 ins.)
Overall length of valve ..	135.0 mm. (5.315 ins.)
Number of springs per valve ..	One.

Free length of spring	60.0 mm. (2.36 ins.)
Length of spring in position (no lift)	46.00 mm. (1.81 in.)
Mean diameter of coils	34.0 mm. (1.34 in.)
Diameter of wire	4.0 mm. (0.157 in.)
Ratio length of spring/lift of valve	4.6 : 1.
Weight of valve complete with spring	0.5 lb.
Weight of spring bare	0.16 lb.

Exhaust valve opens	45 degs. early.
Exhaust valve closes	7 degs late.
Period of exhaust	232 degs.
Exhaust valve tappet clearance ..	0.304 mm. (0.012 in.)

INERTIA FORCES, BEARING LOADS, ETC.

Weight of piston complete with rings and gudgeon pin	4.18 lbs.

Valves and Rockers.

Parts of Carburetter.

AUSTRO-DAIMLER—*continued.*

INERTIA FORCES, BEARING LOADS, ETC.—*continued.*

Weight per sq. in of piston area ..	0.188 lb.
Weight of connecting-rod complete	4.84 lbs.
Weight of reciprocating part of connecting rod..	1.66 lb.
Total reciprocating weight per cyl. .	5.84 lbs.
Weight per sq. in. of piston area ..	0.263 lb.
Length of con. rod (centres) ..	315.0 mm. (12.40 ins.)
Ratio con. rod/crank throw ..	3.6 : 1.
Inertia lbs./sq. in. piston area top centre	63.8 lbs./sq. ins.
Inertia lbs./sq. in. piston area bottom centre..	36.2 lbs./sq. ins.
Inertia lbs./sq. in. piston area mean	25.0 lbs./sq. ins.
Weight of rotating mass of con. rod	3.18 lbs.
Total centrifugal pressure	610 lbs.
Centrifugal pressure lbs./sq. in. piston area..	27.5 lbs./sq. ins.
Mean average fluid pressure including compression	47.0 lbs./sq. ins.
Mean average loading on crank pin bearing, total from all sources in terms of lbs./sq. in. piston area.	91.0 lbs./sq. ins.
Diameter of crank pin	56.0 mm. (2.20 ins.)
Rubbing velocity	13.42 ft. per sec.
Effective projected area of big-end bearing	32.4 sq. cm. (5.02 sq. ins.)
Ratio piston area/projected area of big-end bearing	4.42 : 1.
Mean average loading on big-end bearing	402 lbs./sq. ins.
Load factor on big-end bearing ..	5400 lbs./ft. sec.

CYLINDERS.

Overall height of bare cylinder from top of base chamber	365.0 mm. (14.370 ins.)
Depth of spigot at base of cylinder	15.0 mm. (0.590 ins.)
Diameter of cylinder over water jacket	160.0 mm. (6.29 ins.)
Thickness of flange at base of cylinder	11.0 mm. (0.433 in.)
Number of holding-down bolts per cylinder	Eight.
Diameter of holding-down studs ..	4 of 14.0 mm. 4 of 19.0 mm.
Thickness of water jacket	1.00 mm. (0.039 in.)
Mean thickness of combustion chamber wall	5.0 mm. (0.197 in.)
Thickness of cylinder barrel (top)..	4.0 mm. (0.157 in.)
Thickness of cylinder barrel (centre)	3.0 mm. (0.138 in.)
Thickness of cylinder barrel (bottom)	4.0 mm. (0.157 in.)
Diameter of water connections between cylinders	36.0 mm. (1.42 in.)

Inside view of Base Chamber and Filter Plates.

View of Base Chamber from beneath, showing Air Passages and Cover Plate.

AUSTRO-DAIMLER—continued.

PISTON.

Type of piston	Aluminium ; internal ribs
Diameter at top	134.0 mm. (5.275 ins.)
Diameter at bottom..	134.58 mm. (5.277 ins.)
Length	110,5 mm. (4.35 ins.)
Ratio, piston length cylinder bore..	0.82 : 1.
Number of rings per cylinder ..	Three.
Position of rings	Above gudgeon pins.
Width of rings	7.0 mm. (0.275 in.)
Gap of rings in cylinder ..	0.48 mm. (0.019 in.)

CONNECTING-ROD.

Length between centres	315.0 mm. (12.40 ins.)
Ratio connecting rod/crank throw..	3.6 : 1.
Little-end bearing, type	Plain phosphor bronze.
" " " diameter ..	28.0 mm. (1.10 in.)
" " " length ..	67.0 mm. (2.64 ins.)
" " " projected area..	18.70 sq. cm. (2.90 sq. ins.)
Ratio piston area/projected area little-end bearing	7.66 : 1.
Big-end bearing, type	Bronze shell white lined metal.
" " " diameter.. ..	56.0 mm. (2.20 ins)
" " " length (actual) ..	67.0 mm. (2.63 ins.)
" " " length (effective) ..	58.0 mm. (2.28 ins.)
" " " projected area ..	28.4 sq. cm. (5.02 sq. ins.)
Ratio piston area/projected area big end bearing	4.42 : 1.
Number of big-end bolts	Four.
Full diameter of bolts	10.0 mm. (0.39 in.)
Total cross sectional area bottom of threads	2.04 sq. cm. (0.316 sq. in.)
Pitch of threads	1.5 metric.
Maximum load due to inertia at 1400 r.p.m...	1390 lbs.
Maximum load due to inertia at 1600 r.p.m...	1815 lbs.
Load due to centrifugal force at 1400 r.p.m...	370 lbs.
Load due to centrifugal force at 1600 r.p.m...	485 lbs.
Total load on bolts at 1400 r.p.m.	1760 lbs.
Total load on bolts at 1600 r.p.m.	2300 lbs.
Stress per sq. in. at 1400 r.p.m ..	5570 lbs./sq. ins.
Stress per sq. in. at 1600 r.p.m.	7280 lbs./sq. ins.

Semi-Diagrammatic sectional views of Carburetter.

Power, Throttle, and Consumption Curves.

CRANKSHAFT.

Number and type of main bearings	Seven, bronze cage, lined white metal.
Cylinder centres	166.0 mm. (6.53 ins.)
Crankpins	
Outside diameter	56.0 mm. (2.20 ins.)
Inside diameter	30.0 mm. (1.18 in.)
Length	68.0 mm. (2.67 ins.)
Journals.	
Outside diameter	58.0 mm. (2.28 ins.)
Inside diameter (front two) ..	21.0 mm. (0.82 in.)
" " (others) ..	30 mm. (1.18 in.)
Length airscrew end..	56.0 mm. (2.20 ins.)
" rear end	43.5 mm. (1.71 in.)
" centre	50.0 mm. (1.97 in.)
" intermediate ..	50.0 mm. (1.97 in.)
Crank Webs.	
Width	74.0 mm. (2.91 ins.)
Thickness (front two)	24.5 mm. (0.96 in.)
" (others)	24.4 mm. (0.94 in.)
Radius at ends of journals and crank pins	4.5 mm. (0.17 in.
Weight of complete shaft ..	96.5 lbs.

WORKING CLEARANCES.

Piston clearance top (total) ..	1.00 mm. (0.039 in.)
Piston clearance bottom (total) ..	0.42 mm. (0.016 in.)
Side clearance of con. rod in piston (total)	2.50 mm. (0.098 in.)
Side clearance of con. rod on crank-pin (total)	1.00 mm. (0.039 in.)
End clearance of crankshaft in main bearings	2.00 mm. (0.079 in.)

LUBRICATION SYSTEM.

Number and type of oil pumps ..	One plunger.
Oil consumption per hour ..	7.0 pints.
Oil consumption per b.h.p. hour ..	0.035 pt.=0.039 lb.
Oil pressure	50 degs. C.
Oil temperature	5 lbs. per sq. in.
Specific gravity of oil	0.899.
Ratio pump speed/crankshaft speed	1 : 15.

IGNITION.

Number and type of magnetos ..	Two Bosch Z.H.6.
Firing sequence of engine ..	Airscrew 1-5-3-6-2-4.
Ignition timing (fully advanced) ..	20 degs. E. to 40 degs. E., variable.
Number of plugs per cylinder ..	Two.
Type of plugs	Bosch.
Ratio magneto speed/crankshaft speed	1.5 : 1

AUSTRO-DAIMLER—*continued.*

COOLING SYSTEM.

Number and type of water pumps..	One centrifugal.
Diameter of inlet pipe	36.0 mm. (1.42 in.)
Diameter of. outlet pipe	36.0 mm. (1.42 in.)
Diameter of rotor	112.0 mm. (4.40 in.)
Number and type of radiators ..	One Honeycomb.
Ratio water pump speed/engine speed	1.894 : 1.
Water temperature inlet	54.5 degs. C.
Water temperature outlet	60.0 degs. C.

AIR PUMP.

Type of air pump	Cam operated plunger.
Bore	38.0 mm. (1.496 in.)

WEIGHTS.

Weight of complete engine, dry, with airscrew boss and exhaust manifold	720.5 lbs.
Weight per b.h.p. ditto	3.64 lbs.
Weight of fuel per hour	100.00.
Weight of oil per hour	7.86 lbs.
Total weight of fuel and oil per hour	107.86 lbs.
Gross weight of engine in running order, less fuel and oil (cooling system at 0.65 lb. per b.h.p.) ..	858.50 lbs.
Weight per b.h.p. ditto	4.29 lbs.
Gross weight of engine in running order, with fuel and oil for six hours' running (tankage at 10 per cent. weight of fuel and oil) ..	1570.4 lbs.
Weight per b.h.p.	7.85 lbs.

OVERALL DIMENSIONS.

Height..	1150 mm.
Length	1724 mm.
Width	568 mm.

GENERAL ANALYSIS OF WEIGHTS.

Description of Part.	No. per Set.	Average Unit weight in lbs.	Weight of complete Set in lbs.	Percentage of total weight.
Cylinders, bare ..	6	18.43	110.62	15.30
Detachable Inlet valve pockets	6	1.06	6.37	0.87
Pistons complete with rings	6	3.52	21.12	2.90
Gudgeon pins	6	0.66	4.00	0.54
Connecting rods ..	6	4.84	29.04	3.98
Crankshaft	1	96.50	96.50	13.24
Inlet valves	12	0.34	4.12	0.56
Exhaust valves ..	12	0.34	4.12	0.56
Inlet exhaust valve springs	24	0.16	3.88	5.53
Valve collars and locking cones	24	0.09	2.19	0.30
Valve rockers (with bearings)	12	1.25	15.00	2.06
Camshaft	1	10.25	10.25	1.40
Camshaft casing complete	1	34.50	34.50	4.74
Half compression gear	1	2.69	2.69	0.36

GENERAL ANALYSIS OF WEIGHTS—*continued.*

Description of Part	No. per Set.	Average Unit weight in lbs.	Weight of complete Set in lbs.	Percentage of total weight.
Vertical camshaft driving spindle (complete)	1	6.81	6.81	0.93
Vertical spindle housing	1	1.62	1.62	0.22
Camshaft bevel sprocket	1	3.15	3.15	0.43
Crankcase, top half ..	1	107.00	107.00	14.68
Crankcase, bottom half	1	73.50	73.50	10.09
Bearing caps	7	2.27	15.93	2.19
Main holding - down bolts	14	0.75	10.50	1.44
Thrust race complete..	1	5.28	5.28	0 72
Airscrew hub	1	11.31	11.31	1.55
Carburetters	1	24.06	24.06	3.30
Induction pipes ..	2	4.25	8.50	1.16
Exhaust pipes.. ..	6	2.33	14.00	1.92
Oil pump	1	11.81	11.81	1 62
Oil leads with relief valve..	1	4.56	4.56	0.62
Magnetos	2	14.37	28.75	3.94
High tension leads with casing	1	4.75	4.75	0.65
Magneto and throttle controls	1	2.12	2.12	0.29
Water pump	1	7.62	7.62	1.04
Water pipes	1	6.56	6.56	0.90
Air pump	1	1.62	1.62	0.22
Rev. counter drive ..	1	0.75	0.75	0.10
Gun gear with case ..	1	5.81	5.81	0.80
Miscellaneous parts ..	1	28.09	28.09	3.85
Total.. ..			728.50	100.00

200 H.P. AUSTRO-DAIMLER.

BORE 135.　STROKE 175.

BASSÉ & SELVE (German).

BASSE & SELVE, Altena in Westphalia.

THE 270-300 BASSÉ-SELVE AERO-ENGINE.

(This Report is published by courtesy of the Controller, the Technical Department, the Department of Aircraft Production.)

INTRODUCTORY NOTE.

The following report on the design of the 270 h.p. Bassé-Selve engine is based on a detailed examination of the engine (No. 550) taken from the remains of a German Rumpler two-seater biplane (R.A.F. identification No. G/5BD/14), which was shot down and destroyed in France on May 31st, 1918.

Unfortunately, this is the only engine of its type which has been captured up to the time of writing, and as it was seriously damaged, it was impossible to carry out any power and consumption tests of the engine : consequently, the following report deals with design and construction only.   Certain figures connected with the performance have, however, been calculated by assuming the engine speed and Brake Mean Effective Pressure to correspond approximately with those of other German engines of about the same capacity.   The figures adopted for these items are as follows :—

Normal engine speed   ..   ..   1,400 r.p.m.
Normal B.M.E.P. at 1,400 r.p.m.   110 lbs. per sq. in.

All the figures in the data at the end of this report, which are based on the above assumption (and therefore only to be accepted with reserve) are marked with an asterisk.   Actual figures and test reports on the running of these engines will be issued as soon as an engine of this type is obtained in good condition.

GENERAL DESCRIPTION.

These engines, manufactured by Bassé and Selve, Altena, Westphalia, have but recently appeared in the field.   In most of their leading details of construction they closely resemble both the 260-h.p. Mercédès and 230-h.p. Benz engines, on which the design is evidently based.   Markings on the engine indicate the year of manufacture to be 1917, the crankshaft being marked "A.G. Krupp, Essen, 1917."   The nominal rating of the engine according to a cast plate on the crankcase is 270-h.p., and the normal engine speed would probably be about 1,400 r.p.m. Assuming the B.M.E.P. to be 110 lbs. per sq. in. at 1,400 r.p.m., the power developed would be approximately 269 b.h.p.

The accompanying photographs show the engine to be of the usual six-cylinder water-cooled type, the bore being 155 mm. and the stroke 200 mm., i.e., 5 mm. less in the bore and 20 mm. longer in the stroke than the 260 h.p. Mercédès engines.

Owing to the damaged condition of the cylinders and pistons it has been difficult to ascertain the exact clearance volume.   This is approximately 1,130 c.c., giving a compression ratio of 4.34 : 1, which is lower than any of the previous enemy engines.

The Bassé-Selve Aero-Engine.   Three-quarter View from Airscrew End.

BASSÉ & SELVE—*continued.*

Twin inlet and exhaust valves are fitted in the head of each cylinder, and the method of water cooling the exhaust valve stems by an annular passage, which completely surrounds the valve stem guides, is a novel detail of construction in enemy engines.

The valves are operated by an overhead camshaft, running in bronze bearings in a cast aluminium casing ; the design of the valve rocker and valve gear is worthy of notice.

An unusual type of compression release gear is used, which is of remarkably simple construction. Aluminium pistons are fitted. These are machined all over, inside and out. The slightly convex crowns are supported by conical pillars which bear upon the centre of the gudgeon pins through the slotted small ends of the connecting rods. This construction, together with the design of the tubular connecting rods, is essentially Benz practice, whilst the construction of the steel cylinders is taken from the 260-h.p. Mercédes design, but incorporates several improvements.

A large oil-cooling radiator is attached to the bottom of the crankcase, and is used in conjunction with a new design of duplex-plunger oil pump, which works vertically at the rear end of the crankcase. The design of the oil pump is somewhat similar to that now used on the new 200-h.p. Austro-Daimler engines.

Two separate two-jet carburetters fitted with annular floats are employed. These are apparently equipped with some form of altitude adjustment. Unfortunately, only one incomplete carburetter was found on the engine.

No details can be given of the construction of the water pump, as this component was missing from the engine.

The crankshaft is of ordinary, but exceptionally heavy design. The main journal bearing shells are machined with a screw-thread bedding for the white metal linings in a similar manner to the 300-h.p. Maybach engines. The propeller hub is fitted to a detachable tapered extension piece, which is bolted by a flange to the end flange of the crankshaft.

Further details of the design are given in the following description, and the leading particulars of the engine are shown in the accompaying data, which are as complete as the condition of the engine allows.

DETAILS OF CONSTRUCTION.

CYLINDERS.

A sectional drawing showing most of the construction of the steel cylinders is given.

This construction is similar to the 260-h.p. Mercédès, as also are the eight ribs machined on the outside of the barrels.

The cylinder heads are of cast steel, and the four valve pockets in each cylinder are cast integrally with the head. The formation of the combustion chamber and the unusual inclination of the valves at 23.5 deg. to the vertical axis of the cylinder are interesting points.

The valve guides are steel tubes lined with phosphor bronze ; they are pressed into the valve pockets, and are acetylene welded in position top and bottom.

View of a Complete Cylinder, from Exhaust Side. The curious gargoyle-face effect of this View is interesting. 26b

Section of one Cylinder, Bassé-Selve engine.

BASSÉ & SELVE—continued.

VALVES.

The inlet and exhaust valves are of the same diameter in the heads and stems, and of similar section.

VALVE GEAR.

The general layout of the valve gear is shown in the cross-sectional arrangement drawing, and presents some interesting details of design. The camshaft runs in eight comparatively short plain bearings of phosphor bronze, which are held in split aluminium housings of hollow section and large diameter. These are carried in the halves of a cast aluminium camshaft casing, and are located by dowel pegs in the usual way. The camshaft is made in two parts, joined together at the centre by two flanges and four short bolts. This valve gear is very similar to that used on the Peugeot racing cars (four valves per cylinder) about seven years ago.

Each pair of valves is depressed by a rocker lever mounted on ball bearings. The inner arm of each rocker lever is operated by its cam through a tappet in the top half of the camshaft casing.

The tappets are made in the form of stirrups which encircle the cams, and are supported in bronze bushes at the top and bottom ends. The cams and their tappets are case-hardened, and the camshaft bearings and tappets are lubricated under pressure through the hollow camshaft.

COMPRESSION RELEASE.

A simple form of compression release gear is used in place of the usual half compression cams and mechanism. This is operated by means of a rod which lies horizontally along the outside of the camshaft casing directly underneath the exhaust valve rocker arms. This rod has slots cut in it which lift the exhaust valve rockers when the rod is partially rotated by means of the hand-lever fixed to the rear end of the horizontal rod. The purpose of this compression release is apparently to facilitate swinging the propeller.

PISTONS.

The pistons are of aluminium.

The crowns are considerably domed and the pistons are machined all over, both inside and out. Both the material and the machining are excellent.

No bushes are provided as liners in the gudgeon pin bosses. The gudgeon pin is fixed in position by a large hollow set-pin which passes through both sides of the boss and gudgeon pin as shown.

CONNECTING RODS.

These are of tubular section, and closely resemble the Benz connecting rods in design, but are of considerably larger proportions throughout. These rods are particularly heavy, the weight of the complete connecting rod being 9.0 lbs.

CRANKSHAFT.

The crankshaft is of normal design, and, apart from its massive proportions, requires no special description.

A large double-thrust ball-race is fitted to the front end of the crankshaft by means of a shoulder machined on a flange just behind the propeller hub ; the thrust races are threaded on over the cranks, and are secured by a large screwed collar and spring locking ring. The main distribution bevel gear floats on the splined rear end of the crankshaft, and is fitted with a thrust ball race between the bevel and the rear end of the journal bearing.

PROPELLER HUB.

This is of the standard 260-h.p. Mercédès type, and fitted to a short tapered extension of the crankshaft. This extension is detachable, being bolted to a flange on the crankshaft. The standard Mercédès locking device is used.

View of part of Camshaft and Casing, Bassé-Selve engine.

D 2

BASSÉ & SELVE—*continued*.

CARBURETTERS AND INDUCTION.

Unfortunately, only one incomplete carburetter was found on the engine. The carburetters, which are quite separate, are of unusually light and simple construction compared with previous German design. The floats and float chambers are of the annular type, and encircle the main air intakes directly below the throttles, which are of the ordinary butterfly type. The body of each carburetter and throttle is made of cast aluminium, and the main jet is formed by a hole drilled in a tube which is screwed diagonally into the water-jacketed body of the carburetter, and lies across the choke tube directly beneath the throttle. The jet tube is open at the bottom end, and projects into the bottom of the annular float chamber, which is made of pressed sheet steel of very light gauge.

The pilot jet is formed by a second tube of small diameter inside the main jet tube. This pilot jet tube is also open at the bottom end, and is drilled radially with a small hole, just above the main jet. It communicates with the mixing chamber just above the throttle by a passage drilled in the carburetter body.

An altitude compensating control is fitted. This takes the form of a pipe opening into a passage drilled in the top of the float chamber.

Each carburetter feeds three cylinders through a branched induction manifold, the vertical part of which is water-jacketed.

The total weight of each carburetter complete should not exceed 2 lbs.

CRANKCASE.

The design of the top half of the crankcase requires no description, being constructed on Mercédès lines. The lower half also closely follows standard Mercédès design, with the exception of the oil reservoir and oil-cooling radiator on the bottom of the rear end. The construction of this cooler may be seen in a photograph. It consists of a cast aluminium oil chamber, having a number of thin aluminium tubes (12 mm. diameter) running longitudinally in three rows, and expanded at the ends. The cooler is bolted to the bottom flange of an oil reservoir below the base chamber, and is not an oil sump, inasmuch as there are no oil connections between it and the base chamber.

Two air intake passages are cast on each side of the crank chamber (see photograph); they are arranged to communicate with the carburetter through passages in the top and bottom halves between the transverse box-housings of the main bearings.

OIL PUMP AND LUBRICATION SYSTEM.

The oil pump is attached to the bottom half of the crankcase at the rear end, and driven by a worm gear off the rear end of the crankshaft through a short transverse layshaft.

Most of the details of construction of the oil pump may be seen in the photograph of the pump, which has been specially sectioned to show as much as possible.

The pump consists of two double-acting steel plungers, which work vertically in the barrels formed in the ends of the cast aluminium pump body. In action, the plungers are rotated by means of the worm gear, and are simultaneously reciprocated

Three-quarter View from Pump End, showing Clutch and Belt Pulley for Wireless Generator.

28b

BASSÉ & SELVE—continued.

by the action of the scroll-cam cut in the spindle, and operated by a hardened steel roller working on a pin screwed into the pump body.

At every stroke of the two double-acting plungers, oil is drawn from the cooler tank and sumps in the base chamber, and is delivered to the main bearings and camshaft or returned to the oil cooler respectively, through the four distributing ports in the pump plungers. These ports when in action coincide with the drilled passages in the body casting of the oil pump, which are connected to the various leads as shown in the lubrication diagram.

The functions of the oil pumps and circuits are as follows :—

1. MAIN PRESSURE CIRCUIT, by the two inner pumps to crankshaft and connecting rod bearings and also to the hollow camshaft, returning by gravity to the two sumps at either end of the base chamber. The oil for this circuit is drawn from the supplementary oil cooler tank, which is replenished by fresh oil from the service oil tank.

2. SCAVENGER CIRCUIT.—Oil is drawn by the two outer pumps from the two oil sumps in the bottom of the base chamber, and is returned to the oil cooler.

The total weight of the oil pump complete is 5 lbs.

The water pump was evidently driven by the short transverse shaft which drives the oil pump at the rear end of the engine.

The air pump, which was driven by a small crank fixed in the front end of the camshaft, was probably similar in design to the 260-h.p. Mercédès.

IGNITION.

Ignition is by two Z.H. 6 magnetos, which are driven obliquely to the crankshaft axis by bevel gears off the camshaft driving spindle at the rear end of the engine.

Two Bosch 3-point plugs are fitted to each cylinder, and are situated just below the induction valves. Provision is also made for fitting one sparking plug on the exhaust side of the cylinders, the holes not in use being plugged.

The machine-gun interrupter-gear triple drive is bolted to the camshaft bevel gear case, and is driven off the rear end of the camshaft as shown in Fig. 2. The wireless dynamo is driven off the rear end of the crankshaft by a standard type of friction-clutch belt pulley described in a previous report

Photograph of the Bassé-Selve Oil Pump sectioned, showing the spiral groove which reciprocates the pistons, and the oil passages in the body.

Diagram of the Lubrication System.

Lower Half of Crankcase, showing the Oil-cooler, Oil-pump in Position, and the Air Vents in Crankcase-side. 270-h.p. Bassé-Selve engine.

BASSÉ & SELVE—continued.

GENERAL ANALYSIS OF WEIGHTS.

Description of Part.	No. per set.	Average unit weight in lbs.	Weight of complete set in lbs.	Percentage of total weight.
Cylinders (bare) ..	6	35.67	214.05	24.20
Pistons, with rings ..	6	5.18	31.12	3.51
Gudgeon pins	6	1.00	6.00	0.68
Connecting rods ..	6	9.0	54.0	6.10
Crankshaft	1	138.50	138.50	15.05
Inlet valves	12	0.50	6.00	0.68
Exhaust valves ..	12	0.50	6.00	0.68
Inlet and exhaust valve springs	24	0.25	6.00	0.68
Valve collars and locking nuts	24	0.03	0.74	0.08
Valve rockers with bearings	12	1.43	17.22	1.94
Camshaft, with bearings	1	18.75	18.75	2.12
Camshaft tappets ..	12	0.31	3.75	0.42
Camshaft casing, with air pump and rev. counter drive ..	1	35.77	35.77	4.04
Vertical shaft driving spindle	1	4.50	4.50	0.51
Ditto, casing	1	2.30	2.30	0.26
Crankcase (top half) ..	1	97.50	97.50	11.00
Crankcase (bottom half)	1	112.00	112.00	12.67
Propeller hub, complete	1	29.43	29.43	3.33
Carburetters	2	2.00	4.00	0.45
Induction pipes ..	2	2.00	4.00	0.45
Oil pump	1	5.00	5.00	0.56
Oil leads	1	4.56	4.56	0.51
Magnetos	2	14.37	28.75	3.25
High tension leads and case	2	2.12	4.24	0.48
*Water pump (estimated)	1	8.00	8.00	0.90
*Exhaust manifold (estimated)	1	15.00	15.00	1.70
Miscellaneous parts ..	1	27.82	27.82	3.15
Total			885.0	100.00

GENERAL DATA.

Type number	No. 550.
Number and arrangement of cylinders	Six, vertical.
Bore	155.0 mm. (6.10 in.).
Stroke	200.0 mm. (7.87 in.).
Stroke/Bore ratio	1.29 : 1.
Area of one piston	188.7 sq.cm. (29.24 sq.in.).
Total piston area of engine ..	1132.2 s.cm. (175.44 s.in.).
Stroke volume of one cylinder	3774.0 cu.c. (230.21 cu.in.

Total stroke volume of engine ..	22644.0 c.cm.(1381.28c.in
Clearance volume of cylinder ..	1130 cu.cm. (68.96 cu.in.)
Compression ratio (approx.) ..	*4.34 : 1.
Normal B.H.P. at 1,400 R.P.M. ..	*269 B.H.P.
Maximum B.H.P. at 1,600 R.P.M. ..	*302 B.H.P.
Direction of rotation of crankshaft and propeller	R.H.T.
Type of valve gear	Overhead camshaft.
Type of starting gear	Compression release.
Weight of complete engine, dry ..	*885 lbs.
Weight per normal B.H.P., ditto ..	*3.29 lbs.

CARBURETTERS.

Number and type of carburetters ..	Two, 2 jets.
Diameter of choke tube	50.0 mm. (1.96 in.).
Bore of main jets	2.59 mm. (0.0102 in.).
Bore of pilot jets	1.17 mm. (0.0046 in.).

VALVE AREAS, GAS VELOCITIES, ETC.

Diameters :—
Induction pipe	58.0 mm. (2.28 in.).
Inlet and exhaust effective valve ports (each)	56.0 mm. (2.20 in.).

Cross sectional areas :—
Induction pipes	10.4 sq. cm. (4.10 sq. in.).
Inlet valve (π dh) and exhaust valve (π dh) (each)	17.6 sq. cm. (2.72 sq. in.).

MEAN GAS VELOCITIES (1,400 R.P.M.).

Piston speed	*1837 ft. per min.
Induction pipe	*219 ft. per sec.
Inlet valve	*164 ft. per sec.
Exhaust valve	*164 ft. per sec.

INLET AND EXHAUST VALVES.

Number per cylinder (each) ..	Two.
Largest diameter	61.0 mm. (2.40in.).
Effective valve port diameter ..	56.0 mm. (2.20 in.).
Angle of seating	45 deg.
Lift of valve	10.0 mm. (0.39 in.).
Diameter of stem	11.0 mm. (0.43 in.).
Length of valve guide	90.0 mm. (3. 54 in.).
Overall length of valve	146.0 mm. (5.74 in.).
Number of springs per valve ..	One.
Free length of spring	80.0 mm. (3.14 in.).
Length of spring in position (no lift) inlet	58.0 mm. (2.28 in.).
Length of spring in position (no lift) exhaust	55.0 mm. (2.16 in.).

Photograph of the Carburetter of the Bassé-Selve engine. This carburetter appears to be of a type known in Germany as the "Pallas" and manufactured by the German makers of the "Zenith" carburetter.

Section of the Airscrew Hub, and of the thrust-bearing of the Bassé-Selve, showing clearly the coupling between the crankshaft and the separate nose-piece.

BASSÉ & SELVE—continued.

Mean diameter of coils (top) ..	36.0 mm. (1.41 in.).
Mean diameter of coils (bottom) ..	28.0 mm. (1.10 in.).
Diameter of wire	4.0 mm. (0.157 in.).
Ratio, length of spring/lift of valve (inlet)	5.8 : 1.
Ratio, length of spring/lift of valve (exhaust)	5.5 : 1.
Weight of valve complete with spring	0.75 lb.
Weight of spring	0.25 lb.

INERTIA FORCES, BEARING LOADS, ETC.

Weight of piston, complete with rings and gudgeon pin	6.187 lbs.
Weight per sq. in. of piston area ..	0.211 lb.
Weight of connecting rod, complete	9.00 lbs.
Weight of reciprocating part of connecting rod	2.25 lbs.
Total reciprocating weight per cylinder	8.437 lbs.
Weight per sq. in. of piston area ..	0.288 lb.
Length of connecting rod (centres)	360.0 mm. (14.17 in.).
Ratio, connecting rod/crank throw	3.6 : 1.
Inertia lbs./sq. in. piston area :—	
top centre	80.7 lbs. sq. in.
bottom centre	45.7 lbs. sq. in.
mean	31.6 lbs. sq. in.
Weight of rotating mass of connecting rod	6.75 lbs.
Total centrifugal pressure ..	1480 lbs.
Centrifugal pressure lbs./sq. in. piston area	50.7 lbs. sq. in.
Mean average fluid pressure, including compression	44 lbs. sq. in.
Mean average loading on crankpin bearing, total from all sources in terms of lbs./sq. in. piston area ..	115.7 lbs. sq. in.
Diameter of crankpin	70.0 mm. (2.75 in.).
Rubbing velocity	16.8 ft. per sec.
Effective projected area of big-end bearing	53.9 sq. cm. (8.35 sq. in.).
Ratio, piston area/projected area of big-end bearing	3.50 : 1.
Mean average loading on big-end bearing	405 lbs. sq. in.
Load factor on big-end bearing ..	6800 lbs. ft. sec.

CYLINDERS.

Depth of spigot at base of cylinder ..	8.0 mm. (0.31 in.).
Thickness of flange at base of cylinder	10.0 mm. (0.39 in.).
Number of holding-down studs per cylinder	Six.
Diameter of holding-down studs ..	Four of 16.0 mm. ; two of 14.0 mm.
Thickness of water jacket	1.0 mm. (0.039 in.).
Mean thickness of combustion chamber wall	7.0 mm. (0.27 in.).
Mean thickness of cylinder barrel ..	3.0 mm. (0.118 in.).

PISTON.

Types of piston	Aluminium (convex crown).
Diameter of top	154.5 mm. (6.08 in.).
Diameter of bottom	154.75 mm. (6.09 in.).
Length	130.0 mm. (5.11 in.).
Ratio, piston length/cylinder bore ..	0.838 : 1.
Number of rings per piston	Four.
Position of rings	3 above pin, 1 below.
Width of rings	6.0 mm. (0.23 in.).
Type of joint in rings	Stepped.

CONNECTING ROD.

Length betewen centres	360 mm. (14.17 in.).
Ratio, connecting/crank throw ..	3.6 : 1.
Little-end bearing, type	Phosphor bronze.
Little-end bearing, diameter ..	35.0 mm. (1.37 in.).
Little-end bearing, length	80.0 mm. (3.14 in.).
Little-end bearing, projected area ..	28.0 sq. cm. (4.34 sq. in.)
Ratio, piston area/projected area of little-end bearing	6.74 : 1.
Big-end bearing, type	Bronze shell lind.wh.met.
Big-end bearing, diameter ..	70.0 mm. (2.75 in.).
Big-end bearing, length (effective) ..	77.0 mm. (3.03 in.).
Big-end bearing, projected area ..	53.9 sq. cm. (8.35 sq. in.).
Ratio, piston area/projected area of big-end bearing	3.50 : 1.
Number of big-end bolts	Four.
Full diameter of bolts	12.0 mm. (0.47 in.).
Total cross-sectional area bottom of threads	0.460 sq. in.
Pitch of threads	1.75 mm.
Weight of big-end cap, with two bolts and bearing shell	2.562 lbs.
Total load on bolts at 1,400 R.P.M.	3460 lbs.
Total load on bolts at 1,600 R.P.M.	4530 lbs.
Stress per sq. in. at 1,400 R.P.M. ..	7500 lbs. sq. in.
Stress per sq. in. at 1,600 R.P.M. ..	9850 lbs. sq. in.

CRANKSHAFT.

Number and type of main bearings	7,br'ze shell lin'd wh.met.
Cylinder centres	210.0 mm. (8.26 in.).
Crankpins :—	
Outside diameter	70.0 mm. (2.75 in.).
Inside diameter	40.0 mm. (1.57 in.).
Length	85.0 mm. (3.34 m.).
Journals :—	
Outside diameter	70.0 mm. (2.75 in.).
Inside diameter	40.0 mm. (1.57 in.).
Length (propeller end) ..	60.0 mm. (2.36 in.).
Length (rear end)	95.0 mm. (3.74 in.).
Length (intermediate) ..	63.0 mm. (2.48 in.).
Webs :—	
Width	84.0 mm. (3.30 in.).
Thickness (front one) ..	37.0 mm. (1.45 in.).
Thickness (others)	31.0 mm. (1.22 in.).
Radius at ends of crankpins and journals	4.0 mm. (0.158 in.).
Weight of complete shaft	138.5 lbs.
Length of complete shaft	820 mm. (38.28 in.).

Cross-Sectional End Elevation, 270-h.p. Bassé-Selve engine.

BASSÉ & SELVE—continued.

IGNITION.

Number and type of magnetos	Two, Bosch Z.H. 6.
Firing sequence of engines	Prop. 1, 5, 3, 6, 2, 4.
Number of plugs per cylinder	Two.
Type of plugs	Bosch 3-point.
Ratio, magneto speed/engine speed	1.5 : 1.

LUBRICATION.

Number and type of oil pumps	One, duplex(double actg.)
Bore	45.0 mm. (1.77 in.).
Stroke	12.0 mm. (0.47 in.).

F.G.C., Ap.D. L.

J. G. WEIR, Brigadier-General,
October, 1918.   Controller, Technical Department.

R.A.E. METALLURGICAL REPORT.

CHEMICAL ANALYSIS.

The chemical compositions of the crankshaft and piston are as follows :—

Crankshaft.		A 1. Piston.	
Carbon	0.48 per cent.	Silicon	0.45 per cent.
Silicon	0.32 per cent.	Iron	1.06 per cent.
Sulphur	0.061 per cent.	Copper	1.90 per cent.
Phosphorus	0.016 per cent.	Tin	Nil.
Manganese	0.32 per cent.	Zinc	15.62 per cent.
Nickel	2.59 per cent.	Manganese	Nil.
Chromium	1.17 per cent.	Aluminium	
Vanadium	Nil.	(by diff.)	80.97 per cent.

MECHANICAL TESTS.

Mechanical tests on the crankshaft gave values stated below :—

Mark.	A Web Longitudinal.	B Web Transverse.	C Pin.
Diameter	.249 in.	.253 in.	.249 in.
Yield Point, Tons/sq. in.	44.6	44.5	46.3
Ultimate Stress, Tons/sq. in.	55.5	54.4	56.4
Elongation on 4 $\sqrt{A}$	19.5 p.c.	12.8 p.c.	20.8 p.c.
Reduction of Area	48 p.c.	24 p.c.	56 p.c.
Impact, ft. lbs.	28 / 25	26 / 25	41 / 41

R.A.E., Dec. 5th, 1918.

270 HP BASSE-SELVE. 1

Part sectional side Elevation, the Bassé-Selve engine.

BEARDMORE (British).

THE BEARDMORE AERO ENGINE, Ltd.

Chief Office : Parkhead, Glasgow, Scotland.

Registered Office : 36, Victoria Street, Westminster, London, S.W. London Agency and Show Rooms : 112, Great Portland Street, W.

Manufactured by : Arrol-Johnston, Ltd., Dumfries, Scotland, and by various sub-contractors.

Have concentrated on the 160 h.p. type engine illustrated herewith.

160 h.p. type.

B.H.P. at normal revs. : 166 h.p.
Normal R.P.M. : 1250.
Bore : 142 m/m.
Stroke : 175 m/m.
No. of cylinders : 6.
(Set desaxé 18 m/m.)
Petrol consumption, pints per B.H.P. hour : .57.
Oil consumption, pints per B.H.P. hour : .03.
Weight complete with magnetos, carburetters, piping, oil and water pumps, propeller boss, hand starting magneto and switch. } 600 lbs.
Weight of water in cylinder jackets : 4 lbs. 7 ozs.
(But without radiators and water therein.)

This engine is a greatly improved and refined version of the pre-war Austro-Daimler, which itself was in its time one of the most efficient engines in being.

Inlet side of the 160 h.p. Beardmore aero engine.

33b

End View of the 160 h.p. Beardmore aero engine.

E

Cross Section of 160 h.p. Beardmore Engine.

General Arrangement of 160 h.p. Beardmore Engine.
(Seen from rear.)

Part Sectional Diagram of the 160 h.p. Beardmore Engine.

BENZ (German).

BENZ. & CIE, Mannheim.

THE 230-H.P. BENZ ENGINE.

[The following particulars of the 1917 Benz Engine, together with photographs and drawings, have been kindly supplied by the Technical Department of the Air Ministry, to whom the Editor desires to express his thanks.]

This detailed description of the 230-h.p. Benz engines is based on an investigation and tests of the engine (No. 30127) taken from the German Aviatik biplane G.40, captured on May 20th, 1917, and includes a report on the power and consumption tests carried out at the Royal Aircraft Factory, together with chemical analyses of the principal parts of the engine.

LEADING FEATURES OF THE ENGINE.

Following the usual German aero-engine practice, the 230-h.p. Benz is of the six cylinder-vertical water-cooled type. Each separate cylinder is bolted to the crankcase by long studs, which pass through the crank-chamber top half and secure the crank-shaft bearings between the top and bottom halves of the crank-chamber.

Two inlet and two exhaust valves are fitted in the head of each cylinder. The valves are operated by overhead valve rockers working on ball bearings and by push rods on either side of the cylinders. The two camshafts, which run on plain bearings, are neatly arranged inside the top half of the crank-case, and the floating exhaust camshaft is provided with half compression cams.

The pistons are of cast-iron, fitted with three exceptionally wide rings, and the piston heads, following usual Benz practice, are supported by conical steel forgings riveted and welded to the piston crown, which bear on the centre portion of the gudgeon pins, through slots cut in the connecting rod small ends.

As in the 160-h.p. Benz engines, two separate two-jet carburetters are fitted, each having their air intake passages through the top half of the crankcase casting. Each carburetter supplies three cylinders through an independent branched induction pipe, built up of light aluminium tube.

The lubrication of the crankshaft and connecting rod bearings is effected by a very neatly designed gear pump working in an auxiliary oil reservoir formed in the bottom of the air-cooled base chamber.

An oil-sealed petrol pump of interesting design supplies petrol to the carburetters in conjunction with a supplementary pressure reservoir enclosed in the main petrol tank. The petrol pump is driven off the rear end of the inlet camshaft. The same driving spindle also operates the machine-gun interrupter gear and the tachometer drive.

CONSTRUCTIONAL DETAILS.

Cylinders.—Except for the steel water-jackets, the cylinders are made entirely of cast-iron. The water-jacketed heads, including the twin inlet and exhaust valve passages, are cast integral with the cylinder castings.

The bore of the cylinders is 145 mm. and the thickness of the cylinder walls tapers from 5.5 mm. at the base flanges to 6.5 mm. at the top of the cylinder barrels. The water-jackets are of die-pressed sheet steel, built up from half sections and welded both at the vertical joints and at the bottom of the water-jackets to flanges machined on the outside of the cylinder barrels. The water-jackets are exceptionally long, extending to within .45 millimetres of the cylinder base flanges. Seven annular corrugations are formed in the water-jackets to allow for expansion, and three transversely in the sheet steel crown of the water-jackets. The general construction of the cylinders and water jackets with their water connections is clearly shown in the photographic views of the cylinders and in the sectional drawings. Figs. 3 and 4.

The water spaces formed in the cylinder-heads and the cooling of the valve pockets are well carried out. Dished plates are welded in position in the water space above the crown of each

Fig. 1.—Inlet Side of the 230 h.p. Benz Engine.—145 mm. Bore × 190 mm. Stroke.

BENZ—*continued.*

cylinder to deflect the flow of water onto the exhaust valve pockets. The diameter of the cylinder-head water connections is 60 mm.

The cylinder registers extend to 10 mm. below the base flanges into the crank-chamber, and are held down by four 12-mm. studs, and also by dogs at four points. The dogs are secured by long studs which pass through the top half of the crank-chamber and are screwed into the bottom halves of the main bearing housings, which are cast integral with the bottom half of the base chamber. The parts of the holding-down studs which screw into the aluminium are of larger diameter and of coarser pitch. The nuts which secure the cylinder holding-down clamps are of interesting design, being of circular cupped formation and drilled radially with four 12-mm. holes for screwing up with a " Tommy Bar."

The total weight of each cylinder complete with valves, valve springs and valve rocker-supports = 44.25 lbs.

PISTONS.—The pistons, with the exception of the small conical pillars, are made entirely of cast-iron, and weigh 7.62 lbs. each, complete with rings and gudgeon pin.

Three rings are provided above the gudgeon pin, the lower one being a scraper ring. The width of each ring is 8 mm. and the width of gap in cylinder = 0.45 mm. The space between the two top rings is 4.25 mm., whilst the scraper ring is 10 mm. below the middle ring ; 4-mm. pegs are provided to locate the radial position of each ring, and six 2-mm. holes are drilled in the piston below the scraper ring.

The slightly domed head of each piston is supported by a hollow conical pillar, which is machined from a steel forging and is riveted onto the under side of the piston, as shown in the sectional drawings of the piston, Figs. 6 and 7. The lower end of the conical pillar, which is machined at the same time as the holes in the gudgeon-pin bosses are bored, bears on the centre part of the gudgeon-pin, and to allow for this the centre portion of the top of the connecting rod small end and gudgeon-pin bush is cut away. By this construction the greater part of the force of the explosion is transmitted from the head of the piston directly to the connecting rod.

The gudgeon pins are 38 mm. diameter and are bored 30 mm. inside diameter. The centre portion of the gudgeon pin is 25 mm. bore for a length of 20 mm., where the conical piston head support bears on the centre of the gudgeon pin. The piston ring side clearance = 0.004 in. The diameter at the top of the piston = 144.15 mm. The diameter at the bottom of the piston = 144.67 mm.

CONNECTING RODS.—The very clean design of the tubular connecting rods is apparent in the photographic views.

The whole of the connecting rod, including the lugs for the four bolts securing the halves of the big end, is machined all over from a steel forging. The outside diameter of the tubular rod is 36 mm. and the inside is bored with a 30 mm. hole from the crank-pin end to within 6 mm. of the gudgeon-pin bush—the bottom end of the bore being fitted with a screwed plug.

A 6 mm. steel pipe, for lubricating the gudgeon pin, is fixed inside the centre of the connecting rod and the pipe is supported in the centre by two flanged discs, as shown in the drawing. The weight of the big end is lightened by four 12-mm. holes and one 30-mm. hole drilled radially through the big end. Two semi-circular oil grooves are machined in the white metal of the big end bearing caps and one lateral groove is cut in the top portion of the big end bearing. The total weight of the complete connecting rod is 7 lbs. 1 oz. ; the big end weighing 4 lbs. 12 ozs., and the small end 2 lbs. 5 ozs.

Total big end side clearance = 0.15 mm. and the float of the small end bush between the gudgeon-pin bosses = 14 mm.

Fig. 2.—Exhaust Side of the 230 h.p. Benz Engine.

THE 230. H.P BENZ AERO ENGINE
SECTIONAL ELEVATION
BORE 145 ⅓ STROKE 190 ⅓

Fig. 3.—Sectional General Arrangement.

CRANKSHAFT.—The six-throw crankshaft runs in seven plain bearings, and weighs 109.25 lbs., including the airscrew boss.

The cranks are, of course, set at 120°, and the diameter of all the journals is 62 mm., whilst that of the crank-pins is 60 mm. The length of the front journal bearing (propeller end) = 79 mm., and the length of the other journal bearings = 54 mm., with the exception of the rear end bearing, which is 55 mm.

The crankshaft journals and crank-pins are bored for lubrication, the webs being drilled with communicating holes in the usual manner. The internal diameter of the holes bored in both crank-pins and journals is 27 mm. The ends of the holes are plugged with sheet-steel discs sweated into the recessed ends, and all the discs which plug the rear ends of the holes in both the crank-pins and journals are drilled with a central 5-mm. hole presumably with the idea of lubricating the camshafts with the oil thrown out by the cranks.

A double-thrust ball race, 120 mm. diameter, is fitted at the front end of the crankshaft behind the front flange to which the propeller hub is bolted. The thrust races are large enough to be assembled over the cranks, and are secured in position by a split collar which is screwed on to the crankshaft. The halves of the split collar are held together on the screw thread on the shaft by a recess cut in the split collar. This recess holds a corresponding flange turned on the crankshaft.

Fitted to the rear end of the crankshaft is a friction clutch for operating the wireless drive, which is designed so that the driving brake-shoes of the clutch can be thrown in or out of

Fig. 4.—Cross Section. General Arrangement.

Fig. 5.—Views of Piston and Connecting Rod.

Fig. 6.—End view of Gudgeon, with Piston shown in section in same aspect.

Fig. 7.—Sectional Details of Piston and Gudgeon viewed Broadside to the Engine.

engagement with the driving pulley from the pilot's seat, through the action of two wedges, which operate the friction shoes through ball-ended levers.

The propeller boss is attached to the crankshaft by a flange which is bolted to a corresponding flange on the end of the crankshaft by eight 14-mm. bolts.

VALVES AND VALVE GEAR.—The twin inlet and exhaust valves work vertically in the cylinder heads, and are operated as previously mentioned by rockers mounted on ball bearings, carried by supports screwed into the cylinder head. The general design of the complete valve-gear is clearly shown in the sectional drawings (Figs. 3 and 4), and the arrangement of the valves and valve springs, etc., on the cylinder head in Fig. 9.

The rocker levers operate the valve stems through hardened steel rollers which are mounted on eccentric bolts. These, in conjunction with adjustable spherical joints screwed into the top ends of the vertical push rods on each side of the cylinders, give a fine adjustment for the tappet clearances. The spherical joints on the valve rockers are evidently provided to simplify the alignment of the valve rocker supports which are screwed into the cylinder heads.

Semi-spherical joints are also provided at the bottom ends of the push rods, which work in steel cups inside the hollow tappets, and it should be noted that the hardened steel rollers of the

tappets, are slightly off-set from the camshaft centres and each pair of tappet guides is held in position by a steel bridge clamp.

The dimensions of both the inlet and exhaust valves are the same, each valve weighing 1.25 lbs. The lift of the inlet valve = 0.465 in. and lift of the exhaust valve = 0.443 in. Clearance of inlet tappet = 0.009 in., exhaust 0.015 in.

CAMSHAFTS.—The hollow camshafts each run in three plain phosphor-bronze bearings, and are arranged inside the top half of the crank-chamber. The camshaft bearing bushes, which are hollow, are 53 mm. outside diameter, and are split on the camshaft axis and held together by wire rings on either side to allow the camshafts to be easily inserted in the crankcase. The bearings are located by grub screws screwed in from the outside of the crank-chamber.

The camshafts are driven by gears from the intermediate gear wheel which meshes with the crankshaft distribution pinion, and arranged inside a casing formed at the rear end of the crank case. The camshaft gears are bolted to the camshafts by drilled flanges, which provide a vernier adjustment for setting the camshafts.

Half compression cams are arranged on the exhaust camshaft in the usual manner. The lateral movement of the floating camshaft is effected by a small lever at the rear end of the crankcase which operates a two start square thread screw of

Fig. 8.—**General View of Crankshaft, with Connecting Rods and Airscrew Boss.**

Fig. 9.—**Top of Cylinder Showing General Arrangement of Valve Gear.**

24 mm. pitch. The camshaft is returned to its normal running position by a spring arranged inside the front end of the hollow camshaft.

The half compression cams open the exhaust valves at 35° E., and close 22° L.

CRANKCASE. The general design of the crankcase is shown in the longitudinal and cross sectional drawings of the engine (Figs. 3 and 4.)

The method of cooling the interior of the crank-chamber and sump indicates the fact that this matter has received most careful consideration in design. In the top half of the crankcase six of the seven main bearing housings are cast so that the webs form air passages transversely across the engine. Two of these passages form the air intake passages for the two carburetters—similarly to those of the 160-h.p. Benz engines—as already stated.

The bottom half of the crank-chamber is extended to form an oil sump and is of unusual design. The lower portion is cooled by eighteen 30-mm. aluminium tubes fixed transversely across the base chamber, the air being scooped into the cooling tubes by a large sheet aluminium louvred cowl on the induction side of the engine. A corresponding but reversed cowl is fitted on the exhaust side.

Breathers are also fitted into the top half of the crank-chamber. The simple type of wire spring clip fitted to the breathers should be noted.

CARBURATION SYSTEM.—Two separate carburetters are fitted each feeding three cylinders. These are attached by flanges to the side of the top half of the crank-chamber.

The combined jet is screwed obliquely into the bottom of the float chamber casting and not into the body of the carburetter. The float chamber is attached to the body of the carburetter by two bolts, and the throttle is of the horizontal barrel type.

_____

September 4th, 1917.

ROYAL AIRCRAFT FACTORY TEST REPORT ON 230-H.P. BENZ ENGINE.

The engine was run up to 1700 r.p.m., the peak of the power curve occurring at 1650 r.p.m., at which 250 h.p. was developed.

The maximum brake m.e.p. reached 119 lbs. per square inch at 1100 r.p.m.

The results of a one-hour test run were as follows :—

R.P.M.	1400
B.H.P.	229
Petrol Consumption	150 pints.
Oil Consumption	4.5 pints.
Water Inlet Temperature (average)	62°C.
Water Outlet Temperature (average)	71°C.
Oil Temperature (Max.)	50°C. steady.
Oil Pressure (Min.)	28 lbs. sq. in. steady.

The engine was erected on a test bed and coupled to a Heenan and Froude Water Dynamometer.

230-H.P. BENZ ENGINE DATA.

Number and arrangement of cylinders	6 vertical.
Bore	145 mm. (5.71 ins.).
Stroke	190 mm. (7.48 ins.).
Stroke/bore ratio	1.31-1.
Stroke volume of one cylinder	3137.476 cub.cms.(191.386 cub. ins.).
Total stroke volume of engine	18824.856 cub. cms. 1148.316 cub. ins.).
Area of one piston	165.13 sq. cms. (25.59 sq. ins.).
Total piston area of engine	990.78 sq. cms. (153.57 sq. ins.).
Clearance volume of one cylinder	796 cub. cms. (48.66 cub. ins.).
Compression ratio.	4.91-1.
Normal B.H.P. and speed	230 B.H.P at 1,400 r.p.m.
Piston speed	1,744 ft. per min.
Brake mean effective pressure	113 lbs. per sq. inch at 1,400 r.p.m. ; 119 lbs. per sq. inch at 1,100 r.p.m.
Cub. inches of stroke volume per B.H.P.	4.99.
Sq. inches of piston area per B.H.P.	.667.
H.P. per cub. ft. of stroke volume	346.3 h.p.
H.P. per sq. ft. of piston area	215.9 h.p.
Direction of rotation of crank	R.H.T.
Direction of rotation of propeller	R.H.T.
Normal speed of propeller	Engine speed.
Lubrication system	Forced to main bearings from reservoir in sump.
Brand of oil	50 per cent. Vacuum Heavy and 50 per cent. Sternol.
Oil pressure	28 lbs. normal, 50 lbs. max.
Oil temperature	50° C., max.
Oil consumption per hour	4.5 pints.
Oil consumption per B.H.P. hour	.02 pints.
Specific gravity of oil	.9.
Type of carburetter	2 Benz each feeding 3 cylinders (2 jet)
Mixture control	Automatic
Fuel consumption per hour	150 pints.
Fuel consumption per B.H.P. hour	.65 pints.
Specific gravity of fuel	.720.
Type of Magneto	2 Bosch Z.H.6.
Firing sequence of engine	Prop. : 1-5-3-6-2-4.
Numbering of cylinders	Prop. : 1-2-3-4-5-6.
Speed of magneto	2/3rds. engine speed.

Direction of rotation of magneto, facing driving end of armature	Anti-clockwise.
Magneto timing	30° E. 18 mm. on stroke.
Inlet valve opens. Deg. on crank	10° E.
Inlet valve closes. Deg. on crank	55° L.
Maximum lift of inlet valve = h	11.8 mm. (.465 in.)
Diameter of inlet valve = d (smallest diam.)	Two of 52 mm.
Area of inlet valve port = $\pi \times d \times h$	19.27 sq. cms. each.
Mean gas velocity through inlet valve	124 ft. per sec.
Clearance of inlet tappet	.009 in.
Exhaust valve opens. Deg. on crank	60° E.
Exhaust valve closes. Deg. on crank	20° L.
Maximum lift of exhaust valve = h	11.25 mm. (.443 in.)
Diameter of exhaust valve ports=d (smallest diam.)	Two of 52 mm. dia.
Area of exhaust valve ports = $\pi \times d \times h$	18.37 sq. cms. (each) = 2.84 sq ins.
Clearance of exhaust tappet	.015 in.
Direction of rotation of revolution counter drive, facing driving shaft on engine	Anti-clockwise.
Speed of revolution counter drive	½ E.S.
Weight of engine complete with propeller hub, less water, fuel and oil and exhaust manifold	848.32 lbs.
Weight per B.H.P. ditto	3.68 lbs.
Weight of exhaust manifold	15 lbs.
Weight of oil carried in engine	18 lbs.
Jacket capacity of one cylinder	1873 c.c.
Weight of water carried in engine	30.9 lbs.
Weight of radiators, less water	136 lbs.
Weight of fuel per hour	135 lbs.
Weight of oil per hour	5.06 lbs.
Total weight of fuel and oil per hour	140.06 lbs.
Gross weight of engine in running order, less fuel and oil. Cooling system at 0.65 lbs. per B.H.P.	996 lbs.
Weight per B.H.P. ditto	4.33 lbs.
Gross weight of engine in running order with fuel and oil for six hours. (Tankage reckoned at 10 per cent. weight of fuel and oil)	1920.89 lbs.
Weight per B.H.P. with fuel and oil for six hours.	8.35 lbs.

ENGINES.

WEIGHTS OF PARTS.

LISTS OF COMPARATIVE WEIGHTS OF PARTS AND THEIR PERCENTAGE OF TOTAL WEIGHT OF ENGINE.

Description of Part.	Lbs.	Per cent. Total Weight.
Cylinders, complete, including supports for rocker levers (six at 44.25) ..	265.5	30.753
Pistons, complete, with rings and gudgeon pins (six at 7.62 lbs. each)	45.72	5.296
Connecting rods, complete (six at 7.13 lbs. each)	42.78	4.955
Valves and springs complete (twenty-four at 1.14 lbs. each)	27.36	3.169
Tappets, push rods and rocker levers (twelve sets at 3.2 lbs. each) ..	38.4	4.447
Induction pipes, complete (two at 2.625 lbs. each)	5.25	.608
Carburetters, complete (two at 6.54 lbs. each)	13.08	1.515
Crank-chamber, top half	103.25	11.959
Crank-chamber, bottom half (including cylinder studs and oil pump shaft)	110.25	12.77
Crankshaft, complete	109.25	12.66
Propeller boss, complete	19.32	2.236
Camshafts, complete, with bearings less gear-wheels (two at 8.25 lbs. each)	16.5	1.912
Magnetos, complete (two at 10.75 lbs. each)	21.5	2.490
Ignition wiring, complete (two at 2.12 lbs. each)	4.24	.491
Water pump, complete	8.75	1.013
Oil pump, complete	2.89	.335
Petrol pump, complete	6.75	.782
Exhaust manifold	15	1.737
Miscellaneous parts	7.53	.872
Total weight of complete engine	863.32	100

CHEMICAL ANALYSES.

Chemical analyses have been made on parts of the Benz engine with the following results :—

	Carbon Per cent.	Silicon Per cent.	Sulphur Per cent.	Phosphorus Per cent.	Manganese Per cent.	Nickel Per cent.	Chromium Per cent.
Water jacket ..	0.07	0.03	0.046	0.0027	0.35	Nil	0.02
Crankshaft.....	0.13	0.31	0.026	0.0014	0.48	3.21	0.87
Connecting rod	0.15	0.21	0.027	0.0026	0.37	4.02	1.21
Gear wheel	0.23	0.25	0.014	0.0027	0.53	3.58	0.81
Camshaft	0.14	0.23	0.029	0.0026	0.95	4.68	1.48
Inlet valve.....	0.26	0.28	0.012	0.0020	0.40	5.36	1.06
Valve spring ...	0.40	0.02	0.033	0.0085	0.55	Nil	0.01

	Graphitic Carbon. Per cent.	Combined Carbon. Per cent.	Silicon. Per cent.	Sulphur. Per cent.	Phosphorus Per cent.	Manganese Per cent.
Cylinder	1.90	0.77	1.68	0.122	0.176	0.48
Piston.........	1.85	0.50	1.46	0.130	0.210	0.77

	Graphitic Silicon Per cent.	Combined Silicon Per cent.	Iron Per cent.	Tin Per cent.	Copper Per cent.	Zinc Per cent.	Lead Per cent.	Aluminium Per cent.
Crankcase	0.18	0.89	0.93	Trace	6.20	9.59	Trace	82.21

	Antimony. Per cent.	Tin. Per cent.	Copper. Per cent.	Lead. Per cent
Bearing metal	11.95	78.57	8.10	0.90

The analyses of gear wheel and camshaft were made on drillings taken from the cores, as these were case-hardened parts.

MECHANICAL TESTS.

Mechanical tests gave results as under :—

	Yield Point. Tons per square in.	Ultimate Stress. Tons per square in.	Elongation. Per cent.	Reduction of Area. Per cent.	Impact. Ft./lbs.
Crankshaft	55.2	62.5	21.3	59.75	26
Cylinder	—	8.36	Nil	Nil	—
Connecting rod	41.9	48.1	14.0	—	—
Crankcase	—	8.91	—	—	—

B.H.P. (British).

Initials stand for Beardmore-Halford-Pullinger.

Made by :—

The Galloway Engine Co., Ltd., Dumfries.

The Siddeley-Deasy Motor Co., Ltd., Coventry.

The original design of 6 cylinder water-cooled engine was produced by Major (then Captain) F. B. Halford, in collaboration with Sir William Beardmore, Bart. and Mr. T. C. Pullinger (Managing Director of Arrol Johnston & Co. Ltd.)

The work was started in the Spring of 1916, when the situation on the Western Front made it vital that the Royal Flying Corps should have machines with engines of considerably higher power than had been used to that date. Although the Germans had adopted the 6 cylinder type of engine as their standard, the only engine of the same type which had been consistently used by the British Flying Services up to that time, was the 120 h.p. Beardmore.

As the situation was serious, it was considered that there was insufficient time to design and try out and produce an entirely new design of engine. Arrol Johnston & Co. Ltd. then set to work to modify the 120 h.p. Beardmore to give over 160, as was eventually proved. This latter engine completely replaced the 120 h.p. and has done extraordinarily good work on long distance bombing and reconnaissance machines.

A new Company, the Galloway Engineering Co. Ltd., was formed to exploit the new B.H.P. Engine, and a new factory was built to assist it's production. The size of the cylinder proposed, i.e. 145 m/m bore was considered by many to be too

Induction Side of the B.H.P. Galloway "Adriatic" engine.

Oil Pump, Water Pump and Valve Gear Drive of the Galloway "Adriatic" engine.

B.H.P.—continued.

large to embody in a 6 cylinder engine, but as has been happily proved, the critics proved wrong.

The first engine was running in June, 1916, and after satisfactory non-stop endurance tests on the bench, was fitted into a D.H.4 Aeroplane, which had been specially designed for the engine by Captain Geoffrey de Haviland, of the Aircraft Manufacturing Company.

The results in the air with this combination proved extremely satisfactory, in that although the best performance of this type of machine had been approximately 95 m.p.h. the D.H.4 resulted in 115 m.p.h. at 1000 feet.

The machine was officially tested by the Central Flying School and decision made by the Authorities to order the engine in larger numbers than had been proposed before with any other type.

Realising the facilities that would be required to produce 100 engines per week and spares, which was the figure suggested, and in view of the important part played by the Beardmore engine (which occupied the whole production of Arrol Johnston and Co. Ltd.), Siddeley-Deasy, of Coventry, were asked to take over the production of the B.H.P. and to take such steps as would ensure the maximum output per week.

Although this Firm was only then producing some 25 to 30 engines per week, the results of their efforts are best realised

Airscrew End of the Galloway "Adriatic" engine.

Exhaust and Magneto Side of the Galloway "Adriatic" engine.

B.H.P.—continued.

when it is stated that at the time of the Armistice the production of Siddeley-Deasy's Works of the B.H.P. Engine, better known as the "Puma," was equivalent, including spares, to 200 engines per week.

The engine was made the standard 6 cylinder water-cooled used by the Royal Air Force, and has been consistently used by the Independent Air Force in the bombing of Rhine Towns.

Before the aluminium cylinder block reached the satisfactory stage the Galloway Engineering Co. Ltd., tried out a cast iron construction, in order to ensure engines being turned out in the quickest possible time. This type was dropped when the Siddeley engines reached the production stage.

Realising again the necessity for considerably higher powered engines, the Galloway Engineering Co. Ltd. set to work to design and produce a 12 cylinder B.H.P. Engine.

To eliminate as many experimental features as possible a double B.H.P. was made, incorporating two pairs of cylinder blocks with cast iron construction. This engine was known as the "Atlantic" B.H.P. and gave 500 h.p. at 1500 r.p.m.

As in the case of the 6 cylinder B.H.P. no gear reduction was fitted, and the fact that the weight per h.p. of 2¼ lbs. was obtained with an engine running at only 1400-1500 r.p.m. was very creditable. This engine, the "Atlantic" was tested out on the bench, and also flown in another of the Aircraft Manufacturing Company's machines, the D.H. 9A, which was designed for the "Liberty."

A short time before the Armistice when it became imperative that a high power engine should be standardised for bombing machines, one of the engines chosen for mass production was the "Atlantic"; but for production purposes as the "Puma" cylinder blocks were then on the satisfactory production basis and being turned out in very large numbers, it was decided to pool the resources of several of our largest firms in the mass production of the engine, which was then rechristened the "Siddeley Pacific." Some thousands were ordered, and but for the Armistice no doubt would have been produced. It is thus interesting to see the order in which the four engines came forward.

THE 500 H.P. B.H.P. "ATLANTIC" AERO ENGINE.

Specification.

Bore	145 mm.
Stroke	190 mm.
Normal b.h.p.	500.
Direction	Right hand tractor.
Petrol consumption per b.h.p. hour	.588 pints.
Oil consumption per b.h.p. hour ..	.060 pints.

Weight (dry)	1210 lbs.
Weight per b.h.p. (dry)	2.42 lbs.
Weight in running order with 6 hours fuel and oil	3508 lbs.
Weight per b.h.p. ditto	7.02 lbs.
Compression ratio	4.9 : 1.
Maximum lift of exhaust valve ..	12 mm.
Clearance of inlet tappet	.25 mm.

Front End of the Galloway "Atlantic" engine, 500 h.p.

B.H.P.—*continued*.

Rear View of the Galloway "Atlantic" engine, 500 h.p.

Rear End of the Galloway "Atlantic" engine, 500 h.p.

B.H.P.—*continued.*

Front View of the Siddeley " Pacific " engine, 500 h.p.

Side View of the Siddeley " Pacific " engine, 500 h.p.

Connecting Rod Arrangement of the Siddeley " Pacific " engine.

B.H.P.—*continued.*

Rear View of the Siddeley "Pacific" engine, 500 h.p.

Rear End of the Siddeley "Pacific" engine, 500 h.p.

B.H.P.—continued.

THE 230 H.P. SIDDELEY "PUMA."

Specification.

Type : 6 cylinder water-cooled vertical. Aluminium, with steel liners.
Bore : 145 mm.
Stroke : 190 mm.
B.H.P. : 230 at 1400 r.p.m.
Weight (dry) : 680 lbs. (including airscrew boss, carburetters, magnetos, etc.).
Fuel consumption : .55 pints per B.H.P. hour.
Oil consumption : .025 pints per B.H.P. hour.
Lubrication : Force feed at 30 lbs. per sq. in. to main bearings.
  Force feed at 10 lbs. per sq. in. to camshaft.
Dry sump : One suction pump, one pressure pump.
Ignition : Dual magnetos. 2 plugs per cylinder. Hand starter magneto.
Carburetters : 2 Zeniths, with altitude control.
Valve gear : 2 exhaust, and 1 inlet.
Camshaft set *désaxé*, operating direct on exhaust valves and by overhead rockers to inlet valves.

Rear End of the B.H.P. Siddeley " Puma " Engine, 230 h.p.

B.M.W. (German).

Bayerische Motor Werke, Munich.

The motor appears to follow general Mercédès design, with overhead camshaft.

49b

G

B. R. (British).

Bentley Rotary.

Designed by Mr. W. R. Bentley for the Air Department, Admiralty. Originally known as the A.R. (Admiralty Rotary) and afterwards as the B.R. (as above).

Generally very similar to the Clergét Rotaries, from which it differed in having cylinders of aluminium alloy with pressed-in steel liners,

Made in two types—B R. 1, 150 h.p., and B.R. 2, 250 h.p.

Manufactured by Humber, Ltd., Coventry; Gwynne's, Ltd., Hammersmith.

THE B.R. 1 ROTARY AERO ENGINE.
Specification.

No of cylinders ..	.. ..	9.
Bore	.. ..	120 m/m.
Stroke	.. ..	170 m/m,
Normal b h.p. ..	.. ..	150
Normal r.p.m. ..	.. ..	1250
Weight per b.h.p.	.. ..	2.67 lbs.
Fuel consumption	.. ..	11 galls. per hour.
Oil consumption ..	.. ..	12 pints per hour.

THE B.R. 2 ROTARY AERO ENGINE.
Specification.

No of cylinders ..	.. ..	9
Bore	.. ..	140 m/m.
Stroke	.. ..	180 m/m.
Normal b.h.p. ..	.. ..	250
Normal r.p.m. ..	.. ..	1250
Weight per b.h.p.	.. ..	1.9 lbs.
Fuel consumption	.. ..	20 galls. per hour.
Oil consumption	.. ..	16 pints per hour.

Front View of the B.R. 1 engine, 150 h.p.   *(From a photograph supplied by Humber, Ltd.*

Front View of the B.R. 2 engine, 250 h.p.   *(From a photograph supplied by Humber, Ltd.)*

Side View of the B.R. 2 engine, 250 h.p.   *(From a photograph supplied by Gwynne's, Ltd.)*

Half Rear View of the B.R. 2 engine, 250 h.p.   *(From a photograph supplied by Gwynne's, Ltd.)*

KING-BUGATTI (Italo-American).

BUGATTI ENGINE.

The American version of the engine designed and built in France by Signor Bugatti and made in America by the Duesenberg Motor Corporation, Edgewater, N.J., Chicago, Ill.

The following particulars of the Americanised version of the 400-h.p. Bugatti aero-engine are due to the " Aerial Age Weekly," of New York.

Generally speaking, the main features and dimensions of the American engine and of the original appear to be very similar.

The cylinders are in two vertical rows, each of eight cylinders, each row driving a separate crankshaft revolving in the same direction. Each crankshaft drives through a pinion at its end a spur-wheel on the common airscrew shaft.

The crankshaft of each row of cylinders is made in two halves, each half being of the standard type for a four-cylinder vertical engine. That is to say, the two central crank-pins of each set of four are in line one with the other, and the two outer crank-pins are also in line one with each other, but displaced 180 deg. from the two central pins. The pair of four-throw shafts for each line of eight cylinders are coupled together 90 deg. out of phase, and the two lines are geared together with an angular displacement between them of 45 deg.

The engine is, therefore, so far as regularity of turning movement is concerned, equivalent to four four-cylinder engines coupled together with a displacement of 45 deg. between each crankshaft, and gives eight equally-spaced impulses per revolution.

The following general specification is given :—

GENERAL DATA.

No. and arrangement of cylinders ..	16 vertical, 2 rows of 8 in blocks of 4.
Material	Cast iron.
Bore	4.33 ins. (110 mm.).
Stroke	6.3 ins. (160 mm.).
Stroke-bore ratio	1.455 : 1.
Area of one piston	14.725 sq. ins.
Total piston area	235.6 cu. ins,
Swept volume of one cylinder ..	92.768 cu. ins.
Displacement of motor	1484.288 cu. ins.
Compression ratio	5 : 1.
Normal brake h.p.	410 at 2,000 r.p.m.
Ratio propeller to crankshaft speed	2 : 3.

Three-quarter view from Airscrew end, 410-h.p. Bugatti Engine.

KING-BUGATTI—*continued*.

Section through cylinder head, showing valve ports.

VALVES.

Number per cylinder	Two inlet and one exhaust.
Outside diameter, inlet	1.535.
Outside diameter, exhaust ..	2.263.
Port diameter, inlet	1 27/64 in.
Port diameter, exhaust	2 3/64 ins.
Angle of seat	10 deg.
Valve lift, inlet	653 ins.
Valve lift, exhaust	700 ins.
Number of springs per valve, inlet and exhaust	2 concentric.
Length of spring in position, inlet (small)	2 7/64 ins.
Length of spring in position, inlet (large)	2 15/64 ins.
Length of spring in position, exhaust (small)	2 27/64 ins.
Length of spring in position, exhaust (large)	2 27/64 ins.
Valves parallel to centre line of cylinder bore.	

CYLINDERS.

Overall height of cylinders	10 27/64 ins.
Length of projection in crankcase ..	3 1/16 ins.
Thickness of flange (base)	7/16 in.
Number of studs per block of four cylinders	20.
Diameter of stud	5/16 in.
Thickness of water-jacket wall side and head	5/32 in.
Thickness of combustion chamber wall	13/64 in.
Thickness of cylinder barrel, above flange at water-jacket	3/16 in.
Thickness of cylinder barrel, above flange below water-jacket ..	7/32 in.

PISTONS.

Length	4 1/16 ins.
Length to diameter ratio	0.938 : 1.
Width of rings	1/8 in.
Distance from bottom to centre of gudgeon pin	2 1/6 ins.
Thickness of head at centre ..	1/4 in.
Thickness of head at edge	3/8 in.
Thickness of wall at bottom ..	1/8 in.

GUDGEON PIN.

Diameter of gudgeon pin	1 5/64 in.
Thickness of wall	0.164

CONNECTING ROD.

Length between centres	10 7/16 ins.
Ratio length to crank throw ..	3.313 : 1.
Width	5/8 in.

CRANKSHAFT.

Number of crankshafts	2.
Number of bearings (Plain) per crankshaft	9.
Number of bearings (Ball) per crankshaft	1.
Cylinder centres (in block)	4 17/32 ins.
Cylinder centres (between blocks) ..	7 15/32 ins.
Crank pins, outside diameter ..	2 3/16 ins.
Inside diameter	1 1/8 in.
Length	2 11/64 ins.
Main Bearings :	
Outside diameter Nos. 1, 2, 3, 4, 6, 7, 8, 9	2 3/16 ins.
Outside diameter No. 5	2 5/8 ins.
Inside diameter, Nos. 1, 2, 3, 4, 6, 7, 8, 9	1 1/8 in.
Length, Nos. 1, 2, 3, 4, 6, 7, 8 Bearing Bushings	1 9/16 in.

Longitudinal Section, the American Bugatti.

KING-BUGATTI—*continued.*

Length No. 9 Bearing Bushing .. 2 19/32 in.
Length No. 5 Bearing Bushing .. 1 31/32 ins.
Ball Bearing .. .. Hess-Bright Monarch No.
6211.

Crank Webs :
Width .. .. 3 17/32 ins.
Thickness .. .. 43/64 in.
Radius of fillets .. .. .. 3/32 in.
Weight of one complete shaft, for 8
cylinders, with propeller drive gear
bolts and nuts, bevel gear and oil
passage shells .. .. .. 96½ lbs.

CAMSHAFT.

Diameter of shaft .. .. .. 1 in.
Inside diameter .. .. .. 11/16 in.
Number of bearings .. .. .. 10.
Number of cams per cylinder .. 3.

CAMSHAFT BEVEL GEAR.

Pitch diameter .. .. .. 3 3/4 ins.
Number of teeth .. .. .. 30.
Pitch .. .. 8.
Width of face .. .. .. 3/4 in.

CAMSHAFT DRIVING SHAFT.

Diameter .. .. 3/4 in.
Wall thickness .. .. .. 1/8 in.

CRANKSHAFT UPPER HALF.

Material .. .. Aluminium.
Thickness of wall .. .. .. 3/16 to 5/16 in.
Thickness of supporting flange .. 3/8 to 7/16 in.
Centre distance of support bolts .. 24 3/4 ins.
Number of support bolts .. .. 12.
Diameter of support bolts .. .. 3/8 in.
Centre to centre of crankshaft .. 10 1/4 ins.
Height of case .. .. .. 9.055 ins.

CRANKCASE LOWER HALF.

Material .. .. Aluminium.
Thickness of wall .. .. .. 3/16 in.

IGNITION.

Type .. .. Magneto.
Number .. .. 4.
Make .. .. "Dixie 800."
Firing order 1L, 7R, 5L, 4R, 3L, 8R,
7L, 2R, 4L, 6R, 8L,
1R, 2L, 5R, 6L, 3R.

Advance .. .. 38 deg.

REDUCTION GEARS.

Crankshaft airscrew drive gear :
Pitch diameter .. .. .. 5.6 ins.
Pitch .. .. 5.
Number of teeth .. .. .. 28.
Width face .. .. 2 3/8 ins.
Diameter bolt circle .. .. .. 3 17/32 ins.
Number of bolts .. .. .. 9.
Diameter of bolts .. .. .. 7/16 in.
Airscrew shaft gear :
Pitch diameter .. .. .. 8.4 ins.
Pitch .. .. 5.
Number of teeth .. .. .. 42.
Width face .. .. 2 3/8 in.
Number of splines .. .. .. 8.
Width of splines .. .. .. 0.405.
Height of splines .. .. .. 0.094.

PROPELLER SHAFT.

Number of bearings .. .. .. 3.
Type of bearings .. .. .. Two ball, one plain.
Plain bearing .. .. Bronze babbitt lined.
Outside diameter at gear (over splines) 3 3/4 ins.
Outside diameter at rear end .. 3 5/16 ins.

Outside diameter at propeller .. 3 31/64 ins.
Inside diameter .. .. .. 2 61/64 ins.
Diameter airscrew flange .. .. 9 3/4 ins.
Diameter of bolt circle .. .. 7 7/8 ins.
Diameter of bolts .. .. .. 5/8 in.
Number of bolts .. .. .. 8.

The following further details have been extracted from the same source :—

CYLINDERS.

The cylinders are of cast iron in blocks of four. The water jackets are integral with the cylinder blocks, but open on each side below the inlet and exhaust ports. These openings are covered by screwed-on aluminium plates.

Three vertical valves are used per cylinder. The relative positions of these valves are shown in a figure, from which it is seen that each of the large exhaust valves is provided with a separate port, and that the four inlet valves of each pair of cylinders have a common inlet port.

All valve stems and seatings are amply water-jacketed.

Two ignition plug sockets are fitted to each cylinder in the side of the combustion chamber on the inlet side.

Crankshaft assembled, 410-h.p. American Bugatto.

Camshaft and Casing Assembly.

KING-BUGATTI—*continued*.

VALVE GEAR.

The valves are driven through rocking levers by overhead camshafts, one centrally over each row of cylinders.

Actually there are four separate shafts, one for each block of four cylinders, but the pair of camshafts for each line of cylinders are coupled together between the two cylinder blocks.

At this coupling a bevel wheel is attached, which engages with a gear at the head of a vertical shaft, which is in turn driven by the centre of the crankshaft.

Cross-section showing Oiling System of the American Bugatti.

Upper half of crankcase, American Bugatti engine.

Each camshaft with its gear and the attendant rocking levers is carried in a cast aluminium housing, which completely encloses the valve gearing.

PISTONS.

These are aluminium castings, with cut-away skirts.

CONNECTING RODS.

The connecting rods are steel forgings of I section, machined all over. The small ends have bronze bushes pressed in. The big ends are bronze-bushed and white metal lined.

CRANKSHAFTS.

As has already been stated, each of the two crankshafts is made in two pieces coupled together.

The junction is a fine taper cone, keyed and held tight by a nut on the small end. At this junction is a bevel wheel which drives a vertical shaft from which the magnetos and the camshaft of that line of cylinders are both driven.

Airscrew Shaft of the American Bugatti engine.

KING-BUGATTI—*continued.*

CRANKCASE.

Both upper and lower halves are aluminium castings. All crankshaft bearings are carried entirely by the upper half of the crankcase.

The lower bearing caps are carried by bridge pieces which pass nearly across the crankcase and support both crankshafts. The central bridge is a steel forging, as the bearings at this point are arranged to take any end thrust which may come on the crankshafts. All the other crankshaft bearings have end play, and the corresponding bridge pieces are aluminium castings.

All the main bearings are plain, bronze-bushed and white metal lined, but at the airscrew end of each shaft, beyond the pinion for the airscrew drive one ball-race journal is used.

THE AIRSCREW SHAFT.

This is a steel forging, with one airscrew hub flange solid with the shaft.

This shaft is bored out to a sufficient diameter to permit of firing a 37 m/m. Q.F. gun through it, and a clear passage through the crankcase in line with it is provided for the same purpose.

The spur wheel through which the shaft is driven from the crankshafts is carried by 9 bolts passing through a flange on the shaft.

Bugatti engine with Exhaust Pipes.

Sectional End View American Bugatti engine.

KING-BUGATTI—continued.

Deep grooved ball-races support the shaft on each side of the spur wheel and these races take the whole of the airscrew thrust.

IGNITION.

Four magnetos, each firing eight cylinders, are fitted. Two are placed on each side of the engine between the carburetters, with their shafts parallel to the crankshafts. Upon the vertical shaft driving the camshaft a bevel wheel is mounted inside the crankcase, and this drives a horizontal shaft at right angles to the crankshaft, passing out through the side of the crankcase. At its outer end this shaft carries another bevel wheel which drives the two magnetos on its own side of the engine. The magnetos appear to be fitted with an advance and retard mechanism of the spiral coupling type, which secures maximum spark intensity at all magneto timings.

LUBRICATION.

The oiling system is arranged on the dry sump system, with one pressure and one scavenging oil pump. One of these pumps is driven from the airscrew end of each crankshaft.

CARBURATION.

A separate carburetter is provided for each block of four cylinders. Gas is led to the inlet ports through water-jacketed manifolds.

The modifications from the original model are solely to points of detail design, the most important probably being an alteration to the cylinder head, providing freer water circulation, better valve cooling, and a slight increase in the distance between valve centres.

The original engine was fitted with an overhung airscrew shaft, with bearings inside the spur gear only, and the adoption of bearings on both sides of the gear should undoubtedly improve the engine.

Longitudinal Section of the Bugatti engine, showing the Oiling System.

H

CLERGÊT (French & British).

France :—CLERGÊT BLIN ET CIE, 37, Rue Cavé, Levallois (Seine).

Great Britain :—GWYNNES, Ltd., Hammersmith Iron Works, London, W.

THE CLERGET ENGINE.

This successful engine of the rotary type is the outcome of years of investigation and experiment carried out by the firm of Clerget Blin & Cie, of Paris, who, working from the lesser to the greater, have successively perfected more and more powerful models.

The sole licence and manufacturing rights for the British Empire are held by Gwynnes Ltd., of Hammersmith and Chiswick, who have the distinction of being the first constructors in this country, after the outbreak of war, to lay down the necessary and suitable plant, in entirely new works, for the manufacture of aeroplane engines.

The earlier types of Clerget engines being of small power, have now become obsolete, except for demonstration purposes, and the smallest engine now manufactured is an 80 h.p. with seven cylinders, which was at the time of its introduction a distinct advance upon previous models. It has done excellent service, and is still a useful and reliable engine for purposes where greater power is not demanded.

The advent of the 9-cylinder 110 h.p. type immediately placed the Clerget in a high position amongst engines of the rotary class, a position it has deservedly maintained by subsequent improvements introduced in the 130 h.p. and one later model.

The 110 h.p. and higher power motors have the advantage of great accessibility, the whole of the working parts being easily removable from the front end without the necessity of disconnecting the engine from the aeroplane. A trained mechanic can easily open up the engine for examination of the pistons, rods, valve cam gear, etc., and re-assemble the parts removed ready for flight well within 30 minutes.

Front View of the Gwynne-Clerget engine.   Type 7 Z.   80 h.p.

Front View of the Gwynne-Clerget engine.   Type 9 Z.   110 h.p.

CLERGÊT—continued.

From a cursory glance at the accompanying illustrations, the Clerget appears to have a strong family likeness to other engines of the rotary type, but a more careful examination will disclose distinctive features peculiar to this particular engine.

Whilst the success it has attained is partly due to its mechanical construction, there can be no doubt it has been rendered more certain by the great care and attention bestowed on the design of the various details, to make them particularly suitable for the duties they have to perform under the special flying conditions demanded of light high-speed aeroplanes ; quite a different matter to designing a showy test bench engine.

VALVE GEAR,

As to details, an essential feature of the Clerget design is the valve tappet driving gear, which is distinctly ingenious.

The inlet and exhaust tappets are actuated independently by two cam gear wheels which run on ball bearings centred on fixed eccentrics ; the cam gear wheels are driven by crown wheels fixed in the cam gear box, each crown wheel having twice as many teeth as the number of tappets to be operated. The cam gear wheel has two teeth less than its driving crown wheel, and one tooth in every four in the cam gear wheel is extended to form a cam tooth for actuating the tappets.

Owing to the decelerated rotary motion of the cam tooth during the short period it is in contact with the tappet, and to the special form of the tooth and tappet foot, there is very little sliding motion between them, friction and wear being reduced to a minimum.

CYLINDERS AND PISTONS.

The steel cylinders and connecting rods and aluminium pistons are all carefully proportioned in accordance with the demands of experience in order to obtain the desired results ; the crankshaft is more amply proportioned than is usual in rotary engines.

Half-Side View of the Gwynne-Clerget engine   Type 9 Z.   110 h.p.

Rear View of the Gwynne-Clerget engine.   Type 9 Z.   110 h.p.

CLERGÊT—continued.

It is interesting to note in this connection that in cases where machines driven by Clerget engines have crashed or had bad landings, the crankshafts have given a good account of themselves. The thrust has been calculated on sound mechanical principles, and the thrust bearing is of ample proportion and quite independent of either of the journal bearings.

The main particulars of the various types are given below in list form, and they show that the Clerget is an excellent example of modern rotary engines.

THE CLERGET ENGINE. TYPE 7Z. 80 H.P.

Specification.

No. of cylinders	7.
Bore	120 mm.
Stroke	150 mm.
Weight complete	234 lbs.
Compression ratio	4 : 1.
Normal h.p.	80.
Effective h.p.	85.
R.P.M.	1200.
Oil consumption per h.p. hour ..	.10 pints.
Petrol consumption per h.p. hour ..	.74 pints.

THE CLERGET ENGINE. TYPE 9Z. 110 H.P.

Specification.

No. of cylinders	9.
Bore	120 mm.
Stroke	160 mm.
Weight complete	397 lbs.
Compression ratio	4 : 1.
Normal h.p.	110.
Effective h.p.	115.
R.P.M.	1180.
Oil consumption per h.p. hour ..	.14 pints.
Petrol consumption per h.p. hour ..	.75 pints.

Front View of the Clerget engine.   Type 9 B.F.   140 h.p.

Side View of the Gwynne-Clerget engine.   Type 9 B.F.   140 h.p.

CLERGÊT—continued.

THE CLERGET ENGINE. TYPE 9B. 130 H.P.
Specification.

No. of cylinders	9.
Bore	120 mm.
Stroke	160 mm.
Weight complete	381 lbs.
Compression ratio	4 : 1.
Normal h.p.	130.
Effective h.p.	135.
R.P.M.	1250.
Oil consumption per h.p. hour ..	.09 pints.
Petrol consumption per h.p. hour ..	.74 pints.

THE CLERGET ENGINE. TYPE 9BF. 140 H.P.
Specification.

No. of cylinders	9.
Bore	120 mm.
Stroke	172 mm.
Weight complete	381 lbs.
Compression ratio	5.3 : 1.
Normal h.p.	140.
Effective h.p.	153.
R.P.M.	1250.
Oil consumption per h.p. hour ..	.11 pints.
Petrol consumption per h.p. hour ..	.59 pints.

THE CLERGET ENGINE. TYPE 11EB. 200 H.P.
Specification.

No. of cylinders	11.
Bore	120 mm.
Stroke	190 mm.
Weight complete	507 lbs.
Compression ratio	5 : 1.
Normal h.p.	200.
Effective h.p.	210.
R.P.M.	1300.
Oil consumption per h.p. hour ..	.11 pints.
Petrol consumption per h.p. hour ..	.68 pints.

Rear View of the Gwynne-Clerget engine. Type 9 B.F. 140 h.p.

General Arrangement Diagram of the Clerget engine. Type 9 B.F. 140 h.p.

CLERGÊT—continued.

THE CLERGET ENGINE. TYPE 16X. RADIAL. 400 H.P.

Specification.

No. of cylinders	..	..	..	16.
Bore	..	..	..	130 mm.
Stroke ..	..	..	..	130 mm.
Weight complete	..	..	..	750 lbs.
Compression ratio	..	..	..	5 : 1.
Normal h.p.	..	..	..	400.
Effective h.p.	..	..	..	420.
R.P.M.	..	..	..	1600.
Oil consumption per h.p. hour	..			.05 pints.
Petrol consumption per h.p. hour	..			.63 pints.

Half-Front View of the Gwynne-Clerget engine. Type 11 E.B. 200 h.p.

Front End View of the Gwynne-Clerget engine. Type 11 E.B. 200 h.p.

62b   **General Arrangement Diagram of the Water-cooled Clerget engine. Type 16 x. 400 h.p.**

THE COSMOS (British).

THE COSMOS ENGINEERING Co., Ltd. Offices :—Orient House, 42, 45, New Broad Street, London, E.C.2. Works :—Fishponds, Bristol.

One of the firms who have specialised in the radial engine and have pinned their faith to the type is the Cosmos Engineering Co., Ltd., of Bristol, formerly known as Brazil, Straker & Co., Ltd. To those who know their car histories little more need be

said. The Cosmos Co. is not entirely identical with the car people, but it is not far removed, as offspring go.

Research and experiment have led to the production of two radial engines by the firm—the " Mercury " of 315 h.p. and the "Jupiter" of 500 h.p., of fourteen and nine cylinders respectively. Other engines will be, and, indeed, are being, designed and produced, but upon the success of these two engines the makers have decided to commit themselves definitely to a programme of peace-time production.

THE " MERCURY " ENGINE.

The " Mercury " engine—two rows of seven cylinders each—was introduced to satisfy Air Board Scheme A issued in April, 1917. Its main details are :—Maximum diameter, 41⅝ ins. ; bore, 4¾ ins. ; stroke, 5 13-16 ins. ; power output, 315 b.h.p. at 1,800 r.p.m. (normal) and 347 at 2,000 r.p.m. (maximum) ; total weight, without fuel and oil tanks, but with the engine absolutely complete, even to the gun synchronising gear, 582 lbs.

Front View. " Mercury " engine.

Rear View. " Mercury " engine.

THE COSMOS—*continued*.

Front and rear view illustrations are reproduced herewith, which make quite clear the general lay-out of the unit, including the ignition apparatus of two 7-cylinder M.L. magnetos and Remy 14-cylinder distributor and the two carburetters bolted to circular induction chambers on the crankcase. The mixture is conducted from these chambers by separate induction pipes to each cylinder and admitted through one inlet valve. The three overhead valves per cylinder may be seen in the front view of the engine; the tappet gear is of the roller type arranged in a circular unit, which can be assembled complete before attachment to the crankcase.

As regards constructional details not apparent in the illustrations, the cylinders are turned from a solid billet, the fins integral with the barrel. Separate aluminium heads are bolted onto the cylinder barrels. These heads are so designed as to obtain effective cooling of the valve seatings and ports, and to avoid all distortion. The crankshaft is of the two-throw type on roller bearings throughout. The rollers of the big-end bearings run direct on the crank-pin, and each connecting-rod has its own crankshaft bearing, so that the seven rods of each row of cylinders lie side by side on their respective crank-pins. An interesting feature of this part of the engine is that the whole crankshaft assembly can be withdrawn complete, with the connecting-rods in position. The tappet gear is of the roller type, the tappets operated by two cam rings, each having three cams and working at one-sixth engine speed.

Front View. " Jupiter " engine.

Rear View. " Jupiter " engine.

THE COSMOS—*continued*.

Lubrication is on the dry sump principle, and the oil is drawn by one pump from the tank mounted in the fuselage, delivered under pressure to the hollow crankshaft, and, after being led by separate leads to all necessary parts, is returned to the tank by another pump.

On this engine the airscrew is ungeared, the airscrew boss being driven direct through serrations on the crankshaft. The airscrew boss is to Air Board standard design.

On the Bristol Scout Type "F" this engine has been given exhaustive flying tests, and has given extremely satisfying results.

THE 300 H.P. "MERCURY" RADIAL AERO-ENGINE.

Specification.

No. of cylinders	14.
Bore	$4\frac{3}{8}$ ins.
Stroke	$5\frac{13}{16}$ ins.
Normal b.h.p.	315 b.h.p.
Maximum b.h.p.	347 h.p.
Normal revs. per min.	1800.
Maximum revs. per min.	2000.
Total weight	587 lbs.
Maximum dia. of engine	$41\frac{5}{8}$ ins.
Ignition	2 M.L. magnetos and a 14-cylinder Remy distributor and coil.

THE "JUPITER" ENGINE.

The rear view of the "Jupiter" engine makes clear many of its constructional features. There are nine cylinders made on lines similar to those of the "Mercury," but the bore and stroke are $5\frac{3}{4}$ ins. and $7\frac{1}{2}$ ins. respectively, while the power output is 450 h.p. at 1,800 r.p.m. as an ungeared engine or 500 at 2,000 r.p.m. with a geared down airscrew. The weight of the ungeared model is 662 lbs. complete, including electric starter, but without fuel and oil tanks.

AN IMPORTANT FEATURE.

From the illustration the engine might be taken to be of the rotary type, owing to the arrangement of the inlet pipes, which form part of a very interesting induction system. As will be seen, three carburetters are bolted to the crankcase cover, which also forms one side of the induction chamber.

This induction chamber is annular, and into it is fitted a spiral fluted aluminium casting which acts as a gas distributor to the cylinders. Each of the three carburetters supplies three cylinders *via* the spiral, which delivers the carburetted charge to the correct cylinder in turn, with the advantage that each cylinder is more efficiently supplied with mixture, and, if one cuts out, none of the others is affected. On bench tests the arrangement has proved itself a success.

Two inlet and two exhaust valves are fitted per cylinder, operated by two cam rings, each with four cams running at one-eighth engine speed, through tappets mounted in the front of the engine. Ignition is by two 9-cylinder Thompson Bennet magnetos driven by bevel gearing from the crankshaft and mounted on the back cover of the crankcase—i.e., the cover of the induction chamber—in such a position that the contact breakers are readily accessible.

With the exception of the connecting-rod assembly, the engine is, in essentials, similar to the "Mercury." A master connecting-rod with articulated rods is used. The bearing of the master rod is white metal lined, all other bearings in the engine are of the roller type. It is hardly necessary to point out that the crankshaft in the "Jupiter" engine is of the single throw type.

Spiral Fluted Induction Ring. Induction chamber removed. "Jupiter" engine.

65b

THE COSMOS—*continued.*

THE 500 H.P. "JUPITER" RADIAL AERO-ENGINE.
Specification.

No. of cylinders	9.
Bore	$5\frac{3}{4}$ ins.
Stroke	$7\frac{1}{2}$ ins.
Normal b.h.p.	450 h.p. (Mark i). 500 h.p. (Mark ii geared).
Normal revs. per min.	1800 (Mark i). 1300 (Mark ii geared).
Total weight	662 lbs. (Mark i).
Ignition	2 9-cylinder Thompson Bennett magnetos..

In addition to these engines, the Cosmos firm are to manufacture a light cheap 3-cylinder engine, to be known as the "Lucifer," and are experimenting with a much larger engine than the two already described.

Back Cover Unit, "Jupiter" engine.

CURTISS (American).

THE CURTISS AEROPLANE CO., Buffalo, New York.

British Representative : Clun House, Surrey Street, Strand, W.C.

250 h.p. Model.

Type : Water-cooled " V."

No. of cylinders : 12.

Bore : 5 in.   Stroke : 7 in.

R.P.M. : 1,400–1,500.

Cylinders : High carbon steel, cast separately.

Valves : Overhead.   Inlet, nickel steel ; exhaust, tungsten steel.

Carburetters : 4 Zenith, each supplying 3 cylinders.

Ignition : Two 12-spark magnetos.

Lubrication : Pressure feed from reservoir.

Weight : Engine, 1,125 lbs.   Radiator, 120 lbs.   Water : 100 lbs.

Dimensions : Length, 84⅝ in. ; width, 34⅛ in. ; depth, —— in. ; width at bed, 30½ in. ; height from bed, 21¼ in. ; depth from bed, 18½ in.

Other models on same lines, but with only eight cylinders, with the following bores and strokes :—

	Bore.	Stroke.	r.p.m.	Wt. in lbs.
90 h.p.	100 m/m.	125 m/m.	1,200	325
100 h.p.	105 m/m.	125 m/m.	1,250	340
160 h.p.	125 m/m.	180 m/m.	1,100	700

In 1918 produced the K–6 and K–12 models, designed by Mr. Kirkham.

The feature of this engine is that the cylinders and the top part of the crank-case are cast of aluminium alloy in one unit.

Pressed steel cylinder-liners are used.   The cylinder heads are cast in one unit and bolted to the top of the other casting.

Made in two models :—

K–6—6 cylinder vertical—150 h.p. direct drive.

K–12—12 cylinder Vee—375 h.p. gear drive.

The 250 h.p. Curtiss engine.

CURTISS—*continued*.

Side View of the Curtiss K–12, minus exhaust manifold.

Side View of the Curtiss engine, Type K-6.   150 h.p.

CURTISS—*continued.*

Front End of the Curtiss engine, Type K–6. 150 h.p.

Side View of the Curtiss engine, Type O X–5. 100 h.p.

THE 150 h.p. CURTISS-KIRKHAM AERO ENGINE.

Specification :

Type	K–6
No. of cylinders	6
Bore	$4\frac{1}{2}$ in.
Stroke..	6 in.
B.H.P.	150
Engine speed	1700 r.p.m,

THE 375 h.p. CURTISS-KIRKHAM AERO ENGINE.

Specification :

Type	K–12
No. of cylinders	12
Bore	$4\frac{1}{2}$ in.
Stroke..	6 in.
B.H.P.	375
Engine speed..	2250 r.p.m.

69b

DUESENBERG (American).

THE DUESENBERG MOTORS CORPORATION

Edgewater, New Jersey and Chicago, Ill.

Made the following types in 1917-18:—

4 Cylinder Vertical.
Bore : 4¾ in.   Stroke : 7 in.
Weight (all on) : 509 lbs.
(Without demultiplication gear 436 lbs.)
H.P. : 125 at 2,100 r.p.m. (propeller speed 1,210 r.p.m.)
Also 300 h.p. " V " type, as shown in end view drawing.

Have recently produced the 16-cylinder Vee engine, stated to be of 850 h.p.   Illustrated herewith.

End view of the Duesenberg 300 h.p. " V " type engine showing valve-rockers and horizontal valves.

The 850 h.p. Model H. Duesenberg 16-cylinder Aero engine.

FIAT (Italian).

Societa Anonyma F.I.A.T., Turin.

The Fiat 300 h.p. aviation engine, officially known as the A-12, is a 6-cylinder water-cooled vertical type of 160 × 180 mm. bore and stroke.

The cylinders are separate steel forgings, each one carrying four inclined valves in the head and fitted with a welded-on sheet steel water-jacket, having a patented flexible joint at the base.

The cylinders are mounted on an aluminium crank chamber with detachable "dry" sump, all the oil, which is delivered to the bearings under pressure, being contained in a tank independent of the engine.

Valves are inclined in the head and are operated by an overhead enclosed camshaft.

There is a single cam with forked rocker for each pair of valves—two inlets, or two exhausts.

Pistons are aluminium, and connecting rods are I-section.

All the valve operating mechanism is at the rear of the engine. This consists of an enclosed vertical shaft, driven by bevel gearing from the crankshaft, and operating the camshaft by means of a pair of bevel pinions.

At the base of the vertical shaft, and to left and right of it are two 6-cylinder magnetos. Thus the charge in each cylinder is fired by a pair of plugs.

At the base of a downward extension of the magneto driving shaft is the centrifugal water pump contained with an aluminium housing.

The carburetter is a dual Fiat type, with independent float chambers and mixing chambers, but forming a common aluminium casting and having a common water-jacket around the mixing chamber.

The airscrew is mounted direct on the crankshaft and rotates anti-clockwise at a normal speed of 1,700 revolutions a minute.

The 300 h.p. Fiat engine is used by all the Allied air services. Among its most notable performances are the non-stop flight of 1,040 miles from Turin to Naples and return, and a flight from Turin to London with passenger, guns, ammunition, provisions and mail.

In addition to the 300 h.p. 6-cylinder vertical engine, the Fiat Company produces a 12-cylinder V-engine of 700 h.p.

Fiat 300 h.p.
Bore : 160 m/m.
Stroke : 180 m/m.
No of cylinders : 6.
R.P.M. : 1,700.
H.P. : 300.

No details are available as to the Specifications of the 400 h.p., and 700 h.p. Engines.

Rear End of the Fiat 300 h.p. 6-cylinder engine (1918 type).

FIAT—*continued*.

THE FIAT AIRSHIP ENGINES.

The majority of Italian airships were equipped with Fiat engines. The size and type of engine varied with the airship, but a very popular installation was a twin group composed of two four cylinder engines placed side by side, and as close together as possible, in a channel section frame.

These engines have a bore and stroke of 110 by 190 mm.

The cylinders are a block casting, with enclosed valves in the head, and large aluminium water jacket plates on the sides and the ends.

The overhead camshaft is operated by means of an enclosed vertical shaft and bevel gearing, and advantage is taken of this shaft to mount the starting gear by means of a lever and bevel gearing.

The carburetter is placed on the outside of each engine, and the exhaust is on the inside.

At the base of the vertical shaft the water pump and the high-tension magneto are driven by means of bevel gearing. These two organs are opposed, so that the magneto distributors and contact breakers are on the outside in each case.

Each engine is fitted with a light fly-wheel and a spiral spring clutch, the control of which is by means of a lever at the forward end of the engine.

From the clutch shaft the airscrew shaft is driven by means of bevel gearing, this shaft having an inclination of about 45 deg. from the vertical.

Front end of the 12-cylinder Fiat engine. 400 h.p.

FIAT—*continued.*

Rear View of the 12 cylinder Fiat engine.   700 h.p.

Rear end of the 12 cylinder Fiat engine.   700 h.p.

73b

FIAT—*continued.*

Front View of thc Fiat Twin Airship engines.

Rear end of Fiat Twin Airship
Engines.

GANZ-FIAT AERO MOTOR CO. LTD. (Austrian)

Formed in 1916 with a capital of £100,000 by the Anglo-Austrian Bank, the Maschinen-und-Schiffbau A.G., Ganz-Danubius, at Budapest, and the Austrian Fiat Motor Works, Ltd., originally a branch of the Italian Fiat company.

It may in this respect further be mentioned that the rest of the Austrian-Hungarian automobile industry (Laurin & Clement, Alpha, M.A.G.F.A., Hungarian Benz Co.) has, similarly to the conditions of the other belligerent countries too, supplied aero engines (all of vertical, water-cooled type and general automobile engine features).

GENERAL ORDNANCE (American).

THE GENERAL ORDNANCE COMPANY, Derby, Connecticut.

Were constructors in 1917 of a new engine of water-cooled " V " type.

No. of cylinders : 8.

Bore : $4\frac{3}{4}$ in.   Stroke : $6\frac{1}{2}$ in.

H.P. : 200.

Weight all on : $876\frac{1}{4}$ lbs.

GNÔME & RHÔNE (French & British).

SOCIÉTÉ DES MOTEURS GNÔME & RHÔNE, 3, Rue la Boétie, Paris.

GNÔME & LE RHÔNE ENGINE Co., Ltd., 47, Victoria St., S.W.

Also made by THE GENERAL VEHICLE CO., Long Island City, Long Island, U.S.A.

Also made by LA SOCIETA ITALIANA MOTORI GNÔME & RHÔNE, 73, Strada Veneria, Madonna di Compagna, Italy.

GNÔME ENGINES.

Monosoupape type :—

(Type A)   80 h.p. 7 cylinders, 110×150 m/m (1200 r.p.m.).

(Type B 2) 100 h.p. 9 cylinders, 110×150 m/m (1200 r.p.m.), 260 lbs.

(Type N) 160 h.p. 9 cylinders, 150×170 m/m (1350 r.p.m.), 340 lbs.

Petrol consumption of Type B Mono. giving 106 h.p. at 1230 revs., is ·778 pints per h.p. per hour.

LE RHÔNE ENGINES.

80 h.p. 7 cylinders, 105×140 m/m (1200 r.p.m.), 199 lbs.

120 h.p. 9 cylinders, 112×175 m/m (1200 r.p.m.), 308 lbs.

Side and front view of 100 h.p. Monosoupape Gnôme engine.

GNÔME & RHÔNE—*continued.*

SOCIÉTE DES MOTEURS GNOME

MOTEUR MONOSOUPAPE Type B

9.Cylindres — Alésage 110 — Course 150

The internal arrangement of the Monosoupape Gnôme engine of 1914. This has since been improved by altering the valve gear and removing the hand-control device.

Side view of 110 h.p. Le Rhône engine, showing valve rockers and attachment of inlet pipes ; also arrangement of magneto and main shaft.

GNÔME & RHÔNE—*continued.*

Front view of 110 h.p. Le Rhône engine.

Back view of 110 h.p. Le Rhône engine.

GNÔME & RHÔNE—*continued.*

MOTEUR

LE RHONE

TYPE. J-110 HP

alèsage 112 – course 170

Section of the 110 h.p. Le Rhône.   112 mm. bore × 170 mm. stroke.

GRADE (German).

GRADE made only engines for his own monoplanes.

GREEN (British).

THE GREEN ENGINE Co., Ltd., 166, Piccadilly, W.

100 h.p. Model.
Type : Water-cooled vertical.
No. of cylinders : 6.
Bore : 140 m/m.   Stroke : 152 m/m.
R.P.M. : 1,200.
Cylinders : Steel, copper water jackets.
Valves : Overhead camshaft.

150 h.p. Model.
Type : Water-cooled vertical.
No. of cylinders : 6.
Bore : 142 m/m.   Stroke : 178 m/m.
R.P.M. : 1,200.
Cylinders : Steel, copper water jackets.
Valves : Overhead camshaft with vertical gear drive.

300 h.p. Model.
Type : Water-cooled " V."
No. of cylinders : 12
Bore : 142 m/m.   Stroke : 178 m/m.
R.P.M. : 1,200.
Cylinders : Steel, copper waterjackets.
Valves : Overhead camshafts with vertical gear drive.
Carburetter : Twin.
Ignition : Twin magnetos.
Lubrication : Forced feed.

Part top view of the 300 h.p. Green engine.

79b   **A batch of the 300 h.p. Green engines ready for delivery.**

GREEN—*continued.*

Front End of the 450 h.p. Green engine.

Rear End of the 450 h.p. Green engine, which is practically a " Broad Arrow " version of the 300 h.p. type.

HALL-SCOTT (American).

THE HALL-SCOTT MOTOR CAR Co., Inc.   Gen. Offices :
Crocker Building, San Francisco.

Built in 1917, the following model.   No further information
available.

212 b.h.p., at 1,666 r.p.m.
Bore and stroke, 5 in. and 7 in.
Weight, 502 lbs.

HIERONYMUS (Austrian and German).

ESSLER, WARSCHALOWSKI & Co., Vienna.

Designed by Hieronymus, the famous racing motor driver. The
Warschalowski Brothers were early pilots and manufacturers of
the *Autoplan* biplanes (*Henry Farman* box kite type with steel-
tube landing chassis).

Also made under license by the Loeb Motor Works in Berlin.

Exhaust–side View of the L. 6 type Hall-Scott 6–cylinder engine.

Inlet–side View of the L. 6 type Hall-Scott.   6 cylinder.

HISPANO-SUIZA (Spanish, French, British and American).

Head Office :—LA SOCIEDAD HISPANO-SUIZA, Barcelona. Spain.

U.S.A :—THE WRIGHT-MARTIN AIRCRAFT CORPORATION Simplex Works, New Brunswick, New Jersey, U.S.A.

Also manufactured in France and in England.

One of the most successful engines in the world, being light for its weight, reliable, and designed so as to fit neatly into an aeroplane.

The distinguishing feature of the engine is the use of aluminium Monobloc cylinder castings into which steel liners are screwed.

Made in three sizes :—

180 h.p. 8-cylinder. V-type, direct drive.
220 h.p. 8-cylinder. V-type, geared drive.
300 h.p. 8-cylinder. V-type, geared drive.

Model A. 180 h.p.

Bore : 4.7245" } 4 cylinders in each block of the " V."
Stroke : 5.1182" }
Piston Displacement : 718 cubic inches.
H.P. : 180, at 1750 r.p.m.
Weight, without radiator, water, oil or exhaust pipes: 445 lbs.
Fuel consumption : .5 lbs. per h.p. per hour.
Oil consumption : 3 quarts per hour.

The 220 h.p. type is the same as the 180 h.p., but running at 2,200 r.p.m.

The 300 h.p. type is as the 220 h.p., but with bigger bore and longer stroke.

THE WRIGHT-MARTIN HISPANO-SUIZA AERO ENGINE.

Specification :

Type	..	..	..	Model 1.
No. of cylinders	..	..	8 (Vee type)
Bore	..	..	..	120 m/m. (4.724 in.)
Stroke	..	..	..	130 m/m. (5.118 in.)
Normal b.h.p.	..	..	150
Normal r.p.m.	..	..	1,500
Maximum b.h.p.	..	..	170
Maximum r.p.m.	..	..	1,700
Weight (with airscrew)	..	455 lbs.
Fuel Consumption	..	..	.51 lbs. per h.p. per hour
Oil „	..	..	.03 lbs. per h.p. per hour

Type A. Hispano-Suiza engine, as built by the Wright-Martin Corporation at the New Brunswick Works, New Jersey, U.S.A.

HISPANO-SUIZA—*continued*.

Longitudinal Part Section of the Standard Hispano-Suiza engine.

Cross–Section of the Hispano-Suiza Engine.

ISOTTA-FRASCHINI (Italian).

IL FABRICA AUTOMOBILI ISOTTA FRASCHINI, Via Monte Rosa 79, Milan.

The Isotta Fraschini firm are famous as motor car, aeromotor and big marine motor builders. Their aeromotors were used first on the hydro-aeroplanes of the Italian Navy, and later on biplanes of *Voisin* type before Italy came into the war, and they have since been used successfully on *Caproni* triple engine biplanes. The newer Isotta-Fraschini engines, type V6 have been adopted also in the Italian " chaser " aeroplanes. Moreover, the Isotta-Fraschini is the only Italian firm that has made a speciality in the manufacture of big marine motors from 300 to 800 h.p. which have been adopted in a large scale by the Italian Navy on the " chaser " boats against submarines.

No fresh particulars are available since last year.

190 h.p. Model.—Type V4B.

Type : Water-cooled vertical.
No. of cylinders : 6.
R.P.M. : 1,450 (direct drive).
Cylinders : In pairs—steel water-jackets.
Valves : Overhead camshafts and valves.
Carburetters : Twin.
Ignition : 2 six-spark magnetos.
Lubrication : Forced feed.

245 h.p. Model.

Type : Water-cooled vertical.
No. of cylinders : 8.
Bore : 130 × 190 m/m.
R.P.M. : 1,300 (direct drive).
Cylinders : In pairs—copper water-jackets
Valves : Overhead camshafts.
Carburetter : Twin.
Ignition : 2 eight-spark magnetos.
Lubrication : Forced feed.

245 h.p. Model.—Type V5.

Type : Water-cooled vertical.
No. of cylinders : 8.
R.P.M. : 1,400 (direct drive).
Cylinders : In pairs—steel water-jackets.
Valves : Overhead camshafts and valves.
Carburetter : Twin.
Ignition : 2 eight-spark magnetos.
Lubrication : Forced feed.

A Later type Isotta-Fraschini 6-cylinder model.

LAWRENCE (American).

LAWRENCE MOTOR Co.,

Make the engine described and illustrated herewith.

THE LAWRENCE 60 h.p. RADIAL ENGINE.

Specification :

Type	L–1.
No. of cylinders	3 (Y–type).
Bore	4.25 in.
Stroke	5.25 in.
Normal B.H.P.	60.
Maximum B.H.P.	63.
Normal r.p.m.	1900
Maximum r.p m.	2100
Weight complete (with air-screw hub) ..	130 lbs.

LOEB & CO. AUTOMOBILE WORKS.

Berlin, Charlottenburg.

Manufacturers of the Austrian Hiero aero engines by licence. Said to have made aeroplanes also.

Side View of the Lawrence 60 h.p. Air-cooled Radial engine

Front and Rear View of the Lawrence 60 h.p. engine.

LIBERTY (American).

Manufactured wholly and in part by a number of automobile firms in the U.S.A.

The Liberty engine, or parts of it, is being made by every motor factory in the United States. It is an officially designed engine, intended to fulfil all purposes in air war.

THE OFFICIAL ACCOUNT.

The following account of the origin of the engine was published officially in 1917.

It was designed by Major Vincent, of the Packard Co., and Major Hall, of the Hall-Scott Co., under circumstances herein-after officially related.

The first hand-made engines have given good results and good weight for power.

The successful completion of the U.S.A. or Liberty aircraft engine was announced in an official statement issued by the Secretary of War, on August 12th, 1917. The statement reads :—

" The United States aviation engine has passed its final tests. They were successful and gratifying. The new engine, designated by the Signal Service as the ' Liberty engine,' is now the main reliance of the United States in the rapid production in large numbers of high-powered battle planes for service in the war. In power, speed, serviceability and minimum weight the new engine invites comparison with the best that the European war has produced.

" I regard the invention and rapid development of this engine as one of the really big accomplishments of the United States since its entry into the war. The engine was brought about through the co-operation of more than a score of engineers, who pooled their skill and trade secrets in the war emergency, work-ing with the encouragement of the Aircraft Production Board, the War Department and the Bureau of Standards.

" The story of the production of this engine is a remarkable one. Probably the war has produced no greater single achievement.

" One of the first problems which confronted the War Department and the Aircraft Production Board after the declaration of hostilities was to produce a dependable engine. Two courses were open. One was to encourage manufacturers to develop their own types, the other to bring the best of all types together and develop a standard.

" The necessity for speed and quantity of production resulted in a choice of the latter course, and a standard engine became our engineering objective.

" Two of the best engineers in the country, who had never before seen each other, were brought together at Washington, and the problem of producing an all-American engine at the earliest possible moment was presented to them. Their first

conference, on June 3rd, lasted from the afternoon until half-past two o'clock in the morning.

" These two engineers were figuratively locked in a room in a Washington hotel and charged with the development of an aeroplane engine for use by American aviators over the battle-fields of Europe. For five days neither man left the suite of rooms engaged for them. Consulting engineers and draughts-men from various sections of the country were brought to Washington to assist them. The work in the draughting room proceeded continuously, day and night. Each of the two engineers in immediate charge of engine development alternately worked a twenty-four hour shift.

The Liberty Engine.   Three-quarter View—Airscrew End.

(*Photograph by courtesy of the Technical Department (Aircraft), Ministry of Munitions.*)

LIBERTY—*continued.*

" An inspiring feature of this work was the aid rendered by consulting engineers and motor manufacturers, who gave up their trade secrets under the emergency of war needs. Realising that the new design would be a Government design and no firm or individual would reap selfish benefit because of its making, the motor manufacturers patriotically revealed their trade secrets and made available trade processes of great commercial value. These industries have also contributed the services of approximately 200 of their best draughtsmen.

" The two engineers locked together in a hotel room in this city promised the Government, if given an opportunity, they would design a satisfactory aero-engine before a working model could be brought from Europe.

" A remarkable American engine was actually produced three weeks before any model could have been brought from Europe. It was promised that this engine would be developed before the Fourth of July. Twenty-eight days after the drawings were started the new engine was set up. This was on July 3rd.

" In order to have the engine in Washington and in actual running order at the nation's capital on Independence Day the perfected engine was sent from a Western city in a special express car. The journey was made in twenty-one hours, and four young men guarded the engine *en route* to Washington and personally attended to its transfer from one railroad to another.

" With the need for speed as an incentive, tools for building the first engine were made even before the drawings were finished —on the assumption that they would be correct.

" Parts of the first engine were turned out at twelve different factories, located all the way from Connecticut to California. When the parts were assembled the adjustment was perfect and the performance of the engine was wonderfully gratifying. This in itself demonstrated the capabilities of American factories when put to the test and when thoroughly organised for emergency work of this sort.

" One of the chief rules outlined at the beginning of the designing work was that no engineer should be permitted to introduce construction which had not been tried out. There was no time for theorising. The new engine is successful because it embodies the best thought of engineering experience to date. Not only did this country furnish ideas through celebrated consulting engineers, but the representatives in the United States, of England, France and Italy co-operated in the development of this motor.

" Thirty days after the assembling of the first engine, preliminary tests justified the Government in formally accepting the engine as the best aircraft engine produced in any country. The final tests confirmed our faith in the new engine in every degree.

(*Photograph by courtesy of the Technical Department (Aircraft), Ministry of Munitions.*)

The Liberty Engine—Ignition End.

" Both the flying and altitude tests of the new engine have been gratifying. One test was conducted at Pike's Peak, where the United States aviation engine performed satisfactorily at this high altitude. One of the engines in an aeroplane broke the American altitude record in a recent flying test.

" While it is not deemed expedient to discuss in detail the performances and mechanics of the new engine, it may be said that standardisation is a chief factor in the development of the

LIBERTY—*continued*.

Government's engine. Cylinders, pistons and every other part of the engine have been standardised. They may be produced rapidly and economically by a great many factories operating under Government contracts. They may be as rapidly assembled, either by these plants or at a central assembly plant.

"The new engine amounts practically to an international model. It embodies the best there is in American engineering and the best features of European models, so far as it has been possible to adapt the latter to American manufacturing methods.

"The two engineers most directly connected with the production of the United States aviation engine had before them not only the blueprints and models of the most successful engines the war has produced, but also every available American suggestion. Men skilled in the invention of motors, both automobile and aeroplane, advised these engineers, who were charged with the duty of providing rapidly and unerringly an engine which would embody every essential of war-time use. Non-essential complexities were consistently discarded by these engineers. The result was a composite design of maximum power, minimum weight, great speed capability and adaptability to quick production.

"The standardisation of parts materially simplifies the problem of repair and maintenance. Spare parts will be promptly available at all times. Even the cylinders are designed separately. It is possible to build the new engine in four models, ranging from four to twelve cylinders, and under the standardisation plan now worked out an eight-cylinder or a twelve-cylinder model can be made, using the same standard cylinders, pistons, valves, cam shafts, and so on.

"With the completion of final tests of the engine—tests which satisfied and gratified both expert engineers and army officers—progress already has been made toward organising industry for the manufacture of the new machines and deliveries will begin within a comparatively short time."

THE LIBERTY ENGINE.

The first official technical announcement concerning the Liberty was made by the War Department on May 15th, 1918. The statement read :—

"The design of the parts of the Liberty engine were based on the following :—

"Cylinder.—The designers of the cylinders for the Liberty engine followed the practice used in the German Mercédès, English Rolls-Royce, French Lorraine Dietrich, and Italian Isotta Fraschini before the war and during the war. The cylinders are made of steel inner shells, surrounded by pressed steel water jackets. The Packard Company by long experiment had developed a method of applying these steel water jackets. The valve cages are drop forgings welded into the cylinder heads.

The principal departure from European practice is in the location of the hold-down flange, which is several inches above the mouth of the cylinder, and the unique method of manufacture evolved by the Ford Company. The output is now approximately 1,700 cylinder forgings per day.

"Cam Shaft and Valve Mechanism Above Cylinder Heads.—The design for the above is based on the Mercédès, but was improved for automatic lubrication, without wasting oil, by the Packard Motor Car Company.

"Cam Shaft Drive.—The cam shaft drive was copied almost

FRONT ELEVATION

Elevation of the Liberty "Twelve"—Airscrew End.

Elevation of the Liberty "Twelve"—Pump End.

LIBERTY—*continued.*

entirely from the Hall-Scott motor ; in fact, several of the gears used in the first sample engine were supplied by the Hall-Scott Motor Car Company. This type of drive is used by Mercédès, Hispano-Suiza, and others.

"Angle Between Cylinders.—In the Liberty engine the included angle between the cylinders is 45 degrees ; in all other existing 12-cylinder engines it is 60 degrees. This feature is new with the Liberty engine, and was adopted for the purpose of bringing each row of cylinders nearer the vertical and closer together, so as to save width and head resistance. By the narrow angle greater strength is given to the crank case and vibration is reduced.

"Electric Generator and Ignition.—A Delco ignition system is used. It was especially designed for the Liberty engine, to save weight and to meet the special conditions due to firing 12 cylinders with an included angle of 45 degrees.

"Pistons.—The pistons of the Liberty engine are of Hall-Scott designs.

"Connecting Rods.—Forked or straddle type connecting rods, first used on the French De Dion car and on the Cadillac motor cars in this country, are used.

"Crank Shaft.—Crank shaft design followed the standard 12-cylinder practice, except as to oiling. Crank case follows standard practice. The 45 degree angle and the flange location on the cylinders made possible a very strong box section.

"Lubrication.—The first system of lubrication followed the German practice of using one pump to keep the crank case empty, delivering into an outside reservoir, and another pump forcing oil under pressure to the main crank shaft bearings. This lubrication system also followed the German practice in allowing the overflow in the main bearings to travel out the face of the crank cheeks to a scupper, which collected this excess of crankpin lubrication. This is very economical in the use of oil and is still the standard German practice.

"The present system is similar to the first practice, except that the oil, while under pressure, is not only fed to main bearings, but through holes inside of crank cheeks to crank pins, instead of feeding these crank pins through scuppers. The difference between the two oiling systems consists of carrying oil for the crank pins through a hole inside the crank cheek, instead of up the outside face of the crank cheek.

"Propeller Hub.—The Hall-Scott propeller hub design was adapted to the power for the Liberty engine.

"Water Pump.—The Packard type of water pump was adapted to the Liberty.

"Carburetter.—A Carburetter was developed by the Zenith Carburetter Company for the Liberty engine.

"Bore and Stroke.—The bore and stroke of the Liberty engine is 5 by 7 ins., the same as the Hall-Scott A5 and A7 engines, and as in the Hall-Scott 12-cylinder engine.

"Remarks.—The idea of developing Liberty engines of 4, 6, 8, and 12 cylinders with the above characteristics was first thought of about May 25th, 1917. The idea was developed in conference with representatives of the British and French missions, May 28th to June 1st, was submitted in the form of sketches at a joint meeting of the Aircraft (Production) Board and the joint Army and Navy Technical Board, June 4th. The first sample was an 8-cylinder model, delivered to the Bureau of Standards, July 3rd, 1917. The 8-cylinder model, however, was never put into production, as advices from France indicated that demands for increased power would make the 8-cylinder model obsolete before it could be produced.

"Work was then concentrated on the 12-cylinder engine, and one of the experimental engines passed the fifty-hour test August 25th, 1917.

"After the preliminary drawings were made, engineers from the leading engine builders were brought to the Bureau of Standards, where they inspected the new designs and made suggestions, most of which were incorporated in the final design. At the same time expert production men were making suggestions that would facilitate production.

LONGITUDINAL SECTION

Longitudinal section of the Liberty Twelve

LIBERTY—*continued*.

"The Liberty 12-cylinder engine passed the fifty-hour test, showing, as the official report of August 25th, 1917 records, that the fundamental construction is such that very satisfactory service, with a long life and high order of efficiency, will be given by this power plant, and that the design has passed from the experimental stage into the field of proven engines.

"An engine committee was organised informally, consisting of engineers and production managers of the Packard, Ford, Cadillac, Lincoln, Marmon and Trego companies. This committee met at frequent intervals, and it is to this group of men that the final development of the Liberty engine is largely due."

The prime consideration of the designing engineers was to have a motor that would be efficient from every modern standpoint, and at the same time suitable for production on a rapid basis. Both results have apparently been achieved.

The following dimensions and characteristics are of interest :—

GENERAL DATA.

Number and arrangement of cylinders	Twelve-Vee
Included angle	45 deg.
Bore	5 in.
Stroke	7 in.
Stroke-bore ratio	1.4 : 1
Area of one piston	19.635 sq. in.
Total piston area	234.62 sq. in.
Swept volume of one cylinder	137.445 cu. ins.
Displacement of motor	1649.5 cu. in.
Compression ratio (Army)	5 4 : 1
Compression ratio (Navy)	5. : 1
Normal brake h.p.	400 at 1750 r.p.m.
Type of Valve gear	Overhead cam shaft and valve rockets
Number of carburettors	Two Duplex Zenith

VALVES.

Number per cylinder	One inlet and one exhaust
Outside diameter	$2\frac{3}{4}$ in.
Port diameter	$2\frac{1}{2}$ in.
Width of seat	$\frac{1}{8}$ in.
Angle of seat	30 deg.
Valve lift (inlet)	7/16 in.
Valve lift (exhaust)	$\frac{3}{8}$ in.
Diameter of stem	7/16 in.
Length of valve	6 3/16 in.
Number of springs per valve	2 concentric
Length of spring in position	2 3/16 in.
Mean diameter of coils (large spring)	1 7/16 in.
Mean diameter of coils (small spring)	1 in.
Inlet rocker clearance	.015 in.
Exhaust rocker clearance	.020 in.
Included angles of valves	27 deg.

Three-quarter Top View from Airscrew End, Liberty Engine.

Three-quarter Top View from Pump End, Liberty Engine.

LIBERTY—continued.

CYLINDERS.

Overall height of cylinders	16 13/16 in.
Length of projection in crankcase ..	57/64 in.
Diameter of cylinder over water-jacket	$6\frac{3}{8}$ in. max.
Diameter of cylinder over water-jacket	5 13/16 in. min.
Thickness of flange (base)	$\frac{1}{4}$ in.
Number of studs	10
Diameter of stud	$\frac{3}{8}$ in.
Thickness of water-jacket	3/64 in.
Thickness of cylinder head	3/16 in.
Thickness of combustion chamber-wall	5/32 in.
Thickness of cylinder barrel ..	$\frac{1}{4}$ in.
Number of reinforcing ribs ..	8
Thickness of valve ports	$\frac{1}{4}$ in.
Diameter of port at valve	$2\frac{1}{2}$ in.
Diameter of port at flange	$2\frac{1}{8}$ in.
Number of spark plugs	2 per cylinder

PISTONS.

Type of piston (Army)	Crowned
Type of piston (Navy)	Flat
Material	Aluminium
Length of piston	5 in.
Length to diameter ratio	1 : 1
Number of rings per piston ..	3
Position of rings	Above gudgeon pin
Width of rings	$\frac{1}{4}$ in.
Width of lands	$\frac{1}{8}$ in.
Distance from bottom to centre of gudgeon pin	2 in.
Thickness of head	$\frac{3}{8}$ in.
Thickness of wall at bottom ..	3/16 in.
Diameter of gudgeon pin	$1\frac{1}{4}$ in.
Thickness of gudgeon pin wall ..	$\frac{1}{8}$ in.

CONNECTING RODS.

Type	Forked
Length between centres	$11\frac{7}{8}$ in.
Ratio length to crank throw ..	3.49 : 1
Small end bearing	Bronze bushing
Outside diameter of bushing ..	$1\frac{3}{8}$ in.
Outside diameter	1 11/16 in.
Type of section	"I"
Depth	1 5/16 in.
Width	15/16 in.
Thickness of flange	3/32 in.
Large end bearing	Bronze, babbit lined
Inside diameter	$2\frac{3}{8}$ in.
Outside diameter	2 13/16 in.
Length	$2\frac{1}{8}$ in.
Thickness of babbit	1/16 in.

CRANKSHAFT.

Number of bearings (Main) ..	7
Cylinder centres	$6\frac{1}{2}$ in.
Crank pins :	
Outside diameter	$2\frac{3}{8}$ in.
Inside diameter	$1\frac{1}{4}$ in.
Length diameter	$2\frac{1}{2}$ in.
Main bearings :	
Outside diameter	$2\frac{5}{8}$ in.
Inside diameter	$1\frac{3}{8}$ in.
Length	2 in.
Length (propeller end) ..	$4\frac{1}{2}$ in.
Crank Webs :	
Width	$2\frac{3}{4}$ in.
Thickness	1 in.
Radius of fillets	$\frac{1}{8}$ in.
Weight of shaft	103 lbs.

CAMSHAFT.

Diameter of shaft	1 in.
Inside diameter	11/16 in.
Number of bearings	7
Length of bearing (5 intermediate)	$3\frac{1}{8}$ in.
Length of bearing (gear end) ..	$2\frac{3}{4}$ in.
Length of bearing (front end) ..	$3\frac{1}{4}$ in.
Width of cam face	$\frac{3}{8}$ in.
Number of cams per cylinder ..	1 inlet and 1 exhaust
Diameter of gear flange	$2\frac{5}{8}$ in.
Thickness of gear flange	3/16 in.
Diameter of bolt circle	2 in.

Number of bolts	7
Diameter of bolts	$\frac{1}{4}$ in.
P. D. of gear	6 in.
Number of teeth	48
Width of face	$\frac{1}{2}$ in
Camshaft housing	Barrel type
Material	Aluminium
P. D. of pinion	2 in.
Number of teeth	16
Width of face	$\frac{1}{2}$ in.
Diameter of inclined drive shaft ..	$\frac{3}{4}$ in.

CRANKCASE (UPPER).

Material	Aluminium
Thickness of wall	3/16
Thickness of cylinder pads	$\frac{1}{8}$ in.
Thickness of supporting flange ..	3/16 in.
Centre distance of motor support bolts	$16\frac{3}{4}$ in.

CRANKCASE (LOWER).

Material	Aluminium
Thickness of wall	$\frac{1}{8}$ in.

LUBRICATION.

Type	Forced feed
Type of pumps	Rotary gear
No. of pumps	1 double pressure and 1 scavenging
Ratio of pump speed to crankshaft speed	1.5 : 1

Circuit diagram of ignition on the Liberty Twelve

IGNITION.

Type	Battery and generator
Firing order	L 1-9-5-11-3-7,
	R 8-4-12-6-10-2
Number of plugs per cylinder ..	2
Type of plug..	A, C.
Ratio of generator speed to crank-	
shaft speed..	1.5 : 1

COOLING SYSTEM.

Type	Water cooled
Pump	1 centrifugal

Diameter of inlet pipe	2 in.
Diameter of outlet pipe	1⅜ in.
Number of outlets	2
Diameter of rotor	3⅛ in.
Ratio of pump speed to crankshaft	
speed	1.5 : 1
Water temperature inlet	155° F.
Water temperature outlet	175° F.

Ignition Connections of the Liberty Engine.

Transverse Section through Cylinders.

Section through Valve Gears.

MAYBACH (German).

MAYBACH MOTORENBAU G.m.b.H., Friedrichshafen.

Constructed by the Canstatt-Daimler Co., Canstatt.

Herr Maybach was formerly of the Daimler Motor Co., and collaborateur of Gottlieb Daimler. Maybach developed and specialized in the German airship engine, which is exclusively used on the *Zeppelin, Schütte-Lanz* and *Parseval* craft.

THE 300 H.P. MAYBACH ENGINE.

The following is extracted from the Official Report on the 300 h.p Maybach engine and is published by courtesy of Technical Department of the Air Ministry, to whom the thanks of the Editor are due.

INTRODUCTORY NOTE.

The general distinctive features of the design of the Maybach Aero Engines are comparatively speaking, as well known amongst aeronautical engineers in this country as any of the enemy aero engines in service ; firstly, by reason of the adoption of the old Wolseley-Maybach aero engines, the designs of which was acquired before the war for airship work, and which was based on the design of the original Maybach engine ; and, secondly, through the publication of the somewhat incomplete details of construction of the Zeppelin-Maybach engines and their installation, which were collected under great difficulties from the remains of the several Zeppelin airships brought down during the war.

These engines, in almost every case, were so badly damaged by fire that it was found almost impossible at the time to compile any really detailed report on their design, or of their power and general performance.

A new and more powerful type of Maybach engine is now being used in service by the enemy, which, according to French reports, develops over 300 h.p., and which possesses great efficiency.

During the past few months several of the latest type of Rumpler machines have been captured fitted with the new 300 h.p. Maybach engines. These engines in their general design follow more or less the principle of the Zeppelin-Maybach 240 h.p. engines, and a detailed report, together with a full description of the constructional details and the general running performance of the new engine, is herewith given.

The following report on the design of the 260/300 h.p. Maybach engines is based on a detailed examination of the engine (No. 1261) taken from a Rumpler two-seater biplane (G. 120), known as the C.4 type. This machine was brought down in France by a shot which perforated the carburetter and water pump, on Jan. 18th, 1918. The machine was, unfortunately, completely destroyed by fire on landing, but the engine was captured intact and little damaged. After slight repairs this

Induction side view of Engine

(*Note.—The Airscrew Hub Flange Bolts are not those normally used.*)

MAYBACH—*continued.*

engine has been put into running condition and tested for power, consumption, etc., at R.A.E. The results of these tests are given in the following report, together with metallurgical analyses and mechanical tests of materials and alloys used in the principal parts of the engine.

Compared with the 260 h.p. Mercédès engines, fitted in these machines, the new Maybach engines are credited with attaining an increase of 200 r.p.m. at altitudes above 2,000 ft., and also possess greater efficiency in speed and climb in the Rumpler biplanes.

Total weight of machine fully loaded, approx. = 3,439 lbs.

GENERAL FEATURES.

The 300 h.p. Maybach presents several unusual and interesting details, and as compared with the old 240 h.p. Zeppelin-Maybach design, the new engines are undoubtedly a great improvement in general design and efficiency. The quality of the workmanship of every part, including the exterior finish throughout, is exceptionally good, and the working clearances are carried to very fine limits. Compared with any other of the types of enemy engines, the workmanship is undoubtedly of a very much more finished nature ; every part, nevertheless, shows the usual German characteristics of strength and reliability, combined with standardisation of parts and ease of manufacturing, in preference to the saving of weight

The general lay-out of this engine follows the usual German six-cylinder vertical type. The compression ratio is exceptionally high, viz., 5.94 : 1, which necessitates the use of very heavy pistons and connecting rods ; in these particulars this engine follows the previous Maybach practice, but the adoption of a cast-iron floating bush in the little end bearing is an interesting development.

Four overhead valves per cylinder are fitted—*i.e.,* two inlet and two exhaust. These are operated by rocker levers mounted on roller bearings in brackets fixed to the cylinder heads, as shown in Fig. 2, and by push rods on each side of the cylinders actuated by separate inlet and exhaust camshafts.

The camshafts run in plain bronze bearings in the crank-chamber, and are splash lubricated.

Little alteration has been made in the design of the massive crankshaft, which runs on plain white-metal lined bearings throughout, and is provided with the well-known Maybach type centrifugal pressure lubrication system to the crank-pins, thence to the gudgeons pins through small pipes, inside the hollow connecting rods.

The three separate and detachable gear oil pumps, which are situated in the bottom of the base chamber, are of new design.

Exhaust side view of Engine, showing rear end carburetter and throttle indicator, water pump, magnetos, wireless dynamo clutch-pulley, petrol pump and gun gear, and also the crankcase ventilator, which has been cut open to show oil trap.

MAYBACH—*continued*

300 HP MAYBACH AERO ENGINE

BORE 165 M/M   STROKE 180 M/M

MAYBACH—*continued*.

The pump driving shaft at the front end is driven through a ratchet gear on the front scavenger pump, apparently with the object of preventing an air lock in the lubrication system in the event of back-firing.

A double-acting, oil-sealed petrol pump of unusual design is now fitted. This is driven off an extension of the main oil pump spindle at the rear end of the base chamber, and works, of course, in conjunction with the two separate carburetters. These are of the well-known Maybach type, and have been only slightly modified; as shown in Figs. 1 and 2, they are attached, as in the Zeppelin engines, to the front and rear cylinder water jackets. A full description of the functions and workings of this interesting type of carburetter is given towards the end of this report.

The well-known Maybach induction type starting gear is fitted, but is slightly modified in design.

The whole of the induction system and the oil-condensing crankcase ventilating system is an interesting point in the design of this engine, as is also the method of attaching the airscrew-hub driving flange on the tapered front end of the crankshaft.

Practically no alteration has been made to the general design of the very simple and efficient type of water pump, which delivers directly into the bottom of the rear end carburetter water jacket as in the old Maybach engines. Ignition is by two Z.H.6 type Bosch magnetos, which are driven directly off the rear ends of the camshafts; the position of the sparking plugs in the cylinder heads is a point of interest dealt with in detail in the following description.

ENGINE TEST REPORT AT ROYAL AIRCRAFT ESTABLISHMENT. 5-4-18.

CALIBRATION AND ENDURANCE TESTS.

The Maybach engine (No. 1261), after several slight repairs had been carried out to the cylinders and propeller hub flange and coupling, was erected on a test bed, coupled to a Heenan and Froude dynamometer, and submitted to the following power and consumption tests, including a one hour's duration test at normal speed. The results of the calibration tests are as follows :—

R.P.M.	..	..	1,200	1,300	1,400	1,500
B.H.P.	..	..	258	279	294.5	304.5
Brake, M.E.P.	..	..	120.5	120.3	118	113.9
Petrol consumption in pints b.h.p. hour			0.53	0.52	0.526	0.545

The results of these tests are shown graphically on the diagram.

ONE HOUR TEST.

At the conclusion of the above tests a run of one hour's duration at normal revolutions (1,400 r.p.m.) was carried out with the following results :—

Cylinder, complete.

Cross Section of engine.

AYBACH—continued.

Calibration Curves. R.A.E. Tests.

erage b.h.p. ..	290
trol consumption ..	20 gallons = 0.55 points per b.h.p. hour.
consumption ..	11 pints = 0.038 pints per b.h.p. hour.
pressure	5 lbs./sq. in.
temperature ..	67°C.
ater temperature (inlet)	57°C.
ater temperature (outlet)	68°C

VALVE TIMING DURING TESTS.

Inlet.	Exhaust.
O. 8°E.	O. 33°E.
C. 35°L.	C. 7°L.
Magneto advance	38°E.

Running was steady at all speeds between 900 and 1,400 p.m., but owing to the fact that the propeller hub flange on e crank-shaft was damaged, and was running slightly out of ruth, the vibration became excessive above 1,400 r p.m.

Considerable trouble was experienced with the water onnection between the cylinders on the exhaust side. The unning became unsteady below 900 r.p.m.

DISTRIBUTION.

Owing to the exhaust manifold being fitted as part of the ngine starting gear, it was not possible to form an idea of the distribution.

GENERAL DATA.

Make of engine and rated h.p. ..	Maybach 300 h.p.
Type number..	1261
Number and arrangement of cylinders	Six vertical
Bore	165.0 mm. = 6.50 ins.
Stroke	180.0 mm. = 7.09 ins.
Stroke/Bore ratio	1.09 : 1.
Area of one piston	213.825 sq. cm. = 33.2 sq. ins.
Total piston area of engine.. ..	1282.95 sq. cm. = 199.2 sq. ins.
Swept volume of one cylinder ..	3848.85 cu. cm. = 235.3 cu. ins.
Total swept volume of engine ..	23093.1 cu. cm. = 1412.0 cu. ins.
Clearance volume of one cylinder ..	778.9 cu. cm. = 47.54 cu. ins.
Compression ratio	5.95 : 1.
Normal b.h.p. and speed ..	294.0 b.h.p. at 1400 r.p.m.
Maximum b.h.p. and speed..	304.5 b.h.p. at 1500 r.p.m.
Normal b.m.e.p.	117.7 lbs. per sq. in. at 1400 r.p.m.

Cross Section through Crankcase, showing method of holding Cylinders and Journal Bearings.

Details of Pistons, gudgeon pins and floating small-end bushes.

Lubrication Diagram, also showing petrol system and water circulation.

MAYBACH—*continued.*

Maximum b.m.e.p.	120.5 lbs. per. sq. in. at 1200 r.p.m.
Piston speed	1654.0 ft. per min. at 1400 r.p.m.
Mechanical efficiency (calculated) ..	86.0%
Indicated mean pressure (calculated)	137.0 lbs. sq. in.
Fuel consumption per b.h.p. hour ..	0.526 pint = 0.473 lbs.
Brake thermal efficiency	28.9%
Indicated thermal efficiency ..	33.6%
Air standard efficiency	51.0%
Relative efficiency	65.9%
Cu. in. of swept volume per b.h.p.	4.80 cu. ins.
Sq. in. of piston area b.h.p. ..	0.678 sq. ins.
H.p. per cu. ft. of swept volume ..	360.0 b.h.p.
H.p. per sq. ft. of piston area ..	212.4 b.h.p.
Direction of rotation of crankshaft	Anti-clockwise (facing propeller).
Direction of rotation of propeller ..	Anti-clockwise (facing propeller).
Type of Valve gear	Overhead valve rockers and push-rods
Type of starting gear	Maybach of special design.
Number of Carburetters	Two Maybach.
Bore of main jets	Variable from 0.0 to 2.5 mm.
Bore of pilot jets	Variable from 0.0 to 1.1 mm.
Fuel consumption per hour.. ..	19.33 gallons

VALVE AREAS AND GAS VELOCITIES.

Diameters.

Induction Pipe	62.0 min. = 2.44 ins.
Inlet port	45 × 67 mm.=1.77 × 2.64 ins.
Exhaust port	45 × 67 mm.=1.77 × 2.64 ins.
Exhaust branch pipes	66.0 mm. = 2.60 ins. (approx.).

Cross Sectional Areas.

Induction pipe	29·26 sq. cm=4.67 sq. ins.
Inlet port	30.15 sq. cm.=4.67 sq. ins.
Inlet valve (π dh.)	4.416 sq. ins. (total)
Exhaust valve (π d·h.) ..	4.366 sq. ins. (total)
Exhast port	30.15 sq. cm.=4.67 sq. ins.
Exhaust branch pipes	34.11 sq. cm.=5.31 sq. ins.

Gas Velocities.

Induction pipe	196.1 ft. per sec.
Inlet port	196.1 ft. per sec.
Inlet valve	208.0 ft. per sec.
Exhaust valve	210.0 ft. per sec.
Exhaust port	196.1 ft. per sec.
Exhaust branch pipes	172.5 ft. per sec.

INLET VALVES (Two per cylinder).

Outside diameter	54.0 mm.=2.126 ins.
Port diameter (in cylinder head) ..	48.0 mm. = 1.89 in.
Width of seating	3.5 mm. = 0.137 in.
Angle of seating	30°
Radius under valve head	20.0 mm. = 0.787 in.
Lift of valve	9.45 mm. = 0.372 in.
Diameter of stem	11.0 mm. = 0.433 in.
Over-all length of valve	136.5 mm. = 5.373 ins.
Number of springs per valve ..	One.
Free length of spring	52.5 mm. = 2.066 in.
Length of spring in position (no lift)	39.5 mm.= 1.55 in.
Mean diameter of coils	51.0 mm. = 2.00 in.
Gauge of wire	No. 6 B.W.G.
Ratio length of spring/lift of valve	4.21 : 1.
Weight of valve complete with spring	0.843 lb.
Weight of spring bare	0.281 lb.
Inlet valve opens, deg. on crank ..	8° early.
Inlet valve closes, deg. on crank ..	35° late.
Period of induction	223°
Inlet tappet clearance	0.3 mm. = 0.012 in.

EXHAUST VALVES (Two per cylinder).

Outside diameter	54.0 mm.=2.126 ins.
Port diameter (in cylinder head) ..	48.0 mm. = 1.89 in.
Width of seating	3.5 mm. = 0.127 in.
Angle of seating	30°.
Radius under valve head	9.0 mm. = 0.354 in.
Lift of valve	9.34 mm. = 0.368 in
Diameter of stem	11.0 mm. = 0.433 in.
Length of valve guide	80.0 mm. = 3.149 ins.
Over-all length of valve	152.5 mm. = 6.00 in.
Number of springs per valve ..	One.
Free length of spring	52.5 mm. = 2.06 ins.

WEIGHTS OF RECIPROCATING MASSES.

				SPRING.	
WEIGHT OF 2 VALVES	15 OZS	WEIGHT OF TAPPET ROD	8 OZS	EFFECTIVE COILS	3
HALF WEIGHT OF 2 SPRINGS	4½ OZS	,, PLUNGER	6½ OZS	THICKNESS OF WIRE (DIA)	55%
WEIGHT OF 2 SPRING CAPS	3 OZS	,, ROLLER	1 OZS	MEAN DIAMETER	310%
EQUIVALENT WEIGHT OF ROCKER	4 OZS		15½ OZS	FREE LENGTH	520%
	26½ OZS		30 OZS	MINIMUM LENGTH	230%
MULTIPLY BY RATIO OF 55:31			43½ OZS		
	30 OZS			133 LBS PRESSURE AXIALLY WHEN VALVE FULL	
TOTAL RECIPROCATING MASS AT CAM.	2 LBS 13½ OZS			32 TONS STRESS ..	

VALVE GEAR OF

300 H.P. MAYBACH AERO ENGINE.

Crankshaft.

MAYBACH—*continued.*

Length of spring in position (no lift)	39.5 mm. = 1.55 in.
Mean diameter of coils	51.0 mm. = 2.00 ins.
Gauge of wire	No. 6 B.W.G.
Ratio length of spring/lift of valve	4.21 : 1.
Weight of valve complete with spring	0.881 lb.
Weight of spring bare	0.281 lb.
Exhaust valve opens, deg. on crank	33° early.
Exhaust valve closes, deg. on crank	7° late.
Period of exhaust	220°.
Exhaust tappet clearance	0.4 mm.

INERTIA FORCES, BEARING LOADS, ETC.

Weight of piston, complete with rings and gudgeon-pin	14.05 lbs.
Weight per sq. in. of piston area ..	0.4235 lb.
Weight of connecting-rod complete	8.93 lbs.
Weight reciprocating part of connecting-rod	3.305 lbs.
Total reciprocating weight per cylinder	17.355 lbs.
Weight per sq. in. piston area ..	0.538 lb.
Length of connecting-rod (centres)	310.0 mm. = 12.20 ins.
Ratio. Connecting-rod/crank throw	3.445 : 1.
Inertia, lbs. sq. in. piston area, top centre	137.0 lbs. sq. in.
Inertia, lbs. sq. in. piston area, bottom centre	75.5 lb. sq. in.
Inertia, lbs. sq. in. piston area, mean	53.25 lbs. sq. in.
Weight of rotating mass of connecting rod	5.625 lbs.
Total centrifugal pressure	1106 lbs.
Centrifugal pressure, lbs. sq. in. piston area..	34.4 lbs. sq. in.
Mean average fluid pressure, including compression	48.0 lb. sq. in.
Mean average loading on crankpin bearing, total from all sources in terms of lbs. sq. in. piston area..	118.0 lbs. sq. in.
Diameter of crankpin	66.0 mm. = 2.598 ins.
Rubbing velocity	15.85 ft. sec.
Effective projected area of big end bearing	43.23 sq. cm. = 6.70 sq. ins.
Ratio. Piston. area/projected area of big end bearing	4.96 : 1.
Mean average loading on big end bearing	585 lbs. sq. in.
Load factor on big end bearing ..	9270 lbs. ft. sec.

CYLINDERS.

Over-all height of bare cylinder from top of base chamber	479.5 mm. = 18.87 ins.
Depth of spigot at base of cylinder	3.5 mm. = 0.13 in.
Diameter of cylinder over water jacket	185.0 mm. = 7.28 ins.
Valve centres (between inlet and exhaust)	63.0 mm. = 2.48 ins.

Top half of Crankcase.

Inside view of Crankcase, top half, shown upside down.

ENGINES.

MAYBACH—continued.

Thickness of flange at base of cylinders	12.0 mm. = 0.47 in.
Number of holding-down studs per cylinder	Four.
Diameter of holding-down studs	19.0 mm. = 0.74 in.
Thickness of water jacket	1.0 mm. = 0.039 in.
Mean thickness of combustion chamber wall	8.0 mm. = 0.31 in.
Mean thickness of cylinder barrel	3.0 mm. = 0.11 in.
Tensile stress	6.640 lbs. sq. in. (approx.) (Assumed maximum pressure 450 lbs. sq. in.)

PISTON.

Type of piston	Cast-iron (flat crown.)
Diameter at top	164.25 mm. = 6.466 ins.
Diameter at bottom	164.75 mm. = 6.486 ins.
Length	151.00 mm. = 5.944 ins.
Ratio. Piston length/cylinder bore.	0.914 : 1
Number of rings per piston	Three piston rings, one scraper ring.
Position of rings	All above gudgeon-pin.
Width of rings	6.5 mm. = 0.255 in.
Gap of rings in cylinder	1.39 mm. = 0.055 in.

CONNECTING ROD.

Length between centres	310.0 mm = 12.205 ins.
Ratio. Connecting rod/crank throw	3.44 : 1.
Little end bearing type	Floating cast iron bush.
Floating bush, diameter, inside	38.0 mm. = 1.496 in.
Floating bush, diameter, outside	44.3 mm. = 1.743 in.
Floating bush, effective length inside	93.0 mm. = 3.661 ins.
Floating bush, projected area of bearing on gudgeon-pin	35.35. sq. cm. = 5.48 sq. ins.
Ratio. Piston area/projected area of little end bearing	6.06 : 1.
Big end bearing. Type	Bronze shell lined white metal.
Big end bearing. Diameter	66.0 mm. = 2.598 ins.
Big end bearing. Length (actual).	73.56 mm. = 2.893 ins.
Big end bearing. Length (effective)	65.5 mm. = 2.580 ins.
Big end bearings. Projected area.	43.23 sq. cm. = 6.700 sq. ins.
Ratio. Piston area/projected area of big end bearing	4.96 : 1.
Number of big end bolts	Four.
Full diameter of bolts	14.0 mm. = 0.551 in.
Diameter at bottom of threads	12.0 mm. = 0.472 in.
Total cross sectional area, bottom of threads	4.520 sq. cm. = 0.70 sq. in.

Pitch of threads	1.5 mm.
Total load on bolts at 1,400 r.p.m.	5,824 lbs.
Total load on bolts at 1,600 r.p.m.	7,602 lbs.
Stress per sq. in. at 1,400 r.p.m.	8.320 lbs. sq. in.
Stress per sq, in. at 1,600 r.p.m.	10.860 lbs. sq. in.

CRANKSHAFT.

Number and type of main bearings	Seven bronze shell lined white metal
Cylinder centres	187.0 mm. = 7,362 ins.
Crank-pins—	
Outside diameter	66.0 mm. = 2.598 ins.
Inside diameter	38.0 mm. = 1.496 in.
Length	74.0 mm. = 2.913 ins.
Journals—	
Outside diameter	66.0 mm. = 2.598 ins.
Inside diameter	36.0 mm. = 1.417 in.
Length, propeller end	68.0 mm. = 2.638 ins.
Length, rear end	67.0 mm. = 2.638 ins.
Length, centre	67.0 mm. = 2.638 ins.
Length, intermediate	67.0 mm. = 2.638 ins.
Crank Webs—	
Width	95.0 mm. = 3,740 ins.
Thickness	23.0 mm. = 0.906 in.
Radius at ends of Journals and crank-pins	4.5 mm. = 0.171 in.
Weight of complete shaft	99.9 lbs.

WORKING CLEARANCES.

Piston clearance, top (total)	0.75 mm. = 0.029 in.
Piston clearance, bottom (total)	0.25 mm. = 0.009 in.
Side clearance of connecting rod in piston (total)	11.8 mm. = 0.464 in.
Side clearance of big end on crank-pin (total)	0.44 mm. = 0.0173 in.
End clearance of crankshaft in main bearings	3.0 mm. = 0.118 in.
Clearance of valve stem in guide (inlet)	0.12 mm. = 0.00472 in.
Clearance of valve stem in guide (exhaust)	0.15 mm. = 0.0059 in.

LUBRICATION SYSTEM.

Number and type of oil pumps	Three, rotary gear.
Oil consumption per hour	11.0 pints.
Oil consumption per b.h.p. hour	0.037 pint.
Oil temperature	65° Centigrade.
Oil pressure	5.0 lbs. per sq, in.
Specific gravity of oil	0.899 s p.g.
Ratio, Pump speed/crankshaft speek	1 : 2.
Pump delivery (calculated at 100% volumetric efficiency	91 gallons per hour of normal engine revs.

IGNITION.

Number and type of magnetos	Two Bosch.
Firing sequence of engine	1-5-3-6-2-4.
Ignition timing (fully advanced)	38° early.
Number of plugs per cylinder	Two.
Type or plugs	Bosch 3 point.
Ratio. Magneto speed/engine speed	1.5 : 1.

COOLING SYSTEM.

Number and type of water pumps.	One centrifugal.
Diameter of inlet pipe	54.0 mm. = 2.126 ins.
Diameter of outlet pipe	50.0 mm. = 1.966 ins.
Diameter of rotor	111.0 mm. = 4.36 ins.
Water capacity of one cylinder	1284.0 cu. cm.

The front oil pump, showing ratchet drive and section of detachable oil sump in Chamber.

MAYBACH—*continued.*

Number and type of radiators ..	One semicircular honeycomb.
Ratio. Water pump speed/engine speed	2 : 1.
Water temperature, inlet	57° Centigrade.
Water temperature, outlet.. ..	68° Centigrade.

PETROL PUMP.

Number and type of petrol pumps	One Maybach double acting.
Bore	15 0 mm. = 0.59 in.
Stroke	17 0 mm. = 0.66 in.
Normal delivery	264 pints per hour at 800 r.p.m.
Maximum delivery	630 pints per hour at 1.275 r.p.m.
Ratio. Pump speed/crankshaft speed	1. : 2.

WEIGHTS.

Weight of complete engine, dry, with propeller boss & exhaust manifold.	911 lbs.
Weight per b.h.p., ditto	3.10 lbs.
Weight of fuel per hour	139 lbs.
Weight of oil per hour (s.p.g. 0.899).	12.36 lbs.
Total weight of fuel and oil per hour	151.36 lbs.
Gross weight of engine in running order, less fuel and oil (cooling system at 0·65 lbs. per b.h.p. ..	1102.0 lbs.
Weight per b.h.p., ditto	3.79 lbs.
Gross weight of engine in running order, with fuel and oil for six hours (tankage at 10% weight of fuel and oil)	2100.9 lbs.
Weight per b h.p., ditto	7.14 lbs.

Radiator fitted to centre section of Rumpler biplanes, as used with 300 h.p. Maybach and 260 h.p. Mercédès engines.

Diagrammatic section of carburetter.

Fig. 18.—Sectional arrangement of the carburetter.

MAYBACH—*continued.*

GENERAL ANALYSIS OF WEIGHTS.

Description of Part.	No. per Set.	Average unit in lbs.	Weight of complete set in lbs.	Percentage of total weight.
Cylinders (bare)	6	32.75	196.50	21.59
Pistons, complete with rings and gudgeon-pin set screws ..	6	12.30	73.80	8.11
Gudgeon-pins	6	1.75	10.50	1.15
Connecting rods and floating bushes	6	8.93	49.12	5.39
Crankshaft, complete with oil rings	1	99.90	99.90	10.98
Crankshaft extension, with nut and pin	1	4.00	4.00	0.44
Inlet valves	12	0.43	5.25	0.57
Exhaust valves	12	0.47	5.70	0.62
Inlet and exhaust valve springs ..	24	0.28	6.74	0.74
Inlet and exhaust valve collars, with cotters and locking device ..	24	0.12	3.00	0.32
Thrust, complete with ball races propeller hub flange, and camshaft driving sprocket	1	17.68	17.68	1.94
Camshafts	2	10.00	20.00	2.20
Overhead valve rockers, complete..	12	1.08	12.99	1.42
Overhead rocker bearings, complete	24	0.42	10.50	1.15
Valve tappets and guides	12	0.93	11.25	1.23
Crankcase, top half	1	94.30	94.30	10.36
Crankcase, bottom half ..	1	41.32	41.32	4.54
Bearing caps.. ..	6	2.68	16.12	1.77
Front bearing cap	1	5.56	5.56	0.61
Crankcase holding-down bolts, with clamps, nuts, and washers ..	14	2.40	33.60	3.70
Induction pipe complete	1	9.09	9.09	1.00
Propeller hub, with bolts and nuts	1	21.00	21.00	2.30
Inlet valve push rods	6	0.48	2.90	0.32
Exhaust valve push rods	6	0.49	2.97	0.33
Inlet and exhaust stiffening plates..	2	2.00	4.00	0.44
Oil pumps, with drive and pipe ..	1	9.00	9.00	0.98
Rear cover plate	1	6.06	6.06	0.66
Front cover plate	1	4.00	4.00	0.44
Water pump, complete	1	8.50	8.50	0.93
Camshaft, oil and water pumps driving gears	1	13.65	13.65	1.50
Wireless clutch	1	5.06	5.06	0.55
Revolution counter gear	1	2.62	2.62	0.28
Machine-gun interrupter gear ..	1	1.82	1.82	0.20
Petrol pump	1	3.50	3.50	0.38
Magnetos	2	10.75	21.50	2.36
Magneto wiring	1	4.75	4.75	0.52
Oil pipes	1	4.00	4.00	0.44
Self-starter gear	1	6.60	6.00	0.66
Exhaust manifold	1	27.00	27.00	2.96
Carburetters..	2	16.00	32.00	3.51
Miscellaneous			3.85	0.41
Total weight of engine			911.00	100.00

ENGINES.

METALLURGICAL ANALYSIS OF PRINCIPAL PARTS. MECHANICAL TESTS.

	Carbon.	Graphite Carbon.	Combined Carbon.	Silicon.	Manganese.	Sulphur.	Phosphorus.	Nickel.	Chromium.
	p.c.	p.c.	p.c.	p.c.	p.c.	p.c.	p.c.	p.c.	p.c.
Cylinder head .		2·57	0.91	1.60	0.70	0.131	0.34		
Cylinder barrel	0.49			0.33	1.01	0.028	0.054		
Cylinder water jacket ..	0.25			0.27	0.63	0.032	0.037		
Piston.. ..		2.42	0.83	1.29	0.83	0.111	0.30		
Gudgeon pin floating bush		2.39	0.65	1·43	0.76	0.146	0.47		
Gudgeon pin ..	0.28			0.23	0.48	0.028	0.022		
Connecting rod	0.15			0.33	0.31	0.027	0.010	1.42	0.49
Inlet valve ..	0.53			0.30	0.48	0.032	0.044	4.01	0.51
Exhaust valve.	0.10			0.20	0.26	0.019	0.023	3.62	1.16
Crankshaft ..	0.31			0.31	0.63	0.030	0.015	4.01	0.83
Camshaft ..	0·40			0.25	0.23	0.022	0.040	3.46	0.68
Camcore ..	0.17			0.23	0.75	0.036	0.014		0.47

	Lead.	Iron.	Tin.	Copper.	Zinc.	Antimony.	Silicon.	Manganese.
	p.c.	p.c.	p.c.	p.c.	p.c.	p.c.	p.c.	p.c.
Big-end bearing metal ..	3.51		80.05	6.34				
Main journal bearing ..	0.92		77.65	10.00				
Crankcase ..		0.99		0.87	12.01	Aluminium (by difference 86.57)	2·56	trace

MECHANICAL TESTS.

Mechanical tests were made on the crankcase and crankshaft, the results of which are given below :—

CRANKCASE.

Mark.	Diam.	Max Stress.	Elongation, p.c.
T	0.253	.... 11.65	 1
L	0.254	.... 11.28	 1

CRANKSHAFT.

Position.	Mark.	Diam.	Yield Stress. Tons/sq. in.	Max. Stress. Tons/sq. in.	p.c. Elang. on 4A.	R. of A. p.c.	Impact Ft. lbs
End	1	0.254	59.0	63.1	14.3	56.3	17.21
Journal ..	2	0.254					
Web	3	0.254	61.6	64.1	15.1	54.6	16.121
Long... ..	4						
Cank-pin, long.	5	0.254	63.6	67.1	15.1	55.7	12.12
	6						
Web. trans...	7	0.254	61.4	65.3	7.2	10.5	5.5

TEST N° 844

POWER CURVE CORRECTED FOR BAROMETER

Calibration Curves. R.A.E. Tests.

MERCÉDÈS (German).

MERCÉDÈS-DAIMLER MOTOREN GESELLSCHAFT, Stuttgart-Untertürkheim.

Turned out early an aviation engine, which was not favoured by the German aviators, though excellent design work—for which the engine was awarded the prize of the Automobile Technic Society, as best in the B-Z £5,000 competition, 1911.

Was brought into limelight by Hirth in numerous flights, and universally adopted from 1912 even to 85-90 per cent. Is a very reliable motor.

Daimler engines were employed in the first *Zeppelin* and other early German airships, but the former Oberingenier of the company and collaborateur of Daimler, Maybach, catered for special airship wants, and Maybach airship motors are now exclusively used (see latter).

The 100 h.p. Model won the chief prize in the Kaiser engine Competition, and an upside-down hanging cylinder type, never further developed, was once tried.

TYPES.

100 h.p., 6-cyl.	220 h.p. 6-cyl.
160 h.p., 6-cyl.	250 h.p. 8-cyl.
180 h.p., 6-cyl.	260 h.p. 6-cyl.
200 h.p., 6-cyl.	

160-70 h.p. Mercédès engine :

No. of cylinders : 6.
Bore : 140 m/m.
Stroke : 160 m/m.
Cylinders : Steel, cast in single units, with integral water-jackets.
Ignition : Twin Bosch magnetos.
Valves : Overhead, with overhead camshaft, bevel driven from mainshaft.
Lubrication : Forced feed.
H.P. : 160 at 1250 r.p.m.

THE 260-H.P. MERCÉDÈS ENGINE.

[The following details of the 260-h.p. Mercédès Engine have been supplied, together with the photographs and drawings, by the Technical Department of the Air Ministry, to whom the Editor desires to express his thanks.]

INTRODUCTORY NOTE.

The details of the following report on the latest type Mercédès engines and the accompanying scale sectional drawings have been collected from an investigation of the twin engines taken from the captured German aeroplane G.23, a three-seater "Gotha" biplane of the pusher type, which was brought down near Vron by Lieut. Breadner on April 23rd, 1917.

The machine was set on fire by the occupants after landing and partially destroyed, one engine being scrapped and the crankcase melted. The other engine, No. 29870, however, was little damaged, with the result that after certain repairs had been carried out, this engine was able to be put through a bench test at the Royal Aircraft Factory, where the following particulars regarding B.H.P., consumption, etc., were taken.

LEADING PARTICULARS OF THE 260-H.P. MERCÉDÈS ENGINE.

Number and arrangement of cylinders	6, vertical
Bore	160 mm., 6.30 in.
Stroke	180 mm., 7.09 in.
Stroke/Bore ratio	1.125—1.
Stroke volume of one cylinder	3,620 cub. cms., 220.82 cub.in.
Total stroke volume of engine..	21,720 cub. cms., 1,324.92 cub. in.
Area of one piston	20.1062 sq. cms., 31.164 sq. in.

Fig. 1.—Inlet Side of 260-h.p. Mercédès engine.

MERCÉDÈS—*continued.*

Total piston area of engine ..	1,206.372 sq. cms., 186.984 sq. in.
Clearance volume of one cylinder	920 cub. cms., 56.12 cub. in.
Compression ratio	4.94—1.
Normal b.h.p. and speed ..	252 at 1,400.
Piston speed	1,653 ft. per min. at 1,400. 1,775 ft. per min. at 1.500.
Brake mean effective pressure..	107.5 lbs. per sq. in.
Cub. in. of stroke volume per b.h.p.	5.25.
Sq. in. of piston area per b.h.p.	0.74
H.P. per cub. ft. of stroke volume	329.14 h.p.
H.P. per sq. ft. of piston area	194.6.
Direction of rotation of crank	Anti-clock.
Direction of rotation of propeller	,,
Normal speed of propeller ..	E.S.
Lubrication system	Forced feed to all bearings and camshaft.
Brand of oil recommended ..	Sternoil (air cooled) on test.
Oil pressure recommended ..	No indicator.
Oil temperature recommended	Not above 60° C.
Oil consumption per hour ..	8.125 pints.
,, ,, ,, b.h.p. hour	.032 pints.
Specific gravity of oil	:9.
Type of carburetter	1 twin jet Mercédès.
Mixture control	Automatic.
Fuel consumption per hour ..	125 pints.
,, ,, ,, b.h.p. hour	.605 pints.
Specific gravity of fuel ..	.720.
Type of magneto	2 Z H 6.
Firing sequence of engine ..	Prop. 1 5 3 6 2 4.
Numbering of cylinders ..	Prop. 1 2 3 4 5 6.
Speed of magneto	1.5 engine speed.
Direction of rotation of magneto, facing driving end of armature	Anti-clock.
Magneto timing	31° E.
Inlet valve opens, degree on crank	1° L
Inlet valve closes, degree on crank	49° 3′ L.
Maximum lift of inlet valve ..	10.125 mm.
Diameter inlet valve	55.25 mm.
Area of inlet valve opening (2 valves)	35.12 sq. cm., 5.44 sq. in.
Mean gas velocity through inlet valve	151.1 ft. per second.
Clearance of inlet tappet ..	.018 in.
Exhaust valve opens, degrees on crank	50.6° E.
Exhaust valve closes, degrees on crank	17.6° E

Maximum lift of exhaust valve	10 mm.
Diameter exhaust valve ..	55.25 mm.
Area of exhaust valve opening (2 valves)	34.70 sq. cm., 5.4 sq. in.
Clearance of exhaust tappet ..	.018 in.
Speed of revolution counter drive	Camshaft speed.
Weight of engine complete without water, fuel or oil ..	936 lbs.
Weight per b.h.p. without water, fuel or oil	3.71 lbs.
Weight of exhaust manifold ..	26 lbs.

Weight of starting gear not integral with engine	Nil.
Weight of fuel per hour ..	136.8 lbs.
,, of oil per hour	9.14 lbs.
Total weight of fuel and oil per hour	145.94 lbs.
Gross weight of engine in running order, less fuel and oil ..	1,099 lbs. approx.
Weight per b.h.p., less fuel and oil	4.36 lbs

Fig. 2.—Exhaust Side of 260-h.p. Mercédès engine.

MERCÉDÈS—*continued*.

Gross weight of engine in running order, with fuel and oil for six hours .. .. .. 2,072 lbs.

Weight per b.h.p., with fuel and oil for six hours .. .. 8.2 lbs.

Period of induction .. .. 228°.

„ exhaust .. .. 247°.

Half compression cam opens exhaust .. .. 12° A.B.C.

Half compression cam closes exhaust .. .. 44° B.T.C.

Diameter of induction pipe branch .. .. .. 75 mm.

Diameter of induction pipe main .. .. 100 mm.

Diameter of choke tube .. 32 mm.

Length of connecting rod between centres .. .. 326 mm.

Diameter of crank pin .. .. 64 mm.

Length of crank pin bearing .. 80 mm.

Diameter of journals .. .. 64 mm.

Length of journal bearings .. 64 mm.

Length of front journal bearing 104 mm.

Connecting rod side-clearance (total) in piston .. .. 2.25 mm.

Fig. 3.—Magneto and Carburetter End.

Fig. 4.—Airscrew End.

ENGINES.

MERCÉDÈS—continued.

Total capacity of each petrol tank	95 galls.
„ „ „ oil tank	7.25 galls.
„ „ water in system	6.5 galls.
Weight of complete cylinder with valves and springs ..	34.25 lbs.
Weight of complete piston with rings and gudgeon pin ..	10.725 lbs.
Total weight of complete connecting rod with gudgeon pin bush	7 lbs.
Weight of connecting rod, big-end, complete	4 lbs. 14 oz.
Weight of connecting rod, small-end, with bush	2 lbs. 2 ozs.
Weight complete valve with spring washer and nut (inlet and exhaust)	.759 lbs.
Weight of valve rocker complete	1.246 lbs
Total weight of engine with water, including radiator, etc.	1,099 lbs. approx.
Weight of crankshaft with propeller boss	139.5 lbs.
Diameter of piston at top ..	159.258 mm.
„ „ bottom	159.715 mm.
Width of rings	5 mm.
Width of gap in rings in cylinder	16/1000 mm.
Diameter of water pump inlet..	44 mm.
Diameter of water pump outlet	44 mm.

GENERAL DESCRIPTION.

In many respects these engines resemble the 160-h.p. Mercédès and are of the usual German aero-engine design, being of the six-cylinder vertical type, water cooled, with a massive six-throw crankshaft running in plain bearings, the design throughout aiming at strength and reliability combined with ease of manufacture in preference to the consideration of weight per b.h.p. as the primary factor in design.

The salient features of the 260-h.p. Mercédès are briefly as follows :—Notwithstanding its abnormal size, the whole engine is of very proportionate and clean design throughout, as shown in the accompanying photographs and detail drawings of the engine. The complete engine, including the propeller boss, measures 6 ft. 5½ in. overall, and from the bottom of the sump to the top of the overhead camshaft casing measures approximately 3 ft. 10 in. The bore of each cylinder is 160 mm. and the stroke 180 mm. Four valves, i.e., two inlet and two exhaust, are fitted in the head of each cylinder, and are operated by an overhead camshaft, running in a detachable casing of malleable cast iron supported on brackets screwed into the head of each cylinder. All the valves are interchangeable.

A half compression gear, employing a sliding camshaft device similar to that in the 160-h.p. Mercédès, is fitted to the rear end of the shaft casing.

A single carburetter employing a main jet and a slow running jet is attached to the rear end of the base chamber, taking its air supply from the interior of the base chamber through a 4-in. diameter passage cast in the bottom of the crank chamber, which is constructed with a false bottom.

The bottom halves of the crankshaft main bearing housings, or bearing caps, are cast integral with the bottom half of the crankcase ; the long bolts which secure the bearing caps pass

Fig. 5.—The Mercédès Cylinder.

106b

Fig 6.—Cross Section through Cylinder and Crankcase.

Fig. 7.—Cross Section through Cylinder and Valve Gear.

ERCÉDÈS—*continued.*

ough the top half of the crankcase, and are used to secure cylinders in position by triangular clamps, a design of stionable merit, but a method which undoubtedly adds eased stiffness to the crankcase construction.

he lubrication system is forced to all bearings through the led crankshaft from a four-throw eccentric-driven plunger np, which is an improved design on the 160-h.p. form of rcédès type. The scheme embodies an " auxiliary " sump in front end of the crankcase, and small supplementary pump ngers, which work in conjunction with the main oil pump the purpose of feeding fresh oil into the system from the vice oil tank.

Full details of this lubrication system, and also of the some-at complicated Mercédès oil pump, are given in the following scription. Two Bosch Z.H. 6 magnetos are used, driven off e camshaft vertical driving shaft, one being a starter magneto. plugs are fitted on the induction side of the cylinders.

The water-pump driving spindle is lubricated whilst in flight a rachet-driven grease lubricator worked by a cable and ver from the pilot's seat. An electric tachometer is driven at gine speed from the rear end of the camshaft through a xible shaft.

DETAILS OF CONSTRUCTION.

CYLINDERS (Fig. 5).—The construction of the built-up ylinders, which are composed entirely of steel forgings and heet steel, pressed to the form of the water jackets, is an interesting example of expert acetylene steel welding.

The method of building up the cylinders, and their general onstruction, is shown in the scale cross-sectional drawing. Fig. 7).

The steel cylinder barrels are screwed into the cylinder head, the pitch of the thread being 1.75 mm.

The cylinder barrels are machined from steel forgings, the thickness of the cylinder walls being 3.5 mm., this dimension being increased to 6 mm. at the holding-down base flange.

Six rectangular ribs are machined on the outer diameter of the cylinder barrel, the distance between the ribs increasing towards the base of the cylinder. The cylinder barrels extend 35 mm. below the base flanges and are of 3 mm. thickness for a depth of 12 mm. ; the extension is reduced to 2.75 in thickness at the lowest part (Fig. 7).

The cylinder heads are machined from steel forgings, into which are built the four valve pockets and inlet and exhaust ports.

The valve face seatings are machined in the cylinder heads, the thickness of the crown of the cylinder head being 11 mm. The valve pockets, which are machined from steel forgings, are acetylene welded into the cylinder heads, and steel valve stem guides are pressed into the valve pockets and welded.

The valve stem guides are bushed with phosphor-bronze liners, which are pressed into the guides.

It will be noticed that the exhaust valve stem guide is considerably longer than the inlet valve stem guide.

The water-jackets are built up in four sections from sheet steel pressings 1.25 mm. in thickness, the lower section of the jacket being of barrel formation, and welded to the flange joint on the cylinder walls.

The top sections are in halves, and encircle the valve pockets, the joints being welded vertically on the centre line of the valve ports.

The top of the water-jacket is a sheet steel disc which is welded on to the flanged top sections, and the water circulation pipe connections are welded into the top and bottom of the jackets on the exhaust side.

Fig. 8.—**Double Branch Valve Tappets and Rockers.**

Fig. 9.—**Connecting Rod, Piston, Gudgeon Pin, and Bush.**

o 2

MERCÉDÈS—*continued*.

Fig. 10.—Valves and Valve-Springs.

The sparking plug bosses are fitted and welded into the cylinder barrels on the induction side just below the inlet valves.

As in the 160-h.p. Mercédès engines, the exhaust valve stem guides are water-cooled by recesses formed in each of the exhaust valve pockets, so that the water is led right up to the valve stem guides.

Considering the size of the cylinders, they are remarkably light in weight. The complete cylinder with valves, valve springs, etc., including the two brackets screwed into the cylinder head to carry the camshaft, weighs 34.25 lbs.

The PISTONS are constructed in two parts, the head which carries the gudgeon pin in projecting lugs, and the skirt of the piston, into which the head is screwed.

The head of the piston is a steel forging machined all over, the thickness of the crown being 8.5 mm. The skirt of the piston is screwed onto the head and acetylene welded at the joint ; the head of the piston is slightly domed.

The skirt of the piston is of cast-iron. Three compression rings are fitted in grooves cut in the cast-iron skirt above the gudgeon pin, and a scraper ring at the base of the piston, the width of the rings being 5 mm.

All the rings are split at a diagonal gap of 45° and no locating pegs are fitted to maintain the positions of the rings. The gudgeon pin, which is 37 mm. in diameter, projects through the lugs on the piston head, and fits into the piston skirt, flush with the outside diameter. The gudgeon pin is fixed by an 8 mm. set screw, screwed into the end of the gudgeon pin through the boss and locked with a split pin on the inside.

The weight of the complete piston with gudgeon pin and bush is 10.93 lbs.

VALVES AND VALVE GEAR.—As previously mentioned, the twin inlet and exhaust valves are interchangeable. The maximum diameter of the head of all valves is 60 mm. ; the lift of both the inlet and exhaust valves is 10 mm. ; and the clearance between the end of valve stem and adjustment screw of the arm rocker is 0.018 in. The general arrangement of the valves and rocker arms is clearly shown in the cross-sectional scale drawing (Fig. 7). In this drawing the section is taken through the centre of the cylinder as far as the top of the cylinder barrel,

Fig. 11.—Arrangement of Camshaft and Half Compression Gear.

MERCÉDÈS *continued.*

and above this point the section is shown through one inlet and one exhaust valve, and valve gear.

The valves are operated by a single overhead camshaft, working in a detachable casing of special alloy machined all over, which is supported on twin T brackets which are screwed into the head of each cylinder.

The camshaft runs on seven phosphor-bronze plain bearings, which are mounted in aluminium bushes fitted into the bore of the camshaft casing, each bush being located by a tapered grub-screw.

The method of operating the twin valves off one cam and the general design of the camshaft and camshaft casing is of interesting design. The details of this are shown in the sectional drawings (Fig. 11).

The spindle of each rocker lever is mounted on three bearings in the camshaft casing, and so designed that the cam operates the arm of the rocker lever inside the camshaft casing, whilst the other arm of the rocker operates the valve outside the casing. This arm works between two outer bearings of the rocker spindle and is situated between the separated compartments of the camshaft casing.

On the end of the outer rocker arm a double branch tappet arm is fixed which operates the twin valves (Fig. 8).

Although these branch arms do not swivel upon the valve rocker, they are not secured by a set screw or pin, being merely pressed on to the ends of the rocker arm and easily driven off.

The spindles of the valve rockers are carried directly in the camshaft casing, no gun-metal bearing liners being fitted.

The inner arms of the rocker levers, which are worked by the cams, are fitted with hardened steel rollers. The diameter of the valve stem is 11 mm., and each valve works in a phosphor-bronze bush in the valve stem guide, as already mentioned. Each valve works at an angle of 15° to the perpendicular axis of the cylinder centre line. Single helical valve springs are fitted and measure 39 mm. at the base of the coil, tapering to 31 mm. at the top.

Conical based adjusting nuts are provided inside the valve spring washers for adjusting the valve springs. Details of these are shown in the sectional drawings.

CAMSHAFT DRIVE AND HALF COMPRESSION GEAR.—The camshaft is driven through a vertical shaft by the main distribution bevel gear mounted on the end of the crankshaft by four splines.

The method of attaching the small driving bevel gear to the top end of the vertical driving shaft is interesting. The bevel gear pinion is detachable from the shaft, and is designed so that it may be adjusted for the correct mesh in the teeth of the camshaft-driven bevel wheel. Full details of this gear are shown in the sketch Fig. 11.

The driving end of the shaft is machined and ground parallel to 23 mm. diameter, and is fitted with a key, onto which is

driven a ground taper on the bottom extension of the bevel pinion, which is split by four saw-cuts. A collar, screwing on to the lower extension of the bevel pinion, locks it securely on the vertical driving shaft.

HALF COMPRESSION GEAR.—In order to allow these large engines to be more easily turned over, a half compression gear is provided.

This is similar in design to that fitted on the 160-h.p. Mercédès engines.

In this type of compression release gear the camshaft is designed to slide longitudinally in its bearings, and in doing so, it brings into operation a small cam situated on the mid neutral axis of the exhaust cam, but not of course on the actual cam face.

To allow for the sliding movement of the camshaft in its bearings without disturbing the mesh of the driving bevel gears, the large driven bevel gear is provided with six rectangular serrations, which engage with corresponding serrations cut in the end of the camshaft. The bevel gear is mounted in a split

Fig. 12.—Details of Connecting Rods.

109b

Fig. 13.—Airscrew Boss and Locking Device.

gun-metal bearing which is driven into the rear end of the camshaft casing. The sliding movement of the camshaft is effected by means of a hand lever, which is set at right angles to the axis of the camshaft, and attached to a gun-metal collar, having a five start square-thread screw of 23 mm. pitch cut on its inner diameter.

This collar, which is located in an aluminium housing, operates a corresponding screw thread cut on the outer diameter of a steel sleeve, and inside the sleeve is contained a double thrust ball race and collar, which is fixed to the rear end of the camshaft. (See Fig. 11.)

In action the partial rotation of the half compression lever on the axis of the camshaft rotates the quick-thread screw of the sleeve, which pulls or pushes the end of the camshaft in its bearings through the serrated bore of the driven bevel gear. When the camshaft is drawn towards its limit of movement to the rear, the half compression cam is drawn into line with the roller end of the exhaust valve rocker arm, thus giving a slight lift to the exhaust valve as the camshaft rotates.

The half compression cam is so positioned on the camshaft as to open the exhaust valve 12° after bottom dead centre on the compression stroke, and to close it 44° before top dead centre.

The hardened steel rollers on the cam rocker arms are bevelled off at 45° on one side to allow of easy engagement of the half compression cam, which is also bevelled at 45°.

The details of this gear are clearly shown in the scale longitudinal sectional drawing of the rear end of the camshaft driving gear (Fig. 11).

CONNECTING RODS.—The connecting rods are of normal design and are of H section forgings machined from steel forgings, and measure 326 mm. between centres. The total weight of the complete connecting rod, including the small-end bush, is 7 lb. The weight of the big end complete is 4 lb. 14 oz., and the weight of the small end 2 lb. 2 oz. [Presumably the connecting rod was cut exactly midway and the weights represent each half of the rod.—Ed.]

MERCÉDÈS—continued.

The thickness of the centre web of the H section is 2.5 mm., and that of the two outer webs is 3.5 mm. The diameter of the big end bearings is 64 mm., and the length 80 mm. These are split in the usual manner and held by four 12-mm. bolts.

The distinctive feature of the connecting rods is the floating gudgeon pin bush, the design of which is similar to that used on the 160-h.p. Mercédès. The bush is of hardened steel ground 2.5 mm. in thickness, the outside diameter being 42 mm., and the inner diameter 37 mm. The bush is a perfect working fit in the small end, and also on the gudgeon pin ; and is lubricated by 14 holes of .5 mm. drilled radially in the bush, oil being supplied by a 6-mm. pipe leading upwards from the big end bearing. The pipe, which is of soft mild steel, is attached to the central web of the connecting rod by two riveted clips. Details of the connecting rods and floating gudgeon pin bush are given in Fig. 12.

CRANKSHAFT.—The six-throw crankshaft, which is of very massive design, weighs no less than 139 lb., including the propeller boss. The cranks are set at 120°, and the diameter of both crankpins and journals is 64 mm. The length of the front journal bearing next to the propeller is 140 mm., and the other crankshaft bearings is 64 mm.

The thickness and the width of the crank webs increase towards the front end of the crankshaft. The thickness of the front web is 29 mm., that of the second is 28 mm., whilst the remainder are all 27 mm. in thickness.

The crankshaft is bored and the webs drilled with oil passages leading from the hollow journals to the crankpins for lubricating the big end bearings in the usual manner. The holes bored in the journals and crankpins are of decreasing diameters, according to their distance from the oil pump and main delivery, as follows :—

Internal diameter of Hollow Crankshaft Journals.

Prop. end.	1	2	3	4	5	6
	35 mm.	35 mm.	35 mm.	38 mm.	40 mm.	41 mm.

Oil pump.

Internal diameter of Hollow Crankpins.

Prop. end.	1	2	3	4	5	6
	32 mm.	33 mm.	35 mm.	38 mm.	41 mm.	43 mm.

Oil pump.

The ends of the hollow journals and crankpins are plugged with sheet steel caps which are driven into the cranks, and then expanded into an annular groove cut inside the holes bored in the cranks.

To take the propeller thrust, a single thrust ball race 110 mm. in diameter is provided on the front end of the front journal bearing, and mounted in a split cage which is held in the housing of the crankcase halves.

PROPELLER BOSS.—The propeller boss, which is mounted on a taper of the crankshaft, is secured by a single key 120 mm. long and 13 mm. wide, which is sunk in the crankshaft parallel to the taper.

The front flange is fitted on to the boss by six stepped serrations or grooves, each 29 mm. wide, and is clamped to the propeller by six 18-mm. bolts on a 230 mm. diameter circle.

The propeller boss and the front flange are both locked on the shaft by the usual Mercédès locking device, shown in the drawings of the boss (Fig. 13).

CRANKCASE.—The very clean design of the crankcase casting is evident in the photographic views of the engine. It is of very light section considering the size of the engine, the average thickness of the walls of the casing being 6 mm. The top and bottom halves are bolted together in the usual way by 26 10-mm. hollow bolts through the flange on the centre level of the crankshaft.

The crankshaft main bearing caps are cast as part of the bottom half of the crank chamber. The long 20-mm. bolts which secure the bearing caps at the bottom pass through the top half of the crankcase and act as the holding-down bolts for the cylinders, which are held in position by triangular bridge clamps.

The bottom ends of the cylinder barrels extend past the base flanges, and fit into the top of the crankcase ; the holding-down bolts clamp each cylinder base flange at four points by the bridge pieces between each pair of cylinders.

Below the crank chamber, at the rear end is situated the mail oil sump, which contains the oil pump. In the front end of the base chamber casting below the false bottom is an auxiliary service oil sump, into which the return oil from the circulation system drains through a wire gauze filter.

The central chamber of the base chamber casting between the two sumps is used as an air chamber for the dual purpose of cooling the oil and warming the air supply to the carburetter.

Air is led by two ventilating funnels on each side of the crankcase into two oval ports in the base chamber casting, and a number of fins are cast on the under side of the false bottom inside the base chamber for cooling purposes.

The air intake to the carburetter is a large passage 4 in. in diameter, cast in the left-hand side of the crank chamber and base, as shown in the sectional arrangement drawings of the engine.

Cooling fins are also cast on the under side of the sump, and four breathers are fitted into the top half of the crank chamber between the webs of the main-bearing housings.

LUBRICATION.

Although the general lubrication system of the 260-h.p. Mercédès engines is arranged on normal principles it is necessary to deal with the various details of the somewhat complicated construction of the plunger type oil pump, and to describe their

different functions and the method of lubricating the engine as a whole.

The system of lubrication may be subdivided into three circuits :—

(a) The main pressure circuit, in which oil is drawn from the main oil sump at the rear of the engine and forced to the main crankshaft and connecting rod bearings, and also to the camshaft bearings.

(b) The supplementary pressure system, in which two auxiliary plungers of the main oil pump draw a small charge of fresh oil from the service oil tank at every stroke, and supply the main circulation with fresh oil.

(c) A suction "scavenger" circuit, which supplies the main oil sump from the auxiliary drain sump at the front of the base chamber. The working oil level is maintained in the rear sump by a secondary suction pump, which draws off the oil above the oil level through an overflow pipe and returns it to the service oil tank.

OIL PUMP.—The oil pump is attached to the bottom of the oil sump and is of the plunger type, being somewhat similar in design to that used on the 160-h.p. Mercédès.

Two main plunger pumps for suction and delivery are employed, and three auxiliary needle plunger pumps, suspended from one of the main pump plungers, work in conjunction with piston valves on plungers at the sides of the main pumps.

Each pump and valve plunger is operated by an eccentric, and the eccentric spindle is driven transversely to the engine crankshaft by a worm gear from a lay shaft, which is driven by bevel gearing from the vertical driving shaft of the water pump ; this shaft is in turn driven from the main distribution gear pinion on the rear end of the crankshaft, as shown in the sectional elevation of the engine (Fig. 6).

In its passage through the hollow camshaft the oil under pressure is fed through small holes and oil grooves cut in each of the camshaft bearings.

The camshaft rocker arm spindles are lubricated by oil thrown off the revolving cams, which deliver oil into two holes drilled side by side in the upper portion of the hollow rocker arm spindles and communicating with the bearings by small holes drilled radially in the spindle.

The lubrication of the rocker arm does not appear to have been very efficiently carried out, as it was noticed that one or more of the spindles had commenced to seize in their cast-iron brackets in the camshaft casing.

No outlet holes are provided in the rear end of the camshaft for the egress of oil, consequently the camshaft is entirely under a constant oil pressure, which finds its way through the bearings into the troughs in the bottom of the camshaft casing. The overflow oil returns to the crankcase through a 12-mm. pipe at

MERCÉDÈS—continued.

the front end of the engine from the bottom of the air pump crankcase, and also at the rear end of the camshaft casing down the hollow vertical shaft, oil channels being cut in the under side of each of the camshaft bearing bushes.

The oil which has returned by gravity to the crankcase is led into the oil sump at the rear through two holes 30 mm. in diameter drilled in the false bottom of the base. At the forward end of the crank-chamber the oil flows into the front auxiliary sump through a wire gauze filter, already mentioned.

In action, the pulsations of the oil pump plungers are damped out in the delivery pipe by the cushioning effect of the spring loaded plunger, which communicates direct with the pump on its under side. The bottom face of the plunger is prevented from touching the bottom of the barrel by a small set screw in the base.

The lubrication of the crankshaft and connecting rod bearings is standard practice and has already been referred to. Details of this are shown in the sectional elevation of the engine.

CARBURETTER AND INDUCTION SYSTEM.—Notwithstanding the large size of these engines only one carburetter is employed; this is situated low down at the rear end of the crankcase.

Below the float chamber is attached a petrol filter chamber, the petrol entering through a gauze cylindrical filter tube, which is screwed into the top filter chamber.

Petrol enters the bottom of the float chamber, which is of the ordinary balanced needle valve type.

The main jet, which is a plain tube with an orifice of 2.33 mm. diameter, is situated in the centre of the intake pipe, inside the choke tube. The choke tube is 32 mm. in diameter at the waist and 45 mm. at the largest diameter, top and bottom.

The throttle valve, which is of the barrel type, is 80 mm. in diameter and is mounted on ball bearings at each end; the races are 35 mm. in diameter, and are supported in recesses turned in the end covers of the gun-metal throttle valve liner, which is pressed into the cast aluminium body of the carburetter.

The dimensions of the semi-elliptical ports in the throttle valve are 80 mm. long by 50 mm. wide at the bottom side and 80 mm. × 55 mm. at the top.

The pilot jet, which is the same length as the main jet, is .89 mm. bore at the orifice. It is situated at the side of the intake passage, and communicates with an annular groove machined around the outer end of the throttle valve liner in the body of the carburetter. From this annular channel a passage communicates with the induction pipe just above the throttle valve, which when closed draws air through a V slot cut in the barrel of the throttle.

A conical suction valve supplies extra air automatically through eight holes 14 mm. in diameter drilled in the annular seating which surrounds the base of the choke tube.

Air is taken into the carburetter, as already mentioned, from the interior of the air chamber cast in the base chamber. The diameter of the air intake passage is 100 mm., and it extends inside the crankcase to the centre of the engine.

INDUCTION PIPE.—The diameter of the induction pipe at its joint with the carburetter is 70 mm.; this diameter increases to 100 mm. as it leads upwards to the engine in a right angle bend, which is lagged with asbestos cord.

The throttle valve is water heated by pipes leading from the main water circulation pipe to a water space cast in the body of the carburetter around the throttle valve.

No device for altitude adjustment is provided on the engines examined.

The design of the induction pipe is interesting; the gas is led to the centre of the engine by the 100-mm. pipe; the gas then enters a branch pipe 70 mm. in diameter through a port 100 mm. in diameter. Thence the two branch induction pipes lead outwards to the six inlet ports of the cylinders, which are 85 mm. long and 50 mm. wide.

IGNITION.—Two Bosch magnetos, type Z.H.6, are mounted on a transverse bracket at the rear end of the crankcase, one being a starter magneto, used in conjunction with a hand starter dynamo.

The magnetos are driven direct by bevel gears off the vertical camshaft driving shaft, the direction of rotation being anti-clockwise in both cases.

All 12 sparking plugs are fitted on the inlet side of the engine, and are situated directly below the inlet valves; the H.T. wires are carried in two fibre tubes attached to the sides of the cylinders on the inlet side.

AIR PUMP.—The air pump is driven off the front end of the camshaft, the bore being 26 mm. and the stroke 27 mm.

An adjusting screw is fitted above the release valve of the pump for regulating the strength of the spring, the released pressure being taken through the hollow stem of the adjusting screw. An oil trap is provided just below the air pump to retain any surplus oil which may find its way past the air pump valve and into the pressure pipe.

WATER PUMP.—The water pump extension shaft is driven through a vertical shaft off a bevel gear on the end of the crankshaft, and in the same vertical axis as the camshaft driving shaft; it is attached by a flange to the bottom of the sump, next to the oil pump.

The pump is of the centrifugal type, employing a rotary vane disc, the water entering below the bottom flanged cover through a 44-mm. port, below the rotor, and the water is delivered centrifugally from the vanes between the top and bottom of the rotor, which is also fitted with vanes upon its top side to throw the water away from the spindle.

Instead of packing glands, a hardened steel friction washer is let into a recess machined in the upper face of the rotor, and is kept in uniform contact with the face of the phosphor-bronze

spindle bush by the action of a light spring, which is fitted under a ball thrust race at the driving end of the spindle.

The diameter of the outlet passages from the water pump to the cylinders is 44 mm.

Double inlet water connections between each of the six cylinders supply the water-jackets at top and bottom, the diameter of the circulation hole in the steel water-jacket being 40 mm.

[THE FIGURES IN THE FOLLOWING COLUMNS ARE EXACTLY AS GIVEN IN THE OFFICIAL DOCUMENT.—ED.]

Tests on 260-h.p. Mercédès Engines at R.A.F. 14.7.17.

Power readings were taken at full throttle from 950 r.p.m. to 1600 r.p.m., simultaneous fuel consumption readings being taken. During this test the water outlet temperature varied from 75° to 81° C.

The water brake was then set to absorb full power at 1400 r.p.m. and the engine was gradually throttled down to 900 r.p.m. power and consumption readings being taken.

The results of these tests are shown graphically on the appended chart (C. 335).

At the conclusion of the above tests, a run of one hour's duration at 1400 r.p.m., full throttle, was made with the following results :—

Average b.h.p.	252
Petrol—pints per hour	15.25
pints per h.p. hour	0.605
Oil—pints per hour	8.125
pints per h.p. hour	0.032
Oil temperature at end of run	54.5° C.
Water outlet temperature	80° C.

It was noticed that at speeds below 1150 r.p.m. the vibration was rather excessive.

No adjustments were made to the engine during these tests.

Material Specification of Parts of 260 h.p. Mercédès Engine, No. 30111.

Analysis shows the chemical composition of the parts to be as follows :—

Gear Wheel.

Carbon	0.30	per cent.
Silicon	0.27	,,
Manganese..	0.74	,,
Sulphur	0.025	,,
Phosphorus	0.030	,,
Nickel	4.17	,,
Chromium	1.39	,,
Vanadium	Nil.	,,

ENGINES.

MERCÉDÈS—continued.

Connecting Rod.

Carbon	..	..	0.13 per cent.
Silicon	..	..	0.19 ,,
Manganese..	..	..	0.52 ,,
Sulphur	..	..	0.033 ..
Phosphorus	..	..	0.014 ,,
Nickel	..	..	2.83 ,,
Chromium	..	..	0.29 ,,

Camshaft.

Carbon	..	..	0.16 per cent.
Silicon	..	..	0.27 ,,
Manganese..	..	..	0.60 ..
Sulphur	..	..	0.052 ..
Phosphorus	..	..	0.014 ..

Camshaft Case.

	Body.	Cover.
Carbon	0.24 per cent.	—
Graphite carbon	—	2.97 per cent.
Combined carbon	—	0.62 ,,
Silicon	0.02 per cent.	1.81 ,,
Manganese	0.46 ,,	0.53 ,,
Sulphur	0.041 ,,	0.118 ,,
Phosphorus	0.012 ,,	0.085 ,,

Valves.

	Exhaust.	Inlet.
Carbon	1.75 per cent.	1.82 per cent.
Silicon	0.58 ,,	0.52 ,,
Manganese	0.10 ,,	0.10 ,,
Sulphur	0.048 ,,	0.048 ,,
Phosphorus	0.013 ,,	0.010 ,,
Nickel	Nil.	Nil.
Chromium	10.85 ,,	10.47 ,,
Vanadium and Tungsten	Nil.	Nil.

Crankcase.

Total Silicon	..	..	0.96 per cent.
Graphitic Silicon	..	..	0.35 ,,
Copper	..	..	4.22 ,,
Zinc	..	..	3.65 ,,
Iron	..	..	0.81 ,,

Valve Springs.

Carbon	..	..	0.52 per cent.
Silicon	..	..	0.07 ,,
Manganese	..	..	0.59 ,,
Sulphur	..	..	0.060 ,,
Phosphorus	..	..	0.031 ,,
Nickel and Chromium	..	..	Nil.

Crankshaft.

Carbon	..	..	0.41 per cent.
Silicon	..	..	0.29 ,,
Sulphur	..	..	0.052 ,,
Phosphorus	..	..	0.042 ,,
Manganese..	..	..	0.64 ,,
Nickel	..	..	2.36 ,,
Chromium	..	..	0.86 ,,

MECHANICAL TESTS.

Mechanical tests on the valve spring gave the following results :—

Outside diameter of spring	..	1.250 to 1.352 in.
Diameter of wire	..	1.56 in.
		[Probably a misprint for .156.—Ed.]
Number of free coils	..	7
Length of spring	..	3 in.

Compression in inches.	Load in lbs.	Unloading.
0	0	0
.1	6	4¾
.2	12	10¼
.3	18	16¾
.4	24	23
.5	30	29¼
.6	36	35⅓
.7	42	41
.8	48	47
.9	54¾	53¼
1.0	60⅜	59⅜
1.1	66¾	65⅞
1.2	73½	72½
1.3	81	79¾
1.4	88½	88
Closed 1.5	97⅛	—

Permanent Set, Nil.

Crankcase.

Tensile Tests :—

Yield point	..	..	8.7 tons per sq. in.
Maximum stress	..	..	9.35 ,, ,,
Elongation	..	..	3.55 per cent. on 2 in.
Reduction of area	..	..	3.5 per cent.
Specific gravity	..	..	2.867

Crankshaft.

Tensile Test :—

Yield point	..	..	55.7 tons per sq. in.
Maximum stress	..	..	62.0 ,, ,,
Elongation	..	..	13.5 per cent. on 2 in.
Reduction of area	..	..	23.5 per cent.

Impact Test on Crankshaft :—
23 ft. lbs. } on boss in direction
16 ft. lbs. } of shaft.

B. M. DEPARTMENT, R.A.F.

July 16th, 1917.

ENGINE DATA.

Number and arrangement of cylinders	..	6 (vertical, separate).
Bore	..	6.30 in.
Stroke	..	7.09 in.
Stroke/Bore ratio	..	1.125—1.
Normal b.h.p.	..	252.
Normal speed	..	1,400 r.p.m.
Piston speed	..	1,655 ft. min. (27.6 ft. sec.)
Area of one piston	..	31.17 sq. in.
Total piston area of engine	..	187.02 sq. in.
Swept volume of one cylinder	..	221 cub. in.
Total swept volume of engine	..	1,326 cub. in.
Volume of clearance space	..	56.10 cub. in.
Compression ratio, total vol./clearance vol.	..	4.94—1.
Air standard efficiency	..	47.30 per cent.
Brake mean pressure	..	107.50 lbs.
Mechanical efficiency (calculated)		87.90 per cent.
Indicated mean pressure (calculated)	..	122.35 lbs. sq. in.
Fuel consumption (lb. per b.h.p. hour)	..	0.541 lb.
Brake thermal efficiency (18,500 B.T.U.'s lb.)	..	25.46 per cent.
Indicated thermal efficiency	..	28.98 ,,
Relative efficiency	..	61.20 ,,

FRICTION LOSSES (CALCULATED).

(In terms of lbs. per sq. in. of piston area.)

Bearings, valve gear and auxiliaries		2.50 lbs. per sq. in
Fluid pumping losses	..	4.50 ,, ,,
Piston friction	..	7.85 ,, ,,
Total losses	..	14.85 ,, ,,
Brake mean pressure	..	107.50 ,, ,,
Mechanical efficiency, 107.50/122.35		87.90 per cent.

MERCÉDÈS—*continued*.

GAS VELOCITIES, VALVE AREAS, ETC.

Gas Velocity.

Choke tube	302.0 ft. per sec.
Vertical induction pipe	70.2 ,,
Induction manifold	125.6 ,,
Inlet port	115.6 ,,
Inlet valve	158.0 ,,
Exhaust valve	158.0 ,,
Exhaust port	115.6 ,,

Cross Section Area.

Choke tube	Total, 2,850 sq.in.
	[Probably a misprint for 2.850.—Ed.]
Vertical induction pipe	12.18 sq. in.
Induction manifold	6.86 ,,
Inlet port (total)	7.44 ,,
Inlet valve (total) (dh.) ..	5.45 ,,
Exhaust valve (total) (dh.) ..	5.38 ,,
Exhaust port (total)	7.44 ,,

Diameter.

Choke tube	
Vertical induction pipe	3.937 in.
Induction manifold	2.953 ,,
Inlet port (each)	2.175 ,,
Exhaust port (each)	2.175 ,,

Inlet valve (two per cylinder) :—

Outside diameter of valve ..	2.362 in.
Lift of valve	0.398 ,,
Width of seating	0.0787 ,,
Diameter of stem, in guide ..	0.433 in.
Diameter of stem, below guide ..	0.433 ,,
Radius under valve head	0.394 ,,
Length of valve guide	3.818 ,,

Length of spring, valve closed ..	2.362 in.
Ratio—Length of spring lift of valve	5.95—1

Exhaust Valve (two per cylinder) :—

Outside diameter of valve ..	2.362 in.
Lift of valve	0.394 ,,

[Compare with inlet lift. Possibly a micrometer error of 0.004 in.—Ed.]

Width of seating	0.0787 in.
Diameter of stem, in guide ..	0.433 ,,
Diameter of stem, below guide ..	0.433 ,,
Radius under valve head ..	0.394 ,,
Length of valve guide ..	3.818 ,,
Length of spring, valve closed ..	2.362 ,,
Ratio—Length of spring lift of valve	5.99—1.

INERTIA STRESSES.
LOADING ON CRANK-PIN BEARINGS, ETC.

Weight of piston, complete with rings, gudgeon pin, etc.	10.725 lbs.
Weight per sq. in. piston area ..	0.344 lb.
Weight of connecting rod, complete with bearings	7.00 lbs.
Total reciprocating weight per cylinder	13.225 lbs.
Weight per sq. in. piston area ..	0.424 lb.
Length of connecting rod between centres	12.835 in.
Ratio, connecting rod / crank-throw (l./r.)	3.62—1.

Inertia pressure, lbs. per sq. in. piston area—

Top centre	106.70 lbs. sq. in.
Bottom centre	60.50 lbs. sq. in.
Mean	83.60 lbs. sq. in.
Weight of rotating mass of connecting rod	4.50 lbs.

Total centrifugal pressure	887 lbs.
Centrifugal pressure, lbs. sq. in. piston area	28.45 lbs. sq. in.
Total loading due to inertia and centrifugal pressures	112.05 lbs. sq. in.
Mean average fluid pressure, including compression and pumping strokes ..	44.00 lbs. sq. in.
Mean average loading on connecting rod bearing, total from all sources in terms of lbs. per sq. in. on piston area ($\frac{2}{3}$ inertia)	128,120 lbs. sq. in. [?—Ed.]
Diameter of crank-pin	2 520 lbs. [?—Ed.]
Rubbing velocity	15.40 ft. per sec.
Projected area of big-end bearing ..	8.80 sq. in.
Ratio, piston area/projected area big-end bearing	3.545—1.
Mean average pressure on big-end bearing	454.00 lbs. sq. in.

Loading on connecting rod big-end bolts :—

Maximum load due to inertia at 1,400 r.p.m.	3,328 lbs.
Maximum load due to inertia at 1,600 r.p.m.	4,338 lbs.
Maximum [!—Ed.] load due to centrifugal force at 1,400 r.p.m. ..	887 lbs.
Maximum loads due to centrifugal force at 1,600 r.p.m.	1,163 lbs.
Total load on bolts at 1,400 r.p.m. ..	4,215 lbs.
Total load on bolts at 1,600 r.p.m. ..	5,501 lbs.
Number of bolts	Four.
Full diameter of bolts	0.4724 in.
Total cross-sectional area at bottom of thread	0.580 sq. in.
Stress per sq. in. at 1,400 r.p.m. ..	7,270 lbs. sq. in.
Stress per sq. in. at 1,600 r.p.m. ..	9,990 lbs. sq. in.

THE 180 H.P. MERCÉDÈS ENGINE.

ENGINE DATA.

Number and arrangement of cylinders	Six, vertical, separate.
Bore	140 mms.=5.51 ins.
Stroke	160 mms.=6.30 ins.
Stroke/bore ratio	1.142 : 1.
Area of one piston	23.84 sq. ins.=153.9 sq. cms.
Total piston area of engine ..	143.04 sq. ins.=924 sq. cms.
Stroke volume of one cylinder ..	150.28 cu. ins.=2463 cu. cms.
Total stroke volume of engine ..	901.68 cu. ins.=14778 cu. cms.
Volume of clearance space	41.3 cu. ins.=676.64 cu cms.
Compression ratio. Total volume/ Clearance volume	4.64 : 1.
Normal B.H.P. and speed	174 B.H.P. at 1400 r.p.m.
Piston speed	1470 ft. per min.
Brake mean pressure	109.1 lbs. sq. in.
Cu. ins. of stroke volume per B.H.P.	5.18 cu. ins.
Sq. in. of piston area per B.H.P. ..	0.823 sq. in.
B.H.P. per cu. ft. of stroke volume	334.0.
B.H.P. per sq. ft. of piston area ..	175.0.
Direction of rotation of crank and airscrew	Anti-clockwise facing airscrew.
Lubrication system	Forced, multiple plunger pumps.
Oil consumption per hour	7.3 pints=8.21 lbs.
Oil consumption per B.H.P. hour ..	0.642 pint=0.047 lb.
Oil pressure	20 lbs. sq. in.
Volume of oil carried in base chamber	17 pints.
Number and type of carburetters ..	One dual Mercédès, twin-jet.
Diameter of chokes	0.945 in.=24 mms.
Bore of main jets	0.058 in.=1.472 mms.
Bore of pilot jets	0.022 in.=0.559 mms.
Fuel consumption per hour ..	94.83 pints=85.32 lbs.
Fuel consumption per B.H.P. hour	0.545 pint=0.491 lb.
Inside diameter of induction pipes	2.126 ins.=54 mms.
Number and type of magnetos ..	Two, Bosch, Z.L.6.
Firing sequence of engine	1, 5, 3, 6, 2, 4.
Ignition timing (fully advanced) ..	30 deg. early.
Speed of magnetos	1.5 engine speed.
Inlet valve opens	Top dead centre.
Inlet valve closes	40 deg. late.
Diameter of inlet valve (smallest diam.)=d.	2.677 ins.=68 mms.
Lift of inlet valve=h	0.453 in.=11.5 mms.
Area of inlet valve opening (π.d.h.)	3.81 sq. ins.=24.58 sq. cms.
Mean gas velocity through inlet valve	153.4 ft. per sec.
Clearance of inlet tappet	0.017 in.=0.432 mms.
Exhaust valve opens	40 deg. early.
Exhaust valve closes	10 deg. late.
Diameter of exhaust valve (smallest diam.)=d	2.677 ins.=68 mms.
Lift of exhaust valve=h	0.453 in.=11.5 mms.

Photograph by courtesy of the Technical Department, R.A.F.

Magneto end of the 180 h.p. Six Cylinder Mercédès. High Compression Type.

MERCÉDÈS—continued.

Area of exhaust valve opening
(π.d.h.) .. .. 3.81 sq. ins. = 24.58 sq. cms.
Clearance of exhaust tappet .. 0.014 in. = 0.355 mms.
Diameter of inlet and exhaust ports 2.165 in. = 55 mms.
Diameter of water-pump inlet .. 1.692 in. = 43 mms.
Diameter of water-pump outlet .. 1.575 in. = 40 mms.
Ratio of water-pump speed to crankshaft speed .. .. .. 1.5 .1.
Delivery of water-pump at normal speed .. .. 41.4 gallons per min.
Inlet water temperature .. .. 64 deg. Cent.
Outlet water temperature .. .. 64 deg. Cent.
Outlet water temperature .. .. 74 deg. Cent.
Water-jacket capacity of one cylinder 1280 cu. cms.

GENERAL ANALYSIS OF WEIGHTS.

Description of Part.	No. per set.	Average unit weight.	Weight of complete set.	Percentage of total weight.
Cylinders (bare) ..	6	19.25	115.50	17.5
Pistons, complete with rings and gudgeon pins	6	6.85	41.10	6.23
Connecting rods, with gudgeon pin bushes	6	5.00	30.00	4.55
Valves, complete with springs, etc. ..	12	1.31	15.74	2.39
Crankshaft (bare) ..	1	70.00	70.00	10.60
Camshaft (bare) ..	1	7.75	7.75	1.17
Camshaft casing with bearings and covers	1	27.63	27.63	4.18
Valve rockers	12	.87	10.50	1.59
Half compression gear (complete) ..	1	7.00	7.00	1.06
Vertical driving shaft (complete, including casing, oil pump, drive, and floating bevel) ..	1	17.50	17.50	2.66
Base chamber (top half)	1	72.25	72.25	10.92
Base chamber (bottom half)	1	100.00	100.00	15.16
Carburetters	one dual	16.75	16.75	2.54
Induction pipes (lagged asbestos)	2	5.00	10.00	1.52
Water pump (complete)	1	7.75	7.75	1.17
Oil pump (complete) ..	1	13.25	13.25	2.00
Air pump (complete) ..	1	4.75	4.75	.72
Magnetos (complete) ..	2	14.00	28.00	4.25
Water piping	—	3.25	3.25	.49
Propeller hub (complete)	1	12.50	12.50	1.90
Ignition wiring (complete)	2	2.00	4.00	.61
Exhaust manifold ..	1	13.00	13.00	1.97
Miscellaneous parts ..	—	31.78	31.78	4.82
Total weight of complete engine (dry) (with propeller hub and exhaust manifold)		660 lbs.		100.00

WEIGHTS.

Weight of engine complete, dry, including propeller hub and exhaust manifold .. .. 660.0 lbs.
Weight per B.H.P. .. .. 3.79 lbs.
Weight of exhaust manifold .. .. .. 13.0 lbs.

P 2

Weight of oil carried in engine .. .. .. 19.125 lbs.
Weight of fuel and oil per hour .. .. .. 93.53 lbs.
Gross weight of engine in running order, less fuel, oil and tanks, but including cooling system at 0.65 lbs. per B.H.P. .. .. 773.0 lbs.
Weight per B.H.P. .. .. 4.44 lbs.
Gross weight of engine in running order, with fuel, oil and tanks for six hours. (Tanks at 10 per cent. weight of fuel and oil) .. .. .. 1390.3 lbs.
Weight per B.H.P. .. .. 8.00 lbs.

Airscrew end of the 180 h.p. (High Compression) 6 Cylinder Mercédès. *Photograph by courtesy of the Technical Department, R.A.F.*

115b

MERCÉDÈS—*continued.*

THE 200 H.P. HIGH COMPRESSION MERCÉDÈS ENGINE.

The following particulars are published by courtesy of the Controller, Technical Department, Department of Aircraft Production :—

The following report on the running performance of the 200-h.p. High Compression Mercédès Engine is based on an examination and tests carried out at R.A.E. on the engine (No. 775) taken from a *Fokker D.*7 biplane (*G/2 B/14*) brought down in France on June 6th, 1918.

It is of interest to note that this is the first Mercédès engine to be fitted with an altitude compensator carburetter. This compensator, which is here fully described, is so arranged that it is impossible to run the engine all out on the ground.

In most respects this engine is identical in design with the standard 180-h.p. Mercédès engine already reported on, except as to the following points :—

1. New design of pistons giving increased compression.
2. Carburetter—fitted with altitude control.
3. Induction manifolds—water-jacketed.
4. Duplex horizontally opposed air pumps.
5. Wireless dynamo mounted on induction side of crankcase, driven by gearing from rear end of crankshaft.

PISTON DESIGN AND COMPRESSION RATIO.

The pistons used in these engines are of the usual Mercédès construction, being built up with steel crowns which carry the gudgeon pins. The crowns are screwed and welded into their cast-iron skirts, and, as shown in the sectional drawing (Fig. 2), are considerably domed as compared with the concave heads used in the standard 180-h.p. Mercédès engines, thus giving a compression ratio of 5.73 : 1, *i.e.*, an increase of 23.54 per cent.

Standard 180-h.p. Mercédès connecting rods are fitted, and the distance from the gudgeon-pin centre to the top of piston is the same as before.

CARBURETTER.

The carburetter fitted to this engine is of the standard Mercédès type, with the exception of the throttle barrel, which is slightly modified to provide the automatic altitude control. This device consists of two extensions on the bottom of the barrel diametrically opposite to each other, of the shape shown in the sketch.

A section of the complete carburetter is shown diagrammatically in a figure.

Slots are cut in the sliding air valve to correspond with the extensions on the throttle barrel. The throttle control lever is marked for opening out to its maximum ground level position, and at all throttle openings up to this mark the lift of the sliding air valve is restricted, owing to its coming in contact with the extensions on the throttle barrel. Immediately the throttle is opened past the mark on the control lever, the extensions on the throttle barrel come in line with the slots in the

Three-quarter View from Airscrew End, 200 h.p. High Compression Mercédès engine.

MERCÉDÈS—*continued*.

sliding air valve, allowing the air valve to lift to its maximum position and uncover extra air holes, thus weakening the mixture to such an extent that the engine stops if the throttle is fully opened on the ground.

INDUCTION MANIFOLDS.

The induction manifolds are fitted with welded steel water jackets in place of the usual asbestos lagging. The jackets are each in direct communication with a feed from the water pump to the carburetter, the respective outlets being connected to the rear end cylinder jacket. Circulation is controlled by a cock on the return pipe (presumably for use in hot weather) which does not affect the water supply to the carburetter jackets.

AIR PUMP.

A double acting air pump of the usual plunger type is now fitted in place of the standard Mercédès air pump used hitherto on these engines. Both plungers are operated by a small common crank attached to the front end of the camshaft, the construction of which is shown in a sketch.

COMPARATIVE DATA.

In view of the similarity of design of the 160-h.p., 180-h.p., and 200 h.p. (high compression) Mercédès engines, the following brief comparison of the leading data is interesting :—

	160 H.P.	180 H.P.	200 H.P. (H.C.)
Bore	140 mm.	140 mm.	140 mm.
Stroke	160 mm.	160 mm.	160 mm.
Compression ratio	4.5 : 1	4.64 : 1	5.73 : 1
Normal B.H.P. and speed	162.5 at 1,400	174 at 1,400	204 at 1,600
B.H.P. per c.f. Stroke vol.	312 B.H.P. r.p.m.	334 B.H.P. r.p.m.	391 B.H.P. r.p.m.
B.H.P. per sq. in. Piston area	163.5 B.H.P.	175 B.H.P.	205.4 B.H.P.
Normal B.M.E.P.	102lbs. sq. in.	109lbs. sq. in.	112lbs. sq. in.
Fuel consumption per B.H.P. per hour	0.58 pt. =0.522 lb.	0.545 pt. =0.491 lb.	0.629 pt. =0.566 lb.
Diameter of choke tube	24.0 mm.	24.0 mm.	24.0 mm.
Capacity of main jets	355 cc. per min.	355 cc. per min.	450 cc. per min. (test jet) 250 cc. per min. standard jet)
Oil consumption per B.H.P. per hour	0.031 pt. =0.025 lb.	0.042 pt. =0.047 lb.	0.029 pt. =0.032 lb.

VALVE TIMING.

Inlet opens	2 deg. L.	Top dead centre.	1 deg. L.
Inlet closes	35 deg. L.	40 deg. L.	40 deg. L.
Exhaust opens	63 deg. E.	40 deg. L.	46 deg. E.
Exhaust closes	13 deg. L.	10 deg. L.	8 deg. L.

TAPPET CLEARANCES.

Inlet		0.017 in.	0.017 in.
Exhaust		0.014 in.	0.015 in.
Magneto timing	30 deg. E.	30 deg. E.	30 deg. E.

TESTS.

Three sets of calibration curves were taken in the following order :—

(a) With the carburetter opened out to its maximum position for ground level running.

(b) With the sliding air valves fixed at the base of the choke tubes and the throttle fully opened.

(c) With a 180-h.p. Mercédès carburetter (which had no altitude control) fitted in place of the standard carburetter, the jets being opened out to suit the engine, and the curves being taken with the throttle fully opened.

In the last test a fair amount of trouble was experienced with over-heating, due to the high compression ratio employed, but this was overcome at the expense of petrol consumption.

From the general running it is assumed that the normal speed of the engine is in the region of 1,500-1,600 r.p.m., as these are the best running speeds. Below 1,400 r.p.m. the engine is very rough, and it has a very bad period between 1,000-1,200 r.p.m.

SUMMARY OF POWER CURVES.

R.P.M.	1,200			1,400			1,600		
Para. as above	(a)	(b)	(c)	(a)	(b)	(c)	(a)	(b)	(c)
B.H.P.	148.5	144.5	151	164	174	180	171	186	204
B.M.E.P.lbs./in.	108.5	105.5	110	102.5	109	112.5	94	102	111.9
Petrol consumption pt. B.H.P./hr.	.515	.650	.680	.511	.590	.645	.520	.590	.629

Maximum power recorded—217 B.H.P. at 1,750 r.p.m.

Induction pipe depressions were taken between Nos. 1 and 2 cylinders.

Details of Piston—200 h.p. High Compression Mercédès engine.

MERCÉDÈS—*continued.*

Subsequently two one hour duration tests were carried out—
1 at 1,500 r.p.m.
1 at 1,600 r.p.m.

R.P.M.	1,500	1,600
Average B.H.P.	168	171
Average water inlet temperature	60 deg. C.	58 deg. C.
Average water outlet temperature	67 deg. C.	63 deg. C.
Average oil pressure	20 lbs. sq. in.	20 lbs. sq. in
Average oil temperature in tank	23 deg. C.	20 deg. C.
Oil consumption	4 pts. per hour = .024 pt./h.p./hr.	5 pts. per hour = .029 pt./h.p./hr.
Petrol consumption	91 pts./hr. = 35 pt./h.p./hr.	96.5 pts./hr. = .565 pt./h.p./hr.

F.G.C., Lieut., R.A.F. Ap.D. (L.).
J. G. WEIR. Brigadier-General, Controller, Technical
Department.

Section of Carburetter.

Part Sectional View of Carburetter Barrel, showing Altitude Control.

NAPIER (British).

D. NAPIER & SON, LTD., 14, New Burlington Street, London, W. 1. Works, Acton, London, W.

THE 450 H.P. NAPIER "LION."

The all-British "Lion" aero engine has many points of interest. The most noticeable novelty in the latest model is the new type of water jacket. There is now a separate jacket to each cylinder instead of a multiple jacket for each block of four cylinders. Undoubtedly, this is an improvement. Weight is saved, and the new method of making a water-tight joint between the cylinder and jacket is preferable to the old method which was used in the type produced in 1917, which could not then be described owing to the war. In the war former models the lower joint was made by a rubber ring; in the latest type the jackets are welded to the cylinders.

The "Lion" engine, which develops 450 B.H.P. at 2,000 r.p.m., and weighs only 1.86 lbs. per B.H.P. (without water, fuel, or oil), is in its entirety a highly creditable British production. Its twelve cylinders are arranged in three sets in the "broad arrow" method. Each cylinder has two inlet and two exhaust valves, the seatings of which are screwed through the head of the cylinder into the head casting. The valves are operated by two overhead camshafts, and the cams act directly upon the tappet heads, the stems of which are screwed into the valve stems so that the clearance may be adjusted. A spring locking ring secures the tappet head when the adjustment has been made.

The Self-Starting Device.

The engine is started by pumping an explosive mixture into the cylinders and firing it by means of a hand-starting magneto. By means of linked control levers the two forward valves of each cylinder are opened by hand pressure. The air-pump is mounted in the cockpit, and by means of a two-way cock it can be used first to pump pure air to the cylinders to expel any foul gasses that there may be in the combustion chambers, and then the explosive mixture is ready for firing. The mixture is formed by pumping air through a petrol vaporiser which is a form of spray carburetter.

The three rows of cylinders are supplied with mixture, when running, by two carburetters, a single and a duplex type. The gas passages are water-jacketed. So far as the throttles, diffusion jets and altitude control cocks are concerned the carburetters resemble the H.C.7 type, but modifications have been made to adapt them to the "Lion" engine.

The altitude control system is that of reducing the supply of petrol as the machine climbs. This is, of course, necessary, because as the air becomes rarified the percentage of air to petrol would become incorrect if the flow of fuel were not

View of complete Engine from Airscrew End.

[*The Editor desires to express his indebtedness to the Technical Department of the Air Ministry for assistance in compiling this description.*]

NAPIER—*continued.*

checked. There is a safety device, which causes the control when open to shut automatically when the throttle is closed. This prevents the mixture being too weak when the pilot makes a long dive and flattens out.

LUBRICATION.

Oil pumps of the spur wheel type are fitted and the lubricant is fed under pressure to both ends of the crankshaft and from thence along the inside of the shaft to the crank-pins and to the big-ends and gudgeon pins. Oil is also supplied under pressure to one of the camshafts on each set of cylinders and to the reduction gears. The cylinders are lubricated by oil splashed from the connecting-rod big-end bearings and gudgeon. Two scraper rings are fitted to each piston and the oil from the upper scraper ring is drained through holes cut in the piston,

IGNITION.

Two 12-cylinder magnetos are fitted. They are of the A.V.12 type manufactured by the British Thomson-Houston Co., Ltd. Both rotate anti-clockwise and one has a special distributer rotor for starting purposes. They are driven at one-and-a-half times the speed of the crankshaft in order to give six sparks for each revolution of the engine, as this type of magneto gives four sparks to each revolution. Two plugs are, of course, fitted to each cylinder. Those recommended by Messrs. Napier and Sons are the K.L.G. type F.10.

THE CRANKCASE.

The crankcase of the "Lion" is a fine casting of aluminium alloy. The top halves of the housings for the crankshaft plain and roller bearings are contained in the two ends and four internal cross-webs. The lower halves of the housings for the roller bearings are steel caps carried in studs in the rear and crosswebs.

The casing for the reduction gear is formed at the front end of the crankcase. The gearing is clearly shown in one of the diagrams. It will be seen that the arrangement is extremely neat. There are six camshafts—two for each set of cylinders, one operating the exhaust and one the inlet valves. Only one camshaft on each set of cylinders is driven by the reduction gear, the other camshaft is geared to this. Consequently, there are three shafts driven by the bevel gear wheel attached to the crankshaft. The diagram also shows how one shaft has two bevel wheels, one of which engages with the bevel wheel that drives the centre shaft. The compact arrangement by which the six camshafts, water pumps, oil pumps, and two magnetos are driven is clearly shown.

The following general particulars and dimensions are of interest :—

The new type Water Jacket in Place.

Upper Half of Crankcase—The Napier "Lion."

Crankshaft and Bearing Components of the Napier "Lion."

CYLINDERS.

Steel forgings machined all over. Water-jackets of steel. Detachable aluminium cylinder head, containing inlet and exhaust passages, valves and valve-actuating mechanism.

PISTONS.

Of aluminium alloy, fitted with two gas and two scraper rings. Gudgeon pins of large dimensions and hollow, working in steel bushes.

CONNECTING RODS.

Machined from special high-grade steel. The master rod, coupled to the pistons of the vertical block of cylinders, is formed with lugs on either side, to which are attached the short auxiliary rods for the pistons of the right and left groups of cylinders. The big ends are white metal lined, anchor pins and other parts work in bushes of ample size.

CRANKSHAFT.

Machined from a solid steel forging. The four throws are in one plane, and all journal bearings and crank pins are of large diameter and bored out. The shaft is carried in five substantial roller bearings and a large plain bearing at the forward end.

Connecting Rod Assembly.

WATER-PUMP.

Centrifugal type, mounted to rear end of engine and running at half crankshaft speed. The spindle is fitted with a metallic packed gland and a screw-down greaser. Water is delivered through a separate outlet to each of the three cylinder blocks.

Specification.

Number of cylinders	Twelve.
Arrangement	Three sets of four each, one vertical, two at 60 deg.
Bore..	5½ in.
Stroke	5⅛ in.
Horse-power, normal	450 at 1925 revs.
Direction of rotation of pro- peller shaft	Clockwise viewed from propeller end.
Speed of ditto	Reduction ratio 1 to 1.52 of crankshaft.
Ignition..	Two special dual magnetos; anti- clockwise rotation.
Oil consumption	0.02 pint approximately per B.H.P. hour, at full load.
Fuel Consumption..	6.51 pint approximately per B.H.P. hour, full load.
Self Starter	Napier Patent Air Petrol System
Weight of engine	850 lbs. approximately, complete with propeller boss, carburet- ters, induction pipes, etc.
Weight per h.p.	1.89 lbs.
Length over-all to centre of propeller	4 ft. 8 in. approximately.
Width over-all	5 ft. 6 in approximately.
Height over-all	3 ft. approximately.

The 450 h.p. Napier " Lion " engine.

NAPIER—*continued*.

Distribution End of the Napier "Lion."

26

Exhaust Camshaft

Inlet Camshaft

Propeller Shaft

Exhaust Camshaft.

Inlet Camshaft

Tachometer Drive.

Camshaft Drive

Camshaft Drive (Right)

Inlet Camshaft

Exhaust Camshaft

Magneto Drive

amshaft Drive (Left)

Pump Drive

Magneto Drives

Main Crankshaft Drive

Oil Pump Drives.

Diagram of Distribution Gears.

Sectional End Elevation of the 450 h.p. Napier "Lion."

Sectional Elevation of the Napier "Lion."

NEILSEN & WINTHER (Danish).

NEILSEN & WINTHER, A/S. Presundsvej, Copenhagen.

The only Danish aero-engine makers. Have produced the engine illustrated herewith. It appears to be almost purely Mercédès in type, plus a Benz arrangement of carburetters and inlet pipes.

OBERURSEL (German).

OBERURSEL MOTOREN GESELLSCHAFT, Oberursel by Frankfurt. German licensees for the Gnôme engine.

The fate of the Gnôme motor in Germany is an interesting record. The well-known automobile manufacturer and sportsman, Mathis—an early owner and pilot of an *Antoinette*—being the first agent. The Gnôme was used to a large extent on early German aircraft—*Albatros* constructed *Farman* box-kites and *Antoinette* monoplanes, some "Taubes," and *Euler* aircraft. Owing to national competition conditions, Gnôme disappeared but from Euler, who stuck faithfully to it as pure manufacturer and never entering competitions.

Later agents got small profits from the agency till the Oberurseler Motor Co. took up Gnôme manufacture by license, likely because they constructed already a stationary motor for agriculture service named Gnôme. The Deutsche Motoren Bebricles Gesellschaft were selling agents and found brisk business before and during the war for fighting aircraft of the star turn pilots, as *Ago*, *Fokker*, *Pfalz* and *Rex* mounts.

Same models as the French Gnôme Co. and later as the Le Rhône.

OPEL (German.)

OPEL MOTOR Co., Berlin.

Well-known motor-car firm now making aero-engines of more or less conventional Mercédès type. The Opel engine captured early in 1918 by the R.F.C. gives good results but particulars are not yet available.

OTTO (German).

OTTO-WERKE, Munchen.

200 h.p., 8-cyl. vertical water-cooled.

PACKARD (American).

THE PACKARD MOTOR COMPANY, Detroit, Mich.

This well-known motorcar firm devoted their aeroplane engine department to manufacturing engines for the U.S. Government, and consequently no information is available as to the most recent developments. However, the firm has made an 8-cylinder V engine, of alleged 160 h.p. which is illustrated herewith.

Side View of the 160 h.p. Packard Engine.

R. A. F. (British).

ROYAL AIRCRAFT FACTORY (Now "Royal Aircraft Establishment" to avoid confusion with initials of the Royal Air Force), South Farnborough, Hampshire.

Have experimented with engines for many years. Produced various types at various times.

Best known are the 8-cylinder 70 h.p., 8-cylinder 90 h.p. and 12-cylinder 140 h.p. All air-cooled. V type. General design and layout very similar to *Renault*.

R.A.F.—*continued.*

Later types have been built in large numbers by motor manufacturers in various parts of Great Britain.

Have also experimented with water-cooled V-type engines, and obtained interesting and educative results. A certain number of the water-cooled type had been manufactured for active service use, up to the end of 1917, but the engine is now obsolescent.

RAPP (German).

RAPP MOTORENWERKE G.m.b.H., München, Schleissheimerstrasse 211.

Started aero engine manufacture shortly before and have extended during the war. One of the first samples of this sound-looking design was the power of the well-known German aviator, Bruno Büchner's *Pfalz* biplane, brought to German East Africa for attaining colonial experience before the war and active during the campaign there.

6-cyl., 125 h.p. Weight : 474 lbs.
6-cyl., 150 h.p.
And higher powers.

Features :—
Vertical, water-cooled.
Steel cylinders in pairs.
Detachable inlet and exhaust valves.
Petrol consumption (150 h.p. Model) : 40 litres per hour.

REX (German).

REX Flugmaschine Rex Gesellschaft G.m.b.H., Kölln on Rhine, 1, Antwerpenerstrasse Has turned out a single-valved rotary engine for their own light aircraft.

RHEINISCHE (German).

RHEINISCHE AEROWERKE G.m.b.H., Euskirchen. Never constructed their own types, but in few copies, and selling to experimenters.

RHENANIA MOTOR WORKS, Ltd.,
Mannheim.

Manufacturers of apparently 11-cylinder rotary engines for fighting aeroplanes.

RICHARD & HERING (German).

RICHARD & HERING (Rex-Simplex Automobile Works) have likely dropped their own designs, or may manufacture on small quantity scale for school machines or even the leading types under royalty.

RENAULT (French & British).

France :—LOUIS RENAULT, 15, Rue Gustav-Sandoz, Billancourt (Seine).

These engines are made in the types illustrated hereafter but the firm has not vouchsafed any specifications.

Side View of the Renault engine, 190 h.p.

Rear View of the 300 h.p. Renault engine.

126b   Side View of the Renault engine, 300 h.p.

RENAULT—*continued.*

Side View of the Renault Aero engine, 450 h.p.

Rear View of the Renault engine. 450 h.p.

THE ROBERTS (American).

THE ROBERTS MOTOR MANUFACTURING Co., 151, Roberts Building, Sandusky, Ohio.

Two-stroke engines, made in two models, 6-cylinder, 100 h.p. and 12-cylinder, 350 h.p., as follows :—

	Model 6-X	Model E-12
Number of cylinders	6	12 V Type
H.P.	100	350
Bore and stroke	5″ × 5½″	6″ × 6½″
Speed (r.p.m.)	400 to 1500	400 to 1500
Speed (normal).	1200	1200
Weight	368 lbs.	990 lbs.
Propeller	8′3″ × 5′	as required
Piston pins (hollow)	1⅛″ dia.	1⅜″
Bearings (number of)	7	13
Bearings (size of crankshaft)	2½″ × 2½″ dia.	1¾″ × 3½″ dia.
Crankpin bearings	1¾″ × 2½″	2″ × 3½″

No fresh particulars have been received.

Roberts engine, type 6X, 100 h.p.   Inlet side, with carburetters and one magneto.

ROLLS-ROYCE—*continued.*

ROLLS-ROYCE, Ltd., Derby, and Conduit Street, London, W.

Four types are made, the "Hawk," 100 h.p.; the "Falcon," 280 h.p; the "Eagle," 360 h.p.; and the "Condor," 600 h.p.

The makers have kindly supplied the specifications and installation diagrams which follow hereafter.

One is permitted by courtesy of the Technical Department of the Air Ministry, to publish the accompanying photographs of the "Eagle" type.

Photographs of the other engines and of details are not available.

THE 100-H.P. ROLLS-ROYCE "HAWK."

Type	6-cylinder ungeared vertical water-cooled.
Bore	4 ins.
Stroke	6 ins.

The airscrew is carried by a shaft bolted to the crankshaft. This shaft runs in a nose bearing carried by an extension of the crankcase. By this means the heavy stresses due to the reaction of the porpeller when the machine is turning or diving, which occur in the end crank where the propeller is carried directly on the crankshaft, are avoided.

NORMAL POWER AND SPEED, AND FUEL CONSUMPTION.

Normal b.h.p.	100.
Normal engine speed	1500 r.p.m.
The maximum speed of the engine should not exceed	1700 r.p.m.
Fuel consumption at normal power and speed, using a mixture of 80% petrol and 20% benzole ..	6.5 gallons per hour.
Weight, including airscrew hub, carburetter, magneto, engine feet, etc., but excluding exhaust boxes, radiator, oil, fuel, and water ..	405 lbs.

IGNITION.—The ignition is provided by a 6-cylinder magneto serving one ignition plug in each cylinder.

Owing to the simple fact that the engine has only one single carburetter, it is capable of easy starting and of throttling down on slow running, more reliably and efficiently than is obtained by the common arrangement.

The oil consumption should be taken as ½ gallon per hour.

The quantity of water carried in the cylinder water-jackets, water pipes, and pump is 1.4 gallons.

The water system is completed to two points, at which pipes or couplings joining to the radiator may be affixed. These consist of one inlet connection to the water pump, and one outlet connection from the cylinders.

STARTING OF ENGINE.

It is usual, when starting this small engine, to turn it by means of the propeller for filling the cylinders after the induction pipes have been primed. The operation of the hand magneto (supplied by Messrs. Rolls-Royce) then starts the engine.

The Rolls-Royce Patented Device is supplied for priming. This is a light and simple apparatus, embodying a hand pump, which can be fixed in any convenient position near the pilot's seat, or as desired. One priming device may serve two or more engines with the use of a change-over cock.

When required, a starting handle can be supplied, arranged in line with the crankshaft at the timing gearcase end of engine, and connected thereto by a reduction gear. This apparatus is specially suitable for airship installations.

AIRSCREW HUB.

The airscrew hub is a specially Rolls-Royce design, but it conforms as far as the dimensions of the propeller boss to the design standardised by the Engineering Standards Committee. To overcome the troubles which are known to occur with propeller hubs on 6-cylinder engines, due to the comparatively irregular turning moment of this type of engine, Messrs. Rolls-Royce use a taper serration for connecting the hub to the propeller shaft, which is entirely successful in action.

General Arrangement Diagram of the Rolls-Royce "Hawk." 100 h.p.

ROLLS-ROYCE—continued.

THE 280 H.P. ROLLS-ROYCE "FALCON."

Type .. .. 12-cylinder vee water-
cooled.
Bore .. .. 4 ins.
Stroke .. .. 5.75 ins.

With an epicyclic reduction gear driving the airscrew at the most efficient speed.

NORMAL POWER AND SPEED, AND FUEL CONSUMPTION.

Normal b.h.p. .. .. .. 280.
Normal engine speed .. .. 2250 r.p.m.
Normal airscrew speed with reduction gear of 56/95 ratio .. .. 1327 r.p.m.
The maximum speed of the engine
should not exceed .. .. .. 2500 r.p.m
Fuel consumption at normal power
and speed, using a mixture of 80%
petrol and 20% benzole .. .. 18.5 gallons per hour.

WEIGHT.

Weight of engine, including airscrew
hub, carburetters, magnetos, engine
feet, etc., but excluding reduction
gear, exhaust boxes, radiator, oil,
fuel and water .. .. .. 630 lbs.
Weight of engine as above, but including reduction gear of 56/95 ratio 686 lbs.

IGNITION.

The ignition is effected by two six-cylinder magnetos, one firing each side of the engine, each cylinder being provided with one ignition plug.

OIL CONSUMPTION.

The oil consumption should be taken as .75 gallons per hour.

WATER COOLING SYSTEM.

The quantity of water carried in the cylinder water-jackets, water pipes, and pump is 2.5 gallons.

General Arrangement Diagram of the Rolls-Royce "Falcon." 280 h.p.

ROLLS-ROYCE—*continued*.

THE 360 H.P. ROLLS-ROYCE " EAGLE."

Type	12-cylinder vee water-cooled.
Bore	4.5 ins.
Stroke	6.5 ins.

With an epicyclic reduction gear driving the airscrew at the most efficient speed.

NORMAL POWER AND SPEED, AND FUEL CONSUMPTION.

Normal b.h.p.	360.
Normal engine speed	1800 r.p.m.
Normal airscrew speed, with reduction gear of .6 ratio	1080 r.p.m.
The maximum speed of the engine should not exceed	2000 r.p.m.
Fuel consumption at normal power and speed, using a mixture of 80% petrol and 20% benzole	24 gallons per hour.

WEIGHT.

Weight of engine, including airscrew hub, carburetters, magnetos, engine feet, etc., but excluding reduction gear, exhaust boxes, radiator, oil, fuel, water, and starter battery ..	836 lbs.
Weight of engine as above, but including reduction gear of .6 ratio	900 lbs.

VIRTUES OF THE 12-CYLINDER VEE ENGINE.

The 12-cylinder vee, having an angle of 60° is the type " par excellence " for high-power aero-engines. It possesses a superior mechanical balance, and an evenness of turning moment not found in any other known arrangement of cylinders at present in use. These factors, combined with the excellent power for weight ratio of this type of engine, enables it to excel over all others in meeting commercial requirements.

CYLINDERS.

The cylinders are such an essentially important feature of the engine that there should be no doubt about the reliability of the materials used in their construction.

The Rolls-Royce Cylinders are made entirely of wrought steel to a special patented design, the most reliable and efficient construction yet known for light aero-engines.

OTHER ENGINE PARTS.

The unmeasured attention which has been given to the other parts of the engine, such as pistons, connecting rods, crankshaft, etc., in respect to design, has resulted in great strength and reliability for the minimum weight and complication.

All material used in the manufacture of these pieces is rigorously tested to see that it is of consistent quality and conforms to the requisite standards.

The "Eagle" Rolls.

ROLLS-ROYCE—*continued*.

IGNITION.

The ignition is effected by four six-cylinder magnetos, two firing each side of the engine, each cylinder being provided with two ignition plugs.

It is generally known that magneto ignition is to be preferred where economy in running cost is required, as it is capable of firing those mixtures which are found to give the least fuel consumption.

This ignition being in duplicate and independent of a battery or a single electric conductor is arranged to give the greatest degree of reliability.

SAFETY FROM FIRE.

The four carburetters are specially arranged so as to be particularly free from risk of fire. No petrol can accumulate anywhere internally or externally in the engine, and the carburetters are arranged to drain away from the engine to a point outside of the cowling in the best known manner.

ROLLS-ROYCE REDUCTION GEAR.

With the epicyclic gear, as arranged on the Rolls-Royce Aero-Engines, there is no pressure on the crankshaft bearings due to reaction of the drive, and an efficiency is obtained which is far greater than can be got with any other type of gear, principally owing to the direction of motion not being reversed, and owing also to the gear only having to convert part of the horse power. This arrangement also avoids a great many heavy stresses in the casing.

FUEL, FUEL FEED AND CONNECTIONS.

It is specially recommended that the " Eagle " Engine be run on a mixture of 80% petrol and 20% benzole. This mixture gives slightly more power, and its characteristic manner of burning is specially suitable for an engine of this size.

Fuel is fed to the carburetters through the medium of the usual float feed, which performs satisfactorily through a pressure range of 1 to 4 lbs. per square inch, correspondingly, roughly, to a head variation of 3 to 12 feet.

The fuel feed connections to the carburetters are joined together by a system of piping having flexible joints which connects them to one single point on the engine. A suitable nipple and nut is provided at this main connection, for fixing the petrol pipe from the tank when completing the installation.

OIL CONSUMPTION, OIL FEED SYSTEM AND CONNECTIONS.

The oil consumption should be taken as 1 gallon per hour. The quantity of oil carried in the engine is negligible. The lubrication system of the " Eagle " Engine is of the type in which one oil pump supplies pressure oil to the main bearings, and other parts, while one scavenger pump evacuates the accumulation of oil in the crankcase to the oil tank, which should be provided in the installation. Each oil pump is protected by a strainer, which can be easily detached and cleaned. Connections, for which suitable nuts and nipples are provided, should be made at two points on the engine from the oil tank.

WATER COOLING SYSTEM.

The quantity of water carried in the cylinder water-jackets, water pipes, and pump is 3.1 gallons.

The water system is completed to three points, at which pipes or couplings joining to the radiator may be affixed. These consist of one inlet connection to the water pump, and two outlet connections, one from each group of six cylinders.

HIGH ALTITUDES.

The Rolls-Royce Carburetters are fitted with a control so that the delivery of petrol may be adjusted from the pilot's seat. This not only serves as a means of correcting the effects of decreasing atmospheric pressure with increasing altitude, but can also be used to obtain extremely economical running, and also to obtain a rich mixture for starting. Furthermore, the adjustable jet of the control serves as a very easy means of setting the carburetters for correct running on the bench.

CONTROL GEAR FOR CARBURETTERS AND MAGNETOS.

All controls, *e.g.*, throttle, altitude, and magneto, are brought to one common location on the engine, to facilitate connection to the plane. Only those control connections and levers which are fitted to the engine are supplied. If it is desired to operate the engine from a distance, control wire pulleys instead of levers may be supplied on the final engine connections.

The carburetter throttles are fitted with springs, which, in the event of a breakage of the control, are intended to open the throttles to the full extent.

ENGINE FEET.

The engine feet are designed for use with tubular bearers. One pair of feet should be located endways on the bearers, with suitable collars, while the other pair should be allowed to remain free.

STARTING GEAR.

An electric motor is fitted, arranged to turn the engine at about 25 r.p.m. through a reduction of 100 to 1 after the

General Arrangement Diagram of the Rolls-Royce " Eagle." 360 h.p.

132b

ROLLS-ROYCE (British).

induction pipes have been primed. The operation of the hand magneto (supplied by Messrs. Rolls-Royce) then starts the engine.

The control gear operating the starter, finishes with a wire pulley on the engine, so that connection can be made to it from a distance, if desired.

The Rolls-Royce Patented Device is supplied for priming. This is a light and simple apparatus embodying a hand pump,

which can be fixed in any convenient position near the pilot's seat, or as desired. One priming device may serve two or more engines with the use of a change-over cock.

A detachable handle is incorporated for turning the engine over by hand, through part of the reduction gear which serves the electric motor.

The electrical starting gear is complete in every way, except for the battery, which is not supplied.

**Side view of the " Eagle "
Rolls-Royce engine.**

*Published by courtesy of the Technical
Department of the Air Ministry.*

**End and top view of the " Eagle " type Rolls-Royce engine, showing
gear-box of air-screw shaft.**

ENGINES.

ROLLS-ROYCE—*continued*.

THE 600 H.P. ROLLS-ROYCE "CONDOR."

Type .. .. 12-cylinder vee water-cooled type.

Bore .. .. 5.5 ins.

Stroke .. .. 7.5 ins.

With an epicyclic reduction gear driving the airscrew at the most efficient speed.

NORMAL POWER AND SPEED, AND FUEL CONSUMPTION.

Normal b.h.p. .. .. .. 600.

Normal engine speed .. .. 1750 r.p.m.

Normal airscrew speed, with reduction gear of .666 ratio suitable for machines of moderate size and high speed .. .. .. 1167 r.p.m.

Normal airscrew speed, with reduction gear of .554 ratio, suitable for large machines of moderate speed 970 r.p.m.

The maximum speed of the engine should not exceed .. .. 1900 r.p.m.

Fuel consumption at normal power and speed, using a mixture of 80% petrol and 20% benzole .. .. 39 gallons per hour.

WEIGHT.

Weight of engine, including airscrew hub, carburetters, magnetos, engine feet, etc., but excluding reduction gear, exhaust boxes, radiator, oil, fuel, water, and starting battery .. 1200 lbs.

Weight of engine as above, but including reduction gear of .666 ratio 1300 lbs.

CRANKCASE.

The crankcase is of Rolls-Royce patented cellular construction, which increases the strength and simplicity of the cylinder attachments, and has not the weak points which appear in vee engine crankcases of conventional design.

IGNITION.

The ignition is effected by two complete and independent magnetos, each of which fires the whole of the cylinders.

SAFETY FROM FIRE.

The two carburetters are specially arranged in position and form so as to be particularly free from risk of fire.

Owing to the simple fact that this engine has only two single carburetters, it is capable of easy starting and of throttling down on slow running more reliably and efficiently than is obtained by the more common arrangement.

OIL CONSUMPTION.

The oil consumption should be taken as 1.6 gallons per hour.

WATER COOLING SYSTEM.

The quantity of water carried in the cylinder water-jackets, water pipes, and pump is 5 gallons.

General Arrangement Diagram of the Rolls-Royce "Condor." 600 h.p.

SALMSON (French & British).

SOCIÉTÉ DES MOTEURS SALMSON, 9, Avenue des Moulineaux, Billancourt.

British Address :—THE DUDBRIDGE IRON WORKS, Ltd., 37, Victoria Street, London, S.W.

(Salmson engines are built under the Canton-Unné Patents, and are in consequence frequently called Cantons, or Unnés.)

THE 250 H.P. SALMSON AERO-ENGINE.

Compared with the former Canton-Unné motor of radial type, dropped in 1917 and 1918, the new edition of the Salmson shows improvements and simplicity in many ways.

The development of high performance engines for war aeroplanes leads, undoubtedly, from the vertical model to the radial edition. Because of this development the new Salmson aero engine is very suggestive, and thus worth while to describe at some length.

The engine in question has a normal number of r.p.m. of 1400-1500 with nine cylinders of 125 mm. bore by 170 mm. stroke, and a nominal performance of 250 h.p.

The connecting-rods are attached to a master rod on the well-known principle of the Gnôme rotary engine. The great length of the connecting-rods favours this arrangement without any drawback in respect to the uniformity of the stroke, and offers good balancing of the masses.

The number of r.p.m. has been chosen as high as is possible with direct airscrew drive. Yet measures appear to have been provided for a possible use of the reduction gear, to increase the number of revolutions, as is intimated by the performance curve in Fig. 1.

The cylinders, arranged radially, are mounted round a two-part crankcase. The crankshaft rests on each side in a ball-bearing, and is at the rear end provided with a double-thrust bearing to take the airscrew pressure. On the front side of the crankcase the timing gear wheel box is mounted, enclosing a second bearing for the support of the airscrew shaft. The back half of the crankcase is provided with brackets for the mounting of the water and oil pumps and of the two magnetos.

The carburetter is arranged below the two pumps and is connected with a gas distributing channel, cast in the rear part of the crankcase, by means of two tubes, heated by the radiator water. From the gas channel nine suction tubes lead to the single inlet valves.

Nine tubes bring the exhaust tangentially to a collector, formed as a ring and arranged in front of the cylinders, which corresponds well with the circular fuselage form.

The engine is mounted by means of a centre plate with fixing eyes on the back part of the crankcase.

The general arrangement is evident from the Figs. 2 and 3. Further, it is apparent that the total apparatus is made very compact by the use of a ring-form exhaust collector, and of a round front radiator, long tubes, and other projections being thus avoided.

Figs. 4 to 6 give the general dimensions, which come out very favourably in relation to performance, as well as in regard to diameter and even more in respect to length.

Further details are shown in Figs. 7 and 8.

THE CRANKCASE.

The crankcase is made of an aluminium alloy, and is divided at the level of the connecting rods. Though it should apparently receive no greater strains than a single-cylindered engine, many ribs are provided as well as long guides for the centring of the cylinders. The housings for the ball bearings are strengthened by linings of a harder material. The front part has a centring for the mounting of the gear-wheel case and of an oil sump for the return suction pump.

Fig. 2. **Fig. 3.**

The 1917 Salmson Engine showing how the exhaust manifold is arranged to fit the front of a fuselage of circular form.

SALMSON—*continued*.

The back half has inside an arrangement for supporting the thrust-block with double ball bearings and its lubrication system. Outside is the centering with fixing eyes for the mounting in the aeroplane. The gas collector has been cast in one piece with the back half of the crankcase.

THE CYLINDERS.

The cylinders are made of steel, and are provided with welded water jackets of sheet steel. Much attention has been paid to giving the compression space the right form, and the valves sufficient area. The valve spindle guides are partly cooled.

The plugs are specially protected against oiling and overheating.

The cylinders rest in the crankcase by means of a base with large jointing surfaces, and are secured by stay bands of key section.

The pistons are cast of a special aluminium alloy, suitable for this purpose in respect to lightness, strength and anti-friction. The inner ribs are reduced to a minimum number, but are of specially large dimensions to avoid any deformation. Four cast iron piston rings, 3 mm. thick, are provided, the fourth being arranged in the opposite end of the piston, as a scraper.

The gudgeon pin turns in the piston bearings, so that the pin cannot cause a deformation of the piston. The connecting rods are made of compensated silver steel. Their length is sufficiently great to give a small deviation. Only the main connecting rod turns on the crank pin, while the eight others are attached in the well-known way. The section of the main connecting rod is a double-T form, that of the other ones circular.

THE CRANKSHAFT.

The crankshaft is made of chrome nickel steel in two pieces. The airscrew hub is mounted on the front part. The coned front part is connected with the rear part by means of a sort of head screw through a cone ground in at the crank pin.

The diameter has been very amply chosen, and drilling is employed to a fair extent for the purpose of lightening. To attain a balancing of the masses minutely counter weights are arranged on the crank webs. Each engine is specially tested with all its moving masses for complete balancing.

All main bearings are amply dimensioned and are on ball bearings.

Though this arrangement turns out heavier than journal bearings it has been preferred owing to its smaller sensibility to insufficient lubrication and because of the smaller oil consumption.

The connecting-rod bottom end bearings have ball-races with a special form of cage, and are tested separately under double

load before the mounting. The thrust ball-bearing mounted on the stern end of the crankshaft will take up the load of either a propeller or tractor airscrew.

THE VALVE GEAR.

As is evident from Fig. 8, one valve each is provided in the cylinder head for the inlet and the exhaust, being manipulated by means of rocker levers and adjustable tappets from one single camplate. The latter is mounted free on the front crankshaft pin, and is provided with six cams, each two of which lie in one level. Each pair of cams operate in turn the inlet and exhaust valves of three cylinders. During one turn of a pair of cams each valve of the group of three cylinders is operated twice. As two valve openings correspond in the four-cycle operation with four

Fig. 1.—**Power Curve of the 250 h.p. Salmson aero engine, showing powers developed at normal, full throttle and highest permissible speeds. The last would seem to refer to the possible addition of a reduction gear.**

Fig. 7.—Sectional side view.

ENGINES.

SALMSON—*continued*.

turns of the crankshaft, the gear ratio is thus 1 to 4 between cam and crankshaft. The cam is driven by means of a gearing cut in the crankshaft and two intermediate gear-wheels, mounted on the crankcase.

The transmission of the lift of the tappets by the cams is carried out by means of rocker levers and well-supported valve guides, all of which is housed in an aluminium chamber on the front side of the crankcase.

As the cams are accurately cut in the machining operation, it suffices to adjust one cylinder to regulate the whole cam operation.

LUBRICATION.

The lubrication takes place by means of oil circulating under pressure from a piston pump, mounted on the rear side of the engine below the water pump.

This pump has two cylinders, one to force the oil into the crankshaft and a second to bring the oil back to the oil tank from the sump cast in the front part of the crankcase. The oil-pump operates completely immersed in oil in an enclosed chamber that is connected with the oil tank by an amply dimensioned pipe from which the one piston sucks direct. The drive takes place by means of a worm-drive, lying inside the pump through an outer gear drive from the water-pump gear driving wheel. The wheel engaging in the worm is provided with a crankpin that operates direct on the two pistons, the pistons developing with the corresponding cylinders an oscillating movement whereby the inlet and ou let sections are operated. Thus valves and slides are avoided.

The motor is supplied with oil through the back crankshaft pin by means of a sort of casing running therefrom to the connecting pins wherefrom it is distributed farther on by the centrifugal force.

The inner drilling of the main connecting-rod big end bearing head is, in spite of the ball-bearing, formed as a journal surface, provided at the points of the main and auxiliary rods with drillings, through which the oil gets to the connecting and piston pins, as is usual with stationary engines. The oil coming out by the various bearings is slung round by the moving parts in the crankcase and lubricates in this way the cylinders.

The oil flung by the crankshaft and the pistons is again picked up by corresponding pockets to lubricate the cams, the crankshaft bearings and the thrust bearing. The supply of the camshaft case with the oil from the corresponding oil-catching pocket goes through two lines of piping.

The excess supply of oil from the pump is sucked away from the oil sump, cast in the front half part of the crankcase, and returned to the oil tank.

WATER CIRCULATION.

The water is circulated by means of the usual centrifugal pump, which is mounted on the back half of the crankcase and

driven by gears from the crankshaft. In leaving the radiator the water enters the pump through the cap, disperses through tube branches to the two lower cylinders 1 and 9, and therefrom flows through the rest of the cylinders, which are connected with each other by means of rubber sockets. This connection between the various cylinders is so worked out that the formation of steam-pockets is impossible.

The two water currents meet in the top cylinder No. 5, from which the water goes to the radiator. An exchangeable filter is provided between the motor and the radiator to prevent incrustation.

The tachometer is driven from the crankshaft by a gearing reduction of 2 : 11, and is mounted on the water-pump cap.

IGNITION.

There are two magnetos for the ignition, of Salmson manufacture, having stationary armatures and rotating casing. As the magnetos produce four sparks in one revolution, the relation of the revolution number to that of the crankshaft is 9 : 8. The magnetos are driven by a spur wheel transmission gear from the crankshaft. No spark variation arrangement is provided. Further details of this simple and interesting magneto are to be seen in the wiring diagram.

Finally, a combined drive for the timing the fixed machine-gun and for an alternating current generator is provided on the rear crankcase half appearing pretty voluminous, so far as the

Fig. 4.   **Fig. 5.**   **Fig. 6.**

GENERAL ARRANGEMENT DRAWING.—Kühlwasserein füllstutzen=Water inlet pipe connections. Wasserfilter=Water filter. Von Mitte, etc.=From middle of cylinder to backplate level. Centrierung etc.=Centring of rear mounting. Maschinengewehr Steuerung=Machine-gun timing. Aüspuffkopf=Exhaust head. Kühler=Radiator. Drehzähler=Tachometer. Wasserpumpe= Waterpump. Saugrohrheizung=Hot water jacket on inlet pipe. Olpumpe=Oilpump. Vergaser=Carburetter. Grösster Durchmesser=Greatest diameter.

8

machine-gun timing is concerned, while the drive of the wireless generator is by means of a simple belt pulley with a cone friction clutch.

CARBURATION.

The carburetter is a Zenith twin model with gas regulation for great altitudes, and with a common float chamber. The method of operation is the same as in the rest of the well-known Zenith carburetters with main and slow-running jets and compensator. The arrangement of these jets has been chosen so that the various positions of the aircraft do not influence the ratio of mixture. At the same time the jet arrangement permits a very simple adjustment of the carburettor without dismantling.

Besides the above-mentioned jet arrangement, the carburetter is further provided with an equipment for the regulation of the ratio of mixture for altitude, a simple cock effecting connection of the channel between the fuel jets and the inner air nozzle with the air pressure outside. When this cock is opened the pressure at the mouths of the jets rises, *i.e.,* the pressure gradient between the float chamber and the jet mouths is reduced ; less fuel therefore leaving and the mixture becoming thereby weaker. This cock remains closed on the ground and is opened in relation to the climb of the aeroplane up to a greater altitude. As this cock to some degree reduces the fuel supply in the jets, it may well be called a mixture reduction cock. Similar is the effect of the German Pallas carburetter, only in this case the air reduction section provided with a calibrated nozzle has a fixed adjustment. The piping scheme for petrol and oil is of interest, and will be understood without further explanation. It seems only worth mentioning how a pressure-free supply of the fuel has been attempted, to which end the somewhat elaborate installation of an air-pump in connection with a membrane petrol pump has been made.

Fig. 8.—Part sectional diagram of engine.

Fig. 17.

Luftschraube

Anlassmagnet

Masse

Ausschalter

Magnet 1

Magnet 2

Sicherheits funkenstrecke

Sicherherheits funkenstrecke

Masse

Unterbrecher

Unterbrecher

Masse

Masse

WIRING DIAGRAM.—**Sicherheitsfunkenstrecke=Safety-spark gap.** **Unterbrecher=Contact-breaker.**
Ausschalter=Switch. **Masse=Earth.** **Anlassmagnet=Starting magneto.**

Fig. 9.—Sectional view of Valve-timing gear.

SCHWADE (German).

OTTO SCHWADE & Co., of Erfurt, made Gnôme-copied Stahlherz motors for his *Henry Farman* type biplanes.

S.P.A. (Italian).

SOCIETA PIEMONTESE AUTOMOBILI, Turin.

200 h.p. Model (6A).

Type : Water-cooled vertical.
No. of cylinders . 6.
Bore : 5.31 in.
Stroke : 6.69 in.
R P.M. : 1,600.
H.P. : 220.
Valves : Overhead.   Overhead camshaft.
Carburetters : Two Zenith.
Ignition : Two type N2 Marelli magnetos.

The S.P.A. 200 h.p. aero engine.   Magneto end view.

The S.P.A. 200 h.p. aero engine.   Exhaust side.

SPYKER (Dutch).

TROMPENBURG–SPYKER WORKS, Amsterdam, Holland.

Make a 9-cylinder Rotary Engine of Clergèt type.

Specification.
9 Cylinders.
135 h.p. at 1100/1200 revolutions per minute.
Bore 120.

Stroke 160 m/m.
Mechanically operated valves by push rods, one exhaust, one inlet.
Aluminium pistons. Hollow connecting rods with fixed gudgeon pins floating in bronze bushings in piston.
Cylinders all steel with ribs integrally machined.
Dual ignition.
Total weight 138 K.G.

STŒWER AUTOMOBILE WORKS (German.)

Stettin.

Manufacturers of 6-cylinder vertical aero-engines of 125, 150 and 180 h.p. to own design.

Front End View of the Spyker Rotary engine. 135 h.p.

Front View of the Spyker Rotary engine. 135 h.p.

STURTEVANT (American).

THE B. F. STURTEVANT Co., Hyde Park, Boston, Mass., U.S.A.

210 h.p. Model 5A—4-1/2.

Type : Watercooled V.
Bore : 4½ in. = 114 m/m.
Stroke : 5½ in. = 140 m/m.
Cylinder capacity : 700 cub. in.
No. of cylinders : 8.
Arrangement of cylinders : "V."
Cooling : Water circulation by centrifugal pump.
Cycle : 4 stroke.

Ignition : Double.
Magnetos : 2—8-cylinder "Dixie" magnetos.
Carburetter : Zenith Duplex, water-jacketed manifold.
Oiling system : Semi dry sump, complete forced feed.
Normal engine speed : 2,250 r.p.m.
Propeller speed : 1,350 r.p.m.
Rated H.P. : 210.   Maximum H.P. 240.
Weight, with all accessories, but without water, petrol or oil : 480 lbs.
Weight of water contained in engine : 35 lbs. = 16 kilos.
Weight per B.H.P. dry : 2.4 lbs. = 1.09 kilos.
Fuel consumption, full speed, full load : .55 lbs. per H.P. hr.
Oil consumption : 8 lbs. per hr.

Rear view of the Sturtevant Model 5A.

Front End view of Sturtevant Model 7.   300 h.p.

Side View of the Sturtevant engine.   Type 5A—4½.   210 h.p.

SUNBEAM (British).

THE SUNBEAM MOTOR CAR Co., Ltd., Wolverhampton.

THE SUNBEAM "ARAB" ENGINE.

The issue of Dec. 20th, 1918, of the German motor and aero paper, "Der Motorwagen," contains an illustrated article by Civil Engineer Otto Schwager, of Charlottenburg, on "A New English Aero Motor of Unknown Manufacture," of which an abstract follows.

An eight-cylinder high-speed engine, resembling the Hispano-Suiza engine in appearance and arrangement, made its appearance some time ago on the Western Front. The engine is apparently made by the English Sunbeam firm at Wolverhampton.

The main data of this new motor are as follows :—

Cylinder bore = 120 mm.
Stroke = 130 mm.
Total cylinder capacity = 11.8 litres.
Compression ratio = 5.39.

The engine appears to be designed for a similar rotation speed to the Hispano-Suiza 2,000 r.p.m., and the performance, assuming mean effective pressure of 8.4 kg. per sq. cm., works out at 220 h.p. Between the camshaft and the airscrew a spur-gear has been installed with a reduction ratio of 5.3, the airscrew running thus at 1,200 r.p.m. for 2,000 r.p.m. at the crankshaft. The weight of the motor without water and oil, airscrew boss and exhaust manifold amounts to 240 kg., which corresponds with 1.09 kg. h.p.

All these figures correspond almost exactly with those of the 220 h.p. Hispano-Suiza engine, with which latter its exterior has much in common. Yet it shows quite a number of novel features, some being improvements upon the Hispano-Suiza, although, taken on a whole, it cannot be considered a serious development of its prototype. Its creation must rather be considered a superfluous increase of the types. Nevertheless, this engine possesses many noteworthy details, distinguishing it from its model and affording the designer many hints.

The engine is mounted on an aluminium crankcase, fundamentally different from that of the Hispano-Suiza. The crankshaft is carried entirely by the upper half, as is the practice in various German motors. There is even more reason for choosing this design, as with each set of four cylinders cast together in a block and bolted to the crankcase, an arrangement giving the greatest resistance to torsional stresses can be used. Furthermore, the designer has displaced the joint between the top and bottom parts of the case as far as possible below the crankshaft, still further stiffening the upper half against such

stresses, which are always pretty low in V-type motors with block cylinders. The bearing brasses are lined with white metal and bolted to the top part of the case, through cast aluminium covers.

The bearing covers are further supported by fish-plates of a rolled aluminium alloy, apparently duralumin, and the whole is bolted to the top part of the crankcase.

There is less reason for this design than for that of the upper crankcase, as it should be possible to make the bearing covers considerably more torsion-proof for the same weight. The gear-casing is well strengthened by ribs cast direct on the front part of the case. For mounting in aircraft a continuous ledge, cross-ribbed upwards and downwards, is cast level with the crankshaft centre line. Immediately above this ledge a channel for the oil-supply to the crank bearing is cast in, thus dispensing with oil-pipings, but making the oil-supply depend on accurate

The "Arab" Sunbeam-Coatalen engine, 235 b.h.p. at 2,000 r.p.m.

142b

SUNBEAM—*continued.*

moulding. The bottom part of the crankcase is formed mainly as a light oil sump, and is divided from the top part by means of an oil-filter for most of its length. Thus cleaning the oil-filter is only possible when the motor is taken down, which is apparently unimportant, owing to the large free section of the filter. The weight of the whole crankcase amounts to about 47½ kg. against 36 kg. by the Hispani-Suiza engine. The advantages of the original design seem thus not to have been turned to full effect.

Including the support in front of the small gear wheel the crankshaft has six main bearings. The diameter of these main journals is 59 mm., that of the connecting-rod bearings is 50 mm. The centre crankshaft bearing is much longer than the rest. Though the crankshaft appears stronger than that of the Hispano-Suiza one, its weight is only 16.2 kg., against 23 kilos. of the Hispano-Suiza shaft. This result is achieved by ample boring of the shaft to the extent of 38 mm. diameter between the gear wheel and the first crank, to 42 mm. in the rest of the crankshaft bearing, and to 32 mm. in the crank-pins.

Taking the most unfavourable condition that the piston pressure is distributed on two main bearings 48 mm. long, the surface load = 72 kg. sq. cm. at 30 atmospheres maximum explosion pressure, which corresponds at n = 2,000 r.p.m. to a value for the friction loss x of = 436 m. kg. per sq. cm. per sec.

The connecting rods (illustrated here), contrary to the Hispano-Suiza, have been formed as articulated rods. In spite of the resulting uneven piston movement the articulated rod is to be preferred to the forked rod on the score of reliability, though the latter represents undoubtedly a more elegant design. It renders possible a strong design of connecting-rod bearing cap ; and, secondly, the friction at these bearing connecting-rods can be better dealt with, though care must be taken not to attain this advantage at the cost of too heavy a main connecting-rod. In the present case weight is saved by leaving out brasses in the connecting-rod bearing and casting the white metal in the rod head, with the attendant risk of greater damage to the crankshaft if a bearing runs. The auxiliary connecting-rod is attached to the main rod in the usual way by a bolt 30 mm. diameter and 40 mm. bearing length. The two rods are both of double T-section. The rod end for the bronze gudgeon-pin bush of 30 mm. diameter and 51 mm. bearing length shows the usual form, and is provided with a number of weight-reduction holes. The lubrication of the gudgeon-pin, contrary to the Hispano-Suiza practice and to the rest of the well-known motor designs, is by oil splashing, which simplifies the lubrication system, but does not increase the reliability.

Assuming the maximum explosion pressure, but neglecting the inertia forces, the various bearing loads will be as shown in the following table :—

Bearing	Diameter. Cm.	Bearing length. Cm.	Surface load. kg. per cm.
Main connecting rod pin	5.0	5.2	130.5
Joint pin	3.0	4.0	283
Gudgeon-pin	—	5.1	222

The friction losses for the connecting-rods at 2,000 r.p.m. work out at 681 kgm. per sq. cm. sec. Taken altogether, the design and construction of the connecting-rods must be considered successful, especially considering their weight, which for a complete set of two is 2.075 kg. against 2.57 kg. in the Hispano-Suiza motor.

An astonishing feature of the piston design is its small height, amounting only to 73 mm. against 105 mm. in the Hispano-

The "Arab 2" Sunbeam-Coatalen with ungeared airscrew drive. End View.

143b

Suiza motor. This small height has been chosen to reduce the weight of the reciprocating masses and thereby keep the horizontal inertia forces low. The weight of the finished piston with rings and pin amounts only to 1.165 kg., against 1.4 kg. in the Hispano-Suiza, or 10.2 grammes per sq. cm. of piston surface, as against 12.3 in the prototype. The piston is an aluminium die casting, which practice appears to play an increasing part in foreign aero-motor manufacture, and justifiably so. Firstly, the die casting produces a most exact blank, thus relieving the designer from providing a margin to cover core eccentricities, allowing him to choose the dimensions, giving the necessary stiffness ; and, secondly, die-cast metal possesses better strength qualities than usual sand-castings (about 20-22 kg. sq. mm. and 4-4½ per cent. extension against 10-15 kg. sq. mm. and 1-2 per cent. extension), thus permitting a further reduction of the wall thicknesses, which are reasons for the greater employment in Germany of this casting process. The piston-head is stiffened by two cross-ribs reaching nearly to the bottom of the piston-skirt. Furthermore, a support reaching to the gudgeon-pin has been provided in the middle of the head, a practice employed in some German engines.

Three piston rings are provided above the gudgeon-pin. A fourth ring at the other end of the piston is fitted to scrape off surplus oil. The gudgeon-pin is locked against side displacement by spring rings and studs resist turning. Where the gudgeon-pin bearings penetrate the body of the piston, the latter has been milled flat to avoid seizing caused by distortion of the piston.

The cylinder block is another interesting design item. As in the Hispano-Suiza motor the four cylinders are united in a single aluminium casting. In this case the cylinder casing is extended to the crankcase to which it is fixed through very strong flanges, which renders the whole construction rigid indeed. The steel liners of 2 mm. wall thickness are not screwed in, but are held and prevented from moving by a collar, turned at the bottom. Two small exhaust valves and one large inlet valve are mounted in the cylinder head, inclined slightly in relation to the cylinder shaft, with bronze seats screwed into the aluminium casing. Inserted cast iron bushes serve as valve-stem guides. Special steel bushes are provided on both sides for the plug-threads. Below the plug socket the water-jacket casting is open, with aluminium sheet covers, strengthened by pressed ribs, and fixed with 16 screws to flanges on the block. The top side of the cylinder block is provided with a straight through tunnel carrying the camshaft bearings.

The weight of the cylinder block, ready for erection, with all studs is 35.6 kg., somewhat heavier than in the Hispano-Suiza engine.

The valve gearing differs fundamentally from that of the Hispano-Suiza, this motor being equipped, as already mentioned, with two small exhaust valves of 36 mm. diameter, and one large inlet valve of 53 mm. diameter per cylinder. The valves

SUNBEAM—*continued.*

are operated by the camshaft through twin-armed levers for the exhaust valves, and single-armed ones for the inlet valve. There are no cam-rollers, the rocking levers bear direct on the cams. The lever end does not press direct on the head of the valve stem, but on an inserted thrust-jacket. The play between the latter and the lever can only be readjusted by inserting sheet discs in the jacket. A better arrangement might have been devised here. The whole valve-gearings is enclosed in an oil and dust-proof casing as in the Hispano-Suiza. The lubrication takes place through the hollow camshaft.

The camshaft drive is by an auxiliary shaft, running in a casing cast on at the end of each cylinder block parallel to the cylinder.

The twin-carburetter, mounted between the cylinder blocks, is a Claudel-Hobson, with altitude regulation, much used by enemy aero-motors, with no special features. As in the Hispano-Suiza the incoming air is pre-heated by the radiator, the carburetter intake is fitted with a heating jacket, and the induction pipes are without any heating device. With induction pipes of greater area, combined with the amply dimensioned inlet valve, the charging of the cylinders is better provided for than in the Hispano-Suiza, and the performance, stated at the beginning of the article, should be surpassed.

The ignition arrangements correspond both as regards to position and drive with Hispano-Suiza practice.

The circulating pump is of the usual centrifugal type, and is driven direct from the rear end of the crankshaft. From the pump the cooling water enters the water-jacket of each cylinder block on the inner side of the cylinders between the third and fourth cylinder in each block. To obtain an equal distribution of the water inside the water-jacket, each cylinder block is provided with three gutters, any steam pocket formation being avoided by their favourable position.

Airscrew end of " Arab " Sunbeam engine.

Magneto end of " Arab " Sunbeam engine.

144b

SUNBEAM—*continued*.

The lubrication system is a simple circulation system with a pump extracting the oil from the lowest point of the very deep sump. The oil is pumped by a circulating pump into the already described oil ways in the upper half of the crankcase, thence distributed to the different bearings. At the front end of this oil channel a branch pipe to the gear box leads oil to the gear wheels. The oil collected in the lower part of the crankcase is then returned by the suction pump to the oil tank, which may be replaced by an oil radiator.

The reduction gear is of the usual spur wheel type, and of the following main dimensions :—

Gear ratio, 2,000/1,500 ; gear teeth, 27/45 ; gear diameters, 110.97 m./194.95 mm.

The shaft of the large wheel serves at the same time as air-screw hub. the rear flange of which is in one piece with the shaft. A cam ring, operating the machine-gun control, is screwed to the hub.

Briefly, it may be said that the motor is a somewhat belated, partly improved, edition of the Hispano-Suiza motor, but shows no great development of the original, though in many details it can give German aero-motor designers hints. Specially the use of aluminium die castings should be emphasised.

Specification.

8 cylinders.
120 m/m bore by 130 m/m stroke.
90 degrees Vee.
3 valves per cylinder.
Volume of cylinders : 12,260 ccs.
The camshaft drive is by means of bevel gearing.
Approximate weight per horse power : 2.3 lbs.
Normal revolutions 2,000 per minute.
Articulating connecting rod system.
Maximum B.H.P. is 235 at 2,000 R.P.M.
Variable ignition by two 8 cylinder magnetos.
Claudel Hobson carburetter type H.C.7 set inside.
Lubricant consumption : average 6.5 pints of castor oil per hour.
Normal oil pressure to main engine details at full power : 45 lbs. per square inch.
Some of these engines are fitted with hand starters.
Propeller shaft driven direct from the crankshaft.

A Section through a Cylinder of the Sunbeam " Arab."

Connecting Rods of the Sunbeam " Arab."

Crankshaft of the Sunbeam " Arab."   The dimensions are in millimetres.

The Assembled Crankcase, Sunbeam " Arab."

SUNBEAM—*continued.*

THE "MAORI 4" SUNBEAM-COATALEN AIRCRAFT ENGINE.

(Specially designed for airship use.)

12 cylinders.
100 m/m. bore by 135 m/m. stroke.
60 degrees Vee.
4 overhead valves per cylinder.
2 overhead camshafts per block of cylinders, driven by a train of gears.
Volume of cylinders : 12,270 ccs.
Direct drive to propeller shaft. A flywheel is also fitted to these engines.
Articulating connecting rod system.
Normal revolutions 2100 per minute.
275 B.H.P. at normal revolutions of engine.
Approximate weight per h.p. : 3.3 lbs.
4 Claudel Hobson carburetters B.Z.S. 38.
Pressure feed to carburetters.
Ignition is by two 12 cylinder magnetos.
A hand starter and electric starter are fitted.
The exhaust pipes are provided with a special arrangement for water cooling.
The water pumps are of specially large dimensions, and a governor is fitted to the engine to prevent over-running. When the engine speed reaches 2,500, the governor automatically comes into operation, and similarly when the oil pressure falls below 20 lbs. per square inch.

The " Maori 4 " Sunbeam-Coatalen engine (Direct Drive for Airships). 275 Nominal h.p.

SUNBEAM—*continued.*

General Arrangement of the " Maori 4 " Sunbeam-Coatalen engine.

SUNBEAM—*continued*.

THE "COSSACK" SUNBEAM-COATALEN AIRCRAFT ENGINE.

12 cylinders.
110 m/m bore by 160 m/m stroke.
60 degrees Vee.
4 valves per cylinder.
Volume of cylinders : 18,246 cubic centimeters.

Articulating connecting rod system.
Normal revolutions 2,000 per minute.
Geared drive to propeller shaft.
Reduction ratio : 2 to 1.
Approximate weight per h.p. : 3.7 lbs.
350 B.H.P. at 2,000 R.P.M.
Average petrol consumption : 0.54 per h.p. per hour.
4 Claudel Hobson carburetters, type C.Z.S. 42, set outside cylinder blocks.

Pressure feed to carburetters.
Ignition is by two 12 cylinder magnetos.
Lubricant consumption : average 6.5 pints of castor oil per hour.
Normal oil pressure to main engine details at full power : 45 lbs. per square inch.
A compressed air starter and hand starter are fitted to these engines.

The " Cossack " Sunbeam-Coatalen engine, 350 b.h.p. at 2,000 r.p.m.

End View of the " Cossack " Sunbeam-Coatalen engine.

THOMAS (American).

THE THOMAS AEROMOTOR COMPANY, Inc., Ithaca, New York.

150 h.p. Model 88.
Type : Water-cooled " V."
No. of cylinders : 8.
Bore : 4 ins. Stroke : 5½ ins.
R.P.M. : 2,100. (Propeller shaft : 1,200 r.p.m.)
Cylinders : Cast in pairs, integral jackets, with detachable heads. Cylinders and heads of aluminium alloy, with steel liners to cylinders.

Valves : Side by side, central valve gear.
Carburetters : Duplex Zenith, hot air intake, water heated.
Ignition : 2 four-spark magnetos.
Lubrication : High pressure.
Water feed : Pump operated.
Weight : 525 lbs., including self-starter.
Oil consumption : 1½ gals. per hour.
Petrol consumption : 15 gals. per hour.

UNION (American).

THE UNION GAS ENGINE COMPANY, Oakland, California, U.S.A.

Produce the 6-cylinder engine illustrated, which is believed to have been used on certain small American Airships. No data available.

Exhaust Side of the Union Aero engine.

Pump End of the Union Aero engine.

Inlet Side of the Union Aero engine.

WISCONSIN (American).

WISCONSIN MOTOR MFG. Co., Sta. A., Dept. 335, Milwaukee, Wis.
Engaged entirely on aero engines for U.S. Government. No fresh details available.

140 h.p. Model.
Type : Water-cooled vertical.
No. of cylinders : 6.
Bore : 5 in. Stroke : 6½ in.
R.P.M. : 1,400.
Cylinders : Cast in pairs.
Valves : Overhead. Overhead camshaft

Carburetter : Single
Ignition : 2 six-spark magnetos.
Lubrication : Forced feed.
Weight (claimed) : 600 lbs.

250 h.p Model, as above, but :—
No. of cylinders : 12.
Weight (claimed) : 1,000 lbs.

WOLSELEY (British).

WOLSELEY MOTORS, Ltd. (Proprietors : Vickers, Ltd.)
Head Office : Adderley Park, Birmingham.

London Office : York Street, Westminster.

Have made numerous engines during the war, chiefly Renaults and R.A.F.'s. Later developed the "Viper" engine, a modified Hispano-Suiza, with raised compression and a special type of piston, which gave excellent results.

Plan View of the Wolseley "Viper II."

Front End View of the Wolseley "Viper II."

CHARACTERISTICS OF LEADING AERO ENGINES.

Engine	Rated H.P.	Type	No. of Cyls.	Bore Mm.	Bore Ins.	Stroke Mm.	Stroke Ins.	Bore and Stroke Ratio	B.H.P. Normal B.H.P.	R.P.M.	Maximum B.H.P.	R.P.M.	Compression Ratio	Piston Speed, Ft. Min.	Order of Firing	Method of Cooling	M.E.P. Lbs. per Sq. In.	Inlet No.	Dia., Ins.	Total Area, Sq. Ins.	Lift, Ins.	Exhaust No.	Dia., Ins.	Total Area, Sq. Cms.	Lift, Ins.
ABC Dragon-Fly	320	Radial	9	140	5.5	165	6.5	1.18 −1	320	1650	350	1750	4.025	1785.5 1650	1, 3, 5, 7, 9, 2, 4, 6, 8	A	114	1	2.6559	5.4537	.6535	2	1.6929	2.2992	.4330
ABC Wasp	170	Radial	7	114.3	4.5	.....	5.9	1.31 −1	170	1750	200	1850	4.025	1690	1, 3, 5, 7, 2, 4, 6	A	115	1	2.17	3.33	.4700	2	1.338	2.4800	.2950
BR 1..............	150	Rotary	9	.....	6.72	.....	6.66	1.42 −1	154	1250	156	1300	5.9 −1	1394	1, 3, 5, 7, 9, 2, 4, 6, 8	A	94	1	1.77	2.41	.4300	1	2.000	2.7300	.4300
BR 2	200	Rotary	9	.....	5.51	.....	7.08	1.285−1	238	1300	242	1350	5.3 −1	1475	1, 3, 5, 7, 9, 2, 4, 6, 8	A	95.2	1	2.47	3.9554	.5100	1	2.28	3.6510	.5100
Beardmore	160	Vert.	6	142	.....	175	.....	1.23 −1	178	1350	192	1450	4.56−1	1435	1, 5, 3, 6, 2, 4	W	103	1	2.559	.....	.....	1	2.5590	.....	.....
Benz	220	Vert.	6	145	.....	190	.....	.....	230	1400	252	1650	4.93	1745	.....	.....	113	.	2.244	.....	.....	.	2.244	.....	.....
Clerget 92	110	Rotary	9	120	4.72	.....	6.30	1.33 −1	122	1250	123	1300	4.36−1	1260	1, 3, 5, 7, 9, 2, 4, 6, 8	A	78	1	1.5743	1.9423	.3937	1	1.9685	2.8031	.4528
Clerget 92	130	Rotary	9	120	4.72	.....	6.30	1.33 −1	127	1250	.....	.....	4.56−1	1312	1, 3, 5, 7, 9, 2, 4, 6, 8	A	81	1	1.692	2.24	.3900	1	1.9685	3.038	.4527
Curtiss OX5	90	V-90°	8	101.5	4	127	5	1.25 −1	93	1400	95	1450	4.5	1166	1L, 1R, 2L, 2R, 4L, 4R, 3L, 3R	W	111	1	1.9094	2.0823	.3437	1	1.9094	2.3267	.3878
Curtiss VX	160	V-90°	8	127	5	177.8	7	1.41 −1	206	1350	214	1450	4.71	1575	1L, 1R, 2L, 2R, 4L, 4R, 3L, 3R	W	110	1	2.7559	3.2366	.3740	1	2.7559	3.2366	.3740
Fiat A12bis	275–300	Vert.	6	160	6.3	180	.....	1.12	304−290	1600	325	1760	4.31−1	1653	1, 5, 3, 6, 2, 4	W	105	2	2.00	5.5180	.4300	2	2.0078	5.518	.4375
Fiat A14	600	Vert.	12	.....	6.69	.....	8−27	1.235−1	700	1500	725	1600	.....	.....	.....	W	108	.	.....	.....	.....	.	.....	.....	.....
Galloway	240	Vert.	6	145	5.71	190	7.48	1.31	236	1400	250	1500	4.96−1	1558	1, 5, 3, 6, 2, 4	W	116	1	2.7165	4.0455	.4724	2	1.8110	4.2346	.4724
Gnome	100	Rotary	9	110	4.33	150	5.90	1.36 −1	103	1200	110	1300	4.0 −1	1180	1, 3, 5, 7, 9, 2, 4, 6, 8	A	88.7	0	.....	.....	.....	1	.....	.....	.....
Hispano	150	V-90°	8	.....	4.72	.....	5.12	1.08 −1	156	1500	165	1600	4.8 −1	1280	1, 4, 2, 3, 4, 1, 3, 2	W	114.75	1	1.9685	2.4350	.3937	1	1.9685	2.4350	.3900
Hispano	180	V-90°	8	.....	4.72	.....	5.12	1.08 −1	220	2000	225	2100	5.3 −1	1707	1, 4, 2, 3, 4, 1, 3, 2	W	121.8	1	1.9685	2.4350	.3937	1	1.9685	2.4350	.3900
Hispano*	180	V-90°	8	.....	4.72	.....	5.12	1.08 −1	208	2000	225	2100	5.3 −1	1707	1, 4, 2, 3, 4, 1, 3, 2	W	121.8	1	1.9685	2.4350	.3900	1	1.9685	2.4350	.3931
Hispano*	200	V-90°	8	.....	4.72	.....	5.12	1.08 −1	220	2000	215	2100	4.8 −1	1707	1, 4, 2, 3, 4, 1, 3, 2	W	115	1	1.9685	2.4350	.3900	1	1.9685	2.4350	.3937
Hispano Suiza	150	V-90°	8	120	4.72	130	5.12	1.08 −1	150	1450	170	1700	4.8 −1	1240	1L, 4R, 2L, 3R, 4L, 1R, 3L, 2R	W	114	1	1.9685	2.4350	.3937	1	1.9685	2.4350	.3937
Hispano Suiza	180	V-90°	8	120	4.72	130	5.12	1.08 −1	180	1700	205	1800	5.3 −1	1450	1L, 4R, 2L, 3R, 4L, 1R, 3L, 2R	W	122	1	1.9685	2.9350	.3937	1	1.9685	2.4350	.3937
Hispano Suiza	300	V-90°	8	140	5.5	150	5.90	1.07 −1	300	1600	340	1800	5.3 −1	1578	1L, 4R, 2L, 3R, 4L, 1R, 3L, 2R	W	125	1	.....	.....	.....	1	.....	.....	.....
I.F. V5	200	Vert.	8	130	.....	190	.....	.....	250	1400	268	1600	5	1995	.....	W	107.6	.	.....	.....	.....	.	.....	.....	.....
LeRhone	80	Rotary	9	106	4.13	140	5.51	1.32 −1	80	1200	85	1300	1.33−1	1100	1, 3, 5, 7, 9, 2, 4, 6, 8	A	81	1	1.5629	1.7317	.3593	1	1.5629	1.4492	.2952
Liberty 8	270	V-45°	8	127	5	177.8	7	1.40 −1	270	1700	285	1850	18%	1980	1L, 6R, 5L, 2R, 3L, 4R, 6L, 1R. 2L, 5R, 4L, 3R.	W	115	1	2.5	3.4344	.4375	1	2.5	2.9437	.3750
Liberty 12A	400	V-45°	12	127	5	177.8	7	1.40 −1	400	1700	430	1800	18%	1980		W	115	1	2.5	3.4344	.4375	1	2.5	2.9437	.3750
Lorraine Dietrich	275	V-90°	8	120	4.72	175	6.89	1.46 −1	278	1650	...	.....	.....	.....	.....		.....	.	.....	.....	.....	.	.....	.....	.....
Maybach	200	Vert.	6	150	.....	190	.....	.....	200	1200	...	.....	.....	1496	.....	W	107.4	.	1.8998	.....	.....	.	1.3779	.....	.....
Mercedes	160	Vert.	6	140	.....	160	.....	.....	150	1250	...	.....	4.8−4.52	1312	.....	.....	105.2	.	.....	.....	.....	.	.....	.....	.....
Mercedes	260	Vert.	6	160	.....	180	.....	.....	252	1400	260	1500	4.94	1635 at	.....	.....	107.5	.	2.3622	.....	.....	.	2.3622	.....	.....
Oberursel	110	.....	..	.....	.....	.....	.....	.....	.....	.....	.....	.....	.....	.....	.....		.....	.	.....	.....	.....	.	.....	.....	.....
Rolls-Royce Falcon 3	220	V-60°	12	.....	4.00	.....	5.75	1.44 −1	270	2200	280	2300	5.3 −1	2108	Rht. 1, 2, 5, 4, 3, 1, 6, 5, 2, 3, 4, 6	W	114	1	1.7496	2.4211	.4437	1	1.7496	2.4211	.4400
Rolls-Royce Eagle 8	360	V-60°	12	.....	4.5	.....	6.5	1.44 −1	350	1800	360	1900	5.3 −1	1950	Rht. 1, 2, 5, 4, 3, 1, 6, 5, 2, 3, 4, 6	W	124	1	2.0000	2.9155	.4850	1	2.0000	2.9155	.4800
Siddeley	240	Vert.	6	.....	5.71	.....	7.48	1.31	240	1400	250	1500	5 −1	1558	1, 5, 3, 6, 2, 4	W	118.1	1	2.5984	3.9060	.4724	2	1.7322	5.2080	.4724
Spa 6A	200	....	6	135	.....	170	.....	.....	210	1600	225	1700	5	1895	.....	.....	116.6	.	.....	.....	.....	.	.....	.....	.....
Sunbeam Arab.......	200	V-90°	8	120	4.72	130	5.12	1.08 −1	217	2000	224	2100	5.3 −1	1710	1, 1A, 2, 2A, 4, 4A, 3, 3A	W	115	1	2.126	2.3631	.3543	2	1.2598	2.8088	.3543
Sunbeam Cossack	320	V-60°	12	.....	4.33	.....	6.30	1.45 −1	350	2000	364	2100	5 −1	2100	1, 5, 3, 6, 2, 4	W	121	2	1.6142	3.6952	.3543	2	1.6142	1.8476	.3500
Sunbeam Maori	250	V-60°	12	.....	3.95	.....	5.31	1.35 −1	265	2100	280	2200	5.6 −1	.....	1 5, 3, 6, 2, 4	W	125	2	.....	.....	.3543	2	.....	.....	.3500

CHARACTERISTICS OF LEADING AERO ENGINES.—*continued.*

Engine	Total Fuel & Oil per Hr. Pts.	Lbs.	Pints Fuel	Pints Oil	Lbs. Fuel	Lbs. Oil	Combined Pts.	Combined Lbs.	Dry Lbs.	Dry Lbs./B.H.P	Running Order Lbs.	Running /Lbs./B.H.P.	With Fuel 6 Hrs. Lbs.	With Fuel Lbs./B.H.P.	Torque in Lbs. Ft.	B.H.P. 6000 Ft.	10,000 Ft.	15,000 Ft.	20,000 Ft.	Fuel 6000 Ft.	10,000 Ft.	15,000 Ft.	20,000 Ft.
ABC Dragon-Fly		191.5			.56	.02			600	1.88	600	1.88			1019	256	218	176	138	149	134	116	100
ABC Wasp	94.8	85	.55	.026	.495	.019	.567	.514	260	1.53	260	1.53	820	4.82	510	138.11	122.24	104.37	89.67	83.53	78.56	72.68	67.34
BR1	118.2	109.75	.661	.097	.59	.109	.758	.699	405	2.6	405	2.6	1129.35	7.8	655	129	114.2	97.5	83.7	93.7	88.1	81.5	75.5
BR 2	176.2	162	.7	.066	.63	.074	.766	.702	475	2	475	2	1544	6.5	961	196.8	174.2	148.75	127.8	146.2	137.5	127.2	117.8
Beardmore	108.5	98.96	.52	.032			.609	.552	592	3.3	713	4	1366	7.6	692	147.2	130.3	111.25	95.6	93.7	88.1	81.5	75.5
Benz					.653	.02			829	3.68													
Clerget 92	97.5	91.35	.667	.131	.6	.147	.798	.747	367	3	367	3	970	8	512	101	89.3	76.25	65.5	74	69.6	64.4	59.6
Clerget 92	99.05	92.26	.67	.109	.60	.123	.779	.723	400	3.15	400	3.15	1009	8	533	105	93	79.4	68.2	77.3	72.7	67.3	62.3
Curtiss OX5	48.66	44.16	.51	.018	.46	.02	.528	.48	285	4.2	445	4.8	676.5	7.3	371	76	67.3	57.5	49.4	42.6	40.1	37.1	34.4
Curtiss VX																							
Fiat A12bis	162.8	147.6	.55	.024	.49	.027	.574	.517	928	3.32	1110	3.96	2084	7.44	920	215	190.3	162.5	139.6	141.6	133.2	123.2	114.2
Fiat A14	396.7	363.7	.52	.042	.47	.047	.562	.517	1565	2.36	2020	2.9	4420	6.3	2450	580	512.4	430.75	370.6	306.2	313.7	290.25	268.9
Galloway	143.2	130.45	.58	.027	.52	.03	.607	.55	690	2.95	843	3.57	1704	7.2	885	195.2	172.75	147.5	126.7	124.2	116.8	108	100.1
Gnome					.72	.18		.90	270	2.7													
Hispano	96.5	88.2	.58	.038	.52	.043	.618	.563	455	2.9	657.4	4.29	1239.5	7.9	546	129	114.2	97.5	83.8	82.2	77.3	71.5	66.25
Hispano	138.6	127.8	.58	.05	.52	.056	.63	.576	510	2.32	653	2.97	1492	6.67	583	182	161	137.5	118	115.8	109	100.8	93.5
Hispano*	138.6	127.8	.58	.05	.52	.056	.63	.576	510	2.32	653	2.97	1492	6.67	583	182	161	137.5	118	115.8	109.0	100.8	93.5
Hispano*	137.8	126.9	.6	.06	.54	.067	.66	.607	503	2.42	638	3.1	1475.6	7.8	546	172	152.25	130	111.7	113.3	106.6	98.6	91.3
Hispano Suiza		85.5			.52	.05		.57	440	2.93													
Hispano Suiza		127.2			.52	.056		.576	485	2.69													
Hispano Suiza									596	1.98													
I.F. V5					.485	.033			825	3.95													
LeRhone					.56	.19		.75	245	3.05													
Liberty 8	182.24	182.2	.606	.0214	.547	.050	.627	.597	575	2.12						260	181	148	116	112	100	87	75
Liberty 12A	192.8	192.8	.565	.0199	.509	.037	.585	.546	845	2.11	1151.5	2.88				320	272	220	172	163	144	125	108
Lorraine Dietrich																							
Maybach																							
Mercedes					.6	.029			618	3.86													
Mercedes					.605	.032			935	3.75													
Oberursel																							
Rolls-Royce Falcon 3	161.15	146.6	.56	.026	.53	.026	.586	.559	723	2.68	912	3.38	1880	6.9	694	227.4	201.3	171.8	147.6	139.8	131.5	121.6	112.7
Rolls Royce Eagle 8	204.7	186.2	.56	.025	.5	.028	.585	.528	933	2.66	1177	3.37	2406	6.9	1020	289.5	256.2	218.75	188	178	167.4	154.8	143.5
Siddeley	147.6	135.85	.56	.055	.50	.062	.615	.562	625	2.6	781	3.25	1677.6	7.0	900	198.5	175.7	150	129	122	114.7	106.2	98.4
Spa 6A					.473	.033			539	3.21													
Sunbeam Arab	116.3	106.46	.50	.036	.45	.04	.536	.49	550	2.5	686	3.16	1389	6.4	570	179.5	158.8	135.6	116.5	98.5	92.6	85.7	79.4
Sunbeam Cossack	208	189.9	.56	.034	.50	.038	.594	.538	1118	3.2	1345	3.8	2598	7.4	919	289.5	256.2	218.75	188	178	167.4	154.8	143.5
Sunbeam Maori	161.2	141.97	.56	.023	.51	.026	.583	.536	890	3.3	1065	3.95	2002	7.8	662	219	194	165.6	142.3	136.2	128.1	118.5	109.8

Engine	Carburettor No.	Type	Weight Each, Lbs.	Magneto No.	Type	Speed x E.S.	Weight Each, Lbs.	Oil Pump No.	Type	Weight, Lbs.	Water Pump No.	Type	Weight, Lbs.	Air Pump No.	Type	Weight, Lbs.	Ratio of Gear Reduction	Speed of Propeller	Tractor or Pusher	Overall Dimensions Length, M/M.	Width, M/M.	Height, M/M.
ABC Dragon-Fly	2	H. C. 8	......	2	M. L. 9	1.18	13.5	1	Plunger Distributed	......	.	....	.	.	......	.	....	E.S.	T.	1070	1232	1207
ABC Wasp	2	A. B. C. Injectors		2	P. L. 7. M. L. P.	1.75	......	1	Gear		.	....		.	......		Nil	E. S.	T.	35.7″	42.20″	42.20″
BR1..............	1	Block Tube	5	2	A. D.S. M. L.	2.25	10	1	Plunger	6.63	.	Nil		1	Plunger	4.7	Nil	E. S.	Either	43.5″	47.50″	41.57″
BR 2	1	Block Tube	......	2	M. L.	......	10	1	Plunger	6.63	.	Nil	......	1	Plunger	......	Nil	E. S.	Either	57.08″	19.92″	31.88″
Beardmore	2	Zenith	5.75	2	D. U. 6 S.	1.5	16	1		......	1	Centrif.	4.9	.	....		Nil	E. S.	Either			
Benz			......	2	2H6 Bosch			.	Gear	......	.	Centrif.			....							
Clerget 92	1	Block Tube Bush D.A.L.	4.41	2	A.D.S.	E. S.	9–10	1	Gear	6.63	.	....		1	Plunger	4.8	....	E. S.	Either	36.22″	40.15″	40.15″
Clerget 92	1	Block Tube	5.0	2	A.D.S.	2.25	9–10	1	Plunger	6.63	.	Nil	......	1	Plunger	4.7	Nil	E. S.	Either	36.22″	40.15″ Dia.	40.15″
Curtiss OX5	1	Zenith Duplex	4.2	1	Berling	2	21	1	Gear	.....	1	Centrif.		.	Nil		Nil	E. S.	Either	1408	753	841
Curtiss VX	2	Zenith Duplex	......	1		2		3	Gear	.....	1	Centrif.	......	.	Nil		Nil	E. S.				
Fiat A12bis	1	Siemens.............		2	6-cyl. Dixie 60-V.	1.5	......	3	Gear	.....	1	Centrif.		1	Plunger		Nil	E. S.	Either	......	......	......
Fiat A14											1	Centrif.										
Galloway	2	48 Zenith RA.........	3.25	2	E. M. 6	1.5	15	1	Rotary	4.06	1	Centrif.	6.51	1	Plunger	.88	Nil	E. S.	Either	67.32″	20.07″	42.91″
Gnome	1	Mixing Valve		1		9/4		2	Two Plunger	.....	.	....		.	Nil		Nil	E. S.	Either			
Hispano	1	Zenith Duplex 48 D.C.	7.0	2	1A8S	E. S.	17.75 18.12	1	Eccentric Vane	.....	1	Centrif.	2.69	1	Plunger	15 oz.	Nil	E. S.	Either	51.53″	33.46″	32.67″
Hispano	1	Zenith Duplex 58 D.C.	9.5	2	1A8S. 1AB	E.S.	18.12 17.75	2	Eccentric Vane	.....	1	Centrif.	2.69	.	Plunger		Nil	E. S.	Either	47.24″	33.46″	33.34″
Hispano*	1	Zenith Duplex 58 D.C.	9.5	2	1ABS. 1AB	E. S.	18.12 17.75	2	Eccentric Vane	.....	1	Centrif.	2.69	1	Plunger	15 oz.	Nil	E. S.	Either	47.24″	33.46″	33.34″
Hispano*	1	Zenith Duplex 58 D.C.	9.5	2	S.E.V.	E.S.	16–3	1	Eccentric Vane	.....	1	Centrif.		1	Plunger	13 oz.	24x41 or 21x28	1170 or 1500	Either	51.18″	33.46″	33.26″
Hispano Suiza	1	Zenith Duplex 48 D.C.	7.0	2	8-Cyl. Dixie Transverse	2	......	1	Eccentric Vane Type		1	Centrif.		1	Plunger	......	Nil	E. S.	Either	1308	851	832
Hispano Suiza	1	Zenith Duplex 58 D.C.	9.5	2	8-Cyl. Dixie Transverse	2	......	1	Eccentric Vane Type		1	Centrif.		1	Plunger		Nil	E. S.	Either	1308	851	832
Hispano Suiza	1	Zenith Duplex 58 D.C.	9.5	2	8-Cyl. Dixie Transverse	2	......	1	Gear		1	Centrif.		1	Plunger		Nil	E. S.	Either			
IF. V5				2				.	....		.	....		.	......			1400	Either			
LeRhone	1	Mixing Valve ..	4.19	1	A.D.S. 26° Early	9/4	9.10	1	Plunger	4.125	.	....		.	......		Nil	E. S.	Either			
Liberty 8	1	Zenith Duplex	7	1	Twin Delco Generator, 8-volt	1.5	......	3	Gear	.....	1	Centrif.		1	Plunger	......	Nil	E S.	Either	......		1020
Liberty 12A	2	Zenith Duplex U.S. 52	......	1	Twin Delco Generator, 8-volt	1.5	......	3	Gear	.....	1	Centrif.		1	Plunger		Nil	E. S.	Either	1755		1020
Lorraine Dietrich								.	....		.	....		.	......							
Maybach	2	Maybach	......	2	2H6 Bosch	......		1	Plunger	......	.	Axial Turb.		.	......							
Mercedes	.	Duplex	......	2	2H6 Bosch	......		2	Plunger	......	.	Axial Turb.		.	......							
Mercedes	1	Mercedes	......	2	Bosch	......			Mercedes 4-Plunger		.	Axial Turb.		.	......							
Oberursel				2				.	....		.	....		.	......							
Rolls-Royce Falcon 3	2	R.R.C.H. 38M.	......	2	Watford	1.5	14.25	1	Rotary	.....	1	Centrif.		2	Plunger	2.75	.59–1	1300 r.p.m.	Either	72.04″	37.24″	42.00
Rolls-Royce Eagle 8	2	R.R.C.H. Duplex 42 m/m.	13.000	4	Watford	1.5	14.25	2	Gear	8.75	1	Centrif.	4.625	1	Plunger	2.875	.6–1	1080	Either	75.98″	42.52″	48.03
Siddeley	2	Zenith	4.2	2	E. M. 6	1.5	15	2	Gear	4.1	1	Centrif.	7.2	1	Plunger	.7	Nil	......	Either	69.88″	24.09″	43.62″
Spa 6A				2				.	....		.	....		.	......			1600	Either			
Sunbeam Arab.	1	C.H.H.C. 7 ..	......	2	B.T.H. A8S	E. S.	12.8	3	Gear	.....	1	Centrif.	3	1	Plunger	......	45–27	1200	T.	1105	810	903
Sunbeam Cossack	4	C.H.B.Z.S. 42 m/m.	......	4	B6 or W.B.G.	1.5	19.1	3	Gear	.....	1	Centrif.	......	1	Plunger	......	2–1	½ E. S.	Either	61.81″	37.79	38.89
Sunbeam Maori	4	C.H.B.Z.S. 42 m/m.	......	4	W.B.G.	1.5	19.1	3	Gear	.....	1	Centrif.	......	1	Plunger	......	2–1	½ E. S.	Either	55.11″	35.46	33.85

THE WORLD'S AIRSHIPS.

ARRANGED IN ALPHABETICAL ORDER

OF COUNTRIES,

WITH AN INTRODUCTORY ARTICLE AND A NOTE ON
AIRSHIP MOORING BY

PETER GEOFFREYS.

At the time of compiling this volume, when many of the restrictions of war are still observed, it is obvious that the task of collecting details of the world's airship fleets is one of difficulty, and the matter which follows must necessarily be incomplete so far as it concerns foreign nations. However, it will give a general idea of the lines on which airships are being developed, containing as it does many details that were unpublished during the war.

AIRSHIPS IN THE WAR—AND THE FUTURE.

By PETER GEOFFREYS.

BEFORE the war it was not unusual to regard the airship as something in the nature of an extravagantly impracticable mammoth, possessing a large and costly appetite, a delicate constitution and negligible utility. It was also thought that the airship, like the mammoth, would meet an early termination of its existence as the inevitable consequence of misevolution. Nevertheless the airship is still with us.

THE NAVAL ASPECT.

In the naval side of the war to which the activities of airships have been generally confined, the results produced by airships in their proper sphere, have not only justified their existence, but have earned for them an established place in naval strategy, with possibilities for future development wider and very much more easily realisable than those in prospect for heavier-than-air machines.

Unhappily, during the war, the enemy enjoyed the advantage of preponderating strength in rigid airships capable of extended action with a fleet at sea, and hostilities ended just too soon to allow the British effort to take effect.

For three years Germany was able to maintain almost unhindered aerial reconnaissance with Zeppelins over the North Sea, excluding coastal patrols. Lord Jellicoe in his book has indicated the extent to which this advantage might have assisted a more offensively inclined enemy.

In certain circumstances, Lord Jellicoe pointed out, a rigid airship may have the value of two cruisers. This comparison, one might add, refers to the highly developed modern cruiser in relation to the present type of rigid airship, which has scarcely passed from its teething stage.

IN THE ATLANTIC ?

Naval warfare of the future, it may reasonably be supposed, will be subject to modification. The capital ship must always be a decisive factor, but it is probably correct to prophecy that the duties of the smaller fry of seacraft will be increasingly usurped by aircraft ; primarily by rigid airships by virtue of their superior air endurance.

The rate of development, as regards airships, may be partially dependent upon a rather indeterminable factor—non-inflammable gas. According to official announcements in the United States, helium gas is already being produced in fairly large quantities in Texas. Whether supplies will be available for British airships, and whether other sources for its production, as yet unknown, may be discovered are questions for the future. Newspaper reports suggest that helium has been recently found in Canada.

The future of non-rigid airships in war is less easy to predict. The non-rigid type appears to have little value for any other naval or military purposes than submarine hunting,

in military operations against semi-civilised tribes and to a limited extent for training the personnel of rigids. As it is possible that submarine warfare may in future be banned by the League of Nations, the most important of these functions may cease to exist. In any case, non-rigids can be built by one country as fast as another can turn out submarines. Possibly the development of a satisfactory system of towing non-rigids from seacraft might create a new and important function for small airships.

In peacetime, Service non-rigid airships may, it is proposed, be employed in connection with colonial photographic surveys, for which purpose they are very well suited. The field for activity in this direction is enormous. India alone among the Dominions and Crown Colonies has as yet received exact topographical survey, and incidently, of the whole land surface of the world only about one-sixth has been exactly surveyed.

BRITISH NON-RIGID DEVELOPMENT.

British progress in airship design has proceeded in two parallel lines, allied but virtually independent, in the development of the non-rigid and rigid types.

To those associated with the non-rigid school the more credit is due, for as a result of their work, conducted without contemporary assistance or influence, the British non-rigid is the finest for its size in the world, superior in many respects to the Italian semi-rigid vessels of considerably longer pedigree.

It has often been said, apropos of locomotive design, that when an English engineer sets out to improve his engine he contrives to take something off it, whereas the Frenchman devises something new to put on. The same principle has applied to airship design. Simplicity is the chief characteristic of the British types, while refined complexity marks the majority of Continental models.

The requirements of the anti-submarine patrol have demanded from our airships high speed, reliability and endurance, with which is included comfort for the crew ; height has been an unimportant factor. There are the qualities which distinguish British non-rigids and generally speaking will respond to the needs of commercial air transport.

As the Admiralty has announced its intention of selling a number of non-rigid airships, one presumes that it is permissible to mention that during the war a new and highly satisfactory method has been developed for protecting the outer surface of non-rigid airship envelopes.

This process is applied in conjunction with the rubber proofing, and consists of depositing a mixture of rubber and aluminium powder on to the fabric in a thin layer, by means of a form of rotary printing machine. Most of the non-rigid envelopes are made of this aluminium-faced fabric, which, whilst combining the good qualities of impermeability and durability, requires no dope.

IMPORTED LUXURIES.

Whilst it is true that the lead of twelve years which Germany had gained with rigid airships has to-day been reduced to two, this achievement cannot be attributed to originality on the part of our rigid airship designers.

Extraordinary progress has nevertheless been made in constructional technique and in minor detail design, despite the limitations imposed by war conditions, and it is probable, therefore, that $R\,33$ and $R\,34$, launched since the Armistice, are superior to their prototype, the $L\,33$, brought down at Little Wigborough.

The previous British efforts, $R\,9$, the $R\,23$, $R\,23X$ and $R\,31$ classes, were not remarkable for any particular virtues. On the other hand, only one instance is to be recorded of an utter failure, and that was the result of defective material and the lack of time available for preliminary tests, rather than faulty conception. The plywood airship, $R\,31$, is that to which one refers.

Even though the early rigid airships failed to fulfil many hopeful expectations, they satisfactorily served the purpose for which they were rightly intended—that of training the multi-graded personnel in readiness for airships capable of Fleet work.

Altogether eleven rigid airships had been completed or were nearing completion at the close of the War. At the time of writing, in May, 1919, it is freely reported that a new class of rigid airship has been laid down which will have a volume approaching 3,000,000 cubic feet of gas. From comparative data, such an airship might be presumed to develop a speed of about 70 miles an hour, with an endurance of upwards of 8 days. With the German constructors reduced to a state of impotency, this new airship will be the largest existent.

WAR RECORDS.

Figures relating to the work of the Airship Service have already appeared in the Press, and one's excuse for repeating them here is that they may be readily available for reference.

A sum total of 2,245,800 miles has been flown on service during the war, representing an air endurance of 87,700 hours ; the bulk of this flying has been carried out over the sea, with a total loss of life from all causes of 16 officers and 32 men.

At the beginning of the War, seven airships, two only of which could be regarded as effective, were in commission. One airship station was in working order and another in an unfinished condition, excluding a few privately-owned sheds. The airship constructing industry in this country was to all intents and purposes non-existent.

On October 31st, 1918, 103 airships of all types were in operation, a chain of airship base stations and mooring-out stations had been created around the coasts of England and part of Scotland, and an almost continuous patrol was maintained over the War Channels from the Scillies to Scapa Flow. The British airship industry was in 1919 the most powerful of its kind in the world. Whether it remains so is a matter for Parliament and the Treasury to décide.

ALLIED ACTIVITY.

ITALY :—Considering first the work of Italy, as befits the most insistent of our allies, it is interesting to observe that in Europe the Italians stand alone in maintaining a military airship service. Moreover, the Italian airship represents a striking power of considerable value against a neighbour ill equipped with heavier-than-air machines. In addition to the military airships, a certain number of vessels are operated by the Italian Navy.

During the War, numerous raids were carried out by Italian airships on Pola, Trieste, St. Marco Docks, and various points of importance behind the Austrian lines. Further, it is reported that the bombing operations of the airships during the big Italian retreat in 1917 contributed materially to the success of the withdrawal.

In design, the Italians have adhered to the semi-rigid system, which has been brought to a high pitch of perfection in the M. type.

The conditions underlying design in Italy are fundamentally different to those in this country. Height has been the primary object in view, owing to the necessity for evading hostile gunfire. Endurance has been a secondary consideration, because the raiding flights performed were seldom or never of long duration. That speed has been neglected, is evident from the bulky unfaired cars and the multiplicity and length of rigging cables of most Italian craft. In Italy the winds are considerably less in average force than in Britain, and therefore a relatively high rate of speed has not been essential.

The Italian designers have sacrificed all other qualities in order to increase the maximum ceiling of their vessels, and in this object they have been enormously assisted by the superabundance of skilled labour at their disposal, which has permitted extreme structural lightness to be obtained and, incidentally, truly Latin excellence of craftsmanship.

Contrary to popular belief, the *Forlanini* and *Usuelli* types have not been very extensively employed, although the *Forlanini*, at least, has well kept pace with contemporary progress.

FRANCE :—French interest in the airship appears to have languished since the War proved the vulnerability of lighter-than-air craft in modern conditions of warfare on land against a well-armed enemy.

A useful type of non-rigid airship has been evolved with which to operate against enemy submarines around French ports, but the necessity for energetic measures has been less urgent, and comparably the progress of development has been less rapid than in this country.

UNITED STATES :—The Americans can be congratulated on acquiring, amongst other valuable information imported into the United States during the past two years, the knowledge which has enabled them to produce helium and has given them the means of applying it with the best effect in practice.

It is presumably permissible to mention that numerous Americans have undergone training at Airship Stations in this country and in France, returning to the United States with complete information as to the manner in which years of experience direct that airship services should be conducted. Moreover, both British and French airships have been purchased and conveyed to America, where designers have had the opportunity of gleaning the latest ideas from Old World construction.

The American building programme, as disclosed to the Senate with the introduction of the Naval Estimates on November 28th last year, provided for the construction of three large rigid airships, in addition to a host of non-rigid vessels. Possibly this scheme has since been modified, but there is reason to believe that America, in pursuance of her Naval policy and enjoying at present an important advantage as the sole producer of helium gas, will make a strong bid for supremacy with airships, both in peace and war.

THE SPIRITUAL HOME OF THE RIGID.

It is scarcely necessary to recount the work of the German airships in the war, beyond emphasising the importance of their activities as sea scouts. The development of the Zeppelin, however, is an interesting and little known subject.

Strange as it may seem when comparing the performance of the pre-war types with that of the latest airship of the *L 70* class, Zeppelin development has made apparently not more than four distinct advances since 1914, and only two of these have been accompanied by a material change in dimensions.

In 1916, the serial numbers of the "L" airships broke off abruptly at *L 24*. This was not, as might have been supposed, an indication that the Germans intended to cease construction, for before long appeared the first vessel of a new and enlarged type with a capacity of two million cubic feet. This airship had a considerably improved form (closely similar in silhouette to the *Schutte-Lanz*) and six 240 h.p. Maybach engines, producing a maximum speed of 60-62 m.p.h.

Following upon this achievement, the German designers proceeded diligently to elevate and to improve the new model. Elevation was the principal object in order to enable the ships to rise above the range of anti-aircraft gunfire. As a result, the next type, commencing at the beginning of 1917 with *L 40*, came to be known as the "height-climbing" class—this is the type illustrated in the photograph elsewhere.

Broadly speaking, the dimensions, capacity and general arrangement of *L 10* were identical with those of *L 30*. The hull structure was considerably lightened, smaller fish-form

gondolas were fitted and five engines were installed instead of the six in *L 30*, involving the deletion of the "wing" propellers driven from the after car. These modifications not only raised the ceiling of the class to about 20,000 feet, but actually resulted in an increase in speed.

Next, towards the end of 1917, came the "long range" class of Zeppelin, probably beginning with *L 57*. It may be remembered that *L 57* was the airship with which an attempt was made to fly from Transylvania to East Africa with medical stores. The "long range" class was slightly larger than its predecessors, containing approximately 2,200,000 cubic feet of gas when full. Probably five 300 h.p. Maybach engines were installed.

Retiring once more to refine the new breed, the Zeppelin designers delivered the highly efficient *L 70*, a ship more or less of the same tonnage as the *L 57*, but equipped with seven 300 h.p. Maybach engines. This airship was reported to be capable of a full speed of more than 77 miles per hour and of a static rise to 21,000 feet.

From the beginning, the system of development has been thoroughly characteristic of the Teutonic mind. Each advance has been the result of laborious experiment. In fact, it may be said that each airship produced has been experimental.

This principle of step by step progression has been particularly noticeable in the design of the hull structure. Airships belonging to each separate class and built to the same general specification have rarely been identical in detail composition. Generally, the aim has been to lighten each successive ship to the uttermost degree, until indeed a point has been reached where a breakage in the air has necessitated re-strengthening, and weight has again had to be added. As a means of rapidly attaining maximum practical efficiency, irrespective of other considerations, the system has much to commend it.

AIRSHIPS IN COMMERCE.

In the light of present knowledge, the question of the employment of aircraft in commercial or postal undertakings, as distinct from advertisement and ornamental displays and pleasure flying, is an uncertain one.

After the first rather hysterical manifestation of enthusiasm for air transport, there has appeared a realisation of the many difficulties which must be faced in developing commercial aeronautics.

So far as aeroplanes are concerned, it is generally considered that long distance communication over land constitutes the most fruitful field for activity, but even so it appears that the time is not yet ripe for extensive development. The use of seaplanes and flying boats for overwater traffic is equally dependent upon advances being made, although less affected by competition from existing methods of transport than is the case with aeroplanes operating over land.

The position was summed up in a lecture, in May of this year, to the Liverpool Chamber of Commerce by Major General Sir Fredk. Sykes, Controller General of Civil Aviation, when he said " There seems to be what I can only describe as a gap in front of us. We can mentally pick up the probable future curve of progress some little way ahead. But there is some very important missing link somewhere."

Turning to airships, General Sykes continued " It is possible that the airship may help us to advance in many directions whilst the ' gap ' is being bridged. At all events, both the heavier and lighter-than-air types of aircraft have their appropriate places in aviation."

For long distance flying over wide expanses of sea or land unsuitable for aeroplane traffic, the airship has many definite advantages, and this is certainly its appropriate function. Moreover, there are many arguments in favour of employing airships for journeys such as, for example, London to India and Australia, which are frequently considered to be the prerogatives of aeroplanes.

The large rigid airship, capable of flights of 2000-3000 miles carrying a commercial load, could lay a direct course, avoiding high mountains, of course, to any destination, without regard to the suitability of the intervening terrain for landing and re-fuelling purposes. India could be reached with one stop at Cairo. A prolongation of the flight, *via* Singapore, would take the vessel to Australia in one nearly straight line throughout the journey. Compare this with the suggested aeroplane route to the East, which involves the formation of scores of repair and re-fuelling depots, intermediate landing grounds and emergency alighting grounds in all sorts of inaccessible places, constituting the links of a deviously winding chain across three continents.

Considering the question of speed, the fastest type of aeroplane at all likely to be useful for load carrying would attain a maximum speed of 125 miles per hour. The Handley Page machines are limited to approximately 95 m.p.h. It is customary service practice when estimating average ground speed to deduct at least 25% from the maximum air speed of a machine on account of adverse winds. Also, fully 10% can further be deducted for the time lost at stopping places. This allows a halt of 30 minutes every 400 miles—certainly a reasonable amount. Therefore, 80 m.p.h. is probably the maximum speed now attainable with aeroplane transport.

On the other hand, the commercial airship would be designed to have a full speed of 80 m.p.h. and a cruising speed of 60 m.p.h. at half power. Her course would be direct, and in the aggregate the time for a long journey would not be so very much greater.

It would be ridiculous to pretend that the airship can never be so fast as the aeroplane, but the loads carried in comparison with the unit cost of machine, unit cost of man power engaged and unit cost of h.p. used, would be less, and this factor has a most important bearing on the question. It should be noted that the assumed costs referred to above are dependent upon the provision and use of a practical scheme of mooring rigid airships in the open ; a certain development in the near future.

In connection with General Sykes' views as to the probable lines of future progress, it is important to remember certain basic laws which govern the development of airships and aeroplanes, and will exert an ever-growing influence on their future relations.

With airships we are on the threshold of great advances. Every increase in the size of rigid airships is accompanied by a very much greater proportionate increase in efficiency. Although a rigid airship of ten million cubic feet capacity would have five times the gross lift and more than five times the useful lift of the present two million cubic feet vessel, the dimensions of the larger airship would be only 70% greater, and the horse power required to obtain the same speed only about three times greater. Accordingly its prime cost would be less in proportion to unit lift, and its running costs would be less still in proportion to its load-carrying ability, or with the same running costs its speed would be greater as compared with the smaller airship of to-day. With aeroplanes, design upon present lines is nearing what appears to be a limit, and increase in size results in no automatic increase in efficiency. The proportion of h.p. required is nearly constant for all sizes, and structurally the weight of the aeroplane tends to become proportionately greater with increased dimensions, incurring a reduction of efficiency.

What is perhaps of greater interest in regard to commercial aeronautics is the fact that the airship will always retain the characteristic of safety, derived from its independence of engine power for support in the air, whereas the heavier-than-air flying machine will always be subject to risk from engine breakdown. Stress is often laid upon the risk of fire present in airships. One can only repeat the official statement that during the whole period of the War, in the course of some two and a half million miles of flying, only one airship was destroyed by the accidental outbreak of fire in the air. This was on the occasion of the trial trip of an experimental vessel, and the responsible cause was ascertained and eliminated.

An S.S. Twin and two S.S. Zero airships berthed at a mooring-out station.

AIRSHIP MOORING.

In view of the fact that the solution of the problem of mooring airships safely in the open will have more importance than any other development in increasing the utility of airships, the accompanying photograph is particularly interesting.

It depicts a small non-rigid airship anchored experimentally above the ground, by means of a "three-wire" mooring gear, during a period of severe weather in which the wind force reached 52 miles per hour. Attached to the wind scoop and trailing leeward is a fabric hose used for conveying air to the ballonets from an air blower on the ground, to maintain envelope pressure.

In the course of another experiment, made with a mooring mast instead of cables, a similar airship was exposed for an unbroken period of six weeks, during this time riding safely at her moorings through all weathers.

Experiments with small non-rigid airships, however, no matter what measure of success may be achieved, cannot in themselves be regarded as evidence that the same methods of mooring will be equally effective when applied to large rigid airships such as would be required for long-distance commercial flying.

The difficulties experienced in mooring rigid airships are more complicated. Not least among them is that of maintaining without large changes the buoyancy of the moored vessel, and with this is involved the problem of counteracting the effects of rapid rises in gas temperature due to the sun.

That the mooring of rigid airships is mechanically practicable was demonstrated so long ago as 1911 with the British rigid airship No. 1 ("Mayfly"), which was moored to a mast for many hours in Cavendish Dock, Barrow, and withstood, without mishap, winds attaining speeds of 36-45 miles per hour. Subsequent events proved the airship to be structurally weak, so emphasising, if emphasis is required, the soundness of the scheme employed for mooring.

A small non-rigid airship anchored experimentally by means of a three-wire mooring gear.

BRITISH AIRSHIPS.

Owing to the recent war and the continued existence of the Defence of the Realm Act and the Official Secrets Act, it is impossible to give full details concerning all types of airships in use.

The accompanying illustrations and particulars give a general idea of modern British airships, all of which have been from time to time exhibited to the populace of London and of other large towns, so it is unlikely that any undesirable person will derive from the illustrations any information which should not be known.

The details given concerning each airship are only such as can be published without doing a disservice to the King's Armed Forces.

An S.S. P. Non-rigid Airship.   The band encircling the envelope is a drip-flap.

S.S. P. class.

An airship of small size, now used for training purposes, representing an intermediate stage of development between the original " Blimp " type S.S. and the more refined *Zero* type.

The nacelle is reminiscent of that of a pusher aeroplane, but considerably larger. The air pipe from the air ballonets is arranged to collect the slipstream from the airscrew, which is mounted at the rear of the nacelle, behind the engine. The landing skid underneath the nacelle is noteworthy.

Control is effected by a rudder and two elevators placed behind the stabilizing fins.

Petrol is carried in cylindrical tanks, suspended in fabric slings, one on either side of the envelope.

X

S.S. ZERO class.

The *S.S. Zero* followed the *S.S.*, *S.S.—M.F.*, and *S.S.P.* in the genealogical sequence ot the Submarine Scout class of non-rigid airships. The type was standardised for production and considerable numbers were built and put in commission during 1917 and 1918 for patrol duties.

The envelope is made of two-ply rubber-proofed fabric. The suspensory cables of the car are attached with stuck-on "Eta" patches, so called because they were first used on the Military Airship "Eta," in 1913.

To maintain pressure in the envelope and compensate for loss of gas volume, air is blown into two internal ballonets. When full, the ballonets contain a volume of air equivalent to about one third of the total capacity of the envelope, which in normal conditions is sufficient to permit of a rise to about 8000 feet. A sloping air scoop interposed in the propeller slip stream keeps the ballonets inflated at the required pressure.

Directional control is effected by a rudder placed behind the vertical fin and by a pair of elevators placed behind the horizontal fins.

A strongly-built boat-shaped car, having an engine mounted upon a gantry at the after end, is the chief distinguishing feature of the *S.S. Zero* airship. Foremost in the car is the compartment for the W/T. operator. Next is the pilot's cockpit. A wheel bearing on a transverse bar actuates the elevators and foot steering pedals operate the rudder. Within easy reach of the pilot's hand are the controls for the gas and air valves, controls for the "crabpot" valves in the air ducts and the tricing line with which the airscoop is raised out of the propeller slip stream. Arranged in front of the pilot are the necessary aerostatic and navigational instruments.

Behind the pilot's seat is a separate compartment for the engineer. A starting handle for the engine with chain and sprocket gear is so adapted that it may be utilised to rotate a hand blower for maintaining pressure in the envelope in the event of engine defect and consequent failure of the air supply from the propeller slip stream.

The *S.S. Zero* is normally capable of a flight of 12 hours' duration at full speed, and 24 hours at half-power (three-quarter speed). Two flights were made during the War of over 50 hours' duration with full war equipment.

CHARACTERISTICS.

Capacity	70,000 cu. ft.
Length	143 ft.
Width (overall)	32 ft.
Height (overall)	46 ft.
Engine	Rolls-Royce "Hawk," 75 h.p.
Gross lift	2.2 tons.
Disposable lift	.33 tons.
Full speed	42 kts. (48.37 m.p.h.)
Cruising speed	30 kts. (34.5 m.p.h.)
Crew	3.
Cost (war price)	£5000.

A British Airship of the S.S. Zero Class. Note the petrol tank and parachute case on the side of the envelope.

S.S. TWIN class.

An airship produced during 1918, incorporating improvements suggested by experience with the *S.S. Zero* type.

No attempt has been made to depart from the simple characteristic principles of the preceding *S.S.* airships, either as regards the envelope design, Eta patch suspension, or air pressure system. In the "Twin," however, the ballonets are duplicated and dual air ducts and scoops are fitted—a feature by which it may be readily recognised.

The car contains accommodation for a crew of five, and two engines are installed in outrigger bearers on either side.

The *S.S. Twin* has a full speed of 50 kts. (57.5 m.p.h.) with petrol capacity for 12 hours at this speed. At the cruising speed of 37 kts. (42.5 m.p.h.), the endurance is estimated to be 30 hours.

CHARACTERISTICS.

Capacity	100,000 cu. ft.
Length	165 ft.
Width	35 ft. 6 ins.
Height	49 ft.
Engines	2—75 h.p. Rolls-Royce "Hawk."
Gross lift	3.12 tons.
Disposable lift	1.00 ton.
Full speed	50 kts. (57.5 m.p.h.)
Cruising speed	37 kts. (42.6 m.p.h.)
Crew	4.
Cost (war-price)	£8,200.

An airship of the S.S. Twin class landing.   Later models are equipped with a circular section car of ply-wood construction.

" COASTAL " Class.

A medium-sized airship of the *Astra-Torres* type, with an envelope of trefoil section. The suspensory rigging is attached along the lines of intersection of the top and side lobes and passes through the bottom of the envelope to the car.

The air ballonets are inflated by the propeller slip-stream through the large metal pipe to the rear of the car. In addition, an auxiliary power-driven air blower is installed in the car.

The vessel is driven by two large four-bladed airscrews driven by independent engines, which are placed respectively at the bow and at the stern of the car.

The controls are the ordinary arrangement of fins, rudder and elevators. A machine-gun platform is placed on top of the envelope.

CHARACTERISTICS.

Capacity	..	..	..	.. 170,000 cu. ft.
Length	..	..	..	.. 196 ft.
Width (overall)		..	..	.. 39 ft. 6 ins.
Height (overall)	..		..	.. 52 ft.
Engine and h.p.		..	..	.. 2—150 h.p. Sunbeam.
Gross lift	..		..	.. 4.94 tons.
Disposable lift	..		..	.. 1.6 tons.
Speed (full)	..		..	.. 52 m.p.h.
Crew	..	..	..	.. 5.

The " Coastal " Astra-Torres type airship C. 12. A sister-ship, C. 9, during the war was maintained in commission for 2 years and 3 months, averaging three hours in the air per day.

C. STAR class.

In accordance with a custom of Naval terminology, the designation "C. Star" indicates a modification of the "C," i.e., the Coastal type of airship. Airships of this class were intended primarily for convoy escort duty over greater distances than could be undertaken by the *S.S. Zero* craft.

The envelope is rigged on the *Astra-Torres* tri-lobe principle, and is practically a replica on a smaller scale of the *N.S.*, which made its advent at an earlier date.

The capacity of the *C. Star* is 210,000 cubic feet, as compared with the 170,000 cubic feet of the Coastal, producing an increase in lifting power of approximately one ton and a quarter.

The car remains substantially the same as the Coastal car, but is fitted with engines of a different type. A Berliet of 110 h.p. is installed in the forward mounting, where the efficiency of the propeller is impaired by the large car in its wake, and a 260 h.p. Fiat is placed in the mounting aft. Both these engines are designed on the lines of the Mercédès, and are remarkably reliable.

No gun-platform is fitted on the top of the envelope, as in the Coastal.

In order to assist in distributing the weights evenly along the envelope and to reduce the tensions in the car suspensory cables—some of which are acutely inclined forward and aft—the petrol is carried in tanks suspended inside the gasbag.

The equipment of a *C. Star* airship includes W/T. installation, emergency power driven air blower, floatation bags, and a collapsible lifeboat, to be inflated with air, as well as the usual airship grapnel, drogue and signalling appliances.

CHARACTERISTICS.

Capacity	.. .. ..	210,000 cu. ft.
Length ..	.. .. ..	218 ft.
Width (overall)	.. ..	49 ft. 3 ins.
Height (overall)	.. ..	57 ft. 6 ins.
Engines ..	.. ..	1—110 h.p. Berliet forward.
		1—260 h.p. Fiat aft.
Gross lift	.. .. ..	6.46 tons.
Disposable lift	.. ..	1.8 tons.
Full speed	.. .. ..	50 kts. (57.5 m.p.h.).
Cruising speed	.. ..	35 kts. (40.3 m.p.h.).
Crew ..	.. .. ..	5.
Cost (war price)	.. ..	£12,750.

C. Star 1. The first of the revised coastal airships with a stream-lined "Astra Torres" type envelope.

N.S. class.

The "North Sea" type airship, which was designed for long range reconnaissance, perpetuates the *Astra-Torres* principle in a vessel of considerable size. It is most readily recognised from the *C. Star* type by the large enclosed car and the arrangement of the twin engines behind the car, and placed side by side. Conspicuous also are the large twin air pipes which scoop the slipstream from the airscrews to the air ballonets, along big air ducts running fore and aft.

The vessel has no landing carriage, but floats are provided for alighting on the water if necessary. The control planes are of conventional type.

Petrol is carried inside the envelope in cylindrical tanks suspended at intervals from the internal rigging girdles at the top "ridges" of the envelope. This method of suspension results in more equitable load distribution, relieving the envelope of the stresses that would be set up were the weight of petrol concentrated in the car, and so reducing the liability of the envelope to lose its longitudinal alignment at low pressure. As petrol is consumed from various tanks, air may be blown into contiguous ballonets to trim the ship.

In the latest model of the *N.S.* airship, the car has the same height from end to end to give head room. An engineer's cabin is situated in the space between the engines at the rear. Sleeping bunks and means of heating food by the engine exhaust are provided.

Many notable duration flights have been performed in the course of patrol duties by *N.S.* airships, including a non-rigid endurance record of 101 hours, 50 minutes.

CHARACTERISTICS.

Capacity	360,000 cu. ft.
Length	262 ft.
Width (overall)	56 ft. 9 ins.
Height (overall)	69 ft. 3 ins.
Engines and h.p.	2—260 h.p. Fiat.
Gross lift	10.85 tons.
Disposable lift	3.8 tons.
Full speed	50 kts. (57.5 m.p.h.)
Cruising speed (½-power) ..	37 kts. (42.6 m.p.h.)
Crew (two watches)	10.

A British non-rigid airship (N.S.7), built on the Astra-Torres principle.

View looking aft above the navigating car of an N.S. class airship, showing the arrangement of the two 260 h.p. Fiat engines and interposed engineers' cabin.

RIGID 23 class. (R 23—R 26.)

R 23, designed and constructed by Vickers, Ltd., was put into commission in 1916 as a training airship.

R 24 (built by Wm. Beardmore and Company, Ltd.), *R 25* (Armstrong, Whitworth and Company, Ltd.), and *R 26* (Vickers, Ltd.), followed in 1917, and were also utilised for training and experimental purposes.

The hull, composed of Vickers type duralumin lattice girders, is divided by transverse frames into 18 gas compartments, the gasbags containing a total of 942,000 cubic feet of gas when full.

A V section keel, built of duralumin and steel tubes, extends under the hull from near the bows to join the lower vertical fin at the tail. A portion of the forward half of the keel is widened to form a cabin in which the W/T cabinet and quarters for the crew are located.

Each gasbag is fitted with one automatic gas valve discharging to one side and a top manœuvring valve actuated from the control cabin.

The outer cover is of doped linen.

As originally produced, the forward and aft gondolas were each partitioned into two compartments, a control cabin and an engine room. The main control position was in the leading gondola. Each of these gondolas was equipped with a 250 h.p. Rolls-Royce engine, driving a pair of 4-bladed swivelling propellers through suitable gearing.

Subsequently, the after gondola was removed and its place taken by a light power-car containing an engine with direct transmission to a single 2-bladed propeller.

The car suspended amidships accommodates two engines, also of the Rolls-Royce 250 h.p. type, each coupled through bevel gearing to a 4-bladed propeller on either side of the car. Swivelling gear is not provided for these propellers.

Above the bows of the airship is a gun platform, which is reached by a climbing shaft passing between gasbags two and three.

Cruciform stabilising fins are fitted, and balanced rudders and elevators of high aspect ratio.

R. 23. A Rigid type Training Airship (deleted).

R. 25.—A sister ship of the R23, R24 and R26—of the external girder keel type. 14c

Judging from the standard of the more modern rigid airships, the performance of the *R 23* class is poor. The best flight which has been accomplished is one of slightly over 50 hours. The value of the class has been principally manifested in the experience afforded to those concerned with its construction and operation.

CHARACTERISTICS.

Capacity	..	..	..	942,000 cu. ft.
Length	..	..	..	535 ft.
Diameter	..	..	..	53 ft.
B.H.P.	..	..	..	1,000.
Gross lift	..	..	..	23.6 tons.
Disposable lift	..	..	..	5.8 tons.
Maximum speed	..	..	..	45.2 kts. (52 m.p.h.)
Cruising speed	..	..	..	35 kts. (40 m.p.h.)

R 23 X class.

This class comprised two airships, R 27 and 29, constructed in 1917-18 to Admiralty designs by Wm. Beardmore & Co., Ltd. (R 27) and Armstrong, Whitworth & Co., Ltd. (R 29). It was originally intended to build four airships of this type, but as a result of the acquisition of L 33, R 28 and R 30 were cancelled.

In many essentials the R 23 X class airships are similar to R 23. The dimensions are nearly the same, and the only obvious point of difference is the omission of the keel.

It should be understood that the function of the keel in rigid airships is primarily that of distributing the weights of petrol, oil and water-ballast between the transverse bulkheads of the hull, and as a rule it contributes little more than 5% to the total strength of the hull structure.

In the R 23 X class, these weights are concentrated at the bulkheads, where they are suspended from the radial wiring which maintains the polygonal shape of the hull. A keel is therefore unnecessary, and a considerable saving of weight is secured.

To enable the crew to pass from one gondola to another, a ∩-shaped corridor of light tubular construction is carried through the interior of the airship, and the gasbags are shaped to fill the surrounding space. In all other details, these airships follow closely the lines of R 23. The gondolas and power plant are arranged similarly to those of R 23 as first designed, with swivelling gear for the forward and aft propellers.

CHARACTERISTICS.

Capacity	..	..	..	990,600 cu. ft.
Length ..	..	..	..	539 ft.
Diameter	..	..	..	53 ft.
B.H.P. ..	..	..	..	1000.
Engines ..	..	..	..	Four Rolls-Royce " Eagle," Mark III, 250 h.p.
Gross lift	..	..	..	30.1 tons.
Disposable lift ..	..	..	..	8.2 tons.
Maximum speed	..	..	..	48 kts. (55 m.p.h.).
Cruising speed ..	..	..	..	37 kts. (42.75 m.p.h.).

R 27.—The first of the R23X class, British rigid ships without external keel. The centre car has been replaced by "wing" cars containing one engine apiece.

R 29, sister ship of R27, of the keelless R23X class.

R 31 class.

R 31 and R 32 were constructed by Messrs. Short Bros., at Bedford, to designs based upon *Schütte-Lanz* principles furnished by the Admiralty. Owing to the effects of dampness on the plywood used in the construction of *R 31*, this airship has been condemned.

It is to be noticed that the construction of the hull bears no resemblance to that of the pre-war *Schütte-Lanz* trellis system, and is analogous to the Zeppelin arrangement, which was adopted for the later *S.L.* ships.

Each of the principal girders in *R 31* consisted of three plywood sides, lightened with slots at regular intervals, which were glued to spruce angle-members more or less of V section. The triangular girder thus formed was strengthened internally by plywood diaphragms. This method of construction was used for all varieties of girders, including square and rectangular sections. Casein cement, known as Kaltleim, was adopted as an adhesive.

The gasbags, 25 in number, were made of rubber-proofed cotton fabric, lined with goldbeaters' skin.

A keel corridor extended from end to end inside the bottom of the hull, serving to support and distribute the weights of petrol, water ballast, etc.

The control car under the bows of the airship was divided into three compartments ; forward the navigating cabin, next the wireless room, and aft the officer's sleeping quarters.

As initially tested, *R 31* had six boat-built power gondolas, arranged in pairs. Subsequently, however, one of the rear gondolas was removed and the remaining one slung parallel with the centre line.

Each gondola contained a 250 h.p. Rolls-Royce engine, driving through clutch transmission a two-bladed propeller. Reversing gears were fitted to those amidships.

CHARACTERISTICS.

Capacity	.. .. ..	1,553,000 cu. ft.
Length ..	.. ..	615 ft.
Diameter	.. ..	65.5 ft.
Engines and h.p.	.. ..	5—250 h.p. Rolls-Royce (1250).
Gross lift	.. ..	47.1 tons.
Disposable lift ..	..	16.4 tons.
Maximum speed	.. ..	65 m.p.h.
Cruising speed ..	..	46 m.p.h.
Crew ..	.. ..	21.

R 31—the first of the two wooden airships built by Short Bros.—with the original twin power cars aft, which have since been replaced by a single car.

H.M. Airship R32.   Built by Short Bros., at Bedford.

16c

R 33 class.

Two airships of this class, completed in 1919, were constructed by Armstrong, Whitworth & Co., Ltd. (*R 33*) and Beardmore & Co., Ltd. (*R 34*). The designs were prepared by the Admiralty from data acquired from the wreck of *Zeppelin L 33*, brought down at Little Wigborough in 1916.

The hull, streamlined over the greater part of its length, has the sectional shape of a 25-sided polygon, and is composed of 20 main circumferential girder frames and 25 longitudinal girders, one at each corner of the polygon. An auxiliary circumferential frame is interposed between each pair of main frames, and the whole is braced diagonally by high tensile steel wire. There are 19 gas chambers.

At each bulkhead, radial wires of steel wire rope are connected centrally to an axial plate, and a jackstay runs from plate to plate, bracing the bulkheads together longitudinally.

Along the inside of the bottom of the hull is a keel-corridor, formed of A-shaped girder frames. As well as accommodating the petrol, water ballast and bombs, the keel provides means for the crew to pass from one gondola to another, for which purpose a walking-way girder is interposed between the two lower longitudinals of the hull.

A top gun platform is situated above the third main frame, near the bows, and at the after end of the airship a lightly built prolongation of the corridor gives access to a gun-pit at the extremity of the stern.

The tail fins and control surfaces are cruciform in arrangement and constructed of duralumin girders, covered with doped linen.

The gasbags are shaped to fill as completely as possible the interior of the hull, surrounding the sides of the corridor when full. They are made of a single thickness of rubber-proofed cotton fabric lined with goldbeater's skin; finished weight not more than 160 grams per square metre. An automatic gas release valve is fitted to each bag, discharging near the bottom through exhaust shafts running to the top of the airship between each alternate pair of gasbags. Certain bags are also furnished with hand-controlled manœuvring valves.

The outer cover is made of doped linen, tightly stretched between each pair of main circumferential frames.

The forward gondola, although apparently homogeneous, is built in two parts separated by a small gap. In the leading section are the controls and wireless cabinet, and in the section behind is an engine coupled through a clutch to a propeller at the rear.

R 33 on the landing ground.

The forward gondola of R33, comprising: control compartment, W/T cabinet, and adjoining, an engine room.

R33 Class—*continued.*

Approximately amidships, two small "wing" gondolas are attached to the hull side by side, each one housing an engine. Reversing gears, for use in braking the airship whilst landing, are fitted between the engines and propellers in these cars.

The sternmost gondola accommodates two engines, geared to drive one large propeller. In this respect, the *R 33* class airships are similar to the German *L 40* and differ from *L 33* by the omission of the shaft-driven "wing" propellers and one of the three engines installed in the after gondola of that ship.

CHARACTERISTICS.

Capacity	..	..	.. 1,950,000 cu. ft.
Length ..	..	..	.. 643 ft.
Max. diameter	..		.. 78.75 ft.
Engines and h.p.	..	..	.. 5-250 h.p. Sunbeam "Maori" (1250).
Gross lift	..	..	.. 59.2 tons.
Disposable lift	..		.. 30 tons.
Maximum speed	..		.. 62 m.p.h.
Cruising speed	..	..	.. 45 m.p.h.
Crew	..	..	.. 22.

After gondola of R34. It contains two engines and auxiliary controls.

The Beardmore built R34.

The stern showing gunpit, fins, balanced control planes and tail skid.

R 35-40 class (projected).

Beyond a statement in the House of Commons to the effect that six rigid airships of improved types are being built to the order of the Admiralty, little official information has been vouchsafed as to the size and capabilities of the new vessels.

From reports which have appeared in the newspapers, however, it is to be deduced that two airships, *R36* and *R37*, are being built of practically the same type as the *R33*, each with a capacity of about 2,000,000 cu. ft., and three larger vessels.

Since no mention is made of a possible *R35*, it appears that this number has not been allocated, or has been cancelled. Thus, the total of six airships presumably comprises *R80*, *R36* and *37*, and a new class *R38*, *R39* and *40*.

The "R38 Class" is referred to in the official "Notes on Airships for Commercial Purposes," in which it is stated that the capacity will be 2,720,000 cu. ft. and that the cruising endurance at 45 miles per hour is estimated to be 211 hours, or 34 hours greater than the German *L70*.

Some figures relating to the dimensions and lifting capacity of these new airships have been published in the Press, and these, supplemented or checked by obvious calculations, furnish the following details :—

CHARACTERISTICS (R38 CLASS).

Length	695 ft.
Diameter (overall)	87.6 ft.
Capacity	2,720,000 cu. ft.
Engines and h.p.	Four 350 h.p. Sunbeam "Cossack"; Two 275 h.p. Sunbeam "Maori."
Gross lift	82 tons.
Disposable lift (estimated) ..	50 tons.
Speed, full (estimated) ..	70 m.p.h.
Crew (estimated)	30.

In connection with the specifications given above the attached diagram, reproduced by courtesy of Sir W. G. Armstrong, Whitworth & Co., Ltd., and representing to a uniform scale the airships so far built by that firm, gives a graphic idea of the evolution of British-built rigids in the last two years.

R 80 class.

A rigid airship designed and put into construction in November, 1917, by Vickers, Ltd., at Barrow. It is to be completed during the latter half of 1919, and, unless employed for commercial demonstrations, will probably be taken over by the Admiralty.

Compared with contemporary rigid airships it is small in size, having a gas capacity of 1,250,000 cubic feet. It is, however, designed on up-to-date lines, and may be expected to prove highly efficient within the limitations imposed by its small dimensions.

An advance upon other rigid airships is the shape of the hull, which has no parallel portion amidships, but is a symmetrical streamline form throughout its length. The construction and general arrangement of the hull, including the internal keel-corridor, conforms generally with the recognised principles of rigid airship design, but incorporates several minor improvements in detail devised by Vickers, Ltd. Patent bow mooring attachments are fitted.

The gasbags are 15 in number. Cruciform tail fins and balanced elevators and rudders are fitted and two gun positions, one above the bows and one in tip of the stern, these features are reminiscent of the practice in *R33*.

A point of recognition is the arrangement of the gondolas, of which there are three—one large gondola forward and a pair of "wing" power cars approximately amidships. The fore gondola is composed of two sections, flexibly connected, the leading section containing all the controls for the airship and the W/T cabinet.

Four 240 h.p. Wolseley-Maybach engines provide propulsive power, two engines being installed en echelon in the after section of the forward gondola, and one each in the twin "wing" cars. A propeller is mounted at the rear of each gondola, and the transmission is such that the forward propeller can be driven by either of its two engines separately or both together, whilst the "wing" car propellers may be reversed.

It is stated that *R80* will have a full speed of over 60 miles per hour, and be capable of crossing the Atlantic. The endurance at cruising speed of 45 m.p.h., with a maximum load of fuel, will presumably be about 75 hours.

CHARACTERISTICS.

Length	535 ft.
Diameter (overall)	70 ft.
Capacity	1,250,000 cu. ft.
Engines and h.p.	Four 240 h.p. Maybach.
Gross lift	36.5 tons.
Disposable lift (estimated) ..	15 tons.
Full speed (normal) ..	60 m.p.h.
Cruising speed	45 m.p.h.
Crew	20.

H.M.A. R.80. Overall Length 530.0'

R 80. A Vickers ship of the latest type.

R25 — Capacity: 900000 cub ft. No of engines 4-250 H.P. Speed: 50 M.P.H. Disposable lift 4 tons. Net weight of ship: 25.75 tons.

534'-11.6"

R29 — Capacity: 980000 cub ft. Speed: 55 M.P.H. Disposable lift 8.63 tons. Net weight of ship: 21.16 tons.

640.29 feet — R33 — Capacity: 2000000 cub. ft. No of engines 5-275 H.P. Disposable lift: 29 tons. Net weight of ship: 26.7 tons.

672'-5" — XR35 — Construction commenced, but abandoned.

694.5 feet — R39 — Capacity: 3000000 cub ft. No of engines {4-350 H.P. / 2-275 H.P. Disposable lift 48 tons (About 60% of capacity @ 68 LBS. per 1000 cub ft)

LEONARD BRIDGMAN '19.

FRENCH AIRSHIPS.

MILITARY AIRSHIP FACTORY.

(Chalais Meudon).

Construction, on a large scale, both of non-rigid airships and kite balloons, has been undertaken by the Chalais-Meudon Establishment, in addition to experimental work and tests.

During the first three years of the War, airships were built for the French Army alone. Notably among these vessels are the "Lorraine" and "Tunisie" (1916), of about 10 tons displacement, and the "Capitaine Caussin" (1917), of 9 tons. In their general features, these airships are akin to Zodiac practice of the same period.

The Zodiac system of rigging has been adopted, comprising an external girdle along both sides of the envelope and tangential cables to the car.

In each case the car is short, constructed of steel tubing. Twin propellers are mounted upon brackets on opposite sides, driven by engines enclosed in the car, through shafts and bevel reduction gears.

Pressure in the envelope is maintained by a power blower in the car, from which air passes up to the ballonets through a vertical pipe.

CHARACTERISTICS.

	"Lorraine" & "Tunisie" (1916).	"Capitaine Caussin" (1917).
Capacity	370,000 cu. ft.	312,000 cu. ft.
Length	305 ft.	267 ft.
Width	50 ft.	46 ft.
Engines and h.p.	2—220 h.p. Clement Bayard	2—240 h.p. Canton Unné.
Gross lift	10.6 tons.	9.2 tons.
Disposable lift	4.4 tons.	4.9 tons.
Maximum speed	43 m.p.h.	50 m.p.h.
Crew	5.	6.

T class.

Following upon the *Capitaine Caussin* in 1917, appeared a smaller type of airship, known as the *T*.

Six vessels at least were produced of this pattern and taken over by the Navy for anti-submarine patrol duties.

The envelope form of the *T* class is distinguishable by its extremely high fineness ratio—in the order of 8 : 1. In conjunction with the manner of rigging the car, a short one, close under the envelope, this long envelope must certainly involve the use of an inordinately high internal gas pressure to keep it in alignment. Consequently, the envelope fabric must be heavy, and this is probably the chief reason for the fact that the ratio of disposable lift of this type is low.

The car is streamlined, constructed of duralumin, and provides good protection for the crew. The two power units installed are Salmson-Canton-Unné engines of 160 h.p. As they are of radial type, it has been possible to economise space and weight by embodying the engines in the framework on opposite sides of the car, each engine facing outboard and driving through direct shaft transmission and bevel reduction gearing, a two bladed propeller.

CHARACTERISTICS.

Capacity	194,000 cu. ft.
Length	230 ft.
Overall width	46 ft.
Engines and h.p.	2—160 h.p. Canton-Unné.
Gross lift	5.4 tons.
Disposable lift	1.7 tons.
Maximum speed	50 m.p.h.
Crew	5.

A French airship of the "T" class notable for the fineness of its lines.

FRENCH AIRSHIPS.

C.M. class.

A non-rigid airship of medium size on the same general lines as the *T* class, but with a shorter envelope of more conventional shape. The *C.M.* class was specifically designed for submarine hunting, and towards the end of the War, appears to have become the standard French airship for sea patrols

The car is constructed of duralumin, and is carefully faired throughout. In this respect the method of mounting the twin Canton-Unné engines flush with the sides of the car is noteworthy.

The propellers, carried on outrigger brackets on each side, are driven through bevel gearing by shafts directly coupled to the engines.

A Q.F. gun of light calibre is mounted forward.

Biplane horizontal fins are attached to the tail of the envelope, and a large triangular fin below forms the foundation for the "box" type elevator and rudder control surfaces.

CHARACTERISTICS.

Capacity	..	..	176,500 cu. ft.
Engines and h.p.	..	..	2—160 h.p. Canton-Unné.
Gross lift	..	..	5.2 tons.
Disposable lift	..	..	1.8 tons (est.)
Maximum speed	..	..	52 m.p.h.
Crew	..	..	5.

ASTRA class.

Astra Société de Constructions Aeronautique 13, Rue Couchot and 121, Rue de Bellevue, Billancourt, Paris.

British representative : "Airships, Ltd.," 47, Victoria Street, London, S.W.

This firm was founded by M. Surcouf for the production of ordinary balloons. Constructed early *Lebaudys*, later *Astras*, and finally the *Astra-Torres* type, noted principally for the unique trefoil section of the envelope.

Large vessels built by the firm have been used during the War by the French Government. Vessels with one and two cars have been constructed, of which details are available concerning the sister ships *Alsace* and *Pilatre de Roxieres*, built in 1915.

In general appearance, these airships are similar to the British *N.S.* class

CHARACTERISTICS.

Capacity	..	..	495,000 cu. ft.
Length	..	..	295 ft.
Diameter	..	..	54 ft.
Engines and h.p.	..	..	2—220 h.p. Cheau.
Gross lift	..	..	14.2 tons.
Disposable lift	..	..	6.5 tons.
Maximum speed	..	..	40 m.p.h.
Cruising speed	..	..	80 m.p.h.
Crew	..	..	6.

A French C M. (Chalais Meudon) class airship. The arrangement of the tail is characteristically French.

A LARGE ASTRA-TORRES AIRSHIP, with four engines arranged in pairs.

FRENCH AIRSHIPS.

ASTRA class—*continued*.

LATER TYPES.

Two later types of Astra non-rigid airships of smaller volume were constructed in 1917 for anti-submarine operations. The first vessel of this new series was reported to have a capacity of approximately 210,000 cu. ft. and two 170 h.p. Renault engines. The second type was somewhat larger, with a capacity of 234,000 cu. ft., giving a total lift of 6.7 tons and a disposable lift of 2.4 tons. With two 200 h.p. Hispano-Suiza engines, this type of airship attained a full speed of 50 m p.h., and an endurance of 10 hours.

CLEMENT BAYARD class.

Usines Clement-Bayard, Quai Michelet, Levallois-Perret, (Seine).

The principal products of this firm, before the outbreak of war, were large non-rigid airships, with streamlined shaped envelopes from which was suspended a girder nacelle of great length intended to distribute the load.

The Car of a French C.M. type airship. The mounting of the Salmson engines should be noted.

AN ASTRA-TORRES AIRSHIP, with twin nacelles.

Reproduced from La Guerre Aérienne.

FRENCH AIRSHIPS.

C.M. class.

A non-rigid airship of medium size on the same general lines as the *T* class, but with a shorter envelope of more conventional shape. The *C.M.* class was specifically designed for submarine hunting, and towards the end of the War, appears to have become the standard French airship for sea patrols

The car is constructed of duralumin, and is carefully faired throughout. In this respect the method of mounting the twin Canton-Unné engines flush with the sides of the car is noteworthy.

The propellers, carried on outrigger brackets on each side, are driven through bevel gearing by shafts directly coupled to the engines.

A Q.F. gun of light calibre is mounted forward.

Biplane horizontal fins are attached to the tail of the envelope, and a large triangular fin below forms the foundation for the " box " type elevator and rudder control surfaces.

CHARACTERISTICS.

Capacity	..	..	..	176,500 cu. ft.
Engines and h.p.	..	..	2—160 h.p. Canton-Unné.
Gross lift	..	..	..	5.2 tons.
Disposable lift	..	..	1.8 tons (est.)
Maximum speed	..	..	52 m.p.h.
Crew	..	..	..	5.

ASTRA class.

Astra Société de Constructions Aeronautique 13, Rue Couchot and 121, Rue de Bellevue, Billancourt, Paris.

British representative : "Airships, Ltd.," 47, Victoria Street, London, S.W.

This firm was founded by M. Surcouf for the production of ordinary balloons. Constructed early *Lebaudys*, later *Astras*, and finally the *Astra-Torres* type, noted principally for the unique trefoil section of the envelope.

Large vessels built by the firm have been used during the War by the French Government. Vessels with one and two cars have been constructed, of which details are available concerning the sister ships *Alsace* and *Pilatre de Roxieres*, built in 1915.

In general appearance, these airships are similar to the British *N.S.* class

CHARACTERISTICS.

Capacity	..	..	..	495,000 cu. ft.
Length	..	..	..	295 ft.
Diameter	..	..	..	54 ft.
Engines and h.p.	..	..	2—220 h.p. Cheau.
Gross lift	..	..	..	14.2 tons.
Disposable lift	..	..	6.5 tons.
Maximum speed	..	..	40 m.p.h.
Cruising speed	..	..	80 m.p.h.
Crew	..	..	..	6.

A French C M. (Chalais Meudon) class airship. The arrangement of the tail is characteristically French.

21c   **A LARGE ASTRA-TORRES AIRSHIP, with four engines arranged in pairs.**

ASTRA class—continued.

LATER TYPES.

Two later types of Astra non-rigid airships of smaller volume were constructed in 1917 for anti-submarine operations. The first vessel of this new series was reported to have a capacity of approximately 210,000 cu. ft. and two 170 h.p. Renault engines. The second type was somewhat larger, with a capacity of 234,000 cu. ft., giving a total lift of 6.7 tons and a disposable lift of 2.4 tons. With two 200 h.p. Hispano-Suiza engines, this type of airship attained a full speed of 50 m p.h., and an endurance of 10 hours.

CLEMENT BAYARD class.

Usines Clement-Bayard, Quai Michelet, Levallois-Perret, (Seine).

The principal products of this firm, before the outbreak of war, were large non-rigid airships, with streamlined shaped envelopes from which was suspended a girder nacelle of great length intended to distribute the load.

The Car of a French C.M. type airship. The mounting of the Salmson engines should be noted.

AN ASTRA-TORRES AIRSHIP, with twin nacelles.

Reproduced from La Guerre Aérienne.

22c

ZODIAC class.

Société Francaise des Ballons Dirigeables et d'Aviation Zodiac, 10, Route du Havre, Puteaux, Seine.

The Zodiac Company maintained a fair output of successful airships during the War period.

Two non-rigid airships, built to the order of the French Army during 1915-16, are notable as being the largest non-rigids constructed in recent years. They are the "D'Arlandes" and Champagne, each of 530,000 cu. ft. volume. When the French Military Airship Service was disembodied, these vessels passed to the Naval Authorities.

A distinguishing feature of Zodiac design, is the method of attaching the car suspension cables to the envelope by means of long reinforced fabric girdles attached to the envelope on both sides. Considerable success has been achieved in rigging the car close up to a long, finely streamlined gasbag, despite the natural difficulties of this system. Gas pressure is doubtless high.

The stabilising surfaces of the Zodiac closely resemble those of the productions of the Chalais-Meudon establishment, illustrated in the photographs of the C.M. type airships. In brief, the arrangement consists of a large vertical fin below the tail, carrying box elevators and rudders, with one or more small supplementary horizontal fins attached to the sides of the envelope immediately above.

All Zodiac airships are equipped with a power-driven blower in the car, to maintain pressure in the internal ballonets. An air duct, of large diameter, through which the air passes from the car to the envelope, is a recognisable feature of the make.

"D'Arlandes" and "Champagne."
CHARACTERISTICS.

Capacity	.. .. ..	530,000 cu. ft.
Length ..	.. .. ..	335 ft.
Diameter	.. .. ..	49 ft.
Engines and h.p.	.. ..	2—220 h.p. Zodiac.
Gross lift	.. .. ..	15.2 tons.
Disposable lift ..	.. ..	7 tons.
Maximum speed	.. ..	43 m.p.h.
Cruising speed ..	.. ..	32 m.p.h.
Crew	.. .. ..	6.

LATER TYPES.

"Vedette Zodiac" (1916).

Capacity	.. .. ..	77,600 cu. ft.
Gross lift	.. .. ..	2.23 tons.
Engines and h.p.	.. ..	2—70 h.p. Anzani.
Maximum speed (about)	..	50 m.p.h.

"Vedette Zodiac" (1917).

Capacity	.. .. ..	97,000 cu. ft.
Engines and h.p.	.. ..	2—60 h.p. Renault.
Gross lift	.. .. ..	2.8 tons.
Maximum speed (about)	..	50 m.p.h.

"Eclaireur Zodiac" (1917).

Capacity	.. .. ..	219,000 cu. ft.
Engines and h.p.	.. ..	2—220 h.p. Hispano-Suiza.
Gross lift	.. .. ..	6.3 tons.
Maximum speed (about)	..	50 m.p.h.

"Croiseur Zodiac" (1917-18).

Capacity	.. .. ..	430,000 cu. ft.
Length ..	.. .. ..	331 ft.
Diameter	.. .. ..	50 ft.
Engines and h.p.	.. ..	2—225 h.p. Zodiac.
Gross lift	.. .. ..	13.3 tons.
Maximum speed	.. ..	47 m.p.h.

The "Eclaireur Zodiac" type of French airship.

GERMAN AIRSHIPS.

Note.—A total of about 120 airships are believed to have been constructed by the Zeppelin Company for the German Army and Navy, and about 20 by the Schütte-Lanz Company for the Navy. The German Military Airship Service was disbanded probably during the summer of 1917, and the few Zeppelins that it then possessed passed to the control of the German Admiralty.

The year 1918 was disastrous to the Naval Airship Service, for in addition to war losses, including the practical extinction of Tondern Station by British aeroplanes and the destruction on her first war flight of the *L70*, their latest and best vessel, involving the death of Captain Strasser, the Leader of Airships (Fuhrer der Luftschiffe), six Zeppelins of a new type were destroyed by an explosion at Ahlhorn. Thus it happened that at the time of the Armistice only nine airships—all Zeppelins—were in commission and on the active list.

In the stress of the last few months of Germany's war effort, the production of new vessels appears to have been reduced, but that the Germans had by no means lost faith in rigid airships is shown by the fact that designs had been prepared for Zeppelins of much larger size and greater capabilities than any others yet constructed.

The capacity of these vessels would probably have been somewhere in the region of 5,000,000 cubic feet, and the "ceiling" of the projected vessels would undoubtedly have been very much higher than the 22,000 feet already attained. It is therefore possible that raiding might have again become a practical proposition, though this work was never regarded as the primary function of the German Airship Service—sea reconnaissance was the most important of its duties.

ZEPPELIN Class.

The Zeppelin airship in commission at the close of hostilities belonged chiefly to what is known as the long-range class, with the possible exception of one or two training airships, and the *L71*, which was the second vessel recently constructed of a new and improved class. Included with the training ships may have been the famous *L14*, on which many notable Zeppelin pilots learned their art, a vessel built in 1915 that established a tradition of its own for charmed longevity, and was still heard of well towards the end of the war.

From the appended table of dimensions and performance may be gathered the progress of Zeppelin development from *L1* to *L70* of the naval classes, and the following notes furnish additional particulars of the airship latterly employed.

ZEPPELIN L40 (Height-Climbing) Class.

Airships of this class were constructed in 1917. The capacity (2,000,000 cu. ft.), overall dimensions, and general arrangement were almost identical with those of the previous *L30* Class, and, as these features also recur, without material variation, in the British *R33* Class, a detailed enumeration is unnecessary.

With the object of saving weight, however, many improvements were introduced in the construction of the hull, and it may be said that the process of lightening was carried to such a point that these airships were capable of the highest performance with safety only at great altitudes where the aerostatic and

A Stern of a Zeppelin, showing clearly the arrangement of fixed fins, rudders and elevators, which was typical for all vessels from L30 to L71.

24c

aerodynamic forces experienced are less—e.g., at roughly 16,000 feet the principal stresses on a rigid airship are nominally halved.

The truss system of stiffening the main circumferential girder frames was modified and lightened and minor economies in weight were effected wherever possible. The gondolas were made considerably smaller and more attention paid to reducing their air resistance by streamlining. This development applied principally to the forward gondola, but it was also evidenced in the wing gondolas, as is shown in the accompanying photographs of the wreck of the *L49*.

The engines installed were five 240 h.p. Maybachs distributed as in the case of *R33*—one in the aft section of the forward gondola, one in each of the twin "wing" gondolas, and two in the sternward gondola. A full speed of 62 miles per hour was attained by these airships, which were capable of a static climb to 21,000 feet. In the raids on Britain a load of bombs was carried amounting usually to about 2½ tons.

ZEPPELIN L57 (*Long Range*) Class.

These airships, commissioned late in 1917 and early in 1918, probably comprised *L57* to *L65*, and were 50 ft. longer than the above-mentioned *L40* class, but not otherwise dissimilar in general appearance.

The gas capacity was increased to 2,200,000 cu. ft. and the extra lift so secured, supplemented by a further addition in disposable lift effected by certain improvements in design, resulted in a better all-round performance.

Four streamlined gondolas, similar to those of the "height-climbing" class, were fitted, but in place of the 240 h.p. Maybach engine the newly-developed 300 h.p. engine of the same make was adopted, five engines being installed as before. Thus the power was increased to a total of 1,500 h.p. and the speed to 65 miles per hour.

Many long flights were accomplished by Zeppelins of this class, including an attempt to fly from Jamboli (Transylvania) to East Africa with 12 tons of medical stores. The airship was ordered back by wireless and landed at her base after covering about 3,000 miles.

ZEPPELIN L70 Class.

Two vessels of a new type, *L70* and *L71*, were commissioned in 1918, *L70* meeting destruction by British Naval forces in August of that year. They were the largest, most powerful, and most efficient airships ever built. Possibly *L71* may fly again under another flag.

In size these airships retained the same dimensions as their predecessors of the "long-range" class, the length being 693 ft., diameter 79 ft., and capacity 2,200,000 cu. ft. The gross lift was 66.64 tons, and the disposable (useful) lift 38.84 tons, which,

One of the German Zeppelins of the "Height-climbing" class. The peculiar painting should be noted. This ship is black below to reduce the effect of searchlights from below and white above to reduce the heating effect of sunshine.

An outline drawing of the German L70 class of rigid airships.

although this type of craft was very heavily engined, amounted to more than 58 per cent. of the total lifting capacity.

The design, whilst displaying no fundamental departure in principle from precedent, represents the highest standard of development yet achieved. It was the product of 12 years of effort on the part of the Zeppelin designers.

A point of recognition was the number of the gondolas, of which there were six, an addition of two "wing" gondolas,

making four in all, having been occasioned by the greater number of engines installed, as compared with former classes.

The gondolas thus comprised one double gondola forward containing, in separate sections as is usual, the controls, W/T and an engine, an after gondola containing the auxiliary control position and two engines, and four "wing" gondolas, each with one engine, arranged in two pairs spaced at equal intervals intermediately.

The engines, seven in number, were the Maybach 300 h.p. type, giving a total of 2,100 h.p., with which a full speed of 77.6 miles per hour was obtainable.

Flying at an economic speed of 45 miles per hour, the *L70* class of airship was capable of cruising for nearly eight days, covering 8,000 miles in still air.

A view down the central keel of a modern Zeppelin, showing the footway or "cat-walk" and petrol tanks.

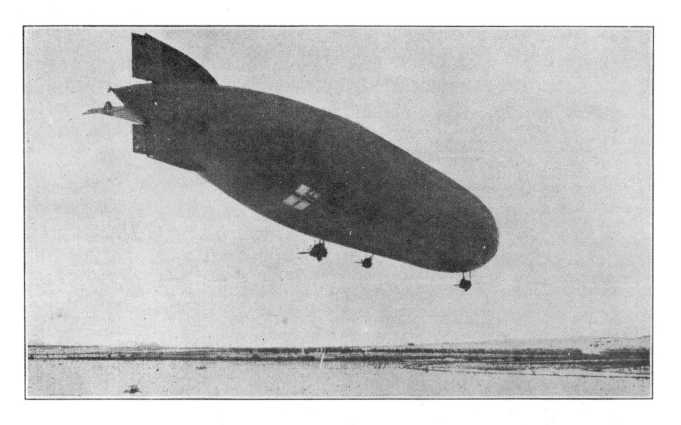

Zeppelin L57 (Long-Range class). Note the horizontal position of the propellers to avoid damage by the gondolas bumping the ground whilst in the hands of the landing party.

The Development of Naval Zeppelin Airships, 1912-1918.

In the following table an attempt has been made to demonstrate the progressive growth in size and performance of the Naval types of Zeppelin airships.

A considerable number of military airships and a few passenger models were produced in the early days of development, with a consequent diversity of characteristics.

As, however, the Naval models during this period were generally similar in dimensions to their contemporaries, it is convenient to confine the figures to the Naval types, as representative of the whole.

Information concerning certain of the Naval series is scanty, and various recorders of Zeppelin data give divergent figures in some instances. There is no means at the present of securing absolute accuracy, and therefore certain of the values in the table below may be incorrect. Generally, they can be accepted as being not far from the mark, erring, if at all, on the side of underestimation.

	1912 L1.	1913 L2.	1914-15 L3—L8.	1915 L11—L19.	1916 L20—L24.	1916 L30—L39.	1917 L40—L56.	1918 L57—L65.	1918 L70.
Capacity, cu. ft.	882,500	918,000	1,059,500	1,130,000	1,235,500	2,000,000	2,000,000	†2,200,000	†2,200,000
Length, ft.	495	525	525	561	561	643	643	693	693
Diameter, ft.	52.1	54	60.7	60.7	66	78-75	78.75	79	79
Gross lift, tons	25.9	28	32	34.3	40.2	59.5	59.5	66.4	66.4
Disposable lift, tons	8.7	8.9	—	15.7	—	27	30.5	—	38.8
Cars	2	3	2*	2*	2*	4*	4*	4*	6*
Engines No. and h.p.	3—180 h.p. Maybach (540)	4—180 h.p. Maybach (720)	3—180 h.p. 1—240 h.p. Maybach (780)	4—220 h.p. Maybach (880)	5—220 h.p. Maybach (1100)	6—220 h.p. Maybach (1320)	5—240 h.p. Maybach (1200)	5—300 h.p. Maybach (1500)	7—300 h.p. Maybach (2100)
Airscrews	Ford 2-2 Bl. Aft. 2-4 Bl.	4-4 Bl. " Wing "	4-2 Bl. " Wing "	2—2 Bl. Pusher. 2—2 Bl. " Wing."	2—2 Bl. Pusher. 2—2 Bl. " Wing."	4—2 Bl. Pusher. 2—2 Bl. " Wing."	4—2 Bl. Pusher.	4—2 Bl. Pusher.	6—2 Bl. Pusher.
Crew	16	17	18	18	18	22	22	†22	30
Speed (full), m.p.h.	47	49	50	55	59	60	62	†65	77.6
Height (max. static rise)	—	6000	9000	10,000	11,500	14,000	21,000	22,000	20,900
Endurance (full speed), hours	—	13	14	25	30	54	46.3	†65	55
Endurance (cruising speed), hours	30(Endurance Test)	20	26	60	x67	110	92.5	†150	177

† Estimated.   * Forward car divided into two separate sections.

27c

ZEPPELIN — *continued.*

The centre section of a Zeppelin, Height-climbing class, with the two streamline " wing " gondola placed side by side underneath the hull.

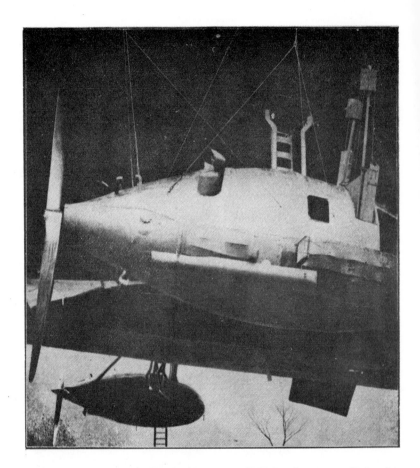

A Zeppelin " wing " gondola, sometimes described as a " power egg," showing arrangement of radiator, exhaust box, etc., etc.

ITALIAN AIRSHIPS.

Note.—The majority of the Italian airships are officially designed and built, or procured, by the "Stabilimento Construzioni Aeronautica" at Rome, which is the aircraft factory of the Italian Government, and provides airships and kite balloons to both the Naval and Military authorities. The official designs emanate from the Institute Centrale dell' Aeronautica adjoining the works.

It is necessary to explain that the semi-rigid in Italy has been developed on two distinct principles. Firstly, there is the official design, having as its characteristic a keel composed of a number of separate rectangular sections, constructed of steel tubing, which are ball-jointed together so that the whole is free to bend in a vertical plane, whilst constituting a beam for the purpose of distributing the suspended weights of the car evenly along the envelope.

The correct shape of the envelope in this design is partially dependent upon internal gas pressure, but the head of pressure necessary is very considerably less than in a non-rigid airship. Consequently, a lighter fabric can be used, and, in the aggregate, sufficient weight may be saved to compensate for the weight of the keel system.

The second principle is represented by the *Forlanini* and in lesser degree by the *Usuelli*. In these airships, the keel is a rigid beam which distributes the suspended weights in a similar manner. The *Forlanini* design has merit in this respect, but it lacks the advantages derived from the flexibility of the official type.

STABILIMENTO CONSTRUZIONI AERONAUTICA.

Four primary classes of airships (excluding the *D.E.* class) were projected, viz. :—the *Piccolo* (P)—small, ————— (M)—medium, the obsolescent *Veloce* (V)—fast, and the *Grande* (G)—large. The latter, a proposed rigid airship, was abandoned during the War, and a large semi-rigid, known as the *A* class, was introduced in its stead.

P and P VELOCE classes.

These are old and obsolescent airships, now mostly used for instruction. In general appearance they are similar to the *D.E.*, *M.* and *V.* types, and represent the intermediate size between the two first mentioned models.

The *P* is the earliest of the official Italian designs. Two 75 h.p. Fiat engines are installed, which are usually carried on outrigged bearers like those of the *S.S. Twin*. With these engines a speed of 40 m.p.h. is obtained.

The *P-Veloce* is the same type of airship fitted with two 225 h.p. Fiat engines. As it attains a maximum speed of 56 m.p.h., it is the fastest of all Italian airships, except, perhaps, the latest Forlanini vessels. Its range of action is limited.

CHARACTERISTICS.
(Common to P and P-Veloce.)

Capacity	..	..	..	176,500 cu. ft.
Length	..	..	..	203 ft. 6 ins.
Width	..	..	..	39 ft.
Height	..	..	..	70 ft. 6 ins.
Gross lift	..	..	..	5.4 tons.
Crew	..	..	..	3.

A PICCOLO SEMI-RIGID AIRSHIP, Front View.

M class.

During the War, the *M* type has undergone considerable modification, and the following notes must be taken to refer to the improved type now being built with two, three, and perhaps four engines. Two engines apparently constitute the standard.

The envelope is divided by diaphragms into six gas chambers, each fitted with two valves. A ballonet extends internally from the bow to near the tail, and is joined to the lower part of the envelope on either side of the keel. At the forward end, the ballonet encloses a valve in the extreme nose, the entrance of air being regulated by shutters on the principle of a Venetian blind.

Perforated diaphragms are inserted in the ballonet. Whilst permitting air to pass, these serve to check the tendency of the air to serge towards the lower end when the airship is inclined.

The keel (sectional hinged type) is attached at the bows to a radial nose-stiffening framework, and at the stern forms the foundation for the attachment of a large vertical stabilising fin and the control planes. A narrow fin is attached to the top of the envelope.

The weight of the car is communicated from the keel to the envelope by means of parabolic wires sewn into the envelope between each keel-joint. Also, circumferential bands pass round the envelope at each of these places, and internal wires connect the keel to two longitudinal canvas girdles along the top of the envelope—producing a small lobe in the centre.

A gun platform is provided above the bows.

The car is short and bulky. Two engines are carried in bearers on the sides of the car, each driving a propeller at the rear through long shafting. These propellers are of variable and reversible pitch. In the accompanying illustration of an *M*-type car, a third engine is shown mounted on a gantry above the others.

CHARACTERISTICS.

Capacity	..	..	..	441,000 cu. ft.	Height	..	..	..	89 ft.
Length	..	..	..	265 ft.	Engines and h.p.	..	..	2—280 h.p. Itala.
Width	..	..	..	59 ft.	Gross lift	..	..	13.8 tons.
					Crew	..	..	..	5.

An Italian Airship of the " M " class.

Car of " M " class airship.

The Tail Surfaces of an Italian Airship of the M class.

V class.

Following the advent of the M class, a limited number of larger semi-rigids were built to a new design, known as the *V*. It appears that the development of this type has lapsed, and some of its proved good points have been incorporated in a revised model of the *M*.

The *V* is distinguishable from other Italian airships of the official series by the absence of a long, single vertical fin below the keel. In lieu thereof it has two small triangular fins and larger vertical control planes. A long top fin is also fitted.

CHARACTERISTICS.

Capacity	..	..	553,000 cu. ft.
Length	..	..	287 ft.
Width	..	..	62 ft. 4 ins.
Engines and h.p.	..	..	4—130 h.p. Itala.
Gross lift	..	..	17 tons.
Maximum speed	..	..	51 m.p.h.

D.E. class.

The *Dirigible Exploratore* type of semi-rigid airship was produced chiefly for submarine-hunting, and corresponds in size and functions with the British *S.S. Zero* type. It is interesting as demonstrating that the semi-rigid principle can be successfully applied to an airship of so small a capacity as 100,000 cubic feet.

The envelope is divided by fabric diaphragms into four gas compartments, to reduce the loss of gas in case of localised damage. One long air-ballonet extends along the inside of the envelope, above the keel. A shutter valve in the nose of the airship (where pressure is relatively high) admits air to the ballonet.

At the after end of the keel, is attached a long stabilising fin, which forms the perpendicular of a number of triangular frames. The control planes are of "box" type, fitted at extremity of this fin.

In each of the above features, the *D.E.* is representative of the officially designed types.

The car is short and, although roomy, appears to afford little comfort for the crew. A Fiat engine of 100 h.p. is mounted on a gantry above the car, and drives directly a propeller of conventional pattern.

CHARACTERISTICS.

Capacity	..	..	..	92,000 cu. ft.
Length	..	..	..	159 ft.
Width	..	..	..	34 ft. 6 ins.
Height	..	..	..	55 ft. 9 ins.
Engines and h.p.	..	..	..	1—100 h.p. Fiat.
Gross lift	..	..	..	2.8 tons.
Maximum speed	..	..	..	42.5 m.p.h.
Crew	..	..	..	4.

An Italian Airship of the " Dirigible Exploratore " class.

FORLANINI class.

Manufacturers : La Società Leonardo da Vinci.
Offices : via Baccacio 21, Milan.

Although limited in number and use, the semi-rigid airships built by the Societa Leonardo-da-Vinci, near Milan, to the designs of Enerico Forlanini, have developed very considerably in size and capabilities during the War. The latest projected model, when completed, will be the largest airship, other than of the rigid type in existence.

An indication of the development of the Forlanini vessels from the beginning, is furnished by the table below :—

Generally, the following characteristics are typical of all airships of Forlanini design :—

A rigid triangular steel girder constructed of light, steel tubing, lattice fashion, extends internally from end to end, along the bottom of the envelope.

The gas is contained in a compartmented gasbag (usually with 12 gas chambers) from which the lift is transferred directly to the top of the keel girder evenly along its length. The whole is surrounded by an outer cover of silk, and the ring space between the inner and outer envelopes constitutes the air ballonet of the airship. Air enters through a valve in the nose.

The car is attached rigidly to the keel, and encloses the control cabin and two or more engines. Two variable pitch propellers are mounted on brackets on the sides of the car and driven through shafting and bevel gears.

A peculiar feature is the installation of a small air compressor actuated by shafting from the engines. From a receiver, air is available at different pressures for operating the gas valves, for the petrol system and for inflating the bumping bags under the car.

In the case of the *F3*, it is stated that biplane elevators are fitted on the sides of the car to increase the dynamic lift of the airship. The " box " control planes of this vessel comprise ten rudders and eight elevating planes attached to a large cambered fin below the tail end of the keel.

The tail arrangement of a Forlanini F 3.

	F1. Leonardo da Vinci.	F2. Citta di Milano.	F3.	F4.	F5.	F6.	*F8.
Capacity, cu. ft.	115,250	416,500	487,000	487,000	628,000	628,000	990,000
Length, ft.	132	238	297	297	295	295	361
Width, ft.	46	59.4	59.4	59.4	65.6	65.6	75.5
Engines and h.p.	40 h.p. Antoinette	2—85 h.p. Isotta-Frachini (170)	4—100 h.p. Fiat (400)	2—160 h.p. (320)	2—240 h.p. Fiat (480)	4—240 h.p. Fiat (760)	4—350 h.p. (1400)
Gross lift, tons	3.32	12	14	14	19.1	19.1	30
Disposable lift, tons	—	—	—	—	9.55	9.36	15.04
Max. speed (sea level) m.p.h. ..	31	40	46	45	43.5	45.8	49.7
Max. speed (at 13,000 ft.), m.p.h.	—	—	—	—	49.7	55	62.2

*As designed.

The Car of the Forlanini F 3, which carries the crew and the engines.

Reproduced from the " Scientific American."

FORLANINI AIRSHIP F3, in which the keel is arranged inside the envelope and the car suspended therefrom.

UNITED STATES AIRSHIPS.

NAVAL AND MILITARY.

A large number of non-rigid airships of diverse types were constructed in America during the last year of the War, mainly for the purpose of submarine-hunting. The designs were prepared by the Bureau of Construction and Repair, Navy Department, and contracts placed with the Goodyear Tyre and Rubber Company, Akron, Ohio; the B.F. Goodrich Company, Akron, Ohio; and the Connecticut Aircraft Corporation. Since the declaration of Armistice, it has been announced that the American Navy will continue to devote money to the development of lighter-than-air craft, and proposals have been published for the construction of three or four rigid airships and a considerable number of new non-rigids.

In addition, the Balloon and Airship Division of the Department of Military Aeronautics contemplates the building up of a fleet of small, single engine airships of the non-rigid type, which it is intended to use for fire control work, and also in connection with coast fortifications and military liaison duties.

An initial order for six airships of about 75,000 cu. ft. has been let, one half in the U.S.A., and the others in Europe.

COMMERCIAL.

Various schemes are on foot to start the construction of commercial airships, but nothing definite has as yet been accomplished.

The Goodyear Tire and Rubber Co. have completed the designs for a 750,000 cu. ft. airship of the semi-rigid type, reminiscent of *Forlanini* practice, which is to be 400 ft. long, 65 ft. in diameter, and is to be driven by two 450 h.p. engines. Accommodation is provided for twenty-four passengers, and the endurance at 60 m.p.h., is estimated at 2,000 miles. This ship has been designed for trans-continental transport.

The Connecticut Aircraft Corporation have tentative plans for the construction of a 300,000 cu. ft. airship of the non-rigid type, with belly-band rigging; which is to accommodate twenty passengers, and be fitted with two engines totalling 400 h.p. A maximum speed of about 60 m.p.h. is expected. The engines will be located in separate cars, rigged forward and aft, while the passenger car will be located amidships.

The B.F. Sturtevant Co., which has had some experience with light structures by building vanadium-steel aeroplanes to Grover C. Loening's designs, is investigating the possibility of building rigid airships and operating them for passenger transport between New York and Chicago.

B class (Naval).

SUBMARINE SCOUT AIRSHIPS.

B.1—B.33 (1917-1918). Built by Goodyear (24), Goodrich (7), and Connecticut Aircraft Co. (2).

A small type of non-rigid airship, proportional in size to the British *S.S.* class. Capacity, 75,000 to 84,000 cubic feet.

The envelope design is conventional. Tangential rigging is employed for the car suspension, the attachment of the cables to the envelope being effected either by a rigging girder or by finger patches.

A United States Naval Airship of the "B" Class.

An American Non-Rigid.—A "B" Class Airship fitted with cruciform fins.

B class—continued.

Air is supplied to the ballonets by a power blower in the car or, alternatively, by a blower pipe interposed in the propeller slip stream.

The arrangement of the stabilising fins varies. A horizontal fin is attached on either side of tail, and in some ships two vertical fins are placed on the under side ; on others, one vertical fin is placed above and one below. All control planes are balanced.

The car follows the lines of a tractor aeroplane fuselage, with accommodation for a crew of two. Floats are provided on the landing carriage to permit of a descent upon water.

CHARACTERISTICS.

	GOODRICH Type A.	CONNECTICUT Type B.
		(Rigging by belly-band.)
Volume	80,000 cu. ft.	75,000 cu. ft.
Length	167 ft.	156 ft.
Width	33 ft.	35 ft.
Height	50 ft.	45 ft.
Total h.p.		100.
Engine	Curtiss OXX-2.	Hall-Scott A-7a.
Airscrew		1 tractor.
Full speed	50 m.p.h.	44–47 m.p.h.
Full speed endurance		10 hours.
Rate of climb		700 ft. per min.
Static ceiling		7,000 ft.

	GOODYEAR Type F (12).	GOODYEAR Type FA (12).
		(Rigging by finger patches.)
Volume	77,000 cu. ft.	84,000 cu. ft.
Length	160 ft.	163 ft.
Width	31.5 ft.	31.5 ft.
Height	45 ft.	45 ft.
Total h.p.	100.	100.
Engine	Curtiss OXX-2.	Curtiss OXX-3.
Airscrew	1 tractor.	1 tractor.
Full speed	45 m.p.h.	49 m.p.h.
Full speed endurance		10 hr.
Rate of climb		700 ft. per min.
Static ceiling		7,000 ft.

C class (Naval).

C.1—C.15 (1919 and building, nine by Goodyear, and six by Goodrich).

Coastal patrol airships designed for escort duties and submarine hunting.

These airships are not remarkable for any particular features, apart from demonstrating the practicability of applying the patch system of suspensory attachment to non-rigid airships of

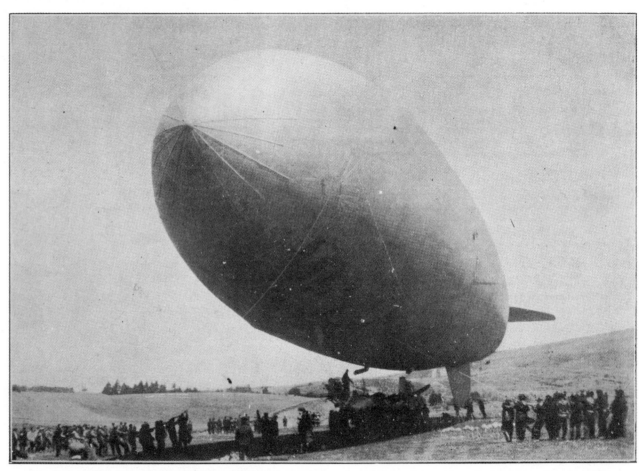

The U.S. Airship Service.—A "C" Class ship on the ground. The method of attaching the head-rope is noteworthy.

C class (Naval)—*continued.*

the fairly large size. Finger patches are used in the *Goodyear* airships, and horseshoe patches in those built by the Goodrich Company.

The envelope has the same silhouette as that used for the British non-rigid airships, and is laid out upon analogous lines.

A large car is fitted with two engines mounted upon outrigger bearers towards the forward end, and twin propellers. Ample accommodation for the comfort of the crew is provided.

The air supply system for maintaining pressure in the ballonets consists of two blower pipes in the wake of the propellers. The bore of these pipes appears to be small, in view of the size of the airship, indicating a slow rate of descent.

A point of recognition is the large single vertical fin under the hull.

CHARACTERISTICS.

Volume ..	..	..	..	170,000 cu. ft.
Length ..	..	..	..	190 ft.
Width ..	..	..	..	43 ft.
Height ..	..	..	..	54 ft.
Total h.p.	..	..	..	300.
Engines ..	..	..	..	Two 150 h.p. Hispano-Suiza.
Airscrews	..	..	..	2.
Full speed (alleged)	..	..	60 m.p.h.
Full speed endurance	..	..	10 hours.
Rate of climb ..	..	..	1,000 ft. per min.
Static ceiling ..	..	..	8,000 ft.
Complement ..	..	..	4.

D class (Naval).

D.1—D.8. Building or to be built, five by the Goodyear Tyre and Rubber Company, Akron, Ohio, and three by the B.F. Goodrich Company, Akron, Ohio.

Medium-sized airships of the non-rigid type, intended for coastal patrol duties.

As in the case of the *C* class, the suspensory rigging is attached to the envelope by stuck-on patches.

CHARACTERISTICS.

Volume ..	..	..	..	180,000 cu. ft.
Length ..	..	..	..	198 ft.
Width ..	..	..	..	43 ft.
Height ..	..	..	..	54 ft.
Total h.p.	..	..	..	250.
Engines ..	..	..	..	Two 125 h.p. 6-cyl. Union.
Airscrews	..	..	..	2.
Full speed (alleged)	..	..	60 m.p.h.
Full speed endurance	..	..	12 hours.
Rate of climb ..	..	..	1,000 ft. per min.
Static ceiling ..	..	..	8,000 ft.
Complement ..	..	..	4.

Description. — Non-rigid type, trimmed by ballonets; external rigging to finger patch (Goodyear) and horseshoe patch (Goodrich). Designs of the Bureau of Construction and Repair, Navy Department.

The Power Plant and Car of an American C Class Naval Airship.

A "C" type Airship belonging to the U S. Navy. Rigged by the "finger-patch method," the product of the Goodyear Tyre & Rubber Co.

E class (Naval).

A refinement of the Submarine Scout class of small non-rigid airship. Actual figures as to the size of this type are not available, but it is presumed to be about 100,000 cu. ft.

The design of the envelope, and the system of car suspension, is based upon standard practice.

A point of interest is the large area of the balanced rudder and elevators, the shape of which is also distinctive. A top fin is fitted.

An air blower pipe in the slipstream of the propeller conveys air to the ballonets, and for use in emergency a power-driven blower is installed in the car.

The car has clean lines and is arranged much in the same way as a " pusher " aeroplane nacelle. An undercarriage, equipped with floats, is fitted at the after end, and under the nose of the car there are two small bumping bags.

The engine is a 150 h.p. Thomas.

OTHER COUNTRIES.

Beyond the nations hereinbefore mentioned none have carried out any airship work of note.

Japan is known to have possessed at one time a curious experimental airship of native design, and it is distinctly likely that during the late war she may have acquired small airships of Allied make and have reproduced them.

Otherwise, so far as can be discovered, the rest of the world has been absolutely inert in the matter of airships.

An Airship of the U.S. Navy's E Class. The balanced rudders and elevators are noteworthy.

ALPHABETICAL INDEX OF AEROPLANES.

Abbreviations :—Aust.=Austro-Hungarian ; Bel.=Belgian ; Brit.=British ; Ger.=German ; Ital.=Italian ; Jap.=Japanese ; Rou.=Roumanian ; Rus.=Russian.

ALPHABETICAL INDEX OF AERO-ENGINES.

ALPHABETICAL INDEX OF AIRSHIPS.

106 adv.